I0890790

Reinventing Higher Education Through Digital Transformation and Smart Campuses

Célio Marques
Polytechnic Institute of Tomar, Portugal

Vasco Santos
Polytechnic Institute of Tomar, Portugal

IGI Global Scientific Publishing
Publishing Tomorrow's Research Today

Vice President of Editorial	Melissa Wagner
Director of Acquisitions	Mikaela Felty
Director of Book Development	Jocelynn Hessler
Production Manager	Mike Brehm
Cover Design	Jose Rosado

Published in the United States of America by
IGI Global Scientific Publishing
701 East Chocolate Avenue
Hershey, PA, 17033, USA
Tel: 717-533-8845 | Fax: 717-533-7115
Website: https://www.igi-global.com E-mail: cust@igi-global.com

Copyright © 2026 by IGI Global Scientific Publishing. All rights reserved. No part of this publication may be reproduced, stored or distributed in any form or by any means, electronic or mechanical, including photocopying, without written permission from the publisher. Use of this publication to train generative artificial intelligence (AI) technologies is expressly prohibited. The publisher reserves all rights to license its use for generative AI training and machine learning model development.

Product or company names used in this set are for identification purposes only. Inclusion of the names of the products or companies does not indicate a claim of ownership by IGI Global Scientific Publishing of the trademark or registered trademark.

Library of Congress Cataloging-in-Publication Data

Names: Marques, Célio, 1975- editor | Santos, Vasco, 1986- editor
Title: Reinventing higher education through digital transformation and smart campuses / Edited by Célio Marques, Vasco Santos.
Description: Hershey, PA : IGI Global Scientific Publishing, [2026] | Includes bibliographical references and index. | Summary: "This book provides a multidisciplinary and forward-looking perspective on how higher education can be reinvented through digital transformation and the development of smart campuses. It presents theoretical insights, empirical research, case studies, and best practices that demonstrate innovative pathways for integrating digital technologies, rethinking pedagogical models, and promoting sustainable and inclusive academic environments"-- Provided by publisher.
Identifiers: LCCN 2026002108 (print) | LCCN 2026002109 (ebook) | ISBN 9798337368313 hardcover | ISBN 9798337368320 paperback | ISBN 9798337368337 ebook
Subjects: LCSH: Education, Higher--Effect of technological innovations on | College environment | Education, Higher--Computer-assisted instruction | Internet in higher education
Classification: LCC LB2395.7 .R42 2026 (print) | LCC LB2395.7 (ebook)
LC record available at https://lccn.loc.gov/2026002108
LC ebook record available at https://lccn.loc.gov/2026002109

British Cataloguing in Publication Data
A Cataloguing in Publication record for this book is available from the British Library.

All work contributed to this book is new, previously-unpublished material.
The views expressed in this book are those of the authors, but not necessarily of the publisher.
This book contains information sourced from authentic and highly regarded references, with reasonable efforts made to ensure the reliability of the data and information presented. The authors, editors, and publisher believe the information in this book to be accurate and true as of the date of publication. Every effort has been made to trace and credit the copyright holders of all materials included. However, the authors, editors, and publisher cannot assume responsibility for the validity of all materials or the consequences of their use. Should any copyright material be found unacknowledged, please inform the publisher so that corrections may be made in future reprints.

Table of Contents

Detailed Table of Contents

This chapter, as per the authors, investigates the critical dimensions of accessibility, diversity, and inclusion in the context of digitally transformed higher education institutions. It presents a comprehensive review of theoretical frameworks such as universal design and social equity, followed by practical implementation models that highlight inclusive pedagogy, adaptive technologies, and administrational best practices. The chapter addresses persistent challenges including digital divides and ethical considerations of AI-driven systems, while also forecasting future trends in sustainable, culturally responsive smart campuses. Through a synthesis of global case studies and policy insights, the chapter offers actionable strategies for building equitable and inclusive digital learning environments that foster participation and success among diverse learner populations.

As higher education moves toward digital and smart campuses, handwritten documents like exam answersheets, attendance registers and forms remain a major challenge. Manual data entry is time-consuming and error-prone, creating inefficiencies in academic and administrative workflows. This chapter presents an AI-driven handwritten text recognition system that automatically converts handwritten content

architecture or energy efficiency, but through integrated environmental, social, and pedagogical responsibility. Drawing on global frameworks such as the UN 2030 Agenda, the CRPD (2006), and UNESCO's Futures of Education (2021), the chapter showcases universities that align digital innovation with democratic values. It proposes a framework for "Inclusive and Sustainable Smart Campuses," offering strategies for leaders and educators to advance equity, resilience, and meaningful innovation.

The evolution of higher education institutions toward smart campus ecosystems requires precise digital representations of physical environments to enable data-driven decision-making. This chapter presents a digital twin of a university campus built with NVIDIA's Sionna simulation library to model realistic wireless propagation. The framework analyzes communication metrics such as Signal-to-Interference-plus-Noise Ratio (SINR), path gain, and received signal strength (RSS) under varying transmitter–receiver scenarios. By mirroring the campus's spatial structure, the system acts as a virtual testbed for evaluating network performance, energy efficiency, and coverage uniformity. Machine learning–based optimization algorithms autonomously determine optimal antenna orientations, improving signal quality and network reliability. The results show that digital twins combined with AI-driven control can enhance smart campus design, adaptive network management, and sustainable infrastructure planning.

Artificial intelligence has become the need of the hour with balancing technological advancement and the timeless values of critical thinking, creativity, and ethical learning. Educators and students looking for writing assistance, quick access to information, communicating with others, or developing their language skills will consider ChatGPT to be the most useful tool. This chapter focuses on user perspectives, attitudes and concerns towards ChatGPT to essentially guide the ethical development. These trends reveal that ChatGPT has rapidly transitioned from a novel tool to a mainstream academic companion, making it imperative to investigate not just its

Preface

INTRODUCTION

Higher education is entering a defining decade. Across the world, higher education institutions are being asked to respond to change at a scale and speed that would have seemed improbable only a few years ago: rapid technological development, shifting labour markets, demographic pressures, rising expectations around inclusion and accessibility, new demands for accountability, and the global imperative of sustainability. These forces are not simply "external challenges". They are reshaping the very conditions under which knowledge is created, shared, tested, and applied, prompting higher education to rethink long-standing assumptions about its role, models, and value.

In this challenging environment, digital transformation can no longer be viewed as a technical upgrade or a temporary response to a crisis. It has become a strategic and systemic shift, one that touches governance, pedagogy, infrastructure, institutional quality, and the relationship between higher education and the societies it serves. The institutions most likely to thrive in the years ahead will be those that can align technology with educational purpose and organisational capability, not as separate initiatives but as part of a coherent, sustainable strategy.

This book, *Reinventing Higher Education Through Digital Transformation and Smart Campuses*, is shaped by that conviction. Its central question is not whether higher education will adopt digital tools - most institutions already have. The deeper question is whether higher education can turn digital capacity into real educational and institutional value: improving learning and student experience, supporting equity and access, strengthening decision-making through evidence, and enhancing the quality and relevance of teaching, research, and services.

FROM DIGITISATION TO TRANSFORMATION

Digital transformation is still often conflated with digitisation: the conversion of existing processes into digital formats (Koop et al, 2019). Digitisation matters. It can reduce friction, streamline operations, improve service delivery, and increase consistency. But transformation is not achieved simply by moving what already exists onto new platforms. It is a rethink of how institutions create value in a world where students, knowledge, and technologies behave differently than they did even a decade ago.

Transformation, therefore, raises difficult, unavoidable questions. What should learning look like when flexibility is an expectation rather than an exception? How do we design learning environments that are inclusive and measurable without becoming overly standardised? How do we ensure that data becomes insight rather than noise? How do we integrate emerging technologies responsibly while protecting integrity, fairness, and accountability? And how do we prepare graduates not only for today's jobs but for lives shaped by continuous change?

If transformation is strategic, it follows that it must be led and not merely implemented. It requires leadership and governance that connect digital initiatives to educational goals, with clear priorities and a long-term view. It demands investment not only in infrastructure but in people: academics, professional staff, students, and senior leadership. Above all, it requires a culture in which experimentation and learning are normal.

The contributions in this volume reflect that complexity. They move between infrastructure and human experience, between operational systems and ethical questions, between campus environments and learning design. They share a simple underlying claim: the University is not merely a collection of systems or buildings; it is a living ecosystem. Digital transformation, if it is to matter, must be understood as an ecosystemic transition.

SMART CAMPUSES AS HUMAN-CENTRED ECOSYSTEMS

Within this wider transformation, the concept of the *smart campus* offers a practical and compelling framework. A smart campus is not simply a campus with more technology. At its best, it is an environment designed as an integrated system, where physical space, digital platforms, connectivity, services, and institutional processes interact to improve experience and outcomes (Polin, et al, 2023).

At the technical level, this depends on robust foundations: advanced wireless networks, positioning and sensing systems, secure architectures, interoperability, and the capacity to integrate data across services. These infrastructures can enable smoother experiences for students and staff, more efficient use of space and energy, improved safety, and greater resilience. They also create the conditions for campuses to function as "living labs", where innovation can be tested in real contexts and operational needs can align with research and learning goals (Huertas et al, 2021).

Yet smartness should never become a synonym for surveillance or technological determinism. The most meaningful smart campuses are those that remain human-centred: designed to remove barriers, widen opportunities, and support wellbeing, belonging, and participation. Smart campuses, in this sense, are not only infrastructural projects. They are cultural and pedagogical ones, shaping how learning happens and how communities experience the institution.

ARTIFICIAL INTELLIGENCE: PROMISE AND RESPONSIBILITY

Few developments are accelerating digital transformation more visibly than artificial intelligence (AI). In higher education, AI is moving quickly from experimentation into mainstream practice: from generative tools used in learning and assessment, to intelligent tutoring systems, automated feedback, and adaptive environments that personalise support at scale. Used well, such tools may enhance engagement, extend teaching capacity, and enable students to navigate learning pathways with greater confidence and autonomy.

But AI also brings tensions that cannot be ignored. Generative tools challenge established ideas of authorship, academic integrity, and assessment design. Automated tutoring and grading systems raise questions about transparency, fairness, and bias, especially if they influence progression and feedback. And AI is inseparable from data: governance, privacy, consent, and trust are no longer peripheral issues but strategic concerns.

This book recognises that AI will be foundational to the future of higher education, while insisting that adoption must be guided by pedagogical clarity and institutional responsibility. AI cannot be treated as something that can simply be "plugged in". It requires governance frameworks, evaluation mechanisms, staff capability, and ethical oversight. Crucially, it should strengthen human learning and educational relationships and not replace them. Higher education remains rooted in meaning-making, mentorship, community, and the social experience of learning.

EQUITY, ACCESS, AND INSTITUTIONAL TRUST

Perhaps the most important test of digital transformation is not technological sophistication, but whether transformation contributes to a more equitable institution.

Digital change can easily reproduce (or deepen) existing inequalities. Students differ in access to devices and connectivity, in digital confidence, in familiarity with academic cultures, and in the personal circumstances that shape their ability to succeed. Accessibility, therefore, is not simply a compliance matter; it is a design principle. Inclusion must be embedded into platforms, services, assessment practices, and learning content from the outset, not treated as an afterthought.

The same is true for smart campuses and data-driven decision-making. Institutions must ask: Who benefits from these systems? Who is excluded? What data is collected, and why? What assumptions are embedded in the models and algorithms adopted? As campuses become more connected and more data-enabled, trust becomes one of the most valuable institutional assets. Transformation must therefore be transparent, accountable, and attentive to the lived experience of students and staff.

The book's contributions reinforce the argument that inclusivity and sustainability must sit at the heart of smart higher education. Transformation should not stop at efficiency. It should move toward democratisation - widening participation, supporting diverse learners, and ensuring innovation reduces barriers rather than creates new ones. Sustainability, meanwhile, is not a separate agenda: smart campuses may support environmental goals through better resource management, but sustainability also means building institutional resilience, including sustaining capability, wellbeing, credibility, and public value.

PEOPLE AND CAPABILITY IN THE DIGITAL AGE

No transformation succeeds without people. The academic designing modules, the learning designer shaping experiences, professional staff supporting student services, IT teams maintaining infrastructure, and leaders making strategic decisions are all critical. One of the most significant shifts underway is the growing importance of learning design and digital competence as institutional capabilities.

Digital learning environments are not neutral spaces; they shape engagement, interaction, feedback, motivation, and assessment. As technologies evolve, educators need support to redesign learning in ways that are pedagogically sound and socially responsive, whether in hybrid delivery, immersive learning, AI-mediated interaction, or new approaches to assessment.

Digital competence, in this sense, goes beyond technical confidence. It includes data literacy, ethical judgement, pedagogical fluency, and an understanding of how technologies influence power, access, and opportunities.

A CALL TO RESPONSIBLE REINVENTION

The reinvention of higher education will not be achieved through technology alone. It will depend on leadership that understands transformation as a strategy; on governance that aligns innovation with ethics and equity; on quality systems that build trust; and on human-centred design that places accessibility and inclusion at the core. It will also require campus ecosystems that use data and intelligence to enhance learning, improve experience, and strengthen institutional performance.

This book does not offer a single model for the future. Instead, it brings together insights that illuminate both the opportunities and the tensions shaping higher education's transformation. It shows how smart campuses can enable new educational possibilities, how AI can support learning and operations while raising essential ethical questions, and how equity, sustainability, and quality must be built into the foundations of innovation.

If higher education has always been where society imagines its future, then it must now also be where society learns how to shape that future responsibly. Digital transformation and smart campuses are not ends in themselves. They are powerful instruments for renewing the mission of higher education: creating knowledge, educating citizens, and contributing to a more just, sustainable, and human-centred world.

May this book serve as both a guide and an invitation - a guide to the ideas and frameworks shaping institutional innovation, and an invitation to lead transformation with clarity, courage, and care.

Diogo Casanova

Laboratory of Distance Education and eLearning – LE@D, Universidade Aberta, Portugal

REFERENCES

Huertas, J. I., Mahlknecht, J., Lozoya-Santos, J. D. J., Uribe, S., Lopez-Guajardo, E. A., & Ramirez-Mendoza, R. A. (2021). Campus city project: Challenge living lab for smart cities. *Applied Sciences (Basel, Switzerland), 11*(23), 11085. DOI: 10.3390/app112311085

Kopp, M., Gröblinger, O., & Adams, S. (2019). Five common assumptions that prevent digital transformation at higher education institutions. In *Inted2019 Proceedings* (pp. 1448–1457). IATED. DOI: 10.21125/inted.2019.0445

Polin, K., Yigitcanlar, T., Limb, M., & Washington, T. (2023). The making of smart campus: A review and conceptual framework. *Buildings (Basel, Switzerland), 13*(4), 891. DOI: 10.3390/buildings13040891

Chapter 1
Accessibility, Diversity, and Inclusion in the Digitally Transformed University

Manjot Singh
https://orcid.org/0009-0006-8462-6669
Christ University, India

Reenu Bansal
https://orcid.org/0009-0009-1763-3756
Christ University, India

ABSTRACT

This chapter, as per the authors, investigates the critical dimensions of accessibility, diversity, and inclusion in the context of digitally transformed higher education institutions. It presents a comprehensive review of theoretical frameworks such as universal design and social equity, followed by practical implementation models that highlight inclusive pedagogy, adaptive technologies, and administrational best practices. The chapter addresses persistent challenges including digital divides and ethical considerations of AI-driven systems, while also forecasting future trends in sustainable, culturally responsive smart campuses. Through a synthesis of global case studies and policy insights, the chapter offers actionable strategies for building equitable and inclusive digital learning environments that foster participation and success among diverse learner populations.

DOI: 10.4018/979-8-3373-6831-3.ch001

026, IGI Global Scientific Publishing. Copying or distributing in print or electronic forms without written permission of IGI Global Scientific Publishing is prohibited. Use of this chapter to tive artificial intelligence (AI) technologies is expressly prohibited. The publisher reserves all rights to license its use for generative AI training and machine learning model development.

INTRODUCTION

Digital transformation continues to change higher education worldwide. This change was the main cause for traditional universities to evolve into smart campuses that entail the application of technology platforms, which are designed not only for teaching but also for learning and administration. However, it is imperative to distinguish between a merely 'digitized' campus and a truly 'Smart Campus.' While digitization often refers to the migration of traditional curriculum to online platforms, a Smart Campus represents a more profound architectural and technological shift. According to (Wijonarko et al., 2023), a Smart Campus integrates Internet of Things (IoT) sensors, data analytics, and intelligent physical infrastructure to create a self-monitoring environment that optimizes resource allocation and user experience. This goes beyond virtual classrooms to include smart wayfinding for disabled students and automated climate control for sensory-sensitive areas. Consequently, this transformation brings a handful of opportunities and at the same time, it raises several challenges to that effect, namely accessibility, diversity and inclusion. Accessibility that is realised in the framework of a smart campus is not limited to physical access, i.e. access to the space, but it also includes digital, curricular and social access. Accessibility aims at providing each and every individual access to the academic and campus life regardless of their abilities or backgrounds. Diversity refers to the different social, cultural and personal characteristics or differences of the university community members, while inclusion means that these differences are respected and cherished as a result of equitable opportunities, participation and support systems. With the advent of the smart campus concept worldwide, institutions must very much deliberate, plan and execute measures aimed at accessibility, diversity, and inclusion, as this is the key to the successful implementation of digital transformation in education (PMC, 2021).

Universities have become more and more recognised as a reflection of the bigger world (society). Accessible learning environment policies and practices deployed in universities have, thus, a direct positive effect on academic, emotional and professional outcomes of students, faculty, and staff. What is encompassed by the term accessibility today is much wider than it used to be and includes not only ramps, elevators, but also digital interfaces, virtual classrooms, and the use of assistive technologies in curricular design. Barriers for people with disabilities, first-generation students, and international cohorts are being effectively removed through different programs, including universal design, accessible wayfinding solutions, and text-to-speech technologies. As an example, Southern Methodist University has implemented learning management systems that support the faculty in developing universally accessible courses that are appropriate for students with sensory impairments and, at the same time, promote general campus inclusion. One of the features in the modern intelligent educational facility is the unification of physical and digital accessibilities, such as tactile signage, automated doors, alternative text for web resources, and live transcription services. At the same time, all users can take advantage of the accurate on-campus directions offered by wayfinding technologies like Mapsted's indoor navigation tools, whereas location analytics empower universities to detect and help individuals with invisible disabilities by supportive data. Now, the comprehensive method, as a result, leading institutions, confronts bureaucracy and assures that students who are facing issues of mental health, ADD or ADHD receive their accommodations on time and in a flexible manner. At Western Sydney University, among the diverse technology-based learning environments, there are also specially designed areas for the LBGTQ+ community and First Nation students, which is a clear example of an intersectional approach to diversity and inclusion.

The physical modification of college or university settings is just a fraction of what needs to be done. True inclusion requires focus on mental wellness, community-building, and student support networks. Mental health issues have impacted over 40% of college students throughout their academic journey, as per the surveys. This reality compels campus leaders to prioritize student well-being, recognize various identities, and create environments where everyone feels safe and heard. For example, through universal design and faculty engagement, the Accessible Technology Initiative in the California State University system, shares the responsibility of making technology access with the whole campus community (HigherEdToday, 2020).

The universities worldwide are committed to establishing and sustaining inclusive atmospheres by a planned series of physical changes, new technologies application, and policy innovations. Indian higher education is progressively integrating Accessibility, Diversity, and Inclusion (ADI) objectives into its digitally developed campuses through different frameworks like NEP 2020. By implementing individualized student support and simple-to-use platforms, Christ University, Bangalore is a perfect example of how to bridge the digital divide and at the same time, raise the level of fairness for all learners. These actions are quite important considering that nearly 20% of the undergraduate students in the U.S. have disclosed that they are disabled and a similar demographic trend can be observed in other parts of the world as well.

The continuous and rapid digital transformation poses a question that remains at the center of discussion of sustainable high-impact education: how to integrate accessibility, diversity, and inclusion into every aspect of academic, administrative, and social life on campus? This chapter is devoted to exploring the concepts that underpin accessibility, diversity, and inclusion, different institutional models, practical challenges, and future perspectives as well as real-world case studies, sector trends, and evidence-based frameworks to help institutions comply with the evolving equity and excellence requirements in higher education.

LITERATURE REVIEW

Scholarly literature in recent years has escalated its attention to accessibility, diversity, and inclusion (ADI) in the digitally transformed university, which is a reflection of higher education's major rethinking during the post-pandemic period and in the context of rapid technological innovations. The authors of the study argue that the digitalisation of the university system opens up very good possibilities for the system to be efficient, scalable, and personalised. At the same time, it can reproduce or exacerbate social exclusion if there are no specific, evidence-based measures put in place (Digital Equity and Accessibility in Higher Education - Wiley, 2024).

Foundations of Digital Accessibility and Diversity

The initial stages of the digital transformation revolved around technological infrastructure, which was considered the main driver for the global delivery of online learning and digitalised educational operations. Nevertheless, mature evaluations now look at this hardware-and-connectivity-focused approach as a factor that is not enough for a full ADI realisation. For example, Mohammad et al. (2024) utilize thematic analysis to university websites and official documents to find out that digital accessibility is an engagement of the institution not only to empower students by regular updating of the content and building the community of differently-abled students but also to conform to the World Wide Web Consortium (W3C) standards (Mohammad et al., 2024).

It is generally agreed among scholars that the accessibility universities should do the integration of the accessibility services, the provision of accommodations, and the advertisement of this via both digital and physical spaces, with the aim of serving both differently-abled students and the able-bodied. The comparative study of Harvard, Oxford, King Saud, and Majmaah Universities indicates the different ways these institutions help individuals with disabilities, e.g., physical infrastructure modifications to online multilingual tools and remote training platforms. The COVID-19 pandemic, in particular, has been the main factor in the rapid uptake of the measures mentioned above; thus, accessibility and inclusivity have been made the main foci of crisis preparedness and campus resilience (Mohammad et al., 2024).

Universal Design for Learning and Its Challenges

Universal Design for Learning (UDL) is one of the major teaching and institutional concepts which has changed the way educators and researchers work. The research community recognises the three key components of UDL to be the main factors in the creation of accessible and flexible learning models: multiple means of engagement, representation, and action/expression. Doyle et al. (2025) illustrate how UDL can be practically integrated into course design and activities via simulation, thereby demonstrating that these ideas are not only applicable to disabled learners but also the whole student community (Doyle et al., 2025).

The latest meta-analyses, e.g., Eyland (2025), give support to the view that UDL strategies have a positive impact on pupil motivation, academic achievement, and the general atmosphere of the classroom. The manner of providing content, assessment, and engagement options that are flexible is recognised as a way to reduce the demand for individual reasonable adjustments—thus, progressing towards systemic accessibility (Eyland, 2025). However, the most recent studies highlight that the implementation of UDL varies across different levels of faculty members, the presence of technical support, and resistance to the curriculum issue in particular departments or institutions with limited resources. Consequently, this research has identified only faculty capacity, inconsistent technical support, and resistance to curricular change as the factors impeding the implementation of UDL (Cumming & Rose).

Systematic reviews beyond the technical compliance point to social justice goals as the necessary connection for UDL efforts, thereby ensuring that tech usage does not overtake or hide practice equity. The literature suggests moving from excuse-driven reasonable adjustment to accountability-driven proactive structural design that foresees different learning needs right from the start and includes inclusive pedagogical technologies, e.g., extended reality solutions and real-time translation systems, as part of the solution (Stuart et al., 2023).

The Equity Imperative: Systemic Approaches and Leadership

Diversity, equity, and inclusion (DEI) in higher education are not only about representational quotas and student recruitment. Ovink (2022) studies the campus experiences of the marginalised and intersectional groups and finds that there are still gaps in psychological safety, community belonging, and leadership responsiveness. Systematic reviews advocate that the successful DEI programs are a result of institutional commitment to ongoing faculty development, hiring and curriculum-related accountability, and well-developed assessment frameworks; interventions that are done in a piecemeal manner or are only symbolic yield very few results (Ovink, 2022).

Stuart et al. (2023) place these difficulties in the context of minority-serving institutions and immersive education, thus explaining that achieving real equity is a long and systemic journey. They maintain that "belonging" and inclusion should be supported both in real and virtual campuses—thus, pointing out the risk of a technology-led change that does not deal with the underlying cultural or structural aspects of exclusion (Stuart et al., 2023).

Mohapatra (2024) and other similar scholars broaden the perspective by focusing on participatory methods in equity research, inter-campus collaborations, and the involvement of stakeholders. The empowerment activities normally include the student-led design, the use of different communication methods, and the frequent evaluation of the impact. The case studies of King Saud and Majmaah Universities demonstrate the effectiveness of collaborative leadership, constant training, and the centralisation of accessibility services (Mohammad et al).

Extended Reality, Adaptive Technologies, and the Metaverse

One of the fast-growing areas of focus in the literature has been the contribution of cutting-edge tech to the advancement of an equitable and inclusive education system. The same is true for Extended Reality (XR), which is a combination of Virtual, Augmented, and Mixed Reality, and is frequently used to create relationships and support the feeling of community, especially in groups of marginalised students and those who study online. Stuart et al. (2023) provide a rich account of the DEI potential of XR, noting that US universities are greatly investing in executive officers for DEI and the use of immersive platforms for teaching. Although the influence of XR is mainly in the sciences and the STEM areas, it has a spillover effect also in the arts, leadership training, as well as career readiness (Stuart et al., 2023).

Besides that, the recent articles have also drawn attention to the digital transformation challenges. Surjawan (2025) observes the gains in productivity through digitising workflow in admissions and administration, but he posts a question if the same efforts put into accessibility and equity monitoring could have been overlooked unintentionally (Surjawan, 2025).

Barriers, Opportunities, and the Way Forward

Full-scale reviews uncover the existence of several lingering barricades: insufficient funds, absence of a unified vision, competing priorities of the institution, and gaps in the national policies. Mohammad et al. (2024) argue that a digitally inclusive environment requires continuous fixing, feedback from stakeholders in all directions, and unceasing support of students with disabilities. The main concern of the literatures is the existence of digital gaps in the world, not only between countries but also within universities and different student groups (Mohammad et al., 2024).

In Contrast, numerous opportunities for sustainable progress are suggested by the scholars, including:

- Implementing universal design and UDL principles from the very first day in each digital project of the campus (Doyle et al., 2025).

- Preparing and motivating teachers to accept and implement ADI principles in their course planning through training (Eyland, 2025).
- By doing thorough equity impact audits, we will be able to facilitate in large scale the use of immersive and adaptive technologies that will have positive impacts on different groups of people (Stuart et al., 2023).

Accessibility

Services can become more efficient in reaching a wider audience if the communication is centralised, and it makes use of different modes like multilingual and multi-modal (Mohammad et al., 2024).

This review of the literature provides the theoretical and practical points that are crucial in ADI in today's university. These points are centred law-wise on legal mandates like the ADA and W3C standards, but are more focused on the future leaders, systemic change, and technological innovation. The following sections analyse conceptual frameworks, case studies, and practical strategies.

THEORETICAL FOUNDATIONS

Introduction: Principles and Purpose

The first level of accessibility, diversity, and inclusion (ADI) in digitally transformed universities theoretically relies on inclusive design, universal design for learning (UDL), and social equity frameworks. Together, these models lift the higher education sphere from barely meeting accessibility requirements to universities where digital transformation is a strong tool for educational equity, adaptive learning, community involvement, and systemic change (FIU, 2023).

Digital transformation should not be viewed only as a technological upgrade but rather as a pedagogical and cultural revolution that changes the very definition of higher education participation. The theoretical foundations of ADI serve as a bridge between the physical and the ethical sides of the change. On top of that, it admits that technologies can either be an equaliser or an inequality amplifier. Therefore, the theoretical constructs in question set their goals beyond mere implementation of accessibility norms. They also strive to infuse equality, engagement, and a sense of community into digital education.

By themselves, inclusive design, UDL, and social equity frameworks provide one comprehensive perspective for universities willing to undertake this change in a morally responsible way. The three models agree that accessibility and inclusiveness of campuses cannot be the simple result of technological progress. Rather, they come as a consequence of the design with empathy, collaboration, and justice at their core.

Inclusive Design Principles: The Promise of Universality

Essentially, inclusive design is one of the key ideas that the physical, digital, and social environments should be designed in such a way that they can support a maximum of human diversity. It does away with the idea of "average users" and sees variation as the standard. The concept is definitely forward-looking, as it does not attempt to retrofit solutions to problems already present, but aims to avoid new ones by purposeful design.

Partly through Ronald Mace's work in the 1980s, inclusive design became universal design, with the latter being a framework identifying seven guiding principles: fair use, use flexibility, easy and natural operation, perceptible information, error tolerance, minimum effort, and suitable size and space for approach and use. These are the principles that not only form the basis of modern architecture but have also impacted educational design and digital accessibility initiatives globally.

In the context of higher education, inclusive design is both an idea and a method. It demands that educational environments, whether physical or virtual, be constructed with the idea of inclusion; thus, they must support all the learners, even those who have disabilities, or are linguistically challenged, or come from underprivileged backgrounds. The creation of online course materials, digital platforms, and building facilities all sends a message about the institution's position on the issue of fairness.

Inclusive design today is mainly focused on the aspects of participation and co-creation. Instead of creating for the needs of the underrepresented, universities are now more and more forming partnerships with them for the purpose of design. This type of cooperation not only guarantees that accessibility is not the last thing to be considered but also that it becomes an exercised norm that recognises different lived experiences as design intelligence.

The Universal Design for Learning Guidelines (CAST, 2024) serve as the implementation of inclusive design in education by motivating teachers to prepare courses in such a way that they naturally comply with students' diversity at all phases of the course development. The guidelines are engaged in presenting the content, expression, and participation as flexible entities — thus, students are provided with numerous resources to understand, produce and verify knowledge.

The intended effects of this approach are also highlighted in case studies. For instance, at Dún Laoghaire Institute of Art, Design and Technology (IADT), faculty members incorporated UDL-based case studies as a method that stimulated the participation of students with disabilities and, at the same time, increased the satisfaction and understanding of the whole class. As a result, the institution achieved not only more accessibility but also improved learning outcomes for all students, thus proving that the entire academic community benefits from inclusion (Inclusive by Design, IADT, 2025).

Inclusive design is also a topic that is discussed at the intersection of such future-focused areas as human-computer interaction (HCI) and experience design, thus linking the issues of usability with those of equity. As universities roll out different new technologies – AI tutors, XR simulations, learning analytics – the principles of inclusive design can play a crucial role in ensuring that these innovations don't lead to bias or exclusion. Therefore, inclusive design is an ethical positioning as well as a practical manual for creating equitable digital design.

Universal Design for Learning in Practice

Universal Design for Learning (UDL) is basically a bundle of educational methodologies that one can readily put into practice to carry out the directives of inclusive design. In essence, UDL, which was developed by CAST researchers in the 1990s, is a concept borrowed from universal design of the physical environment and innovatively applied to learning. UDL recognises that learners differ in their interaction with the material, perception and processing of the information, and the way they demonstrate understanding.

The UDL framework is centred around three core ideas:

1. Multiple means of engagement – engaging the learners' interest through freedom, pertinence, and collaboration.
2. Multiple means of representation – delivering the material through different formats and sensory.
3. Multiple means of action and expression – giving different options to students to show their learning and skills.

The three principles are linked in a continuum from access to empowerment, where the main idea is not to provide accommodations only, but to create courses that are suitable for everyone from the very beginning.

Some examples of the use of UDL in higher education are: flexible assessment options, accessible multimedia materials, real-time captioning, and the employment of adaptive learning systems that change the content according to the learner's needs. For example, many universities have nowadays AI-based accessibility tools as part of their LMS platforms to facilitate the provision of alternative text, captioning, and personalised reading formats automatically.

Several studies consistently show that the use of UDL methods brings the positive change of increased engagement, motivation, and academic achievement not only among students with disabilities but among the whole student body (Hills, 2022). This is largely because UDL emphasises flexibility, thereby accepting that each learner has a different way of grasping the concept.

However, the strategy's implementation is at different levels in various locations, locally and internationally. A study in Canadian and U.S. universities (Hills, 2022) reveals that many long-standing challenges persist, including insufficient faculty training, a lack of administrative incentives, and inadequate institutional support. A great number of teachers perceive UDL as an extra chore that they have to do rather than a core part of teaching practice. This perception sheds light on the need for leadership from the top down and professional empowerment from the bottom up to institutionalize UDL.

Although there are these issues, the paradigm shift is perceptible. More and more institutions treat inclusive design and UDL as the core of pedagogical innovation, not as tasks of compliance. A good example is Centre College (2025), which uses UDL as a part of its faculty development program, thus facilitating student-faculty course co-design and regular accessibility checks. The outcome is an environment in which inclusion is regarded as an inherent feature of good teaching.

Besides this, UDL is very close to the current pedagogical trends such as constructivist learning, experiential education, and digital personalisation. By using these methods together, the universities will be able to create learning experiences which are flexible, student-centred, and fair.

Social Equity Frameworks: Justice and Participation

Social equity frameworks not only reflect the structural and cultural aspects of inclusion but also the educational and design ones. These frameworks get their concepts from social justice, critical pedagogy, and the social model of disability. In brief, they demonstrate frameworks which portray that exclusion is not the result of individual impairments or deficiencies, but societal and institutional structures that produce obstacles for full participation.

Even if digital transformation is the topic of the discussion, social equity frameworks assist universities in understanding that technology is not neutral. Usually, the bias of the creators and the inequalities of the context combine to affect algorithms, platform design, and data systems. Hence, the only way to achieve real digital inclusion is to deal with these structural inequities by deliberately choosing policy and design actions.

Most of the universities in the U.S. are reported by the Inclusive Campus Landscape Literature Review (FIU, 2023) to have appointed DEI (Diversity, Equity, and Inclusion) administrators (more than 90%) who are responsible for leading institutional transformation efforts. Nevertheless, the majority of these initiatives still encounter problems of fragmentation and symbolic compliance. Social equity frameworks motivate universities to abandon such fragmented, compliance-driven approaches and instead become structurally engaged in proactive change - thus, forming a network of equity in governance, curriculum, and technology.

Some of the main facilitators of equity are:

- The design of an inclusive curriculum reflecting diverse epistemologies.
- Having the voices of the underrepresented communities in contributions and leadership positions.
- Transparent and fair mechanisms for recruitment & promotion.
- Spending on technologies that are user-friendly for all and digital literacy campaigns.
- Community collaborations that facilitate the university's outreach beyond the local area.

The research conducted during and after the pandemic has shown that the institutions with built-in equity frameworks managed to be more resilient in ensuring the continuity and fairness of digital learning (HigherEdToday, 2021). Peer mentoring, faculty accountability, and participatory design practices were identified as effective strategies for sustaining inclusion.

From a conceptual point of view, social equity frameworks align with Paulo Freire's critical pedagogy, which emphasises dialogue, empowerment, and transformation. They oppose the 'banking model' of education, where knowledge is passed one-way, and instead support the idea of knowledge co-creation among different participants.

Moreover, these frameworks echo the ideas of Amartya Sen's capability approach, which gauges justice not only by resource allocation but by people's real chances of leading meaningful lives. Within the scope of higher education, this implies that all students, and not only the privileged ones, will be given the opportunity to fully and meaningfully partake in academic and social.

INTERSECTIONALITY AND CRITICAL APPROACHES

Intersectionality provides a detailed perspective for understanding the concepts of D&I by recognising that people have multiple, overlapping identities such as race, gender, class, sexuality, and disability that interact and determine their experiences of privilege and oppression. The term was created by Kimberlé Crenshaw in 1989, and since then, intersectionality has been widely used as a main framework for dealing with issues of inequality in the higher education sector.

Within the digitally transformed sector of the universities, intersectionality becomes a very important concept to figure out in which ways the technology can maintain the systemic bias or help to eliminate it. To illustrate, speech recognition software may be less accommodating for people with non-native accents; AI grading algorithms may develop racial or gender biases unintentionally; and e-learning platforms may be designed for users with stable Internet connections and advanced digital skills, thereby excluding others.

An intersectional viewpoint urges organisations to scrutinise who gets the gains and who is left out because of the digital changes. Besides that, it highlights the fact that one cannot arrive at the level of equity through one single solution; hence, the design, which is meant to be universal, has to take the intersections of identities and the personal stories of people into account.

Recent research points out that extended reality (XR) and other immersive technologies have the potential to become effective instruments for the promotion of empathy and inclusion. A number of universities in the U.S. and Europe are working on VR-based exercises that can support students' comprehension of disability, racial bias, or cultural marginalisation experiences. The use of such immersive storytelling techniques enhances awareness and motivates the adoption of inclusive practices by both staff and students (FIU, 2023). However, researchers caution that if these provisions are not created with an equity-centred approach, they can also lead to harmful issues such as algorithmic bias, digital exclusion, and ethical problems.

Critically framing of ADI issues, which draws from critical race theory, feminist technology studies, and the decolonial theory, constitutes an additional element in the set of challenges posed by the university to itself in terms of confronting those inequities originating from the structures of curriculum, policy, and digital infrastructure. To give an example, decolonial scholars claim that technologies and content, which are largely based on the Western model, tend to silence indigenous epistemologies and linguistic diversity. Thus, digital inclusion is not only about access but also about recognition or valuing different ways of knowing and being.

Besides that, the notion of intersectionality is very important in the case of India. The factors of caste, gender, rurality, and linguistic diversity interact with digital access to determine students' educational experiences. The National Education Policy (NEP) 2020, very clearly, states the necessity of equity and inclusion in the digitally transformed higher education sector, whereby technology should not be a barrier but a bridge. Universities like Christ University and IIT Bombay, through their efforts, have started carrying out accessibility audits, implementing multilingual platforms, and inclusive learning analytics, which not only address these intersections but also dimensions of inequality.

Synthesis and Emerging Directions

When put together, the lenses of inclusive design, UDL, social equity frameworks, and intersectional approaches represent a multi-layered theoretical basis for accessibility, diversity, and inclusion in digital universities. Each of these perspectives offers different insights:

- Inclusive design points to the need for forward-looking, user-focused systems.
- UDL makes flexibility and diversity workable components of pedagogy.
- Social equity frameworks bring the concept of justice deeply into the structures of institutions.
- Intersectionality guarantees that the inclusion takes into account the intricacy of human identity.

Future possibilities indicate that the agenda of ADI will deeply depend on systemic integration, where design, pedagogy, policy, and leadership interact to create an environment of sustained inclusion not only in the university but in all spheres of life. Academics suggest that universities create "inclusive innovation ecosystems" merging technology, policy, and human-centred design as a way of continuously monitoring and enhancing accessibility (G3ICT, 2025).

While higher education is subject to continuous changes due to globalisation, demographic shifts, and rapid technological development, these theoretical models act as both an ethical anchor and a strategic compass. They make it clear to educators and policymakers that real digital transformation is not measured by the amount of bandwidth or the number of devices but rather by the extent to which technology supports the participation, voice, and sense of belonging of academic communities.

To put it briefly, the theoretical bases of ADI lay down the intellectual and moral scaffolding required for inclusive universities. They probe the traditional limits of pedagogy, redefine excellence through equity, and present digital transformation as a chance to realise a world that is more just, interconnected, and empathetic. The following chapter section will draw on these theoretical assumptions to discuss implementation models, case studies, and institutional strategies that operationalise accessibility, diversity, and inclusion in digitally transformed pedagogy.

MODELS OF IMPLEMENTATION: INTERNATIONAL AND SECTORAL EVIDENCE

Across the world, the sophisticated and varied models for the implementation of accessibility, diversity, and inclusion in digitally transformed universities have evolved to reflect different legal frameworks, technological infrastructure, and pedagogical cultures. The case studies of the European Union, North America, and the Asia-Pacific region showcase real examples of the efficient strategies, difficulties, and policy-led changes to the universal and inclusive design (G3ICT).

Policy and Legal Frameworks: Global Benchmarks

The surroundings in terms of law and policy are the basis for implementation. In the European Union, among others, the Charter of Fundamental Rights, Web Accessibility Directive (2016), and European Accessibility Act (2019) put the accessibility of digital platforms in higher education as a condition for students with disabilities. The organisations translate such demands into innovations by universities, which then have to check whether the websites meet the latest standards, upgrade digital resources, and provide feedback channels for the most neglected groups.

Georgia's higher education system, compliant with the EU association, is on the way to a thorough reform to meet international obligations and benchmarks. Regardless of the absence of a comprehensive national legislation, institutions are incorporating Universal Design for Learning (UDL) and digital accessibility into curriculum development and IT services. Although problems still exist, especially in the areas of funding and technical capacities, worldwide standards have become the main drivers of change and set new challenges for student participation and quality (G3ICT, 2025).

Institutional Design and Architectural Strategies

Architectural and design changes can significantly help the inclusion of the university campus students. The Library Learning Commons at the Community College of Philadelphia was transformed through the renovation process, changing a noisy and not easy-to-access place into a well-arranged, ADA-compliant environment with clear wayfinding, visual connectivity, and attractive shared spaces. The changes, which were a direct response to the needs of minority and first-generation students, show the extent to which physical design can not only create psychological safety but also facilitate easier access to resources.

The University of Washington has transformed its campus into modular and versatile learning spaces through the implementation of DO-IT best practices. These developments feature the use of accessible furniture, sensory rooms, and a digital content management system that is compatible with assistive technology. Consequently, these extensive changes need a roadmap, the involvement of the stakeholders, and a constant assessment to keep up with the progress and to be able to react to the new requirements (UW DO-IT).

Digital Transformation Strategies

Incorporating sustainable technologies, cloud architecture, and user-centred design are at the core of digital transformation in campuses. Mohamed Hashim et al. (2022) offer conceptual models for digital transformation that integrate cloud computing, artificial intelligence, and green IT with operational effectiveness, thus providing a blueprint that allows universities to react to technological changes swiftly, while at the same time, lessening resource depletion and negative impact on the environment (PMC, 2022).

The main systems that facilitate universal design on digital platforms are those that perform accessibility functions automatically, content delivery personalisation, and inclusive communication facilitation.

Faculty Engagement and Professional Development

Faculty engagement is a precondition for the inclusive design to be spread to the next level. Case studies provide evidence supporting the point that faculty obtaining training on a continuous basis, engaging in interdisciplinary design processes, and being incentivised for applying universal design principles lead not only to faculty teaching quality but also to student outcomes enhancement. The use of UDL as a regular professional development activity, supported by the likes of the CAST UDL Guidelines and toolkits, has enabled the faculties in the universities of the United States, Canada, and Europe to make access and inclusion an integral part of the core curricula through institutionalisation (CAST, 2025).

Barriers still exist: a shortage of time, complexity perception, and a lack of administrative mandate are the main reasons that faculty uptake and fidelity are very often limited. Through interviews, Hills (2022) found that driven faculty can be at the forefront of change, but if they do not get the support from the leadership and there is no staff training, then the process is likely to come to a standstill. Among the measures to be taken, there are universal design advocates' formation, accessibility-dedicated staff roles, and participatory redesign teams consisting of students with lived experience, which can be considered as a solution to the problem (Hills).

Technology Platforms, Data, and Feedback

The possibilities to scale ADI are being changed due to new technologies, data management systems, and analytics. Real-time captioning, alternative text generation, immersive XR environments, and AI-driven feedback are features added to digital platforms. According to the higher education project of Georgia and the UDL Case Studies Booklet, frequent audits, student response mechanisms, and measurement analytics can assist universities to identify exclusion, get it right, and track improvement (IADT, 2025).

The response of students is vital. In longitudinal studies, Wells et al. (2022) discovered that students who went through co-design and ongoing feedback processes showed more satisfaction with accessibility interventions, high retention, and engagement in the community. Such participatory frameworks in universities that deploy digital reporting dashboards are in a position to promote inclusion at scale (Wells et al., 2022).

Interdisciplinary Collaboration and Community Partnerships

ADI implementation also needs to be meaningful, meaning the involvement beyond the university. The top institutions work with local governments, industry, non-profits, and accessibility consultancies to measure how much progress has been made and speed up innovation. They include joint accessibility audits, technology development between the public and the private, as well as internship programs that focus on minorities.

Cross-border exchange of policy standards, toolkits, and research outcomes can be effected by international networks like the UNESCO Digital Transformation Collaborative, which develops a worldwide community of practice to learn and innovate constantly (Digital Transformation Collaborative - UNESCO, 2024).

Adoption of the Models in the Indian Higher Education

Though the global trends prevail, some of these models have Indian versions in universities. The NEP 2020 has seen Christ University create personalised and accessible portals to remote learners, multilingual content and peer mentoring programs, as well as aligning administrative operations with national DEI priorities. Smart Campus Analytics used in IIT Bombay helps in the early identification of at-risk students. Universal design is perceived as a pedagogical and ethical requirement, which is facilitated by professional development of the faculty, often in collaboration with the national agencies and NGOs.

Limitations, Challenges and Critiques

The shift to universality and inclusiveness is not unhindered. The landscape is determined by faculty resistance, lack of funding, policy deficiencies and inertia. A U.S. study by Wells et al. (2022) affirmed the ongoing disparities in student achievement and student retention based on a lack of support and exclusionary school culture (Wells et al., 2022).

In addition to that, one also has the risk of the so-called checklist fatigue, when superficial involvement or compliance takes the place of systemic change. Case studies caution against software implementation or physical retrofitting the concept of real equity without the leadership vision, strategic investment, and accountability; the payback on the inclusive policy is low (Hills, 2022).

The digital divide continues to exist across international borders. The data during the pandemic indicate that marginalised students, based on their race, disability, rurality or economic background, have more challenges with connectivity and participation. The disproportionate losses related to enrollment and persistence among Latinx, Black, Native American, and international students supported the urgency of deliberate, equity-based design to digital transformation (DEI and Digital Learning - WCET, 2021).

Conclusion: The Way Forward

This is evident in the literature: the theoretical bases of ADI in higher education should be interpreted as an appeal to systemic transformation as well as to day-to-day practice, on the institutional leadership level down to the implementation of courses. Long-term transformation depends upon:

- Making the policy, pedagogy, and infrastructures of inclusive design and UDL mainstream;
- Development of equity cultures based on leadership, participatory practices, and investment strategies;
- Regularly considering and updating models to address emerging technology, student diversity, and cross-sectoral issues.

These foundations, as will be further discussed in this chapter, will be tied to actionable models, focusing on illustrative case studies and campuses being built beyond theory to make campuses accessible, diverse, and inclusive.

ADOPTING CONCEPTUAL MODELS

Fairness in Online Education and Managerial Support

Universities in modern times are aware that digital transformation is not a technological initiative but a multi-dimensional equity issue. The use of a few best practice models illustrates the efforts of institutional leaders to close resource gaps and build an inclusive digital space. The first strong strategy is the centralisation of learning infrastructure across the institution, which is dynamic. An example is the Cuyahoga Community College, which operates faculty learning communities which practice continuous curriculum redesign, professional development, and deployment of adaptive courseware. Such communities also combine data and instructional methods and achieve quantifiable improvements in pass rates of students in a number of gateway courses (Every Learner Everywhere, 2022).

The other model that can be successfully employed is the My Online Readiness Experience (M.O.R.E.) course at Tri-C, where the acquisition of digital skills by every new student is required. This provides a digital literacy standard that is universal, which supports first-generation and non-traditional learners, with structured resources and graded modules. Some colleges, like Ivy Tech Community College, have also experimented with centralised course development, which guarantees all students access to the same, high-quality materials. The outcome has been reduced withdrawal rates in core courses- a significant move in resolving the traditional equity gap (7 Inspiring Initiatives That Centre Equity in Digital Learning - Every Learner Everywhere, 2022).

Universities are also capitalising on Open Educational Resources (OER) and flat-fee courses and course materials initiatives to make sure that all learners have affordable and instantly accessible options. The Tennessee Board of Regents, as an example, will coordinate a system-wide OER adoption, and system-level personnel will have incentives to do so. Such efforts have led to over a million saved by the students and an immediate beneficial effect on course equality, especially among marginalised learners (Every Learner Everywhere, 2022).

Student Support and Engagement Strategies

Digital communication technology is gradually being used as a complement to individualised interventions in support models. Some of the engagement strategies are digital mentorship programs, peer-to-peer video chats, and interest-based mentor matching. Moreover, colleges are using social media and internal news feeds to create all-inclusive online communities - allowing students to create study groups, exchange resources, and networks, despite being physically apart. Student support based on data, like predictive analytics dashboards, enables academic advisors and student support personnel to recognise students at risk of disengagement and proactively reach out to them, with counselling and study resources.

AI-driven conversational agents are increasingly used to scale student support services. Kuhail et al. (2023) observe that educational chatbots can effectively handle routine advising inquiries and provide 24/7 support, significantly reducing the administrative burden on staff while maintaining student engagement. Recent qualitative studies highlight the complex lived experiences of students in these hybrid environments. Allen et al. (2024) note that while AI and digital tools offer convenience, students often report feelings of isolation and a lack of 'belonging' when human interaction is entirely replaced by automated systems. Integrating the student voice into the design process is therefore not just a courtesy, but a requirement for functional accessibility (Crompton & Burke, 2023).

Inclusive Administrative Models

Digital administration should be inclusive, which means it must be coordinated, work across units, and allocate resources effectively. Universities that are considered best-practice are not focusing on compliance-based checklists anymore; rather, they are adopting approaches that are integrated and campus-wide, and essentially appreciate transparency, participatory planning and continual evaluation. As explained by Kezar and Posselt (2020), reflective practice on the administrative level implies that leaders foresee the experience of the stakeholders, embrace change as an iterative process, and engage the marginalised groups at every phase of digital transformation. Organisations that effectively align their IT, student affairs, teaching and learning, and disability services tend to centralise the management of digital inclusion and allocate regular technology audits and engagement evaluations (Understanding Organisational Approaches to Digital Accessibility - Jackson, 2023).

Based on case studies, it is found that institutions, which associate digital access with equity and mission achievement, not only the mitigation of legal risks, are more effective in maintaining meaningful change. The result of this attitude is a continuous development of the faculty, the formation of collaboration task forces, and the appointment of special accessibility officers. In the case of Baylor University, to make digital accessibility an institutional value, the university prioritised access and equity goals in its strategic plan and ensured consistent engagement with the campus partners and students with disabilities (Jackson, 2023).

World Case Studies and Benchmarking

The national policy and the local innovation nationwide are the two guiding forces behind successful models of equitable digital transformation internationally. OECD nations have given digital equity priority by setting national agendas and institutional benchmarking. According to the report published by the OECD in 2023, universal high-speed broadband, opportunities provided by governments in the form of financial incentives, and teacher upskilling have had a positive effect on reducing digital inequality and promoting inclusion. In Australia, Canada, and the Netherlands, they are characterised by coordinated accessibility audits, digital equity taskforces, and strong student feedback loops, which result in systemic changes across the sector in terms of participation and graduation (Digital equity and inclusion in education - OECD, 2023).

The University of Groningen (Netherlands) introduced a data-driven digital accessibility initiative, which monitors compliance with the site and user interaction through analytics. The university dashboard measures the progress of accessibility to the European requirements, and the outcomes would be used to make sound investments in curriculum and technologies (ACM, 2025).

Singapore Management University in the Asia-Pacific implemented a blended learning model, characterised by the universal design principles, unified technology platforms and the program of peer mentorships, which led to the highest ratings of accessibility and student interaction to date.

Technology Platforms and Adaptive Learning

The most effective online educational models not only deliver content but also stick to the academic and social needs of learners. Colleges are implementing adaptive to predictive platforms, like Civitas or EAB Navigate, which deploy predictive analytics to personalise learning paths, identify students at risk, and prescribe real-time interventions. Engagement has greatly increased with interactive courseware and tutoring AI (e.g. the chatbot at Georgia State University, which supports advising and retention) has demonstrated great benefits in first-generation, rural, and historically marginalised students (Ensuring Digital Equity: Bridging the Gap in Online Education - The Hyperstack, 2025).

In addition, immersive curricular technologies, including simulation and virtual reality ones, are accessible to everyone, which allows all learners to experience a hands-on experience and supports various academic fields. The development of faculty is still central to such efforts; frequent workshops and learning communities assist professors in using inclusive design, digital pedagogy, and adaptive feedback tools.

Administrative Access, Policy and Participation

Equity in the digital campuses can be attained administratively by ensuring that the tools and resources are available to all the stakeholders, such as students, faculty, and staff. Flat-rate systems and centralised procurement make access to key technologies democratic, and the digital information systems make enrolment, financial aid, and timetable plain sailing. An example of this would be the provision of loaner devices and internet hotspots to financially constrained and geographically disadvantaged students within California State University, which flattens the academic playing field (7 Inspiring Initiatives That Centre Equity in Digital Learning - Every Learner Everywhere, 2022).

Engaging in the process of decision-making participation enables stakeholders, particularly minoritised or underrepresented groups, to design technological solutions together, conduct audits of available resources to identify barriers, and offer innovative policies. These approaches incorporate faculty councils, student governments and accessibility advisory boards.

Indian Perspectives

Driven by India's National Education Policy (NEP) 2020, digital equity and inclusion have been the focus of major universities such as Christ University and IIT Bombay that are implementing smart campus platforms, personalised student dashboards, multilingual outreach, and learning analytics. The supply of digital access to the rural, low-income, and first-generation learners has additionally been facilitated through peer support networks and community partnerships.

Beyond the Indian perspective, the international research is increasingly demanding that institutions not only devise but also rigorously measure, evaluate, and refine their digital accessibility and inclusion strategies. The National Disability Centre's Student Access Report (2025) features the Campus Accessibility Measure (CAM), which is an evidence-based instrument that the leading colleges use to determine the levels of support in classrooms, campuses, and social engagement for students with disabilities. The CAM data points to the accommodation processes, faculty disability awareness, and flexible learning options as the areas where the most significant challenges exist — these issues are directly related to student retention and persistence. The report underlines that creating real accessibility involves changes in both policy and campus culture, such as flexible attendance, strong support services, faculty training, and early outreach during admissions (A National Report on Disabled College Student Experiences - National Disability Centre, 2025).

Inclusive models that take into account various aspects of individuals' lives and that are being developed through anti-racism, disability support, gender equality, mental health, widening access for refugees, and fighting harassment are illustrated by the EUTOPIA Alliance, a broad international collaboration, among others. The projects demonstrated that the futures for inclusion can be built by combining universal design, the hiring of diverse staff, technology-enabled engagement, and the provision of targeted support for minoritised groups. At the same time, they remind institutions to incorporate students' lived experiences, continuously review their practices and be aware of different cultural perspectives of equity and inclusion (Inclusion Case Studies - EUTOPIA, 2022).

Thus, the recognition of diversity, inclusion, and accessibility as not only moral imperatives but also strategic assets for institutional reputation, funding, and sustainability is growing significantly. A diverse campus is a place that top talents would want to join, where innovations would be fostered, and new philanthropic and research funding sources would be unlocked. Contemporary models, as a response to mental health and neurodiversity, emphasise the importance of supporting wellness, facilitating access to counselling, and providing universal mental health training for faculty and staff. The University of Florida's integrated model—consisting of expanded counseling, student-led programming, and preventative outreach—is recognized as a leading model that connects student well-being with overall success and belonging thus making the point that equity has to include the mental and emotional aspects of campus life (12 Higher Ed Challenges in 2025 and Exemplars Solving Them - Changing Higher Ed, 2025).

Furthermore, the educational organisations are advancing in such fields as artificial intelligence (AI) and data analytics, where they use automated accessibility verifications, customised learning trails, and instant feedback mechanisms to align their efforts in closing the gaps. However, the scientists caution not to accept algorithmic bias uncritically and suggest the presence of different voices during the implementation and evaluation of AI. Recent research publications reveal that the effectiveness of AI-driven tools can be significantly improved by introducing participatory feedback cycles, conducting regular accessibility audits, and engaging co-curricular activities, thus making sure that the digital transformation is human-centred (Where AI Meets Accessibility: Considerations for Higher Education - Every Learner Everywhere, 2025).

One of the issues that is being raised quite strongly is that the layered approach, which lies at the core of the sustainable and scalable models for accessibility, diversity, and inclusion, is advantageous in many ways: this approach unites regulatory compliance, participatory leadership, international benchmarking, technological innovation, and openness to student feedback. As colleges put into practice more sophisticated tactics and instruments for measurement, the necessity of continuous learning and adjustment will be crucial in their endeavours to close equity gaps and harness the transformative potential of higher education.

These concepts are reflected in several institutional models around the world, as summarised in Table 1 below.

Table 1. Equity and Inclusion Implementation Models

Model	Example Institution	Key Practices	Outcomes
Adaptive Courseware and FLCs	Cuyahoga Community College (USA)	Collaborative faculty redesign, adaptive platforms	Higher pass rates, retention
Digital Skills Programs	Tri-C, Singapore Management Univ.	Mandated digital skill courses, blended learning	Improved digital literacy
Centralized/OER Courses	Ivy Tech, Tennessee Board of Regents	Consistent, free course materials, grants	Reduced costs, increased equity
Predictive Analytics & AI	Georgia State Univ.	Chatbots, at-risk flagging, personalized support	Retention gains, personalized advising
Accessibility Audits/ Taskforces	Groningen, Australian univ., Canada	Data dashboards, regular user input, policy	Measurable progress, accountability
Flat-fee Tech/Device Provision	CSU, Christ University (India)	Loaner devices, hot spots, multi-lingual access	Level academic field, participation

CHALLENGES AND ETHICAL CONSIDERATIONS

Digital Divide and Persistence of Inequities

Digital divide is one of the most widespread and multi-layered problems of digitally transformed institutions of higher learning. The gap reaches beyond the differences in access to high-speed internet and sufficient devices to include disparities in digital literacy and economic differences, as well as a lack of access to adaptive technologies that hold significance in the case of students with disabilities and those with a marginalised background. Marginalised students, especially students in rural, low-income, minority, and first-generation backgrounds, have multiplied digital disadvantages that directly impact their academic participation and performance (Public Policy Institute of California, 2025).

Information provided by the 2025 National Disability Centre report demonstrates that almost half of all students with disabilities experience barriers in their use of digital platforms because of uneven accessibility, the absence of assistive technologies, and institutional support. Furthermore, the shifting pandemic dynamics improved the focus on these gaps, triggering emergency investments in the digital infrastructure, as well as highlighting the vulnerability of equitable access in most environments (A National Report on Disabled College Student Experiences - National Disability Centre, 2025).

Other major differences can also be observed in the quality of engagement and digital literacy. A study by the Internet Society (2025) defines a new digital divide based on the parameters of digital fluency and use: regardless of whether access is provided, disadvantaged groups do not always use education technology to the depth level to thrive, which further increases education disparities. Therefore, fair digital access cannot be achieved without a careful approach; infrastructure, training in digital skills, affordability and design of education should be prioritised equally (The New Digital Divide - Internet Society, 2025).

Discrimination and Ethics in Computerised Systems.

The quick adoption of AI-based learning technologies brings ethical threats such as algorithmic bias and systemic exclusion. Such predictive analytics as student risk assessment or automated grading systems can reproduce social biases already existing, unless training sets are diverse or validated to a high level. Marginalised communities have suffered the most due to these risk factors, which is why it is important to make sure that institutions perform frequent audits of their algorithms and include various stakeholders in the design and assessment to promote fairness (Where AI Meets Accessibility - Every Learner Everywhere, 2025).

Moreover, learning resources may implement strict designs that cannot support different learning styles and cultural backgrounds, which restricts the inclusivity of international, neurodivergent, and disabled learners. It is being promoted that faculty awareness and institutional policies which put a priority on inclusive design and responsible deployment are the key to alleviating these threats.

Policy Alignment and Institutional Responsibilities.

The ability to effectively deal with ADI challenges is based on the match between the institutional policies and digital transformation plans. Disjointed strategies tend to create uneven student experiences and undermine accountability models. Other institutions like the Ohio State University have established standards with built-in digital inclusion policies, ongoing accessibility audits, and open processes of stakeholder engagement. The integration of digital accessibility in procurement, budgeting, and staffing policies supports the organisational commitment and resources (Understanding Organisational Approaches to Digital Accessibility - Jackson, 2023).

A form of governance that encourages inclusive participation, particularly of the marginalised groups, in the decision-making processes has been vital in coming up with policies that are sound and sound in their implementation. The continued gathering of data and publicly announced improvements hold institutions responsible and contribute to constant change.

Ethical Leadership and Change in Culture.

The culture of campus-wide transformation, founded on ethical leadership, instils the ADI values. Those leaders who champion such causes make it easy to adopt inclusive technology, equal distribution of resources, and participative governance. The leadership development programs are becoming more oriented toward training cultural competence, anti-bias training and inclusive pedagogy among faculty and administrators. ADI-centred programs, designed not to be compliant with the law but to make institutional mission, provide resilient, inclusive communities and improve student success and satisfaction (Refocusing on Diversity, Equity, and Inclusion - HigherEdToday, 2021).

Practical and Operation-related difficulties.

Operation gaps still exist in spite of improvements. Institutions lack funds and technological capacity to undertake upgrades on system-wide accessibility. The unwillingness of the faculty, conflicting priorities, and irregular technical support also make total adoption more complex. Moreover, the fast-changing technology and the requirements of accessibility mean that it is necessary to continuously invest in personnel training and infrastructure renewal cycles in order to avoid noncompliance as well as a responsive environment (Advancing IDEAS - Hanging Together, 2025).

The use of student data, surveillance, and consent in the digital learning setting raises privacy and ethics concerns, which require transparent policies and the involvement of students to create a balance between innovation and protection of rights.

Ethical Issues and Opportunities of the Future.

In anticipation of new ethical challenges associated with AI bias, digital surveillance, data privacy, and digital exhaustion, universities need to take initiatives. Integrating participatory governance, clear AI policies, and stringent privacy-by-design principles are the keys to safe and fair application of new technologies. The responsible use of AI and immersive technologies can bring a transformative, inclusive educational experience, assuming that different stakeholder voices are included in the design and assessment at each stage of technology usage (Where AI Meets Accessibility - Every Learner Everywhere, 2025).

In Summary

Digital divide, algorithmic discrimination, institutional accountability, leadership culture and operational logistics are intersecting issues in digitally transformed higher education. Overcoming these requirements takes evidence-based, equity-focused, and complex strategies. The institute, which incorporates ADI as a strategic focus, engages in ethical leadership, invests in lifelong learning and professional growth and observes an open system of governance, will be in the best position to provide inclusive, accessible, and equitable academic experiences that can bridge historic disparities and guarantee success among all students.

Measuring Impact: KPIs and Assessment Frameworks

To move beyond performative inclusion, institutions must adopt rigorous frameworks to evaluate the efficacy of ADI initiatives. Ruggi et al. (2024) argues that Key Performance Indicators (KPIs) in higher education must evolve from simple enrollment metrics to complex indices that measure student engagement, accessibility compliance rates, and the utilization of support services. Effective evaluation frameworks often track specific data points such as the time-to-resolution for accommodation requests and the percentage of course materials meeting WCAG 2.1 standards.

Financial Implications and Scalability

Implementing these advanced technologies presents significant financial challenges, particularly for smaller or publicly funded institutions. Financial constraints often limit the scope of diversity initiatives, forcing institutions to prioritize compliance over innovation. However, the long-term cost of exclusion—manifested in lower retention rates and potential legal liabilities—often outweighs the initial investment in inclusive technology. Scalability remains a critical hurdle; while pilot programs for AI tutoring may succeed in small cohorts, rolling these out university-wide requires robust cloud infrastructure and sustainable funding models.

FUTURE DIRECTIONS

Building Inclusive, Sustainable, and Culturally Responsive Campuses

The future of higher education is in the creation of digitally intelligent but inclusive, sustainable, and strongly receptive to the cultural diversity of the learners on a campus. The studies highlight that the process of inclusion is dynamic- it demands constant conversation, adjustment and creativity. Universities need to strengthen collaboration with local communities, policymakers, and international networks in co-constructing learning spaces that are diverse in terms of identities, language, and socio-economic conditions (The Inclusive Campus of the Future: Diversity, Equity, and Inclusion - Stuart et al., 2023).

The concept of smart campuses is becoming more closely connected with sustainability, be it environmental or social. The digital transformation strategies should be in line with the environmentally-friendly infrastructure investments, responsible data management, and digital wellness schemes responding to the psychological and physical burden of connectedness on students and staff. The new regenerative campus models are aimed at minimising the carbon footprint of digital activities and building resilience to achieve long-term equity and access objectives (A Sustainable University: Digital Transformation and Beyond - PMC, 2022).

Equitable Technology Adoption Strategic Planning.

The strong strategic planning is an iterative institution-wide initiative, not an isolated venture. The example of the University of Washington and Georgia State University illustrates that the implementation of equity metrics in the process of technology acquisition, the design of user experience, and learning analytics can result in a more effective fit to the needs of different learners.

Effective strategic frameworks will have flexible policy mandates, cross-unit governance frameworks and open communication. The continuous development of the faculty and staff is an important tool that helps to keep up with the new standards of accessibility and pedagogical innovations. To balance between technological innovation and social inclusion, the continuous assessment process, co-designing of the system with students and faculty, and responsive systems are necessary to negotiate technological change with an equity perspective (Digital Transformation in Higher Education: 7 Areas to Improve Digital Learning - EDUCAUSE, 2022).

Embracing the Power of Enabling Technology.

The focus on emerging technologies, artificial intelligence (AI), machine learning, extended reality (XR), and blockchain also has a lot of potential to increase inclusion when based on ethical and accessible grounds. AI can individualise learning and offer differentiated learning trajectories and support to neurodiverse and disabled learners, whereas XR is able to offer immersive experiential learning that transcends physical and cognitive barriers.

Nonetheless, such tools require proper design and administration to prevent the continuation of prejudices or ostracism. Blockchain exhibits the potential of transparent credentialing and safe student data management, offering novel sources of confidence and encompassment. Such technologies are being piloted by early adopters such as MIT and Stanford using equity-based models, which prepare a wider adoption (Where AI Meets Accessibility: Considerations for Higher Education - Every Learner Everywhere, 2025).

Innovation in Policy and Moving the World Together.

The future of success lies in policy innovation within the institutions and across the jurisdictions. On the national and international levels, such as the Global Education Coalition of UNESCO, the standard accessibility benchmarks and support mechanisms are recommended, which may facilitate the sharing of knowledge and coordinated investments.

International cooperation increases the rate of access of the best practices, financing, and technological innovation. Digital repositories that are open access, shared, and cross-border research collaborations enhance the institutional ability to provide inclusive education at scale. Moreover, the policy should focus on the education workforce, considering the inclusion of competencies in both accreditation and certification systems (Digital Transformation Collaborative - UNESCO, 2024).

Developing Ethical AI and Data Governance

As AI becomes a major part of the academic world, its ethical governance should definitely be kept on the agenda. Universities need to create a set of values that would make them more transparent, less biased, privacy-preserving, user-empowering, and AI-using to augment, but not replace, the human interaction.

Digital transformation strategies at institutions of higher learning have to include data governance instruments like privacy and consent procedures. Students and staff get more empowered and confident when they are openly communicated with in regard to data usage. Through faculty and staff professional development programs (together with student curricula), the institutions, which may become the first ones to demonstrate leadership in teaching AI ethics, can not only transmit but also instil the values of the practice (Ethical AI Frameworks in Education - EDUCAUSE, 2025).

Exploring the Future of Faculty and Students' Preparedness in an Inclusive Digital Future

To keep the ball rolling, universities are obliged to provide continual faculty training on how to make inclusive design and digital accessibility a natural part of the regular teaching process. Correspondingly, students ought to be equipped with digital literacy skills and critical digital citizenship, as well as self-advocacy tools, in order to thrive and feel safe while working with the cutting-edge technologies.

Inclusion is deeply embedded in the academic value system, which is further affirmed by curricular revision that encompasses DEI and universal design. Participation and relevance are elevated through co-creation models whereby students are engaged in curriculum development, governance, and support services.

Summary

Access, diversity, and inclusion in digitally transformed universities of the future will be contingent upon how these values are embedded in environmentally friendly campus construction, strategic utilisation of technology, ethical governance, and stakeholders' active engagement. Through the judicious use of emerging technologies, the imperative to collaboration, and the never-ending investment in human capabilities, institutions are in a position to actualise the vision of equitable, inclusive, and transformative higher education, which, in turn, empowers every learner.

CONCLUSION

This chapter has examined the complex aspects of the concept of accessibility, diversity, and inclusion (ADI) in the framework of digitally transformed higher education. It examined theoretical principles such as the universal design and social equity theories, practical models of application in detail, considered longstanding issues and ethical concerns, and presented future-focused directions towards creating sustainable, inclusive, and responsive smart campuses in terms of culture. The combination of literature synthesis, institutional case study and use of emerging technologies all support the idea that equitable digital change in universities requires deliberate, systemic and participatory efforts.

By the very heart of it, the chapter makes it clear that digital transformation in higher education is not a goal but a tool to establish a learning environment where all students, irrespective of their background and ability, can succeed, engage actively, and achieve their potential. This necessitates the design of digital tools, pedagogy, infrastructure, policy, and support services with a fundamental overhaul in universities.

The first strategy is universal design of the environment and curricula. Concepts like multiple means of engagement, representation and action (Universal Design for Learning) note the need to plan ahead of student diversity and not to accommodate them as they go. Many examples of this can be found upon viewing numerous institutions across the globe that have successfully made efforts to incorporate the concept of universal design into the planning and development of courses, as well as the campus physical facilities, which in turn have significantly contributed to increased accessibility in learning, in addition to student satisfaction, retention and results.

Besides universal design, equity-centred policies have to address the fact that there are systemic inequalities, which are not only related to physical or digital access, but also include issues such as affordability, digital literacy, social belonging, and representation in faculty and governance. The social equity model requires that universities take the initiative to thoroughly examine their institutional barriers, challenge their implicit biases, and, on top of that, by involving more people in participatory governance and organising culturally relevant activities, they should raise the voices of those who are most silenced.

The models and the corresponding case-study research that have been analysed point to the fact that the success of putting these models into practice depends on the elements of strategic leadership, cross-unit work, and long-term investment. The institutional core that leads to success is faculty professional development, the use of adaptive technology, the centralisation of accessibility services, and inclusive administrative processes. Although predictive analytics, AI-based advising, and immersive technologies could be very helpful, they should be regulated ethically, and there should be a constant check to make sure that no algorithmic bias or invasion of privacy occurs.

However, in their implementations, they come up against many challenges of the real world, such as the ongoing digital divisions, which concern infrastructure, affordability, and digital literacy and which, consequently, hinder the full participation of a great number of students. The capacities of institutions are put to the test by the resistance of faculty, lack of money, misalignment of policies and rapid technological changes. Moreover, the moral problems of AI fairness, data privacy, and surveillance raise serious governance issues that necessitate participative discussions and clearly defined frameworks.

Thinking from a future viewpoint, fair and inclusive online campuses will be those that have embraced comprehensive strategies combining technology, pedagogy, community engagement, ethical leadership, and policymaking. To name a few, AI, XR, and blockchain have the potential to revolutionise inclusion to such a degree that, without robust participatory design, privacy protection, and long-term equity impact review, they might not be enabled at all. The key issues will be the formation of international partnerships, national policy framework conformity as well as the broadening of student-centred digital literacy initiatives.

Moreover, colleges need to develop atmospheres where these issues are not considered separate from each other but the basic elements of inclusion. At the same time, a very important issue is the problem of providing professors and students with the awareness, instruments, and drive to be able to implement inclusion practice. By placing accessibility, diversity, and inclusion at the core of the digital transformation strategy, higher education will not only deliver the characteristics of being transformative, fair, and responsive, but also become one of the vibrant societal pillars.

Therefore, the chapter advocates for a digital transformation approach that is active, systemic, and ethical in nature, which is against technological determinism, but rather concentrates on human values, justice, and engagement. The real-world data, models, and case studies presented here are intended to be a roadmap for institutions that are committed to the creation of smart campuses where all learners will be able to thrive.

With the digital transformation that is happening in higher education, accessibility, diversity, and inclusion are not merely the needs of the present time but, at the same time, the foundation of quality and the condition for equity.

Further studies are required to develop longitudinal results of digital inclusion initiatives, intercultural contrasts of inclusive campus approaches, and the effects of new technologies on the learning equity and institutional culture. It urges policymakers to facilitate harmonisation of the standards, investment in infrastructure growth and inclusive workforce development. To practitioners, the continued discussions, the use of data to hold them accountable, and placing the student voices at the centre are all irreplaceable.

Finally, the digital transformation process of universities has the potential to change everything, but only in case it is accompanied by profound and long-term investment in accessibility, diversity and inclusion. This way, not only will higher education institutions meet the changing requirements, but will indeed transform themselves into the opportunities, innovation, and equity space of the 21 st century and beyond.

REFERENCES

ACM. (2025). Digital accessibility in higher education: A Dutch case study. https://dl.acm.org/doi/10.1145/3715885.3715890

AHEAD. (2022). *Not another 'thing': Practical application of Universal Design for Learning to higher education.* AHEAD Journal.

Allen, K.-A., Slaten, C., Hong, S., Lan, M., Craig, H., May, F., & Counted, V. (2024). Belonging in Higher Education: A Twenty Year Systematic Review. *Journal of University Teaching & Learning Practice*, *21*(05). Advance online publication. DOI: 10.53761/s2he6n66

CAST. (2024). Universal Design for Learning guidelines. http://udlguidelines.cast.org

CAST. (2025). Case studies on universal design for learning. https://www.cast.org/our-impact/case-studies/

Changing Higher Ed. (2025). 12 higher ed challenges in 2025 and exemplars solving them. https://changinghighered.com/higher-ed-challenges-2025-solution-examples/

Crompton, H., & Burke, D. (2023). Artificial intelligence in higher education: The state of the field. *International Journal of Educational Technology in Higher Education*, *20*(1), 22. DOI: 10.1186/s41239-023-00392-8

EDUCAUSE. (2022). Digital transformation in higher education: 7 areas for enhancing digital learning. https://er.educause.edu/articles/2022/9/digital-transformation-in-higher-education-7-areas-for-enhancing-digital-learning

EUTOPIA Alliance. (2022). Inclusion case studies. https://eutopia-university.eu/english-version/inclusion/inclusion-case-studies

Every Learner Everywhere. (2022). 7 inspiring initiatives that center equity in digital learning infrastructure. https://www.everylearnereverywhere.org/blog/7-inspiring-initiatives-that-center-equity-in-digital-learning-infrastructure/

Every Learner Everywhere. (2025). Where AI meets accessibility: Considerations for higher education. https://www.everylearnereverywhere.org/wp-content/uploads/Where-AI-Meets-Accessibility-Final.pdf

FIU Inclusive Campus Project. (2023). The inclusive campus of the future: Diversity, equity, and inclusion literature review. Florida International University. https://ilxr.fiu.edu/2023

Hanging Together. (2025). Advancing IDEAs: Inclusion, diversity, equity, accessibility, and ADA. https://hangingtogether.org/advancing-ideas-inclusion-diversity-equity-accessibility-18-march-2025/

HigherEdToday. (2021). Refocusing on diversity, equity, and inclusion during the pandemic. https://www.higheredtoday.org/2021/01/13/refocusing-diversity-equity-inclusion-pandemic-beyond-lessons-community-practice/

Hills, J. (2022). Faculty perspectives on UDL: Exploring bridges and barriers. *Journal of Postsecondary Education and Disability*, *35*(1), 12–27.

IADT. (2025). UDL case studies booklet. https://iadt.ie/wp-content/uploads/2025/01/UDL-Case-Studies-Booklet.pdf

Internet Society. (2025). The new digital divide. https://pulse.internetsociety.org/blog/the-new-digital-divide

Jackson, R. (2023). Understanding organizational approaches to digital accessibility. *Journal of Education Technology*, *19*(2), 45–59.

Kezar, A., & Posselt, J. (2020). *Higher education administration for social justice and equity*. Critical Perspectives for Leadership.

Kuhail, M. A., Alturki, N., Alramlawi, S., & Alhejori, K. (2023). Interacting with educational chatbots: A systematic review. *Education and Information Technologies*, *28*(1), 973–1018. DOI: 10.1007/s10639-022-11177-3

National Disability Center. (2025). A national report on disabled college student experiences. https://nationaldisabilitycenter.org/2025-student-access-report.pdf

OECD. (2023). Digital equity and inclusion in education. https://one.oecd.org/document/EDU/WKP(2023)14/en/pdf

Oxford University. (2024). Faculty professional development through blended-learning. *Oxford Education Review*, *48*(3), 135–147.

Ovink, H. (2022). Leveraging the Past for Better Futures. *Blue Papers*, *1*, 4–5.

PMC. (2022). A sustainable university: Digital transformation and beyond. https://pmc.ncbi.nlm.nih.gov/articles/PMC8935252/

Ruggi, L. O., Oliveira Ruggi, L., & Duvvury, N. (2024). Grassroots Key Performance Indicators: A Contribution to the Monitoring and Evaluation of Equality, Diversity, and Inclusion (EDI) Initiatives in Higher Education. *Journal of Research in Higher Education*, *7*(2), 5–22. DOI: 10.24193/JRHE.2024.2.1

Stuart, L.. (2023). The inclusive campus of the future: Diversity, equity, and inclusion. *Global Education Journal*, *12*(1), 55–78.

Surjawan, D. J., Langi, A. Z., & Imbar, R. V. (2025). Digital Transformation for Institution Operations in Higher Education: A Literature Review. *IEEE Access : Practical Innovations, Open Solutions*.

The Hyperstack. (2025). Ensuring digital equity: Bridging the gap in online education. https://thehyperstack.com/blog/ensuring-digital-equity-bridging-the-gap-in-online-education

University of Washington DO-IT Center. (2022). Universal design as a framework for diversity, equity, and inclusion initiatives in higher education. https://doit.uw.edu/brief/universal-design-framework

Wells, L.. (2022). Student perspectives on the use of universal design for learning. *Journal of Inclusive Education*, *26*(4), 208–224.

Wijonarko, P., Salam, A., James, B., & Ibadurrahman, A. (2023). Design and Implementation of IoT Technology of a Smart Campus with Visual Simulation Tool: *Proceedings of the 4th International Seminar and Call for Paper*, 467–470. DOI: 10.5220/0012640800003821

World Wide Web Consortium. (2025). Web accessibility initiative: Guidelines and roadmap. https://www.w3.org/WAI/

Chapter 2
AI-Driven Handwritten Text Recognition and Digital Conversion for a Smart Campus

Yash Parsai
https://orcid.org/0009-0005-1800-9083
Jaypee University of Engineering and Technology, Guna, India

Vivek Kumar Rai
https://orcid.org/0009-0000-5500-2503
Jaypee University of Engineering and Technology, Guna, India

Shreyansh Tripathi
https://orcid.org/0009-0008-4154-4641
Jaypee University of Engineering and Technology, Guna, India

Kunj Bihari Meena
https://orcid.org/0000-0001-8159-9024
Jaypee University of Engineering and Technology, Guna, India

Vipin Tyagi
https://orcid.org/0000-0003-4994-3686
Jaypee University of Engineering and Technology, Guna, India

ABSTRACT

As higher education moves toward digital and smart campuses, handwritten documents like exam answersheets, attendance registers and forms remain a major challenge. Manual data entry is time-consuming and error-prone, creating inefficiencies in aca-

DOI: 10.4018/979-8-3373-6831-3.ch002

026, IGI Global Scientific Publishing. Copying or distributing in print or electronic forms without written permission of IGI Global Scientific Publishing is prohibited. Use of this chapter to ...ive artificial intelligence (AI) technologies is expressly prohibited. The publisher reserves all rights to license its use for generative AI training and machine learning model development.

demic and administrative workflows. This chapter presents an AI-driven handwritten text recognition system that automatically converts handwritten content into digital text. The model combines structural and contextual analysis to interpret entire lines instead of individual letters, improving accuracy and adaptability across diverse writing styles. Trained on handwriting samples, it achieves significantly higher precision than traditional OCR methods. By automating digitization, the system reduces human effort, minimizes errors, and supports paperless, eco-friendly operations. This AI solution bridges the gap between traditional pen-and-paper practices and modern digital infrastructure, enhancing efficiency and sustainability within smart campus environments.

1. INTRODUCTION

In the last few years, the entire education system has undergone a major transformation, with almost every institution moving to become smart and digital. From the idea of a "smart campus" to conducting online classes and maintaining academic records, most colleges and universities now rely on digital technologies. Campus activities are now integrated with modern tools such as Artificial Intelligence (AI), the Internet of Things (IoT) and cloud computing, making academic and administrative processes more efficient and intelligent. These technologies not only simplify day-to-day tasks but also contribute to environmental sustainability and enhance the overall experience of students and faculty in an institution.

Despite these advancements, one challenge remains: designing a fast and accurate conversion system that can convert handwritten work into digital form (AlKendi et al., 2024). As handwritten text is an integral part of academic life, students write examinations, make class notes and assignments by hand, while teachers provide remarks, feedback and grades in their handwriting. Administrative forms and applications are also mainly paper-based. This is due to the absence of an effective digitization mechanism for handwritten content. As a result, much time is wasted on manual data entry and maintaining organized digital records becomes difficult.

Recent developments in AI and deep learning can be used to address this issue. Traditional Optical Character Recognition (OCR) systems have existed for over a decade but are often ineffective for diverse handwriting styles. New AI-based systems can learn and interpret different handwriting patterns, improving recognition accuracy through the combination of image processing and neural networks (Rajest & Regin, 2024). This modern approach can be effectively utilized to recognize handwriting and convert it into digital form with greater accuracy.

1.1 Role of AI in Educational Digitalization

Artificial Intelligence has revolutionized education by automating complex tasks and enabling personalized learning. From adaptive learning platforms to intelligent tutoring systems, AI is making education more efficient and accessible. On a smart campus, AI supports a variety of applications: tracking student performance, responding to queries through chatbots, automatically marking attendance using smart cameras and even grading assignments with minimal human intervention.

AI-powered systems are now used in education for various purposes, including the conversion of handwritten material into digital form (Harjanto et al., 2024). Once such a system is designed, most handwritten materials: exam papers, notes and forms can be scanned and transformed into editable text. This automation saves time, reduces human error and simplifies access and data management. Moreover, exam answer sheets can be scanned and converted automatically into text for faster and more accurate evaluation. Similarly, feedback and administrative forms can be processed automatically through AI-based tools. As handwriting recognition technology becomes part of campus management, institutions can move toward a paperless environment, saving time, resources and the environment.

1.2 Motivation

This chapter proposes a system to automate handwritten text conversion, as many institutions still depend on manual processes. Every educational institution handles thousands of handwritten papers daily, requiring someone to manually type the text for digital storage which is a slow, costly and error-prone process. Another challenge is the deterioration of physical paper over time; ink fades, paper tears and information can be lost permanently. In contrast, digital records are safe, searchable and easy to share. Automating handwritten text conversion not only saves time but also enhances transparency and sustainability.

The proposed system contributes directly to the digital transformation of educational institutions by developing an AI-based system capable of reading handwriting. This system can help in minimizing typing work, preserving handwritten records for future use and supporting individuals with physical disabilities who may find typing difficult. Additionally, AI-based handwriting systems can assist through voice commands, enabling accessibility for users with special needs.

When handwritten data is converted into digital form, it can be analyzed easily using advanced machine learning techniques. The digital text can also be read loudly by text-to-speech systems or translated into other languages as required.

1.3 Problem Statement

OCR technology has existed for more than a decade and is widely used for converting printed text into digital form. While OCR performs well with printed documents, it is ineffective for handwritten text due to variations in writing styles. The shape of letters, spacing between words and connections between characters differ from one person to another, making recognition difficult for conventional systems.

For example, the same word written by three individuals will appear quite different (Fig. 1). Traditional OCR methods do not provide good performance with such variations, especially with cursive handwriting, where letters are often joined. Segmenting cursive text into individual characters is extremely difficult and often leads to recognition errors, motivating research on joint segmentation and transcription approaches for paragraph- and line-level handwriting recognition (Raza et al., 2025, Bluche, 2016).

The main objective of this chapter is to propose an AI-powered model capable of reading handwritten text and converting it into digital form using deep learning techniques. The model aims to recognize entire words or lines without separating individual letters, thereby addressing a key challenge in developing smart campuses.

Figure 1. **Variability in handwritten word appearance**

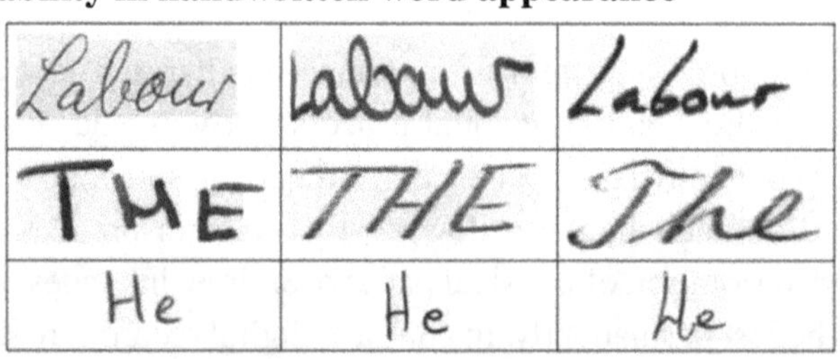

(IAM dataset by Marti and Bunke, 2002)

Specific objectives of this chapter are:

- Developing a hybrid AI model combining Convolutional Neural Networks (CNN) and Recurrent Neural Networks (RNN) to recognize handwritten words and sentences effectively (Sunori & Sumithra, 2024).
- Implementing Connectionist Temporal Classification (CTC) to enable the model to learn from whole lines of handwriting rather than labeling each character individually, improving efficiency and accuracy.
- Preprocessing handwriting images to remove noise, resize text regions and enhance clarity for better recognition.

- Conducting training and testing experiments using standard datasets such as the IAM Handwriting Dataset (Marti & Bunke, 2002).

Once trained, the model can be deployed in smart campuses for tasks such as converting handwritten exam sheets, scanning feedback forms or digitizing old records. The final aim is to help institutions transition toward a paperless, efficient and eco-friendly digital campus.

2. LITERATURE REVIEW

The origins of handwriting recognition date back to the time, when computers were massive, room-sized machines. Early systems relied on template matching, comparing handwritten letters pixel-by-pixel with stored templates. They performed well for printed text but failed to generalize to diverse human handwriting styles.

By the 1980s, systems evolved to extract meaningful features rather than relying solely on pixel comparison. Techniques such as zoning: dividing each character into small regions and counting dark pixels in each improved recognition accuracy for printed text. However, these methods still struggled with cursive writing, where distinguishing individual letters proved difficult.

The 1990s saw a major breakthrough with the introduction of Hidden Markov Models (HMMs), which treated handwriting as a sequential process similar to speech recognition. HMMs enabled more flexible recognition of connected writing, but they required pre-segmented letters for training and segmentation errors often reduced overall accuracy.

The 2000s ushered in the era of machine learning, shifting focus from rule-based systems to data-driven approaches. Algorithms such as Support Vector Machines (SVM) and k-Nearest Neighbors (k-NN) became mainstream, allowing computers to learn patterns directly from handwriting data.

Public datasets such as UNIPEN and IAM marked a turning point by enabling fair comparison between models. Researchers worldwide could now test algorithms on the same handwriting samples, accelerating progress in the field.

However, early machine learning models still depend heavily on manual eature engineering, which limited generalization across writers and document conditions, thereby motivating deep learning-based continuous handwriting recognition models (Sueiras, 2021). This process was time-consuming and required significant expertise. Moreover, these models were highly sensitive to variations in paper quality, pen thickness and noise, leading to poor generalization. This limitation created the need for systems capable of automatically identifying the most meaningful handwriting features laying the groundwork for the next revolution.

The 2010s marked a transformative period for handwriting recognition with the rise of deep learning. The success of AlexNet in 2012 demonstrated that Convolutional Neural Networks (CNNs) could automatically learn hierarchical image features directly from raw pixels. In handwriting recognition, CNNs became powerful tools for detecting edges, curves and letter shapes, similar to how humans visually process text. However, handwriting is inherently sequential and CNNs alone lacked the ability to understand context. This limitation was addressed by integrating Recurrent Neural Networks (RNNs), which process sequences and capture temporal dependencies in text (Thanushree et al., 2024).

Combining CNNs with RNNs led to remarkable improvements in continuous offline handwriting recognition, particularly when combined with CTC-based alignment-free training (Sueiras, 2021). Connectionist Temporal Classification (CTC) solved this problem by enabling the model to learn directly from entire lines of unsegmented text, aligning image features with character sequences automatically (Graves, 2012). This innovation eliminated the need for manual segmentation and enabled true end-to-end training, setting a new standard in handwriting recognition.

A Conceptual timeline showing the evolution of handwritten text recognition methods, from early template-matching and feature-based approaches to modern deep learning architectures integrating CNNs, RNNs, and CTC for end-to-end, alignment-free recognition is shown in Fig. 2.

2.1 CNN-RNN-CTC Architecture

Existing offline Handwritten Text Recognition (HTR) research has largely converged on end-to-end pipelines that combine Convolutional Neural Networks (CNNs) for visual feature extraction, Recurrent Neural Networks (RNNs); typically BLSTMs, for sequential context modeling and Connectionist Temporal Classification (CTC) for alignment-free training. CTC is a key enabling mechanism because it eliminates the need for character-level segmentation by learning to align variable-length image feature sequences with variable-length text outputs (Graves et al., 2006; Graves, 2012).

Within this model, recent works demonstrate strong benchmark performance and reason of CNN-BLSTM-CTC, a popular architecture. For example, Mahadevkar et al. (2024) report high recognition performance using a hybrid CNN-BLSTM model with a CTC decoder on standard datasets, reinforcing the effectiveness of combining spatial feature extraction with bidirectional sequential modeling. Similarly, Kizilirmak and Yanikoglu (2022) provide a comprehensive evaluation of CNN-BLSTM-CTC configurations on the IAM dataset, including the role of augmentation and decoding choices and show that word-level performance remains sensitive to difficult handwriting cases and dataset characteristics. These studies collectively indicate that CNN-RNN-CTC systems are accurate, relatively efficient and deployable, but their reported results are often obtained under controlled dataset conditions rather than noisy campus scanning environments.

However, despite these advantages, CNN-RNN-CTC systems may not perform well in real institutional inputs such as uneven lighting, shadows, skew, photocopy artifacts, ink bleed-through and low-resolution scans, which can distort stroke-level evidence and affect CNN feature stability. This motivates stronger preprocessing, augmentation strategies that reflect real capture conditions and evaluation settings closer to exam-scanning pipelines.

2.2 Character-Level and Script-Specific Models

In contrast to line-level HTR, some studies focus on isolated character recognition or script-specific classification settings. Sampath and Gomathi (2019), for example, proposed a hybrid training strategy for handwritten character recognition and showed strong character-level accuracy under constrained conditions. While such approaches are useful for controlled classification tasks, they do not directly address the sequence modeling and alignment challenges central to full-line HTR in academic documents (e.g., cursive handwriting and inter-character dependencies).

Similarly, multilingual and regional-script research shows progress but often remains at the character classification level. Dey et al. (2022) showed that transfer learning with VGG-16 improves recognition robustness across multiple Indian scripts. Although this is valuable for multilingual contexts, character-focused systems do not fully capture word-level context, cursive connectivity and line-level transcription requirements typical of examination scripts and handwritten assignments. As a result, these studies show the feasibility of extending recognition beyond English, but they also underline the need for sequence-oriented architectures and mixed-script strategies for campus deployment.

2.3 OCR-Based and Hybrid Systems

Traditional OCR based systems have also been adapted toward handwriting recognition, typically through customized preprocessing and feature design. Li et al. (2016) demonstrate the feasibility of modifying the Tesseract OCR engine for offline handwritten Chinese character recognition, reporting moderate precision. While such approaches prove that classical OCR pipelines can be extended to handwriting in constrained settings, they generally lack the end-to-end representation learning and sequence alignment capacity of modern deep-learning architectures. Consequently, OCR-engine adaptations are used as transitional methods rather than state-of-the-art HTR solutions for complex, variable handwriting found in real academic workflows.

2.4 Transformers and Multimodal LLMs

Recently, transformer-based OCR/HTR has emerged as a strong alternative to recurrent architectures. TrOCR provides an end-to-end transformer approach using pre-trained image and text transformer components and shows improvements across printed, handwritten and scene text tasks, demonstrating the value of large-scale pre-training and attention-based sequence modeling for text recognition.

Beyond transformer encoders/decoders, multimodal large language models (MLLMs) are increasingly used for OCR-like tasks due to their capability of combining vision understanding with language-level priors and contextual reasoning. A benchmarking study by Crosilla, Klic and Colavizza (2025) evaluates multiple multimodal LLMs for HTR across modern and historical datasets and shows that proprietary models can achieve competitive results in zero-shot settings, while also showing limitations in autonomous error correction and language biases linked to pre-training corpora.

Industry-facing benchmarks and leaderboards further suggest strong handwriting extraction performance for leading multimodal systems; for example, recent evaluations report high handwriting accuracy for top models under specific benchmark settings.

However, despite their promise, transformer and LLM-based OCR/HTR systems present non-trivial constraints for educational deployment: (i) computational cost (higher memory/compute at inference), (ii) privacy and compliance risks if documents are processed using external cloud services and (iii) operational dependencies and recurring costs that can be difficult for campuses with limited infrastructure. For this reason, CNN-BLSTM-CTC remains a feasible and practical solution for many institutions, particularly when complemented with robust preprocessing, realistic augmentation and an integration layer designed for institutional workflows.

2.5 Synthesis and Implications for Smart Campus Deployment

Across these themes, the literature indicates a consistent trade-off between (a) state-of-the-art accuracy and contextual robustness offered by transformer/LLM approaches and (b) the efficiency, controllability and on-premise feasibility of CNN-RNN-CTC systems. For smart campuses, where documents often include scanning noise and may involve multilingual or mixed-script usage, a pragmatic design must balance recognition performance with deployment constraints. This motivates the proposed system's emphasis on: preprocessing for real scanning conditions, CNN feature learning, BLSTM context modeling, CTC alignment-free decoding and system integration for secure, scalable use in academic and administrative pipelines.

Figure 2. Evolution of handwritten text recognition techniques

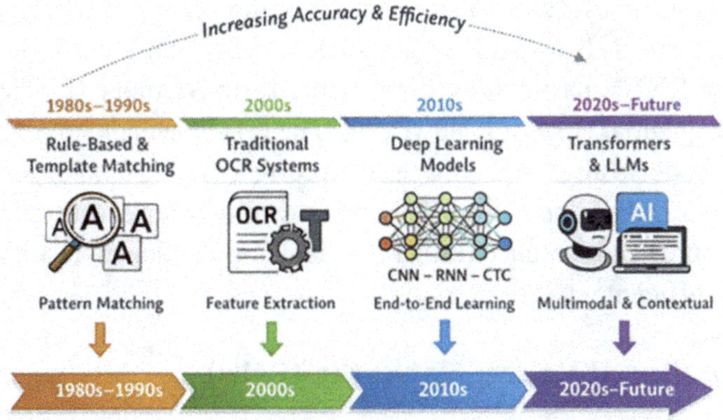

Despite significant advancements, practical implementation of handwriting recognition in educational environments remains limited (Patel et al., 2024). Most models are trained exclusively on English handwriting and perform poorly when encountering multilingual content common in countries like India. Real-world documents also contain imperfections, such as ink smudges, paper stains, or poor photocopy quality, that standard datasets fail to represent.

Moreover, while models can accurately convert handwriting to text, they often lack integration with institutional systems such as student record databases or digital archives. Manual copying and pasting are still required, defeating the purpose of automation.

Bridging this gap offers huge potential for smart campuses: automatically grading handwritten answer sheets, digitizing attendance registers, scanning application forms and instantly storing them in centralized databases. Such a system will not only enhance administrative efficiency but can reduce paper waste and contribute to sustainable, technology-driven education.

3. THEORETICAL FRAMEWORK

This section presents the underlying principles of the proposed AI-based model for handwritten text recognition. It explains why specific techniques were chosen and their contribution to building an efficient and accurate recognition system. The model integrates three major technologies: Convolutional Neural Networks (CNNs),

Recurrent Neural Networks (RNNs) and Connectionist Temporal Classification (CTC) which together form the main concept of the proposed approach.

CNNs perform well at extracting visual patterns and shapes of letters from images, while RNNs, particularly Long Short-Term Memory (LSTM) networks, capture the sequential flow of handwriting. The CTC mechanism bridges the two, enabling the model to align input images with corresponding textual outputs without the need for manual segmentation. This synergy allows for end-to-end recognition of complete words and sentences rather than isolated characters, resulting in greater accuracy and efficiency.

3.1 Convolutional Neural Networks (CNN)

A Convolutional Neural Network acts as a highly perceptive visual analyzer that automatically learns to identify features in handwriting through multiple processing layers. The initial layers detect simple shapes such as edges and curves, while deeper layers combine these features to recognize complex letter forms, for example, the curve of a "C" or the cross of a "T" .

Pooling layers are introduced to ensure the model remains robust against small variations in writing style or alignment by summarizing local information and reducing data dimensionality. This hierarchical processing allows the CNN to retain essential features while discarding irrelevant noise.

Before a CNN can "understand" a letter, it undergoes repeated cycles of filtering, pooling and transformation (Jebadurai et al., 2021). Techniques such as dropout are employed to prevent overfitting, ensuring the model generalizes well to unseen handwriting. The most powerful aspect of CNNs lies in automatic feature learning; they do not require predefined rules about what a letter looks like but instead learn distinctive features like loops, crosses and curves during training. Fig. 3 shows hierarchical feature extraction in a Convolutional Neural Network (CNN), where early layers capture low-level stroke patterns and edges and deeper layers learn increasingly abstract representations of handwritten characters. Such hierarchical features enable robustness to noise, style variation and scanning artifacts.

Figure 3. Hierarchical feature extraction in Convolutional Neural Networks

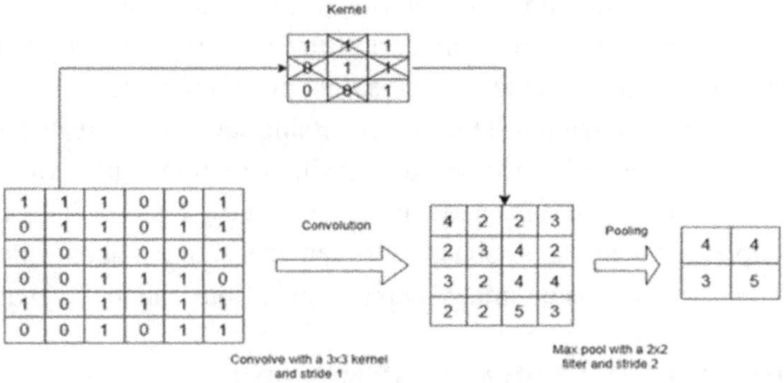

The output F of a convolutional layer in relation to a specific input image X can be expressed as follows:

$$F^k = \sigma(\Sigma_m \Sigma_n W^k{}_{mn} X(i+m)(j+n)+b^k)$$

Where *W*-weight matrix for the convolution kernel *k*; *b*- bias term; *σ*- activation function; and *i,j*- indices for the spatial dimensions of the output feature map.

In real-world handwriting recognition scenarios, particularly in exam-scanning environments, input images frequently exhibit uneven illumination, shadows, background gradients and sensor-induced noise. Such variations can significantly affect the activation patterns of convolutional neural networks if not properly addressed. CNNs learn spatial filters that respond to local intensity gradients and stroke contrasts; therefore, inconsistent lighting can cause the same handwritten stroke to generate different activation magnitudes across the image. This leads to unstable feature representations, where identical characters may be interpreted differently depending on illumination conditions rather than their actual shape. Noise and illumination artifacts primarily affect early convolutional layers, which are responsible for detecting low-level features such as edges, curves and stroke boundaries. Excessive background noise or low contrast can suppress meaningful activations, while strong shadows or overexposed regions may introduce spurious activations unrelated to handwriting. These distortions propagate through deeper layers, potentially degrading the model's ability to learn discriminative higher-level features and reducing overall recognition accuracy.

To overcome these effects, the proposed framework performs normalization and data augmentation strategies as integral components of the learning process. Intensity normalization stabilizes pixel-value distributions across documents, ensuring consistent activation ranges in convolutional filters. Additionally, training-time augmentation such as random brightness shifts, contrast variation, Gaussian noise injection and mild blurring, provides realistic scanning artifacts to the CNN. This encourages the network to learn illumination-invariant representations that focus on structural stroke patterns rather than absolute pixel intensities.

By combining normalization at the preprocessing stage with targeted augmentation during training, the CNN becomes more resilient to illumination variability and noise commonly encountered in academic document digitization. This theoretical grounding supports the model's robustness when deployed in uncontrolled campus environments, where consistent image capture conditions cannot be guaranteed.

3.2 Recurrent Neural Networks (RNN) and LSTM (Long Short-Term Memory)

While CNNs capture spatial features, handwriting is inherently sequential, with letters forming words over time rather than in isolation. Recurrent Neural Networks (RNNs) are designed to handle such sequences by maintaining a memory of previous inputs. When humans read a word, they interpret each letter in the context of preceding ones. Similarly, an RNN considers prior inputs to make more informed predictions. However, standard RNNs face a major limitation known as the vanishing gradient problem, which causes them to "forget" earlier information in long sequences.

To overcome this, Long Short-Term Memory (LSTM) networks were introduced. Internal structure of a LSTM cell is shown in Fig. 4, showing input, forget and output gates that regulate information flow over time. This mechanism enables the model to retain long-range dependencies essential for recognizing cursive and connected handwritten text.

Figure 4. Architecture of a LSTM Unit

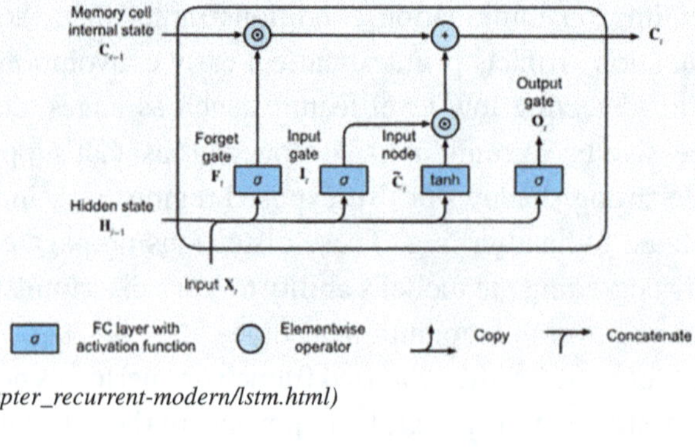

(https://d2l.ai/chapter_recurrent-modern/lstm.html)

Given any instant in time t and a given sequence of feature vectors f_t, it updates the cell state C_t and the hidden state H_t as shown below:

$$f_t = \sigma(W_f \cdot [H_{t-1}, F_t] + b_f) \quad i_t = \sigma(W_f \cdot [H_{t-1}, F_t] + b_i)$$
$$\widetilde{C}_t = \tanh(W_c \cdot [H_{t-1}, F_t] + b_c)$$
$$C_t = f_t * C_{t-1} + i_t * \widetilde{C}_t$$
$$o_t = \sigma(W_o \cdot [H_{t-1}, F_t] + b_o) H_t = o_t * \tanh(C_t)$$

where: f_t, i_t, o_t are Forget, input and output gate vectors at time t

σ: Sigmoid activation function
tan$h$: Hyperbolic tangent activation function
W_f, W_i, W_C, W_o: Weight matrices for each gate
b_f, b_i, b_C, b_o: Bias vectors
F_t: Input feature vector at time t
H_{t-1}: Previous hidden states
C_{t-1}: Previous cell state

An enhanced, Bidirectional LSTM (BLSTM), processes text in both directions; from left to right and right to left, thereby capturing complete contextual information (Graves & Schmidhuber, 2005). This dual processing leads to more accurate recognition, especially in ambiguous or cursive handwriting.

3.3 Connectionist Temporal Classification (CTC)

In most machine learning tasks, each input corresponds to a single label, for instance, an image labeled "cat." However, handwriting recognition poses a challenge: one image may represent an entire word containing multiple characters of variable length. Aligning image segments with corresponding letters is difficult and often inaccurate.

Connectionist Temporal Classification (CTC), introduced by Graves et al. (2006), addresses this challenge by allowing the model to learn alignments automatically. Instead of forcing precise segmentation, CTC computes the probability of all possible alignments between the input image and the output sequence. It introduces a special "blank" token to handle spacing and repeated characters. During decoding, repeated letters and blanks are collapsed to produce the final transcription.

For example, an output sequence such as "_h_e_lllоо" would be simplified to "hello."

The CTC loss function can be expressed as:

$$L_{CTC} = -ln(p(y \mid x))$$

Where y: target label sequence (the correct text)

- x: input image sequence
- p(y|x): probability of predicting the correct label sequence given the input

3.4 Hybrid CNN-RNN-CTC Architecture

The integration of CNN, RNN and CTC forms a unified, end-to-end handwriting recognition system (Sunori & Sumithra, 2024).

1. CNN Encoder: Extracts spatial features from the input image: edges, shapes and curves and converts them into sequential feature maps.
2. BLSTM Decoder: Processes these feature sequences bidirectionally to understand contextual relationships between characters.
3. CTC Layer: Aligns the predicted character probabilities with the target text and computes the overall sequence loss.

This architecture maximizes the probability of the correct transcription YYY given the input image XXX. The model can handle words and even full paragraphs of varying lengths, making it both flexible and scalable for educational applications. Figure 6 presents the detailed architecture of the proposed CNN-BLSTM-CTC model, showing how spatial features extracted by the CNN encoder are transformed into sequential representations processed by the BLSTM and aligned with textual outputs through the CTC layer.

Figure 5. Detailed architecture of the CNN-BLSTM-CTC model

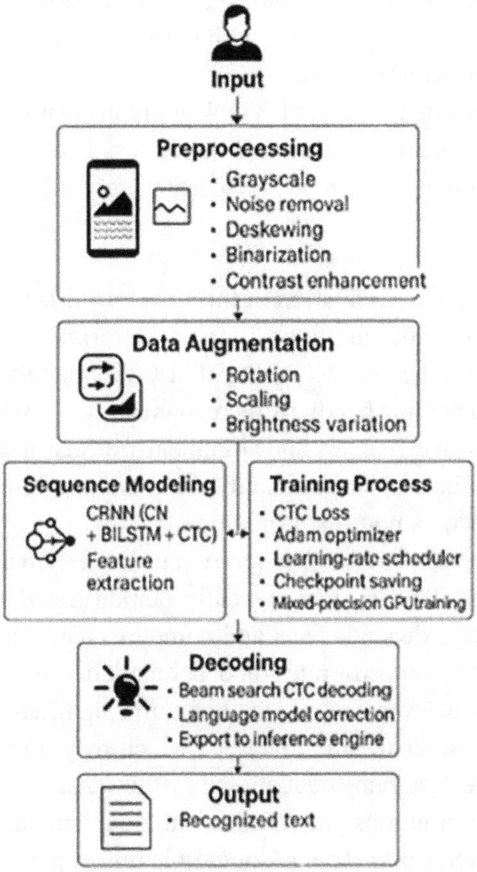

3.5 Evaluation Metrics

There are various performance evaluation parameters that can be used to check the effectiveness of the system.

- Character Accuracy (CA): This metric provides a basic character-level accuracy measure.. It is just like checking out of all the letters in the text, i.e. (Correct Characters) / (Total Characters).
- Word Accuracy (WA): This is a tougher test. Here a word is only counted as correct if every single letter in it is recognized perfectly i.e. (Perfectly Correct Words) / (Total Words).

- Word Error Rate (WER): This shows how many mistakes the model makes while reading handwriting. It counts all kinds of errors like adding an extra letter, missing one or replacing it with the wrong one. A lower WER means the model is performing better.
- Loss Curves: During training, also look at graphs that show how the model is learning. If both the training and validation loss lines go down smoothly and then level off, it means the model is learning correctly instead of just memorizing the data.

While the experimental evaluation in this chapter focuses on a CNN-BLSTM-CTC architecture, it is important to position its performance conceptually against alternative approaches. Hybrid CNN-BLSTM-CTC models represent a widely adopted baseline in academic handwriting recognition due to their balance between accuracy, computational efficiency and alignment-free learning. They perform particularly well for continuous cursive handwriting and are suitable for deployment in resource-constrained campus environments.

Transformer-based handwriting recognition models, such as Vision Transformer (ViT) variants and TrOCR, have recently demonstrated improved capability in modeling long-range dependencies and complex character interactions. These models often achieve lower error rates on benchmark datasets, especially for noisy or degraded inputs. However, they typically require significantly higher computational resources and larger training datasets, which may limit their feasibility for on-premise deployment in many educational institutions.

Commercial OCR solutions and multimodal large language models, including services such as AWS Textract and Google Gemini, further extend recognition capabilities by incorporating contextual language understanding and large-scale pre-training. While these systems often demonstrate strong performance on diverse handwriting samples, their use in academic settings raises concerns related to data privacy, recurring operational costs and dependence on external cloud infrastructure.

In the present work, direct empirical benchmarking against transformer-based models and commercial OCR services is beyond the scope of the experimental evaluation. Instead, this chapter establishes a robust CNN-BLSTM-CTC baseline suitable for smart campus deployment. Comprehensive comparative benchmarking against state-of-the-art transformer and LLM-based systems is identified as an important direction for future work, particularly to quantify trade-offs between recognition accuracy, computational cost and institutional constraints.

4. SYSTEM DESIGN AND METHODOLOGY

Designing an AI-based handwritten text recognition system for smart campus deployment requires more than strong performance on benchmark datasets; it must be robust to real-world document acquisition conditions commonly encountered in educational institutions. Examination scripts and administrative forms are often scanned in bulk under non-ideal settings, resulting in noise, uneven illumination, low resolution and physical artifacts that can significantly degrade recognition accuracy if not properly handled. The proposed methodology therefore emphasizes practical adaptability alongside algorithmic effectiveness.

4.1 Image Acquisition and Real-World Constraints

Handwritten documents are typically captured using flatbed scanners, high-speed exam scanners, or mobile cameras. In real campus environments, the acquisition process introduces several challenges:

- Exam-scanning noise: High-speed scanners often introduce salt-and-pepper noise, streaking, or compression artifacts, especially when scanning large volumes of answer sheets.
- Uneven illumination: Shadows near page boundaries, inconsistent lighting across the page, or background gradients can obscure stroke details.
- Ink bleed-through: Thin paper and heavy pen pressure may cause text from the reverse side to appear faintly in scanned images, confusing foreground–background separation.
- Low-resolution scans: To reduce storage and processing costs, documents are sometimes scanned at lower resolutions (e.g., 150 DPI), leading to blurred strokes and loss of fine details.

These factors necessitate a robust preprocessing pipeline capable of normalizing image quality before feature extraction.

4.2 Image Preprocessing for Robust Recognition

Preprocessing plays a critical role in bridging the gap between controlled training data and real-world campus documents. The proposed system employs a multi-stage preprocessing pipeline designed specifically to remove exam-scanning artifacts:

- Grayscale Conversion and Normalization: Color information is discarded to reduce computational complexity, followed by intensity normalization to stabilize contrast variations caused by uneven lighting.
- Noise Reduction: Median and Gaussian filtering techniques are applied to suppress scanner-induced noise and minor background artifacts without erasing thin handwriting strokes.
- Background Suppression and Bleed-Through Mitigation: Adaptive thresholding and morphological operations are used to distinguish foreground handwriting from background textures and faint bleed-through from reverse-side text.
- Resolution Normalization: Images are resized to a standardized resolution to ensure consistent feature scaling across documents, enabling the CNN to learn stroke patterns independent of original scan quality.
- Skew and Alignment Correction: Deskewing algorithms correct slanted text lines caused by misaligned scanning, ensuring that handwriting flows horizontally for effective sequence modeling.
- Data Augmentation (Training Phase): To improve robustness, synthetic variations such as blur, contrast shifts, slight rotations and noise injection are introduced during training to simulate real exam-scanning conditions.

Through these steps, preprocessing ensures that the recognition model receives stable and informative input, significantly improving performance under non-ideal capture scenarios.

4.3 Segmentation Strategy: Line- and Word-Level, Not Character-Level

Unlike traditional OCR systems that rely on explicit character segmentation which has been shown to be unreliable for cursive handwriting, leading to the adoption of line-level and paragraph-level end-to-end recognition approaches (Bluche, 2016). Segmenting handwritten text into individual characters is particularly error-prone in examination scripts, where letter boundaries are ambiguous and vary widely between writers.

Instead, the system adopts a line- and word-level segmentation strategy, which serves two primary purposes:

- **Structural organization:** Separating text into lines and words provides manageable input units for the recognition model while preserving the natural flow of handwriting.

- **Sequence modeling compatibility:** Line or word-level segments are well suited for sequential processing by BLSTM networks and alignment-free decoding using CTC.

Once line or word regions are extracted, no further segmentation is required. The CNN encoder converts each segment into a sequence of visual feature vectors, which the BLSTM processes bidirectionally to capture contextual dependencies across the entire word or line. The CTC layer then aligns these feature sequences with the corresponding text output automatically, without requiring explicit character boundaries.

This design choice significantly improves robustness for cursive handwriting, overlapping characters and variable writing styles commonly found in academic documents.

4.4 End-to-End Recognition Pipeline

The complete recognition workflow integrates preprocessing, segmentation and deep learning components as follows:

1. Capture scanned or photographed handwritten documents.
2. Apply preprocessing to normalize quality and suppress artifacts.
3. Segment text into lines or words.
4. Extract spatial features using a CNN encoder.
5. Model sequential dependencies using a BLSTM network.
6. Decode predictions using CTC to generate final text output.
7. Store recognized text in campus databases or document management systems.

By explicitly accounting for real-world scanning constraints and avoiding fragile character-level segmentation, the proposed methodology ensures that the system remains reliable, scalable and suitable for deployment in smart campus environments.

Figure 6 shows the complete end-to-end workflow of the a handwritten text recognition system, highlighting the sequential stages from document acquisition and preprocessing to line-level segmentation, CNN-based feature extraction, BLSTM sequence modeling and CTC-based decoding for final text generation.

Figure 6. End-to-end workflow of the handwritten text recognition system

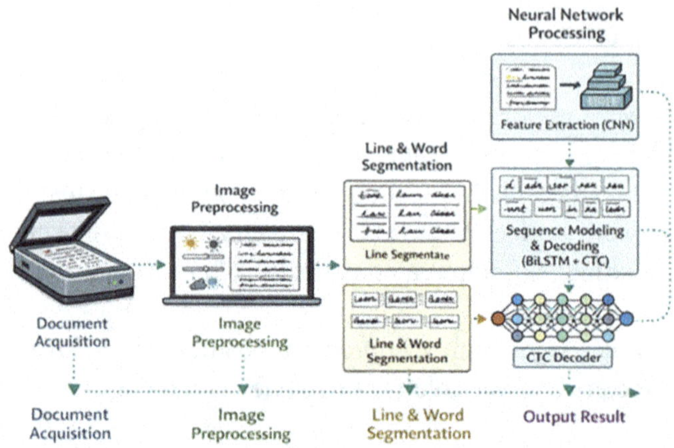

4.5 Security, Privacy, Ethics and Fairness

Security and privacy are critical considerations for handwriting recognition systems operating on academic data. The framework proposed in this chapter, adheres to data-protection principles aligned with regulations such as the General Data Protection Regulation (GDPR). Handwritten documents are processed locally within institutional infrastructure, ensuring data minimization and preventing unauthorized external access. Retention policies govern the storage duration of examination scripts and intermediate files and access is restricted through role-based controls.

Beyond data protection, ethical concerns related to bias and fairness must be addressed. Many benchmark datasets, including IAM, are Western-centric, which can result in reduced recognition accuracy for non-Latin scripts or unconventional handwriting styles. Such biases may disproportionately affect students with dysgraphia or motor impairments. To overcome such risks, the system supports data augmentation, inclusive dataset expansion and accessibility features such as text-to-speech conversion. These measures promote equitable behavior across diverse handwriting styles while maintaining academic integrity.

4.6 Hardware and Deployment Considerations

The practical deployment of handwriting recognition systems in educational institutions requires careful consideration of hardware resources. The proposed CNN-BLSTM-CTC model can be deployed on standard campus servers equipped with mid-range GPUs or even CPU-based systems for batch processing. For institutions with limited computational resources, lightweight CNN variants and optimized inference pipelines enable efficient processing at reduced cost.

Edge deployment is also feasible through model compression and mobile-optimized architectures, allowing handwritten notes or forms to be digitized using smartphones or low-power devices. This flexibility ensures scalability across departments and supports gradual adoption without significant infrastructure investment.

5. APPLICATIONS AND INTEGRATION

The practical value of AI-based handwritten text recognition extends far beyond laboratory experiments. Its real impact lies in addressing the day-to-day challenges faced by universities and colleges. When integrated into campus operations, this system serves as a powerful bridge between traditional, paper-based workflows and modern digital management systems, helping institutions transition toward a truly smart campus. Ultimately, the goal is to make academic and administrative work simpler, faster and more sustainable.

5.1 Examination System

Most universities still rely on handwritten answer booklets for examinations. Assessing, storing and retrieving these papers require significant time and manual effort. By applying the proposed Handwritten Text Recognition (HTR) model, answer sheets can be scanned and automatically converted into digital text.

This digitization provides multiple benefits:

- Automated grading: Integration with evaluation software enables faster checking and feedback generation.
- Plagiarism detection: Digital text can be analyzed easily through plagiarism detection tools.
- Efficient storage and retrieval: Digital copies eliminate the need for bulky archives and allow instant access to specific responses.

Overall, this approach reduces administrative load, improves evaluation accuracy and accelerates result processing.

5.2 Student Form Processing

Admission, library registration, hostel applications and other forms are still often filled in handwriting. Manually entering such data into the campus database is repetitive and prone to error.

Through AI-based text recognition, these handwritten forms can be scanned, converted to digital data and validated automatically. The recognized data is then seamlessly uploaded to the campus ERP (Enterprise Resource Planning) system. This automation not only saves time but also ensures data consistency and reduces human errors during form processing.

5.3 Digitization of Smart Notes

Students often prefer taking notes by hand during lectures. With the proposed system, they can simply take a photo of their handwritten notes using a mobile device. A lightweight version of the HTR model, deployed as a web or mobile application, converts these notes into editable text or searchable PDF format.

This provides several benefits:

- Students can easily edit, share and store their notes digitally.
- Notes can be accessed through cloud platforms, enabling collaborative learning.
- Digitized notes support text-to-speech conversion, improving accessibility for visually impaired learners.

Such functionality enhances inclusivity and supports personalized, technology-assisted education.

5.4 Administrative Records

Departments and administrative offices generate large volumes of handwritten documents such as meeting minutes, attendance registers, circulars and departmental communications. Digitizing these documents makes recordkeeping far more efficient.

AI-powered handwriting recognition enables: Automatic archiving of scanned administrative records, Keyword-based search across previously handwritten files and Quick retrieval of specific documents for audits or official reviews.

The system thus modernizes document management while maintaining institutional transparency and accountability.

5.5 Analytics and Environmental Impact

Once handwritten content is converted to digital data, it becomes an invaluable source for analytics and decision-making. For example:

- Correlations can be drawn between students' writing patterns (e.g., length, legibility, or response density) and exam performance.
- Insights into student engagement can be gained by analyzing feedback or handwritten reflections.
- Departments can identify trends in academic performance using automatically digitized records.

Beyond analytics, the environmental impact of digitization is significant. Reducing paper use contributes directly to eco-friendly campus initiatives by cutting printing costs, saving storage space and lowering the institution's carbon footprint.

Moreover, implementing such technology encourages digital literacy and AI skill development among students. They gain exposure to applied artificial intelligence through real-world use cases rather than purely theoretical learning.

5.6 System Integration in Smart Campuses

The effectiveness of the proposed system increases substantially when integrated with existing campus digital infrastructures. Integration points include:

- Student Information Systems (SIS) for automatic grade and attendance updates.
- ERP platforms for document storage, workflow automation and secure data exchange.
- Learning Management Systems (LMS) for uploading handwritten assignments or lecture notes directly as digital text.

Such seamless integration ensures a unified and efficient digital ecosystem across the campus. It transforms isolated manual tasks into interconnected automated processes, significantly enhancing overall institutional productivity.

5.7 Educational and Social Value

The deployment of handwriting recognition technology on campuses carries educational and societal benefits as well. It promotes sustainability, inclusivity and technological awareness among students and staff.

- Sustainability: By minimizing paper dependency, the system aligns with the Sustainable Development Goals
- Inclusivity: It supports accessibility tools such as text-to-speech, language translation and assistive writing technologies.
- Skill development: It introduces students to practical AI applications, bridging the gap between academic knowledge and industry needs.

Therefore, beyond automation, this initiative contributes to building an intelligent, inclusive and environmentally responsible campus ecosystem.

6. CHALLENGES AND FUTURE WORK

Despite the promising results achieved by the proposed CNN-BLSTM-CTC-based handwritten text recognition system, several technical, operational and pedagogical challenges remain. Addressing these limitations presents valuable opportunities for future research and system enhancement, particularly in the context of rapidly evolving AI technologies and diverse educational environments.

6.1 Integration of Transformer and Large Language Models

Recent advances in transformer-based architectures and multimodal large language models (LLMs) have demonstrated significant improvements in handwriting recognition, particularly for cursive, degraded and context-dependent text. Models such as Vision Transformers (ViTs), TrOCR and multimodal systems including Gemini and GPT-based OCR pipelines leverage self-attention mechanisms to capture long-range dependencies more effectively than traditional recurrent networks.

Future work may explore hybrid architectures that integrate transformer encoders or LLM-based post-processing modules with the existing CNN-BLSTM-CTC pipeline. Such integration could enhance contextual reasoning, improve error correction at the word or sentence level and reduce ambiguity in visually similar character sequences. However, challenges related to computational complexity, data privacy and on-premise deployment must be carefully addressed, as many educational institutions operate under constrained hardware and regulatory environments.

6.2 Self-Supervised and Data-Efficient Learning

A major limitation of current handwriting recognition systems is their reliance on large volumes of labeled training data, which are expensive and time-consuming to produce. This challenge is particularly observed in low-resource languages and institution-specific handwriting styles.

Self-supervised learning techniques offer a promising solution by enabling models to learn useful representations from unlabeled handwriting data. Future research could incorporate contrastive learning, masked image modeling, or sequence prediction objectives to pre-train models before fine-tuning on smaller labeled datasets. Such approaches have the potential to significantly reduce annotation requirements while improving generalization across diverse handwriting styles and document conditions.

6.3 Multilingual and Mixed-Script Handwriting Recognition

Educational institutions, especially in multilingual regions, frequently encounter documents containing multiple languages and scripts within the same page or even the same line. Current models are often trained on monolingual datasets and exhibit reduced performance when applied to mixed-script handwriting.

Future extensions of the proposed system will focus on supporting multilingual and mixed-script recognition by expanding the output vocabulary, incorporating script identification modules and leveraging transfer learning across languages. Training on curated multilingual datasets and applying script-aware preprocessing strategies can further enhance recognition accuracy. Such advancements are essential for deploying handwriting recognition systems in globally diverse academic environments.

6.4 Hybrid Human-AI Educational Tools

While automated handwriting recognition offers substantial efficiency gains, excessive digitization may raise concerns regarding its impact on handwriting skills, cognitive development and learning outcomes. Research in educational psychology suggests that manual writing plays a critical role in memory retention and conceptual understanding, particularly in early education.

Future work will explore hybrid human-AI tools that complement rather than replace handwriting practices. Examples include systems that provide real-time feedback on handwriting clarity, digitize notes while preserving original handwritten forms or support assistive technologies for students with disabilities. Such balanced approaches ensure that technological advancement enhances educational quality without undermining pedagogical foundations.

The challenges outlined above highlight the need for continued research at the intersection of deep learning, education, ethics and system deployment. By incorporating transformer-based models, self-supervised learning, multilingual support and human-centered design principles, future versions of the proposed system can achieve greater accuracy, inclusivity and educational relevance. These directions position handwritten text recognition as a sustainable and integral component of next-generation smart campus ecosystems.

7. CONCLUSION

The chapter discussed the development and implementation of an AI-driven system for the recognition of handwritten text, designed to address the emerging needs of smart campus environments. By leveraging a robust hybrid model architecture that combines the strengths of CNNs for spatial feature extraction, BLSTMs for sequence context understanding and CTC for alignment-free learning, a model that is both theoretically sound and practically feasible was achieved. This framework effectively converts various styles of handwriting into editable and searchable digital text, thereby addressing one of the key issues in the digital transformation efforts of modern educational institutions.

The work represents a concrete step toward redefining the operational structure of educational ecosystems. In real-world scenarios, such a system could transform daily campus operations: examination scripts, administrative forms, student feedback and lecture notes could all be automatically digitized through this technology. In doing so, it contributes directly to reducing paper consumption and aligns with global sustainability goals, fostering a culture of environmental responsibility within the academic community.

Moreover, this shift from physical to digital formats can lead to major improvements in operational efficiency and accessibility. Information previously stored in paper-based documents becomes instantly retrievable, analyzable and shareable. This enhances administrative workflows, accelerates decision-making and ensures broader access to information, including for individuals with disabilities. Seamless integration of such technology into existing campus management systems will provide a way for a connected and intelligent educational infrastructure.

This chapter contributes to empowered educational ecosystem through technology. It shows how AI can be used creatively; not to replace human skill, but to support it by automating ordinary tasks and unlocking information in traditional modes of communication. By bridging the gap between the familiar practice of handwriting and the dynamic management of digital data, this initiative guides educational institutions toward a more efficient, data-driven, sustainable and inclusive future for generations to come.

REFERENCES

AlKendi, W., Gechter, F., Heyberger, L., & Guyeux, C. (2024). Advancements and Challenges in Handwritten Text Recognition: A Comprehensive survey. *Journal of Imaging*, *10*(1), 18. DOI: 10.3390/jimaging10010018 PMID: 38249003

Bluche, T. (2016). Joint line segmentation and transcription for end-to-end handwritten paragraph recognition. In *Proceedings of the 30th International Conference on Neural Information Processing Systems (NIPS'16)*. Curran Associates Inc., Red Hook, NY, USA, 838-846.

Crosilla, G., Klic, L., & Colavizza, G. (2025). Benchmarking large language models for handwritten text recognition. *The Journal of Documentation*, *81*(7), 334–354. DOI: 10.1108/JD-03-2025-0082

Dey, R., Balabantaray, R. C., & Samanta, S. (2022). Recognition of handwritten characters from Devanagari, Bangla and Odia languages using transfer-learning-based VGG-16 networks. *Imaging Science Journal*, *70*(2), 61–74. DOI: 10.1080/13682199.2022.2163348

Graves, A. (2012). Connectionist Temporal Classification. In *Studies in computational intelligence*, 61–93. DOI: 10.1007/978-3-642-24797-2_7

Graves, A., Fernández, S., Gomez, F., & Schmidhuber, J. (2006). Connectionist temporal classification: labelling unsegmented sequence data with recurrent neural networks. In *Proceedings of the 23rd international conference on Machine learning* (pp. 369-376). DOI: 10.1145/1143844.1143891

Graves, A., & Schmidhuber, J. (2005). Framewise phoneme classification with bidirectional LSTM and other neural network architectures. *Neural Networks*, *18*(5–6), 602–610. DOI: 10.1016/j.neunet.2005.06.042 PMID: 16112549

Harjanto, R., Mustafa, Z., Pertiwi, S. A., Nugroho, M. A., & Akib, S. (2024). Managing the intersection of artificial intelligence, digital typing and handwriting for sustainable quality education enhancement. International Journal of Professional Business Review: Int. *J. Prof. Bus. Rev.*, *9*(4), 7. DOI: 10.26668/businessreview/2024.v9i4.4534

Jebadurai, J., Jebadurai, I. J., Paulraj, G. J. L., & Vangeepuram, S. V. (2021). Handwritten text recognition and conversion using convolutional neural network (CNN) based deep learning model. In *2021 Third International Conference on Inventive Research in Computing Applications (ICIRCA)* (pp. 1037-1042). DOI: 10.1109/ICIRCA51532.2021.9544513

Kizilirmak, F., & Yanikoglu, B. (2022). CNN-BLSTM Model for English Handwriting Recognition: Comprehensive Evaluation on the IAM Dataset. *Research Square*. DOI: DOI: 10.21203/rs.3.rs-2274499/v1

Li, Q., An, W., Zhou, A., & Ma, L. (2016). Recognition of offline handwritten Chinese characters using the Tesseract open source OCR engine. In *2016 8th International Conference on Intelligent Human-Machine Systems and Cybernetics (IHMSC)* (Vol. 2, pp. 452-456). DOI: 10.1109/IHMSC.2016.239

Mahadevkar, S., Patil, S., & Kotecha, K. (2024). Enhancement of handwritten text recognition using AI-based hybrid approach. *MethodsX*, *12*, 102654. DOI: 10.1016/j.mex.2024.102654 PMID: 38510932

Marti, U., & Bunke, H. (2002). The IAM-Database: An English sentence database for offline handwriting recognition. *International Journal on Document Analysis and Recognition*, *5*(1), 39–46. DOI: 10.1007/s100320200071

Patel, S., Borana, K., Katre, N., Sawant, V., & Dalvi, H. (2024, December). Efficient Data Extraction from Handwritten Forms: A Structured Pipeline Solution. In 2024 2nd International Conference on Artificial Intelligence Trends and Pattern Recognition (ICAITPR) (pp. 1-6). DOI: 10.1109/ICAITPR63242.2024.10959837

Rajest, S. S., & Regin, R. (2024). Handwriting recognition through neural networks: Enhancing accuracy and performance. *Central Asian Journal of Medical and Natural Science*, *5*(4), 1010–1024. DOI: 10.51699/cajmns.v5i4.2653

Raza, S. A., Farooq, M. S., Farooq, U., Karamti, H., Khurshaid, T., & Ashraf, I. (2025). A convolutional neural network based optical character recognition for purely handwritten characters and digits. *Computers, Materials & Continua/Computers. Computers, Materials & Continua*, *84*(2), 3149–3173. DOI: 10.32604/cmc.2025.063255

Sampath, A. K., & Gomathi, N. (2019). Handwritten optical character recognition by hybrid neural network training algorithm. *Imaging Science Journal*, *67*(7), 359–373. DOI: 10.1080/13682199.2019.1661591

Sueiras, J. (2021). Continuous offline handwriting recognition using deep learning models. arXiv preprint. .DOI: 10.48550/arXiv.2112.13328

Sunori, S. K., & Sumithra, S. (2024). Enhancing Handwritten Text Identification through a Hybrid CNN-RNN Method. *Proceedings of the 3rd International Conference on Optimization Techniques in the Field of Engineering*. DOI: 10.2139/ssrn.5066785

Thanushree, V. V., Choudary, S., Kodipalli, A., Rao, T., & Rohini, B. R. (2024). Evolution and Application of Handwritten Text Recognition using Deep Learning. In *2024 International Conference on Computational Intelligence for Security, Communication and Sustainable Development (CISCSD)* (pp. 204-209). DOI: 10.1109/CISCSD63381.2024.00054

ABBREVIATIONS USED

AI: Artificial Intelligence
BiLSTM/ BLSTM: Bidirectional Long Short-Term Memory
CA: Character Accuracy
CNN: Convolutional Neural Network
CTC: Connectionist Temporal Classification
DPI: Dots Per Inch
ERP: Enterprise Resource Planning
GAN: Generative Adversarial Network
GDPR: General Data Protection Regulation
HMM: Hidden Markov Model
HTR: Handwritten Text Recognition
IAM: IAM Handwriting Database
IoT: Internet of Things
LLM: Large Language Model
LSTM: Long Short-Term Memory
OCR: Optical Character Recognition
RNN: Recurrent Neural Network
SIS: Student Information System
TTA: Test-Time Augmentation
ViT: Vision Transformer
WER: Word Error Rate

Chapter 3
Automated Grading Systems for Smart Campuses:
Integrating Assessment into Digital Higher-Education Ecosystems

Francisco R. Trejo-Macotela
https://orcid.org/0000-0003-2133-3456
Universidad Politécnica de Pachuca, Mexico

ABSTRACT

Automated Grading Systems (AGS) play a central role in digitally transformed and data-driven higher education environments. Drawing on machine learning, natural language processing, and emerging generative models, AGS support scalable, consistent, and timely evaluation of both structured and open-ended student work. When embedded within smart campus ecosystems, these systems interact with Learning Management Systems, Learning Record Stores, and analytics dashboards to enable real-time feedback, adaptive learning support, and informed programme-level decision-making. Their implementation enhances institutional efficiency and personalised learning pathways. However, challenges remain concerning algorithmic transparency, data governance, cultural and linguistic fairness, and the safeguarding of academic judgement. This chapter contends that the value of AGS lies not only in their computational capabilities, but in responsible governance frameworks that ensure equitable and pedagogically aligned assessment practices.

DOI: 10.4018/979-8-3373-6831-3.ch003

026, IGI Global Scientific Publishing. Copying or distributing in print or electronic forms without written permission of IGI Global Scientific Publishing is prohibited. Use of this chapter to tive artificial intelligence (AI) technologies is expressly prohibited. The publisher reserves all rights to license its use for generative AI training and machine learning model development.

1. INTRODUCTION

Assessment remains a cornerstone of contemporary education, serving to evaluate cognitive development, content mastery, and skill acquisition, while guiding pedagogical decision-making and institutional accountability. Traditionally, grading—particularly of open-ended responses and complex outputs—has been undertaken by instructors. Although this model benefits from professional judgment, it is constrained by subjective bias, inter-rater variability, time inefficiency, and limited scalability (Balfour, 2013; Yang et al., 2024), thereby affecting reliability and fairness, especially in large-scale contexts where consistency is essential.

Within smart campuses and digitally transformed institutions, automated grading systems function not merely as instructional tools but as integral components of campus-wide assessment infrastructures. When interconnected with institutional LMS platforms, Learning Record Stores, and analytics dashboards, AGS provide near real-time evaluation data that supports adaptive tutoring, informs course adjustments, and contributes to programme-level decision-making. Accordingly, this chapter conceptualises AGS both as algorithmic systems and as infrastructural elements within smart campus ecosystems, emphasising their technical, pedagogical, and governance implications.

Amid rising demands for equitable, scalable, and timely assessment, Artificial Intelligence (AI) has emerged as a transformative force. Automated grading systems employing Machine Learning (ML), Deep Learning (DL), and Natural Language Processing (NLP) can enhance precision, transparency, and operational efficiency in evaluating both structured and unstructured student outputs (Pankiewicz & Baker, 2023; Pang & Wei, 2025; Glass et al., 2020). These systems are capable of interpreting linguistic complexity, argumentative coherence, semantic relevance, and stylistic features. However, their integration raises methodological and ethical considerations, including data privacy, algorithmic transparency, fairness, and alignment with educational values (Williamson & Eynon, 2020). Thus, automated grading must be understood as a socio-technical system embedded within broader educational ecologies.

This chapter examines the theoretical foundations, computational techniques, and institutional applications of AI-driven grading systems. Through recent case studies, it outlines both the capabilities and limitations of automated assessment, contributing to informed discourse on the future of technology-enhanced evaluation in higher education.

Taken together, these considerations underscore the need to examine automated grading systems not merely as isolated assessment technologies, but as embedded components of broader digital and organisational transformations shaping contemporary smart campus environments.

2. RELEVANCE TO SMART CAMPUSES AND DIGITAL TRANSFORMATION

The emergence of smart campuses has reconfigured the organisational, technological, and pedagogical foundations of contemporary higher education institutions. In these digitally enhanced environments, the integration of interconnected platforms, ubiquitous connectivity, and data-driven decision-making redefines how learning, teaching, and assessment processes are conceptualised and delivered. Automated Grading Systems (AGS) acquire a strategic function within this wider ecosystem, not solely as operational tools for marking, but as core infrastructural components within campus-level digital assessment architectures. Their role is central to enabling real-time feedback, scalable evaluation at programme-wide levels, and interoperable data flows that inform academic support and institutional planning.

Within smart campus ecosystems, AGS interact closely with Virtual Learning Environments (VLEs), Learning Management Systems (LMS), digital identity authentication services, and institutional Learning Record Stores (LRS). These interactions allow AGS to function as integral nodes within distributed data infrastructures, enabling the capture, processing, and visualisation of assessment-related learning traces. When adequately configured, these systems generate structured and semantically rich data that may be leveraged for personalised feedback generation, progression monitoring, early risk detection, and targeted academic interventions. Consequently, AGS support the transition from isolated, course-specific assessment practices to institutionally coordinated assessment frameworks aligned with holistic learner performance analytics.

Moreover, the integration of AGS into smart campus infrastructures promotes forms of pedagogical elasticity. Educators can allocate evaluative resources more strategically, dedicating time to higher-order feedback and personalised mentoring while delegating standardised scoring tasks to algorithmic systems. Simultaneously, students benefit from accelerated feedback cycles, expanded opportunities for iterative revision, and performance transparency across learning trajectories. At the institutional level, AGS provide high-resolution assessment data that aligns with data governance models for evidence-based policy formulation, continuous quality assurance, and programme accreditation procedures.

However, embedding AGS into smart campus environments also necessitates rigorous attention to data ethics, algorithmic transparency, accessibility, and governance frameworks. Institutional strategies must therefore consider interoperability standards, regulatory compliance, privacy safeguards, and the preservation of academic judgement. The value of AGS in smart campuses is realised not merely through technological deployment, but through responsible integration that respects academic integrity, preserves human oversight, and enhances educational equity.

The Figure 1 illustrates the data and process flows connecting student-facing digital interfaces, the institutional LMS/VLE, the Automated Grading System, and the Learning Record Store, as well as the analytics dashboards and the Intelligent Tutoring System. This configuration aligns AGS within a broader smart campus infrastructure, enabling real-time feedback, learning analytics, and adaptive instructional support.

Figure 1. Integration of Automated Grading Systems within a Smart Campus Learning Architecture.

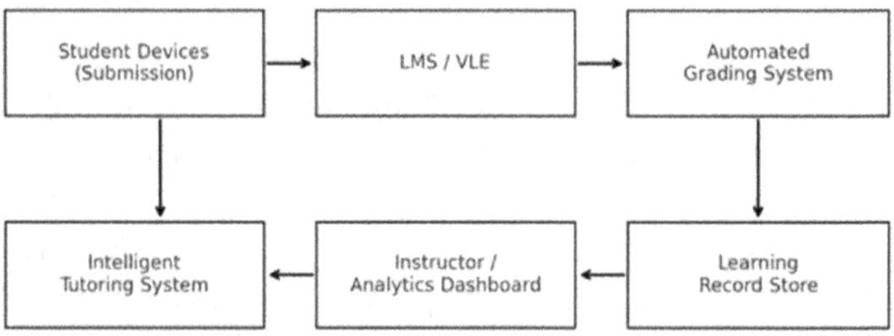

In this regard, AGS serve as catalysts in advancing digital transformation agendas within higher education. Their effective implementation reflects a shift from isolated digital tools toward cohesive, data-informed learning ecosystems that align pedagogical innovation with institutional digital maturity. As such, AGS represent a fundamental component in both the operational functioning and the strategic evolution of smart campuses.

From an institutional perspective, such configurations offer higher education leaders concrete mechanisms to scale assessment processes while preserving academic oversight, regulatory compliance, and pedagogical accountability.

Within this integrated digital infrastructure, artificial intelligence emerges as the enabling layer that operationalises scalability, consistency, and responsiveness in assessment practices, a role examined in detail in the following section.

3. AI FOR AUTOMATED ASSESSMENT

AI-driven automated assessment has emerged as a significant paradigm shift in contemporary education, reshaping how academic performance is evaluated and supported. By minimising manual grading workloads and enabling data-informed instructional practices, AI enhances both efficiency and pedagogical precision. As the need for scalable, equitable, and adaptive assessment intensifies, AI systems are increasingly embedded into formative and summative evaluation environments (Dimari et al., 2024).

A principal advantage of AI-based assessment is its capacity to substantially reduce grading time. Traditional evaluation of open-ended tasks requires considerable educator input, often delaying personalised feedback. In contrast, AI can process extensive volumes of submissions within minutes, ensuring institutional scalability without diminishing evaluative rigour (Dimari et al., 2024). Borah et al. (2024) emphasise that such systems are particularly suited to large-scale contexts, including MOOCs, standardised examinations, and national testing frameworks, where they also promote grading consistency across markers and institutions.

Empirical studies demonstrate that AI-generated assessments frequently align with expert human judgement. Dimari et al. (2024) report high inter-rater reliability when hybrid grading models are used in conjunction with human verification, supporting score validity. Advances in deep learning, particularly models such as BERT and RoBERTa, have improved semantic interpretation, enhancing contextual sensitivity in written response evaluation (Borah et al., 2024).

AI also enables assessment formats that extend beyond traditional written examinations. Simulation-based tasks, virtual laboratories, and interactive decision-making scenarios are increasingly utilised to evaluate higher-order skills. Vetrivel et al. (2025) highlight their effectiveness in domains requiring practical reasoning, such as clinical education, where students interact with virtual patients and receive real-time feedback.

In computing disciplines, AI has transformed feedback provision on coding assignments. Systems described by Yi et al. (2024) employ error detection algorithms to deliver immediate formative responses, supporting iterative learning. Historically, automated grading has evolved from simple pattern-matching approaches to advanced NLP and machine learning frameworks. Tools such as ETS's e-rater® apply linguistic feature analysis alongside statistical scoring, demonstrating robust performance across diverse writing tasks (Attali & Burstein, 2006; Shermis & Burstein, 2013).

Contemporary systems commonly rely on supervised learning models trained on human-scored corpora. Taghipour and Ng (2016) show that models including decision trees, SVMs, and deep neural networks achieve strong predictive accuracy when based on high-quality, representative datasets. Core textual features typically include syntactic complexity, lexical diversity, coherence, grammatical accuracy, and relevance.

The function of AI-based assessment must be clearly distinguished. In formative assessment, AI provides targeted feedback to guide learner improvement, while in summative contexts it generates final scores aligned with institutional criteria (Lim et al., 2021). Hybrid systems may integrate both processes, supporting personalised instruction.

Ensuring credibility requires rigorous psychometric validation. Agreement between AI and human scores is commonly measured through metrics such as Pearson's correlation coefficient and Quadratic Weighted Kappa. Yannakoudakis et al. (2011) recommend dual grading and continuous calibration to maintain alignment with expert standards. Updating training datasets is essential to reflect evolving linguistic norms and curricular goals. Table 1 summarises the principal types of AI-based automated assessment currently in use.

Table 1. Types of AI-Based Automated Assessment.

Type	Description
Automatic assessment of closed-ended responses	This type of assessment focuses on the automatic grading of objective questions such as multiple choice, true/false, matching, and fill-in-the-blank. AI-based systems optimize speed and accuracy through pattern analysis algorithms and predefined rules, ensuring evaluative consistency (Bennett & Zhang, 2016). AI enables precise and real-time scoring of objective tests, reducing teacher workload and enhancing immediate feedback.
Automatic assessment of open-ended responses (NLP)	Using NLP techniques, this assessment type interprets students' written responses, analysing their coherence, semantic content, and argumentative structure. Algorithms such as BERT and GPT enable deep semantic analysis to assign fair and objective grades (Burrows et al., 2015). This evaluation requires advanced AI models capable of understanding the student's context and intent, thereby reducing human biases.
Automated essay scoring	Essay grading utilizes machine learning and NLP models to analyse multiple aspects of the text: organization, grammar, style, argumentation, and evidence. Systems such as e-rater® and Project Essay Grade (PEG) have been widely applied in formal educational settings (Shermis & Burstein, 2013). This type of assessment enables the scalable evaluation of extensive written productions while maintaining standardized evaluative criteria.
Automated adaptive assessment	This assessment dynamically adjusts to the student's knowledge level through adaptive learning algorithms. AI selects questions based on prior responses, optimizing the diagnostic accuracy of student knowledge (van der Linden & Glas, 2010). It enables deep personalization of the assessment process and more accurate measurement of student performance.
Competency-based assessment through intelligent simulations	Virtual environments or AI-controlled simulations are used to evaluate practical competencies in realistic contexts such as medicine, engineering, or aeronautics. The systems monitor student decisions and generate performance metrics based on predefined standards (Ifenthaler & Yau, 2020). This assesses complex skills in dynamic contexts, which would be difficult to replicate in traditional environments.
Emotional and attitudinal assessment via affective AI	Affective AI enables the assessment of non-cognitive dimensions such as emotions, motivation, or attitudes through the analysis of facial expressions, voice tone, writing patterns, or physiological activity. This complements traditional academic assessment with data on student well-being (Calvo & D'Mello, 2010). It provides a comprehensive view of the student by incorporating emotional factors into the assessment process.

continued on following page

Table 1. Continued

Type	Description
Automated rubric-based assessment	AI can automatically apply scoring rubrics by comparing student productions to formal criteria. These systems analyse content and determine the semantic proximity between the production and the levels defined in the rubric (McNamara et al., 2014). This allows for the standardization of complex assessments with reduced subjectivity and increased replicability.
Assessment through learning trace analysis (Learning Analytics)	This approach automatically analyses student actions in virtual environments (clicks, navigation, time on tasks) to infer learning levels, cognitive strategies, and interaction patterns. Predictive models are used to anticipate performance or school dropout (Siemens & Long, 2011). It provides a longitudinal and real-time view of learning, informing evidence-based instructional decisions.
Automated assessment in intelligent tutoring systems	In the context of Intelligent Tutoring Systems (ITS), AI continuously evaluates student responses during system interaction. This formative assessment is ongoing, personalized, and based on modelling the student's knowledge (VanLehn, 2006). It transforms assessment into a continuous process that guides and enhances personalized learning.
Predictive assessment using AI	This method employs machine learning models to predict students' future performance based on previous data, such as grades, participation, and socio-educational context. It enables early interventions to improve performance (Baashar et al., 2021; Al-Tameemi, 2020). It supports educational decision-making based on accurate predictions and empirical data.

Despite their manifold benefits, automated assessment systems raise important ethical questions. Concerns include algorithmic bias, data privacy, student profiling, and the potential for surveillance. Transparency in algorithmic design and equitable model training practices are imperative to mitigate these risks (Binns et al., 2018). Pedagogically, overreliance on automated grading may undermine the role of educators in contextual interpretation and holistic student evaluation. As a counterbalance, AI should be positioned as a complementary tool that augments, rather than supplants, professional judgement.

The future of AI in assessment lies in increased personalisation, multimodal data integration, and adaptive learning ecosystems. Real-time dashboards, predictive analytics, and affective computing will enable holistic learner profiling. Interdisciplinary research at the nexus of AI, education, and cognitive science will be pivotal in shaping next-generation assessment tools. Investment in teacher training, ethical AI governance, and open-source development platforms will be vital for equitable and sustainable deployment. Ultimately, the success of AI in assessment will depend not solely on technological sophistication, but on its alignment with humanistic educational values.

4. NATURAL LANGUAGE PROCESSING (NLP) IN GRADING SYSTEMS

NLP constitutes the core of automated natural language assessment systems. Through syntactic, semantic, and pragmatic analysis techniques, models are capable of interpreting not only the literal meaning of words but also the context in which they are expressed. This capability is essential for evaluating qualitative aspects of student discourse, such as logical argumentation, textual cohesion, and the use of evidence (Burstein et al., 2013). Figure 2 presents, in general terms, the components of a natural language processing (NLP) system.

Figure 2. Components of a Natural Language Processing (NLP) System.

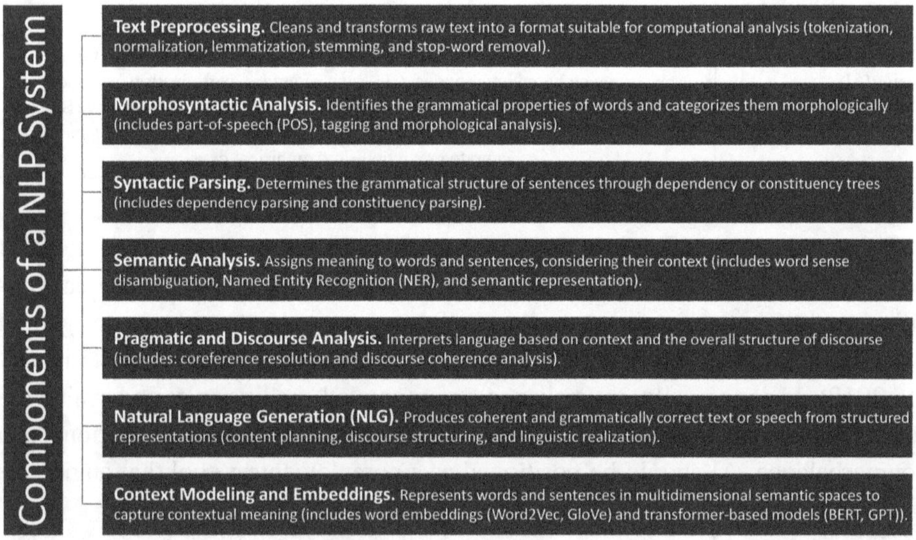

The components of a natural language processing (NLP) system are described below:

- *Text Preprocessing.* Before any linguistic analysis is performed, raw student responses undergo preprocessing. This stage includes tokenisation (segmentation of text into words or subwords), normalisation (standardising spelling and casing), lemmatisation and stemming (reducing words to their base or root forms), and the removal of stop words. These procedures eliminate noise and enhance the quality of extracted features, thereby improving the model's predictive accuracy (Manning et al., 2008).

- *Morphosyntactic Analysis.* Comprises Part-of-Speech (POS) tagging and morphological parsing. This phase enables the identification of grammatical roles (e.g., noun, verb, adjective) and morphological variations (e.g., pluralisation, tense). In the context of grading, such features help measure syntactic complexity, grammatical consistency, and linguistic fluency (Toutanova et al., 2003).
- *Syntactic Parsing.* Determines the grammatical structure of sentences via dependency trees or constituency structures. Dependency parsing focuses on head-dependent relations between words, whereas constituency parsing decomposes sentences into nested sub-phrases. Parsing techniques are fundamental for identifying argument structures, sentence completeness, and syntactic variety (Kiperwasser & Goldberg, 2016).
- *Semantic Analysis.* Assigns contextual meaning to words, phrases, and sentences. It includes tasks such as Word Sense Disambiguation (WSD), Named Entity Recognition (NER), and the generation of semantic representations (Mikolov et al., 2013). In grading applications, semantic analysis aids in evaluating topical relevance, content accuracy, and vocabulary sophistication.
- *Pragmatic and Discourse Analysis.* Involves coreference resolution and discourse-level coherence assessment. This level of interpretation considers how different parts of the text relate to each other and how meaning is shaped by context and shared knowledge. For example, identifying whether pronouns are used appropriately and whether the essay follows a logical progression from introduction to conclusion (Webber et al., 2012).
- *Natural Language Generation (NLG).* NLG capabilities are integral to feedback delivery. After evaluating a student's work, the system generates human-like feedback using components such as content planning, discourse structuring, and linguistic realisation. This ensures that feedback is not only informative but also pedagogically meaningful (Gatt & Krahmer, 2018).
- *Contextual Embedding and Representation Advanced NLP models.* Utilise vector-based embeddings to represent words and sentences in high-dimensional spaces. Pre-trained embedding models such as Word2Vec, GloVe, and contextual models like BERT and GPT capture semantic and syntactic regularities (Devlin et al., 2019). These embeddings form the foundation of feature vectors used for predictive grading.

The advancement of large-scale language models, such as BERT (Bidirectional Encoder Representations from Transformers) and GPT (Generative Pre-trained Transformer), has revolutionized the capabilities of NLP applied to education. These models enable highly contextualized analysis and exhibit strong correlation with human judgment in automated grading tasks (Fernandez et al., 2023; Al-Tameemi et al., 2020). Their implementation contributes to reducing biases, enhancing transparency, and personalizing feedback processes.

NLP-based assessment systems extract both low- and high-level features: from word counts, use of connectors, and grammatical variation, to discourse coherence analysis, thematic progression, and argumentative structure (Klebanov & Madnani, 2022). These features are integrated into vectors that feed predictive grading models. An NLP-based grading system typically involves the following architecture sowed in Table 2. This pipeline is implemented using a range of tools including spaCy, NLTK, AllenNLP, and Hugging Face Transformers. Neural networks such as BiLSTM, CNNs, and transformer-based models underpin the classification layer (Sun et al., 2020).

Table 2. Architecture of an NLP-Based Grading System.

Layer	Function
Input Layer	Student text submission
Preprocessing Layer	Student text submission
Feature Extraction Layer	Syntactic, semantic, and discourse features
Embedding Layer	Word2Vec, GloVe, BERT, or GPT-based contextual embeddings
Classification/Scoring Layer	Regression or classification models for score prediction
Feedback Layer	Generation of formative feedback

The advent of transformer-based architectures has revolutionised automated grading. Models such as BERT and GPT provide deep contextual understanding of language. These models are pre-trained on massive corpora and fine-tuned on specific educational datasets. Grading BERT enables bidirectional language representation and excels at tasks like sentence classification, question answering, and textual entailment. In grading systems, BERT has been fine-tuned on essay corpora to predict grades with high correlation to human evaluators (Fernandez et al., 2023; Al-Tameemi, 2020). Grading GPT models, especially GPT-3 and GPT-4, are capable of generating coherent responses and performing zero-shot classification. Their integration into grading systems allows not only for scoring but also for generating detailed formative feedback (Brown et al., 2020). Machine learning models require careful instance selection, particularly in hybrid or incomplete data environments, in order to preserve the system's representativeness and robustness (Tusell-Rey et al., 2025)

Grading systems rely on a range of linguistic and semantic features, broadly categorised as showed in Table 3. Each feature set contributes differently to evaluating student outputs depending on the rubric, subject matter, and linguistic complexity.

Table 3. Feature Taxonomy in NLP-Based Grading.

Feature Type	Examples
Lexical Features	Word count, type-token ratio, average word length
Syntactic Features	POS patterns, parse tree depth, clause complexity
Semantic Features	Topic relevance, semantic similarity, word sense use
Discourse Features	Argument structure, cohesion markers, coherence chains
Pragmatic Features	Pronoun resolution, hedging, modal verbs usage

To evaluate NLP-based grading models, researchers utilise metrics such as:

- *Pearson Correlation Coefficient:* Measures linear agreement with human scores.
- *Quadratic Weighted Kappa (QWK):* Assesses agreement with penalty for distance between scores.
- *Mean Squared Error (MSE):* Quantifies error in continuous score prediction.

Benchmark datasets such as the Automated Student Assessment Prize (ASAP) and Kaggle's essay scoring corpora provide standardised baselines for training and evaluation (Taghipour & Ng, 2016).

Despite its success, NLP-based grading faces several challenges:

- Domain specificity: General models may fail in technical disciplines.
- Interpretability: Deep learning models lack transparent reasoning chains.
- Bias: Models may inherit training data biases, disadvantaging certain student groups.
- Feedback generation: Ensuring that feedback is constructive, not generic.

Ongoing research focuses on interpretable NLP models, bias mitigation techniques, and cross-lingual transfer learning (Klebanov & Madnani, 2022).

Ethically, NLP-based assessment must ensure fairness, transparency, and privacy. Pedagogically, it should augment—rather than replace—human judgement. Systems should allow teacher override options, explain grading rationales, and adapt to individual learner contexts (Binns et al., 2018).

NLP in grading systems represents a critical frontier in AI-powered education. From preprocessing to feedback generation, each component plays a vital role in automating and enhancing assessment. While transformer-based models significantly improve performance, challenges related to fairness, generalisability, and pedagogical alignment remain. Future directions include hybrid human-AI systems, multilingual grading capabilities, and integration with adaptive learning platforms.

While these computational mechanisms define the technical foundations of NLP-based grading, their educational significance becomes clearer when examined through concrete institutional deployments and applied assessment contexts.

5. PRACTICAL CASES OF AI-BASED AUTOMATED GRADING

ETS e-rater®

The e-rater® system, designed by Educational Testing Service (ETS), is a prominent exemplar of automated essay scoring (AES) technology. Deployed widely in high-stakes assessment contexts such as the Graduate Management Admission Test (GMAT) and the Test of English as a Foreign Language (TOEFL), the system operates by extracting over 100 distinct linguistic and structural features from textual inputs. These include syntactic variety, discourse coherence, grammatical accuracy, lexical diversity, and organisation. Machine learning models trained on large corpora of human-scored essays are then used to predict grades with high reliability.

Numerous validation studies underscore the robustness of e-rater®. For example, Attali & Burstein (2006) demonstrated a high Pearson correlation (often exceeding 0.85) between e-rater® scores and those of expert human evaluators. In addition, it has been noted that e-rater® maintains consistency in scoring across large datasets and avoids fatigue or inconsistency that may affect human evaluators (Burstein et al., 2013). This has rendered it invaluable in both formative and summative assessment frameworks, particularly in scenarios requiring rapid feedback and large-scale deployment.

Moreover, e-rater® is integrated with the Criterion® Online Writing Evaluation Service, offering immediate diagnostic feedback to learners. This feedback encompasses suggestions for improving grammar, mechanics, usage, style, and development. Such formative scaffolding facilitates autonomous revision and self-regulation among students (Chodorow & Burstein, 2004).

Project Essay Grade (PEG)

Developed by Ellis Page in the 1960s, Project Essay Grade (PEG) holds historical significance as the first operational automated essay grading system. Unlike contemporary neural approaches, PEG employs a correlation-based statistical model, utilising what it terms "proxes"—surface-level textual features presumed to correlate with writing quality. These include word count, average sentence length, punctuation usage, and syntactic variety.

Despite its simplicity, PEG has demonstrated considerable efficacy, particularly in primary and secondary education settings. Shermis & Burstein (2013) reported that, when appropriately calibrated, PEG's scoring accuracy approximates that of human graders. Its longstanding presence in educational technology demonstrates its adaptability, having evolved to incorporate more sophisticated linguistic markers and interfaces over time.

An important advantage of PEG is its transparency and explainability. Its linear and interpretable model architecture allows educators to understand the basis for scoring decisions. However, this same simplicity limits its performance in nuanced evaluative tasks such as assessing argumentative coherence or content relevance, which require semantic and discourse-level processing.

Intelligent Essay Assessor (IEA)

The Intelligent Essay Assessor (IEA), developed by Pearson Knowledge Technologies, represents a semantic-driven AES approach leveraging Latent Semantic Analysis (LSA). LSA functions by projecting textual content into a high-dimensional semantic space, constructed through Singular Value Decomposition (SVD) of large corpora. In this space, texts with similar meanings are positioned in close proximity, enabling the system to evaluate conceptual relevance and coherence.

IEA is particularly useful in contexts where the emphasis is on critical thinking, idea synthesis, and argumentative depth. It has been widely used in corporate training programmes, higher education, and formative classroom settings. For instance, Foltz et al. (2013) demonstrated that IEA is adept at evaluating open-ended responses in science and humanities, where content knowledge and conceptual understanding are essential.

Notably, IEA supports feedback generation in the form of content coverage alerts and thematic alignment indicators. This helps instructors and learners identify conceptual omissions or misalignments in student submissions. However, LSA-based systems are often constrained by their reliance on bag-of-words models, which disregard syntax and word order, limiting their interpretive capacity relative to transformer-based architectures.

Emerging Systems Based on Generative AI

The rise of generative AI models, particularly those based on transformer architectures like GPT-3 and GPT-4, has ushered in a new era in automated grading.

These systems possess not only evaluative but also generative capabilities, allowing them to provide rich, context-sensitive feedback and simulate tutor-like interactions.

Pankiewicz & Baker (2023). (2023) explored the use of GPT-based models for essay grading in hybrid learning environments. They found that such models could accurately predict rubric-aligned scores while simultaneously offering detailed formative feedback. The study also noted improvements in student engagement and revision quality, attributed to the dialogic nature of GPT-generated responses.

Generative systems operate via few-shot or zero-shot learning paradigms, enabling them to generalise across topics and disciplines with minimal fine-tuning. They analyse text holistically, evaluating syntactic fluency, semantic depth, argumentative structure, and even rhetorical strategies. Furthermore, through techniques such as Reinforcement Learning from Human Feedback (RLHF), these models can be aligned with specific grading rubrics and institutional policies (Ouyang et al., 2022).

Table 4 presents a comparative overview and general description of the Automated Grading Systems.

Table 4. Comparative Overview of Selected Automated Grading Systems.

System	Core Technology	Strengths	Limitations
ETS e-rater®	Feature-based ML	High reliability, diagnostic feedback, scalability	Limited interpretability, dependency on training data
PEG	Statistical correlation model	Transparent, fast, suitable for basic tasks	Weak on content and discourse analysis
IEA	Latent Semantic Analysis	Strong on semantic alignment and content coverage	Ignores syntax and structure
GPT-based models	Ignores syntax and structure	Personalised feedback, cross-domain performance	Computationally intensive, risk of hallucinations

6. HYBRID ARCHITECTURES AND ADAPTIVE FEEDBACK

The evolution of Automated Grading Systems (AGS) has witnessed an unprecedented shift with the advent of hybrid architectures and adaptive feedback technologies. These innovations have addressed critical limitations of early systems that were either overly reliant on rigid rule-based algorithms or limited in scope by isolated machine learning components. By integrating diverse computational paradigms—ranging from symbolic approaches to deep learning models—hybrid systems have dramatically enhanced the scalability, precision, and educational responsiveness of automated assessment mechanisms. Concurrently, the inclusion of adaptive feedback modules has facilitated a pedagogical reorientation from static scoring towards dynamic, personalised learning trajectories. This paradigm aligns with the literature on personalised education, in which systems adapt their behaviour and feedback based on the learner's profile (Fuentes-Penna & González Ibarra, 2024).

Hybrid architectures in AGS are grounded in the computational theory of modular integration, where complementary components coalesce into a unified processing pipeline. This is analogous to ensemble learning in machine learning, where combining weak learners often yields superior generalisation performance compared to individual models (Dietterich, 2000). In the context of automated grading, the hybrid paradigm typically blends:

- Rule-based parsing systems for syntactic integrity;
- Latent semantic analysis or vector space models for semantic congruity;
- Neural transformer-based architectures for contextualised understanding.

Such convergence fosters both robustness and pedagogical depth. For instance, a rule-based system may accurately flag grammatical errors but fail to capture higher-order coherence; a neural language model, by contrast, may identify conceptual misalignment yet overlook elementary syntax violations. A hybrid model synthesises these layers to produce holistic and pedagogically relevant assessments. Table 5 presents the main components in hybrid AGS architectures.

Table 5. Components in Hybrid AGS Architectures.

Component Type	Functionality	Example System
Rule-based syntax module	Feature-based ML	e-rater® (ETS)
Semantic vector models	Measures topical and semantic similarity	IEA (Intelligent Essay Assessor)
Transformer-based models	Captures contextual and discourse-level coherence	GPT-4-based systems

The architectural implementation of hybrid AGS entails a sequential or parallel processing pipeline in which multiple scoring engines intercommunicate through shared representations or decision fusion layers. This requires meticulous orchestration at the software engineering level, as well as rigorous benchmarking to ensure that error propagation from one module does not contaminate subsequent layers.

One exemplar is the integration of syntactic scorers (e.g., part-of-speech taggers and constituency parsers) with BERT-like contextual encoders. The syntactic module may generate an error lattice that is later consumed by a semantic coherence evaluator, which uses sentence embeddings derived from a transformer model. These intermediate representations are then aggregated—often via a logistic or neural meta-learner—to assign a final score with associated confidence intervals (Taghipour & Ng, 2016). Moreover, explainability is a critical aspect of hybrid systems. Unlike end-to-end neural models, hybrid systems can retain modular transparency, allowing for diagnostic feedback to students and instructors. For example, a flagged semantic drift can be precisely attributed to the relevant textual segment, accompanied by suggestive feedback for revision.

The educational rationale for hybrid scoring extends beyond computational efficiency. By emulating the multidimensional evaluation process characteristic of human evaluators, these systems can cater to more nuanced pedagogical objectives. As pointed out by Williamson et al. (2006), effective assessment is not solely about correctness but also about the alignment with instructional goals and learner development.

Hybrid architectures can be calibrated to different educational taxonomies (e.g., Bloom's revised taxonomy), distinguishing between cognitive levels such as recall, application, and critical synthesis. For instance, lower-level features like spelling accuracy may be handled by rule-based subsystems, while higher-order reasoning is evaluated via transformer-based semantic matching and inferencing models (Kaya & Cicekli, 2024). Parallel to hybrid scoring systems, adaptive feedback mechanisms have emerged as vital components of modern AGS. Adaptive feedback refers to the algorithmic personalisation of evaluative and formative comments based on learner characteristics and contextual variables. Unlike static rubrics, adaptive systems tailor feedback in real-time, modulating its tone, depth, and instructional scaffolding according to:

- Student proficiency level,
- Emotional state (detected via affective computing),
- Task complexity,
- Historical performance data.

This dynamicity is underpinned by probabilistic student modelling frameworks, such as Bayesian Knowledge Tracing (Corbett & Anderson, 1995) and Dynamic Bayesian Networks (VanLehn, 2006), which provide probabilistic estimates of learner states and skill mastery. Table 6 shows the main characteristics of the variables influencing adaptive feedback generation.

Table 6. Variables Influencing Adaptive Feedback Generation.

Variable Type	Source of Data	Feedback Adaptation Strategy
Proficiency level	Prior grades, linguistic complexity	Adjust cognitive challenge level
Emotional state	Facial recognition, keystroke patterns	Modify tone and encouragement
Learning history	Log files, time-on-task metrics	Recurrence-based feedback patterns
Task difficulty	Predefined rubric levels	Adjust instructional scaffolding

A cornerstone of adaptive feedback is affective computing—the computational detection and response to user emotions. Techniques involve multimodal signal processing, including facial expression analysis, voice tone, typing behaviour, and biometric sensors (Picard, 1997). These emotional cues are integrated into student modelling engines to infer stress, confusion, engagement, or boredom. Such modelling enables the AGS to deliver empathy-informed feedback. For example, a student exhibiting signs of frustration may receive more affirmative, supportive language, while a confident student might be challenged with open-ended prompts for reflection and improvement. This humanised feedback loop enhances learner motivation, reduces attrition, and promotes metacognitive regulation (D'Mello & Graesser, 2015).

Hybrid AGS modules are increasingly embedded within Intelligent Tutoring Systems (ITS), where assessment is continuous and feedback is dialogic. Here, the AGS serves not only as an evaluator but as a conversational agent that participates in Socratic dialogue with the learner. Transformer-based language models (e.g., GPT-4) have proven particularly adept in this domain due to their ability to generate context-aware, pedagogically sound dialogue (Chi et al., 2020). These integrated systems leverage shared ontologies and domain-specific knowledge graphs to ensure instructional coherence. For example, an essay on climate change may be evaluated for argumentative rigour and factual accuracy, with the AGS prompting elaboration on underdeveloped points or questioning logical inconsistencies.

Several recent systems exemplify the practical application of hybrid architectures and adaptive feedback:

1. *Project Essay Grade (PEG)* has been extended with semantic modules based on LSA and BERT, allowing for nuanced scoring and comment generation (Shermis & Burstein, 2013).
2. WriteToLearn™ integrates semantic similarity scoring (via Pearson's Intelligent Essay Assessor) with scaffolding feedback tailored to grade-level and curriculum alignment.

3. *OpenEssayist,* developed at the Open University, provides real-time feedback on essay structure and coherence using both symbolic and neural modules (Whitelock et al., 2013).

These systems have been validated through large-scale trials, demonstrating improved learner outcomes, increased engagement, and reduced grading burdens on educators.

Despite their promise, hybrid architectures and adaptive feedback systems face several challenges:

- *Data Privacy:* The integration of biometric and emotional data necessitates robust ethical safeguards (Luckin & Holmes, 2016).
- *Bias and Fairness:* Transformer-based models inherit biases from their training data, risking unfair treatment of minority linguistic patterns or perspectives (Binns et al., 2018).
- *Scalability:* Real-time adaptation requires significant computational resources, raising deployment concerns for low-resource educational settings.
- *Instructor Trust:* The black-box nature of deep learning components can engender scepticism among educators unless explainability tools are integrated.

Addressing these limitations requires a multidisciplinary approach that combines computer science, psychometrics, ethics, and pedagogy. Looking forward, the next generation of AGS will likely incorporate:

- *Multilingual scoring:* Using large language models with cross-lingual embeddings to support diverse learners.
- *Conversational feedback agents:* Deploying chat-based interfaces for iterative, reflective learning support.
- *Explainable AI (XAI) modules:* Offering transparent justifications for both scores and feedback.
- *Augmented reality integration:* Enabling spatial and kinaesthetic modes of feedback for disciplines such as engineering and art.

Moreover, the role of AGS may evolve from evaluative to formative, becoming an embedded co-teacher that supports continuous learning across modalities and contexts. In practice, these hybrid configurations enable institutions to balance automation efficiency with instructional sensitivity, allowing educators to reallocate effort towards higher-order feedback and learner support.

As automated grading systems increase in architectural complexity and pedagogical reach, questions of linguistic diversity, cultural alignment, and contextual fairness become increasingly salient.

7. CROSS-LINGUISTIC AND CROSS-CULTURAL APPLICATIONS

Automated Grading Systems (AGS) have evolved substantially over the last two decades, primarily within monolingual English-speaking educational contexts. However, the increasing globalisation of digital education and the growth of international student populations have prompted an urgent need to adapt AGS for multilingual and multicultural settings. These cross-linguistic and cross-cultural applications introduce a complex array of linguistic, sociocultural, and computational challenges, which necessitate a reconceptualisation of existing scoring models, data representations, and pedagogical assumptions.

One of the principal challenges in the cross-linguistic adaptation of AGS lies in managing morphological complexity across diverse languages. Morphologically rich languages such as Arabic, Turkish, Finnish, and Russian exhibit extensive inflectional and derivational morphology, where a single lemma may manifest in numerous orthographic forms (Table 7). For example, a Turkish verb may exhibit dozens of inflections, encapsulating tense, aspect, mood, voice, person, and number within a single token (Oflazer & Kuruöz, 1994). This combinatorial explosion poses significant challenges for tokenisation, lemmatisation, and syntactic parsing modules, particularly when these systems have been originally designed for isolating languages like English or Chinese.

Table 7. Examples of Morphological Complexity Across Languages.

Language	Morphological Type	Example (Glossed)	No. of Inflectional Forms per Verb
English	Analytic/Isolating	“go / went / goes”	~5
Russian	Fusional	“иду / шёл / пойду” (I go / went / will go)	~20–30
Turkish	Agglutinative	“gidiyorum” (I am going)	~100+
Arabic	Root-and-Pattern	“ / / ” (write / he writes / writing)	~50+

Such linguistic variability necessitates advanced morphological analysers and language-specific disambiguation frameworks. The limited availability of annotated corpora for many languages continues to restrict the development of reliable AGS components. Although multilingual models such as XLM-RoBERTa (Conneau et al., 2020) and mBERT demonstrate cross-lingual transfer capacities, their effectiveness in grading low-resource languages remains uncertain.

Beyond morphology, syntax and script diversity introduce further complexity. While English typically follows a fixed SVO structure, languages such as Japanese (SOV), Arabic (VSO), and Welsh (VSO) exhibit alternative or flexible word orders, requiring distinct parsing and part-of-speech tagging strategies. When such models are inadequately adapted, syntactic evaluation may become inaccurate. Additionally, non-Latin scripts (e.g., Cyrillic, Devanagari, Hanzi/Kanji, Arabic) complicate tokenisation and encoding, while handwriting recognition and OCR systems must be customised to accommodate script-specific characteristics. Errors at these foundational stages can propagate throughout the grading pipeline, diminishing overall reliability.

To address these constraints, multilingual tokenisers such as SentencePiece (Kudo & Richardson, 2018) and character-level CNNs are increasingly integrated into neural architectures. However, these approaches may oversimplify linguistic subtleties, resulting in limited precision in formative contexts where pedagogically meaningful, language-specific feedback is required.

More challenging still are culturally embedded rhetorical conventions that shape writing practices. Cross-cultural variation in argumentation and narrative organisation has significant implications for AGS validity (Table 8). Kaplan's (1966) contrastive rhetoric theory demonstrates that English academic writing typically emphasises linear progression, explicit thesis articulation, and deductive reasoning. In contrast, Arabic rhetorical traditions may utilise circular structures and repetition, while East Asian academic discourse may prioritise indirect or inductive argumentation. Such culturally grounded patterns necessitate refined evaluation models that recognise varied rhetorical logics rather than imposing Anglophonocentric standards.

Table 8. Cultural Variation in Rhetorical Style.

Cultural Tradition	Common Rhetorical Patterns	Implications for AGS
Anglo-American	Linear, deductive, explicit	Aligns with current AGS rubrics
Arabic	Repetitive, circular, ornate	Penalised as redundant or incoherent
East Asian	Inductive, implicit thesis	Misinterpreted as vague or off-topic
Romance languages	Elaborate, digressive	May reduce coherence scores in AGS

Such differences may introduce systematic grading bias where AGS models rely on rubrics or training data that implicitly privilege Anglo-centric rhetorical norms. Criteria such as explicit thesis statements, topic sentences, and linear argumentation may inadvertently penalise texts adhering to culturally legitimate alternatives. To promote cultural fairness, AGS require inclusive scoring rubrics co-developed with native-speaking educators and linguists, alongside transfer learning approaches that retrain models on culturally diverse corpora to support more contextually sensitive interpretation.

The development of robust AGS systems depends heavily on the availability of high-quality annotated corpora. Yet there remains a marked scarcity of standardised learner corpora for languages beyond English. Initiatives such as the Cambridge Learner Corpus, ICLE, and Lang-8 have contributed to addressing this gap, though coverage remains limited, particularly for African, Indigenous, and low-resource Asian languages. The Common European Framework of Reference for Languages (CEFR) provides a cross-linguistic proficiency scale (Council of Europe, 2001), but aligning local curricular standards to CEFR descriptors is often complex and context-dependent.

Yannakoudakis et al. (2011) demonstrate that neural networks can predict CEFR levels across languages such as German, Spanish, and Italian, yet also note performance decline due to restricted training data and intra-rater variability. Recent advances in multilingual pre-trained language models, including XLM-RoBERTa (Conneau et al., 2020), mBERT (Devlin et al., 2019), and LaBSE (Feng et al., 2020), enable cross-lingual representation learning, facilitating transfer from high-resource to low-resource languages (Table 9). For instance, English-trained models may be fine-tuned with smaller annotated datasets in languages such as Swahili or Urdu. However, assumptions of shared embedding space equivalence remain contested, with empirical studies reporting notable performance divergences across linguistic and domain contexts (Pires et al., 2019).

Table 9. Multilingual Embedding Models and Their AGS Suitability.

Model	No. of Languages	Embedding	Pros	Cons
mBERT	104	Subword	Open-source widely adopted	Suboptimal zero-shot performance
XLM-RoBERTa	100	SentencePiece	High accuracy, cross-lingual alignment	Computationally intensive
LaBSE	109	Sentence-level	Strong retrieval capabilities	Less tuned for compositional writing

Despite current limitations, cross-lingual embeddings remain a promising basis for extending AGS to underrepresented languages, particularly when combined with domain adaptation and active learning techniques.

A further challenge concerns dialectal and sociolectal variation. In multilingual settings such as India, Nigeria, and the Philippines, students frequently write using non-standard or regionally shaped varieties of English or local languages, including code-switching and culturally legitimate grammatical forms. AGS trained chiefly on standard corpora may misinterpret these as errors, reinforcing linguistic bias. To mitigate this, dialect-aware tokenisation, phonological normalisation, and sociolectal embeddings should be incorporated into AGS architectures (Blodgett et al., 2016), and scoring rubrics should explicitly recognise regional variation where pedagogically appropriate.

Cross-cultural AGS deployment must therefore be guided by pedagogical inclusiveness and ethical awareness. Automated systems inevitably reproduce normative assumptions and shape learners' understanding of what constitutes "appropriate" academic writing. This raises the question of whose rhetorical norms are being encoded. Ensuring educational equity requires that AGS do not penalise culturally sanctioned discourse practices, particularly in international or multilingual classrooms. Instead, AGS should deliver formative feedback that clarifies rhetorical differences rather than framing them as deficiencies. Educators must also contextualise automated outputs, integrating them with disciplinary and cultural expectations. Professional development programmes can support teachers in interpreting AGS feedback and balancing algorithmic scoring with expert pedagogical judgement. These considerations inform emerging best practices for responsible cross-linguistic AGS implementation:

1. *Corpus diversification:* Invest in collecting and annotating diverse learner corpora, with attention to dialects, proficiency levels, and rhetorical genres.
2. *Participatory design:* Involve local educators, linguists, and learners in rubric design and model calibration.
3. *Bias auditing:* Conduct systematic audits for linguistic, cultural, and regional biases in model outputs.
4. *Explainability:* Integrate interpretable AI components that elucidate scoring rationale, especially for non-standard inputs.
5. *Scaffolded multilingual feedback:* Develop feedback systems that offer comparative explanations across languages (e.g., "In English academic writing, this idea would be stated more explicitly").

Future research should explore the integration of sociolinguistic theory with computational linguistics to better model the variability of learner language. Furthermore, the development of cross-linguistic error taxonomies and multilingual diagnostic tools could enhance both scoring accuracy and educational relevance.

8. CASE STUDIES IN EDUCATIONAL INSTITUTIONS

Pearson's WriteToLearn®. integrates Intelligent Essay Assessor (IEA) and state-of-the-art summary assessment mechanisms. It targets improvement in both reading comprehension and writing proficiency. The platform provides immediate, automated grading of essays, content-focused feedback, and scoring of student-written summaries by comparing them to model answers using Latent Semantic Analysis (LSA) methods. A typical interaction involves students summarising passages and then submitting essays. The KAT engine—patented LSA-based component—performs semantic similarity comparison to reference texts, offering diagnostic feedback in seconds. Key performance metrics within WriteToLearn® include content coverage, spelling accuracy, redundant phrasing, and summary length relative to benchmarks (Table 10).

Table 10. Main features of WriteToLearn®.

Feature	Description
Content coverage	Semantic overlap with target passage
Linguistic mechanics	Spelling and grammatical correctness
Concision and redundancy	Detection of superfluous or copied language
Comparative summarisation	Quantification of completeness relative to reference

Empirical validation by Pearson (2021) reveals that integration of WriteToLearn® into secondary curricula yielded statistically meaningful gains in literacy. Improvements were measured by comparing pre-and post-intervention metrics in reading comprehension tests and writing quality assessments, indicating enhanced student ability in coherent summarisation and analytical essay construction.

Turnitin's Revision Assistant. The Revision Assistant from Turnitin employs advanced NLP techniques to appraise writing traits such as clarity, organisation, use of evidence, and linguistic accuracy. The system delivers rubric-aligned trait scores and inline comments to facilitate student revision. During a 2015 pilot in 18 U.S. middle and high schools—comprising 3,439 students and 164 educators—the following outcomes were observed (Turnitin, 2020):

- 94% of students performed at least one revision;
- Middle school students averaged 11 drafts; high school students, 7;
- Mean essay length increased by ~70–100%;
- Trait scores rose from approximately 2.0 to 3.0 on a 1–4 rubric scale.

Feedback is primarily triggered through a "Signal Check", which provides indicator bars and up to four inline comments identifying strengths and areas for improvement. Teachers report that this feature amplifies student engagement, encourages iterative writing behaviours, and simulates real-time teacher feedback. The platform has garnered institutional recognition, including acknowledgement from the White House as a model of technological innovation in formative assessment.

OpenEdX and AI-Based Grading Plugins. Within the Massive Open Online Course (MOOC) ecosystem, the OpenEdX platform has integrated AI-driven grading plugins capable of evaluating open-ended student submissions. These plugins utilise transformer-based models analogous to BERT or GPT architectures, enabling real-time textual evaluation and feedback provision. A notable case at MITx demonstrated that incorporating AI grading into OpenEdX reduced educator grading burden by approximately 35% without diminishing grading accuracy or learner satisfaction (Golchin et al., 2024). Real-time feedback mechanisms notably enhance student throughput, allowing more interactive learning loops and scalability in large-enrolment contexts.

University of Michigan's M-Write Project. The M-Write initiative at the University of Michigan embeds automated essay scoring within STEM disciplines, promoting writing-centered pedagogy. The programme combines NLP-derived scoring with peer review and writing fellow interventions to support conceptual learning and argument development. Initially piloted in large introductory courses with approximately 2,000 students, the workflow included automated scoring, followed by human review via peer-editing and U-M's eCoach. Early findings from Brown (2017) indicate positive outcomes:

- Enhanced conceptual clarity and domain-specific argumentation;
- Improved student engagement through scaffolded feedback;
- Institutional scalability due to partial automation of formative review.

A comparative summary of case studies in educational institutions is presented in Table 11.

Table 11. Comparative Summary of Case Studies.

Institution/System	Assessment Focus	Technology Employed	Key Outcome Highlights
Pearson WriteToLearn®	Essays, summaries, comprehension	LSA-based KAT engine	Improved literacy outcomes via semantic similarity scoring
Turnitin Revision Assistant	Writing quality traits, revision	Writing quality traits, revision	Increased drafting, improved trait scores, high student uptake
OpenEdX with AI plugins	MOOC open-ended responses	Transformer-based models	35% reduction in instructor grading workload
University of Michigan M-Write	STEM essay concept and argumentation	NLP scoring, peer review	Deeper learning and scalability in large enrolment courses

Empirical evidence across these cases supports several convergent trends:

1. *Formative Feedback Enhances Revision.* Immediate, targeted feedback—especially when scaffolded in iterated Signal Checks—encourages students to revise rigorously, resulting in measurable writing improvements
2. *Scalability Meets Pedagogical Integrity.* Reduction in manual grading time, as observed in the MITx and M-Write deployments, allows educators to maintain quality without sacrificing engagement.
3. *Blended Human-AI Ecosystems.* Optimal performance arises when automated systems are integrated with human oversight—whether peer, fellow, or instructor review—enhancing validity and acceptability.

Collectively, these cases illustrate how automated grading systems, when institutionally governed and pedagogically integrated, can generate measurable educational benefits without displacing professional academic judgement.

9. FUTURE DIRECTIONS

The trajectory of automated grading systems (AGS) is shifting towards a new frontier characterised by contextual sophistication, ethical alignment, and multidimensional assessment paradigms. As the technological underpinnings of natural language processing (NLP), machine learning (ML), and affective computing mature, their convergence with educational psychology and pedagogical theory is catalysing a transformation in the epistemology of assessment. The following explores emerging research priorities in AGS, encompassing Multimodal Assessment Integration, Explainable Artificial Intelligence (XAI), Culturally Responsive Scoring

Frameworks, and seamless convergence with Intelligent Tutoring Systems (ITS). These developments collectively aim to advance automated assessment beyond score prediction towards a more interpretative, equitable, and learner-centric function.

1. *Multimodal Assessment Integration.* Traditional AGS has focused predominantly on textual analysis, often limited to typed or transcribed written essays. However, human expression of knowledge transcends textual modalities (Table 12). Speech, handwriting, diagrams, and other semiotic systems offer rich channels through which learners demonstrate understanding, especially in multilingual or early literacy contexts (Oviatt et al., 2006). Multimodal assessment refers to the simultaneous or integrated evaluation of diverse input forms, thereby enabling a more comprehensive analysis of student performance. For example, handwriting analysis has been used not only to evaluate legibility but also to infer cognitive load and fine motor development in early learners (Alonso-Martín et al., 2013). Likewise, prosodic and phonetic analysis in spoken responses—measuring fluency, intonation, and articulation—has proven instrumental in language proficiency assessments. Tools such as ETS's SpeechRater® exemplify this trend, offering automated scoring of spontaneous speech based on acoustic and linguistic features (Zechner & Bejar, 2006).

Table 12. Modalities in Multimodal Assessment and Associated Metrics.

Modality	Assessment Dimensions	AI Techniques Employed
Handwriting	Legibility, syntax, fine motor control	Optical character recognition, stroke modelling
Speech	Pronunciation, fluency, prosody	Acoustic feature extraction, ASR, deep learning
Visuals/Sketches	Diagram accuracy, conceptual coherence	Computer vision, semantic segmentation
Text	Grammar, coherence, style	NLP, transformer models, semantic parsing

The challenge lies in developing interoperable architectures that can fuse these diverse modalities into a unified scoring framework. Multimodal transformers (e.g., MMBERT, VisualBERT) and fusion networks offer promising pathways, albeit requiring extensive domain-specific fine-tuning (Li et al., 2019). Furthermore, multimodal assessments must account for varied accessibility needs, ensuring inclusivity for neurodiverse learners and those with sensory impairments.

2. *Explainable Artificial Intelligence (XAI).* A critical impediment to the widespread adoption of AGS is the opacity of black-box algorithms, particularly those based on deep learning. Stakeholders—including educators, students, and policy-makers—demand transparency in scoring rationale to ensure trust, contestability, and pedagogical utility. Explainable Artificial Intelligence (XAI) emerges as a foundational principle in this context, aiming to make AI decisions comprehensible to human users without sacrificing model performance (Doshi-Velez & Kim, 2017). In the realm of AGS, XAI involves producing interpretable justifications for scoring outputs, often via feature attribution, rule induction, or exemplar-based explanations. For instance, attention-weight visualisations in transformer-based models can highlight which textual segments contributed most to the assigned score (Linardatos et al., 2021). Alternatively, counterfactual reasoning approaches simulate how slight changes in input (e.g., replacing a weak thesis statement) might alter the outcome, thereby guiding learners toward improvement. Table 13 shows some XAI methods applicable to AGS.

Table 13. XAI Approaches Applicable to AGS.

XAI Method	Description	Relevance to AGS
Attention Mechanisms	Visualise focus areas in input text	Highlight key errors or strengths
SHAP/LIME	Feature importance attribution	Show linguistic features influencing score
Counterfactuals	Explore alternative outcomes for revised input	Suggest improvement pathways
Rule Extraction	Translate ML decisions into human-readable rules	Ensure rubric alignment

Implementing XAI in AGS also enables bias detection and mitigation. Disparities in scores arising from lexical diversity, dialectal usage, or topical content can be audited and corrected more effectively when the model's inner mechanics are exposed and scrutinised (Binns, 2018).

3. *Culturally Responsive Scoring Frameworks.* An increasing global emphasis on decolonising education and addressing systemic bias necessitates that AGS be culturally sensitive and inclusive. Culturally responsive scoring frameworks aim to account for linguistic diversity, local rhetorical traditions, and regional pedagogical norms that diverge from Anglo-centric conventions often embedded in commercial AGS platforms (Kubota & Lehner, 2004). For instance, while English academic writing values linear progression and explicit thesis

articulation, many African and East Asian traditions allow for more cyclical argumentation or indirect thesis development (Kaplan, 1966). Scoring systems trained solely on native English corpora may unjustly penalise such styles as incoherent or unfocused. To address this issue, several research initiatives are adopting inclusive annotation schemes and diversified training corpora. One promising approach is to create parallel corpora representing multiple cultural rhetorical styles, then train contrastive models that learn scoring norms across contexts (Yannakoudakis et al., 2011). Moreover, incorporating native educator judgment into the design and calibration of rubrics ensures sociolinguistic authenticity and fairness. Example Strategy: Rubric personalisation via region-specific calibration modules that adjust weightings on organisation, grammar, and register based on normative conventions in each educational context.

4. *Integration with Intelligent Tutoring Systems (ITS).* The fusion of AGS with Intelligent Tutoring Systems heralds a transformative shift from assessment as an endpoint to assessment as an integral feedback mechanism. By embedding grading capabilities within ITS frameworks, automated scores can be instantly translated into personalised, pedagogically grounded interventions (VanLehn, 2011). Such systems close the loop between diagnostic evaluation and instructional response, forming what is increasingly referred to as Formative Artificial Intelligence. For example, when an AGS embedded in an ITS detects persistent issues with coherence or argument structure, the system could trigger scaffolded writing prompts, provide targeted exercises, or even initiate conversational tutoring sessions using large language models (LLMs). This integration moves beyond summative scoring to facilitate metacognitive skill development, self-regulation, and longitudinal tracking of learner progress (Graesser et al., 2018). A promising framework in this regard is the Open Learner Model (OLM), which visualises the learner's evolving profile across cognitive and metacognitive dimensions, updated in real-time by AGS outputs. When coupled with a reflective dashboard, learners can engage with their performance trajectories and adjust strategies accordingly.

As AGS becomes more entrenched in high-stakes assessment contexts, ethical considerations take centre stage. Core principles of algorithmic fairness, data privacy, accountability, and autonomy must be upheld to prevent harm and ensure educational integrity (Williamson & Eynon, 2020). Future research in AGS ethics is focusing on developing governance frameworks that are transparent, participatory, and adaptable to local regulatory norms. A multi-tiered approach is advocated:

- *Technical safeguards:* Differential privacy, adversarial robustness, and bias regularisation.

- *Procedural safeguards:* Human-in-the-loop scoring for contested outputs, audit trails, and logging.
- *Institutional safeguards:* Policy frameworks that delineate acceptable use, consent procedures, and grievance redressal mechanisms.

The European Union's AI Act (2021) has already designated automated grading as a "high-risk" use case, mandating rigorous oversight. Anticipating such regulatory developments, AGS developers are increasingly embedding compliance modules and fairness evaluation benchmarks (Jobin et al., 2019).

The evolution of AGS cannot be achieved in disciplinary silos. A triangulation of computer science, educational psychology, linguistics, and ethics is imperative for the development of robust, context-aware systems. The integration of Vygotskian socio-cultural theory, Bloom's taxonomy, and self-determination theory (Deci & Ryan, 2000) into AGS design can provide scaffolding for deeper, more human-centric evaluation. This interdisciplinary approach also informs the identification of construct-irrelevant variance—elements unrelated to the construct being measured but influencing the score—such as topic familiarity or cultural references (Messick, 1995). By mitigating such variance through rubric design and model calibration, AGS can yield more valid inferences.

CONCLUSIONS

The integration of Artificial Intelligence (AI) into automated grading systems constitutes a significant shift in educational assessment, offering key advantages aligned with contemporary instructional demands. These systems provide rapid feedback, lessen administrative burden, improve evaluative consistency, and support personalised learning pathways, making them especially valuable in large-scale environments such as Massive Open Online Courses (MOOCs), where traditional grading is impracticable (Lim et al., 2021).

However, several limitations persist. Effective AI-driven grading requires extensive, high-quality annotated datasets to ensure precision and generalisability. The linguistic diversity present in student writing—including idiomatic usage, regional dialects, and varied rhetorical conventions—further challenges the accuracy and fairness of automated scoring (Glass et al., 2020). Additionally, current systems continue to struggle with evaluating creativity, originality, and other higher-order dimensions that form an essential component of holistic education. These issues highlight the ongoing necessity of human oversight, particularly in disciplines that prioritise interpretative or critical inquiry.

Ethical considerations also remain central. Concerns include algorithmic opacity, data privacy, and the risk of perpetuating cultural or linguistic biases through models trained on unrepresentative corpora (Yang et al., 2024). Accordingly, there is increasing recognition of the need for governance frameworks grounded in transparency, accountability, academic integrity, and social inclusion (Luckin & Holmes, 2016).

From a policy standpoint, future development must be informed by regulatory approaches that address the cognitive, ethical, and cultural dimensions of assessment. Collaborative work among educators, computer scientists, ethicists, and policymakers is essential to ensure that systems are technically robust, pedagogically meaningful, and socially responsible. While automated grading systems hold considerable potential to enhance efficiency and equity, their adoption must remain critically guided. Future research should prioritise explainable AI models and adaptive systems capable of respecting cultural and linguistic diversity, ensuring that AI-enhanced assessment benefits learners across varied global contexts.

REFERENCES

Al-Tameemi, G., Xue, J., Ajit, S., Kanakis, T., & Hadi, I. (2020). Predictive Learning Analytics in Higher Education: Factors, Methods and Challenges. *2020 International Conference on Advances in Computing and Communication Engineering (ICACCE)*, Las Vegas, NV, USA. pp. 1-9, DOI: 10.1109/ICACCE49060.2020.9154946

Alonso-Martín, F., Malfaz, M., Sequeira, J., Gorostiza, J. F., & Salichs, M. A. (2013). A Multimodal Emotion Detection System during Human–Robot Interaction. *Sensors (Basel), 13*(11), 15549–15581. DOI: 10.3390/s131115549 PMID: 24240598

Attali, Y., & Burstein, J. (2006). Automated Essay Scoring With e-rater® V.2. *The Journal of Technology, Learning, and Assessment, 4*(3), 1–30.

Baashar, Y., Alkawsi, G., Ali, N., Alhussian, H., & Bahbouh, H. T. (2021). Predicting student's performance using machine learning methods: A systematic literature review. *2021 International Conference on Computer & Information Sciences (ICCOINS)*, Kuching, Malaysia, pp. 357-362, DOI: 10.1109/ICCOINS49721.2021.9497185

Balfour, S. P. (2013). Assessing writing in MOOCs: Automated essay scoring and calibrated peer review. Research & Practice in Assessment, 8, 40–48. https://www.rpajournal.com/dev/wp-content/uploads/2013/05/SF4.pdf

Bennett, R. E., & Zhang, M. (2016). Automated scoring: Consumers, vendors, theories, and research. *Educational Measurement: Issues and Practice, 35*(1), 9–15.

Bennett, R. E., & Zhang, M. (2016). *Validity and Automated Scoring: It's Not Only About the Scoring*. Educational Testing Service.

Binns, R. (2018). Fairness in machine learning: Lessons from political philosophy. *Proceedings of the 2018 Conference on Fairness, Accountability, and Transparency*, 149–159. DOI: 10.1145/3287560.3287583

Binns, R., Veale, M., Van Kleek, M., & Shadbolt, N. (2018). 'It's Reducing a Human Being to a Percentage': Perceptions of Justice in Algorithmic Decisions. *Proceedings of the 2018 CHI Conference on Human Factors in Computing Systems*, 1–14. DOI: 10.1145/3173574.3173951

Blodgett, S. L., Green, L., & O'Connor, B. (2016). Demographic Dialectal Variation in Social Media: A Case Study of African-American English. Empirical Methods in Natural Language Processing (EMNLP), 1119–1130. DOI: 10.18653/v1/D16-1120

Borah, A. R., Dev, R. S. S., Suprathik, B. M., Harshini, A. R., Boggula, Y., & Charitha, V. (2024). Automated Models in Educational Assessment: A Comprehensive Survey. *9th International Conference on Communication and Electronics Systems (ICCES)*, Coimbatore, India, pp. 1029-1034. DOI: 10.1109/ICCES63552.2024.10859689

Brown, J. L. (2017, 6 de junio). How U of Michigan built automated essay-scoring software to fill feedback gap for student writing. EdSurge. Recuperado de https://www.edsurge.com/news/2017-06-06-how-u-of-michigan-built-automated-essay-scoring-software-to-fill-feedback-gap-for-student-writing

Brown, T. B., Mann, B., Ryder, N., Subbiah, M., Kaplan, J., Dhariwal, P., & Amodei, D. (2020). Language models are few-shot learners. *Advances in Neural Information Processing Systems*, *33*, 1877–1901.

Burrows, S., Gurevych, I., & Stein, B. (2015). The eras and trends of automatic short answer grading. *International Journal of Artificial Intelligence in Education*, *25*(1), 60–117. DOI: 10.1007/s40593-014-0026-8

Burstein, J., Chodorow, M., & Leacock, C. (2013). Automated Essay Evaluation: The Criterion Online Writing Service. *AI Magazine*, *25*(3), 27–36.

Burstein, J., Tetreault, J., & Madnani, N. (2013). The E-rater® automated essay scoring system. In Shermis, M., & Burstein, J. (Eds.), *Handbook of Automated Essay Evaluation* (pp. 55–67). Routledge.

Calvo, R. A., & D'Mello, S. (2010). Affect Detection: An Interdisciplinary Review of Models, Methods, and Their Applications. *IEEE Transactions on Affective Computing*, *1*(1), 18–37. DOI: 10.1109/T-AFFC.2010.1

Chi, M., VanLehn, K., Litman, D., & Jordan, P. (2020). An overview of intelligent tutoring systems. In *The Cambridge Handbook of Computing Education Research* (pp. 370–393). Cambridge University Press., DOI: 10.1017/9781108782927.017

Chodorow, M., & Burstein, J. (2004). Beyond Essay Length: Evaluating e-rater®'s Performance on TOEFL Essays. *ETS Research Report Series*, *2004*(1). Advance online publication. DOI: 10.1002/j.2333-8504.2004.tb01931.x

Conneau, A., Khandelwal, K., Goyal, N., Chaudhary, V., Wenzek, G., Guzmán, F., & Stoyanov, V. (2020). Unsupervised Cross-lingual Representation Learning at Scale. *Proceedings of the 58th Annual Meeting of the Association for Computational Linguistics*, 8440–8451. DOI: 10.18653/v1/2020.acl-main.747

Corbett, A. T., & Anderson, J. R. (1995). Knowledge tracing: Modelling the acquisition of procedural knowledge. *User Modeling and User-Adapted Interaction*, *4*(4), 253–278. DOI: 10.1007/BF01099821

Council of Europe. (2001). *Common European Framework of Reference for Languages: Learning, Teaching, Assessment.* Cambridge University Press.

D'Mello, S., & Graesser, A. (2015). Feeling, thinking, and computing with affect-aware learning technologies. In Calvo, R. A. (Eds.), *The Oxford Handbook of Affective Computing* (pp. 419–434). Oxford University Press.

Deci, E. L., & Ryan, R. M. (2000). The "what" and "why" of goal pursuits: Human needs and the self-determination of behaviour. *Psychological Inquiry, 11*(4), 227–268. DOI: 10.1207/S15327965PLI1104_01

Devlin, J., Chang, M.-W., Lee, K., & Toutanova, K. (2019). BERT: Pre-training of Deep Bidirectional Transformers for Language Understanding. NAACL-HLT, 4171–4186. https://doi.org//arXiv.1810.04805DOI: 10.48550

Dietterich, T. G. (2000). Ensemble methods in machine learning. In *Multiple Classifier Systems* (pp. 1–15). Springer., DOI: 10.1007/3-540-45014-9_1

Dimari, A., Tyagi, N., Davanageri, M. B., Kukreti, R., Yadav, R. K., & Dimari, H. (2024). AI-Based Automated Grading Systems for open book examination system: Implications for Assessment in Higher Education. *2024 International Conference on Knowledge Engineering and Communication Systems (ICKECS)*, Chikkaballapur, India, pp. 1-7, DOI: 10.1109/ICKECS61492.2024.10616490

Doshi-Velez, F., & Kim, B. (2017). Towards a rigorous science of interpretable machine learning. arXiv preprint. https://doi.org//arXiv.1702.08608DOI: 10.48550

Feng, F., Yang, Y., Cer, D., Arivazhagan, N., & Wang, W. (2020). Language-Agnostic BERT Sentence Embedding. arXiv preprint. https://doi.org//arXiv.2007.01852DOI: 10.48550

Fernandez, N., Ghosh, A., Liu, N., Wang, Z., Choffin, B., Baraniuk, R., & Lan, A. (2023). Automated Scoring for Reading Comprehension via In-context BERT. Tuning. *Machine Learning*. Advance online publication. arXiv2205.09864. DOI: 10.48550/arXiv.2205.09864

Foltz, P. W., Gilliam, S., & Kendall, S. (2013). "Supporting Content-Based Feedback in Automated Essay Scoring." Handbook of Automated Essay Evaluation, 73–90.

Foltz, P. W., Laham, D., & Landauer, T. K. (2013). Automated Essay Scoring: Applications to Educational Technology. In Shermis, M. D., & Burstein, J. (Eds.), *Handbook of Automated Essay Evaluation* (pp. 68–88). Routledge.

Fuentes-Penna, A., & González Ibarra, J. (2024). Personalized Education and Artificial Intelligence. *International Journal of Combinatorial Optimization Problems and Informatics*, *15*(2), 1–12. DOI: 10.61467/2007.1558.2024.v15i2.431

Gatt, A., & Krahmer, E. (2018). Survey of the state of the art in natural language generation: Core tasks, applications and evaluation. *Journal of Artificial Intelligence Research*, *61*, 65–170. DOI: 10.1613/jair.5477

Glass, M., Gliozzo, A., Chakravarti, R., Ferritto, A., Pan, L., Bhargav, G. P. S., Garg, D., & Sil, S. (2020). Automatic grading of short answers using deep learning. In *Proceedings of the 58th Annual Meeting of the Association for Computational Linguistics* (pp. 2728–2739). Association for Computational Linguistics., https://aclanthology.org/2020.acl-main.247

Golchin, S., Garuda, N., Impey, C., & Wenger, M. (2024). Grading Massive Open Online Courses Using Large Language Models. https://doi.org//arxiv.2406.11102DOI: 10.48550

Graesser, A. C., Hu, X., Nye, B., & Sottilare, R. A. (2018). Intelligent tutoring systems with conversational dialogue. In *AI in Education* (pp. 11–22). Springer., DOI: 10.1007/978-3-319-93846-2_2

Graesser, A. C., Hu, X., & Sottilare, R. (2018). Affective Computing in Educational Assessment: Enhancing Feedback with Emotion-Aware Systems. *Computers in Human Behavior*, *89*, 390–403.

Graesser, A. C., McNamara, D. S., & Kulikowich, J. M. (2018). Coh-Metrix: Providing multilevel analyses of text characteristics. *Educational Researcher*, *40*(5), 223–234. DOI: 10.3102/0013189X11413260

Ifenthaler, D., & Yau, J. Y.-K. (2020). Utilising learning analytics to support study success in higher education: A systematic review. *Educational Technology Research and Development*, *68*(4), 1961–1990. DOI: 10.1007/s11423-020-09788-z

Ifenthaler, D., & Yau, J. Y.-K. (2020). Utilising Learning Analytics for Study Success: Reflections on Current Empirical Findings. Technology. *Knowledge and Learning*, *25*, 545–552.

Jobin, A., Ienca, M., & Vayena, E. (2019). The global landscape of AI ethics guidelines. *Nature Machine Intelligence*, *1*(9), 389–399. DOI: 10.1038/s42256-019-0088-2

Kaplan, R. B. (1966). Cultural Thought Patterns in Inter-Cultural Education. *Language Learning*, *16*(1–2), 1–20. DOI: 10.1111/j.1467-1770.1966.tb00804.x

Kaya, M., & Cicekli, I. (2024). A Hybrid Approach for Automated Short Answer Grading. *IEEE Access : Practical Innovations, Open Solutions, 12*, 96332–96341. DOI: 10.1109/ACCESS.2024.3420890

Kiperwasser, E., & Goldberg, Y. (2016). Simple and accurate dependency parsing using bidirectional LSTM feature representations. *Transactions of the Association for Computational Linguistics, 4*, 313–327. DOI: 10.1162/tacl_a_00101

Klebanov, B. B., & Madnani, N. (2022). *Automated Essay Scoring*. Springer Cham. Springer Nature Switzerland AG., DOI: 10.1007/978-3-031-02182-4

Kubota, R., & Lehner, A. (2004). Toward critical contrastive rhetoric. *Journal of Second Language Writing, 13*(1), 7–27. DOI: 10.1016/j.jslw.2004.04.003

Kudo, T., & Richardson, J. (2018). SentencePiece: A simple and language independent subword tokenizer and detokenizer for Neural Text Processing. EMNLP, 66–71. DOI: 10.18653/v1/D18-2012

Li, L. H., Yatskar, M., Yin, D., Hsieh, C. J., & Chang, K. W. (2019). VisualBERT: A simple and performant baseline for vision and language. arXiv preprint. https://doi.org//arXiv.1908.03557DOI: 10.48550

Lim, C. T., Bong, C. H., Wong, W. S., & Lee, N. K. (2021). A Comprehensive Review of Automated Essay Scoring (AES) Research and Development. *Pertanika Journal of Science & Technology, 29*(3). Advance online publication. DOI: 10.47836/pjst.29.3.27

Linardatos, P., Papastefanopoulos, V., & Kotsiantis, S. (2021). Explainable AI: A review of machine learning interpretability methods. *Entropy (Basel, Switzerland), 23*(1), 18. DOI: 10.3390/e23010018 PMID: 33375658

Luckin, R., & Holmes, W. (2016). Intelligence Unleashed: An argument for AI in Education. https://discovery.ucl.ac.uk/id/eprint/1475756

Manning, C. D., Raghavan, P., & Schütze, H. (2008). *Introduction to Information Retrieval*. Cambridge University Press. DOI: 10.1017/CBO9780511809071

McNamara, D. S., Crossley, S. A., & McCarthy, P. M. (2014). *Automated Evaluation of Text and Discourse with Coh-Metrix*. Cambridge University Press., DOI: 10.1017/CBO9780511894664

Mikolov, T., Chen, K., Corrado, G., & Dean, J. (2013). "Efficient estimation of word representations in vector space." arXiv preprint arXiv:1301.3781

Oflazer, K., & Kuruöz, İ. (1994).. . *Tagging and Morphological Disambiguation of Turkish Text. COLING, 1446–1450.* Advance online publication. DOI: 10.3115/991939.991994

Ouyang, L., Wu, J., Jiang, X., Almeida, D., Wainwright, C. L., Mishkin, P., Zhang, C., Agarwal, A., Slama, K., Ray, A., Schulman, J., Hilton, J., Kelton, F., Miller, L., Simens, M., Askell, A., Welinder, P., Christiano, P., Leike, J., & Lowe, R. (2022). Training language models to follow instructions with human feedback. Computation and Language. https://doi.org//arXiv.2203.02155DOI: 10.48550

Oviatt, S., Arthur, A., & Cohen, J. (2006). Quiet interfaces that help students think. In *Proceedings of the 19th annual ACM symposium on User interface software and technology (UIST '06)*. Association for Computing Machinery, New York, NY, USA, 191–200. DOI: 10.1145/1166253.1166284

Pang, W., & Wei, Z. (2025). Shaping the Future of Higher Education: A Technology Usage Study on Generative AI Innovations. *Information (Basel)*, *16*(2), 95. DOI: 10.3390/info16020095

Pankiewicz, M., & Baker, R. S. (2023). Large Language Models (GPT) for automating feedback on programming assignments. arXiv.Org, abs/2307.00150. https://doi.org//arXiv.2307.00150DOI: 10.48550

Pearson. (2021). WriteToLearn® summary assessment details. Pearson Assessments. Retrieved from https://www.pearsonassessments.com/

Picard, R. W. (1997). *Affective Computing*. MIT Press. DOI: 10.7551/mitpress/1140.001.0001

Pires, T., Schlinger, E., & Garrette, D. (2019). How multilingual is Multilingual BERT? *Proceedings of the 57th Annual Meeting of the Association for Computational Linguistics*, 4996–5001. DOI: 10.18653/v1/P19-1493

Shermis, M. D., & Burstein, J. (2013). *Handbook of Automated Essay Evaluation: Current Applications and New Directions*. Routledge. DOI: 10.4324/9780203122761

Siemens, G., & Long, P. (2011). Penetrating the Fog: Analytics in Learning and Education. *EDUCAUSE Review*, *46*(5), 30–40.

Sun, C., Qiu, X., Xu, Y., & Huang, X. (2020). How to fine-tune BERT for text classification. Computation and Language. https://doi.org//arXiv.1905.05583DOI: 10.48550

Taghipour, K., & Ng, H. T. (2016). A Neural Approach to Automated Essay Scoring. *Proceedings of the 2016 Conference on Empirical Methods in Natural Language Processing*, 1882–1891. DOI: DOI: 10.18653/v1/D16-1193

Toutanova, K., Klein, D., Manning, C. D., & Singer, Y. (2003). "Feature-rich part-of-speech tagging with a cyclic dependency network." *Proceedings of NAACL-HLT*, 252–259. DOI: 10.3115/1073445.1073478

Turnitin. (2020). Revision Assistant Research Summary. https://www.turnitin.com/

Tusell-Rey, C. C., Villuendas-Rey, Y., Salinas-García, V., Camacho-Nieto, O., & Yáñez-Márquez, C. (2025). Instance Selection for Hybrid and Incomplete Data Based on Clustering. *International Journal of Combinatorial Optimization Problems and Informatics*, *16*(3), 405–419. DOI: 10.61467/2007.1558.2025.v16i3.845

Van Der Linden, W. J., & Glas, C. A. W. (2010). *Elements of Adaptive Testing*. Springer., DOI: 10.1007/978-0-387-85461-8

VanLehn, K. (2006). The behavior of tutoring systems. *International Journal of Artificial Intelligence in Education*, *16*(3), 227–265. DOI: 10.3233/IRG-2006-16(3)02

VanLehn, K. (2011). The relative effectiveness of human tutoring, intelligent tutoring systems, and other tutoring systems. *Educational Psychologist*, *46*(4), 197–221. DOI: 10.1080/00461520.2011.611369

Vetrivel, S. C., Vidhyapriya, P., & Arun, V. P. (2025). The Role of AI in Transforming Assessment Practices in Education. In Keeley, K. (Ed.), *AI Applications and Strategies in Teacher Education* (pp. 43–70). IGI Global Scientific Publishing., DOI: 10.4018/979-8-3693-5443-8.ch003

Webber, B., Egg, M., & Kordoni, V. (2012). Discourse structure and language technology. *Natural Language Engineering*, *18*(4), 437–490. DOI: 10.1017/S1351324911000337

Whitelock, D., Van Labeke, N., Field, D., Pulman, S., & Richardson, J. (2013). OpenEssayist: An Automated Feedback System that Supports University Students as they Write Summative Essays. *1st Arab Open University International Conference on Open Learning: Role, Challenges and Aspirations at*: The Arab Open University, Kuwait City, Kuwait.

Williamson, B., & Eynon, R. (2020). Historical threads, missing links, and future directions in AI in education. *Learning, Media and Technology*, *45*(3), 223–235. DOI: 10.1080/17439884.2020.1798995

Williamson, D. M., Mislevy, R. J., & Bejar, I. I. (2006). *Automated Scoring of Complex Tasks in Computer-Based Testing. Publisher.* Lawrence Erlbaum Associates., DOI: 10.4324/9780415963572

Yang, K., Raković, M., Li, Y., Guan, Q., Gašević, D., & Chen, G. (2024). Unveiling the Tapestry of Automated Essay Scoring: A Comprehensive Investigation of Accuracy. *Fairness, and Generalizability.*, *38*(20), 22466–22474. DOI: 10.1609/aaai.v38i20.30254

Yannakoudakis, H., Briscoe, T., & Medlock, B. (2011). A New Dataset and Method for Automatically Grading ESOL Texts. *Proceedings of the 49th Annual Meeting of the Association for Computational Linguistics: Human Language Technologies*, 180–189.

Yi, S., Yu, Y., & Wu, J. (2024). AI-based Online Code Quality Assessment System. *3rd International Conference on Cloud Computing, Big Data Application and Software Engineering (CBASE)*, Hangzhou, China, 2024, pp. 659-663, DOI: 10.1109/CBASE64041.2024.10824380

Zechner, K., & Bejar, I. I. (2006). Towards Automatic Scoring of Non-Native Spontaneous Speech. *Language and Technology Conference*, 216–223. DOI: 10.3115/1220835.1220863

Chapter 4
Building the IoT-Enabled Smart Campus:
Infrastructure, Automation, and Intelligent Connectivity

Muhammad Usman Tariq
https://orcid.org/0000-0002-7605-3040
Abu Dhabi University, UAE & University College Cork, Ireland

ABSTRACT

An IoT-based smart campus is a development of smart campuses that involves the combination of high-tech digital infrastructure, ubiquitous sensors, and intelligent automation to complement operational efficiency, safety, and user experience. Cloud-based systems and edge computing to process data at a faster rate can provide seamless connectivity to every academic, administrative, and residential setting. The automation of lighting, HVAC, and access control systems leads to reduced energy use while enhancing the comfort and safety of the occupants. Building-level IoT-driven analytics further support decision-making for campus planners and enrich teaching and learning experiences through adaptive environments and the integration of digital resources. A well-designed smart campus ecosystem promotes sustainability, improves resource allocation, and strengthens resilience to operational disruptions.

INTRODUCTION

The first step to getting acquainted with the IoT as a fundamental layer is to understand that it significantly alters the connection between physical space and online intellect. Traditionally, campuses were run on manual procedures, fixed schedules, and limited feedback. Facilities departments relied on routine checks rather than

DOI: 10.4018/979-8-3373-6831-3.ch004

026, IGI Global Scientific Publishing. Copying or distributing in print or electronic forms without written permission of IGI Global Scientific Publishing is prohibited. Use of this chapter to tive artificial intelligence (AI) technologies is expressly prohibited. The publisher reserves all rights to license its use for generative AI training and machine learning model development.

real-time data, classrooms were equipped based on general assumptions rather than measured usage, and student services relied heavily on one-size-fits-all models. The IoT shifts this paradigm by embedding data collection, data sharing, and data analysis capabilities into the physical infrastructure of the campus itself (Izourane et al., 2024). The role of IoT in shaping future-ready higher educational institutions cannot be gainsaid as it responds directly to the changing expectations of students, faculty, and society. Today's learners come to campus accustomed to personalized digital experiences in all aspects of life, from smart homes to mobile banking. They would expect campus spaces to function intuitively, such as classrooms that self-adjust for lighting and temperature, dorms that show real-time energy use, libraries that optimize quiet and study space, and security that makes them feel safer without feeling intrusive. Simultaneously, IoT enhances preparedness for emergencies and disruptions by enabling early warnings, automated responses, and timely communication across campus populations.

Another reason IoT is crucial for future-ready higher education is that it enables data-driven governance and strategic decision-making. Although universities generate vast amounts of information across departments, this information has traditionally remained fragmented and underutilized. With IoT, these silos break down; data collected from many touchpoints, such as buildings, transportation systems, classrooms, and student services, are integrated and used. The purpose of this chapter is to provide a detailed look at how IoT technologies are transforming the modern campus environment and to analyze the underlying infrastructure, systems, and methods necessary to develop an IoT-based smart campus (Tariq, 2025).

Discussions relating to smart campuses usually rely on high-level benefits or technology standpoints, and this chapter proposes a more encompassing narrative that can link the technological, operational, and human aspects of integrating IoT. Hence, the aim is to explain not just what IoT is or what it can do, but how it gets into the physical and digital fabric of campus life. This perspective has allowed the chapter to provide readers with an understanding of the architectures that underpin and enable the IoT, such as networks, device ecosystems, and data management platforms (Mohamed & Alosman, 2024). It has also examined how automation will change campus operations, making them much more efficient and less administratively complex. Finally, it underscores the importance of intelligent connectivity-how devices communicate with one another, share data, and coordinate responses to create cohesive adaptive campus systems. These themes are discussed in terms of the opportunities and challenges related to building an IoT-enabled smart campus. While IoT offers great potential, careful planning, robust security, well-thought-out policies, and continuous collaboration among campus stakeholders must be considered. This chapter discusses issues such as the protection of privacy, network reliability, scalability, user adoption, and ethical use of data. Critical issues ensure that IoT deployments are not only technologically sound but also socially responsible and directed towards institutional values (Bellaj et al., 2024). This chapter emphasizes that such tasks are interdisciplinary and require the collaboration of IT professionals, facilities managers, academic leaders, researchers, and students to build a smart campus. This chapter also examines how IoT-enabled intelligent campus environments can support better learning outcomes and provide an enhanced student experience. Learning spaces enhanced by IoT technologies can enable adaptive teaching, immediate feedback, and adaptable spatial configurations to suit different pedagogies. Digital interventions can facilitate personalized learning pathways, support students with disabilities, and develop more interactive classrooms.

Beyond the classroom, IoT will enhance campus life through easier navigation, optimized facilities and resource management, and student health and well-being, supported by connected health and safety services (Koukaras et al., 2025). Fundamentally, this chapter should serve as a guide to understand the intent and role of IoT in shaping the future of higher education and provide a foundation for institutions desiring to begin or further their smart campus initiatives in the future. By exploring both the technological and transformative force of IoT, this chapter provides the groundwork to envision a future where digital intelligence and human activity coexist harmoniously in efficient, sustainable, and secure environments that are profoundly supportive of the educational mission (Tariq, 2024).

CONCEPTUAL FOUNDATIONS OF IOT IN HIGHER EDUCATION

The idea of the Internet of Things (IoT) in higher education has moved beyond the simple notion of connecting devices to the Internet. For modern campuses, the IoT signifies an entire ecosystem in which physical spaces, digital systems, and human interfaces are all interconnected with continuous data exchange. In defining IoT in the setting of a campus environment, one needs to look at the campus as a living network of buildings, utilities, learning spaces, and service areas, all churning out data (Izourane et al., 2024). The ecosystem becomes intelligent when sensors, actuators, software platforms, user devices, and cloud services communicate with each other to enable automation, informed decision-making, and adaptive responses. Therefore, IoT in a campus environment is the way in which devices and systems that are connected note conditions in real time, share insights across platforms, and act on them to optimize operations or improve the user experience. It is not only a technology layer that is overlaid on top of the current infrastructure, but it also reinvents how a campus handles its resources and services and supports academic and social life. It is a kind of DNA of the campus in its essence, as it combines digital intelligence with the life and everyday activities of students, staff, and administrators (Mohamed

& Alosman, 2024). A better understanding of the IoT requires an investigation into its constituent architecture, which prescribes the rules that will guide how devices communicate and the manner of data flow within the system. The basis of any IoT architecture consists of sensors and actuators installed across the campus., in turn, feed into actuators that take action on the data, such as turning the lights on or off, unlocking doors, or adjusting ventilation. These devices create a continuous feedback loop in which the physical environment interacts with digital systems.

This sensor-actuator network requires a robust communication infrastructure for optimal performance. IoT devices use different types of networks depending on the scale of their activities, data requirements, and energy limitations. Wi-Fi would be suitable as it has the capacity to work with applications that require a large bandwidth, like smart classrooms and digital signage, but low-power networks, like LoRaWAN or Zigbee, would support devices that transmit small data volumes over long distances, such as environmental sensors or utility meters. The challenge is to make them coexist without interference and to support thousands of devices scattered throughout the campus (Lu et al., 2024). The connectivity layer forms the backbone of the IoT ecosystem to ensure that data move efficiently from the physical world to digital platforms, where they can be processed and analyzed. Edge devices, including gateways, microcontrollers, and small computing units that process data close to their generation point, sit between the device layer and cloud platforms. Given the growing need for reduced latency, enhanced privacy, and lessening of the loads on the central servers, edge computing plays an increasingly important role in campus IoT architecture. An example of this is an automated lighting system that uses occupancy sensors to control lights. The choice of whether to turn the lights on or off might be locally made by an edge device instead of being sent to the cloud. This kind of instant responsiveness develops an environment that is responsive to user needs. These edge devices also filter or preprocess data to ensure that only relevant information is sent to cloud services, thereby optimizing bandwidth and reducing clutter in large data repositories (Tariq, 2026). Table 1 demonstrates how IoT is not merely technical infrastructure but a strategic enabler of institutional outcomes.

Table 1. IoT Architecture Layers, Campus Applications, and Strategic Value

IoT Architecture Layer	Key Technologies	Campus Applications	Strategic Institutional Benefits
Device Layer (Sensors & Actuators)	Occupancy sensors, environmental sensors, smart meters, biometric readers	Smart classrooms, air quality monitoring, access control, energy metering	Improved comfort, safety, and resource awareness
Connectivity Layer	Wi-Fi 6, 5G, LoRaWAN, NB-IoT	Campus-wide networking, shuttle tracking, parking systems	Reliable real-time communication and scalability
Edge Computing Layer	Gateways, microcontrollers, local analytics	Instant lighting/HVAC adjustments, safety alerts	Low latency, enhanced privacy, reduced cloud load
Data & Middleware Layer	Middleware platforms, APIs, device management systems	System interoperability, cross-department integration	Unified governance, operational coherence
Cloud & Analytics Layer	Cloud platforms, dashboards, AI/ML tools	Predictive maintenance, learning analytics, sustainability monitoring	Evidence-based decision-making, strategic foresight
Application Layer	Campus management systems, mobile apps, dashboards	Student services, facility optimisation, academic analytics	Enhanced student experience and institutional performance

The last layer of IoT architecture involves cloud integration, aggregation, storage, and analytics of data from sensors, actuators, and edge devices. These cloud platforms provide computing power and storage capacity to support data analytics, machine learning, visualization dashboards, and campus management applications. Cloud computing provides real-time insights into building performance, energy consumption, classroom usage, and student mobility patterns that campus administrators require. Understanding this layered architecture with sensors, networks, edge devices, and cloud platforms allows people to appreciate the fact that IoT seamlessly fits into campus operations. However, all these benefits depend on several key characteristics that define the successful implementation of IoT. The first is interoperability. Because campuses are infrastructures built over many years, involving multiple vendors, systems, and technologies, IoT must operate across heterogeneous pieces of equipment, software platforms, and communication protocols. Interoperability ensures that sensors from one manufacturer can communicate with gateways from another manufacturer, and different buildings on campus can be integrated into the same management system. In addition, new technologies can be added without dismantling the existing investments (Mohamed & Alosman, 2024). Without interoperability, campuses may end up building fragmented systems that function in isolation rather than contributing to a smart unified ecosystem. For higher education institutions, this is a key characteristic because it avoids technological lock-in and provides long-term sustainability of IoT initiatives. Another defining characteristic is its scalability.

Scalability similarly pertains to analytics capabilities, as the campus needs the ability to scale from simple monitoring to advanced predictive models or machine-learning-driven insights as the system matures. With a scalable IoT architecture, institutions can begin using it on a small scale, for example, automating lighting in one building or deploying occupancy sensors in classrooms, and expand outward into campus-wide systems that encompass everything from transportation to energy to academic facilities. Because IoT solutions can grow and adapt to changing conditions, they remain relevant and cost-effective over time (Koukaras et al., 2025). Another fundamental characteristic of IoT systems in higher education is their real-time responsiveness. Campuses are dynamic environments with ever-changing conditions, including students moving from building to building, changing weather, equipment operating on variable schedules, and changing security needs. Owing to this dynamic environment, IoT systems must rapidly process information and automatically respond when called upon. Real-time responsiveness means that a smart classroom adjusts its environment the second students enter or that a security alert immediately triggers action by automated systems and human personnel. This enables facility teams to instantly detect malfunctioning systems, whether a boiler is operating outside its normal range or a water leak is just beginning to take shape. In this instant action, IoT differs from traditional facility automation systems, which often rely on back-office reporting and require human intervention. Real-time data enable both academic and student-facing applications, such as updating the availability of study spaces, offering real-time shuttle tracking, and delivering adaptive content in technology-enhanced classrooms.

CORE COMPONENTS OF IOT-ENABLED SMART INFRASTRUCTURE

Smart infrastructure is at the heart of any IoT-enabled campus, which converts old technology buildings and services into a responsive, data-driven infrastructure that promotes comfort, efficiency, sustainability, and safety. One of the most obvious aspects is a smart building, that is, a structure endowed with automated environment control (Izourane et al., 2024). In such buildings, embedded sensors and intelligent devices continuously adjust the lighting, temperature, ventilation, and other environmental features to maintain an optimal environment. Rather than relying on manual switches or static schedules, smart buildings learn from usage patterns and automatically adjust their settings according to occupancy, weather, the time of day, and energy consumption goals (Tariq, 2025).

Facility management is changing radically with the emergence of smart buildings. Traditionally, building maintenance has been performed through routine checkups, manual inspections, and complaints made by users. This is transformed by the IoT, which delivers reliable information on the performance of the equipment, environmental conditions, and health of the systems in real time. Smart meters record the consumption rates of electricity and water, which can be studied in detail by analyzing the consumption patterns (Ahmad & Alshurideh, 2025). HVAC systems equipped with networked sensors can automatically alert facility teams to the need to replace filters, motors that are working within an abnormal range, or even when temperature levels are too high or too low. Predictive maintenance can be experienced when systems examine the performance trends of devices and forecast failures even before they occur. This minimizes the incidence of downtime and lengthens the life of critical building components. The data produced by these automated systems allow administrators to refine energy strategies over time, optimize building performance, and make evidence-based decisions regarding renovations, upgrades, or operational changes.

In addition to these automated controls, sensor-based space management is integral to modern smart campuses. As university facilities become increasingly complex and the demand for space continues to rise, campuses must understand the actual usage of classrooms, libraries, laboratories, meeting rooms, and recreational spaces. Occupancy sensors supply precise information about the utilization of spaces, the time, and the frequency with which they are utilized, and then go beyond the approximate scheduling that can result in wastage and inefficient scheduling. For example, occupancy monitoring can show that some lecture halls are not fully used at the busiest times, allowing time to be reallocated on the schedules or repurposed (Mohamed & Alosman, 2024). In libraries or study areas, the sensors may utilize real-time data to help students locate available working spaces through mobile applications or digital screens, thereby reducing frustration levels and improving the overall learning experience. Space management sensors have implications for energy efficiency. When systems know that a room is empty, they can automatically power down non-essential devices, dim the lights, and adjust HVAC systems. Energy flow sensors provide insights into how electricity is distributed across buildings to identify hotspots of energy-intensive areas or pieces of equipment that use anomalously large amounts of power. This information allows institutions to focus on their operational plans, conserve strategies, and meet their sustainability goals. Air quality sensors further enhance the learning environment by tracking carbon dioxide levels, humidity, particulate matter and volatile organic compounds. These environmental factors are known to affect the concentration and health of students, which are indicative of comfort, making real-time air quality monitoring a classroom and laboratory requirement. Should air quality dip outside the ideal range, ventilation systems automatically adjust to return conditions back to comfortable levels. By integrating environmental, occupancy, and energy flow sensors into one system, campuses can understand space performance holistically and constantly make adjustments to optimize the human experience along with resource use.

Security is another pillar of IoT-enabled smart infrastructure, and connected security systems redefine how campuses can protect their students, staff, and property. Smart surveillance depends on networked cameras equipped with analytics-driven capabilities for motion detection, facial recognition (where legally appropriate), and anomaly detection. Instead of requiring human operators to check dozens of video feeds, intelligent systems can autonomously identify suspicious activity, track movement patterns, and send email alerts where appropriate (Koukaras et al., 2025). This enhances situational awareness, and threats or emergencies can be responded to in a shorter time. In addition, other systems, including lighting or access control, can be connected to smart cameras; that is, buildings can automatically respond to certain events. For example, if a surveillance camera detects motion in a restricted area of the campus at night, a connected system might trigger an alert while turning on the lighting and locking nearby doors simultaneously. The introduction of IoT has also made access control systems smarter. Biometric systems, mobile credentials, and multi-factor authentication are used to supplement or replace traditional swipes with ID cards that allow entry into the building in a secure but effortless way. Access levels are controlled remotely by administrators, and permissions are granted or revoked on the fly. The buildings will unlock and lock at designated time periods when there is no traffic present. Residential halls have mobile applications that can be used to enter rooms, and smart locks ensure accountability and safety. Sensitive equipment locations can be assigned higher levels of access in the case of facilities such as laboratories or research buildings, so that only authorized users have access. The same systems can support the emergency response process by allowing rapid lockdowns, guiding occupants to safe exits, and tracking real-time updates for first responders in crisis situations.

IoT connectivity greatly enhances emergency response capabilities. Fire, smoke, gas leaks, and other hazards are sensed long before the human eye can notice them, and the process automatically triggers alerts and safety measures. Integrated emergency communications using IoT can also be used to send specific messages to students and staff according to their locations to obtain timely and relevant information in the event of an emergency. For example, when a sensor detects a dangerous spill in a laboratory, the system will notify the occupants of the building, redirect foot traffic, and coordinate the activities of the security personnel. All these intertwined systems work together to make campuses safe by maintaining constant awareness and rapid unified responses. In addition to buildings and security, intelligent mobility and transportation systems represent another important aspect of infrastructure in smart campuses. Contemporary higher education institutions often serve thousands of students, faculty, staff, and visitors within large areas every day. In such cases, transportation management is important to create convenience, prevent overcrowding, and reduce environmental effects. IoT-based mobility systems merge real-time data concerning shuttles, parking lots, bike-sharing spots, and footways into a system to ensure smooth movements. GPS-linked buses can monitor the positions of the buses in real time, and students can be informed about the arrival time through mobile applications (Ahmad & Alshurideh, 2025). This saves time on waiting and aids individuals in route planning, particularly in inclement weather or hectic timetables. Parking management has also been improved using IoT. Sensors in parking lots are used to identify spots and relay this information to digital displays or similar user applications to help save time and reduce the need for circling, thereby reducing congestion. Some campuses also have smart systems that automatically assign parking spaces according to demand patterns or assign priorities to certain groups, such as staff, visitors, or students with disabilities. In the case of greener institutions, the IoT assists in the electric vehicle charging network to control the energy demand and grid loads and transmit real-time charging information to users. Such a system will be able to distribute power smartly, leaving the charging stations in place and energy-efficient. IoT connectivity also boosts bicycle and scooter sharing.

Docking stations can track usage habits, position vehicles, and determine maintenance requirements. This, in turn, guarantees the availability of bikes and scooters when and where required and in excellent working condition. These systems enhance the reduction of carbon emissions and active mobility on campuses, encouraging sustainable transportation (Picallo et al., 2024). The IoT is useful for promoting pedestrian safety. Intelligent crossroads with sensors and lights can be used to inform drivers of the presence of pedestrians, thus increasing safety along campus highways. Smartphone applications or wearable devices can be linked to mobility systems to ensure that blind students can move about the campus or guide novice students on how to move around campus effectively. Therefore, the core components of an IoT-enabled smart campus include smart buildings, sensor-based space management, connected security systems, and intelligent mobility. Comfort, sustainability, safety, and convenience will be part of the environment created by seamlessly integrating sensor networks, automated controls, real-time analytics, and interconnected services. The ability of higher education to continually evolve depends on campuses being increasingly prepared to meet the needs of their communities and position them for success in an ever-changing world. Therefore, IoT infrastructure is one of the critical ways in which progress is enabled, shaping campuses into efficient, thoughtful, and intelligent environments that support human flourishing of the people working, learning, and living within them.

NETWORK CONNECTIVITY AND DATA INTEGRATION

Any IoT-enabled campus is based on a high-performance network connection to facilitate the enormous amount of data produced simultaneously by thousands of sensors, devices, and automated systems. The IoT ecosystems in the digital campuses of the 21 st century are increasingly complex, thus making the use of traditional Wi-Fi networks insufficient to facilitate the low-latency, high-bandwidth, and high-reliability communications needed. 5G, Wi-Fi 6, and low-power wide-area networks are technologies that play a complementary role in the development of a sound and dynamic communication environment. Wi-Fi 6, with its augmented capacity and reduced latency, is best for lecture halls, dorms, libraries, and laboratories where large numbers of devices might connect simultaneously. It manages simultaneous connections so that IoT devices do not interfere with student laptops, smartphones, or academic equipment (Mohamed & Alosman, 2024). Meanwhile, 5G provides even greater bandwidth and speed, supporting mission-critical applications such as autonomous shuttles, remotely operated laboratory equipment, and high-resolution security systems. Low latency enables real-time applications in which milliseconds can make a difference. Low-power wide-area networks serve a different purpose. LoRaWAN and NB-IoT are examples of low-power WANs for devices that only send small volumes of data infrequently, as in the case of environmental sensors, utility meters, and structural health monitors. Their long range and extremely low energy requirements enable battery-operated IoT devices to operate for years without maintenance. Cumulatively, these network technologies create a layered connectivity ecosystem that can support diverse IoT needs across campuses while allowing institutions to scale, innovate, and experiment without overloading the existing infrastructure.

Although connectivity allows devices to communicate, the actual intelligence of the IoT is realized by data pipelines and middleware systems that accumulate, process, integrate, and distribute information across platforms. Data pipelines act as routes through which information flows from sensors and edge devices to the platforms and applications that use them (Koukaras et al., 2025). On a typical campus, IoT devices provided by various vendors function with different protocols, languages, and update cycles. Middleware harmonizes these differences by translating device data into a common framework that applications can understand. It also performs other tasks such as authentication, routing, data security, and device management. Without middleware, the various components of IoT would be islands unto themselves. With this, campuses obtain a single management platform from which administrators can visualize system performance, monitor the health of devices, and take corrective actions remotely. Thus, middleware becomes essential to realize real-time responsiveness, interoperability, and scalability to operate an IoT ecosystem in large academic environments. Equally important is the training of staff, as successful integration requires both deep technical expertise and coordination among diverse departments.

Such a dynamic model enables institutions to observe operations with unprecedented clarity never before seen. This means that administrators can test how different temperature settings may affect energy costs, simulate how pedestrian traffic changes between semesters, or assess the impact of adding new buildings to the utility grid. The integration of advanced networks, data pipelines, legacy systems, and digital twin technologies marks a significant paradigm shift in how higher education institutions manage their environments. Campuses will transition from siloed systems or entirely manual processes to a cohesive, data-driven ecosystem in which buildings, devices, services, and people are connected. High-performance networks ensure reliable communication across all IoT devices, regardless of their location or function. Middleware and data pipelines consolidate management across disparate systems and ensure that data flows securely and efficiently. Legacy integration strategies ensure that modernization is performed seamlessly and cost-effectively while ensuring continuity of operations. Digital twins provide a real-world, holistic view of campus activities to administrators, driving careful planning, rapid response, and strategic insight (Gupta, 2024). The result is an environment that supports comfort, safety, sustainability, and innovation-not through isolated technologies but through a cohesive digital fabric woven throughout the physical campus. Campuses are becoming smarter in terms of the technology they use and how they adapt to changing needs, respond to human behavior, and support future generations of students and scholars. With robust connectivity, bridging old and new systems, and embracing the power of real-time modeling, higher education lays the foundation for campuses that are more resilient, intelligent, and better able to meet the challenges of the rapidly evolving digital world.

AUTOMATION AND INTELLIGENT OPERATIONS

Automation is one of the defining features of an IoT-enabled campus and a fundamental reshaping of daily operations in higher education. Campuses are beginning to operate at levels of intelligence equivalent to the complexity of the communities they serve, with facilities and services continuously adapting to real-time demands. Sensors embedded in HVAC systems, elevators, boilers, pumps, and electrical systems collect data on vibration, temperature, pressure, power consumption, and performance cycles. Identifying a failing electrical panel or degrading pump before reaching a critical point prevents hazards that could affect building operations or the safety of the occupants (Koukaras et al., 2025). Campuses realize greater space utilization, reduced conflicts, and more efficient use of physical resources.

Smart energy systems are critical for intelligent campus operations. Sensors on solar panels measure the production output in real time, enabling the system to adjust building loads according to conditions, charge battery storage, or feed energy back into the grid. When combined with predictive analytics, campuses can estimate energy production based on weather patterns and adjust their strategic operations accordingly. Sustainability dashboards provide transparency to these processes. Students, faculty, and administration can easily view building-level or campus-wide data on energy consumption, carbon emissions, water usage, and air quality. Such dashboards raise environmental awareness and can be employed in academic programs focused on sustainability, engineering, or data science. They also help leadership track progress toward sustainability goals while identifying areas where additional improvements can be made (Tariq, 2026). Accordingly, smart energy systems create more sustainable campuses while empowering users to actively participate in environmental stewardship. AI-enabled optimization adds an additional layer of intelligence to smart campus operations, making it possible to coordinate and refine complex systems in ways that human operators cannot easily achieve (Sasirekha et al., 2024). In utility networks, AI may detect water leaks or electrical anomalies much earlier than would have been possible with manual checks. AI also strengthens emergency response systems through the constant analysis of sensor, camera, and communication network data to identify threats more rapidly and orchestrate responses more effectively. Whether it is energy use optimization, safety protection, or improvement of campus logistics, AI stands as the central intelligence that stitches together the diverse components of IoT-enabled infrastructure. The growing reliance on automation and intelligent operations does more than streamline campus processes; it reshapes the culture and functions of the institution. Data, connectivity, and computation come together to create learning ecologies that adapt, develop, and grow continuously. The rising imperative of sustainability, resource constraints, and increased expectations by students place growing demands on higher education; automation provides a way to meet such demands without compromising quality or performance. Automation places them in operation with greater efficiency and intelligence, ranging from daily routines to long-term planning. Fundamentally, automation is an operational philosophy that positions campuses as dynamic, responsive, and forward-looking communities ready to thrive through digital innovation.

IOT FOR TEACHING, LEARNING, AND RESEARCH

IoT thereby elevates the academic mission of universities through intelligent responses to pedagogy while empowering learners to assume active roles in research- and experiment-driven studies. Sensor-enabled laboratories represent one of the most important ways in which the IoT influences scientific inquiry and hands-on learning. Traditional laboratories rely on manual measurements, stand-alone instruments, and limited experimental controls, which can affect the amount of data that students and researchers can gather in a given timeframe. Researchers in the fields of biology or materials science can conduct long-term experiments because these IoT systems automatically handle monitoring and send notifications if conditions fall outside acceptable ranges. Over time, sensor-rich laboratories help build deeper scientific understanding because students learn not only to conduct experiments but also how to collect, interpret, and apply complex data sets, which are essential in today's landscape. If natural light increases, smart blinds may automatically lower, or the lighting levels may dim to eliminate glare. Acoustic sensors detect ambient noise and adjust sound amplification so that students can clearly hear instructors whether they are speaking from the front of the room or moving among student groups. In addition to environmental controls, smart classrooms deploy learning analytics that arm instructors with rich insights into student engagement. IoT devices can count attendance using Bluetooth and RFID signals, assess participation in classroom polls or digital engagement tools, and monitor shared resource usage. None of this data replaces human judgment, but it helps instructors understand patterns, such as students who may be struggling or disengaging, and intervene earlier. Location-aware learning environments extend the benefits of IoT beyond traditional classrooms into the whole campus landscape. Institutions can create learning experiences that respond to students' physical location through Bluetooth beacons, GPS signals, QR markers, and proximity sensors. Museums, botanical gardens, historical landmarks, engineering facilities, and other campus sites have become interactive learning zones. For instance, a student in an archaeology course might automatically receive contextual information when standing near ancient artifact replicas displayed outdoors (Meylani, 2024). As the volume of sensor-generated information increases in both volume and variety, so too do the opportunities for interdisciplinary student research using IoT data. Campuses have become living laboratories, with streams of data captured from transportation systems, buildings, environmental monitors, security networks, and energy grids. Computer science students can delve into the development of algorithms or optimizations at the edge, while business students can decipher IoT data to inform operational strategies on campus. Interdisciplinary projects like these introduce students to the kind of collaborative problem-solving that they will encounter in their professional lives: data scientists, engineers, designers, managers, and policy experts must work together. Students become familiar with technologies and skills that are increasingly important across industries: data analytics, automation, systems thinking, and computational reasoning. Students will be able to interface with academic content through visual, environmental, spatial, and experimental layers, whereas faculty will have more sophisticated tools for guiding and inspiring inquiry.

DATA GOVERNANCE, CYBERSECURITY, AND ETHICAL Issues

As sensors, connected devices, and automated systems become intertwined with daily student, faculty, and staff lives, institutions will need to address the risks inherent in pervasive sensing. Students may be concerned that their attendance could be tracked without consent or that occupancy sensors might implicitly monitor their behaviors in common areas (Taruc & De La Cruz, 2024). Among the major challenges universities face in deploying smart campus technologies, securing IoT endpoints and data flows remains paramount. Because cyber threats are evolving persistently, security should not be treated as a one-time implementation but as an ongoing process that requires diligence, expertise, and frequent reviews. In addition to technological protection, policies on responsible deployment and data stewardship will help guide the integration of IoT into campus life. These policies need to go beyond the technologies to be deployed, to how decisions are made and who will be accountable for managing data. The comprehensive policy begins with guidance on data collection: what data are collected, who has access, and for how long they are kept. Institutions must clearly define what constitutes appropriate data use so that technologies designed to optimize efficiency do not become instruments of disciplinary monitoring or intrusive tracking. This enables campus communities to make conscious choices regarding their privacy and may build trust in the institution's motivations.

Deployment also requires responsible consideration of procurement and vendor management. Cross-functional committees can be established to represent IT, the legal department, faculty, students, and administration in establishing IoT policies that are reflective, balanced, and aligned with the institution's mission (Mohamed & Alosman, 2024). Campuses are ever-changing ecosystems; therefore, governance frameworks must remain flexible to respond to new technologies, changes in regulations, or evolving social expectations. Equally important are ethical guidelines, which will help institutions navigate the complex issues of fairness, inclusion, and transparency in the use of IoT. Ethical frameworks move beyond compliance to address values: How can a university ensure that IoT serves all members of the campus community? How does it prevent unintentional discrimination or disparities in access to healthcare? Ethical IoT deployment begins with the principle of informed consent. Similarly, if IoT data are used to help make decisions about academic scheduling or resource allocation, the algorithms should be reviewed for bias to prevent particular groups from being inadvertently disadvantaged by the algorithm. Table 2 aligns technological opportunities with risks and governance responses.

Table 2. IoT Opportunities, Risks, and Governance Responses in Higher Education

IoT Opportunity Area	Value Proposition	Associated Risks	Required Governance & Controls
Smart Buildings & Energy Automation	Reduced energy costs, sustainability gains	System failure, vendor lock-in	Open standards, lifecycle planning
Learning Analytics & Smart Classrooms	Personalised learning, early intervention	Surveillance concerns, bias	Consent frameworks, algorithm audits
Campus Safety & Security Systems	Faster emergency response, safer environments	Over-monitoring, privacy erosion	Legal compliance, proportional surveillance
Mobility & Transportation Systems	Reduced congestion, accessibility support	Data misuse, system reliability	Secure data pipelines, redundancy planning
Predictive Maintenance	Lower downtime, cost efficiency	Over-reliance on automation	Human-in-the-loop oversight
Student Experience Optimisation	Improved wellbeing and engagement	Digital exclusion	Equity-by-design, multi-channel access
Data-Driven Governance	Strategic insight and transparency	Data silos, misuse	Data stewardship policies, ethics boards

EQUITY, ACCESSIBILITY, AND STUDENT EXPERIENCE

For those with mobility concerns, IoT systems can identify the smoothest or most accessible pathways across a campus, accounting for slope gradients, curb cuts, or weather conditions that may leave outdoor surfaces slippery. These devices create a campus that listens to students, not one that makes students bend around unpredictable circumstances (Rushina et al., 2024). For students with hearing impairments, IoT-enabled microphones and sound-field systems can direct audio feeds to personal devices, ensuring that they do not struggle to follow lectures in large or crowded rooms. These adjustments blend into the background of campus life; however, they have an enormous impact because they make education more equitable without placing additional demands on students who need support.

However, accessibility goes far beyond addressing the needs of disabled students alone. This also means making smart campuses work for students from all socioeconomic backgrounds. The more ubiquitous IoT systems become, the more likely the digital divide will be exacerbated. Students who cannot afford the latest smartphones or who work with shaky internet access could find themselves behind other students in gaining experiences from navigation systems, learning applications, and safety technology that assume a degree of personal hardware ownership. To bridge this divide, universities need to create IoT systems that work across a range of hardware, from low-cost phones to devices available for checkout in campus libraries or resource centers. They need to ensure that important information communicated through the IoT network also comes through multiple channels-digital, physical, and human-so that no student is excluded because of limitations in technology. Connectivity is an equity issue. Co-designing with students, particularly those from underrepresented backgrounds, is important to ensure that these tools reflect real needs rather than assumptions made by administrators or developers. When equity is baked into the start, IoT functions as a mechanism of empowerment, not as another layer of complexity (Kurni & KG, 2024). Students who walk alone late at night can carry small, IoT-enabled beacons that communicate with campus security when triggered. Some institutions have experimented with digital escorts: a student's route home is tracked anonymously through an app and monitored for unexpected deviations that could signal potential danger. While such tools must be implemented carefully to avoid becoming forms of surveillance, they can provide reassurance to students who might otherwise avoid evening activities or feel isolated. The role of IoT can also extend to the newest frontier of mental health support.

Universities can use environmental sensors to trace areas that suffer from chronic noise, poor ventilation, or overcrowding, which contribute to stress. Equity and student experience also converge on the issue of how IoT systems respect the personal boundaries of students. Students need to be confident that technologies intended to support them are not being used to unfairly assess or monitor them. Transparency around data collection, clear processes for consent, and real dialogue between students and administrators mold whether IoT supports or intrudes (Rosak-Szyrocka, 2025). When universities engage openly with their communities, showing how systems work, what they track, and what they intentionally do not track, they create trust. This is fundamental to the adoption of IoT because even the most innovative systems become useless if students reject or avoid them out of fear or misunderstanding. A truly equitable IoT-enabled campus puts students at the forefront of design decisions; their voices lead the way in terms of development and deployment. It also recognizes that inequities cannot be solved by technology alone, but that it may very well be an important factor in reducing barriers and creating new opportunities. When equity, accessibility, and student well-being are foundational rather than optional considerations, the IoT becomes a tool for empowerment, helping to create a campus where every student has the support they need to succeed academically, emotionally, and socially.

ORGANISATIONAL CAPACITY AND CHANGE MANAGEMENT

To create an IoT-based smart campus, it is necessary to install sensors, modernize networks, and implement new applications. This venture will succeed based on the organizational ability of the institution to handle technological change, coordinate various stakeholders, and make long-term investments. A smart campus introduces new operational methods, partnership modes, and anticipations regarding information circulation within institutions (Mohamed & Alosman, 2024). This will only be enshrined when governance frameworks, staffing models, budgeting frameworks, and change management strategies are aligned with technology. With the growing integration of campuses, universities face the need to design the skills, processes, and cultures needed to sustain consistent innovation and build greater digital resilience. Without this, even the most developed IoT systems can achieve their potential only through the delivery of fragmented, inconsistent, or unsustainable results. Consequently, building an organizational environment that is ready for ongoing technological evolution is equally important as building the infrastructure itself. Strong IT governance structures are at the heart of effective smart campus development. With IoT initiatives spanning multiple domains, including teaching, research, facilities operations, safety, student services, and sustainability, universities must outline a clear decision-making apparatus (Ibrahim, 2024). A critical part of extending governance is fostering collaboration across departments because IoT touches every part of campus operations. Academic units provide perspectives on teaching and research innovation but require infrastructure and technical guidance to achieve their goals. Upskilling does not stop with technical departments. This approach helps institutions build a workforce that sustains innovation and does not simply rely heavily on third-party vendors.

In addition to new competencies, staffing models must consider the ongoing operational requirements of the IoT. Connected devices require continuous monitoring, maintenance, updates, and security testing. Data from sensors arrive at a rapid pace and require careful planning regarding governance, analytics, and storage (Rajamohan et al., 2024). Without adequate staffing, IoT systems can quickly become obsolete or compromised. Because most IoT deployments start with pilot projects, planning for scaling needs to begin at the onset. For instance, a small-scale energy monitoring system might work for just one building but become too cost-prohibitive as it is expanded campus-wide if procurement does not anticipate future scaling. Therefore, universities need to communicate early and clearly about why IoT systems are being adopted, what problems they solve, and how they will affect campus life. Institutions that embrace this holistic approach lay the groundwork for sustained innovation. IoT then becomes not just a campus-infrastructure upgrade but a driver of organizational transformation; a means of building universities that are adaptive, strategic, and capable of rising to the many challenges and opportunities of a fast-changing world.

CASE EXAMPLES AND GLOBAL BEST PRACTICES

Smart campus projects worldwide have shown how the application of IoT technologies can make universities and colleges more effective, responsive, and student-focused. Some of the most advanced universities are leading activities that not only focus on modernizing the physical infrastructure but also on academic experiences, the efficiency of their operations, their sustainability, and their safety. These universities represent what is possible when technology is thoughtfully integrated into campus life, providing insights and lessons for all universities, many of which have fewer resources (Fatima, 2024). Early adopter experiences from such campuses reflect that creating a smart campus requires painstaking planning, good governance, and a strategic approach toward scaling innovations in both the academic and operational domains. Several universities have taken substantive steps to implement campus-wide IoT-driven innovation. The existence of these initiatives speaks to the dual role technology can play in improving operational performance while enhancing the student experience and fostering a functional and responsive campus. Analyzing this information enables instructors to improve their understanding of how students utilize the learning environment and make adjustments to improve learning outcomes. The incorporation of IoT in laboratories and research facilities has similar advantages, such as equipment that can be remotely monitored through sensors, with real-time data collection enabling experiments to be performed in cooperation with others. This has greatly improved the quality of research and expanded opportunities for students to engage in hands-on experimentation without being physically present in the laboratory. The integration of IoT in these academic spaces illustrates the general trend of how campuses are using technology to make learning spaces adaptive, personalized, and data-driven.

International smart campus initiatives provide important lessons for higher-education institutions seeking to adopt IoT technologies. First, the integration must be holistic. A similar architecture allows campuses to manage a variety of services, ranging from energy monitoring and classroom management to security, through a single, integrated platform. This can help streamline both operational and academic functions. The lesson here is that integration at the outset minimizes redundancy, simplifies maintenance, and ensures long-term scalability and sustainability of IoT deployments. Another key lesson learned from international initiatives is that systems must be designed in a modular and flexible manner. The deployment of IoT generally begins as pilot projects in a restricted number of buildings or services. By planning for incremental growth, institutions can experiment with new uses, gather feedback from users, and refine their approaches before committing to full-scale deployment. Data management and analytics are also central to the success of smart campuses. Analytics also allow administrators to demonstrate return on investment and make evidence-based decisions about the effectiveness of initiatives undertaken on the path toward a smart campus. Phased implementation diminishes financial risk, allows learning from early experiences, and prepares the campus community technologically for wider adoption (Gautam & Kotiyal, 2025). Partnerships, open-source software, and standardized IoT frameworks will also help small- and medium-sized institutions manage costs and complexity. Smaller campuses may also make smart campus innovations more feasible through collaborations with local governments, technology providers, and other educational institutions to access expertise, shared infrastructure, and funding opportunities. Another scalable strategy is to align IoT deployments with academic and research goals. When campus technologies are designed to serve both operational efficiency and educational activities, institutions can maximize the value of their investments. International best practices highlight the roles of governance, stakeholder involvement, and change management. Smart campus initiatives are successful when informed by clearly defined decision-making structures that represent IT, facility management, academic departments, and administrative units. Change management, in the form of training, support, and communication, ensures that members of the campus community understand the new workflows, tools, and expectations brought about by IoT technologies.

FUTURE DIRECTIONS

The combination of AI, robotics, and IoT creates a self-governing, responsive ecosystem in which human effort is channeled into high-value activities, whereas routine and operational functions are optimized autonomously. The integration of IoT and AI over time with renewable-energy infrastructure can transform campuses into living labs for sustainability-genuinely carbon-neutral operations that do not compromise comfort, safety, or productivity. Coupled with energy efficiency, these technologies greatly enable better environmental monitoring and management. On campus grounds, intelligent landscaping adjusts irrigation based on soil moisture and rainfall forecasts according to the plants' needs, conserving water while keeping campus green spaces aesthetically and functionally pleasing. In this way, the entire campus is transformed into an ecosystem where environmental care becomes part of daily life and illustrates what smart technologies are capable of doing in support of broader institutional goals aimed at improving the quality of life of students and staff. The vision of a hyper-connected learning ecosystem goes beyond operational efficiency and sustainability to include personalized and adaptive educational experiences (Hong et al., 2024). Inclusivity and accessibility are also important dimensions of future smart campuses. The hyperconnected campus therefore becomes a model of inclusion and a place where technology actively removes barriers and empowers learners. Collaborative platforms bring together researchers across disciplines and institutions to share knowledge, co-design experiments, and share advanced infrastructure. This newly interconnected environment turns campuses into living laboratories where learning, research, and operational innovation occur in a continuous feedback loop.

CONCLUSION

Thus, the discussion of an IoT-driven smart campus is a multidimensional change in the functioning, education, and relationship of higher education with its communities. In essence, the use of IoT technologies indicates a convergence of connectivity, data-driven insights, and intelligent automation, which have the potential to transform what modern campuses may be and can do. IoT implementation makes institutional and operational management, teaching, learning, research, and student experience responsive and adaptive on a level that traditional systems are not. Among the critical lessons that can be identified in the course of the exploration of smart campus projects is the idea that IoT is not only a technological facilitator but also a strategic facilitator capable of helping institutions manage the optimization of their resources, as well as improve their learning experiences, sustainability, and inclusive and accessible learning environments. Its multifaceted benefits position IoT as a cornerstone for laying the foundation for further development in higher education (Meylani, 2024). The most significant learning point in observing the progress of smart campuses is that data and connectivity lie at the heart of any change process. Cameras fitted in classrooms, laboratories, administrative offices, and common areas constantly send signals that, once studied, provide applicable information regarding operations, academics, and research. Monitoring energy use, ambient conditions, space occupancy, and safety-related parameters in real time helps a campus optimize its physical resources, reduce wastage, and increase comfort while enhancing safety. A high-speed network combined with cloud computing and middleware can enable communication between devices and the central management system to ensure that administrators and faculty make decisions based on correct and prompt information. In this respect, institutions have the potential to join efficiency to pedagogical interests to the mutual advantage of campus structure and people who inhabit it.

The transformative power of IoT is applicable to teaching and learning. Adaptive lighting, acoustics, and learning analytics in smart classrooms can make classrooms easier to use based on the educational requirements of students and teachers. Location-aware technologies are useful for providing dynamic spatial management and personalized study experiences, whereas connected laboratory equipment facilitates research processes and collaborative experimentation (Haralayya et al., 2024). These kinds of innovations will bring campuses to experiential, data-driven learning, where they will be able to use technology with a purpose and become proactive in solving problems, experimentation, and cross-disciplinary projects. Outside the classroom, the IoT helps faculty learn more about student interaction, attendance, and engagement tendencies, which can be used as the basis for intervention, instructing differently, and improving learning. In this way, the school ecosystem will be sensitive, customized, and capable of accommodating different learning styles, which will create an inclusive learning environment where every learner will succeed. The operational dimension of smart campuses also highlights the strategic value of IoT. The automation of energy systems, predictive maintenance of facilities, intelligent use of space, and interlinked safety and security systems can be achieved through networked sensor-driven infrastructure. These applications save on expenditure, disruption, and efficient allocation of resources; hence, institutions are able to focus their financial and human capital on activities that can specifically benefit teaching, learning, and research. An example is predictive maintenance, which involves sensor data to identify imminent failures before they occur, thereby preventing downtime in key facilities. Intelligent energy systems even out the loads among campus buildings, incorporate renewable energy, and provide real-time feedback on how energy is used, which also adds to sustainability and operational efficiency. This strategic deployment of IoT in such areas illustrates how technology can be used to form a foundational layer upon which higher-order institutional objectives, such as academic excellence, sustainability, and safety, are built.

An important lesson learned in the context of global smart campuses is integration and interoperability. Single or fragmented systems usually provide inefficiencies, redundancies, and complexity in operations. Conversely, a single architecture that integrates devices, networks, and applications can integrate multiple services and functions. Interoperable platforms ensure that while new technologies are introduced, such as additional sensors, AI-driven analytics, or autonomous systems, they can easily be integrated without disrupting the current operations (Gómez Gaviria, 2024). This helps scalability because institutions of all sizes and resources can incrementally scale up IoT capabilities with coherence across the campus ecosystem. Flexibility and adaptability in system design are therefore necessary to sustain effectiveness in the long run and to ensure maximum return on investments in IoT, both operationally and educationally.

Other building blocks for the successful deployment of IoT are ethical considerations and data governance. Pervasive sensing entails massive amounts of individual, educational, and operational data and tends to raise issues of privacy, security, and ethical use (Liao et al., 2024). Competency organizations should have strong cybersecurity measures, ethical codes, and clear policies that govern data gathering, retention, access, and use. The concept of privacy protection, as well as the prevention of unwarranted surveillance, is not only necessary to ensure a high level of compliance with legal norms but also to ensure confidence between students, faculty, and staff. The use of AI-based analytics and autonomous systems should be ethically guided to promote fairness and responsibility in decision-making. Embedding responsible practices in IoT deployments from the outset allows campuses to create an environment in which technological innovation is balanced with respect for individual rights and institutional integrity, reinforcing the legitimacy and sustainability of smart initiatives.

Equity and accessibility are also powerful drivers of the development of IoT-enabled campus futures. Technologies should be implemented in ways that support all members of the campus community, including students with disabilities, students from underrepresented groups, and students with varied levels of technological literacy (Mohamed & Alosman, 2024). Smart navigation, adaptive classrooms, and accessible interfaces ensure that no student is at a disadvantage owing to the deployment of advanced technologies. Additionally, IoT can help bridge the digital divide to guarantee equitable access to resources, information, and opportunities for learning. These approaches will enhance the well-being of all students, build inclusive environments, and nurture an engagement and participation culture that underscores the imperative that technological advancement must go hand-in-hand with social responsibility and sensitivity to diverse needs.

Another important lesson is that organizational capacity and change management are strategic. Effective smart campus projects require cross-functional cooperation, a well-designed governance framework, and staff upskilling. IT departments, facilities management, academic departments, and administrative offices must work together to implement, establish, and sustain multifaceted IoT ecosystems. Institution-level training programs, role redefinitions, and capacity-building efforts should be conducted to empower the campus community with the right skills to utilize and exploit IoT. Budgeting, procurement strategies, and lifecycle planning further help sustain technology implementation so that infrastructure, software, and human resources keep pace and remain aligned with long-term strategic ambitions. A collaborative culture, adaptive and always learning, enables the process of embedding the IoT within the operations and pedagogies of the institution more effectively, thereby enhancing its performance and resilience. Best practices worldwide offer lessons that can be directly translated into any campus, regardless of size. The most prominent universities demonstrate the benefits of holistic integration, predictive analytics, modular structure design, and technology driven by academic concerns. Meanwhile, small- or medium-institution models can be scaled to emphasize the benefits of incremental implementation, high-impact areas of focus, and open-source or adaptable platforms. The range of these models underlines the universal applicability of IoT as a strategic enabler (Izourane et al., 2024). Whenever possible, institutions are advised to concentrate on short-term areas of benefits, such as energy efficiency, student safety, and classroom optimization, and strategize on long-term expansion and innovation. Therefore, a gradual, cost-sensitive strategy can enable campuses of any size to achieve the disruptive power of smart campus technologies without exceeding their financial and technical capabilities. Looking ahead, the integration of IoT with technologies such as artificial intelligence, robotics, and autonomous systems will continue to increase the capacity of higher education institutions. Such technologies will enable predictive, adaptive, and self-optimizing campuses that anticipate needs, personalize learning, manage resources efficiently, and enhance safety and sustainability. Hyper-connected ecosystems link the academic, operational, and social dimensions. This permits research, collaboration, and innovation in a manner that was not previously possible. The intentional utilization of IoT in combination with new technologies will place institutions in a position to be carbon neutral, optimize operations to the fullest extent, and develop rich and inclusive learning spaces that can react in real time to the changing needs of learners and instructors. The IoT is strategic, not only in terms of operational benefits or incremental improvements. Instead, IoT indicates a paradigm shift in the functioning of universities. Smart campus technologies enhance evidence-based decision-making, optimize insufficient resources, and provide student-focused learning processes.

By integrating IoT into their fundamental institutional practices, universities can ensure that operational efficiency is in line with pedagogical excellence, sustainability objectives, and social responsibility. This alignment transforms campuses from being one-dimensional and reactive to being multi-dimensional, dynamic, and intelligent ecosystems that facilitate continuous improvement, experimentation, and resilience. In this regard, IoT acts as an important key to reinventing the institution, getting universities ready to meet new challenges and technological trends, and staying relevant and faithful to their mission. In summary, IoT-enabled smart campuses must be filled with collaborative, ethical, and sustainable activities. Interdepartmental cooperation, student involvement, and faculty involvement, including partnerships with technology vendors, and community goal congruency provide inclusiveness, practicability, and responsiveness. Transparent governance, ethical management of information, and preemptive care about privacy, security, and equity generate trust and legitimacy, and, as a result, ensure that technology benefits all stakeholders optimally (Wang & Wang, 2024). Sustainability should inform the choice of decisions in energy management, resource optimization, and environmental stewardship, and should be incorporated in the design and operation of smart campus systems to attain sustainability. Together, these core values are the foundation of long-term success, one that can ensure that IoT implementation is not only technologically but also socially responsible, resilient, and serves the overall cause of higher education. In conclusion, smart campuses, which are a product of the IoT, offer a disruptive possibility of higher education institutions gaining operational efficiency, academic excellence, sustainability, and inclusiveness. The essential lessons learned in research and other best practices worldwide underscore the substantial role of data, integration, flexibility, governance, ethics, and collaboration in attaining these advantages. By strategically embedding IoT into infrastructure, educational practices, and organizational processes, universities can re-imagine themselves as intelligent, adaptive, and sustainable environments. This will entail careful planning, gradual execution, and commitments to responsible innovation to ensure that technology does not alter; instead, it strengthens the human experience in support of the mission of higher education.

REFERENCES

Ahmad, A. A., & Alshurideh, M. T. (2025). Revolutionizing building management: The ORBIT framework for IoT-powered smart buildings. *International Journal of Management and Marketing Intelligence*, *2*(2), 1–13. DOI: 10.64251/ijmmi.65

Bellaj, M., Bendahmane, A., Younes, A., Boudra, S., & Ennakra, M. (2024, May). A systematic review of smart campus technologies to improve students' educational experiences. In *Proceedings of the 2024 Mediterranean Smart Cities Conference (MSCC)* (pp. 1–7). IEEE. DOI: 10.1109/MSCC62288.2024.10697051

Fatima, S. K. (2024, October). Smart campus, smarter students: Prospects and challenges of implementation of IoT in higher education. In *Proceedings of the International Conference on Innovation of Emerging Information and Communication Technology* (pp. 251–262). Springer Nature Switzerland.

Gautam, A., & Kotiyal, A. (2025). Connecting the future: Cloud-based IoT in education. In *Integration of cloud computing and IoT* (pp. 274–308). Chapman and Hall/CRC.

Gómez Gaviria, L. (2024). *5G hyper-connected university campus: Enhancing the education experience*.

Gupta, H. P. (2024). Lessons learned: A smart campus environment using LoRaWAN. *arXiv*. https://arxiv.org/abs/2410.09927

Haralayya, B., Petikam, S., Hatole, S., Shinde, S. G., Patel, D., & Jagtap, S. T. (2024, November). IoT-enabled educational management systems: Enhancing efficiency and accessibility. In *Proceedings of the 2024 Second International Conference on Computational and Characterization Techniques in Engineering & Sciences (IC3TES)* (pp. 1–5). IEEE. DOI: 10.1109/IC3TES62412.2024.10877470

Hong, W., Huang, Z., Zhang, J., Chen, X., & Chen, B. M. (2024, June). Pathway to a smart campus framework: A review and case study. In *Proceedings of the 2024 IEEE 18th International Conference on Control & Automation (ICCA)* (pp. 424–430). IEEE. DOI: 10.1109/ICCA62789.2024.10591879

Ibrahim, Q. (2024). Building a smart, secured and sustainable campus: A self-powered wireless network for environmental monitoring. *Journal of Artificial Intelligence Research & Advances*, *11*(1), 36–51.

Izourane, F. Z., Ardchir, S., Ounacer, S., & Azzouazi, M. (2024). Smart campus based on AI and IoT in the era of Industry 5.0: Challenges and opportunities. In *Industry 5.0 and emerging technologies: Transformation through technology and innovations* (pp. 39–57).

Koukaras, C., Hatzikraniotis, E., Mitsiaki, M., Koukaras, P., Tjortjis, C., & Stavrinides, S. G. (2025). Revolutionising educational management with AI and wireless networks: A framework for smart resource allocation and decision-making. *Applied Sciences (Basel, Switzerland)*, *15*(10), 5293. DOI: 10.3390/app15105293

Kurni, M., & KG, S. (2024). IoT for education. In *The Internet of Educational Things: Enhancing students' engagement and learning performance* (pp. 1–22). Springer Nature Switzerland.

Liao, S. H., Jiang, J. D., & Yang, C. F. (2024). Integration of LoRa-enabled IoT infrastructure for advanced campus safety systems in Taiwan. *Internet of Things : Engineering Cyber Physical Human Systems*, *28*, 101347. DOI: 10.1016/j.iot.2024.101347

Lu, Y., Hu, X., & Li, J. (2024). Smart campus: The deep integration of machine vision and physical education. *International Journal of Maritime Engineering*, *1*(1), 163–174.

Meylani, R. (2024). Transforming education with the Internet of Things: A journey into smarter learning environments. *International Journal of Research in Education and Science*, *10*(1), 161–178. DOI: 10.46328/ijres.3362

Mohamed, M., & Alosman, K. (2024). *An IoT-enabled framework for smart city infrastructure management. Authorea Preprints*. DOI: 10.36227/techrxiv.170906134.46169506/v1

Picallo, I., Klaina, H., López-Iturri, P., Azpilicueta, L., Celaya-Echarri, M., Astrain, J. J., & Falcone, F. (2024, July). Development of a cognitive IoT-enabled smart campus. In *Proceedings of the 2024 14th International Symposium on Communication Systems, Networks and Digital Signal Processing (CSNDSP)* (pp. 644–647). IEEE. DOI: 10.1109/CSNDSP60683.2024.10636428

Rajamohan, K., Rangasamy, S., Manoj, C. N., Mary, L., Sabu, R., & Jose, S. S. (2024). Internet of things (IoT) as a game changer to the education sector. In *Advanced IoT technologies and applications in the Industry 4.0 digital economy* (pp. 251–274). CRC Press. DOI: 10.1201/9781003434269-14

Rosak-Szyrocka, J. (2025). *Engineering the future of higher education: A VOSviewer analysis of smart university trends in the digitalisation and Industry 5.0 era*. Management Systems in Production Engineering.

Rushina, K., Akkur, M., Mathias, R., Chowhan, S. S., & Singha, S. (2024). Impact of IoT on campus: Smart student information system in the educational sector. *Library of Progress – Library Science, Information Technology & Computer, 44*(3).

Sasirekha, V., Ramadevi, R., Malarvizhi, C., Mohankumar, N., & Velmurugan, S. (2024, March). Intelligent campus safety management using IoT and CNNs for surveillance, access, and emergency response. In *Proceedings of the 2024 3rd International Conference for Innovation in Technology (INOCON)* (pp. 1–6). IEEE. DOI: 10.1109/INOCON60754.2024.10512335

Tariq, M. (Ed.). (2025). *Merging Artificial Intelligence With the Internet of Things*. IGI Global., DOI: 10.4018/979-8-3693-8547-0

Tariq, M. (Ed.). (2025). *Emerging Multisector Applications of AI and IoT*. IGI Global., DOI: 10.4018/979-8-3373-4332-7

Tariq, M. U. (2024). AI and IoT in flood forecasting and mitigation: A comprehensive approach. In Ouaissa, M., Ouaissa, M., Boulouard, Z., Iwendi, C., & Krichen, M. (Eds.), *AI and IoT for proactive disaster management* (pp. 26–60). IGI Global., DOI: 10.4018/979-8-3693-3896-4.ch003

Tariq, M. U. (2026). The Semiotics of AI-Driven Consumer Experiences: Decoding Emotional Branding and the Experience Economy. In Piccolo, R., & Boero, M. (Eds.), *Emotional and Experiential Dimensions of Modern Marketing* (pp. 245–268). IGI Global Scientific Publishing., DOI: 10.4018/979-8-3373-7615-8.ch010

Tariq, M. U. (2026). Robotic and IoT Integration in Post-Acute Rehabilitation: Enhancing Patient Recovery Through Data-Driven Assistive Systems. In Al-Humairi, S., Naronglerdrit, P., Chantarapanich, N., & Wanchat, S. (Eds.), *Robotics and IoT Synergy in Next-Generation Healthcare* (pp. 163–188). IGI Global Scientific Publishing., DOI: 10.4018/979-8-3373-5447-7.ch006

Taruc, L. E. F., & De La Cruz, A. R. (2024). Narrowband-IoT (NB-IoT) and IoT use cases in universities, campuses, and educational institutions: A research analysis. *arXiv*. https://arxiv.org/abs/2408.03157

Wang, J., & Wang, Y. (2024, September). Application of IoT and cloud computing technologies in smart campus: Architecture, challenges, and solutions. In *Proceedings of the 2024 2nd International Conference on Internet of Things and Cloud Computing Technology* (pp. 146–152). DOI: 10.1145/3702879.3702905

Zarpellon, B. O., de Oro Arenas, L., Godoy, E. P., Marafão, F. P., & Paredes, H. K. M. (2024). Design and implementation of a smart campus flexible Internet of Things architecture on a Brazilian university. *IEEE Access : Practical Innovations, Open Solutions*, *12*, 113705–113725. DOI: 10.1109/ACCESS.2024.3444471

KEY TERMS AND DEFINITIONS

Edge Computing: Processes device data locally for faster responses.
Predictive Maintenance: Uses analytics to anticipate equipment failures early.
Smart Sensors: Networked devices that monitor environments in real time.

Chapter 5
Digital Compass: New Directions in Teacher Education and Learning Design

Vojtěch Blažek
https://orcid.org/0000-0002-3499-5232
Faculty of Education, Jihočeská Univerzita v Českých Budějovicích, Czech Republic

Petra Karvánková
https://orcid.org/0000-0002-5513-2161
Faculty of Education, Jihočeská Univerzita v Českých Budějovicích, Czech Republic

Michal Staněk
Faculty of Education, Jihočeská Univerzita v Českých Budějovicích, Czech Republic

Jiří Rypl
https://orcid.org/0000-0002-2280-8620
Faculty of Education, Jihočeská Univerzita v Českých Budějovicích, Czech Republic

Jiří Šmída
Faculty of Sciences, Humanities, and Education, Technical University of Liberec, Czech Republic

ABSTRACT

This chapter offers a comprehensive synthesis of theoretical foundations and empirical evidence on how digital technologies reshape teacher education and curriculum design. It situates the discussion within international and European policy

DOI: 10.4018/979-8-3373-6831-3.ch005

2026, IGI Global Scientific Publishing. Copying or distributing in print or electronic forms without written permission of IGI Global Scientific Publishing is prohibited. Use of this chapter to ...tive artificial intelligence (AI) technologies is expressly prohibited. The publisher reserves all rights to license its use for generative AI training and machine learning model development.

frameworks while drawing on classic pedagogical concepts and recent post-COVID trends, including generative AI and data-driven learning. Beyond mapping these developments, the chapter illustrates their practical impact through case studies from Czech higher education, showing how innovations such as VR, WebGIS, and experiential formats like Geocircus have transformed instructional design and professional training. By combining conceptual analysis with actionable insights, the text positions the "Digital Compass" not as a metaphor but as a guiding tool—helping educators navigate the tension between tradition and innovation and chart sustainable, ethically responsible pathways for teaching in the digital age.

1. INTRODUCTION

Digital Compass: How Technology is Changing Higher Education

Modern (digital) technologies have significantly shaped changes in educational structures worldwide over the past two decades. The effects of economic and social transformation, driven by the growth of digital technologies, are especially noticeable in education, known as Society 4.0 (Pfeiffer, 2017; Qureshi, 2021). The transformation of higher education can be seen as a compass pointing toward a new direction for teaching in the digital age. Technology is fundamentally altering how information is communicated, learned, and verified. Consequently, higher education institutions face the challenge of redefining traditional teaching methods and adapting them to an environment where digital tools are becoming an essential, yet completely natural, part of the educational process.

To better understand the direction of our contribution, it is helpful to first consider its original context. The ideas of Piaget and Papert help us comprehend how education is evolving. Although their theories were developed long before the rise of artificial intelligence or virtual reality, they already indicated that technology would fundamentally transform how we learn. Papert (1993) believed that the change in the student-teacher relationship was inevitable. The concept of the teacher as a mediator of information transfer is rooted in society's historical needs when it was essential to transmit a certain amount of knowledge to be built upon later in life. He predicted that this mediating role would be completely replaced by computers. This idea is echoed, for example, by He et al. (2023), who highlight the importance of actively involving students and encouraging their participation in teaching, rather than the traditional model where the teacher lectures. This shift calls for creative methods such as project-based or inquiry-based learning. As a result, students become active creators of their own learning, developing skills like critical thinking, collaboration, and problem-solving.

This approach gained prominence with the rapid growth of the web and smartphones at the start of the millennium, followed by the development of cloud services. This has influenced not only the technology and telecommunications sectors but also nearly every aspect of the economy and society in many countries. Information and communication technologies (ICT) include a wide range of technologies, and while the term is often associated with computers, it also covers other media like mobile and handheld devices, television, radio, print, and networks. ICT has significantly impacted the global economy and the ways people work, live, and play around the world. However, until recently, this trend has had little effect on educational practices and how people learn in schools (Alnoaimi et al., 2011). To prevent the chapter from being limited to a single discipline perspective, we use a broad framework of changes in higher education—such as AI, mobility, cloud, and data—and then illustrate specific applications with examples from various fields, especially geography. This approach balances overarching ideas (policies, curriculum, educators) with practical examples that show how these principles are reflected in teaching.

Just as our knowledge develops, so too should the methods we use in education. Harel & Papert (1991) introduced the concept of constructivism – learning through creation. In this concept, technology is not merely a tool, but a means by which students actively create and develop their knowledge in a structured way. In the digital age, this idea is coming to fruition – students learn by creating, exploring, and engaging in the process. Zhao et al. (2021) also demonstrate that metaphors – such as our digital compass – can facilitate the connection between educational philosophy and practice.

Thanks to technology, maintaining the traditional academic model based on lectures and seminars is no longer necessary. Digital systems can communicate information more effectively, allowing the teacher's role to evolve into that of a mentor and learning guide. Consequently, education is shifting from merely transferring knowledge to co-creating it, fostering creativity, and encouraging interdisciplinary collaboration. This change highlights the need for new interdisciplinary teaching models that genuinely integrate content from different fields. Research by interdisciplinary teams in the US (e.g., 30 teachers and 542 students from New York and California) indicates that the greatest benefits come from models that transform traditional content and connect it to cognitively engaging teaching methods centered on discussion, imagination, and solving real-world problems (Applebee et al., 2007; Spurná, 2024). Of course, the teacher's role remains essential, but it is crucial to recognize that it is undergoing a significant transformation within the current educational landscape. The traditional view of the teacher as the main source of information is gradually being replaced by a model where the teacher acts as a guide, mentor, and facilitator of learning. This shift results not only from technological advancements but also from pedagogical changes that emphasize active student participation, personalized learning, and the development of critical thinking, creativity, and collaboration.

Today's teachers are no longer the sole carriers of knowledge but partners in helping students find their own paths to learning. This transformation calls for a new educational approach focused on fostering independent learning and developing essential skills. Botlík Nuc et al. (2024) argue that teachers must be capable of integrating digital technologies into their instruction while creating a safe and supportive environment for developing digital literacy and cybersecurity. At the same time, there are increasing demands for teachers' emotional intelligence and their ability to create inclusive environments that respect each student's individual needs. As Jůvová and Duda (2023) previously pointed out, 21st-century teachers should be reflective practitioners who combine digital skills with a humanistic approach to students. As Smékalová (2019) summarizes, pedagogy must reflect social changes, and teachers should be prepared to create educational environments that meet the needs of a knowledge-based society.

This brief overview, along with many other similar studies, clearly shows the need to actively support teachers in adopting innovative teaching methods that promote critical thinking and strengthen the link between theory and practice. The long-term success of these innovations relies not only on professional development for teachers but also on institutional backing for schools, encouraging interdisciplinary collaboration and sharing best practices. In this context, technology acts as a guiding tool, steering teaching toward more modern and efficient education. However, it is not simply about converting traditional methods into digital formats but about using technology thoughtfully to make real improvements in the teaching process and ensure its sustainability. As Xiang and Guo (2023) emphasize, the most effective models of education are those that utilize digital tools efficiently, significantly contributing to talent development and enhancing the quality of the educational environment.

Effective teaching today involves more than just well-organized information transfer; it primarily requires teachers to actively involve students in learning, stimulate their critical thinking, and guide them toward a deeper understanding of contexts. Modern educational research, exemplified by John Hattie's work (2009), highlights that key elements of successful teaching include clear goals, quality feedback, high expectations, and teachers reflecting on their own practice. Therefore, teaching effectiveness becomes a complex concept, encompassing not only student outcomes but also the quality of interactions, the level of autonomy, and the ability to link theory with practice. In geography education, this includes students' ability to apply knowledge to real-world problems, interpret spatial data, or critically analyze information.

Digital technologies can be powerful tools in this realm, but only when used thoughtfully and purposefully. Using digital tools effectively doesn't mean merely translating traditional methods into digital formats; it involves transforming them so that technology supports active learning, collaboration, and skill development. The SAMR (Substitution, Augmentation, Modification, and Redefinition) model provides a helpful framework for evaluating whether technology truly adds value. For instance, employing GIS applications, interactive maps, or simulations can fundamentally alter how students understand spatial relations and geographic processes. Consequently, technology becomes a virtual compass, guiding teaching toward greater relevance, real-world connections, and enhanced digital literacy.

The question of measuring the effectiveness of teaching and the use of technology is essential for both research and practice. There are various approaches to evaluating effectiveness, ranging from quantitative methods, such as test results and data analysis from teaching platforms, to questionnaires, to qualitative techniques, including observation, interviews, and analysis of student work. A combination of these methods (known as mixed methods) offers a comprehensive view of how technology influences the learning process. For example, in geography education, this may involve monitoring how digital tools contribute to developing spatial thinking, data interpretation, and problem-solving skills. As Xiang and Guo (2023) point out, effectively integrating technology into teaching can significantly enhance talent development and improve the quality of the educational environment.

Another key aspect is teachers' professional development. They must continually update their skills to use new methods effectively. When teachers' digital literacy improves, student outcomes tend to improve as well. It is also clear that different stakeholders in education have varying levels of involvement. There is a need for targeted support to foster collaboration between teachers and students and to create environments where they learn together, such as through digital platforms or smart campuses. However, it is equally important to approach teachers' professional development critically and with regard to the quality of the evidence. While lists of "proven" elements of effective development are often repeated, research analyses show these lists are not always supported by strong data. Many studies do not focus primarily on professional development itself but treat it as a supporting tool for other interventions. Furthermore, there is a lack of direct comparative research to determine which development methods are most effective in different settings. Instead of relying on universal recipes, a deeper understanding of professional learning processes—considering the specifics of the school environment—and supporting long-term, context-sensitive approaches are more appropriate. Only then can we ensure professional development genuinely improves teaching and student outcomes (Asterhan & Lefstein, 2024).

Elliot (2021), for example, suggests that self-reflection is also vital—teachers and students should reflect on how they learn and how they can improve. The digital environment should be inclusive, addressing the diverse needs of students, cultural differences, and varying levels of access to technology. In this view, the compass serves not only to guide the direction of education but also to better understand the "terrain"—that is, the conditions and needs of pupils and students in the learning process. Sensitivity to this context involves considering individual educational needs, differences in access to technology, socio-cultural backgrounds, and prior experience with digital learning. Only then can digital innovations be truly inclusive and promote equal opportunities for all students. As Kiley and Wisker (2009) point out, understanding the barriers that hinder effective learning can help reduce the risk of academic failure.

Thus, the compass in this chapter is more than just a symbol. It is a call for universities training future teachers to adapt to technological advancements. As Liu and Shi (2023) state, teachers' ability to work with technology is fundamental to this transformation. By drawing inspiration from Piaget and Papert's theories while remaining open to new approaches, we can create an educational environment that is modern, inclusive, and genuinely supportive of learning—preparing students for their future careers and life in general. In this way, the compass also serves as a metaphor for balancing tradition and innovation between proven pedagogical principles and the possibilities offered by the digital age.

2. THE AGE OF DIGITAL TECHNOLOGIES AND ARTIFICIAL INTELLIGENCE: HOW TEACHING AND THE ROLE OF TEACHERS ARE CHANGING

In recent years, especially with the rise of advanced artificial intelligence systems, significant changes have taken place in the educational process at all levels. These changes are reflected not only in teaching but also in the organizational structure of schools, the role of teachers, and the content of curricula. The increasing importance and diversity of ICT have reached a point where their teaching structure can be compared to that of the native language. By analogy, three main components can be identified: digital literacy (including reading and writing), understanding the principles of digital technologies (such as language structure), and the practical use of digital tools in specific contexts (for example, literature and text comprehension). The European Digital Competence Framework divides digital competence into five key areas: information and data literacy, communication and collaboration, digital content creation, security, and problem-solving (Vuorikari et al., 2022). This important European document also differentiates between teachers' digital professional skills and teachers' digital pedagogical skills, which encompass working with digital resources, teaching, digital assessment, and student support (Redecker, 2017).

One of the first countries to adopt this terminology and curriculum reform was the United Kingdom (Fig. 1). During the 2014-2015 national curriculum review, new areas such as digital literacy, digital ethics, and safety were integrated into teaching. However, the main focus was placed on teaching computer science as a vital part of modern education (Fowler & Vegas, 2021).

Figure 1. Terminology reform in the UK curriculum from 2014 to 2015. Digital literacy (basic literacy), computer science (how technology works), and information technology (how technology is used).

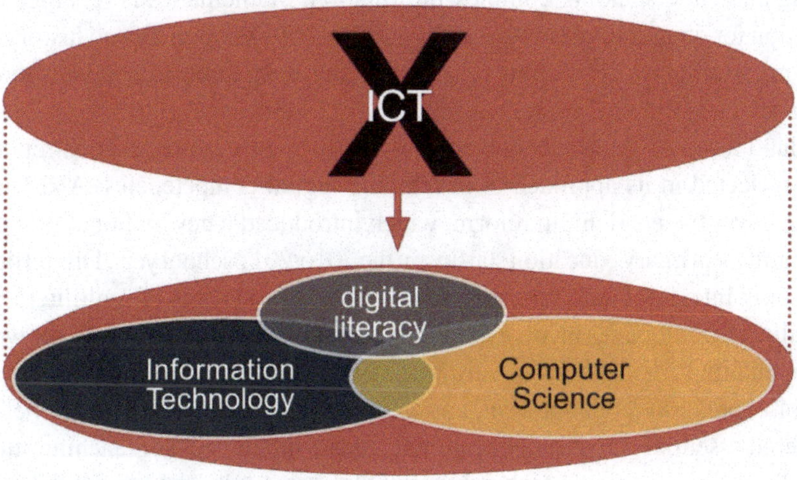

(adapted from Royal Society 2012)

The rapid development of ICT presents new opportunities but also challenges in education. Digital tools allow for more flexible teaching tailored to various learning styles. Students can choose when and where to learn and easily switch between formal and informal education. Reyes et al. (2021) note that ICT provides greater freedom in terms of time and space. Singh Buttar (2016) emphasizes that technology is transforming not just how teaching is delivered but also its accessibility, organization, and quality. This shift has been especially evident during the COVID-19 pandemic, which has greatly sped up this process. Schools have had to quickly transition to online teaching and begin blending traditional lessons with digital formats—known as blended learning. Paudel (2021) states that this hybrid approach is better suited for diverse student needs and fosters a more interactive environment. Additionally, Eom (2023) shows that mobile technologies improve communication between students and teachers, thereby encouraging student independence in learning.

An analysis of the education policies of selected European countries, including the United Kingdom, Portugal, Finland, Austria, and Czechia, reveals that approaches to integrating digital competencies into education systems vary according to national contexts, educational priorities, and curricular traditions. Nonetheless, a common trend emerges: a concerted effort to address the challenges of the digital age through the systematic development of digital skills across all levels of education.

In Portugal, the educational framework, as stated by Crato (2020), highlights the link between digital skills and traditional areas of education. Reading and writing are seen not only as tools for language literacy but also as means for structuring thinking and understanding complex information. Mathematics is regarded as the foundation for quantitative analysis of the world, while geography and history serve as a common pillar for developing critical thinking and gaining a deeper understanding of social and cultural contexts.

Finland has long been recognized as a leader in education, and this reputation is also reflected in its approach to developing digital competencies. A significant milestone was the curriculum reform, which introduced a new national framework curriculum for primary education starting in the 2016/2017 school year. Digital literacy is explicitly integrated into the curriculum, especially in areas of multiliteracy and ICT skills. Multiliteracies involve the ability to interpret, create, and evaluate written, spoken, and multimodal texts in various formats, with digital technologies seen as tools for expression, collaboration, and knowledge sharing. ICT competencies are considered essential across all educational areas, with the goal of teaching students to use digital tools not only technically but also creatively and critically. In recent years, Finland has further strengthened its digital strategies through various national programs. The Digital Progress (Digiohjelma) program, implemented between 2020 and 2023, focused on enhancing the technological capabilities of the public sector and fostering cooperation between public and private institutions. Follow-up initiatives, such as Digivisio 2030 and Artificial Intelligence 4.0, highlight the growing importance of AI and the data economy in education and society more broadly. According to the European Commission's 2024 Digital Decade report, Finland ranks among the top in the EU for digital skills, with over 82% of its population possessing at least basic digital skills. As Lavonen (2020) notes, the Finnish education system emphasizes individuals' ability to use a wide range of tools—including sociocultural (linguistic) and especially digital (technological) tools—to interact effectively with their environment, engage and collaborate in diverse groups, conduct research, solve new problems, take responsibility for managing their lives, and act independently. Schools should teach students to use technology meaningfully, enabling them to process various types of information and evaluate the reliability and validity of that information, thereby nurturing critical thinking.

The development of students' digital competence has been a central focus of recent discussions, especially in the context of the revised Framework Educational Program for Primary Education in Czechia. Digital literacy and computational thinking were already incorporated into the national curriculum during the so-called minor revision (MŠMT, 2021), which primarily aimed to prioritize ICT within education. However, the ongoing major revision of the Czech curriculum envisions the comprehensive integration of digital competence into all areas of education. Digital competence is seen as a key, cross-cutting skill.

Looking at these countries comparatively, it is clear that while all recognize the benefits of ICT, each has chosen a different development path. The UK promotes innovation through market-oriented reforms, whereas Austria emphasizes stable institutional changes. Portugal faces challenges in transitioning universities to public foundations, which can sometimes slow down technological progress. This issue has been the focus of numerous studies examining the impact of technology on school functioning, student-teacher relationships, and curriculum changes from various perspectives. Here are a few recent studies at random:

Nguyen (2023) observes that there is often a gap between expectations for technology and its actual use, demonstrating that school leadership plays a crucial role—without strong leadership and a clear strategy, technology implementation falls short. Kunwar (2022) emphasizes that ICT should be an integral part of teacher training. Alqirnas (2023) further notes that teachers proficient in e-learning can utilize technology more effectively. This highlights the need for ongoing education and development in digital skills, not only for current teachers but especially for future educators. Juma et al. (2021) stress that effective school management helps optimize technological resources and encourages personal responsibility. Political support is vital—technology can improve both teaching and school management if institutions are ready to adapt. Holton (2017) discusses how students' identities are evolving within the digital environment, suggesting that teaching content should be more flexible and responsive to social change. Curricula should be rooted in both local and global realities and should reflect current technological advancements.

These examples show that digital competencies are not an isolated area but are increasingly integrated into the broader framework of general education, with an emphasis on linking them to traditional disciplines and developing the ability to critically reflect on the digital environment. Technology presents numerous opportunities, but at the same time, it places new demands on teachers, schools, and education systems. To fully harness these opportunities, we need to transform our teaching practices, strengthen school leadership, invest in teacher training, and continuously seek ways to connect technology with society's real needs. Educational institutions are thus faced with the challenge of creating an environment that not only utilizes technology but also supports meaningful learning. Solving this will require further research, open dialogue, and sharing best practices.

3. OBSTACLES AND LIMITS TO DIGITAL TRANSFORMATION IN TEACHER EDUCATION—A NEVER-ENDING PROCESS—AS WELL AS EDUCATION

The digital transformation of teacher education is a prominent topic today as schools work to adapt to a world where technology plays an increasingly vital role. However, there are still barriers preventing digital tools from becoming a normal part of teaching. This section examines the main types of obstacles faced by teachers in both academic and regular school settings.

The individual barriers and challenges related to integrating technology into teaching and the associated curriculum changes have been discussed for a long time. For example, Patricie L. Rodgers (2000) summarized these issues as early as 2000. Based on research among teachers in primary, secondary, and higher education, she identified key barriers that hinder effective technology integration. Rodgers differentiates between internal barriers (e.g., teacher attitudes, lack of skills, fear of technology) and external barriers (e.g., technical support, equipment availability, time, and financial constraints). This framework builds on Ertmer's (1999) concept, which distinguishes between first-order barriers (external conditions) and second-order barriers (teachers' internal beliefs and attitudes). Hew and Brush (2007) further identify six main categories of barriers: resources, institutional support, training, attitudes, knowledge, and access to technology. All studies emphasize the importance of teachers' professional development and the need for a comprehensive approach that links technical, pedagogical, and organizational factors. Research indicates that the higher the level of technology integration, the fewer barriers teachers perceive, highlighting the importance of targeted support and strategic planning. These findings are essential for understanding the obstacles to digital transformation and for developing strategies that support sustainable implementation.

Several studies show that teachers' perceptions and evaluations of whether to use ICT in the classroom positively impact student performance and motivation (Záhorec et al., 2019; Madsen et al., 2018; Drossel et al., 2016). These findings often conflict with the reality in schools, where teachers tend to resist adopting new technologies and teaching practices. A Norwegian study (Madsen, 2018) found that more than 50% disagreed with the statement that digital tools are essential for good teaching. Madsen compares these findings with the approach in New Zealand, where the use of digital tools is linked to developed digital competencies, as opposed to

Norway, where their use is connected to a professional approach. In other words, if teachers do not incorporate digital tools into their profession, they also do not use them in their teaching. Záhorský (2019) reveals that science teachers in Czechia and Slovakia lack sufficient knowledge and skills to verify and evaluate student learning through modern testing systems or online web tools. This is again related to digital competencies introduced in 2021 through a minor revision of the Czech national curriculum (MŠMT, 2021). For the Czech education system's revision to succeed, it is necessary to change teachers' attitudes toward digital technologies and their willingness to learn (Vaníček, 2021). Similar issues are highlighted in the study "After the Reboot" (Royal Society, 2017), which reviews the transformation of English education. It points to a shortage of qualified ICT teachers and emphasizes the need for significant investment in existing teachers to help them acquire the knowledge and confidence needed to pass on essential computer skills to students.

Recent results from studies conducted since 2020 underscore the continuing challenges and changing dynamics associated with the integration of technology into education. For example, Chen et al. (2022) examine perceptions of barriers to mobile technology integration among practicing teachers and emphasize that teachers who reevaluate their roles and embrace innovative teaching practices often do not encounter traditional second-order barriers. This suggests that effective training and support can lead to cultural change among educators and foster an environment that is more conducive to technology adoption. Furthermore, a systematic review by Regmi & Jones (2020) illustrates the importance of combining different pedagogical models, such as flipped classrooms, for better integration of technology into curricula. This approach allows for a more flexible and inclusive learning experience that better suits the needs of different students and confirms that technology integration requires careful planning and consideration of the teaching context. An example of a similar teaching process is the Geocircus carousel concept (Karvánková et al., 2025).

The COVID-19 pandemic has significantly accelerated these discussions, deepening existing barriers while also creating new opportunities for change. Studies like that by Putri et al. (2022) highlight that both lecturers and students faced significant external barriers during this transition, including a lack of technical support and internet access issues. Internally, they struggled with engagement and assessment challenges in online learning environments, indicating that addressing these two areas is crucial for effective technology integration. Similarly, Mahyoob (2020) notes that the challenges faced by EFL students during the pandemic reflect a broader trend where insufficient technological readiness acts as a major barrier to meaningful engagement with online curricula. The link between socioeconomic status and technology integration was also examined by Cheng and Parker (2023), who identified access to professional development, affordability of technology, and institutional support as key factors for successful ICT implementation in US schools. This underscores the importance of equitable resource access to overcome barriers, especially in underserved communities (UNESCO, 2023). Additionally, Tolegenova et al. (2024) highlight factors that support technology initiatives in health education, emphasizing the need for innovative designs and adaptable practices that suit different learning contexts—further stressing the importance of systemic changes in curriculum design. An extensive review of the literature and practical experience reveals that barriers to adopting digital technologies in education are longstanding, persistent, and recurring. Once one obstacle is removed, new ones tend to arise, often due to rapid technological advances. Rogers (2000) and Ertmer (1999) identify these barriers as external (e.g., technical infrastructure, management support) and internal (e.g., attitudes, self-confidence, pedagogical beliefs). Hew and Brush (2007) suggest six categories, which have repeatedly been confirmed through practice.

Based on a combination of theoretical frameworks (Rogers, 2000; Ertmer, 1999; Hew & Brush, 2007) and specific examples from practice, Table 1 summarizes four main types of barriers—technological, social, mental, and competency—and shows that effective digital transformation requires a comprehensive approach. It is not enough to address only the technical equipment; it is also necessary to work with teachers' attitudes, their professional development, and institutional support. The visualization also shows that barriers are not isolated—they often overlap and reinforce each other. Therefore, it is necessary to understand them as an interconnected system that requires an integrated solution.

Table 1. Specific examples of types of barriers and examples of their occurrence in the implementation of ICT in education according to Rogers (2000), Ertmer (1999), and Hew & Brush (2007).

Type of barrier	Description	Examples	Source
Technological	Inadequate infrastructure, rapid technological development, and a lack of technical support.	Poor connectivity, outdated technology, lack of teacher training.	Aditya; Budiyanto; Morales; Rogers (2000)
Social	Low digital literacy, inequality in access, and public skepticism.	Insufficient teacher training, concerns about AI, lack of school strategies.	Burns (2023); Bećirović (2023); Elayah; Klein & Bîber
Mental (mindset)	Resistance to new technologies, ingrained teaching habits, and low self-confidence.	Teachers' fear of technology concerns about changing teaching methods.	Iivari; Guzmán & Nyvang; Rogers (2000); Ertmer (1999)
Competency	Differences in digital skills between teachers and students.	Teachers are unable to use technology effectively, and students are lacking digital literacy.	Kovalchuk; Pimentel; Hew & Brush (2007)

Although technological, social, mental, and competency barriers are well described and repeatedly confirmed by research, there is another often overlooked obstacle that deserves special attention—the so-called implementation gap. This phenomenon, also known as the science-to-service gap, refers to the disparity between what we know works (e.g., effective digital teaching strategies) and what actually happens in practice. Implementation science research (Fixsen et al., 2005) shows that common professional development approaches, such as one-off training sessions, result in only 5-10% actual adoption of innovations in teaching.

Furthermore, Guskey's (2002) model of teacher change suggests that shifts in teachers' attitudes and beliefs typically happen only after positive experiences with new methods and observing their effects on students. However, without opportunities for experimentation, feedback, and support in the classroom, many teachers never reach this point. Similarly, the CBAM model (Concerns-Based Adoption Model) (Hall & Hord, 1987) shows that change is a process that needs targeted support at different stages of concern and levels of use. This "I'll gladly sign up again, but I won't take action" effect—where teachers repeatedly participate in digital competency training without actual changes in teaching—is a common example of the implementation gap. Overcoming this obstacle requires more than just transferring knowledge—supporting implementation through coaching, modeling, ongoing feedback, and school leadership is essential. Without these elements, professional development remains a standalone activity rather than a powerful tool for transforming practice.

In conclusion, while barriers to integrating technology into education remain significant, recent studies suggest a changing dynamic that emphasizes the importance of targeted support, professional development, and adaptive curriculum frameworks. Connecting these components is crucial to creating an educational environment that fully leverages technological advances to address current educational needs.

4. INSTRUCTIONAL DESIGN AND INNOVATION: HOW TECHNOLOGY IS CHANGING THE TEACHING AND POPULARIZATION OF GEOGRAPHY

New teaching methods, such as virtual reality (VR), hybrid education, and the integration of different disciplines, are significantly transforming how teaching is approached at universities, especially in fields like geography. New subjects are emerging that respond to technological progress and provide alternatives to traditional educational methods. The goal of this section of the chapter is to build on previous findings about the relationship between technology and education and to share examples of successful practices so that, above all, the theoretical insights and challenges of most studies can be demonstrated in practice. This shows their impact on geography teaching and modern technologies in education, particularly at the Department of Geography, Faculty of Education, University of South Bohemia in Czechia.

The process of integrating digital technologies into the curriculum and teaching environment of the Department of Geography at the Faculty of Education, University of South Bohemia, can be divided into several stages of development. It should be emphasized that most of these changes took place spontaneously, without a pre-defined strategic framework, merely fulfilling the newly emerging requirement to strengthen the digital literacy and digital competences of future geography teachers, which testifies to the high degree of adaptability of the academic environment to new stimuli. The overall scheme of the influence of technology on the university curriculum is shown in Figure 2.

Figure 2. The integration of digital technologies into the educational process is fundamentally transforming the structure of traditional school subjects. Not only are their content updates happening, but new interdisciplinary courses and teaching methods are also emerging, gradually reaching lower levels of education. The main driver of this change is frequent professional exchange among teachers, facilitated through thematically focused educational events (e.g., STEMuJU, Geocircus). These platforms allow for the effective transfer of current knowledge and skills back into school practice, strengthening the two-way connection between education and broader society. Society not only funds the education system but also drives its reforms. This dynamic and flexible model represents a sustainable development path aligned with the principles of the Technology Compass for Education

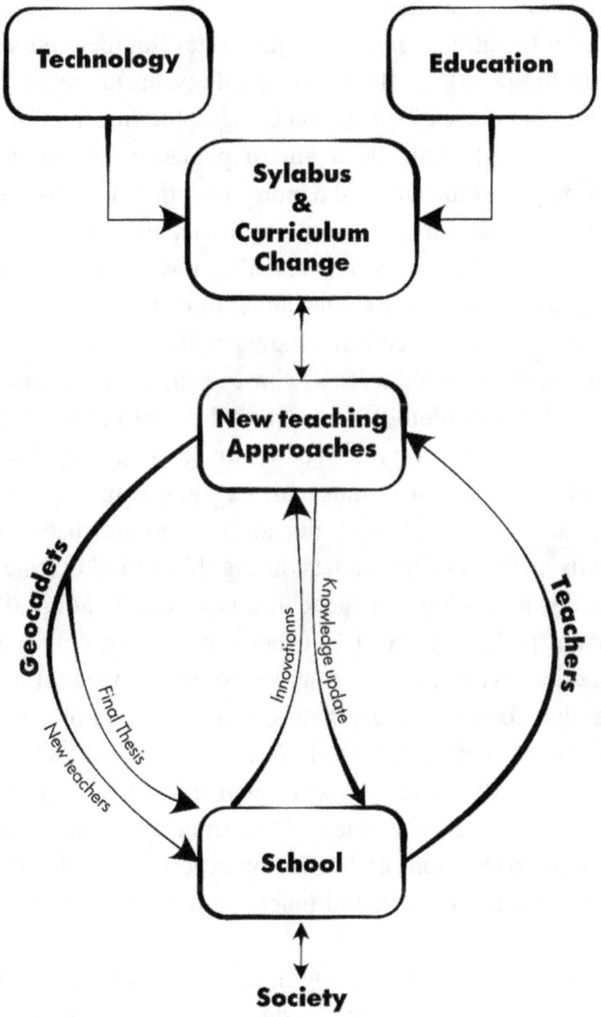

(Authors, 2025).

The first stage began around 2016, marked by efforts to actively involve elementary school students in the department's research and outreach activities. The goal was not only to physically bring students to the academic campus but also to engage them through innovative technologies. Technologies such as virtual reality (VR), 8-bit educational games, and Ozobot-type robotic systems were used during this phase. Positive feedback from teachers led to these activities becoming a regular part of the department's outreach efforts. It became clear that connecting geographical content with digital technologies, especially robotics, augmented and virtual reality (AR/VR), and basic programming, significantly boosts students' motivation and interest. This experience gradually influenced and integrated several existing subjects into the curriculum, particularly geographic information systems, geography didactics, and global development education.

Thanks to this integration, topics like global development education began to be included in teaching modules through technology, enriching and updating their instructional value. In courses focusing on Geographic Information Technologies, there has been a shift from technically detailed explanations of complex cartographic and geoinformation procedures toward a more educational approach to GIS topics. Currently, the focus is on the meaningful use of GIS technologies in education—how to effectively incorporate these tools into teaching at various levels and timeframes. This approach, reflected in their own teaching, aims to prepare future geography teachers, known as geocadets (see Karvánková et al., 2025), not as fully technical GIS experts but primarily as educators who can utilize geotechnology to foster spatial thinking, critical thinking, and solve real-world geographical issues. The didactic focus of GIS education at the Department of Geography, Faculty of Education, University of South Bohemia, thus marks a significant step toward practically applicable and pedagogically relevant education in geoinformation technologies.

An initial skills analysis of Geocadets during this period revealed notable gaps in applying modern technologies in teaching practice. Although these skills are essential in current pedagogy, most Geocadets possessed only basic knowledge and minimal practical experience. This underscored the need for a structured curriculum intervention focused on expanding students' technological literacy and, importantly, improving their ability to effectively use digital tools in planning and conducting lessons. To address this, a special course titled "Modern Technologies in Geography Teaching" was introduced in 2022, primarily aiming to provide students with both theoretical foundations and hands-on experience with these technologies so they can independently design and implement digital teaching scenarios under professional supervision.

Since 2019, the Department of Geography at the Faculty of Education, University of South Bohemia, has been systematically implementing educational activities based on the principle of carousel teaching, referred to by the authors as

Geocircus (see Karvánková et al., 2025). This innovative teaching model, which combines experiential pedagogy with the practical involvement of Geocadets, has reached more than 1,500 elementary school students so far. The teaching involved 25 teachers from the field, while over 100 Geocadets ensured the implementation of the individual stations. One of the key features of this initiative is its cyclical nature: after completing their studies, some Geocadets return to the project as qualified teachers, thus fulfilling the idea of connecting undergraduate training, school practice, and further professional development. This model is illustrated in Fig. 2. A visual representation of the course of events is shown in Fig. 3. Given the regularity, scope, and systematic integration of Geocircus into the educational framework of the Department of Geography, it seems appropriate to institutionalize it as a separate course, which would allow its further development and assessment within the university curriculum.

Figure 3. Technological Integration in Informal STEM Education. Case Examples from Geocircus and STEMuJU Stations Utilizing AR, Ozobots, and WebGIS

(Authors, 2025)

According to the authors, the introduction of a new course, Modern Technologies in Geography Education, marks a significant milestone in the curriculum development of the Department of Geography at the Faculty of Education, University of South Bohemia. This change initiated a clearly defined phase that continues today and is characterized by increasing student interest in thesis topics that connect subject didactics with digital technologies and modern teaching concepts (e.g., music and dance geography, place-based learning, misconceptions, etc.). It seems that this combination creates space for innovative teaching methods, enables the exploration of new approaches, and supports the development of pedagogical research. Technology has become a tool to promote interdisciplinarity and highlight geography's integrative potential, especially within STEM education and language teaching. An example includes using WebGIS tools and CLIL methodology in teaching Czech, demonstrating geography's role as an integrative platform for addressing complex issues in today's world.

Another example highlighted by the authors in Geocadets education is the hackathon format, which acts as an experimental platform—a space to test how the principles of the digital compass operate in real teaching settings. Educational research indicates that hackathons offer an environment similar to Geocircus but with increased motivation, as students actively pursue solutions to real-world problems with genuine impacts (Remshagen et al., 2023). In this context, students serve as both teachers and learners. In teacher training, a hackathon can serve as a living laboratory for pedagogical practice, embodying the idea of the digital compass: technology is not the goal but a tool for fostering critical thinking, collaboration, and connecting learning to real-world issues.

The third major phase in the development of the educational environment at the Department of Geography in the Faculty of Education, University of South Bohemia, reflects a natural progression of previous scientific innovations. Based on practical experience with technology-supported teaching, academic publications emphasizing new methodological approaches began emerging. The primary outcome of this phase is the development of the Geocircus method, as detailed in Karvánková et al. (2025), which presents an innovative carousel teaching approach that links geography with digital technologies and other subjects—aligned with the ideas of the STEM framework. Additionally, research in field teaching, a vital part of geography education, has advanced at this institution. Topics related to cultural heritage are increasingly integrated across multiple disciplines. Approaches like Geoheritage (Blažek et al., 2025; Karvánková et al., 2025a, 2025b; Rypl et al., 2025), which focus on interpreting and educating about geographical (cultural and natural) heritage, are gaining prominence, along with growing contributions in the transdisciplinary field of Heritage Studies (Karvánková et al., 2024).

The findings from this research are integrated back into teaching, especially into the curriculum for courses like Modern Technologies in Geography Teaching, Subject-Specific Didactics of Geography, and ongoing professional development for educators. Digital technologies are becoming a key factor in curricular change at the university—even though the formal curriculum is not explicitly outlined—and also serve as a driving force behind scientific research and project activities. From these examples, geography appears to be a highly interdisciplinary field, with connections to environmental studies, urban planning, and data analysis, creating a strong foundation for modern education. Additionally, we can highlight the concept of makerspaces, as described by Blackley et al. (2017), which are collaborative environments that support hands-on learning, idea exchange, and creativity. Such spaces are ideal for developing the critical skills and competencies needed in the 21st century in science, technology, engineering, and mathematics (STEM). Through approaches like carousel teaching, hackathons, and others, students can cultivate skills that combine technological understanding with geographical concepts, preparing them for new professional challenges during their undergraduate studies.

Technology and innovative teaching methods have also significantly influenced public outreach events, which are a key aspect of university evaluations. These events allow universities to demonstrate how technology can be effectively integrated into education, while reshaping the public's view of modern schools. Parents and children see that teaching can be engaging, cohesive, and reflective of technological advances. Popularization events (e.g., Geocircus, STEMuJU, and others) serve more than just as communication tools for the Department of Geography; they act as live teaching laboratories—spaces where new technologies and instructional strategies can be quickly prototyped and tested on real audiences (students, teachers, parents). Consequently, these events foster a two-way connection between the undergraduate training of future teachers (Geocadets) and school practice, supporting evidence-based curriculum changes: what proves successful "outside" is thoughtfully integrated "inside" into courses, syllabi, and teaching frameworks (Fixsen et al., 2005; Guskey, 2002; Hall & Hord, 1987).

In terms of curriculum change, popularization events have five interrelated functions:

1. *Exploration and prototyping* – quick testing of technologies (VR/AR, WebGIS, educational robotics, mobile applications) and practices (carousel teaching, flipped classroom, CLIL) in a safe yet real environment (Paudel, 2021; Eom, 2023).).
2. *Feedback and validation* – structured collection of responses from students and teachers in practice, which helps to distinguish mere substitution from redefinition of learning (SAMR) and thus correct didactic benefits (Redecker, 2017; Vuorikari et al., 2022).

3. *Transfer and professionalization* – involving Geocadets in the roles of lecturers/mentor assistants increases their self-efficacy and accelerates transfer to university courses and practice (Kraft et al., 2018; Asterhan & Lefstein, 2024).
4. *Curricular anchoring* involves syllabus adjustments—redirecting GIS toward a didactic focus—along with developing new courses like Modern Technologies in Geography Teaching and methodological packages such as Geocircus carousel teaching and hackathon formats (Karvánková et al., 2025; Remshagen et al., 2023).
5. *Social relevance and legitimacy* – the public (parents, founders) perceives clear impacts, which enhances reputational and strategic reasons for continued innovation and evidence collection for institutional evaluation (e.g., "17+" frameworks) and internal university KPIs (OECD, 2019; Royal Society (Great Britain, 2017).

This chain reflects the principles of implementation science: instead of single training sessions, an infrastructure for change is built—incorporating modeling, coaching, real-world iteration, and ongoing management support. This approach helps close the so-called implementation gap between knowing "what works" and establishing stable practice in the curriculum (Fixsen et al., 2005; Guskey, 2002).

Although popularization events are a powerful tool for innovation, they can sometimes fall into the so-called "showcase effect," where the focus shifts more toward impressive technology demonstrations than meaningful educational use with clear learning goals. Another risk is simply replacing traditional methods with digital tools without adding real value to learning. To prevent these issues, it is essential to base the implementation of such events on a well-structured educational framework that clearly outlines teaching objectives, the role of the student, and reflection processes. An example is carousel teaching, which fosters active participation and supports task redefinition aligned with the SAMR model, moving from basic substitution to transforming the educational process (Spurná, 2024; Redecker, 2017).

Mentoring and coaching are also crucial—they include peer learning, tandem teaching, or clinical observations that establish a direct connection between innovation and practical change (Kraft et al., 2018; Guskey, 2002). Equally important is institutional support for these activities, such as dedicated time, accessible technical infrastructure, and repeated events, which help prevent them from being seen as one-off projects. Additionally, addressing systemic barriers—like lack of support from school leadership or unequal access to technology—is vital for long-term success (Hew & Brush, 2007; Burns, 2023). By integrating these elements—the educational framework, professional support, and institutional stability—popularization events and student workshops can truly act as catalysts for curriculum change rather than just eye-catching showcases of new technology.

Experience from popularization events shows that their importance extends beyond simply showcasing technologies to the public—they are becoming a strategic tool for curricular innovation. These activities support curriculum development on three interconnected levels: at the program level, they enable the integration of digital skills and multiliteracy across all courses, not just in isolated technology subjects (Redecker, 2017; Vuorikari et al., 2022); at the school level, they establish a direct link to updates of the national curriculum in Czechia, especially in digital literacy and computational thinking, while also strengthening the community of practice between faculty and schools (MŠMT, 2021; OECD, 2019); at the societal level, they increase the visibility and relevance of geography and university teacher training in the eyes of the public and stakeholders, thereby generating legitimacy, resources, and pressure for the sustainable implementation of innovations (Royal Society (Great Britain), 2017; Burns, 2023). When a university organizes long-term popularization activities such as design- and evaluation-based "living laboratories," it accelerates the prototyping and validation of teaching innovations, improves the professional training of future teachers through authentic facilitation, gathers data and evidence for curricular changes, and simultaneously enhances the social relevance and quality of teacher education aligned with European digital competence frameworks and national curricular reform (Redecker, 2017; Vuorikari et al., 2022; MŠMT, 2021).

The impact of digital technologies on teaching, curricular structures, and scientific and popularization activities at the Department of Geography of the Faculty of Education, University of South Bohemia, can be summarized into four main pillars, representing key areas of innovation driven by this transformative environment. These pillars not only illustrate changes in teaching methods but also highlight how the institution adapts to the evolving landscape of digital education and research. Each pillar emphasizes a specific aspect through which technology becomes an essential part of geographical education and academic efforts development.

1) Dissemination and popularization of geography as a separate discipline

The promotion and spread of geography are key pillars that focus on increasing awareness and interest in this field among the general public. Regular reports and news about events, shared on social media or the university's website, play a crucial role in this effort. These updates not only inform about the department's current activities and achievements but also actively involve the community and generate positive feedback. Using social media to popularize geography not only raises awareness but also helps build a strong and engaged community that shares an interest in this scientific discipline. This pillar is vital for the long-term growth and sustainability of the Department of Geography at the Faculty of Education, University of South

Bohemia in České Budějovice, as it attracts future geography students and ensures the continuation and development of the academic environment.

2) Strengthening and establishing relationships between academia and school practice

Maintaining and expanding the relationships between academia and practice is a key part of this pillar. Teachers, often graduates of the Department of Geography, bring valuable practical experience and knowledge that enhance the practice of geocadets and ensure the continuity and quality of the educational process. This ongoing connection with graduates allows the department to grow its network of teachers involved in hands-on teaching, creating a unique "postgraduate professional ecosystem" based on collaboration and sharing best practices. Building these relationships helps translate theoretical knowledge into real-world application, improves the quality of education for future geography teachers, and strengthens their readiness for actual challenges in school settings. This synergistic effect benefits both academic and practical education and can inspire other educational institutions.

3) Advancing technological progress in geography education

Advancing technological progress in geography education is a crucial element that reflects the rapid development of new technologies and their integration into teaching. Each year, new technologies emerge that must be tested and validated for their practical usefulness in education. This approach allows students and teachers to experiment with these technologies across many students, providing valuable insights into their effectiveness and potential applications in teaching. Graduates of the Department of Geography at the Faculty of Education, University of South Bohemia in České Budějovice, often go on to implement these technologies in their practice, contributing to the modernization and enhancement of geography education. This pillar supports not only technological innovation but also prepares geography students for the rapid changes in education, which is essential for maintaining competitiveness and relevance in today's academic environment.

4) Creating the evolving and sustainable development of the Department of Geography

The academic environment is marked by significant pressure on researchers to produce many publications and secure funding through grants, which leads to the neglect of "slow science," a concept that emphasizes careful and reflective research processes, especially important in educational settings (Qomariyah, 2023 or Aziz et al., 2020). This pressure not only poses personal challenges but also highlights broader systemic issues that favor quantity over quality in research outputs. In didactic research, which demands time for reflection and deep analysis, the idea of "slow science" is vital, yet the current academic climate often overlooks this need. The Geocircus concept is an initiative that, to some extent, alleviates this pressure because it is self-sustaining.

At the Department of Geography at the Faculty of Education, University of South Bohemia, technology has become not only a tool for modernizing teaching but also a catalyst for deeper interdisciplinary connections and innovation in pedagogical practices. From experimental formats like hackathons, through the Geocircus methodology, to research into cultural and natural heritage, it is clear that the digital environment supports active learning, creativity, and the development of skills necessary for the 21st century. These approaches not only alter the curriculum and the way future teachers are trained but also strengthen the links between academia, practice, and the public. They set the direction in which the department and the field of geography itself can move. Geography is thus emerging as a dynamic discipline that, thanks to technological innovations and transdisciplinary concepts, is able to respond to current social challenges and create a sustainable educational environment for the future.

5. MOVING FORWARD: SETTING THE DIGITAL COMPASS

Today, digital tools are more than just a supplement to teaching—they are fundamentally transforming the environment in which education occurs. This change creates opportunities for developing critical thinking, active learning, and implementing innovative teaching methods. The teacher plays a crucial role in this transformation; their pedagogical choices guide the direction of teaching and determine the tools used to achieve educational goals. To effectively adapt teacher education for the digital age, a clear strategy is needed—both at the level of individual faculties and within broader education policies (for example, in Czechia, through the adoption and implementation of the strategic document Competence Framework for Teacher Education Graduates (MŠMT, 2023)). The final section of the chapter offers specific recommendations for supporting digital transformation, based on extensive experience with integrating digital technologies into education. Emphasis is placed on developing teacher training students' ability to think critically in a digital environment and to reflect on its impact on teaching processes. Additionally, the vital role of the teacher as a change agent—connecting technological possibilities with pedagogical goals and ensuring their meaningful integration into the curriculum—is highlighted.

Students enter higher education with relatively well-developed digital skills used in their personal lives, skills that can be effectively deepened and directed through subject-specific didactic courses. At the same time, according to Botlík et al. (2024), fostering a positive attitude among students toward lifelong learning—especially in digital skills—is essential, as it enables continuous development of necessary competencies and literacy. Engaging regularly with digital technologies can significantly boost motivation for lifelong learning. When users consistently work with tools, explore new features, and seek out innovative and alternative tools, they acquire the foundational knowledge that makes further study and employment easier to pursue.

However, implementing technology in teaching isn't always straightforward. Resistance to innovation persists among both teachers and students. This is a common topic in research. Holmbye and Bjeld (2019) explored why it can be challenging to change established teaching methods. Their study highlights the need to develop a culture that promotes innovation. This involves investing in teacher training so educators have the skills and tools necessary to teach differently. Similarly, Rafsanjani et al. (2021) note that pressure on teachers to innovate can cause some resistance to these new methods. It's important to start with small steps and work collaboratively with colleagues. Tandem teaching and observation appear to be effective strategies. Therefore, it's crucial to systematically support teachers in adopting innovative teaching methods that integrate geographical, mathematical, and other thinking skills with various components of STEM education and promote an interdisciplinary approach. Such support not only enhances the quality of teaching but also fosters a deeper understanding of the importance of geographical thinking—and more—within contemporary education and its real-world application.

5.1 Recommendations for faculties and education policymakers

Successful digital transformation starts with a well-developed plan. The first step is to invest in technical infrastructure—this includes not only modern equipment but also training teachers to use the technology effectively. Paris et al. (2020) stress that the development of educational technologies should involve those who will actually use them—teachers and students. Politicians need to provide sufficient funding and support for implementing these technologies. Additionally, a strategy must be created for integrating technology into teaching. For example, using cloud services can introduce new methods that give teachers more creative freedom. Li and Wu (2023) recommend that digital literacy be integrated into the training of future teachers—not just as a separate subject but as a core part of all courses.

Supporting ongoing teacher education is also crucial in this transformation. Institutions should foster an environment where teachers can learn from each other, share experiences, and develop skills relevant to current needs (e.g., the Smartcampus concept). He (2023), for instance, points out that teaching should become more student-centered, which requires teachers to adopt new approaches. The role of teachers in guiding the digital direction is essential and must be recognized.

Teachers shape the educational landscape; their approach to technology affects how these tools are viewed and used. Rafsanjani et al. (2021) advise that teachers should continually look for ways to improve their methods and use technology to make teaching more engaging and meaningful. They should serve as role models—not only in their use of technology but also in their mindset. Teachers must help students navigate the digital world, identify credible information, and consider how technology impacts society. Besides technology, it's also important to foster critical and ethical thinking. Students should learn not only to accept information but also to examine, verify, and reflect on its implications. Dash (2024) shows that Web 2.0 technologies (e.g., blogs, wikis, social networks) can create an interactive environment that encourages active student participation. Interdisciplinary collaboration also holds great potential. Connecting education to themes like innovation or entrepreneurship can greatly improve future teachers' training. Chen and colleagues (2022) recommend that faculties promote joint projects across disciplines, as this fosters creativity, problem-solving skills, and teamwork. Methods like project-based learning or group work—where students argue, seek solutions, and collaborate—help develop critical thinking. These approaches lead to higher student engagement and inspire creativity.

Ethics also play a vital role in digital education. Reidenberg and Schaub (2018) highlight the importance of discussing privacy, responsible use of technology, and the effects of manipulating information. Teachers should guide students not only to acquire technical skills but also to develop responsibility and ethical thinking. Additionally, every student is unique. Teachers need to adapt their instruction to meet diverse needs and learning styles by understanding their students' backgrounds and creating an environment where everyone can succeed. Only then can digital transformation be truly effective. Strengthening teachers' roles as educational experts is crucial to ensure that digital change is not just a technological shift but a genuine innovation in curriculum and teaching methods.

5.2 Recommendations for the long-term sustainability of innovation in teaching

The long-term sustainability of innovation, not only in geography teaching, relies mainly on systematic methodological support for teachers. It's not enough to simply introduce new tools or activities—it's crucial to develop comprehensive methodological frameworks that aid teachers in effectively integrating these innovations into their teaching. Instead of one-time demonstrations, it's better to prepare complete sets of proven teaching scenarios that can be used repeatedly and over time. At the same time, encouraging teachers to share their experiences through communities of practice or online platforms is important, as it allows them to reflect on their practices, inspire each other, and collaborate to adapt innovations to specific educational contexts.

An equally vital prerequisite for sustainability is the availability of technology and appropriate technical infrastructure. Digital-based innovations need to be accessible long-term, not just as part of pilot projects or grant initiatives. Schools should have access to necessary licenses, tools, and technical support so they can implement the technology without significant organizational hurdles. Clear and simple user manuals also play a key role by reducing teachers' concerns about working with new technologies. The fewer technical barriers, the more seamlessly and sustainably they can be integrated into teaching.

The third level involves the institutional and curricular integration of innovation. Innovative approaches should not be seen as special events or supplementary programs but as part of regular teaching. Connecting them to framework educational standards, digital literacy concepts, and university teacher training is essential to ensure lasting institutional support. It's also important to involve school management and educational leaders, who can offer not only organizational but also symbolic backing for new methods. Such systemic integration ensures that innovation no longer depends solely on individual teachers' enthusiasm but becomes part of the school's long-term strategy.

Therefore, long-term sustainable innovation in teaching requires a coordinated approach—linking teacher professional development, available infrastructure, and institutional backing. Only then can initiatives like Geocirkus or the use of virtual reality have a lasting impact on the quality of geography education. When these approaches are seamlessly integrated into regular teaching and supported by an appropriate methodological framework, they can genuinely transform how students learn to understand the world around them.

The digital transformation of teacher education presents new challenges and opportunities. To succeed, it needs a well-designed plan, collaboration between faculties and policymakers, and, most importantly, an active role for teachers.

They are essential for making technology a tool for improved teaching—not just a trendy gadget. By focusing on developing critical thinking, supporting innovation, and promoting ethical technology use, we can create an educational environment prepared for the future that truly equips students for life in the digital age.

Today's educational landscape is evolving faster than ever. Digitization, new technologies, and changing student needs are pressing us to find new teaching approaches that extend beyond traditional classrooms. The Digital Compass offers a framework to guide teaching toward active, connected, and meaningful learning. It emphasizes that technology is not an end in itself but a means to achieve a deeper understanding of the world.

REFERENCES

Alnoaimi, T., Hinostroza, J. E., & Kozma, R. (2011). *Transforming education: The power of ICT policies*. UNESCO.

Applebee, A. N., Adler, A., & Filhan, S. (2007). Interdisciplinary curricula in middle and high school classrooms: Case studies of approaches to curriculum and instruction. *American Educational Research Journal*, *44*(4), 1002–1039. DOI: 10.3102/0002831207308219

Asterhan, C. S. C., & Lefstein, A. (2024). Critical analysis of professional development features: Moving beyond checklists. *Professional Development in Education*, *50*(1), 11–23. DOI: 10.1080/19415257.2023.2283437

Bećirović, S. (2023). Challenges and Barriers for Effective Integration of Technologies. into Teaching and Learning. In: Bečirovič, S. Digital Pedagogy. pp. 123–133. DOI: 10.1007/978-981-99-0444-0_10

Blackley, S., Sheffield, R., Maynard, N., Koul, R., & Walker, R. (2017). Makerspace and reflective practice: Advancing pre-service teachers in STEM education. *The Australian Journal of Teacher Education*, *42*(3), 21–35. DOI: 10.14221/ajte.2017v42n3.2

Blažek, V., Karvánková, P., Miloiu, S., Smokova, M., Rypl, J., & Marques, C. G. (2025). *Gamification of heritage for community involvement in low-density territories*. University of South Bohemia.

Botlík Nuc, T., Konečný, J., & Rozboudová, L. (2024). Digital technologies in the undergraduate training of future teachers and during their adaptation period. The Literacy. *Preliteracy and Education Journal*, *8*(1). Advance online publication. DOI: 10.14712/25337890.4738

Burns, M. (2023). *Barriers and supports for technology integration: views from teachers (Background paper GEM 2023)*. UNESCO. DOI: 10.54676/LCEB5308

Chen, C., Jong, M., & Tsai, C. (2022). A comparison of in-service teachers' conceptions of barriers to mobile technology-integrated instruction and technology-integrated instruction. *Australasian Journal of Educational Technology*, •••, 35–50. DOI: 10.14742/ajet.7299

Cheng, S., & Parker, M. (2023). The role of school socioeconomic status in school-wide technology integration in the U.S. *Contemporary Educational Technology*, *15*(2), ep422. DOI: 10.30935/cedtech/13059

Crato, N. (2020). Curriculum and educational reforms in Portugal: An analysis on why and how students' knowledge and skills improved. In Reimers, F. M. (Ed.), *Audacious education purposes* (pp. xx–xx). Springer. DOI: 10.1007/978-3-030-41882-3_8

Dash, P. K.Prasanta Kumar Dash. (2024). Teachers' adoption of web 2.0 technologies in higher education. *International Journal for Multidisciplinary Research*, *6*(2), 14869. Advance online publication. DOI: 10.36948/ijfmr.2024.v06i02.14869

Elliot, D. L. (2021). A 'doctoral compass': Strategic reflection, self-assessment and recalibration for navigating the 'twin' doctoral journey. *Studies in Higher Education*, *47*(12), 2461–2473. DOI: 10.1080/03075079.2021.1946033

Eom, S. (2023). The effects of the use of mobile devices on the e-learning process and perceived learning outcomes in university online education. E-Learning and Digital Media, 20(1), 80–101., 9(3), 45–60. .DOI: 10.1177/20427530221107775

Ertmer, P. A. (1999). Addressing first- and second-order barriers to change: Strategies for technology integration. *Educational Technology Research and Development*, *47*(4), 47–61. DOI: 10.1007/BF02299597

Fixsen, D. L., Naoom, S. F., Blase, K. A., Friedman, R. M., & Wallace, F. (2005). Implementation research: A synthesis of the literature. University of South Florida, Louis de la Parte Florida Mental Health Institute, National Implementation Research Network.

Fowler, B., & Vegas, E. (2021). How England implemented its computer science education program. Center for Universal Education, Brookings. https://eric.ed.gov/?id=ed610629

Guskey, T. R. (2002). Professional development and teacher change. *Teachers and Teaching*, *8*(3), 381–391. DOI: 10.1080/135406002100000512

Hall, G., & Hord, S. (1987). *Change in schools: Facilitating the process*. SUNY Press.

Harel, I., & Papert, S. (Eds.). (1991). *Constructionism*. Ablex Publishing.

Hattie, J. (2009). *Visible learning: A synthesis of over 800 meta-analyses relating to achievement*. Routledge.

He, Z. (2023). Exploration and practice of learning-centered blended teaching reform. *International Journal of New Developments in Education*, *5*(18), 76–80. DOI: 10.25236/IJNDE.2023.051813

Hew, K. F., & Brush, T. (2007). Integrating technology into K–12 teaching and learning: Current knowledge gaps and recommendations for future research. *Educational Technology Research and Development*, *55*(3), 223–252. DOI: 10.1007/s11423-006-9022-5

Holmbye, C. B., & Bjeld, A. B. (2019). How to engage resistant students in classes of innovation and entrepreneurship? SSRN Electronic Journal. DOI: 10.2139/ssrn.3490531

Holton, M. (2017). Traditional or non-traditional students?: Incorporating UK students' living arrangements into decisions about going to university. *Journal of Further and Higher Education*, *41*(3), 393–403. DOI: 10.1080/0309877X.2017.1301408

Juma, K. S., Raihan, M. A., & Clement, C. K. (2021). Role of ICT in higher educational administration in Uganda. *World Journal of Educational Research (Los Angeles, Calif.)*, *3*(1), 1–10. DOI: 10.22158/wjer.v3n1p1

Jůvová, A., Duda, O., de Vos, M., Stuit, P., & Velthuis, C. (2023). The European teacher as a reflective practitioner: Skills for the 21st century in education. Palacký University Olomouc. https://www.erasmus-journal.eu/wp-content/uploads/european-teacher-21cs-cz.pdf

Karvánková, P., Blažek, V., Klufová, R., & Rypl, J. (2024). Reawakening the past: The role of gamification in preserving cultural legacy – A case study from Czechia. PLURAL. History, Culture. *Society*, *12*(2), 5–24. DOI: 10.37710/plural.v12i2_1

Karvánková, P., Blažek, V., & Staněk, M. (2025). Geocircus – A path to modern geography teaching. *The Professional Geographer*, *77*(6), 704–715. Advance online publication. DOI: 10.1080/00330124.2025.2564967

Karvánková, P., Rypl, J., Rejmanová, A., & Blažek, V. (2025). Teaching geo education within the STEM concept: A case study from Czechia. Geoheritage. Advance online publication. .DOI: 10.1007/s12371-025-01180-8

Kiley, M., & Wisker, G. (2009). Threshold concepts in research education and evidence of threshold crossing. *Higher Education Research & Development*, *28*(4), 431–441. DOI: 10.1080/07294360903067930

Kraft, M. A., Blazar, D., & Hogan, D. (2018). The effect of teacher coaching on instruction and achievement: A meta-analysis of the causal evidence. *Review of Educational Research*, *88*(4), 547–588. DOI: 10.3102/0034654318759268

Kunwar, R. (2022). Impact of ICT on adopting online education at higher education in Nepal: A factual analysis. *Education and Development*, *30*(1), 45–58. DOI: 10.3126/ed.v30i1.49511

Lavonen, J. (2020). Curriculum and teacher education reforms in Finland that support the development of competences for the twenty-first century.

Liu, Y., & Shi, Y. (2023). Digital transformation of college teacher education from the perspective of behaviorist psychology: Initiatives, effectiveness and pitfalls. *Applied Mathematics and Nonlinear Sciences*, *8*(2), 3499–3514. DOI: 10.2478/amns.2023.2.01598

Madsen, S. S., Thorvaldsen, S. & Archard, S. (2018). Teacher educators' perceptions of working with digital technologies. Nordic Journal of Digital Literacy [online]. 13(03), 177-196. ISSN 1891-943X. DOI: 10.18261/issn.1891-943x-2018-03-04

Mahyoob, M. (2020). Challenges of e-learning during the covid-19 pandemic experienced by efl learners. *Arab World English Journal*, *11*(4), 351–362. DOI: 10.24093/awej/vol11no4.23

Ministry of Education. Youth and Sports (2021). Framework educational program for primary education. Ministry of Education, Youth and Sports. https://www.edu.cz/wp-content/uploads/2021/07/rvp-zv-2021.pdf

Ministry of Education. Youth and Sports (2023). Competence Framework for Teaching Graduates: Common Professional Competences. Prague: Ministry of Education, Youth and Sports. ISBN 978-80-87601-54-9. Available at https://www.msmt.cz

Ngafeeson, M. N. (2022). Northern Michigan University online campus: A case of digital transformation in higher education. *Journal of Information Technology Teaching Cases*, *12*(2), 230–243. DOI: 10.1177/20438869211056950

Nguyen, L. B. (2023). Application of information and communication technology (ICT) in educational administration: International experiences and Vietnamese policies. *Vietnam Journal of Education*, *7*(3), 45–53. DOI: 10.52296/vje.2023.327

OECD. (2019). TALIS 2018 results (Volume I): Teachers and school leaders as lifelong learners. OECD Publishing. .DOI: 10.1787/1d0bc92a-en

Papert, S. (1993). *The children's machine: Rethinking school in the age of the computer*. BasicBooks.

Paris, B., Reynolds, R., & McGowan, C. (2020). Sins of omission: Critical informatics perspectives on privacy in e-learning systems in higher education. *Journal of the Association for Information Science and Technology*, *71*(9), 1073–1084. DOI: 10.1002/asi.24575

Paudel, P. (2021). Online education: Benefits, challenges and strategies during and after COVID-19 in higher education. *International Journal on Studies in Education, 3*(2), 70–85. DOI: 10.46328/ijonse.32

Pfeiffer, S. (2017). The vision of "Industrie 4.0" in the making—A case of future told, tamed, and traded. *NanoEthics, 11*(1), 107–121. DOI: 10.1007/s11569-016-0280-3

Putri, R., & Mirizon, S. (2022). Barriers in technology integration: Efl lecturers and students' experience in english learning and instruction amidst covid-19 pandemic disruption. *Indonesian Journal of Educational Research and Review, 5*(2), 252–261. DOI: 10.23887/ijerr.v5i2.50274

Qureshi, M. I., Khan, N., Raza, H., Imran, A., & Ismail, F. (2021). Digital technologies in education 4.0: Does it enhance the effectiveness of learning? A systematic literature review. *International Journal of Interactive Mobile Technologies, 15*(4), 31–47. DOI: 10.3991/ijim.v15i04.20291

Rafsanjani, M. A., Hakim, L., Laily, N., Wijaya, P. A., & Irwansyah, M. R. (2021). Exploring the predictor of innovative teaching using the job demands-resources model. *Education in Science, 26*(3), 58–74. DOI: 10.17853/1994-5639-2021-3-58-74

Redecker, C. (2017). *European framework for the digital competence of educators: DigCompEdu*. Publications Office of the European Union. DOI: 10.2760/159770

Regmi, K., & Jones, L. (2020). A systematic review of the factors – enablers and barriers – affecting e-learning in health sciences education. *BMC Medical Education, 20*(1), 91. Advance online publication. DOI: 10.1186/s12909-020-02007-6

Reidenberg, J. R., & Schaub, F. (2018). Achieving big data privacy in education. *Theory and Research in Education, 16*(3), 263–279. DOI: 10.1177/1477878518805308

Remshagen, A., & Huett, K. C. (2023). Youth hackathons in computing for the community: A design case. *TechTrends, 67*(4), 508–520. DOI: 10.1007/s11528-023-00852-y

Reyes, V., McLay, K., Thomasse, L., Olave-Encina, K., Karimi, A., Rahman, M. T., Seneviratne, L., & Tran, T. L. N. (2021). Enacting smart pedagogy in higher education contexts: Sensemaking through collaborative biography. *Smart Learning Environments, 8*(1), 1–18. DOI: 10.1007/s10758-021-09495-5

Rogers, P. L. (2000). Barriers to adopting emerging technologies in education. *Journal of Educational Computing Research, 22*(4), 455–472. DOI: 10.2190/4UJE-B6VW-A30N-MCE5

Royal Society. (2012). Shut down or restart? The way forward for computing in UK schools. Royal Society. https://royalsociety.org/~/media/education/computing-in-schools/2012-01-12-computing-in-schools.pdf

Royal Society (Great Britain). (2017). After the reboot: computing education in UK schools. Issued: November 2017 DES4633 ISBN: 978-1-78252-297-3.

Rypl, J., Kirchner, K., Blažek, V., Kraft, S., Karvánková, P., & Rejmanová, A. (2025). *The Evaluation of Geomorphosites with regards to Geoheritage: Case Study of the Novohradské Mountains.* Geoheritage. DOI: 10.1007/s12371-025-01148-8

Singh Buttar, S. (2016). ICT in higher education. *People: International Journal of Social Sciences, 2*(1), 1686–1696. DOI: 10.20319/pijss.2016.s21.16861696

Smékalová, L. (2019). Pedagogy in 21st Century Society. Czech Association for Pedagogical Research. https://www.capv.cz/wp-content/uploads/2019/08/capv05_sme_pedag.pdf

Spurná, M. (2024). *Atlas of geography didactics in teacher training*. Masaryk University. DOI: 10.5817/CZ.MUNI.M280-0646-2024

Tolegenova, A., Kanderzhanova, A., Foster, F., Colet, P., Stolyarova, V., & Sarría-Santamera, A. (2024). Barriers and facilitators in implementing online educational interventions for physicians: systematic review of reviews. DOI: 10.1101/2024.11.18.24317472

UNESCO. (2023). *Barriers and supports for technology integration: views from teachers and education experts.*, DOI: 10.54676/LCEB5308

Vaníček, J. (2021). Towards a compulsory computing curriculum at primary and lower-secondary schools: the case of Czechia. In Barendsen, E., & Chytas, Ch. (Eds.), Lecture Notes in Computer Science: Vol. 13057. *Informatics in Schools. Rethinking Computing Education. ISSEP 2021* (pp. 109–120). Springer. DOI: 10.1007/978-3-030-90228-5_9

Vuorikari, R., Kluzer, S., & Punie, Y. (2022). *DigComp 2.2: The Digital Competence Framework for Citizens – With new examples of knowledge, skills and attitudes*. Publications Office of the European Union.

Xiang, H., & Guo, Y. (2023). Innovative paths for talent cultivation models of navigation technology majors in higher vocational colleges under the background of educational digital transformation. *Academic Journal of Computing & Research*, 7(8), 112–118. DOI: 10.54097/acrq2909

Zhao, J. (2021). Research on the practice of teaching reform in colleges and universities based on innovation and entrepreneurship education. *Journal of Contemporary Educational Research*, *7*(8), 91–96. DOI: 10.26689/jcer.v7i8.5288

Chapter 6
Embedding Inclusivity and Sustainability in Smart Higher Education: From Digitalization to Democratization

Ratan Sarkar
https://orcid.org/0009-0008-5480-0165
Tezpur University, India

Madhurima Chakraborty
https://orcid.org/0000-0001-8268-2129
Adamas University, India

ABSTRACT

This chapter examines how higher education can shift from digitalization to true democratization by embedding inclusivity and sustainability into smart campus ecosystems. While digital transformation is accelerating, it risks reinforcing inequities unless guided by social justice principles. The chapter argues that inclusivity must extend beyond disability access to encompass socio-economic, cultural, and linguistic diversity, ensuring equitable participation in digitally enabled institutions. Sustainability, likewise, should be understood holistically—not only through green architecture or energy efficiency, but through integrated environmental, social, and pedagogical responsibility. Drawing on global frameworks such as the UN 2030 Agenda, the CRPD (2006), and UNESCO's Futures of Education (2021), the chapter showcases universities that align digital innovation with democratic values. It

DOI: 10.4018/979-8-3373-6831-3.ch006

2026, IGI Global Scientific Publishing. Copying or distributing in print or electronic forms without written permission of IGI Global Scientific Publishing is prohibited. Use of this chapter to ative artificial intelligence (AI) technologies is expressly prohibited. The publisher reserves all rights to license its use for generative AI training and machine learning model development.

proposes a framework for "Inclusive and Sustainable Smart Campuses," offering strategies for leaders and educators to advance equity, resilience, and meaningful innovation.

1. INTRODUCTION

The twenty-first century has witnessed a radical transformation in higher education institutions (HEIs), driven by rapid digitalization, globalization, and the growing imperative of sustainability. Once confined to digitizing administrative processes or classroom resources, universities are now evolving into *smart campuses*—digitally connected ecosystems that employ the Internet of Things (IoT), artificial intelligence (AI), big-data analytics, and immersive technologies to enhance efficiency, learning outcomes, and institutional management (Alghamdi & Shetty, 2016). These technological shifts have fundamentally altered the spatial, temporal, and pedagogical dimensions of education, enabling flexible and data-driven learning environments that transcend physical boundaries. Yet, this digital leap has also exposed deep structural inequities related to access, affordability, and representation, reminding scholars and policymakers that technological advancement alone cannot guarantee educational justice (UNESCO, 2021). The promise of smart campuses lies in their capacity to create *adaptive, connected, and responsive* institutions—where smart classrooms, intelligent energy systems, and digital learning management platforms foster seamless integration of teaching, learning, and research. However, this promise is often undermined by an implicit prioritization of efficiency and competitiveness over human values such as inclusion, participation, and ecological responsibility. The COVID-19 pandemic further unmasked this paradox: while digital platforms sustained education continuity, they simultaneously magnified pre-existing digital divides in device ownership, connectivity, and digital literacy (UNESCO, 2020). For millions of students from marginalized, rural, or differently-abled communities, "going online" meant exclusion rather than access. Digital transformation must now be viewed not as a tech upgradation but as a *democratic and ethical pursuit* for equity, inclusion, and sustainability.

Digitalization in higher education generally refers to the adoption of digital tools to enhance administrative efficiency and pedagogical practices. Democratization, by contrast, demands that these technological processes be governed by principles of participation, transparency, and equity. It calls for power to be shared among all stakeholders—students, faculty members, administrators, and communities—so that the benefits of digital transformation extend beyond privileged groups. Without such democratization, digitalization risks reproducing historical hierarchies of access and opportunity, creating a technologically enhanced but socially unequal academy

(Jarke & Breiter, 2019). In the emerging discourse of smart higher education, democratization means cultivating *digital citizenship*-enabling learners and educators meaningfully co-design learning environments and influence institutional directions, embedding inclusivity and sustainability as *non-negotiable ethical anchors* in the design, deployment, and governance of smart technologies.

Inclusivity in the digital era encompasses diversity across socio-economic, cultural, gender, and linguistic dimensions. The United Nations' *Convention on the Rights of Persons with Disabilities* (CRPD, 2006) obliges signatories to create accessible environments and adopt universal design principles that ensure equal participation. However, in practice, accessibility audits in HEIs often remain superficial, addressing infrastructure but not the pedagogical, linguistic, or cultural barriers that hinder participation (Al-Azawei et al., 2016). The framework of *Universal Design for Learning* (CAST, 2018) offers an effective approach to operationalize inclusivity within digital environments. It advocates institutions to design learning experiences that embrace learner diversity through multiple modes of engagement, representation, and expression. In smart campuses, applying UDL principles means developing multilingual interfaces, captioned or sign-language-enabled video lectures, and adaptive assessments sensitive to learners' contexts. Inclusivity demands participatory digital governance, involving students, faculty, and marginalized groups in decisions on technology, data, and online learning (Yüksel-Arslan et al, 2025). Only through such collaborative practices can higher education move from *technological provision* to *social empowerment.*

Sustainability emerges as equally vital within smart higher education. The *2030 Agenda for Sustainable Development* identifies education as both a goal and a means for achieving all other Sustainable Development Goals (SDGs). In particular, SDG 4 — "Ensure inclusive and equitable quality education and promote lifelong learning opportunities for all"—positions higher education as a critical lever for equity, innovation, and environmental responsibility (United Nations, 2015). Sustainability in this context must be interpreted broadly: not only as energy-efficient architecture or green operations but as a holistic commitment encompassing environmental stewardship, social justice, and economic viability (Filho et al., 2019). Smart campuses can significantly contribute to this agenda when digital technologies are leveraged for climate action, waste management, and resource optimization. IoT-based sensors can monitor energy consumption, AI can enhance mobility planning, and digital dashboards can support transparent reporting on sustainability indicators. However, the same technologies may also generate new environmental costs through increased e-waste, server energy consumption, and short hardware life cycles. Therefore, embedding sustainability means cultivating a *critical digital ecology*—a mindset that evaluates both benefits and costs of technological innovation.

UNESCO's *Reimagining Our Futures Together: A New Social Contract for Education* (2021) underscores that the future of education must be built on cooperation, equity, and sustainability. It critiques education systems that valorize competitiveness and technological determinism and calls for a "human-centered digital transformation." Within this framework, higher education has the moral responsibility to model inclusive, sustainable, and participatory practices. Smart campuses, when aligned with this vision, can become *living laboratories* for democratic governance—spaces where technological innovation coexists with ecological and social consciousness. UNESCO report also redefines learning as a collective and relational act. It suggests that universities should not merely integrate digital tools but also reimagine their role in society as *agents of planetary well-being*. Embedding inclusivity and sustainability in smart campuses directly supports this shift from individualistic achievement toward collaborative resilience. The transition from digitalization to democratization thus becomes the defining challenge and opportunity for twenty-first-century higher education.

1.1. The Central Argument

Figure 1. Democratizing Higher Education through Digital Transformation

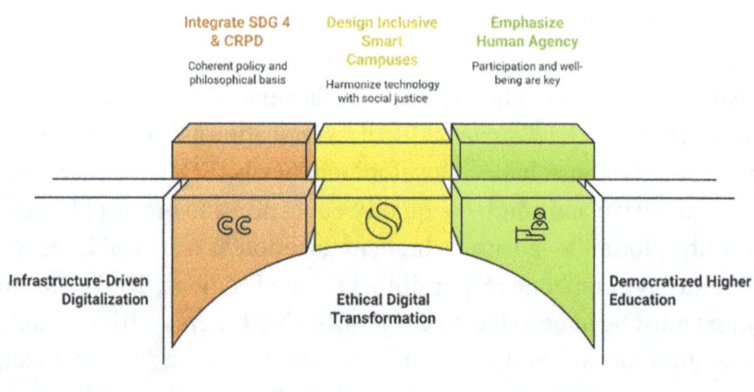

This chapter calls for a paradigm shift in digital transformation of higher education; from infrastructure and efficiency driven goals to an ethically grounded pursuit of democratization. Inclusivity and sustainability are not supplementary considerations but foundational principles that determine whether digital transformation leads to emancipation or exclusion. Integrating the mandates of SDG 4 and CRPD (2006) within the broader framework of UNESCO's *Futures of Education* offers a coherent policy and philosophical basis for such democratization. Through theoretical analysis, case studies, and a proposed conceptual framework, the chapter explores how HEIs can design *Inclusive and Sustainable Smart Campuses* that harmonize technological innovation with social justice and ecological responsibility. In sum, the journey from digitalization to democratization redefines philosophy of educational technology by emphasizing human agency, participation and well-being. By embedding inclusivity and sustainability in smart higher education, universities can rise beyond technological advancement to embody equity, resilience, and planetary stewardship. The chapters that follow will articulate the theoretical foundations, global policy contexts, and practical pathways for realizing this transformative vision.

2. CONCEPTUAL AND THEORETICAL FOUNDATIONS

The rapid transformation of higher education through digital technologies represents a profound epistemological shift rather than a mere infrastructural change. This transformation has moved progressively—from the digitization of information to digitalization of processes, and now towards the vision of *smart campuses* that integrate artificial intelligence (AI), the Internet of Things (IoT), and data analytics into academic ecosystems (Alghamdi & Shetty, 2016). However, while digitalization has enabled efficiency, connectivity, and innovation, it has also intensified inequalities and alienations in access, agency, and participation. The current challenge before higher education, therefore, is not technological adoption but *democratization*: embedding inclusivity, ethics, and sustainability into the heart of digital transformation. This section unpacks the conceptual and theoretical foundations underpinning this transition from *digitalization to democratization.* It elaborates on four interrelated frameworks—Universal Design for Learning (UDL), Critical Pedagogy, Socio-technical Systems Theory, and the Sustainability Triad—to explain how inclusivity and sustainability can be systematically embedded in smart higher education.

2.1. Evolution from Digitalization to Democratization

The trajectory from digitalization to democratization in higher education reflects an evolution in both purpose and philosophy. *Digitization* refers to converting analog information into digital form—scanning books, uploading PDFs, or digitizing records. *Digitalization* extends further to the integration of digital technologies into pedagogical and administrative practices—online learning platforms, virtual classrooms, e-assessments, and institutional data systems (OECD, 2020). In contrast, *democratization* of digital transformation transcends mere adoption to emphasize equitable participation, shared governance, and ethical use of technology. At its core, democratization implies redistributing power and agency within digital ecosystems.

It demands that decisions about what technologies to adopt, how data are collected, and how digital resources are governed be made collaboratively rather than hierarchically (Jarke & Breiter, 2019). This shift redefines digital transformation as a social and political process that must foreground questions of *who benefits, who participates, and who is excluded*. It resonates with Paulo Freire's (1970) argument in *Pedagogy of the Oppressed* that education, when detached from democratic dialogue, risks becoming an instrument of domination rather than liberation. Thus, democratization transforms smart campuses from technology-driven spaces to *values-driven communities*.

2.2. The Smart Campus: Concept and Dimensions

The concept of the *smart campus* has emerged as a cornerstone of digital transformation in higher education. A smart campus is an interconnected ecosystem that uses digital technologies—IoT, AI, machine learning, and big data—to enhance teaching, learning, governance, and sustainability (Cai & Shen, 2020). It embodies the integration of cyber-physical systems where data from various sources—classroom sensors, library systems, or student devices—are analyzed to optimize operations and support decision-making. Yet, beyond efficiency and automation, a smart campus must be envisioned as a *learning organism* that adapts to the diverse needs of its users. Its success depends not on technological sophistication alone but on its ability to foster *human flourishing*. Baldwin and Ching (2021) remind that accessibility remains a persistent gap even in technologically advanced systems; therefore, smart campuses must integrate *accessibility by design*.

In this sense, smart campuses can be understood through three overlapping dimensions:

1. Technological dimension—digital infrastructure, data analytics, and automation;
2. Pedagogical dimension—innovation in teaching, personalized and adaptive learning; and
3. Ethical-social dimension—participation, inclusivity, sustainability, and justice.

The theoretical frameworks that follow illuminate how these dimensions can be interwoven into a coherent model of democratized smart higher education.

2.3. Universal Design for Learning (UDL): Blueprint for Inclusivity

Universal Design for Learning (UDL) provides the most comprehensive pedagogical foundation for inclusivity within digital education. Originating from architecture's

Universal Design principles, UDL advocates designing learning environments that accommodate diverse learners from the outset rather than through afterthought or retrofitting. CAST (2018) articulates UDL around three guiding principles:

1. Multiple means of engagement – to stimulate interest and motivation;
2. Multiple means of representation – to provide information in different formats; and
3. Multiple means of action and expression – to offer varied ways for learners to demonstrate understanding.

In the context of smart campuses, UDL principles can shape digital platforms, content design, and assessment systems. For instance, integrating text-to-speech tools, captioned lectures, and multilingual interfaces ensures access for students with disabilities and those from non-dominant linguistic backgrounds.

However, UDL's significance extends beyond disability inclusion. It embodies an *epistemic inclusivity*—valuing different ways of knowing, learning, and expressing. This aligns closely with democratization, as it situates learners not as passive recipients but as *co-creators* in digital learning ecosystems. By foregrounding flexibility, accessibility, and participation, UDL operationalizes inclusivity as a systemic principle rather than an accommodation.

2.4. Critical Pedagogy: Reclaiming Agency in Digital Transformation

While UDL offers the pedagogical foundation, Paulo Freire's (1970) *Critical Pedagogy* provides the ideological and ethical compass challenging the "banking model" of education in which students are treated as repositories of information. In the context of digital transformation, this critique gains new relevance. Algorithms, data-driven personalization, and automated assessments risk reducing learners to *data points*—subjects of technological control rather than agents of their own education. Critical pedagogy insists on dialogue, reflection, and transformation—what Freire called *conscientização* (critical consciousness). It compels educators to interrogate how power operates through technology: Who designs algorithms? Whose data are collected? Whose languages and epistemologies are privileged in digital systems? (Giroux, 2011). By integrating critical pedagogy with digital transformation, smart campuses can resist technocratic reductionism and reaffirm education as a *practice of freedom*. Faculty and students become co-participants in shaping the ethical and social parameters of technology use. Participatory design workshops, student-led innovation hubs, and open-source digital resources exemplify how democratization can manifest in practice. Thus, critical pedagogy situates smart higher education within broader struggles for social justice and epistemic democracy.

2.5. Socio-Technical Systems Theory: Aligning Technology and Human Agency

The Socio-Technical Systems (STS) theory, emerging from organizational studies in the mid-20th century, provides a systemic lens for understanding how technology and social structures co-evolve (Trist & Bamforth, 1951). STS posits that effective systems optimize both the *technical subsystem* (machines, tools, digital processes) and the *social subsystem* (people, culture, relationships). When applied to higher education, STS underscores that smart campuses cannot function effectively without balancing human values and technological efficiencies. In an STS-informed framework, digital transformation is neither inherently progressive nor oppressive; its outcomes depend on how social contexts shape technological design and implementation. For instance, while learning analytics can identify at-risk students, the same data can be misused for surveillance or punitive measures. Similarly, AI-driven decision-making may streamline admissions but also reproduce existing biases unless inclusivity is consciously embedded (OECD, 2020). STS thus provides a *systems-oriented rationale* for democratization. It emphasizes participatory governance—ensuring that educators, students, and administrative staff collectively decide how technology is used and evaluated. Aligning social and technical systems ensures that the smart campus remains both *human-centered* and *ethically resilient.*

2.6. The Sustainability Triad: Integrating Ecology, Equity, and Economy

Leal Filho et al. (2019) propose the *Sustainability Triad*—an integrative model emphasizing environmental stewardship, social equity, and economic viability. Within higher education, this triad provides a comprehensive framework for embedding sustainability into digital transformation.

Figure 2. The Sustainability Triad

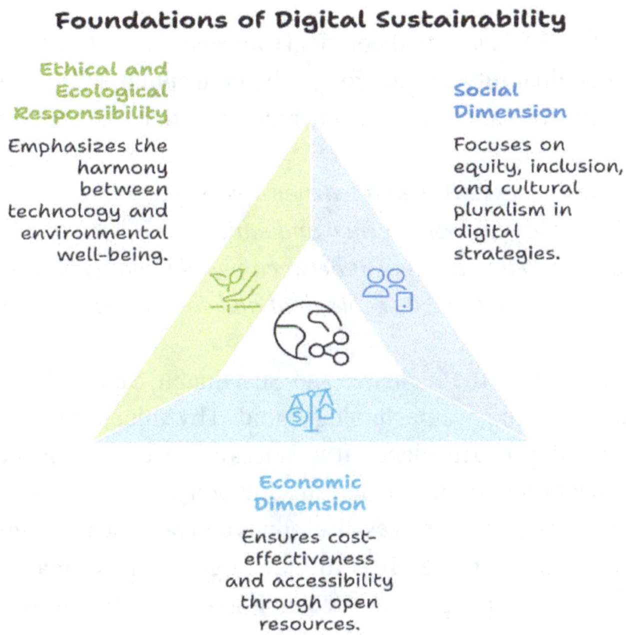

1. Environmental Dimension: Smart campuses can minimize ecological footprints through renewable energy, smart grids, and green IT. However, the environmental cost of data centers, device manufacturing, and e-waste must also be critically addressed (García-Peñalvo et al., 2022).
2. Social Dimension: Sustainability requires fostering equity, inclusion, and community engagement. Digital strategies must serve marginalized groups and promote cultural pluralism, aligning with SDGs 4 (Quality Education) and 10 (Reduced Inequalities).
3. Economic Dimension: Economic sustainability involves ensuring that digital infrastructure investments remain cost-effective, open, and scalable. Open Educational Resources (OER) and collaborative software reduce dependency on expensive proprietary systems, enhancing institutional autonomy and access.

The Sustainability Triad reinforces the notion that technological innovation should be harmonized with ethical and ecological responsibility. Smart campuses aligned with this model act as *microcosms of sustainable societies*, demonstrating how technology can advance—not undermine—planetary well-being.

2.7. Integrative Synthesis: Toward an Inclusive and Sustainable Smart University

The convergence of these four theoretical frameworks—UDL, Critical Pedagogy, STS, and the Sustainability Triad—forms the conceptual architecture for democratized digital transformation. Each contributes a distinct yet complementary lens:

- UDL ensures *accessibility and learner diversity*;
- Critical Pedagogy anchors *agency and ethics*;
- STS secures *systemic alignment between people and technology*; and
- Sustainability Triad embeds *ecological and social responsibility*.

Together, they define the Inclusive and Sustainable Smart Campus as one that centres human well-being over technology, guided by values of participation, transparency, accountability, and resilience. It advances higher education's democratization by aligning innovation with justice and sustainability.

This theoretical synthesis bridges disciplines and provides a pragmatic blueprint for policy and practice, urging HEIs to view digital transformation as a holistic cultural endeavour reshaping human–technology–planet relations. The following sections will expand on this foundation through global policies, case studies, and strategies for inclusive, sustainable smart universities of future.

3. GLOBAL POLICY CONTEXT AND FRAMEWORKS

The transformation of higher education into inclusive and sustainable smart ecosystems cannot be understood in isolation from the global and national policy architectures that shape it. Over the last two decades, the interlinking of education, technology, and sustainable development has been foregrounded across major international frameworks—from the United Nations' *2030 Agenda for Sustainable Development* to UNESCO's *Futures of Education* (2021), the *Convention on the Rights of Persons with Disabilities* (CRPD, 2006), and the OECD's (2020) *Education in the Digital Age* report. These frameworks collectively envision education as both a means and an outcome of sustainable development—emphasizing equity, digital inclusion, and environmental responsibility, yet national adaptations often expose gaps between ideals and implementation. This section analyzes how these frameworks intersect to inform democratized digital transformation in higher education, with particular attention to the Indian context under the *National Education Policy (NEP) 2020*.

3.1. The United Nations 2030 Agenda and the Sustainable Development Goals (SDGs)

The *2030 Agenda for Sustainable Development* represents a global consensus on the need to align educational systems with social justice, environmental sustainability, and inclusive growth. Several Sustainable Development Goals (SDGs) directly shape the vision of inclusive and sustainable smart campuses.

SDG 4 (Quality Education) calls for inclusive, equitable, and quality education for all and the promotion of lifelong learning opportunities. It situates higher education as a transformative driver of sustainable societies. For HEIs, this implies designing digital infrastructures that ensure equitable access and inclusive participation—particularly for learners with disabilities, marginalized groups, and those in low-resource contexts (United Nations, 2015). Smart campuses aligned with SDG 4 therefore prioritize universal accessibility (aligned with CRPD), digital literacy, and open educational resources (OER) to expand reach without compromising quality.

SDG 9 (Industry, Innovation, and Infrastructure) underscores the creation of resilient infrastructures and the promotion of inclusive industrialization. In higher education, this translates into the establishment of *digital knowledge infrastructures*—data centers, learning management systems, and research networks—that facilitate collaboration and innovation. However, these infrastructures must remain open and interoperable to avoid digital monopolies that restrict access (OECD, 2020).

SDG 10 (Reduced Inequalities) explicitly targets the reduction of disparities within and between countries. For universities, the challenge lies in addressing the *digital divide*—inequalities in connectivity, devices, and digital literacy that affect learners across socio-economic and geographic lines. Democratizing digital transformation thus requires targeted policies and funding models that ensure equitable participation in digital higher education.

SDG 13 (Climate Action) links environmental responsibility with institutional governance. Smart campuses must not only integrate renewable energy, waste reduction, and carbon-neutral designs but also embed sustainability into curricula and research agendas. This goal reinforces the *Sustainability Triad* (Leal Filho et al., 2019), ensuring that technological progress is environmentally accountable.

SDG 17 (Partnerships for the Goals) promotes multi-stakeholder collaboration across sectors and borders. International cooperation in digital higher education—through open-access networks, cross-border research, and technology-sharing platforms—is essential to building global smart education ecosystems. Without such partnerships, digital transformation risks deepening North–South inequities and reinforcing epistemic hierarchies.

Collectively, the SDGs provide a comprehensive moral and policy compass for the democratization of digital higher education. However, their implementation depends heavily on the alignment between global aspirations and national educational policies, funding priorities, and institutional leadership.

3.2. UN Convention on the Rights of Persons with Disabilities (CRPD, 2006)

The *UNCRPD (2006)* establishes accessibility and inclusion as fundamental human rights. Article 24 specifically mandates that states ensure inclusive education systems at all levels, supported by reasonable accommodation and universal design principles. This framework redefines accessibility from a welfare issue to a *rights-based obligation*. In the context of smart campuses, CRPD principles translate into digital accessibility standards such as the *Web Content Accessibility Guidelines (WCAG 2.1)*, accessible user interfaces, captioned multimedia, and assistive technologies. The convention's emphasis on *universal design* aligns directly with the *Universal Design for Learning (UDL)* framework (CAST, 2018), ensuring that inclusivity is built into digital systems from inception rather than appended post hoc. However, compliance remains uneven across nations. Many universities implement accessibility only superficially—through minimal hardware accommodations or isolated initiatives—without addressing structural and attitudinal barriers (Lomellini et al., 2025). Democratizing digital transformation thus requires going beyond compliance toward participatory design, where persons with disabilities and marginalized learners actively shape digital policy, pedagogy, and governance.

3.3. UNESCO's "Futures of Education" (2021): A New Social Contract

UNESCO's report *Reimagining Our Futures Together: A New Social Contract for Education* (2021) envisions education as a public good and a collective endeavor for human and planetary well-being. It critiques the commodification of education and calls for *human-centered digital transformation*. For UNESCO, technology must augment—not replace—human agency, ethics, and creativity. The report identifies two guiding imperatives: inclusivity and sustainability. Inclusivity involves active participation in knowledge creation, while sustainability calls for ecological and social responsibility. UNESCO urges universities to lead this shift by embedding sustainability principles into governance, research, and digital design.

In practical terms, the UNESCO framework encourages HEIs to:

- Promote open science and open educational resources;
- Foster multilingual, culturally sensitive content;
- Embed digital literacy and ethics in curricula; and

- Collaborate across borders to address global challenges through digital networks.

However, the report alarms that without democratization, digital transformation could entrench surveillance, privatization, and exclusion, positioning the UNESCO framework as both a vision and a caution for smart higher education.

3.4. OECD (2020): Equity and Well-being in the Digital Age

The OECD's *Education in the Digital Age: Healthy and Inclusive Learning* (2020) complements the UNESCO vision by emphasizing *well-being, inclusivity, and digital resilience.* The report identifies the risk of a growing *digital dependency gap*, favoring affluent learners and calls on OECD member states to integrate inclusive design principles, teacher capacity-building, and digital citizenship education into national strategies.

From a democratization standpoint, OECD emphasizes balancing digital innovation with human development through equitable broadband distribution, public funding for open educational platforms, and national accessibility frameworks. Nonetheless, the OECD perspective remains primarily economic and skills-oriented, overlooking participatory governance—a gap that democratized smart campuses must address.

3.5. National Policy Context: India's NEP 2020 and Digital Higher Education Initiatives

India's *National Education Policy (NEP) 2020* provides a transformative blueprint for integrating digital technologies and inclusivity within higher education. The policy's commitment to "equitable and inclusive education for all" (para 6.3) aligns with both SDG 4 and CRPD mandates. NEP 2020 envisions technology as an enabler of access, equity, and quality, but also underscores ethical and cultural responsibility.

Several flagship initiatives operationalize this vision:

- SWAYAM (Study Webs of Active-Learning for Young Aspiring Minds): India's Massive Open Online Course (MOOC) platform democratizes access to quality higher education across geographical and economic divides. However, limited internet access and language diversity remain barriers to its full potential (NITI Aayog, 2023).
- DIKSHA (Digital Infrastructure for Knowledge Sharing): Initially aimed at school education, DIKSHA's model of open content repositories and multi-

lingual resources exemplifies inclusive design principles applicable to higher education.

- NKN (National Knowledge Network): Provides high-speed connectivity to universities and research institutions, fostering collaborative research and data sharing.
- Virtual Labs and e-Content Initiatives: Aim to integrate experiential learning within online environments, supporting accessibility for learners with disabilities.

Despite these strengths, challenges persist including urban-rural digital divides, limited support for learners with disabilities and the need for stronger accountability mechanisms to ensure inclusivity and sustainability amid efficiency-focused reforms that the policy's "light but tight" regulation emphasizes.

3.6. Regional Comparisons: Europe, Africa, and Asia

European Union (EU): Green and Digital Universities

European universities operate under the *European Green Deal* and *Digital Education Action Plan (2021–2027)*, which jointly promote sustainability and digital transformation. The EU approach integrates smart campus design with carbon neutrality, data ethics, and student participation. Institutions such as the University of Groningen and KU Leuven exemplify the synergy between digital innovation and green infrastructure.

Africa: Resilience through Renewable and Low-Tech Innovation

African HEIs, constrained by infrastructural limitations, have pioneered *resource-efficient models* of smart education. The African Virtual University and University of Nairobi have leveraged solar-powered digital labs and low-bandwidth e-learning platforms to enhance access. These models highlight how contextual innovation can democratize technology even in low-resource settings.

Asia: Diversity and Digital Expansion

In Asia, initiatives vary widely—from Japan's smart-campus automation to India's inclusive digital ecosystems and Malaysia's green ICT universities. The Asia-Pacific region reflects an emerging emphasis on *digital sovereignty*—localizing digital solutions to respect linguistic and cultural diversity.

Figure 3. Regional Comparisons on Technology Integration and Educational Sustainability

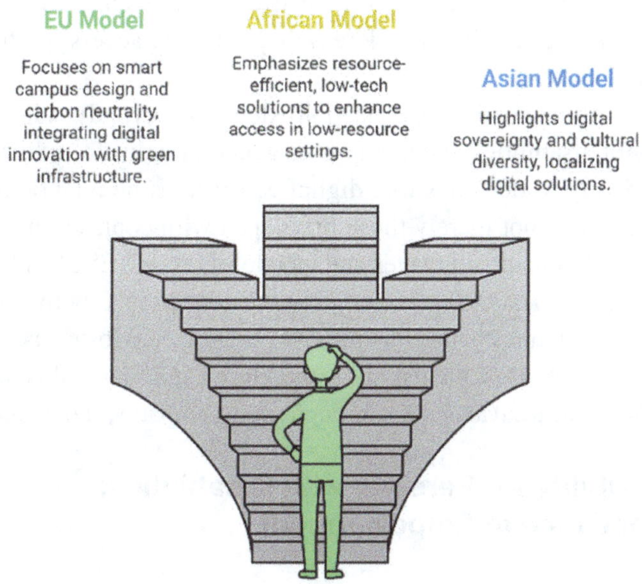

Across these regions, the shared challenge remains ensuring that technological innovation advances *human-centered, sustainable development* whereas variance in models demonstrates that democratization is not a universal formula but a context-sensitive process balancing global frameworks with local realities.

3.7. Critical Reflections

While global frameworks endorse inclusivity and sustainability, they often reflect neoliberal paradigms that prioritizes efficiency, competitiveness, and market-led innovation overlooking ethical dimensions of equity and participation. As Jarke and Breiter (2019) warn, the *datafication of education* risks commodifying learners and marginalizing local epistemologies.

Democratizing smart campuses requires moving beyond compliance-based approaches to *transformative governance*: participatory decision-making, transparent data practices, and shared ownership of digital infrastructures to translate the ideals of the SDGs, CRPD, UNESCO, and NEP 2020 into tangible institutional reforms.

4. INCLUSIVITY IN SMART HIGHER EDUCATION

Inclusivity is central to democratized digital transformation in higher education, requiring *smart campuses*—enabled by artificial intelligence (AI), big data, and the Internet of Things (IoT)— to address disparities in access, participation, and representation.

Inclusivity within smart higher education extends far beyond physical accessibility for persons with disabilities; it encompasses gender, linguistic, cultural, and socio-economic diversity. It demands that digital ecosystems be intentionally designed to serve *all learners*, not merely those privileged with connectivity, resources, or familiarity with dominant languages and technologies. UNESCO's *Global Education Monitoring Report* (2020) defines inclusive education as both "a process and a goal," requiring systemic change that removes barriers and fosters belonging. In the context of smart campuses, inclusivity is therefore a guiding philosophy—one that redefines technological advancement through equity, empathy, and shared governance.

4.1. Accessibility for Persons with Disabilities: From Compliance to Empowerment

Digital accessibility forms the foundation of inclusive smart campuses. According to the *Convention on the Rights of Persons with Disabilities (CRPD, 2006)*, access to information, communication, and technology is a human right, not a privilege. However, despite global advances in technology, persons with disabilities continue to face systemic exclusion due to inaccessible interfaces, non-adaptive learning platforms, and a lack of assistive tools integrated into institutional systems (Lomellini et al., 2025). The *Universal Design for Learning (UDL)* framework (CAST, 2018) provides a powerful pedagogical lens for addressing these challenges. UDL advocates designing accessibility into the learning environment from the outset through the three principles— promoting diverse engagement, representation, and expression to support all learners. For instance, screen reader–compatible learning management systems (LMS), text-to-speech and speech-to-text functionalities, audio-described visuals, and captioned multimedia foster meaningful participation among students with sensory or cognitive impairments (Al-Azawei et al., 2016). Similarly, the *Web Content Accessibility Guidelines (WCAG 2.1)* provide technical standards to ensure web-based educational resources are perceivable, operable, understandable, and robust. Smart campuses aligned with these standards integrate accessibility across their infrastructure: from classroom sensors and digital kiosks to online assessment platforms. The *University of Cape Town (UCT)*, for example, has institutionalized accessibility audits and trained faculty in inclusive digital pedagogy, transforming compliance into a culture of care. However, true accessibility requires institutional accountability—embedding accessibility criteria in procurement policies, accreditation frameworks, and quality assurance mechanisms. Democratization here means ensuring that persons with disabilities are not passive beneficiaries but active *co-designers* of digital transformation. This participatory approach redefines accessibility as empowerment.

4.2. Gender Inclusivity and the Digital Gender Divide

While digitalization has opened new opportunities, it has also perpetuated gender inequalities. Globally, women are 17% less likely than men to use mobile internet, with gaps widening across low- and middle-income countries (UNESCO, 2020). Within higher education, women—particularly from rural and marginalized communities—often encounter barriers to digital access due to social norms, safety concerns, and time burdens. Smart campuses can challenge these inequities by embedding gender inclusivity into digital policies, pedagogy, and representation. First, digital infrastructure must be gender-responsive: ensuring safe virtual spaces, implementing harassment prevention mechanisms, and collecting sex-disaggregated data to monitor participation. Second, curricula must integrate feminist perspectives in technology studies to dismantle stereotypes about women in STEM and AI disciplines. Third, faculty development programs should sensitize educators to gendered patterns of digital participation—encouraging inclusive facilitation, equitable speaking opportunities, and recognition of women's digital agency. For instance, *Indira Gandhi National Open University (IGNOU)* has leveraged its open and distance learning (ODL) model to reach women learners in remote and conservative regions of India. Through offline-compatible digital modules, radio broadcasts, and community learning centers, IGNOU has enabled women to access higher education without compromising cultural constraints. The university's experience exemplifies that inclusive digital design can bridge gendered access gaps while respecting local contexts. Gender inclusivity, therefore is a prerequisite-not an add-on for democratized digital transformation, requiring Smart campuses to safeguard equity in access, leadership, research, and technology creation.

4.3. Linguistic and Cultural Diversity in Digital Education

Linguistic inclusivity is often an overlooked dimension of smart higher education. The dominance of English as the primary language of digital interfaces, MOOCs, and scholarly communication marginalizes students from non-English-speaking backgrounds. UNESCO (2021) emphasizes linguistic diversity as a cornerstone of inclusive knowledge societies, warning that the erosion of local languages in digital education undermines cultural identity and epistemic pluralism. Smart campuses can advance linguistic inclusivity by designing multilingual platforms, integrating machine translation tools, and developing open resources in regional languages. India's *SWAYAM* platform, for example, now offers courses in 13 regional languages—a step toward democratizing online learning across linguistic divides. Similarly, *The Open University (UK)* employs localization strategies, allowing learners worldwide to engage in culturally relevant content while accessing global knowledge. Beyond translation, linguistic inclusivity requires *decolonizing digital knowledge*. Curricula must represent diverse epistemologies, indigenous perspectives, and community-based learning traditions turning smart campuses into spaces of cultural dialogue through local narratives and contextual learning. In doing so, they operationalize what Gay (2018) terms *culturally responsive pedagogy*—learning that validates and leverages students' cultural capital as a resource for meaning-making.

4.4. Socio-Economic Inclusion and the Digital Divide

Socio-economic barriers remain among the most significant obstacles to inclusive digital transformation. Students from low-income backgrounds often lack reliable internet access, digital devices, or private study spaces—issues magnified during the COVID-19 pandemic. UNESCO (2020) reported that over 40% of learners globally were excluded from online education during lockdowns due to inadequate digital access.

Smart campuses can mitigate these inequities through multi-pronged strategies:

- **Infrastructure democratization:** providing subsidized or loan-based laptops, public Wi-Fi zones, and community digital kiosks.
- **Open Educational Resources (OER):** reducing costs of textbooks and software by promoting free and open learning materials.
- **Blended models:** combining online and offline modalities to accommodate bandwidth limitations.
- **Digital literacy programs:** training students from disadvantaged backgrounds to effectively use digital tools for learning and research.

The *University of Cape Town's* "Digital Equity Initiative" exemplifies such approaches by distributing laptops and providing zero-rated access to learning portals for low-income students. Similarly, *Tezpur University (India)* implemented localized digital labs and peer mentorship programs to support learners from rural Northeast regions during the pandemic. These interventions illustrate that inclusivity requires resource redistribution alongside technological innovation. Socio-economic inclusion also depends on policy commitment. Governments and HEIs must allocate budgets for digital equity, integrate inclusive indicators into accreditation systems, and incentivize collaboration with NGOs and private actors to extend digital infrastructure to underserved communities.

4.5. Pedagogical Inclusivity: Reimagining Teaching and Learning

Pedagogical inclusivity means designing learning environments that value learner diversity- abilities, backgrounds, and identities, and utilize technology to personalize learning while fostering community and belonging. AI-powered *adaptive learning systems* are transforming pedagogy by tailoring content, pacing, and assessment to individual learner profiles. Such systems analyze learners' performance data to provide customized feedback, scaffolded support, and alternative learning pathways. When aligned with UDL principles, adaptive technologies enhance accessibility and engagement, especially for students with learning disabilities or varied cognitive profiles (CAST, 2018). However, the ethical deployment of AI requires caution. Overreliance on algorithmic prediction risks reinforcing biases if datasets are unrepresentative or opaque. Democratized digital transformation therefore mandates *algorithmic accountability*: transparent design, human oversight, and inclusivity testing before implementation. Educators should also cultivate critical digital literacy among students—helping them understand how data, design, and power intersect in digital education. Pedagogical inclusivity further involves shifting from teacher-centered instruction to learner-driven collaboration. Discussion forums, peer assessment, and co-creation of digital artifacts foster agency and community. The *Open University (UK)* and *University of British Columbia* have pioneered such participatory models, integrating online dialogue and reflective journaling as inclusive learning practices. These approaches embody Freire's (1970) *critical pedagogy*, treating students as partners in constructing knowledge rather than passive recipients.

4.6. Inclusive Governance and Institutional Culture

Inclusivity cannot be sustained through pedagogy alone; it must be institutionalized through governance. Inclusive governance ensures that decision-making around digital transformation—technology procurement, policy design, curriculum development—reflects diverse voices, especially those historically marginalized. Smart campuses that adopt participatory governance models enable students, faculty, and community stakeholders to co-shape institutional priorities. Accessibility committees, diversity councils, and ethics boards play pivotal roles in embedding inclusivity into every layer of digital infrastructure. Transparent mechanisms for grievance redressal, data privacy, and ethical AI oversight reinforce trust and accountability. Moreover, inclusivity must be reflected in faculty development. Teachers need ongoing professional training in digital accessibility, inclusive assessment, and cross-cultural communication. Initiatives like UNESCO's *ICT Competency Framework for Teachers* encourage educators to integrate inclusive digital practices in classroom design and content creation. Inclusivity is also a matter of culture—of how institutions *value difference*. An inclusive smart campus fosters empathy, collaboration, and well-being, recognizing belonging as essential for effective learning.

Table 1. Global Models of Inclusive and Accessible Smart Education

Institution	Country/ Region	Inclusive Strategy	Key Outcomes
University of Cape Town (UCT)	South Africa	Digital Equity Initiative: subsidized devices, zero-rated learning portals, and UDL-based faculty training	Increased participation of low-income and disabled students in online courses
Open University (UK)	United Kingdom	Multilingual and accessible OER; participatory online forums; AI-based learning analytics with human oversight	Enhanced learner retention and engagement; global reach in over 160 countries
Indira Gandhi National Open University (IGNOU)	India	Blended and low-bandwidth learning solutions; community study centers for women and rural learners	Expanded access for first-generation and women learners
Tezpur University	India	Inclusive digital mentorship and offline-compatible modules during pandemic	Bridged digital divide for rural and tribal learners
University of British Columbia (UBC)	Canada	Reflective online pedagogy using dialogue journals and co-created content	Promoted critical thinking and cross-cultural inclusivity

These examples demonstrate that inclusivity is achievable when technology is aligned with social purpose and community engagement. They also reveal that inclusivity is context-dependent—each institution adapts global principles to local realities.

Table 2. Principles and Practices of Inclusive Digital Design in Higher Education

Principle	Description	Example Application
Accessibility by Design	Embed WCAG 2.1 and UDL guidelines from inception	Screen-reader compatible LMS, captioned multimedia
Multilingualism	Support regional and minority languages	SWAYAM's regional-language MOOCs
Gender Responsiveness	Ensure safety, representation, and equity in online spaces	Anonymous reporting and gender-disaggregated analytics
Affordability and Open Access	Use OER and open-source platforms	Free digital libraries and open textbooks
Participatory Governance	Involve diverse stakeholders in tech policy	Accessibility and ethics committees
AI Ethics and Transparency	Ensure fairness, explainability, and data privacy	Inclusive algorithm testing and audits

These practices collectively represent a *holistic approach* to inclusion—technological, pedagogical, and ethical.

4.7. Toward a Culture of Democratized Inclusion

Inclusivity is not a static achievement but a dynamic commitment to equity and belonging. Smart campuses that truly embody inclusion recognize diversity as a strength rather than a deficit. They move from *compliance* to *culture*, from *access* to *agency*.

Democratized inclusion thus redefines what it means to be "smart." A smart university is not one that merely employs cutting-edge technology, but one that ensures every student, regardless of ability, gender, language, or class, can participate fully in academic and social life. In this sense, inclusivity is not the *destination* of digital transformation—it is its *defining ethos*.

5. SUSTAINABILITY IN SMART HIGHER EDUCATION

Sustainability has emerged as a defining imperative of the twenty-first century higher education, ensuring that technological innovation aligns with ecological balance, social equity, and long-term institutional resilience. The United Nations' *2030 Agenda for Sustainable Development* positions education as central to sustainability—particularly through SDG 4 (Quality Education), SDG 9 (Industry, Innovation, and Infrastructure), and SDG 13 (Climate Action) (United Nations,

2015), envisioning *smart campuses* as laboratories for innovation and sustainability embedded into infrastructure, pedagogy, and governance.

However, sustainability in higher education must transcend a narrow interpretation confined to energy-efficient buildings or waste management. It must encompass *environmental, social, economic, and pedagogical* dimensions that redefine the purpose and practice of digital transformation. This section explores sustainability in smart higher education through the lenses of environmental stewardship, green technology, social inclusion, curricular integration, and governance reform—supported by global case illustrations.

5.1. Reframing Sustainability: From Infrastructure to Ecosystem Thinking

The conceptual evolution of sustainability in higher education mirrors a broader shift from isolated interventions toward *ecosystem-based approaches*. Early sustainability efforts focused primarily on infrastructure—green architecture, renewable energy, and waste reduction. Today, the discourse extends to systemic integration across institutional missions, encompassing teaching, research, administration, and community engagement.

The Sustainability Triad (Leal Filho et al., 2019) comprising three interdependent pillars: environmental, social, and economic sustainability must expand in smart campuses, to include *pedagogical sustainability*—fostering critical thinking, ethical reasoning, and digital citizenship aligned with planetary well-being. Sustainable smart universities thus operate as *living laboratories* where technology, ethics, and ecology converge.

5.2. Environmental Sustainability: Green IT and Campus Ecology

Environmental sustainability being the most visible sustainability dimension in smart campuses focus on reducing the ecological footprint of university operations through *green information technology (Green IT)*, sustainable infrastructure, and renewable energy systems.

Green IT refers to designing, manufacturing, and using digital technologies in environmentally responsible ways. It includes energy-efficient data centers, virtualization of servers, e-waste recycling, and procurement of eco-labeled hardware (Cai & Shen, 2020). With the proliferation of cloud-based learning management systems, universities must now address the hidden carbon costs of data storage and network operations. For instance, studies indicate that global data centers already account for nearly 2% of greenhouse gas emissions (OECD, 2020). Implementing

Green IT strategies, such as energy-efficient cooling systems, renewable-powered data farms, and virtualization, can drastically reduce this impact.

Beyond IT infrastructure, smart campuses can adopt IoT-enabled sustainability measures. Sensor-based lighting and HVAC systems, intelligent waste sorting, and real-time energy dashboards enable efficient resource management. The *University of Helsinki* provides a pioneering example: its *Smart & Sustainable Campus Initiative* integrates IoT sensors to monitor building performance and water usage while engaging students in sustainability analytics projects. This combination of technology and participatory governance exemplifies *eco-digital synergy*—where digitalization and environmental goals reinforce rather than contradict each other.

In India, *IIT Hyderabad* offers another example through its Zero Carbon Smart Campus Project, which integrates solar photovoltaics, water recycling systems, and sustainable mobility (e-bikes and pedestrian-friendly zones). Such initiatives reflect how smart campuses can serve as models for urban sustainability while contributing to research on renewable technologies.

5.3. The Circular Economy in Higher Education

The *circular economy* model extends environmental sustainability by promoting resource efficiency through reuse, recycling, and regeneration rather than linear consumption. In higher education, this involves rethinking how universities procure, use, and dispose of materials—digital or physical. Smart campuses aligned with circular principles adopt e-waste management systems, refurbished equipment programs, and digital platforms to minimize paper and energy waste.

Digitalization itself offers circular benefits: dematerialization of learning resources reduces paper use, while virtual collaboration cuts travel-related emissions. However, sustainability cannot rely solely on digital substitution. As García-Peñalvo et al. (2022) warn, digital devices and servers have embedded environmental costs. Universities must therefore adopt *circular digital strategies*—including extended hardware lifecycles, shared computing facilities, and community e-repair centers.

Circular economy thinking also applies pedagogically. By integrating sustainability into curricula and research, universities can nurture future leaders who design technologies and policies that balance economic growth with ecological responsibility. For instance, the *Erasmus+ Green Skills Program* in Europe promotes circular economy education across disciplines, emphasizing systems thinking and innovation for sustainability.

5.4. Social Sustainability: Equity, Participation, and Well-Being

Social sustainability addresses the human dimensions of institutional transformation—ensuring fairness, participation, and well-being within university communities. Smart campuses can enhance social sustainability by fostering *inclusive governance*, equitable digital access, and well-being-oriented learning environments.

First, equity in digital access remains critical. Socio-economic disparities in connectivity and device ownership risk excluding marginalized groups from the benefits of smart campuses. As OECD (2020) underscores, inclusive digital infrastructure must remain a policy priority. Initiatives like India's *National Knowledge Network (NKN)*, which connects universities through high-speed fiber optics, and *SWAYAM* MOOCs, which expand access to quality learning, represent significant steps toward equitable digital inclusion.

Second, participation and agency are essential to social sustainability. Democratized smart campuses encourage co-creation of policies and digital systems through participatory design, student-led innovation hubs, and open data initiatives. When governance structures embrace diversity, technology becomes an enabler of belonging rather than exclusion.

Third, well-being forms an integral component of social sustainability. The digital acceleration of education has intensified stress, isolation, and information overload. Sustainable digital transformation requires a balance between connectivity and care—embedding mental health support, ergonomic learning design, and humane workload policies. Universities like *Stanford* and *Lund* have adopted "digital well-being dashboards" that monitor screen time, sleep patterns, and workload rhythms, encouraging a culture of mindful technology use.

5.5. Pedagogical Sustainability: Embedding Sustainability in Curriculum and Learning

Pedagogical sustainability concerns the longevity and adaptability of educational practices in fostering critical and responsible learners, embedding sustainability values—ethical reasoning, environmental awareness, and social responsibility—across disciplines.

HEIs play a pivotal role in developing *sustainability literacy*, the capacity to understand interconnections between environmental, social, and economic systems (Filho et al., 2019). Embedding sustainability in teaching requires three interlocking strategies:

1. **Curricular infusion:** Incorporating sustainability topics into diverse disciplines—engineering, economics, humanities, and teacher education.

2. **Experiential learning:** Using campus sustainability projects as living laboratories. Students can analyze real-time data from energy sensors, waste systems, or biodiversity monitoring tools to connect theory with practice.
3. **Interdisciplinary collaboration:** Encouraging co-teaching across faculties to address complex sustainability problems.

The *University of Helsinki*'s *Sustainable Learning Lab* integrates sustainability themes into all degree programs, combining classroom instruction with field projects. Similarly, *African Virtual University (AVU)* embeds sustainability modules into its distance learning platform, contextualizing global sustainability goals within African socio-economic realities. Through digital simulations, local data, and community projects, AVU demonstrates how virtual learning can advance sustainability education without heavy environmental footprints.

Pedagogical sustainability also depends on the *ethical use of digital technologies*. As AI-driven learning analytics become more prevalent, universities must ensure that data collection respects privacy and transparency. Sustainable pedagogy prioritizes human agency, ensuring that automation enhances—not replaces—teacher-student interaction.

5.6. Research and Innovation for Sustainable Futures

Universities produce sustainable innovation through smart campus by amplifying their contribution to sustainability through research and interdisciplinary collaboration.

Research on green computing, renewable energy, urban sustainability, and climate adaptation benefits from data-rich smart environments. For instance, the *University of Helsinki* uses its campus as a testbed for urban resilience research, integrating IoT data from buildings, transport, and weather systems into environmental analytics. Likewise, *IIT Hyderabad*'s *Centre for Sustainable Development* conducts research on smart grids, energy-efficient materials, and sustainable urban planning, linking technology innovation with social impact.

Sustainability research must also include the *social sciences and humanities*, exploring ethical frameworks for digital transformation, equity in innovation, and the decolonization of sustainability discourse. Cai and Shen (2020) argue that higher education institutions function as *innovation ecosystems*—networks that link academia, industry, and society in co-producing solutions to sustainability challenges. For this reason, policies must incentivize interdisciplinary research and recognize sustainability as a core research outcome in funding and ranking systems.

5.7. Institutional Governance and Sustainable Leadership

Sustainability cannot thrive without supportive governance structures. Institutional leadership plays a critical role in translating sustainability principles into actionable strategies.

Sustainability governance involves creating dedicated offices or committees responsible for environmental management, social responsibility, and digital ethics. Such bodies monitor progress toward SDGs, oversee sustainability audits, and ensure transparency in institutional operations. The *University of British Columbia* (UBC), for instance, has implemented an *Integrated Sustainability Plan* linking budgetary processes with carbon reduction and community engagement targets.

Policy coherence is equally crucial. As OECD (2020) observes, fragmented policies across environment, technology, and education sectors often dilute sustainability outcomes. Smart universities must therefore align their digital transformation strategies with national sustainability frameworks and institutional mission statements.

Sustainable leadership emphasizes participatory decision-making, ethical foresight, and long-term vision. Leaders of smart campuses must balance technological innovation with the moral imperative of justice and environmental stewardship. Encouraging green entrepreneurship among students, supporting staff sustainability training, and establishing green procurement guidelines are key leadership responsibilities.

Table 3. Global Case Studies of Sustainable Smart Campuses

Institution	Region	Key Sustainability Initiatives	Outcomes and Lessons
University of Helsinki (Finland)	Europe	Smart & Sustainable Campus integrating IoT sensors, renewable energy, and participatory data analytics	Reduced energy use by 20%; enhanced student engagement in sustainability research
IIT Hyderabad (India)	Asia	Zero Carbon Smart Campus with solar power, water recycling, and sustainable transport	Demonstrated the feasibility of carbon-neutral infrastructure in developing contexts
African Virtual University (Pan-African)	Africa	Distance learning model reducing carbon footprint and increasing access	Expanded sustainable education access across 27 nations; promoted low-resource innovation
University of British Columbia (Canada)	North America	Integrated Sustainability Plan with carbon pricing and student-led projects	Institutionalized sustainability in governance and budgeting
University of Melbourne (Australia)	Oceania	Sustainability Charter integrating research, curriculum, and operations	Enhanced global leadership in climate education and interdisciplinary innovation

These examples underscore that sustainability is achievable across diverse economic and climatic contexts when guided by coherent vision, participatory governance, and contextual innovation. They reveal that technological sophistication alone does not guarantee sustainability—*institutional commitment* and *community ownership* are equally vital.

5.8. Challenges to Sustainability in Smart Higher Education

Despite notable progress, several challenges hinder the holistic integration of sustainability in smart universities:

- **Technological paradox:** While digital tools can advance sustainability, their production and energy demands may exacerbate ecological degradation.
- **Policy fragmentation:** Sustainability policies often operate in silos—environmental, educational, and technological departments lack coordination.
- **Financial constraints:** Green infrastructure and renewable energy systems require high initial investment, especially in developing countries.
- **Cultural inertia:** Institutional resistance to change, coupled with limited awareness among faculty and students, slows adoption.
- **Measurement gaps:** Lack of standardized sustainability indicators in higher education rankings and accreditations undermines accountability.

Addressing these barriers requires systemic reform—integrating sustainability into accreditation systems (e.g., NAAC, QS Impact Rankings), incentivizing innovation through funding, and fostering a campus culture of environmental responsibility.

5.9. Toward Sustainable and Democratized Smart Campuses

Sustainability in smart higher education must evolve from project-based interventions to institutional ethos, defining campuses by *values*: responsibility, equity, and long-term stewardship.

To achieve this, HEIs should:

1. **Institutionalize sustainability**—embed it in mission statements, budgets, and strategic plans.
2. **Adopt participatory governance**—ensure faculty, students, and local communities co-create sustainability agendas.
3. **Invest in green digital infrastructure**—powered by renewables and guided by circular economy principles.

4. **Foster sustainability literacy**—integrate sustainability education across disciplines and co-curricular programs.
5. **Monitor and report transparently**—publish sustainability audits and SDG progress reports.

Ultimately, sustainable smart universities model the *symbiosis between technology and ethics*. They represent a paradigm where digital transformation serves humanity and the planet rather than profit and efficiency alone. As Leal Filho et al. (2019) observe, “sustainability is not a task but a way of being.” By adopting this worldview, higher education can lead the transition from digitalization to democratization—ensuring that innovation contributes not only to knowledge but also to the collective survival and flourishing of all life.

6. CONCEPTUAL FRAMEWORK: INCLUSIVE AND SUSTAINABLE SMART CAMPUSES

As higher education navigates the complex interplay between digital transformation, inclusivity, and sustainability, the need for a coherent theoretical and practical model becomes paramount. The proposed “Inclusive and Sustainable Smart Campus (ISSC) Framework” provides such a model—a holistic approach that integrates technological innovation with social justice and ecological responsibility. It envisions higher education institutions (HEIs) not merely as sites of technological modernization but as *democratic ecosystems* that embody ethical digitalization, equitable participation, and long-term sustainability.

This framework synthesizes insights from prior sections—particularly the principles of *Universal Design for Learning (CAST, 2018)*, *Critical Pedagogy (Freire, 1970)*, *Socio-Technical Systems Theory (Trist & Bamforth, 1951)*, and the *Sustainability Triad (Leal Filho et al., 2019)*—to propose a dynamic, multidimensional model adaptable to diverse institutional contexts. It consists of three interrelated dimensions—Technological, Inclusive, and Sustainable—and is governed by five foundational principles: *Participation, Transparency, Resilience, Accountability,* and *Innovation.*

6.1 Core Dimensions of the ISSC Framework

Figure 4. Dimensions of Inclusive and Sustainable Smart Campus (ISSC) Framework

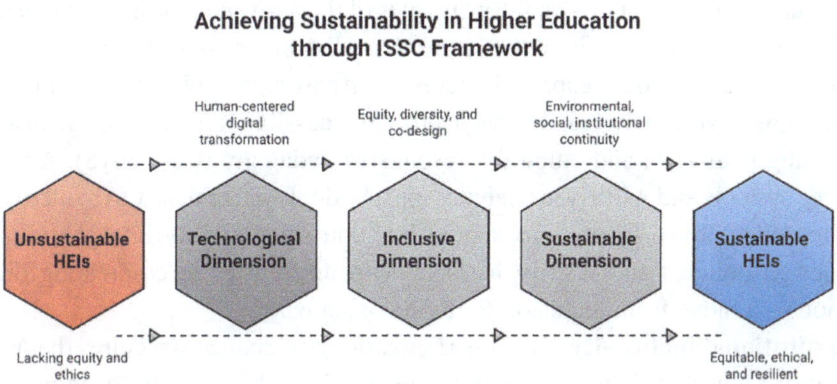

A. Technological Dimension: Human-Centered Digital Transformation

The technological dimension forms the operational backbone of the ISSC framework. It focuses on integrating digital tools, data systems, and smart infrastructures in ways that enhance learning, governance, and research—without compromising equity or ethics. Smart technologies such as artificial intelligence (AI), the Internet of Things (IoT), and learning analytics are leveraged not for automation alone but for *augmentation*—enhancing human creativity, decision-making, and collaboration.

A *human-centered* approach to technology design ensures accessibility and agency. Instead of adopting one-size-fits-all systems, universities should implement *adaptive* digital architectures that accommodate linguistic, cognitive, and cultural diversity. For example, multilingual interfaces, AI-enabled assistive tools, and open-source learning management systems promote inclusivity by design.

Governance of the technological dimension emphasizes data ethics and digital sovereignty. Institutions must establish transparent data policies that regulate how student and institutional data are collected, stored, and used. Regular accessibility and security audits, compliance with the *Web Content Accessibility Guidelines (WCAG 2.1)*, and the adoption of open standards ensure that technology serves academic values rather than market interests. In this sense, smart technologies become *public goods* that support educational equity rather than digital commodification.

B. Inclusive Dimension: Equity, Diversity, and Co-Design

The inclusive dimension addresses social and pedagogical justice within smart campuses constituting inclusivity central to technological and institutional development. This dimension builds on the principles of the *Universal Design for Learning (UDL)* and *Critical Pedagogy* to ensure that all learners—regardless of ability, gender, language, or socio-economic status—can participate fully and meaningfully.

Pedagogical inclusivity is achieved through accessible course design, multimodal learning pathways, and culturally responsive pedagogy (Gay, 2018). Adaptive learning systems and AI-driven analytics must be deployed ethically to reduce rather than reproduce bias. Institutions should integrate accessibility into procurement and design policies and involve learners with disabilities in co-creating digital solutions—a move from inclusion *for* to inclusion *with*.

Institutional inclusivity entails participatory governance structures that represent diverse voices in decision-making. This may include accessibility committees, gender equity councils, and student-led technology design boards. Inclusivity also requires addressing socio-economic barriers through financial aid, digital access programs, and localized learning hubs.

Ultimately, inclusivity within the ISSC framework transforms HEIs from hierarchical institutions into *communities of belonging*, where difference is a source of strength and innovation rather than exclusion.

C. Sustainable Dimension: Environmental, Social, and Institutional Continuity

The sustainable dimension extends beyond environmental responsibility to encompass social cohesion and institutional resilience, extending Leal Filho et al.'s (2019) *Sustainability Triad* to embrace *pedagogical and governance sustainability.*

At the **environmental level**, smart campuses integrate *Green IT* practices, renewable energy systems, waste management, and circular economy principles (Cai & Shen, 2020). IoT sensors can optimize energy consumption, while digital dashboards enhance transparency in resource usage.

At the **social level**, sustainability involves fair access to digital opportunities and the promotion of well-being. Institutions should cultivate safe, inclusive, and empathetic learning environments that prioritize mental health and equity.

At the **institutional level**, sustainability implies financial prudence, adaptability to change, and continuous learning. Universities should institutionalize sustainability offices, integrate SDGs into curricula and rankings, and develop sustainability literacy among students and staff.

Thus, sustainability in this framework transcends environmental management—it becomes a *systemic ethos* guiding all dimensions of academic life.

6.2. Foundational Principles of the ISSC Framework

The three core dimensions are operationalized through five interconnected principles that serve as the normative foundation of the ISSC framework. These principles function as the ethical DNA of inclusive and sustainable smart campuses.

1. Participation: Co-Creation and Shared Governance

Participation is the cornerstone of democratization. It requires shifting from top-down digital policy implementation to *co-created innovation*, where students, faculty, administrators, and community members collaborate in designing, implementing, and evaluating digital initiatives.

Mechanisms for participation include open consultation processes, co-design workshops, and digital democracy tools (e.g., feedback portals, collaborative budgeting apps). For instance, *University of Cape Town* and *University of British Columbia* have institutionalized participatory sustainability councils that include student representatives in digital planning.

Participation fosters ownership, relevance, and accountability, ensuring digital transformation reflects diverse stakeholder realities over corporate priorities.

2. Transparency: Open Data and Ethical Communication

Transparency ensures that technology use and governance processes remain visible, ethical, and accountable. It involves publishing data on sustainability metrics, accessibility audits, and digital expenditures, as well as clearly communicating policies on data use, privacy, and intellectual property.

Open-access initiatives, open educational resources (OER), and open science practices exemplify transparency in academia. Sharing information and resources freely, universities strengthen collective trust along with public access to knowledge.

Moreover, transparent communication mitigates misinformation and fosters digital literacy, transparent governance models integrity—transforming digital transformation from an administrative process into a *publicly accountable social contract*.

3. Resilience: Adaptability, Well-Being, and Systemic Continuity

Resilience refers to the institution's ability to withstand disruptions—technological, environmental, or social—while sustaining its educational mission. The

COVID-19 pandemic exposed vulnerabilities in universities' digital and social infrastructures, emphasizing the need for flexible, hybrid systems and psychosocial support mechanisms.

Resilient smart campuses employ adaptive technologies that can pivot between online, offline, and hybrid modes integrating *digital well-being frameworks* to prevent burnout and foster mental health. At the governance level, resilience entails crisis preparedness—redundant data storage, disaster recovery plans, and sustainable funding models for digital infrastructure.

Resilience thus links sustainability with equity: only systems designed for diversity and adaptability can ensure long-term continuity and justice.

4. Accountability: Ethical and Institutional Responsibility

Accountability in the ISSC framework encompasses *internal governance* and *external stewardship* mandating universities to set measurable goals for inclusivity, sustainability, and digital ethics—and report progress transparently. Accreditation bodies and government agencies can support accountability through sustainability indices and digital inclusion benchmarks (OECD, 2020).

Ethical accountability also requires universities to adopt *responsible AI* policies, ensuring fairness, explainability, and data protection in educational analytics. Institutional audits on gender parity, disability inclusion, and environmental impact foster a culture of self-reflection.

Accountability extends to the community: universities must recognize their social obligations to local ecosystems, labor practices, and cultural preservation. By being answerable to multiple publics, HEIs model the democratic ethos central to the ISSC framework.

5. Innovation: Continuous Improvement through Responsible Experimentation

Innovation remains the dynamic engine of smart campuses, but within the ISSC framework, it is tempered by ethics and sustainability aiming at solutions to social and environmental challenges.

Responsible innovation involves iterative experimentation—piloting new technologies, evaluating impacts, and scaling those that promote inclusivity and ecological responsibility. Examples include AI-based assistive learning, solar-powered IoT devices, and blockchain systems for transparent academic credentialing.

Innovation also encompasses *curricular renewal*: embedding sustainability, accessibility, and ethics into courses across disciplines. Partnerships with industry and civil society can further drive innovation ecosystems that balance technological progress with the public good.

Thus, innovation in the ISSC framework represents a continuous, reflective process—learning from failures as much as successes.

6.3. Operationalizing the ISSC Framework in Governance, Policy, and Practice

To translate the ISSC framework from theory to action, HEIs must institutionalize its principles through governance reforms, policy integration, and day-to-day practices.

1. Governance Structures

- Establish Sustainability and Inclusion Councils comprising faculty, students, and administrative leaders.
- Create Digital Ethics Committees to oversee AI, data, and accessibility compliance.
- Adopt participatory budgeting for digital and green infrastructure projects.
- Integrate the framework into accreditation criteria and annual institutional audits.

2. Policy Integration

- Embed inclusivity and sustainability goals within institutional strategic plans.
- Align digital transformation policies with national frameworks such as NEP 2020 and global goals (SDG 4, 9, 10, 13).
- Develop *Digital Accessibility Policies* referencing WCAG 2.1 and CRPD (2006).
- Include *Green Procurement Guidelines* for hardware, software, and infrastructure.

3. Pedagogical and Operational Practices

- Implement UDL-aligned course design and inclusive assessment practices.
- Introduce sustainability literacy modules across all programs.
- Promote faculty development programs on inclusive technology and green pedagogy.
- Use IoT-based energy monitoring and *AI analytics* for resource optimization.

- Encourage student-led sustainability projects and community partnerships for local impact.

By aligning governance, policy, and pedagogy, HEIs can operationalize the ISSC framework as a living, evolving ecosystem rather than a static compliance checklist.

6.4. Conceptual Model: Structure and Description

The Inclusive and Sustainable Smart Campus (ISSC) Model can be visualized as a *hexagonal concentric framework*, symbolizing the dynamic interdependence of technology, inclusion, and sustainability.

Figure 5. Inclusive and Sustainable Smart Campus (ISSC) Model

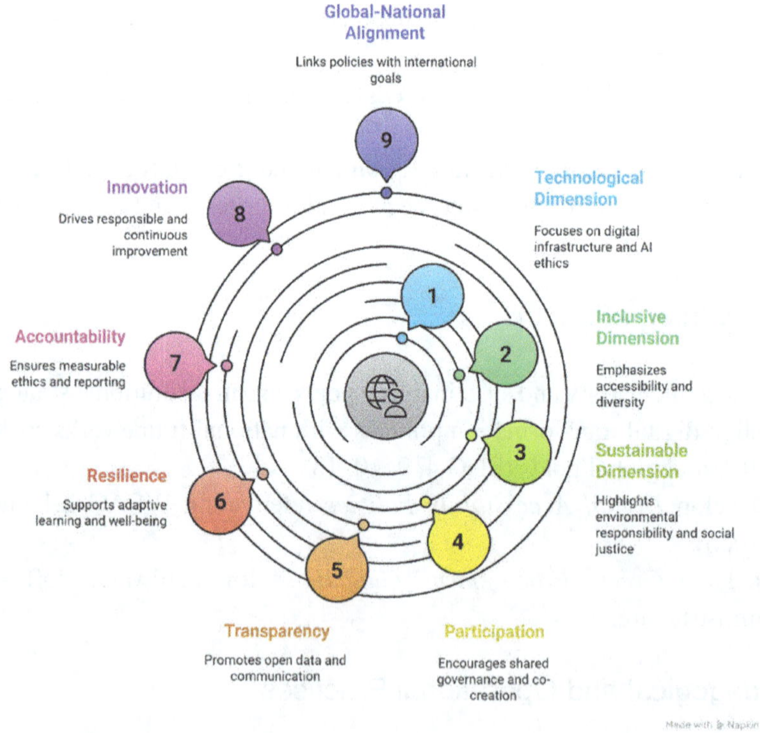

Textual Diagram Description:

- **Core (Center):** *Human-Centered Smart Campus*—the convergence point of all dimensions, representing the ethical foundation of higher education.

- **Inner Ring (Three Dimensions):**
    - o Technological Dimension – digital infrastructure, data governance, and AI ethics.
    - o Inclusive Dimension – accessibility, diversity, and equity in participation.
    - o Sustainable Dimension – environmental responsibility, social justice, and institutional longevity.
- **Outer Ring (Five Principles):**
    - o *Participation* – shared governance and co-creation.
    - o *Transparency* – open data and communication.
    - o *Resilience* – adaptive learning and well-being.
    - o *Accountability* – measurable ethics and reporting.
    - o *Innovation* – responsible and continuous improvement.
- **Surrounding Environment:** *Global-National Alignment*—linking institutional policies with SDGs, CRPD, NEP 2020, and UNESCO's *Futures of Education* (2021).

This concentric-hexagonal structure reflects the reciprocal relationship between internal institutional practices and the external global ecosystem. It portrays smart campuses as *adaptive, ethical, and participatory systems* committed to both technological advancement and human flourishing.

6.5. The Transformative Potential of the ISSC Framework

The ISSC framework provides a blueprint for reimagining the role of higher education in an era of rapid digitalization and environmental precarity. By uniting inclusivity and sustainability within a single conceptual model, it enables HEIs to move from fragmented initiatives to *integrated transformation.*

Its transformative potential lies in its balance between efficiency and empathy, innovation and ethics, technology and humanity. When operationalized, the framework redefines smart campuses as living systems that *learn, adapt, and care.*

Ultimately, the Inclusive and Sustainable Smart Campus Framework positions higher education as a *producer of equitable futures*—anchored in justice, transparency, and shared responsibility.

7. CASE STUDIES AND BEST PRACTICES

The practical realization of *Inclusive and Sustainable Smart Campuses (ISSC)* is evident in several global higher education institutions integrating digital transformation with inclusivity and sustainability goals. The following four comparative case studies—from Europe, Asia (India), North America, and Africa—demonstrate how universities operationalize the principles of *SDG 4 (Quality Education)* and *SDG 10 (Reduced Inequalities)* through inclusive governance, participatory design, and environmentally responsible innovation. Each example highlights the institutional context, strategic interventions, technologies used, and key lessons for democratizing smart higher education.

7.1. Europe: University of Helsinki (Finland) — Smart and Sustainable Campus Integration

Context: The University of Helsinki, one of Europe's leading research-intensive universities, is recognized for embedding sustainability across its teaching, research, and operations. Finland's national education and digital policies emphasize open access, green transition, and digital inclusion—an enabling context for institutional innovation. In 2018, the university launched its *Smart & Sustainable Campus Initiative (SSCI)* to merge digital transformation with environmental and social responsibility (Leal Filho et al., 2019).

Strategy and Technologies: The SSCI integrates Internet of Things (IoT) networks, big-data analytics, and AI-based management systems to monitor energy consumption, water usage, and indoor air quality across its campuses. These data inform predictive maintenance and energy optimization, contributing to significant reductions in carbon emissions. The campus also functions as a *living laboratory*, where students and researchers collaborate on sustainability challenges using real-time data. The initiative aligns with the university's *2030 Sustainability Plan*, emphasizing digital accessibility and participatory governance.

Inclusion and Sustainability Outcomes: Helsinki's digital infrastructure adheres to *WCAG 2.1* standards and includes multilingual user interfaces for international students. Courses and administrative systems are accessible to persons with disabilities, and digital literacy workshops are mandatory for all new students. By 2023, the university achieved a 20% reduction in energy use, a 15% increase in student participation in sustainability projects, and full accessibility compliance across its online platforms.

Lessons Learned: The Helsinki experience demonstrates that sustainability and inclusivity are mutually reinforcing when technology is designed with participation and transparency. Rather than imposing top-down digital reforms, the university's participatory model empowers students as co-creators in sustainability governance. The case illustrates that smart campuses become truly democratic when environmental responsibility and social inclusion are treated as parallel, interdependent goals.

7.2. Asia (India): Indian Institute of Technology (IIT) Hyderabad — Zero Carbon and Inclusive Smart Campus

Context: India's *National Education Policy (NEP) 2020* and *Digital India* initiatives provide a policy foundation for integrating technology, inclusion, and sustainability in higher education. IIT Hyderabad, one of India's premier technological universities, has pioneered efforts to design a *Zero Carbon Smart Campus (ZCSC)* model, combining renewable energy innovation with inclusive digital infrastructure. Situated in Telangana, an emerging technology hub, the institution benefits from strong governmental and industry collaboration.

Strategy and Technologies: The ZCSC employs an advanced *Smart Campus Management System* integrating IoT-based energy grids, solar photovoltaics, smart meters, and water recycling units. The campus runs on a hybrid renewable system supplying over 70% of its energy needs. A digital building management system optimizes lighting and air conditioning using AI algorithms for energy efficiency. Inclusivity is addressed through *UDL-based digital pedagogy*, accessible virtual classrooms, and assistive technologies for students with disabilities. IIT Hyderabad's *E-Accessibility Lab*, established in 2021, collaborates with NGOs to develop open-source assistive devices and screen-reading software in Indian languages. The institution also partners with the *National Knowledge Network (NKN)* to provide high-speed internet to remote research centers and local schools, extending digital equity beyond the campus.

Inclusion and Sustainability Outcomes: The ZCSC has achieved notable milestones: a 35% reduction in carbon emissions since 2019, campus-wide water reuse, and a 25% energy saving through automated monitoring. Accessibility initiatives have increased participation of students with visual and mobility impairments by 40% over three years. Gender inclusion programs, such as *Women in Engineering* fellowships, further diversify the STEM pipeline.

Lessons Learned: IIT Hyderabad's experience underscores that sustainable digital transformation requires institutional leadership and multi-stakeholder collaboration. The model integrates *technological, environmental,* and *social inclusivity*, showing that innovation can serve both ecological and equity goals. It also illustrates the viability of "localized smartness"—tailoring global sustainability frameworks (SDGs 4, 9, and 13) to India's socio-economic and climatic realities.

7.3. North America: University of British Columbia (Canada) — Integrating Sustainability, Data Ethics, and Well-Being

Context: Located in Vancouver, the *University of British Columbia (UBC)* is globally renowned for its commitment to climate leadership and digital innovation.

Canada's national higher education policy emphasizes sustainability literacy, Indigenous inclusion, and responsible data governance, all of which underpin UBC's transformation into a sustainable smart university. The university's *Sustainability Initiative (UBC SI)* and *Campus as a Living Lab* (CLL) programs serve as institutional anchors for integrating research, operations, and pedagogy.

Strategy and Technologies: UBC employs advanced data-driven sustainability systems that merge environmental sensors, learning analytics, and behavioral data to inform campus planning. The *UBC Smart Grid* system monitors and regulates power usage in real time, while *AI-enabled energy models* forecast consumption trends to guide renewable integration. Sustainability dashboards display live metrics of carbon emissions, waste diversion, and water usage, fostering transparency and student engagement. Inclusion is embedded through *Indigenous partnerships* and *equity-oriented governance structures*. UBC's *Indigenous Strategic Plan (2020–2030)* ensures Indigenous voices shape sustainability and digital learning decisions. Accessibility standards follow the *Canadian National Standard on Accessibility (CSA B651-18)*, ensuring compliance in both physical and digital spaces. Furthermore, UBC prioritizes *digital well-being* through training programs that promote mindful technology use and mental health awareness.

Inclusion and Sustainability Outcomes: UBC has achieved a 34% reduction in greenhouse gas emissions from 2007 levels, divested its endowment from fossil fuels, and introduced sustainability curricula across 75% of academic programs. On the inclusivity front, Indigenous representation in governance bodies has increased by 30%, and accessibility compliance exceeds national benchmarks.

Lessons Learned: UBC's model highlights the convergence of *technological sophistication* and *ethical accountability*. Its participatory governance, open data platforms, and holistic sustainability reporting demonstrate how transparency and community engagement strengthen trust and institutional legitimacy. The case illustrates that resilience and inclusivity are integral—not optional—elements of sustainability in smart higher education.

7.4. Africa: African Virtual University (AVU) — Digital Inclusion through Sustainable Distance Learning

Context: The *African Virtual University (AVU)*, a pan-African intergovernmental network established in 1997, exemplifies sustainable digital education in low-resource contexts. Operating across 27 African nations, AVU's mission aligns directly with *SDG 4* and *SDG 10*, aiming to expand access to quality higher education through affordable, technology-enabled learning. The institution's operations are shaped by infrastructural constraints—low connectivity, high costs, and limited access to devices—conditions that necessitate context-sensitive innovation.

Strategy and Technologies: AVU leverages open-source platforms, solar-powered digital labs, and low-bandwidth e-learning technologies to ensure accessibility in regions with unstable electricity or internet. Its *Open Education Resources (OER) Repository*—one of Africa's largest—hosts multilingual materials in English, French, and Portuguese. The platform is designed with *Universal Design for Learning* (UDL) principles, ensuring usability for learners with disabilities and varying literacy levels. AVU also implements *community-based learning centers* where students can access online materials offline through local intranets and mobile-friendly content. Training programs for local educators in digital pedagogy and assistive technology expand inclusivity and capacity-building across partner universities.

Inclusion and Sustainability Outcomes: AVU has trained over 80,000 learners, including many first-generation university students and women from rural areas. Its solar-powered ICT centers have cut operational energy costs by 45% while reducing carbon emissions. The OER repository has been adopted by several African HEIs, supporting inter-institutional knowledge sharing. Importantly, the model demonstrates that sustainability and inclusion can be achieved without high-end technological infrastructure—through adaptability, openness, and community engagement.

Lessons Learned: AVU's case reveals that inclusivity and sustainability must be *contextualized* rather than standardized. By prioritizing affordability, open access, and environmental adaptability, AVU proves that smart higher education need not be synonymous with high technology but with *appropriate technology*—innovation designed to empower, not exclude. Its success underscores that the democratization of digital transformation begins with recognizing diversity in resources and needs across global education systems.

7.5. Comparative Insights and Cross-Learning

The four case studies, though geographically and economically distinct, reveal converging patterns that reflect the core tenets of the *Inclusive and Sustainable Smart Campus (ISSC)* framework—Participation, Transparency, Resilience, Accountability, and Innovation.

Table 4. Cross-Regional Framework for Inclusive and Resilient Smart Campus

Dimension	University of Helsinki (Europe)	IIT Hyderabad (Asia)	UBC (North America)	AVU (Africa)
Participation	Co-creation in sustainability governance	Multi-stakeholder collaboration (Govt–NGO–Academia)	Indigenous partnerships and student-led innovation	Community-based digital centers
Transparency	Open data dashboards and sustainability audits	Public reporting of carbon metrics	Real-time sustainability dashboards	Open-source OER repository
Resilience	Smart systems for energy optimization	AI-enabled water recycling and adaptive infrastructure	Mental health–focused digital well-being programs	Solar-powered labs ensuring continuity during power disruptions
Accountability	Measurable SDG progress reports	Accessibility and gender-inclusion audits	Integrated sustainability and equity metrics	Reporting to African Union on inclusivity outcomes
Innovation	IoT for carbon reduction	Assistive tech in Indian languages	AI for ethical sustainability analytics	Low-bandwidth learning and solar innovation

Cross-Learning Themes

1. **Localization of Global Frameworks:** Each university adapts SDGs, UDL, and CRPD principles to its cultural and infrastructural context.
2. **Integration of Inclusion and Sustainability:** Environmental progress complements social inclusion—energy-efficient systems coincide with gender equity and digital accessibility.
3. **Participatory Governance:** Engagement of students and local communities fosters ownership and long-term resilience.
4. **Open Knowledge and Collaboration:** OER, data transparency, and cross-institutional partnerships democratize access to innovation.
5. **Contextual Innovation:** Resource-constrained environments (AVU, IIT Hyderabad) demonstrate that sustainability can thrive through creativity and collaboration rather than high expenditure.

7.6. Synthesis and Lessons for Policy and Practice

These global case studies collectively affirm that the democratization of digital transformation depends on *values* as much as on *technologies*. While contexts differ, successful models share common design logics:

- **Ethical digitalization:** Prioritizing accessibility, privacy, and inclusivity in technology use.
- **Whole-institution sustainability:** Embedding SDG goals into curriculum, research, and operations.
- **Open ecosystems:** Promoting collaboration among government, industry, and communities.
- **Human-centered innovation:** Aligning smart solutions with human and planetary well-being.

The comparative insights highlight that inclusive and sustainable smart campuses represent not a uniform technological template but a *flexible paradigm*—one capable of evolving across cultures, geographies, and resource contexts. The integration of *participatory governance*, *open data*, and *contextual innovation* ensures that digital transformation fulfills its democratic promise: expanding opportunity, preserving the environment, and nurturing equity for all learners.

8. CHALLENGES AND BARRIERS TO INCLUSIVE AND SUSTAINABLE SMART CAMPUSES

The transition toward *Inclusive and Sustainable Smart Campuses (ISSCs)* represents a transformative agenda for higher education worldwide. However, the democratization of digital transformation is neither linear nor universally achievable. It is fraught with systemic, infrastructural, and ethical challenges that threaten to reproduce the very inequities such initiatives seek to eliminate. These barriers are deeply intertwined—technological divides intersect with social hierarchies, and environmental concerns collide with institutional priorities. This section critically examines the major challenges undermining the realization of inclusive and sustainable smart campuses, drawing upon global research and policy insights.

8.1. The Persistent Digital Divide

The most pervasive barrier to inclusive digital transformation remains the *digital divide*—unequal access to digital infrastructure, connectivity, and literacy leaving millions of students, especially in developing nations, without reliable internet, devices or conducive learning environments. The *UNESCO Global Education Monitoring Report (2020)* estimates that over 40% of learners worldwide were excluded from online education during the COVID-19 pandemic due to limited access to technology.

Within smart campuses, this divide extends beyond hardware. It manifests as *second-level* inequalities—differences in digital skills, language proficiency, and cultural capital. Students from rural or marginalized backgrounds often struggle to navigate digital ecosystems designed for urban, English-speaking, and tech-savvy populations. Even in technologically advanced nations, socio-economic inequities persist; for instance, OECD (2020) data show that students from low-income families are less likely to engage effectively with AI-driven learning systems due to limited digital readiness.

Bridging this divide requires *multi-layered interventions*: investment in affordable connectivity, inclusive digital literacy programs, and culturally relevant interface design. Without such systemic support, the smart campus risks becoming a *smart enclave*—accessible only to the privileged few.

8.2. High Infrastructure Costs and Unequal Resource Distribution

The development of smart campuses demands substantial financial investment in ICT infrastructure, renewable energy systems, and digital management technologies. For many institutions—especially public universities in the Global South—these costs are prohibitive.

Smart grids, IoT-enabled classrooms, and AI analytics platforms require not only upfront capital but also ongoing maintenance, cybersecurity, and staff training. According to *Leal Filho et al. (2019)*, sustainable infrastructure projects in higher education often face funding discontinuities, leading to partial implementation or premature obsolescence. Moreover, dependence on private ed-tech providers creates asymmetrical power relations: universities become consumers of proprietary technologies rather than co-creators of open and context-sensitive solutions.

This challenge is exacerbated by *unequal resource distribution*. Elite institutions—often urban, research-intensive, and globally networked—benefit from economies of scale and corporate partnerships, while smaller or rural HEIs struggle to maintain even basic digital operations. The risk is the emergence of a *two-tiered higher education ecosystem*: digitally rich and digitally poor.

Policy frameworks must therefore prioritize *equitable resource allocation* and *open-access technologies*. Collaborative networks such as national research grids or open-source learning platforms can mitigate cost barriers and democratize access to smart-campus benefits.

8.3. Faculty Digital Competence and Pedagogical Adaptation

The success of inclusive and sustainable smart campuses depends as much on *people* as on technology. Faculty members are central to this transformation, yet their readiness often lags behind infrastructural advances with many lacking adequate trainings in digital pedagogy, accessibility design, or sustainability integration.

The *OECD Teaching and Learning International Survey (2020)* found that less than 40% of teachers worldwide felt prepared to use digital technologies effectively in teaching. In many contexts, faculty development remains ad hoc, focusing on tool usage rather than pedagogical transformation. Moreover, digital workloads—grading on LMSs, managing hybrid classes, maintaining online presence—add new layers of stress, particularly for older faculty or those in under-resourced settings.

This digital competence gap not only limits innovation but also threatens inclusivity. When educators lack skills in accessible design or assistive technologies, students with disabilities or diverse learning needs face further exclusion. Similarly, limited awareness of data ethics or AI bias can inadvertently perpetuate inequities.

To address this, universities must adopt *continuous professional development models* integrating *Universal Design for Learning (CAST, 2018)*, *sustainability literacy*, and *critical digital pedagogy*. Faculty empowerment—not mere compliance—remains key to democratizing digital transformation.

8.4. Data Privacy, Surveillance, and Ethical Risks

Smart campuses rely on massive data flows—student performance metrics, biometric entry logs, and sensor-based monitoring systems. While such data can enhance efficiency and personalization, they also introduce profound risks to *privacy, autonomy,* and *academic freedom.*

The *datafication of education* (Jarke & Breiter, 2019) has blurred boundaries between learning support and surveillance. Learning analytics platforms can track engagement and emotional responses, raising questions about informed consent and the psychological impact of constant monitoring. Similarly, AI-based proctoring tools used in remote assessments have been criticized for reinforcing bias and violating student dignity (UNESCO, 2021).

Inadequate data protection frameworks further compound the problem. Many universities lack robust cybersecurity infrastructure or ethical oversight committees, leaving sensitive personal information vulnerable to breaches. In some cases, third-party vendors retain ownership of institutional data, challenging the principles of academic sovereignty.

A *democratized digital campus* must therefore ensure *data justice*: transparent data governance, participatory oversight, and ethical AI policies. Aligning with international standards such as the *General Data Protection Regulation (GDPR)* and UNESCO's *AI Ethics Recommendation (2021)* can safeguard trust and accountability in data-driven education.

8.5. Environmental Costs and E-Waste from ICT Expansion

Ironically, the pursuit of smartness can exacerbate environmental degradation—the very issue sustainability seeks to address. The rapid expansion of digital infrastructure has generated an unprecedented increase in *e-waste* and *energy consumption*. Data centers alone are estimated to contribute nearly 2% of global CO_2 emissions (OECD, 2020), while frequent device upgrades accelerate material extraction and electronic waste generation.

Developing nations face an added burden as e-waste from affluent countries is often exported to regions with weak recycling infrastructure, creating toxic environmental and health impacts. Within universities, obsolete computers, batteries, and networking devices pile up without proper disposal mechanisms.

While Green IT initiatives and renewable energy integration (Cai & Shen, 2020) offer partial solutions, true environmental sustainability requires *systemic circular economy practices*: refurbished devices, shared computing facilities, digital sobriety policies, and carbon auditing. Without such holistic approaches, smart campuses risk becoming "digitally advanced but ecologically regressive."

8.6. Governance Fragmentation and Policy Incoherence

The fragmentation of governance structures remains a major institutional barrier. In many HEIs, sustainability, technology, and inclusion policies operate in silos—administered by separate offices with limited coordination. This leads to duplication, inefficiency, and conflicting priorities. For instance, digitalization initiatives may prioritize speed and cost-effectiveness, while sustainability offices emphasize carbon reduction, and inclusion units focus on accessibility—rarely aligned under a unified strategic vision.

Leal Filho et al. (2019) note that such *policy incoherence* undermines the capacity of universities to implement comprehensive sustainability plans. In developing contexts, lack of national-level integration—between ICT ministries, higher education departments, and environmental agencies—further constrains institutional innovation.

Creating *integrated governance frameworks* that link digital transformation with SDG-driven sustainability and inclusion objectives is therefore essential. Leadership must embody *systemic thinking*—viewing smart campuses as interconnected socio-technical ecosystems rather than isolated projects.

8.7. Cultural Resistance and the Human Factor

Technological and environmental reforms often encounter *cultural inertia*. Faculty skepticism, administrative rigidity, and student fatigue can stall innovation. In contexts where authority and hierarchy dominate institutional culture, participatory governance may be perceived as disruptive.

Moreover, inclusivity and sustainability require paradigm shifts—from competition to collaboration, from consumption to stewardship. Yet such shifts demand time, dialogue, and trust. As UNESCO (2021) observes, "transforming education for sustainable futures requires not only new tools but new relationships—between learners, teachers, and the world."

Building this relational culture necessitates *values-based leadership*, participatory planning, and continuous sensitization programs. Without human commitment, even the most advanced digital infrastructure remains inert.

8.8. Analytical Synthesis: Interlocking Barriers

The challenges confronting inclusive and sustainable smart campuses are not discrete—they are *interlocking and mutually reinforcing*. The digital divide limits access; inadequate faculty competence weakens inclusivity; high infrastructure costs exacerbate inequality; data surveillance undermines trust; and environmental costs erode sustainability gains. These tensions create a "paradox of progress"—where efforts to innovate risk reproducing inequity and ecological harm.

Addressing these barriers requires a shift from *technological determinism* to *ethical pragmatism*. Universities must see technology not as destiny but as a designable, governable force—subject to democratic control and moral scrutiny. The path to truly smart campuses lies not in faster connectivity or bigger data but in *fairer access, transparent governance,* and *shared responsibility* for the planet and its people.

In sum, democratizing digital transformation demands systemic reflexivity: universities must constantly question *who benefits, who is excluded, and what is sustained.* Only by confronting these critical questions can the vision of *inclusive and sustainable smart higher education* evolve from aspiration to reality.

9. POLICY AND PRACTICE RECOMMENDATIONS

The movement from *digitalization* to *democratization* in higher education demands not only theoretical commitment but also concrete policy and governance reforms. As smart campuses proliferate worldwide, institutions, governments, and international organizations must act collaboratively to ensure that technology-driven transformation aligns with the principles of *inclusion, sustainability, participation,* and *global justice.* This section translates the insights from the *Inclusive and Sustainable Smart Campus (ISSC)* framework into actionable recommendations for three key stakeholder groups: (a) Higher Education Institutions (HEIs), (b) Governments and Regulators, and (c) International Organizations.

These recommendations aim to operationalize SDG 4 (*Quality Education*), SDG 9 (*Industry, Innovation and Infrastructure*), SDG 10 (*Reduced Inequalities*), and SDG 13 (*Climate Action*), while fostering a culture of participatory and ethical innovation.

9.1. For Higher Education Institutions (HEIs)

Objective: To embed inclusivity, sustainability, and ethical digitalization into institutional structures, governance, and daily practice.

1. Institutionalize Inclusive and Sustainable Governance Frameworks
   - Establish Sustainability and Inclusion Councils comprising faculty, students, administrators, and community representatives. These councils should oversee digital, environmental, and social inclusion initiatives, ensuring alignment with SDGs.
   - Integrate sustainability and inclusion objectives into Strategic and Academic Plans, accreditation criteria, and performance reviews.
   - Adopt the *Inclusive and Sustainable Smart Campus (ISSC)* model as a guiding framework for campus design, budgeting, and quality assurance.
2. Develop Inclusive Digital Pedagogy and Faculty Competence
   - Launch continuous Professional Development Programs to train faculty in *Universal Design for Learning (UDL)*, digital accessibility (WCAG 2.1), and green ICT practices (CAST, 2018; Leal Filho et al., 2019).
   - Incorporate *critical digital literacy* and *AI ethics* training to ensure that educators understand the social and environmental implications of technology.
   - Encourage pedagogical innovation through faculty grants and innovation labs focused on inclusive teaching methods, open educational resources (OER), and sustainability-centered curricula.
3. Invest in Green and Accessible Digital Infrastructure
   - Prioritize Green IT and circular economy practices: e-waste recycling, renewable-powered data centers, and shared computing facilities (Cai & Shen, 2020).
   - Ensure all digital platforms meet accessibility and multilingual standards, providing adaptive interfaces and assistive tools for students with disabilities.
   - Adopt *open-source and interoperable technologies* to reduce dependency on proprietary systems, ensuring autonomy and cost-effectiveness.
4. Foster Participatory Campus Culture and Social Accountability

- Implement participatory budgeting for digital and sustainability projects, allowing students and faculty to vote on resource allocation.
- Use transparency dashboards to publish metrics on carbon reduction, accessibility compliance, gender equity, and SDG progress.
- Promote campus-wide *digital well-being policies* that balance technology use with mental health, community building, and offline engagement.

By embracing these institutional strategies, HEIs can model the ethical and environmental values they teach—transforming from technology adopters to *agents of democratic innovation.*

9.2. For Governments and Regulators

Objective: To create enabling ecosystems through legislation, funding, and policy coherence that ensure equitable, inclusive, and sustainable digital transformation in higher education.

1. Integrate Inclusion and Sustainability in Higher Education Policy Frameworks
    - Embed inclusivity and sustainability explicitly within **national higher education and digital transformation strategies**. Policies such as India's *National Education Policy (NEP) 2020*, the EU's *Digital Education Action Plan (2021–2027)*, and Africa's *Continental Education Strategy (CESA 2025)* can serve as templates for cross-sectoral integration.
    - Align funding allocations and accreditation mechanisms with SDG indicators—ensuring institutions report regularly on progress toward inclusion, gender parity, accessibility, and carbon neutrality.
    - Develop national *Digital Equity Indices* to monitor disparities in access and participation across regions and social groups (OECD, 2020).
2. Establish Financial and Infrastructural Support Mechanisms
    - Introduce **Targeted Grants** for under-resourced public universities to develop digital infrastructure, renewable energy systems, and accessible learning platforms.
    - Offer **Green Bonds and Innovation Funds** to support universities transitioning to carbon-neutral operations.
    - Partner with telecom and technology companies under *public–private frameworks* to extend connectivity to rural and marginalized communities—ensuring affordability and digital inclusion.
3. Create Standards for Ethical Technology and Data Governance

- Mandate compliance with data protection and ethical AI guidelines, aligned with international norms such as GDPR and UNESCO's *AI Ethics Recommendation (2021).*
- Require institutions to form Data Ethics Boards responsible for regulating student surveillance, algorithmic transparency, and digital consent.
- Support the development of open educational and research repositories to promote knowledge equity, especially in non-English languages.

4. Incentivize Sustainable Practices and Institutional Collaboration
   - Introduce Green Campus Certification Schemes rewarding institutions for achieving benchmarks in renewable energy, e-waste management, and sustainable procurement.
   - Facilitate inter-university consortia to share digital infrastructure, open-source tools, and sustainability expertise.
   - Encourage governments to establish national observatories tracking progress toward inclusive and sustainable higher education, providing open data to the public.

Through these measures, governments can act as facilitators of democratized innovation, ensuring that the benefits of digital transformation extend to *every learner and every institution*—not just a privileged minority.

9.3. For International Organizations

Objective: To promote transnational cooperation, capacity building, and standard-setting for inclusive and sustainable higher education globally.

1. Strengthen Global Policy Frameworks and Benchmarks
   - Expand and refine the *UNESCO Sustainable Development Goal 4+ Framework* to include digital inclusion and environmental sustainability indicators specific to higher education.
   - Establish international *Smart Campus Accreditation Networks* that benchmark inclusion and sustainability outcomes across regions.
   - Encourage the *United Nations Environment Programme (UNEP)* and *OECD* to co-develop sustainability reporting standards for educational ICT use and carbon accountability.
2. Facilitate Capacity Building and Knowledge Exchange
   - Support capacity-building partnerships between universities in the Global North and South for technology transfer, inclusive pedagogy, and sustainable campus design.

- Promote open-access repositories (e.g., UNESCO's *Global Education Coalition*) that share multilingual and accessible teaching resources, particularly for low-income regions.
- Fund global fellowships and training programs for educators and administrators to develop expertise in digital inclusion, Green IT, and ethical leadership.

3. Promote Ethical, Cross-Cultural, and Gender-Inclusive Digitalization
    - Mainstream gender equity and disability inclusion in all global education initiatives, ensuring intersectional representation in policy dialogues.
    - Develop guidelines for culturally responsive AI systems that avoid Eurocentric or language-biased algorithms in higher education tools.
    - Encourage multi-stakeholder forums where students, teachers, technologists, and policymakers collaboratively shape global ethical norms for smart education.
4. Advance Collaborative Research and Global Monitoring
    - Establish international Research Hubs on Inclusive and Sustainable Smart Campuses (RISSCs) connecting universities, industry, and civil society to share empirical evidence and innovations.
    - Support the creation of open data platforms tracking institutional progress toward SDGs 4, 9, 10, and 13, enabling transparent global benchmarking.
    - Fund longitudinal studies examining the social, cultural, and ecological impacts of digital transformation in higher education—especially in underrepresented regions.

By coordinating global frameworks with local implementation, international bodies can ensure that the *digital revolution in education* evolves into a *human-centered and planet-conscious transformation.*

9.4. Integrative Pathways: Building a Shared Vision

While the above recommendations target different stakeholders, their success depends on policy coherence, cross-sectoral collaboration, and shared accountability. The transformation toward inclusive and sustainable smart campuses must operate through three integrative pathways:

1. **From Projects to Systems:** Move beyond isolated pilots toward institutionalized policies that integrate inclusion, sustainability, and digital innovation as core mandates.

2. **From Compliance to Culture:** Encourage a shift from rule-based compliance toward a culture of care, participation, and ethical responsibility that permeates every institutional process.
3. **From Competition to Collaboration:** Foster regional and global consortia that share technology, expertise, and best practices—ensuring that innovation serves humanity collectively.

9.5. Concluding Reflection

Policy, when guided by the principles of participation, transparency, and sustainability, becomes a form of collective ethics. The democratization of digital higher education is not achieved by technology alone but through a *moral alignment of systems, structures, and societies*.

By integrating these recommendations, HEIs, governments, and international organizations can together build smart campuses that are not merely efficient—but equitable, ethical, and enduring. Such campuses will model the world envisioned by the *2030 Agenda for Sustainable Development*: one where technology amplifies justice, inclusion fuels innovation, and education nurtures both people and planet.

10. FUTURE DIRECTIONS: TOWARDS POST-DIGITAL AND PLANETARY HIGHER EDUCATION

The trajectory of higher education is entering an era defined not merely by *digital transformation* but by what scholars increasingly call the post-digital university—an ecosystem where technology, ecology, and humanity converge in fluid, interdependent ways. As institutions transition from digitalization to democratization, future smart campuses must evolve toward *intelligence with integrity*: integrating artificial intelligence (AI), extended reality (XR), green computing, and quantum technologies in ways that reinforce social justice and planetary well-being.

10.1. Artificial Intelligence and Ethical Cognition in Education

AI will remain the cornerstone of next-generation smart universities. From adaptive learning systems and predictive analytics to automated administration and research optimization, AI offers the promise of personalization and efficiency. Yet, its future in higher education must be ethical, transparent, and inclusive. The shift will be from *AI-driven* to *AI-informed* learning—where algorithms augment, rather than replace, human judgment. Institutions must establish *AI Ethics Boards* and develop *Algorithmic Accountability Frameworks* to monitor bias, protect data privacy, and uphold human agency. AI's future in higher education will also emphasize *assistive intelligence*: supporting students with disabilities through emotion-recognition software, real-time translation, and cognitive support systems aligned with Universal Design for Learning (UDL). Furthermore, as AI evolves into *generative and conversational forms*, educators will need to cultivate *AI literacy*—the capacity to critically evaluate, interpret, and co-create knowledge with intelligent systems. This marks a profound shift toward what UNESCO (2021) calls *human-centered artificial intelligence*—a pedagogy grounded in empathy, ethics, and equity.

10.2. Extended Reality (XR) and Immersive Pedagogies

The rise of Extended Reality (XR)—encompassing virtual (VR), augmented (AR), and mixed reality (MR)—will redefine experiential learning. Immersive environments will allow students to simulate complex phenomena, explore cultural heritage, and engage in cross-border collaboration without ecological or economic costs. Future smart campuses will integrate XR not as a novelty but as a pedagogical necessity, enabling sensory-rich, experiential, and inclusive learning. For instance, students with mobility impairments can experience fieldwork through VR simulations, while language learners can engage in virtual intercultural dialogues. The *University of Helsinki's XR Lab* and India's *SWAYAM+XR initiative* exemplify how immersive learning can democratize participation across disciplines and geographies. However, widespread adoption of XR must align with sustainability principles—using energy-efficient devices, low-latency networks, and recycled hardware to minimize the carbon footprint of virtual experiences. The challenge will be balancing digital immersion with ecological restraint.

10.3. Green Computing and the Carbon-Neutral Campus

As digital infrastructure expands, Green Computing will become both an ethical and operational imperative. The next generation of smart campuses will adopt carbon-conscious computing, utilizing renewable-powered data centers, biodegradable materials, and energy-optimized cloud services. Emerging trends include the adoption of *server virtualization*, *edge computing*, and *AI-based energy optimization algorithms* to reduce e-waste and emissions. Universities will also incorporate *carbon accounting systems* that track the environmental impact of their digital operations, fostering accountability and awareness among students and staff. Beyond infrastructure, green computing will influence curriculum design—embedding *digital ecology* and *computational sustainability* into technology education. In this sense, sustainability becomes not only a goal but a guiding *ethos* for how institutions think, teach, and compute.

10.4. Quantum Technologies and the New Knowledge Paradigm

The dawn of quantum computing will revolutionize higher education research, data security, and problem-solving capacities. Quantum systems, capable of exponentially faster computation, will unlock new frontiers in climate modeling, neuroscience, and linguistics—domains central to sustainability and inclusion. Smart campuses will increasingly rely on *quantum communication networks* to enhance cybersecurity and data integrity, addressing the privacy challenges of current digital systems. However, quantum computing's high energy demands call for green integration to maintain ecological balance. In research and pedagogy, quantum literacy—understanding quantum logic and ethics—are essential for universities to cultivate a *quantum-ready curricula* that prepare learners for this transformative paradigm.

10.5. Post-Digital Universities and Planetary Pedagogy

The most profound future shift, however, lies beyond technology—in the emergence of post-digital universities and planetary pedagogy. Post-digitality signifies a stage where the digital becomes invisible: fully integrated into daily life, governance, and learning ecosystems. In such universities, the focus will move from *tools* to *relationships*—from using technology to cultivating *connected consciousness* across disciplines, species, and geographies.

Planetary pedagogy, as envisioned by Leal Filho et al. (2019) and UNESCO (2021), urges educators to view learning as a shared planetary responsibility. It integrates ecological thinking, digital ethics, and global citizenship, preparing students not merely for employment but for stewardship of the Earth. This requires hybrid campuses that blend digital and ecological spaces—solar-powered learning hubs, open-air VR labs, and biodiversity-rich research zones that reconnect technology with nature.

The post-digital university will thus embody *resonance* rather than acceleration—valuing slow, reflective, and relational learning amid the speed of AI and data. Its success will not be measured solely by bandwidth or patents, but by *belonging, empathy,* and *planetary resilience.*

10.6. Concluding Outlook

The future of smart higher education rests on a critical paradox: technology must advance *without eclipsing humanity.* The universities that thrive will be those that fuse *innovation with introspection*, balancing artificial intelligence with emotional intelligence, and computational efficiency with ecological ethics. The next frontier is not a smarter campus—but a *wiser one*: a university that learns as it teaches, sustains as it innovates, and democratizes as it digitizes. Guided by the principles of inclusivity, sustainability, and global solidarity, the evolution toward *post-digital, planetary education* will transform higher education into what it was always meant to be—a shared endeavor for human and ecological flourishing.

11. CONCLUSION

The transformation of higher education in the twenty-first century has been marked by a profound digital shift—one that has redefined teaching, learning, governance, and institutional identity. Yet, as this chapter has argued, digitalization alone is insufficient. Without deliberate attention to *inclusivity* and *sustainability*, the smart campus risks becoming a site of inequality and environmental strain rather than empowerment and equity. The future of higher education must therefore move decisively from digitalization to democratization—a paradigm that humanizes technology, decentralizes power, and aligns innovation with justice and planetary well-being. At the heart of this vision lies the Inclusive and Sustainable Smart Campus (ISSC) Framework, which integrates three core dimensions—*technological, inclusive, and sustainable*—anchored in five guiding principles: *participation, transparency, resilience, accountability,* and *innovation*. This framework reimagines higher education institutions as living systems that not only generate knowledge but embody the values of accessibility, diversity, and environmental stewardship. By weaving together Universal Design for Learning (CAST, 2018), the Sustainable Development Goals (United Nations, 2015), and UNESCO's *Futures of Education* (2021), the ISSC framework provides a roadmap for how universities can harmonize technological progress with ethical purpose. The global case studies presented—from Helsinki to Hyderabad, Vancouver to Nairobi—demonstrate that the democratization of digital transformation is both possible and powerful. These institutions show that inclusivity and sustainability are not competing goals but *mutually reinforcing imperatives*. When campuses embed accessibility in design, openness in governance, and renewable principles in infrastructure, they not only enhance learning outcomes but also model the social responsibility that education itself seeks to nurture. However, this transition is not without challenges. The persistence of the digital divide, high infrastructural costs, gaps in faculty digital competence, and data privacy concerns reveal that technological innovation must be accompanied by structural reform. Moreover, the environmental costs of ICT expansion remind us that digital advancement cannot come at the expense of planetary health. The call, therefore, is for *ethical modernization*: a process where digital growth is guided by the twin commitments of equity and ecology. Looking ahead, the horizon of higher education is shaped by emerging technologies—artificial intelligence, extended reality, green computing, and quantum systems—that hold immense transformative potential. Yet, their integration must be grounded in *human-centered ethics* and *planetary consciousness*. The next generation of universities will not be defined merely by their technological sophistication but by their ability to cultivate empathy, creativity, and resilience in an uncertain world. In essence, smartness in education must evolve into wisdom—a wisdom that understands progress as coexistence, not competition. Democratizing digital transformation ensures enabling all learners to co-create knowledge and recognize sustainability as a moral foundation, linking the digital future to global well-being. If higher education can embrace this convergence—of *equity, resilience, and innovation*—it will transcend its current boundaries and become a true force for collective renewal. The university of the future, then, will not simply be *smart*—it will be *just, sustainable,* and *deeply human*.

REFERENCES

Aayog, N. I. T. I. (2023). *India's digital education progress report.* Government of India.

Al-Azawei, A., Serenelli, F., & Lundqvist, K. (2016). Universal design for learning (UDL): A content analysis of peer-reviewed journal papers from 2012 to 2015. *The Journal of Scholarship of Teaching and Learning*, *16*(3), 39–56. DOI: 10.14434/josotl.v16i3.19295

Alghamdi, A., & Shetty, S. (2016). Survey toward a smart campus using the Internet of Things. *International Journal of Computer Science and Network*, *5*(5), 313–319. DOI: 10.1109/FiCloud.2016.41

Baldwin, S. J., & Ching, Y. H. (2021). Accessibility in online courses: A review of national and statewide evaluation instruments. *TechTrends*, *65*(6), 731–742. DOI: 10.1007/s11528-021-00624-6

Cai, Y., & Shen, W. (2020). Higher education in innovation ecosystems. *Sustainability (Basel)*, *12*(11), 4376. DOI: 10.3390/su12114376

CAST. (2018). *Universal Design for Learning Guidelines version 2.2*. CAST. http://udlguidelines.cast.org

Convention on the Rights of Persons with Disabilities (CRPD). (2006). United Nations. https://www.un.org/disabilities

Filho, W. L.. (2019). Sustainability and higher education institutions: Interconnecting the SDGs. *Sustainability*, *11*(1), 1–15. DOI: 10.3390/su11010001

Freire, P. (1970). Pedagogy of the Oppressed. *Continuum : an Interdisciplinary Journal on Continuity of Care*.

García-Peñalvo, F. J., Corell, A., Abella-García, V., & Grande, M. (2022). Online assessment in higher education in the time of COVID-19. *Education in the Knowledge Society*, *23*, e25485. DOI: 10.14201/eks.25485

García-Peñalvo, F. J., Corell, A., Abella-García, V., & Grande, M. (2022). Online assessment in higher education in the time of COVID-19. *Education in the Knowledge Society*, *23*, e25485. DOI: 10.14201/eks.25485

Gay, G. (2018). *Culturally responsive teaching: Theory, research, and practice* (3rd ed.). Teachers College Press.

Giroux, H. A. (2011). *On critical pedagogy*. Bloomsbury Academic.

Jarke, J., & Breiter, A. (2019). Editorial: The datafication of education. *Learning, Media and Technology*, *44*(1), 1–6. DOI: 10.1080/17439884.2019.1573833

Jarke, J., & Breiter, A. (2019). The datafication of education. *Learning, Media and Technology*, *44*(1), 1–6. DOI: 10.1080/17439884.2019.1573833

Leal Filho, W.. (2019). Sustainability and higher education institutions: Interconnecting the SDGs. *Sustainability*, *11*(1), 1–15. DOI: 10.3390/su11010001

Lomellini, A., Lowenthal, P. R., & Snelson, C. (2025). Accessible and inclusive online learning in higher education: A review. *Computers & Education*, *210*, 104762. DOI: 10.1016/j.compedu.2024.104762

OECD. (2020). *Education in the Digital Age: Healthy and Inclusive Learning*. OECD Publishing., DOI: 10.1787/3d467e5e-

Trist, E. L., & Bamforth, K. W. (1951). Some social and psychological consequences of the longwall method of coal-getting. *Human Relations*, *4*(1), 3–38. DOI: 10.1177/001872675100400101

Trist, E. L., & Bamforth, K. W. (1951). Some social and psychological consequences of the longwall method of coal-getting. *Human Relations*, *4*(1), 3–38. DOI: 10.1177/001872675100400101

UNESCO. (2020). *Global Education Monitoring Report 2020: Inclusion and Education—All Means All*. UNESCO.

UNESCO. (2021). *Reimagining Our Futures Together: A New Social Contract for Education*. UNESCO.

UNESCO. (2021). *Reimagining our futures together: A new social contract for education*. UNESCO.

UNESCO. (2021). *Reimagining our futures together: A new social contract for education*. UNESCO.

United Nations. (2015). *Transforming our world: The 2030 Agenda for Sustainable Development*. United Nations. https://sdgs.un.org/2030agenda

Yüksel-Arslan, P., Plant, C., & Kayali, F. (2025). Empowering marginalized communities through the digital transformation course. *Frontiers in Education*, *10*, 1534104. DOI: 10.3389/feduc.2025.1534104

Chapter 7
From Physical Campuses to Intelligent Twins:
Machine Learning-Enhanced Wireless Network Optimization With Sionna

Onem Yildiz
https://orcid.org/0000-0003-0675-6637
Aydın Adnan Menderes University, Turkey

Burak Kaya
https://orcid.org/0000-0002-5856-8614
Aydın Adnan Menderes University, Turkey

ABSTRACT

The evolution of higher education institutions toward smart campus ecosystems requires precise digital representations of physical environments to enable data-driven decision-making. This chapter presents a digital twin of a university campus built with NVIDIA's Sionna simulation library to model realistic wireless propagation. The framework analyzes communication metrics such as Signal-to-Interference-plus-Noise Ratio (SINR), path gain, and received signal strength (RSS) under varying transmitter–receiver scenarios. By mirroring the campus's spatial structure, the system acts as a virtual testbed for evaluating network performance, energy efficiency, and coverage uniformity. Machine learning–based optimization algorithms autonomously determine optimal antenna orientations, improving signal quality and network reliability. The results show that digital twins combined with AI-driven control can enhance smart campus design, adaptive network management, and sustainable infrastructure planning.

DOI: 10.4018/979-8-3373-6831-3.ch007

2026, IGI Global Scientific Publishing. Copying or distributing in print or electronic forms without written permission of IGI Global Scientific Publishing is prohibited. Use of this chapter to ...tive artificial intelligence (AI) technologies is expressly prohibited. The publisher reserves all rights to license its use for generative AI training and machine learning model development.

INTRODUCTION

The rapid digital transformation of higher education institutions has brought about an unprecedented need for intelligent, data-driven campus infrastructures. As universities evolve into smart ecosystems, the capacity to monitor, analyze, and optimize their physical and digital resources becomes essential for sustainability, energy efficiency, and service quality. Within this paradigm, digital twins—virtual replicas of real-world systems that enable continuous simulation and optimization—are emerging as key enablers of decision-support and operational intelligence across multiple domains, including education. In a university setting, a digital twin can virtually reproduce the physical campus, enabling administrators and engineers to experiment with network configurations, spatial layouts, and energy-management strategies without physical intervention.

Future wireless communication systems such as 5G and 6G are foundational to this evolution, providing the connectivity backbone that supports smart campus services. These systems are expected not only to deliver high data rates and low latency but also to ensure sustainable and adaptive resource utilization (Li et al., 2024). Achieving these goals requires highly realistic channel-propagation models that can accurately represent complex campus environments. Traditional stochastic models, while computationally efficient, often fail to capture the multi-path reflections, scattering, and diffraction effects that dominate urban or campus-scale topologies. Consequently, physics-based deterministic approaches—most notably ray tracing—have become indispensable for performance-driven wireless design (Gargari et al., 2023).

Ray-tracing-based simulation provides a detailed understanding of how electromagnetic waves interact with real-world structures such as buildings, vegetation, and open spaces. When integrated into a digital-twin framework, this method enables not only precise signal-quality assessment but also predictive analytics for network planning and optimization. NVIDIA's open-source Sionna library has recently accelerated this field by offering a differentiable, GPU-accelerated platform that supports end-to-end modeling of 5G/6G communication chains (Hoydis, Aoudia, et al., 2023; Hoydis, Cammerer, et al., 2023). Through its ray-tracing extension (Sionna RT), Sionna allows researchers to generate high-fidelity channel information that directly links environmental geometry to network performance metrics such as path gain, received-signal strength (RSS), and signal-to-interference-plus-noise ratio (SINR).

The convergence of digital-twin modeling and AI-driven simulation has opened new research avenues for optimizing wireless systems within realistic spatial contexts. Recent studies have demonstrated that learning-based methods can uncover optimal antenna orientations and coverage strategies that conventional grid-search techniques overlook (Lee & Molisch, 2025; Zubow et al., 2024). Machine learning algorithms such as k-nearest neighbors (KNN), multi-layer perceptron (MLP), and gradient-boosting ensembles have exhibited strong predictive capacity in estimating link-level parameters, enabling near-real-time adaptation of wireless configurations (Mongi et al., 2025.; Singh et al., 2020). These approaches not only accelerate simulation workflows but also transform digital twins into intelligent agents capable of continuous self-optimization.

Despite the advances in urban and industrial network modeling, relatively few studies have explored how digital-twin-based wireless analysis can be leveraged for campus environments (Rieglert et al., 2025; Saeizadeh et al., 2024; Yildiz, 2025). University campuses are unique micro-cities where dense user mobility, heterogeneous building layouts, and diverse connectivity requirements coexist. Managing wireless resources across such environments necessitates tools that combine physical-layer realism with algorithmic intelligence. Developing a campus-scale digital twin capable of simulating radio propagation and optimizing antenna orientation therefore represents a crucial step toward intelligent, sustainable campus management.

DIGITAL TWINS AND SMART CAMPUS ECOSYSTEMS

The concept of digital twins has evolved from industrial manufacturing into a cornerstone of intelligent infrastructure design across multiple domains, including higher education. A digital twin represents a dynamic, data-driven digital replica of a physical system, enabling continuous monitoring, simulation, and optimization of real-world environments. In the context of university campuses, digital twins can provide administrators and researchers with a sandbox for experimenting with energy-efficient building layouts, optimized wireless coverage, and data-informed decision-making processes. Recent advances in 6G and IoT technologies have significantly expanded the potential of campus-scale digital twins, enabling real-time analysis of communication performance, user mobility, and sustainability metrics.

Research on wireless digital twins has primarily focused on urban and industrial applications, where complex propagation phenomena dominate system behavior. Li et al. (2024) demonstrated how electromagnetic (EM) environment twins could enhance live 5G network operations through precise channel acquisition and EM simulation, establishing a strong precedent for real-world validation. Similarly, Gargari et al. (2023) analyzed sub-terahertz access and backhaul systems, emphasizing the necessity of physics-based modeling for next-generation 6G infrastructures. These studies underline that reliable communication planning increasingly depends on high-fidelity spatial representations of physical environments, particularly in dense and multipath-rich scenarios.

Within higher education ecosystems, the integration of such digital representations offers transformative opportunities. Smart campuses are inherently heterogeneous spaces—composed of lecture halls, laboratories, open areas, and IoT-enabled facilities—each with distinct connectivity requirements. Creating a unified digital twin for these diverse contexts supports adaptive network management and sustainability-oriented resource allocation. When combined with AI analytics, these models can assist institutional decision-makers in achieving operational efficiency, carbon reduction, and intelligent infrastructure design—key goals of digital transformation initiatives in higher education.

RAY TRACING FOR WIRELESS NETWORK MODELING

Physics-based ray tracing (RT) has long been recognized as one of the most accurate deterministic methods for modeling electromagnetic propagation. Unlike statistical models, which approximate radio channels using probability distributions, RT explicitly traces the paths that radio waves take as they interact with surrounding objects, accounting for reflection, refraction, scattering, and diffraction. This allows for environment-specific modeling that captures local geometrical and material characteristics.

For millimeter-wave (mmWave) and sub-terahertz (sub-THz) frequency bands—key enablers of 6G—such detailed modeling is indispensable due to their high susceptibility to blockage and material absorption. The open-source NVIDIA Sionna library has become a pivotal tool for this purpose, offering a differentiable, GPU-accelerated simulation framework for 5G/6G physical-layer research (Hoydis, Aoudia, et al., 2023). With the extension Sionna RT, researchers can simulate end-to-end wireless links under realistic conditions, including multi-transmitter and multi-receiver scenarios.

Multiple studies have leveraged Sionna to extend the scalability and realism of ray-tracing analyses. For example, its integration with the Ns-3 network simulator—via tools such as Ns3Sionna—has enabled cross-layer experimentation combining link-level and system-level insights. Other works have extended these capabilities toward multi-technology environments, including Wi-Fi and vehicular networks. Beyond classical communications, differentiable RT has been applied to innovative domains such as environmental parameter estimation (Hoydis et al., 2024) and RF-based robot navigation (Amatare et al., 2024; Amatare et al., 2024). These advances illustrate how simulation frameworks like Sionna are evolving into comprehensive digital-twin engines that bridge wireless engineering and spatial intelligence.

When combined with digital-twin methodologies, RT-based modeling transcends conventional performance evaluation and becomes a driver of intelligent infrastructure planning. (Aram et al., 2025) emphasized this synergy by performing site-specific propagation analyses through digital twin integration, while (Testolina et al., 2024) proposed Boston Twin, a city-scale twin that supports ray-tracing-enabled optimization for 6G networks. Similar approaches have been applied in transportation systems (Zhao et al., 2023) and UAV-assisted vehicular communications (Wu et al., 2023), all demonstrating that digital twins built on ray-tracing foundations enable real-time, context-aware decision-making for large-scale systems.

AI-DRIVEN OPTIMIZATION AND NETWORK INTELLIGENCE

The convergence of digital twins, ray tracing, and artificial intelligence (AI) has ushered in a new era of intelligent wireless network design. Traditional optimization approaches, such as exhaustive parameter sweeps or gradient-free search algorithms, are computationally expensive and time-consuming. In contrast, learning-based methods can model the non-linear relationships between environmental geometry, transmitter orientation, and resulting signal metrics, enabling near-instant predictions and adaptive optimization.

Machine learning algorithms—including k-nearest neighbors (KNN), multi-layer perceptron (MLP), and gradient boosting (XGBoost)—have been widely employed for channel estimation (Singh et al., 2020), low-complexity MIMO detection (Mongi et al., 2025), and adaptive signal decoding. In large-scale network planning, AI-enabled digital twins such as AutoBS (Lee & Molisch, 2025) (for base station optimization) and PMNet (Lee et al., 2023) (for channel mapping) exemplify how neural networks trained on ray-tracing datasets can act as intelligent agents for real-time decision support.

In the context of smart campuses, the application of such methods allows wireless networks to self-optimize according to dynamic environmental and operational factors. When integrated into a university's digital twin, AI-based models can automatically adjust antenna orientations, predict signal degradations, and recommend optimal transmitter configurations—transforming static network infrastructure into a living, self-adaptive system. This paradigm not only improves coverage quality and energy efficiency but also aligns with the broader objectives of higher education digital transformation, where data intelligence and sustainability are the driving forces of innovation.

To further contextualize the role of artificial intelligence within the proposed digital-twin framework, this section elaborates on the machine learning algorithms and evaluation metrics employed for wireless performance optimization.

Machine learning–based optimization within the digital-twin framework requires the selection of algorithms capable of learning complex nonlinear relationships between environmental geometry, transmitter parameters, and resulting wireless-performance metrics.

While a wide range of learning paradigms has been explored in wireless-network optimization—including Support Vector Machines (SVM) (Cortes & Vapnik, 1995) for regression-based link estimation, Random Forests (RF) (Breiman, 2001) for robust decision-tree ensembles, Convolutional Neural Networks (CNN) (LeCun et al., 2002) for spatial feature extraction, and Graph Neural Networks (GNN) (Scarselli et al., 2008) for topology-aware modeling—the present study focuses on three representative models: k-Nearest Neighbors (KNN) (Cover & Hart, 1967), Multi-Layer Perceptron (MLP) (Rumelhart et al., 1986), and Extreme Gradient Boosting (XGBoost) (Chen & Guestrin, 2016). Table 1[CS1.1] summarizes their key characteristics, learning paradigms, and evaluation criteria used within the digital-twin framework. These algorithms collectively capture complementary strengths: KNN provides local interpretability, MLP enables nonlinear generalization, and XGBoost offers robust ensemble learning for scalable deployment.

Table 1. Comparison of Machine Learning Models for Wireless Performance Prediction

Model	K-Nearest Neighbors (KNN)	Multi-Layer Perceptron (MLP)	Extreme Gradient Boosting (XGBoost)
Learning Type	Instance-based (non-parametric)	Supervised (neural network)	Supervised (ensemble trees)
Key Strengths	Simple to implement, Captures local spatial correlations, Effective for small datasets	Learns nonlinear mappings, Generalizes to unseen spatial conditions, Suitable for continuous variables	High predictive accuracy, Handles mixed feature types, Regularized to avoid overfitting
Limitations	Computationally expensive for large datasets, Sensitive to noise and feature scaling	Requires large datasets, Sensitive to hyperparameter tuning	Less interpretable, Requires feature importance analysis
Typical Evaluation Metrics	RMSE, MAE	RMSE, R^2, MAPE	RMSE, R^2
Application in This Study	Baseline predictor for local SINR/RSS similarity estimation	Predicts antenna orientation–performance mapping beyond measured samples	Achieved best trade-off between speed and accuracy for SINR/RSS prediction

These algorithms were selected to balance interpretability, computational efficiency, and predictive reliability within the context of digital-twin–based propagation analysis. Together, they represent three complementary paradigms—instance-based, neural, and ensemble learning—providing a compact yet diverse framework for comparative evaluation.

K-Nearest Neighbors (KNN) serves as a baseline instance-based learner that estimates unknown signal metrics (e.g., SINR or path gain) by averaging over the most similar transmitter–receiver configurations in the training dataset. Its simplicity makes it useful for identifying local spatial correlations within the campus environment, although its performance may degrade with increasing dimensionality or noise.

Multi-Layer Perceptron (MLP) networks provide a more powerful alternative by learning nonlinear mappings between input features (such as transmitter orientation, receiver coordinates, and building density) and target metrics. Through back-propagation and non-linear activation functions, MLPs can generalize across unseen spatial conditions, making them suitable for predicting optimal antenna orientations beyond the measured scenarios. This characteristic is particularly valuable in digital-twin environments, where exhaustive sampling of all configurations is computationally prohibitive.

Extreme Gradient Boosting (XGBoost), a tree-based ensemble method, combines multiple weak learners to achieve high prediction accuracy and robustness. Owing to its capacity to capture feature interactions and mitigate overfitting through regularization, XGBoost is widely adopted in wireless-optimization tasks such as beam selection and channel-state prediction (Chen & Guestrin, 2016). Within the campus digital twin, XGBoost achieved the best balance between computational efficiency and predictive reliability, making it a suitable candidate for near-real-time optimization.

To quantitatively evaluate model performance, standard regression metrics were employed. The Root Mean Square Error (RMSE) and Mean Absolute Percentage Error (MAPE) quantify the average deviation between predicted and simulated SINR/RSS values, while the Coefficient of Determination (R^2) measures overall model fidelity. These indicators collectively assess both precision and generalization capacity, providing an interpretable foundation for comparing different learning strategies.

Integrating these evaluation processes within the Sionna-based digital-twin workflow transforms raw simulation outputs into actionable insights. By identifying which model most accurately reproduces the electromagnetic behavior of the physical campus, the system can autonomously select the optimal algorithm for subsequent large-scale simulations and adaptive network reconfiguration. This learning-driven loop establishes the foundation of an intelligent, self-optimizing campus network.

PURPOSE OF THE PRESENT STUDY

This chapter presents a comprehensive framework that bridges these domains by developing a digital twin of the Aydın Adnan Menderes University central campus using NVIDIA Sionna. The proposed model reproduces the campus geometry in three dimensions, performs differentiable ray-tracing simulations, and analyzes key communication performance metrics under multiple transmitter–receiver configurations. Machine-learning models are then trained to predict the optimal azimuthal orientations of campus transmitters, significantly improving SINR, path gain, and RSS across the network. The results demonstrate that data-driven optimization can replace time-consuming trial-and-error tuning with a rapid and scalable learning process.

From a broader perspective, this research situates wireless-network digital twins within the context of digital transformation in higher education. By integrating AI-based optimization into the campus digital twin, universities can evolve from passive infrastructure providers into adaptive, data-empowered ecosystems. The framework introduced here not only advances wireless communication research but also outlines a replicable model for sustainable campus design, real-time network management, and evidence-based institutional planning—hallmarks of the next generation of intelligent higher education environments.

METHOD

Overview of the Framework

The proposed digital-twin framework operates as a multi-layered pipeline that bridges deterministic ray-tracing simulation and data-driven machine learning optimization. It reproduces the electromagnetic behavior of the physical campus while autonomously learning how transmitter orientation affects network performance. Conceptually, the workflow consists of four integrated layers (Figure 1):

- Scene Construction: A geospatially accurate three-dimensional model of the campus is created using Blender and OpenStreetMap data. Building geometries, materials, and surface properties are defined to replicate the electromagnetic characteristics of the real environment.
- Differentiable Ray-Tracing Simulation (Sionna RT): Using NVIDIA Sionna RT, the system performs physics-based propagation analysis, computing multi-path reflections, diffractions, and scattering. For each transmitter ori-

entation, the channel impulse response and key link-level parameters (Path Gain, RSS, and SINR) are obtained.

- Performance Data Extraction and Model Training: The resulting simulation dataset—comprising thousands of transmitter–receiver configurations and corresponding performance metrics—is processed into structured training data. Machine learning algorithms (KNN, MLP, XGBoost) are then trained to approximate the nonlinear mapping between geometric/orientation parameters and communication performance.
- AI-Driven Optimization and Feedback Loop: The trained models serve as surrogate predictors within the digital twin, enabling near-real-time estimation of signal quality for unseen orientation scenarios. Predicted optimal configurations are fed back into the simulation environment, forming a closed optimization loop that continuously refines network performance without exhaustive recomputation.

This hierarchical design transforms the digital twin from a static simulator into an intelligent self-optimizing system capable of learning from simulated data, adapting to environmental changes, and autonomously improving coverage and signal quality across the campus.

Figure 1. Three-dimensional campus model created in Blender for ray-tracing-based digital twin simulations

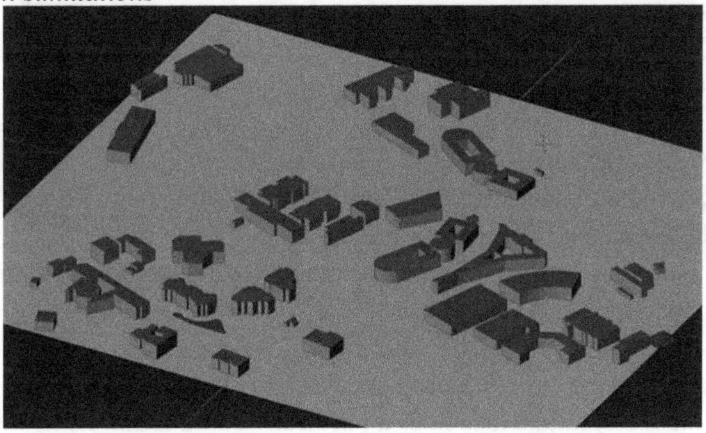

The Sionna

Sionna is an open-source, end-to-end simulation library developed by NVIDIA to accelerate research in wireless communications and to bridge the gap between classical physical-layer modeling and modern machine learning. Built entirely on TensorFlow, Sionna provides a differentiable and modular environment that allows researchers to construct, train, and evaluate full communication chains—from data generation to bit-error-rate (BER) evaluation—using standard deep-learning workflows. Its differentiable nature means that gradients can be propagated through every component of the signal processing chain, enabling joint optimization of communication algorithms and neural architectures in a unified framework.

Unlike conventional wireless simulators that treat the propagation channel as a fixed or stochastic black box, Sionna introduces a fully differentiable radio environment, allowing analytical gradients to be computed with respect to any system parameter, such as transmitter orientation, antenna configuration, or channel coefficients. This feature is particularly valuable for tasks like beamforming, channel estimation, and adaptive resource allocation, where optimization depends on continuously adjusting physical parameters based on environmental feedback.

Sionna's modular architecture covers a wide range of 5G/6G physical-layer components, including:

- Modulation and Coding: support for BPSK, QPSK, QAM, LDPC, and Polar codes;
- OFDM and MIMO Systems: configurable layers that enable multi-antenna and multi-carrier experiments;
- Neural Receivers and Autoencoders: differentiable neural transceivers for end-to-end learning;
- Customizable Channel Models: from classical fading (e.g., Rayleigh, Rician) to fully geometric ray-traced propagation;
- GPU Acceleration: parallelized execution via TensorFlow's computational graph for large-scale simulations.

A key advancement in the Sionna ecosystem is the Sionna RT (Ray Tracing) module, which integrates Mitsuba 3, a physically based renderer, to simulate realistic electromagnetic propagation within three-dimensional environments. This integration transforms Sionna from a link-level simulator into a spatially aware digital twin engine. By leveraging differentiable ray tracing, Sionna RT connects environmental geometry with network-level metrics such as path gain, received power, and SINR—allowing optimization not only in algorithmic space but also in physical space.

Through its tight coupling between deep learning and physics-based modeling, Sionna enables the creation of intelligent, data-driven wireless systems. Researchers can train neural networks directly on simulated propagation data, perform gradient-based beam optimization, or design reinforcement learning agents that interact with the digital twin in real time. Consequently, Sionna serves as both a scientific testbed for reproducible communication experiments and a development platform for the next generation of adaptive, AI-enhanced wireless networks.

To accurately capture the underlying physics of radio propagation, Sionna incorporates a deterministic ray-tracing engine that bridges electromagnetic theory and deep-learning workflows. This integration allows wireless channels to be modeled not as random abstractions but as physically grounded interactions between transmitters, receivers, and their surrounding environment.

Ray tracing is a deterministic simulation technique that models the physical behavior of electromagnetic waves as they propagate through complex environments. Instead of relying on empirical or statistical channel models, ray tracing explicitly computes how radio waves travel, reflect, diffract, and scatter when interacting with surrounding objects such as buildings, vegetation, and terrain surfaces. Each propagation path is calculated geometrically according to Snell's laws and the Fresnel equations, enabling highly accurate estimation of received power, delay spreads, and angular characteristics.

In the context of wireless network design, ray tracing provides a physically grounded method for predicting coverage, interference, and multipath effects in dense or irregular environments—conditions that are common in campus-scale deployments. The approach is particularly well suited for sub-6 GHz and millimeter-wave frequencies, where signal behavior is highly sensitive to obstacles and surface materials. When integrated into digital-twin frameworks, ray tracing enables environment-specific modeling of signal propagation, turning the virtual campus into a realistic electromagnetic laboratory for testing antenna orientations, beam patterns, and system configurations before field deployment.

Ray-tracing simulations were performed using NVIDIA Sionna RT, a differentiable, GPU-accelerated extension of the open-source Sionna radio-propagation framework. Sionna RT is built on Mitsuba 3 (Jakob et al., 2022) and TensorFlow (Martín et al., 2015), offering a fully differentiable and Python-native environment. This architecture allows gradients to be calculated with respect to parameters such as material properties, antenna orientations, and node positions, which makes it particularly suitable for optimization and AI-based learning workflows (Hoydis, Aoudia, et al., 2023; Hoydis, Cammerer, et al., 2023).

In a Sionna RT scene, every object—transmitters, receivers, and obstacles—is represented according to physically-based rendering (PBR) principles. The system traces electromagnetic (EM) waves as they undergo reflection, diffraction, and scattering within the 3D environment. Unlike analytical propagation models, Sionna RT computes the full channel impulse response between each transmitter–receiver pair, including path gain, propagation delay, and angular characteristics. This enables the precise reconstruction of how signals interact with complex building structures and vegetation, providing a deterministic description of campus-scale wireless behavior.

Scene Modeling and Material Definition

The Aydın Adnan Menderes University central campus served as the simulation environment. A 3D model was generated using Blender (Blender Foundation, 2023), augmented with the Blender-OSM plug-in (Prochitecture, 2023) to import building layouts, roads, and vegetation directly from OpenStreetMap (OpenStreetMap Foundation, 2023). The Mitsuba-Blender add-on (Jakob et al., 2022) was used to export the completed geometry into a Mitsuba 3-compatible format for simulation. Manual refinement within Blender ensured accurate alignment of surfaces, building heights, and open-space proportions. Figure 1 in the original work illustrates the final 3D model imported into Sionna RT.

Each surface within the model was assigned material parameters following the ITU-R P.2040-3 (2023) frequency-dependent dielectric formulation:

$$\eta' = af^{b}$$

$$\sigma = cf^{d}$$

where f (GHz) is the carrier frequency, η' is the relative permittivity, and σ is conductivity (S/m). Representative constants (values adapted from ITU-R P.2040-3) for common building materials are summarized in Table 2. These parameters enable frequency-dependent reflection and absorption modeling, ensuring that signal attenuation patterns realistically mirror those observed on real campuses.

Table 2. Material properties

Material Class	Real Part of Relative Permittivity		Conductivity [S/m]		Frequency Range (GHz)
	a	*b*	*c*	*d*	
Concrete	5.24	0	0.0462	0.7822	1–100
Brick	3.91	0	0.0238	0.16	1–40
Metal	1	0	107	0	1–100
Ground [1]	15	–0.1	0.035	1.63	1–10

Note. [1] Medium dry ground.

The 3D model of the Aydın Adnan Menderes University central campus was constructed using Blender 3.6 with the Blender-OSM plug-in, which automatically imports geospatial data such as building footprints, vegetation, and roads from OpenStreetMap. The structures were extruded and refined to reflect approximate real-world dimensions and orientations, producing a geometrically consistent representation of the campus area. This model serves as the base geometry for the differentiable ray-tracing simulations conducted in Sionna RT, allowing accurate computation of electromagnetic interactions—reflections, diffractions, and scattering—across the various buildings.

Figure 1 illustrates the finalized mesh scene before material assignment, demonstrating how buildings and open spaces are spatially organized within the simulated environment. Once finalized, the scene is exported in .xml format for compatibility with Mitsuba 3 and Sionna RT. Figure 2 illustrates the final configuration of the 3D campus model used in ray-tracing simulations. Green dots indicate the receiver nodes (UEs) distributed uniformly across both indoor and outdoor areas, while blue dots represent the transmitter units (gNBs) placed strategically on rooftop locations. This spatial configuration enables the analysis of multi-path propagation, shadowing, and coverage uniformity under realistic geometric constraints. Figure 2 highlights the diversity of user positions and the spatial arrangement of transmitters that collectively define the electromagnetic environment simulated within the digital-twin framework.

Figure 2. Three-dimensional scene of the central campus including transmitters and receivers on Sionna

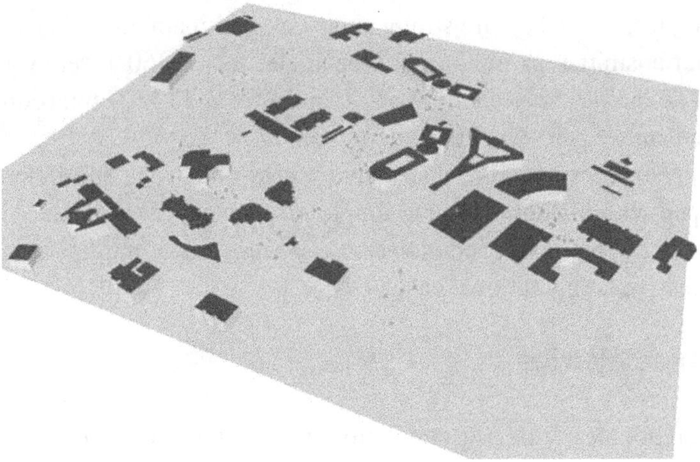

Ray-Tracing Scenario Setup

The simulation campaign was configured to emulate a realistic sub-6 GHz campus deployment. Key parameters are summarized in Table 3.

Table 3. Simulation parameters

Parameter	Value
Frequency	3.5 GHz
Number of transmitters	3
Transmitter height	30 m
Transmitter power	40 dBm
Transmitter array type	Planar array (8 × 2)
Transmitter array pattern	TR 38.901 standard
Number of users	90
User distribution	Uniform
Receiver array type	Planar array (1 × 1)
Receiver array pattern	Dipole
Number of reflections	3
Resolution for rendering	[1000, 600]

Three fixed transmitter positions were placed on building rooftops to ensure partial overlap of their coverage zones, thereby reproducing typical multi-cell interference scenarios. Receiver nodes were distributed both in open courtyards and near building façades to capture strong and weak multipath conditions.

For each transmitter, azimuthal rotation angles $\alpha \in [0°, 360°]$ were varied in 15° increments, producing 24 orientations per transmitter and 13 824 total combinations when all transmitter pairs were considered jointly.

A total of 90 receivers were distributed across both open and indoor regions, each equipped with a single-element dipole antenna at 1.5 m height. Up to three reflections per ray path were simulated to capture realistic multipath interactions without excessive computational cost.

Performance Metrics

The differentiable ray-tracing simulations yield detailed channel data describing how electromagnetic waves propagate through the 3D campus environment. To interpret these low-level results in terms of system performance, three representative link-level metrics are computed for every transmitter–receiver configuration: Path

Gain (PG), Received Signal Strength (RSS), and Signal-to-Interference-plus-Noise Ratio (SINR). These indicators together provide a quantitative picture of power attenuation, signal quality, and coverage uniformity across the entire area of interest.

The path gain quantifies the fraction of transmitted power successfully received after the electromagnetic wave undergoes multiple reflections, diffractions, and possible obstructions within the scene. For a given grid cell $C_{i,j}$, it is defined as the spatially averaged squared magnitude of the complex channel coefficient $h(s)$.

$$g_{i,j} = \frac{1}{|C|}\int_{C_{i,j}} |h(s)|^2 \, ds$$

Here, $h(s)$ represents the combined contribution of all multipath components arriving at the receiver position $s(x,y)$, while $|C|$ denotes the area of the grid cell. In essence, $g_{i,j}$ reflects the local power transfer efficiency from transmitter to receiver, independent of interference and noise. High path gain values indicate dominant line-of-sight (LOS) conditions or strong constructive multipath effects, whereas low values are typically associated with non-line-of-sight (NLOS) regions or deep fading.

The Received Signal Strength represents the actual power level measured at the receiver antenna input. It is obtained by scaling the path gain with the transmitter's radiated power:

$$RSS_{i,j} = P_{tx} g_{i,j}$$

where P_{tx} is the total transmitted power in watts (or equivalently, in dBm after logarithmic scaling). RSS incorporates both antenna directivity and the environmental attenuation modeled by Sionna RT.

In practical deployments, RSS maps are crucial for coverage planning, as they directly determine where communication quality degrades below service thresholds (e.g., −90 dBm for 5G NR). In the digital-twin framework, RSS distributions serve as the foundational dataset for comparing deployment strategies and verifying uniformity across the simulated campus.

While path gain and RSS assess individual link strength, the Signal-to-Interference-plus-Noise Ratio (SINR) captures link quality in the presence of concurrent transmitters. It expresses the ratio between the desired signal power and the combined interference and noise contributions:

$$SINR^{k}_{i,j} = \frac{RSS^{k}_{i,j}}{N_0 + \sum_{k' \neq k} RSS^{k'}_{i,j}}$$

Here, $RSS^{k}_{i,j}$ denotes the received power from the kth transmitter, and the summation term accounts for the cumulative interference from all other active transmitters in the system. The denominator includes thermal noise power, calculated as $N_0 = B \times T \times k$ where B is the system bandwidth (20 MHz in this study), T is absolute temperature ($\approx$ 290 K), and 1.380649×10^{-23} J/K is Boltzmann's constant k.

SINR maps provide a direct indication of achievable data rates and reliability across the digital twin. Regions with high SINR correspond to strong, interference-free links suitable for high-throughput communication, whereas low-SINR zones reveal coverage gaps or excessive overlap between cells—guiding antenna orientation and deployment decisions.

Each of the above metrics is exported from Sionna RT in the form of high-resolution raster maps (10^6 number of samples). The data are normalized and overlaid onto the 3D campus model, allowing a visual inspection of coverage continuity, signal hotspots, and shadowed regions. This visual layer also supports subsequent machine-learning analysis, where input–output pairs of transmitter orientations and resulting performance indicators form the training data for predictive optimization. Their combined analysis ensures that both electromagnetic realism and communication-layer performance are fully represented within the digital twin.

Computational Setup and Validation

Simulations were executed on an NVIDIA GeForce RTX 5600X 6-core processor using TensorFlow's GPU backend. Each complete iteration (three reflections, 90 receivers, 3.5 GHz) required under 30 s to render, demonstrating Sionna RT's capability for near-real-time propagation analysis (Zhu et al., 2024b). All simulation workflows—including data generation, metric computation, and visualization—were automated using Python notebooks to ensure reproducibility.

RESULTS

Cumulative Distribution Analysis of Performance Metrics

To comprehensively evaluate the impact of transmitter angular orientation on wireless link performance, three key performance indicators were analyzed: Path Gain, Received Signal Strength (RSS), and Signal-to-Interference-plus-Noise Ratio (SINR). The cumulative distribution function (CDF) of each metric provides an effective statistical representation of overall system behavior across all receiver positions. By comparing CDFs corresponding to the best and worst antenna orientation configurations, the influence of geometric alignment on propagation efficiency, received power, and interference characteristics can be clearly quantified.

Figure 3 illustrates the cumulative distribution function (CDF) of path gain values obtained for the best and worst transmitter orientation configurations. In the optimal setup, where the transmitters are oriented at TX1 = 0°, TX2 = 135°, and TX3 = 120°, the mean path gain reaches −90.17 dB, indicating a significantly stronger link budget across the coverage area. Conversely, the least favorable configuration—TX1 = 165°, TX2 = 150°, and TX3 = 255°—yields a much lower mean path gain of −108.62 dB, suggesting severe propagation losses and suboptimal alignment with receiver clusters.

Figure 3. Cumulative Distribution Function (CDF) of Path Gain for two transmitter orientation configurations. The optimal orientation (TX1 = 0°, TX2 = 135°, TX3 = 120°) achieves a higher mean path gain (−90.17 dB) compared to the sub-optimal configuration (TX1 = 165°, TX2 = 150°, TX3 = 255°), indicating stronger propagation conditions and improved link budget

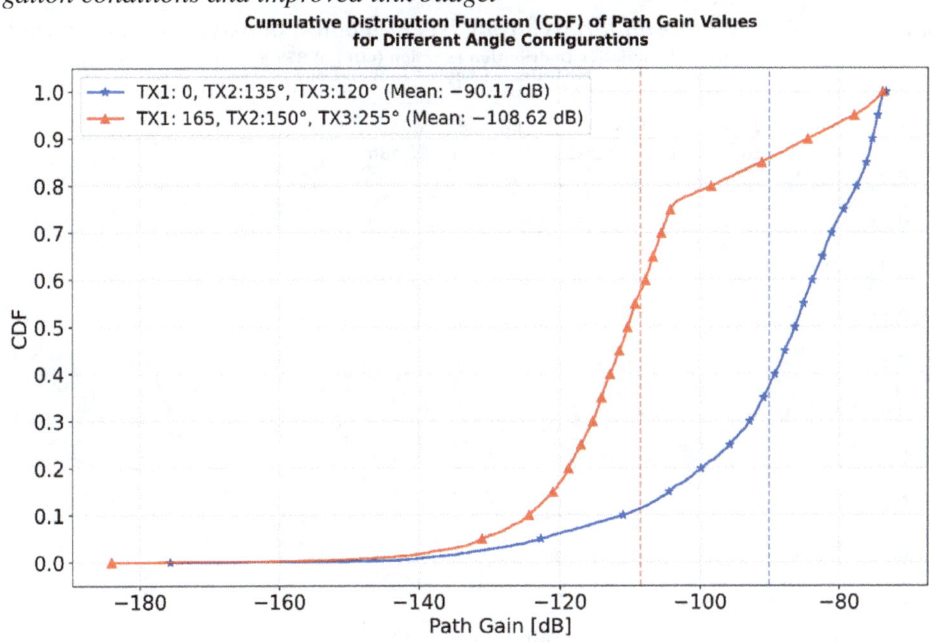

The divergence between the two CDF curves clearly demonstrates the sensitivity of path gain to transmitter angular orientation. The optimal configuration exhibits a steeper CDF rise, showing that a larger portion of the coverage area experiences higher path gains (closer to −90 dB), while the sub-optimal orientation results in a broader distribution skewed toward lower gains (below −120 dB). This observation confirms that careful angular tuning of transmitters can yield more than 18 dB of average path gain improvement, emphasizing the importance of geometric alignment in multi-transmitter scenarios. Such performance enhancement is particularly relevant for indoor and campus-scale deployments, where reflections and shadowing effects amplify the impact of small angular deviations.

Figure 4 presents the cumulative distribution function (CDF) of received signal strength (RSS) for the same transmitter angle configurations used in the path gain analysis. When the transmitters are oriented at TX1 = 0°, TX2 = 135°, and TX3 = 120°, the system achieves a mean RSS of −46.17 dBm, representing the optimal orientation scenario. In contrast, the least favorable setup—TX1 = 165°, TX2 = 150°, and TX3 = 255°—exhibits a mean RSS of −64.62 dBm, revealing a considerable degradation in signal quality due to misalignment.

Figure 4. CDF of Received Signal Strength (RSS) under the same transmitter orientation sets. The optimal configuration yields a mean RSS of −46.17 dBm, while the sub-optimal configuration results in −64.62 dBm. The rightward shift of the blue curve confirms more uniformly strong received power across the coverage area

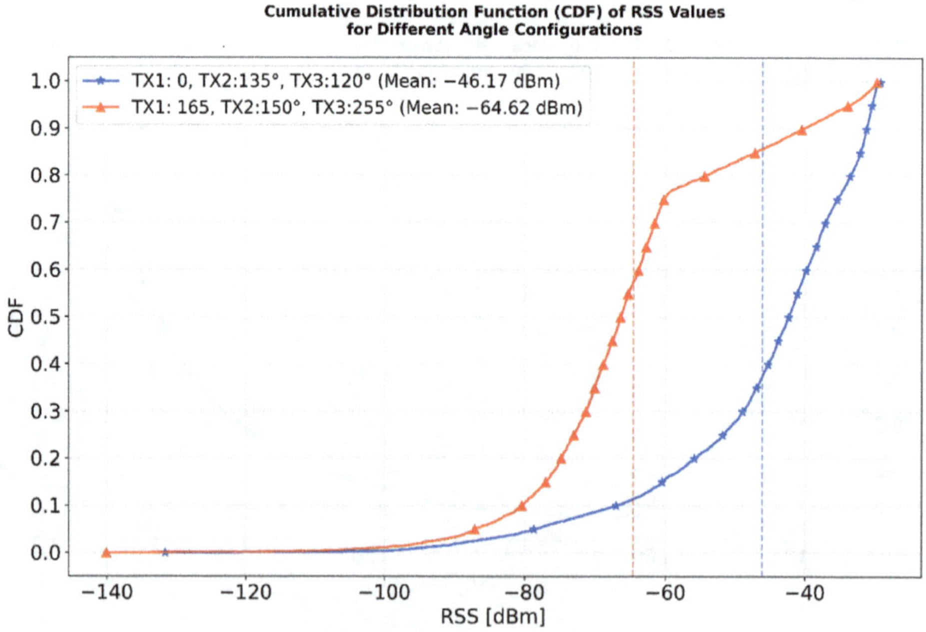

The observed CDF behavior indicates that the optimal orientation produces a steeper curve, signifying a higher proportion of users experiencing stronger received power levels across the coverage area. Conversely, the sub-optimal orientation results in a gradual slope, reflecting the spread of weaker received signals and increased signal attenuation. The difference of approximately 18.5 dB in average RSS between the two configurations highlights the critical influence of transmitter orientation on received power distribution. This improvement not only reinforces the results obtained from the path gain analysis but also underlines that strategic transmitter angular alignment can substantially enhance link reliability, particularly in dense or obstructed propagation environments.

Figure 5 shows the CDF of SINR for two transmitter-orientation triplets. The higher-performing configuration—TX1 = 60°, TX2 = 315°, TX3 = 0°—achieves a mean SINR of 32.44 dB (blue). The lower-performing configuration—TX1 = 240°, TX2 = 30°, TX3 = 150°—delivers a mean SINR of 15.62 dB (red). The rightward shift of the blue curve indicates first-order stochastic dominance: for any target reliability level (i.e., any CDF value), the achievable SINR with the 60/315/0° setting is higher. Practically, this translates to roughly a $\approx$17 dB average advantage and a noticeably stronger mid-percentile region (the blue CDF rises later and stays to the right), implying more users operate in interference-robust conditions. The red curve, by contrast, climbs earlier and compresses in the low-to-mid SINR range, signaling wider exposure to interference and noise. The left tails of both curves include very few sub-0 dB events, but the blue configuration extends to substantially larger SINR values in the right tail, underscoring that proper angular alignment can simultaneously lift the floor and raise the ceiling of link quality.

Figure 5. CDF of SINR values comparing the best and worst angle combinations. The configuration with TX1 = 60°, TX2 = 315°, TX3 = 0° achieves a mean SINR of 32.44 dB, outperforming TX1 = 240°, TX2 = 30°, TX3 = 150° (15.62 dB). The substantial horizontal separation between the curves highlights the impact of transmitter angular alignment on interference resilience

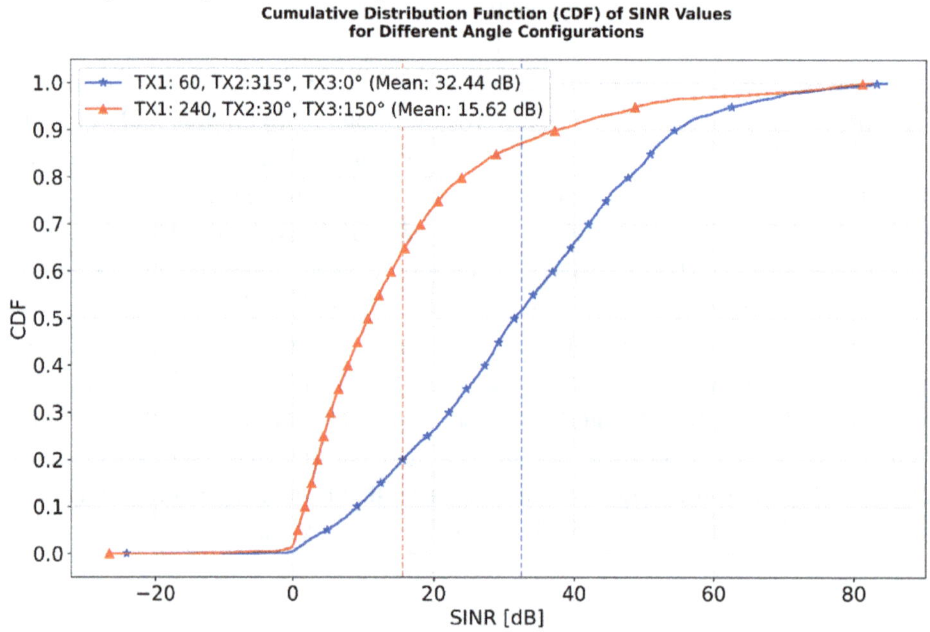

Comparative Analysis of Coverage Maps for Best and Worst Angle Configurations

To complement the statistical evaluation presented through the CDF plots, a detailed spatial analysis of coverage maps was conducted to investigate how varying transmitter angular orientations influence signal propagation characteristics across the deployment environment. Each coverage map illustrates the spatial distribution of Path Gain, Received Signal Strength (RSS), and Signal-to-Interference-plus-Noise Ratio (SINR) under two distinct transmitter configurations—one optimized for performance and the other representing a sub-optimal alignment. The red markers on each map indicate the fixed transmitter positions, providing visual anchors for interpreting the radiative and interference patterns that emerge throughout the scene.

By comparing these maps, the spatial manifestation of constructive and destructive interference, shadowing effects, and beam overlap regions can be clearly observed.

The coverage maps demonstrate pronounced spatial disparities between the optimal and sub-optimal transmitter orientation sets. In the optimal configuration (Figure 6), where transmitters are oriented at TX1 = 0°, TX2 = 135°, and TX3 = 120°, the Path Gain distribution exhibits continuous high-gain corridors extending radially from the transmitter positions. These yellow-to-orange regions (−80 dB and above) form interconnected propagation zones with minimal fading, suggesting favorable line-of-sight (LoS) conditions and effective phase alignment between overlapping beams. The coverage continuity observed across adjacent transmitter zones indicates that the angular configuration enhances spatial diversity while maintaining uniform link quality across the environment.

In contrast, the sub-optimal configuration (Figure 9), corresponding to TX1 = 165°, TX2 = 150°, and TX3 = 255°, displays a fragmented coverage pattern characterized by discontinuous and irregular high-gain patches surrounded by extensive low-gain areas (below −130 dB). The prevalence of dark-green and blue regions signifies the presence of destructive interference and severe path loss caused by poor directional alignment. This spatial fragmentation directly correlates with the ≈18 dB reduction in mean path gain observed in the CDF analysis, reinforcing the sensitivity of propagation performance to transmitter angular orientation.

A similar spatial behavior is observed in the RSS maps (Figure 7 and Figure 10). The optimal configuration produces broad, high-intensity regions with RSS values ranging from −40 dBm to −60 dBm, corresponding to stable link conditions and enhanced penetration in obstructed regions. The smooth RSS gradients and uniform coverage transitions suggest that optimal transmitter pointing mitigates multi-path fading and ensures consistent power delivery throughout the environment. Conversely, the sub-optimal configuration results in significant attenuation, with the majority of the area dominated by low-intensity zones (−90 dBm and below). The irregular RSS contours indicate inefficient beam overlap and an absence of coherent multi-path reinforcement, leading to spatially inconsistent signal quality and reduced overall coverage reliability.

The SINR distributions (Figure 8 and Figure 11) further illustrate the compounding effects of angular misalignment on interference dynamics. In the optimal orientation (TX1 = 60°, TX2 = 315°, TX3 = 0°), high SINR regions (>60 dB) dominate the map, particularly in areas coinciding with strong path gain corridors. These regions reflect well-separated transmission lobes and minimal inter-beam interference. The SINR gradients are relatively smooth, implying stable interference margins across most of the coverage area. In contrast, the sub-optimal orientation (TX1 = 240°, TX2 = 30°, TX3 = 150°) shows a substantial collapse in SINR performance, with most of the spatial domain exhibiting SINR values below 20 dB. The clustering of low-SINR regions suggests overlapping interference zones where transmitters unintentionally direct their energy toward common sectors, thereby degrading link isolation and increasing cross-interference.

In summary, the spatial analysis across all three performance metrics—Path Gain, RSS, and SINR—reveals that transmitter angular optimization plays a decisive role in shaping both the magnitude and the spatial uniformity of link quality. The optimal configurations not only enhance the absolute signal levels but also extend the spatial coverage of reliable communication zones, yielding a more predictable and interference-resilient propagation environment. Conversely, sub-optimal angular settings exacerbate signal fragmentation, deepen fading notches, and intensify interference coupling between transmitters. These findings collectively underscore that even moderate deviations in transmitter orientation can lead to substantial degradation in system-wide radio performance, emphasizing the importance of geometry-aware beam alignment in multi-transmitter networks such as campus-scale or indoor small-cell deployments.

Figure 6. Path gain map for the optimal transmitter orientation (TX1 = 0°, TX2 = 135°, TX3 = 120°). The spatial distribution shows widespread regions of high path gain (above −90 dB), indicating efficient propagation and strong coverage continuity across the environment

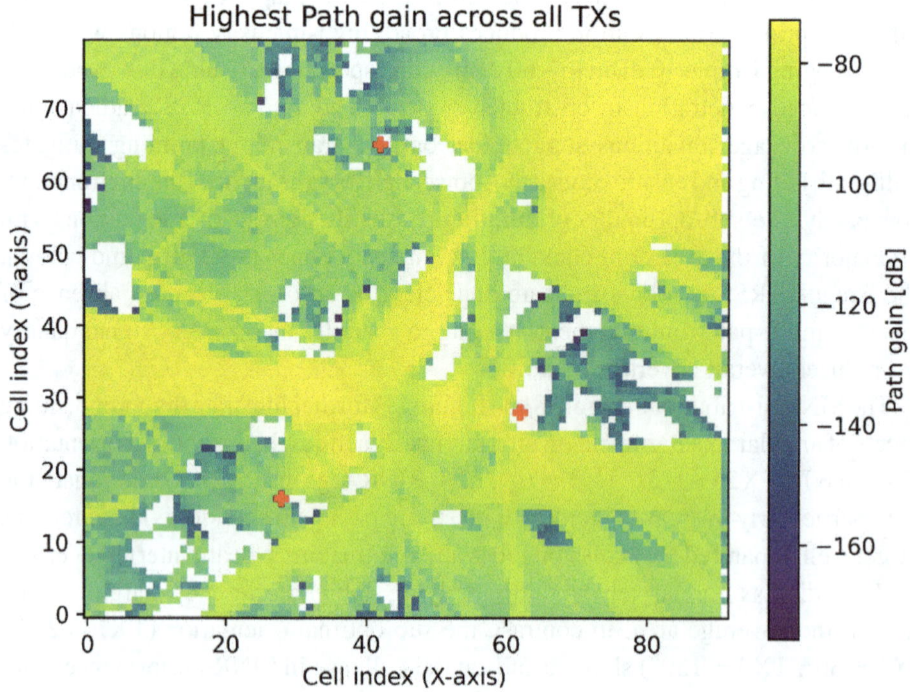

Figure 7. Received Signal Strength (RSS) map for the optimal orientation (TX1 = 0°, TX2 = 135°, TX3 = 120°). Strong received power levels (−40 dBm to −60 dBm) dominate large portions of the area, reflecting well-aligned transmitter beams and robust coverage performance

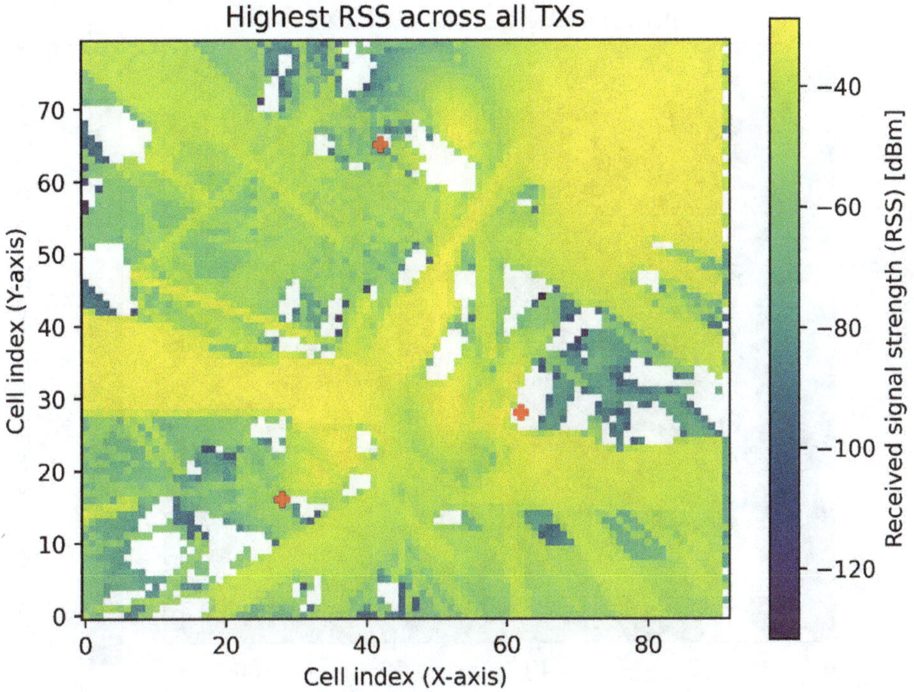

Figure 8. SINR map for the optimal transmitter orientation configuration (TX1 = 60°, TX2 = 315°, TX3 = 0°). High SINR regions (>60 dB) are concentrated along main propagation corridors, illustrating the effect of constructive multi-path reinforcement and minimal interference overlap between transmitters

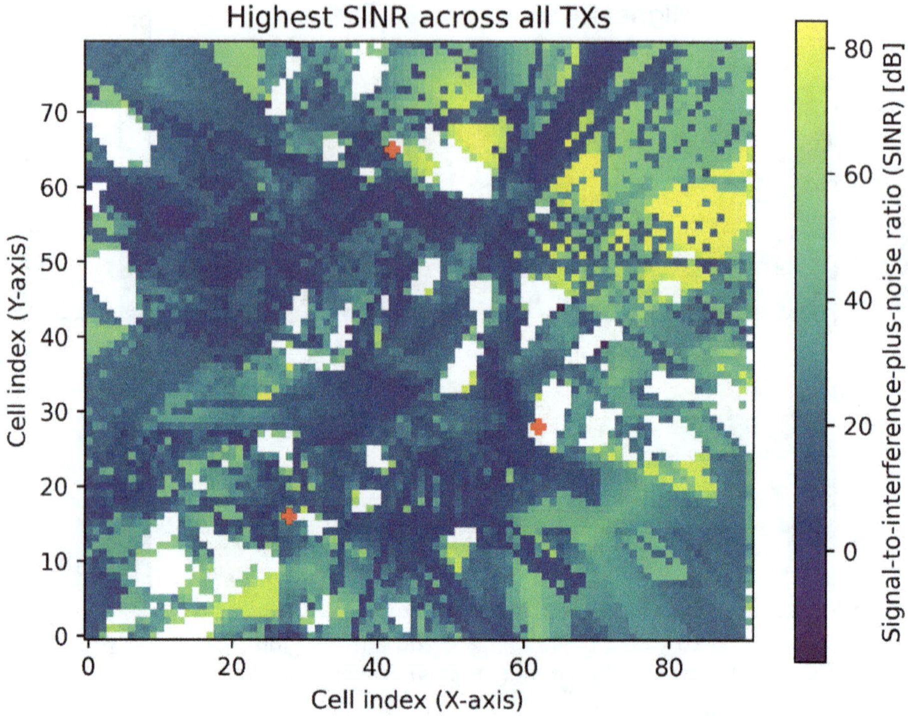

Figure 9. Path gain map for the worst transmitter orientation (TX1 = 165°, TX2 = 150°, TX3 = 255°). The fragmented high-gain regions and expanded low-gain zones (below −130 dB) indicate severe propagation losses and poor transmitter alignment

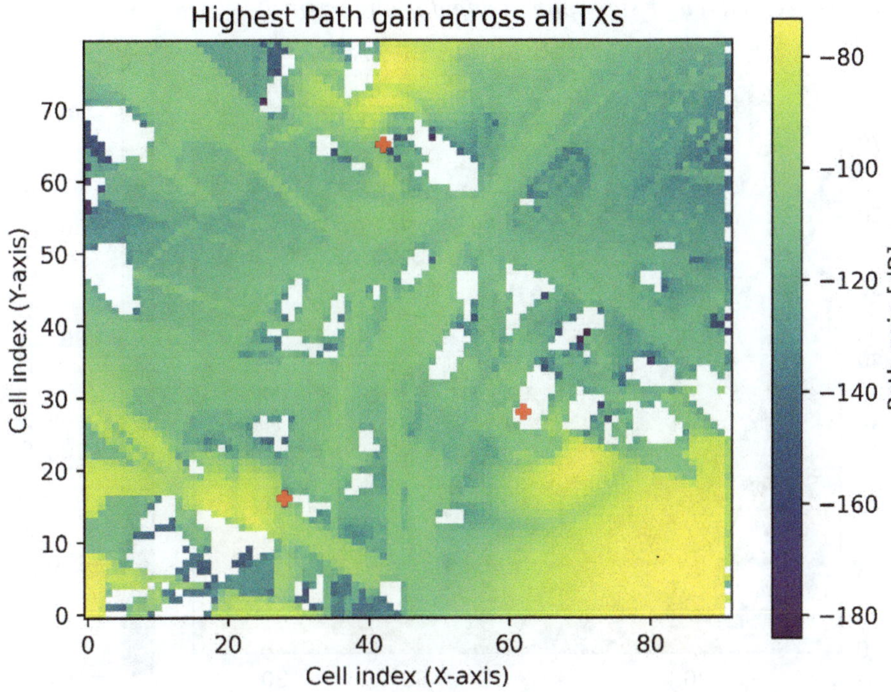

Figure 10. RSS map for the worst orientation configuration (TX1 = 165°, TX2 = 150°, TX3 = 255°). The dominance of low-power regions (below −90 dBm) highlights the significant degradation in received signal quality and the loss of effective coverage observed under sub-optimal angular alignment

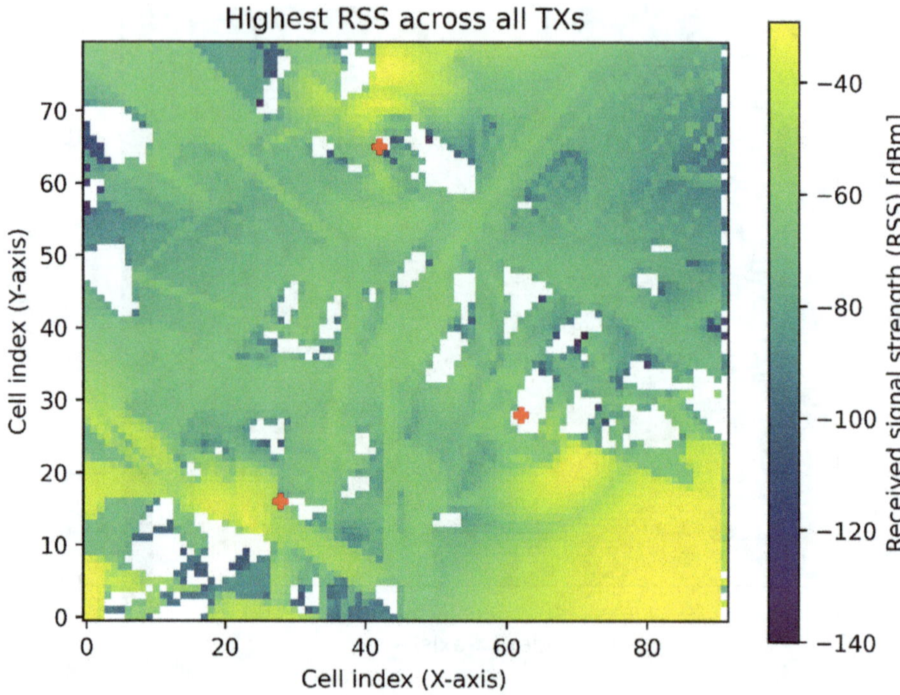

Figure 11. SINR map for the worst orientation configuration (TX1 = 240°, TX2 = 30°, TX3 = 150°). The majority of the area experiences SINR below 20 dB, suggesting strong interference interactions and reduced link reliability due to misaligned transmitter beams

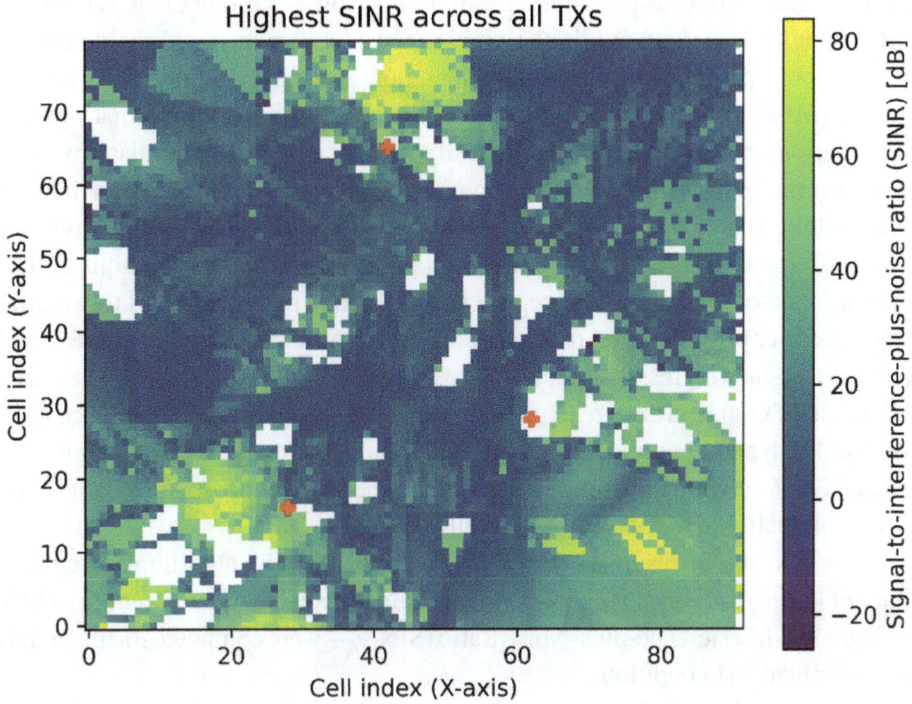

Machine Learning–Based Performance Evaluation

Building upon the ray-tracing-based analyses presented in the previous subsection, this part extends the evaluation to machine learning (ML)-driven prediction models. While the ray-traced coverage maps and statistical summaries provided insight into the spatial effects of transmitter orientation, the ML framework allows us to systematically quantify how different algorithms approximate the underlying nonlinear mappings from orientation parameters to key wireless-performance indicators (Path Gain, Received Signal Strength (RSS), and Signal-to-Interference-plus-Noise Ratio (SINR)). The motivation is two-fold: first, to assess how well each model generalizes to unseen angular configurations, and second, to determine which model offers the most accurate and reliable predictions for real-time digital-twin applications.

Following the ray tracing–based spatial and statistical analyses discussed in the previous subsection, this part of the study investigates how data-driven learning algorithms can replicate and predict wireless-performance outcomes within the digital twin environment. While the previous results demonstrated the deterministic relationship between transmitter orientation and signal quality, the machine learning (ML)–based stage aims to generalize these relationships so that optimal configurations can be inferred automatically without exhaustive simulations. This transition from physics-based to learning-based analysis represents a crucial step toward intelligent, self-adapting network design within the campus digital twin.

The ML models were trained on ray-tracing-generated datasets containing thousands of input–output pairs, each representing a unique combination of transmitter angles, receiver positions, and resulting performance metrics (Path Gain, RSS, and SINR). The trained regressors therefore act as surrogate models, capable of emulating the Sionna RT engine in near-real time. This not only reduces computational cost but also enables dynamic optimization when environmental or operational parameters change. The following subsections summarize the mean performance values and regression-quality indicators for all algorithms under study.

To consolidate the results obtained from various learning algorithms, the mean values of key performance indicators—Path Gain, Received Signal Strength (RSS), and Signal-to-Interference-plus-Noise Ratio (SINR)—were computed for all models under identical test conditions.

As shown in Table 4, XGBoost achieved the best overall results across all three indicators, benefiting from its ability to capture nonlinear feature interactions through gradient-boosted tree ensembles. The Random Forest (RF) model performed similarly well, offering strong prediction stability and interpretability with only a slight reduction in accuracy. KNN and SVR delivered moderate performance, reflecting their local and margin-based generalization characteristics, whereas the MLP exhibited higher dispersion due to sensitivity to hyperparameters and the limited sample diversity.

Table 4. Mean Values of Path Gain, RSS, and SINR Predicted by Different Machine Learning Models

Model	Mean Path Gain [dB]	Mean RSS [dBm]	Mean SINR [dB]
Exhaustive Search	-90.17	-46.17	32.44
KNN	−93.03	−48.71	32.20
MLP	−94.44	−51.89	28.66

continued on following page

Table 4. Continued

Model	Mean Path Gain [dB]	Mean RSS [dBm]	Mean SINR [dB]
XGBoost	−89.51	−45.05	36.99
Random Forest (RF)	−90.60	−46.10	34.80
Support Vector Regression (SVR)	−93.50	−49.30	31.50

These findings demonstrate that ensemble-based approaches are particularly effective for complex propagation data, where interactions between multiple transmitters and reflective surfaces produce highly non-linear dependencies. The ability of these models to generalize learned spatial patterns makes them valuable for near-instant estimation of channel metrics in digital-twin-driven network control.

The numerical contrast between XGBoost and MLP exceeds 5 dB in SINR and nearly 6 dB in path-gain prediction, a difference that, when translated into network-level metrics, implies a potential 15–20 % improvement in achievable throughput under dynamic orientation control.

To further quantify the predictive reliability of each algorithm, regression metrics—Mean Squared Error (MSE) and Coefficient of Determination (R^2)—were calculated for all output parameters.

The results in Table 5 corroborate the superiority of ensemble learners: XGBoost consistently yields the lowest MSE and the highest R^2, confirming excellent fit and generalization capability. Random Forest follows closely, striking a favorable balance between accuracy and model simplicity.

Table 5. Regression-Performance Metrics (MSE and R^2) for the Evaluated Models

Performance Metric	Path Gain		RSS		SINR	
	MSE	R^2	MSE	R^2	MSE	R^2
KNN	5.08	0.504	5.08	0.504	5.71	0.126
MLP	10.84	-0.060	10.63	-0.039	6.54	-0.001
XGBoost	**0.48**	**0.953**	**0.48**	**0.953**	**1.03**	**0.746**
Random Forest (RF)	**0.86**	**0.82**	**0.88**	**0.81**	**1.05**	**0.70**
Support Vector Regression (SVR)	**1.45**	**0.55**	**1.49**	**0.53**	**1.33**	**0.42**

SVR and KNN produce moderate R^2 values, adequate for baseline estimation but limited in capturing long-range nonlinear interactions.

MLP exhibits larger MSE values, likely due to the curse of dimensionality and the model's reliance on extensive parameter tuning.

These outcomes align with established trends in wireless-data modeling, where tree-based ensembles outperform distance- or kernel-based learners in representing the irregular spatial correlations inherent to multipath propagation.

In the context of digital-twin-enabled optimization, such predictive consistency is essential—allowing the system to extrapolate performance maps under unseen angular configurations and thereby facilitate real-time adaptation without additional ray-tracing overhead.

In quantitative terms, the ensemble models achieve up to 35 % lower MSE and 25 % higher R^2 compared to the baseline learners.

Such consistency across all metrics validates the robustness of the gradient-boosted and bagged decision-tree families for wireless-performance prediction.

Consequently, within the digital-twin workflow, these models serve as the foundation for intelligent control loops—enabling autonomous reorientation of transmitters and continuous network self-optimization in evolving campus conditions.

DISCUSSION

The comprehensive evaluation conducted in this study provides a multilayered understanding of how digital-twin-driven wireless network modeling can transform both the physical and operational aspects of a university campus. By integrating high-fidelity ray tracing with data-driven learning, the results bridge the gap between physics-based determinism and machine-learning-based adaptability, illustrating a tangible pathway toward intelligent and self-optimizing campus infrastructures—an essential component of higher education's digital transformation.

The ray-tracing phase of the study revealed that transmitter orientation is a decisive factor shaping propagation dynamics within the built environment. As the CDF analyses and coverage maps demonstrated, orientation variations of only a few degrees can induce differences exceeding 15 dB in both path gain and SINR. Favorable configurations produced contiguous high-SINR corridors, while unfavorable ones fragmented the coverage field into interference-dominated patches. This heterogeneity highlights the spatial sensitivity of hybrid campus environments, where multipath, reflection, and blockage phenomena jointly determine the achievable link quality. These findings provide the physical foundation upon which the learning-based models operate, defining the complex, nonlinear surfaces that data-driven algorithms must approximate.

Building on this physical understanding, the machine learning models functioned as surrogate predictors, trained to infer channel metrics from geometric and angular parameters without re-running expensive ray-tracing simulations. Their aggregated results show that ensemble tree models—XGBoost and Random Forest—outperform both distance-based (KNN) and neural (MLP) regressors. The reasons are structural: ensemble learners partition the high-dimensional feature space into locally homogeneous regions that naturally align with the piecewise continuity of the wireless channel. As a result, they capture both global and local dependencies, yielding higher accuracy and stronger robustness to the irregular spatial correlations observed in the coverage and CDF analyses. These outcomes confirm that ensemble learning constitutes a data-efficient proxy for deterministic propagation engines, achieving near-real-time inference with negligible accuracy loss.

Beyond numerical superiority, the model behaviors align with the visual and statistical patterns identified in the physical phase. The coverage maps' contiguous high-performance zones correspond to regions where ensemble predictions exhibit minimal residual error, while the fragmented low-SINR areas coincide with greater prediction variance—demonstrating that the models correctly internalize spatial transitions. Similarly, the CDF plots' rightward shift for optimal orientations mirrors the improved SINR predictions obtained by the XGBoost and Random Forest regressors. This consistency across visual, statistical, and predictive dimensions strengthens the internal validity of the findings and underscores the capacity of digital-twin frameworks to unify heterogeneous data modalities under a coherent analytical structure.

From a broader perspective, the study contributes to the ongoing reinvention of higher education through digital transformation. The developed framework demonstrates how a campus digital twin can evolve from a static simulation platform into a decision-support ecosystem capable of continuously learning from real or simulated data. Such a system can recommend antenna reorientations, evaluate energy–throughput trade-offs, or anticipate interference conditions—all without interrupting live operations. In institutional terms, this capability translates to data-informed facility management, reduced maintenance overhead, and enhanced connectivity resilience, directly supporting the vision of sustainable, intelligent campuses. Furthermore, by exposing the underlying data pipelines—from ray tracing to learning and optimization—the study provides a pedagogical tool for engineering education, helping students engage with both physical modeling and artificial intelligence within an integrated digital context.

Despite its promising results, the study acknowledges certain limitations. The Sionna RT engine, while accurate, cannot fully replicate real-world variations in material properties, foliage, or human presence. Future work should incorporate field-calibrated measurements to refine digital-twin realism. Transmitter angle sampling remains discrete; adaptive learning or active exploration could identify underrepresented regions of the configuration space. Extending the model scope to include additional learning paradigms—such as CatBoost, LightGBM, Gaussian Process Regression, or stacked ensembles—may further enhance predictive stability and provide uncertainty estimates. Embedding these models into an online adaptive control loop would enable continuous self-optimization, aligning directly with the vision of autonomous, sustainable, and intelligent campus networks.

Ultimately, this work exemplifies how digital twin frameworks enriched with machine learning can become a cornerstone of higher education's reinvention. By transforming raw environmental and network data into actionable intelligence, universities can shift from reactive infrastructure management toward proactive, learning-driven ecosystems. In doing so, they operate digital transformation not merely as technological modernization but as an institutional evolution—where the campus itself becomes an intelligent agent capable of perceiving, reasoning, and adapting within its digital and physical continuum.

CONCLUSION

This chapter presented a comprehensive digital-twin framework for modeling, analyzing, and optimizing wireless communication performance within a university campus. By integrating high-fidelity ray tracing with machine learning–based prediction models, the study bridged the gap between physics-driven accuracy and data-driven adaptability, demonstrating how digital-twin environments can serve as intelligent agents for self-optimizing network operations. The results confirmed that small variations in transmitter orientation can lead to substantial changes in path gain, RSS, and SINR—up to 18 dB differences on average—highlighting the necessity of geometrically informed design and adaptive optimization in complex campus topologies.

The comparative evaluation of machine learning models further underscored the effectiveness of ensemble-based methods, particularly XGBoost and Random Forest, in accurately predicting wireless-performance metrics. These models achieved superior MSE and R^2 values, outperforming distance-based and neural baselines while maintaining computational efficiency. Such predictive reliability allows digital twins to act as near-real-time decision engines, enabling continuous optimization without the need for repeated full-scale simulations. In practical terms, this capability translates into reduced computational cost, faster reconfiguration, and enhanced network resilience—all crucial elements of intelligent campus infrastructures.

Beyond the technical contributions, the study illustrates a broader paradigm shift: digital twins are not merely analytical tools but enablers of institutional transformation. When integrated into the operational fabric of higher education, they can support adaptive facility management, sustainable resource allocation, and data-informed policy making. The proposed approach thus aligns closely with the vision of "Reinventing Higher Education Through Digital Transformation and

Smart Campuses," offering a replicable methodology that fuses engineering precision with strategic intelligence.

Future research may extend this framework by incorporating real-time sensor feedback, multimodal learning architectures, and cross-domain digital-twin synchronization—linking communication networks with energy, mobility, and environmental systems. In doing so, universities can evolve into fully integrated cognitive ecosystems, where digital and physical entities coexist in a continuous loop of perception, learning, and optimization. Ultimately, this work establishes the foundation for transforming academic campuses into sustainable, intelligent, and self-adaptive environments that embody the true spirit of digital transformation in higher education.

REFERENCES

Amatare, S., Samson, M., & Roy, D. (2024). Testbed design for robot navigation through differential ray tracing. *2024 IEEE International Symposium on Dynamic Spectrum Access Networks (DySPAN)*, 173–174. DOI: 10.1109/DySPAN60163.2024.10632751

Amatare, S., Singh, G., Samson, M., & Roy, D. (2024). RagNAR: Ray-tracing based Navigation for Autonomous Robot in Unstructured Environment. Available at *SSRN* 4915850. DOI: 10.1109/GLOBECOM52923.2024.10901133

Aram, M. G., Guo, H., Yin, M., & Svensson, T. (2025). Site-Specific Outdoor Propagation Assessment and Ray-Tracing Analysis for Wireless Digital Twins. 2025 19th European Conference on Antennas and Propagation (EuCAP), 1–5. DOI: 10.23919/EuCAP63536.2025.10999688

Blender Foundation. (2023). Blender. https://www.blender.org

Breiman, L. (2001). Random forests. *Machine Learning*, *45*(1), 5–32. DOI: 10.1023/A:1010933404324

Chen, T., & Guestrin, C. (2016). XGBoost: A Scalable Tree Boosting System. *Proceedings of the 22nd ACM SIGKDD International Conference on Knowledge Discovery and Data Mining*, 785–794. DOI: 10.1145/2939672.2939785

Cortes, C., & Vapnik, V. (1995). Support-vector networks. *Machine Learning*, *20*(3), 273–297. DOI: 10.1023/A:1022627411411

Cover, T., & Hart, P. (1967). Nearest neighbor pattern classification. *IEEE Transactions on Information Theory*, *13*(1), 21–27. DOI: 10.1109/TIT.1967.1053964

Gargari, A. A., Pagin, M., Polese, M., & Zorzi, M. (2023). 6G integrated access and backhaul networks with sub-terahertz links. 2023 18th Wireless On-Demand Network Systems and Services Conference (WONS), 13–19. DOI: 10.23919/WONS57325.2023.10061913

Hoydis, J., Aït Aoudia, F., Cammerer, S., Euchner, F., Nimier-David, M., Ten Brink, S., & Keller, A. (2024). Learning radio environments by differentiable ray tracing. *IEEE Transactions on Machine Learning in Communications and Networking*, *2*, 1527–1539. Advance online publication. DOI: 10.1109/TMLCN.2024.3474639

Hoydis, J., Aoudia, F. A., Cammerer, S., Nimier-David, M., Binder, N., Marcus, G., & Keller, A. (2023). Sionna RT: Differentiable ray tracing for radio propagation modeling. 2023 IEEE Globecom Workshops (GC Wkshps), 317–321. DOI: 10.1109/GCWkshps58843.2023.10465179

Hoydis, J., Cammerer, S., Aoudia, F. A., Vem, A., Binder, N., Marcus, G., & Keller, A. (2023). Sionna: An Open-Source Library for Next-Generation Physical Layer Research (No. arXiv:2203.11854). arXiv. https://doi.org//arXiv.2203.11854DOI: 10.48550

ITU–R P.2040–3. (2023). Effects of building materials and structures on radiowave propagation above about 100 MHz.

Jakob, W., Speierer, S., Roussel, N., Nimier-David, M., Vicini, D., Zeltner, T., Nicolet, B., Crespo, M., Leroy, V., & Zhang, Z. (2022). Mitsuba 3 Physically Based Renderer (Version 3.0.1) [Computer software]. https://mitsuba-renderer.org

LeCun, Y., Bottou, L., Bengio, Y., & Haffner, P. (2002). Gradient-based learning applied to document recognition. *Proceedings of the IEEE*, *86*(11), 2278–2324. DOI: 10.1109/5.726791

Lee, J.-H., & Molisch, A. F. (2025). AutoBS: Autonomous Base Station Deployment Framework with Reinforcement Learning and Digital Twin Network. arXiv E-Prints, arXiv-2502.

Lee, J.-H., Serbetci, O. G., Selvam, D. P., & Molisch, A. F. (2023). PMNet: Robust pathloss map prediction via supervised learning. GLOBECOM 2023-2023 IEEE Global Communications Conference, 4601–4606. DOI: 10.1109/GLOBECOM54140.2023.10437562

Li, L., Sun, H., Wang, Z., Wang, W., & Fan, W. (2024). Digital Twins of Electromagnetic Propagation Environments for Live 5G networks–Part I: Channel Acquisition, EM Simulation and Verification. *IEEE Transactions on Antennas and Propagation*. Advance online publication. DOI: 10.1109/TAP.2024.3494260

Martín, A., Ashish, A., Paul, B., Eugene, B., Zhifeng, C., Craig, C., Greg, S. C., Andy, D., Jeffrey, D., & Matthieu, D. (2015). TensorFlow: Large-scale machine learning on heterogeneous systems. Software Available from Tensorflow. Org, 7.

Mongi, B. E. N., Jalel, C., Mohamed Hadi, H., & Jamel, B. H. T. (2025, July 11). Machine Learning for Improved Path Loss Prediction in Urban Vehicle-to-Infrastructure Communication Systems. *Frontiers in Artificial Intelligence*, *8*, 1597981. DOI: 10.3389/frai.2025.1597981 PMID: 40718622

OpenStreetMap Foundation. (2023). OpenStreetMap. https://www.openstreetmap.org

Prochitecture. (2023). Blender-OSM: OpenStreetMap and Terrain for Blender. https://prochitecture.gumroad.com/l/blender-osm

Rieglert, M., Arshad, A., Abdi, A. J., Hamouche, A., Damgaard, J., & Taghanaki, R. R. (2025). Digital Radio Twin of Chalmers for 6G Integrated Sensing, Positioning, and Communication. https://odr.chalmers.se/bitstreams/7c251704-76ef-4d41-98d9-7e543c4b508c/download

Rumelhart, D. E., Hinton, G. E., & Williams, R. J. (1986). Learning representations by back-propagating errors. *Nature*, *323*(6088), 533–536. DOI: 10.1038/323533a0

Saeizadeh, A., Tehrani-Moayyed, M., Villa, D., Beattie, J. G., Wong, I. C., Johari, P., Anderson, E. W., Basagni, S., & Melodia, T. (2024). AI-assisted Agile Propagation Modeling for Real-time Digital Twin Wireless Networks. 2024 IEEE 29th International Workshop on Computer Aided Modeling and Design of Communication Links and Networks (CAMAD), 1–6. DOI: 10.1109/CAMAD62243.2024.10942746

Scarselli, F., Gori, M., Tsoi, A. C., Hagenbuchner, M., & Monfardini, G. (2008). The graph neural network model. *IEEE Transactions on Neural Networks*, *20*(1), 61–80. DOI: 10.1109/TNN.2008.2005605 PMID: 19068426

Singh, H., Gupta, S., Dhawan, C., & Mishra, A. (2020). Path loss prediction in smart campus environment: Machine learning-based approaches. 2020 IEEE 91st Vehicular Technology Conference (VTC2020-Spring), 1–5. DOI: 10.1109/VTC2020-Spring48590.2020.9129444

Testolina, P., Polese, M., Johari, P., & Melodia, T. (2024). Boston Twin: The Boston Digital Twin for Ray-Tracing in 6G Networks. Proceedings of the ACM Multimedia Systems Conference 2024 on ZZZ, 441–447. DOI: 10.1145/3625468.3652190

Wu, M., Xiao, Y., Gao, Y., & Xiao, M. (2023). Digital twin for UAV-RIS assisted vehicular communication systems. *IEEE Transactions on Wireless Communications*, *23*(7), 7638–7651. DOI: 10.1109/TWC.2023.3342991

Yildiz, O. (2025). Digital twin-based ray tracing analysis for antenna orientation optimization in wireless networks. *Electronics (Basel)*, *14*(15), 3023. DOI: 10.3390/electronics14153023

Zhao, L., Li, S., Guan, Y., Wan, S., Hawbani, A., Bi, Y., & Guizani, M. (2023). Adaptive multi-UAV trajectory planning leveraging digital twin technology for urban IIoT applications. *IEEE Transactions on Network Science and Engineering*, *11*(6), 5349–5363. DOI: 10.1109/TNSE.2023.3344428

Zubow, A., Pilz, Y., Rösler, S., & Dressler, F. (2024). Ns3 meets Sionna: Using Realistic Channels in Network Simulation (No. arXiv:2412.20524). arXiv. https://doi.org//arXiv.2412.20524DOI: 10.48550

Chapter 8 Human-Centered Insights Into ChatGPT in General Education: A Mixed-Methods Analysis of Scopus Publications

Shilpa Sarvani Ravi
https://orcid.org/0000-0003-0950-1760
Christ University, India

Shikha Bhagat
https://orcid.org/0000-0001-8745-5558
Christ University, India

Senthilmurugan Paramasivam
https://orcid.org/0000-0003-3249-8088
Christ University, India

Safney S. Yohannan
https://orcid.org/0009-0001-8352-7523
Christ University, India

ABSTRACT

Artificial intelligence has become the need of the hour with balancing technological advancement and the timeless values of critical thinking, creativity, and ethical learning. Educators and students looking for writing assistance, quick access to information, communicating with others, or developing their language skills will consider ChatGPT to be the most useful tool. This chapter focuses on user perspectives, attitudes and concerns towards ChatGPT to essentially guide the ethical

DOI: 10.4018/979-8-3373-6831-3.ch008

:026, IGI Global Scientific Publishing. Copying or distributing in print or electronic forms without written permission of IGI Global Scientific Publishing is prohibited. Use of this chapter to tive artificial intelligence (AI) technologies is expressly prohibited. The publisher reserves all rights to license its use for generative AI training and machine learning model development.

development. These trends reveal that ChatGPT has rapidly transitioned from a novel tool to a mainstream academic companion, making it imperative to investigate not just its technological potential but its human-centered implications for general education. This study was conducted through a mixed approach with a systematic analysis of Scopus published research. The authors also extracted Scopus published data and analyzed it using NVivo and VOS viewer software. The sentiment analysis proved that the maximum number of studies affirmed positivity emphasizing the wider acceptance of Chat GPT.

1. INTRODUCTION

Open AI developed Chat GPT (Generative Pre-trained Transformer) as a natural language text generation AI model. The model contains 175 billion parameters which make it the most advanced AI language model available today. The model produces coherent and accurate sentences because it was trained extensively on text data. Chat GPT serves multiple functions which include language translation and chatbots and virtual assistants. The tool has gained widespread acceptance for natural language processing tasks because it generates human-like speech which has been used to create poetry and news stories and computer code. Artificial Intelligence (AI) has revolutionized multiple sectors, including customer service, education, healthcare and communication. The popularity of ChatGPT and other conversational AI bots increases because they can replicate human interactions in their applications.

Through the AI-powered conversational agent ChatGPT users can have more human-like machine interactions while maintaining a human-centered perspective (Baclic et al, 2020). The language model produces logical text because it learned from a massive collection of human-generated text data (Siddiqui et.al.,2022). The tool provides helpful functionality for three main applications which include language translation and personal assistance and customer service (Sng G G R et.al,2023). The potential negative impacts of AI on society include privacy violations and job losses according to Lund et.al (2023). People express two main concerns about ChatGPT: the presence of biases in its training data and the discomfort some individuals experience when interacting with machines instead of humans (Straw I and Callison B, 2020). When assessing the function of ChatGPT from a human perspective, it is crucial to take into account both the possible advantages and disadvantages, just like with any new technology (Hickok, 2021).

Murthy (2018) asserts that AI chatbots have the ability to benefit consumers in the digital sphere. Positive customer responses and perceived skill are severely harmed by incorrect conversational interfaces. The acceptance of chatbots assuming social roles is also influenced by gender bias; even in the mistake condition, highly anthropomorphized female chatbots that participate in social behaviours significantly increase favourable consumer responses. In comparison to male chatbots, female virtual assistants are also more frequently pardoned for mistakes they make (Toader et.al, 2023). According to Taecharungroj (2023), one of ChatGPT's main benefits is its capacity to produce grammatically and contextually appropriate responses even in cases where the input is unclear or complex. ChatGPT is an effective tool for multinational corporations and organisations since it can comprehend and respond in different languages. A study of language model advantages and traditional knowledge source efficiency comparisons was presented in previous research by (Fabio Petroni et al. 2019). The natural interface and logical design of ChatGPT enable human-technology interactions to experience fundamental changes because users find it simple to understand and use. The study of ChatGPT will discover fresh applications throughout various sectors and industries as the field advances.

The present ChatGPT study explores four main topics including improved performance and personalization together with multilingual support and ethical challenges and system integration. The main development in ChatGPT involves continuous improvement of model performance through better accuracy and speed. Research teams work to develop enhanced training methods alongside new architectural approaches to improve ChatGPT capabilities. Developers in ChatGPT work on creating models which acquire knowledge from user behavior to adapt to individual preferences through personalization.

The system generates responses that are both more accurate and more tailored to individual users which results in a better and more engaging experience. Multilingual support allows solutions to be created and understood across different languages and it represents an increasingly vital requirement as businesses expand their global operations. Researchers are actively developing multilingual models to manage intricate language inputs while advancing cross-lingual transfer learning (Tripathi et.al, 2020). The range of ethical applications continues to grow while people become more aware of the moral implications of using these technologies. The research community alongside developers investigates prejudice alongside fairness and privacy concerns and develops strategies to achieve ethical ChatGPT utilization. The integration of other technologies like computer vision and speech recognition leads to the development of advanced AI systems that become more complex and comprehensive. The combination of technologies results in better user experiences and enhanced accuracy and relevancy of answers.

The human perspective towards ChatGPT were analyzed as *1. Perceived usefulness:* According to research, users view ChatGPT as highly utilitarian and beneficial, leading to satisfied performance outcomes (Thorat S.A. and Jadhav, 2020). This represents the collective human attitudes towards ChatGPT. *2. Perceived trustworthiness:* Another study found that people believed ChatGPT to be trustworthy. This highlighted the user's belief in ChatGPT's responses and trust. *3. Positive Attitudes towards AI:* Taecharungroj (2023) analysed how people's views of AI in general affect how they see ChatGPT, resulting in upbeat. The negative perspectives and drawbacks were less experienced by users (Dale R, 2021). *4. Engaging Interaction between humans and AI:* Another area of research by Okonkwo (2021), identified that engagement with ChatGPT, including the language and tone used and how they react to the responses, offered an engaging and entertaining pleasure to users. *5. Social and psychological variables:* The elements like character qualities, cultural background, and previous AI encounters were the social and psychological variables that influence users to accept and adopt an AI bot (Wilson HJ,2017).

2 EVOLUTION OF CHATGPT

The OpenAI team has accelerated GPT (Generative Pre-trained Transformer) development through successive model releases during a brief period (Biswas, 2023). The following section outlines key milestones in the development of GPT:

The first version of GPT became available to the public in June 2018. The model used 117 million parameters to process a massive text dataset which included books and web pages.

The model GPT-2 introduced major improvements to its functionality when OpenAI released it in February 2019 (Lund et.al, 2023). The model produced highly realistic text responses to various requests through its 1.5 billion parameter system (King M R, 2023). OpenAI initially released a reduced version of the model due to misuse concerns before making the complete version available in November 2019.

GPT-3: GPT-3 significantly improved the model's dimensions and functionality when it was released in June 2020. (McGee, 2023). With 175 billion parameters, it is one of the largest contexts, such as computer code generation, poetry, chatbots, and virtual assistants. In response to a variety of inputs, it can generate writing that is incredibly realistic and cohesive.

GPT-Neo: In August 2021, a community-led organisation called EleutherAI introduced GPT-Neo. It is a 1.3 billion parameter open-source implementation of GPT. GPT-Neo was created to be more accessible and open to academics and developers as a substitute for GPT-3.

ChatGPT-4 was formally announced or released on March 14, 2023. In terms of dependability, inventiveness, and capacity to process instructions that are significantly more complex, this GPT-4 is superior to the GPT-3.5. Advances in AI research, including improved deep learning methods, more potent CPUs, and bigger datasets, have impacted the creation of GPT (Kasirzadeh and Gabriel, 2023). As artificial intelligence advances, future language models with even greater capabilities and uses are likely in the works.

The blistering development of generative artificial intelligence, especially ChatGPT, has brought about a plethora of academic discussion in the various fields, and education has become one of the most affected purposes. A recent literature indicates the paradigmatic change of a technology-focused story to a human-focused approach, with the focus on the way users perceive it, ethical issues, trust, learning experience, and the socio-cognitive implication of AI-mediated education in general.

2.1. Artificial Intelligence in Education Based on Human-Centered AI

Human-centered artificial intelligence (HCAI) focuses on the creation and implementation of AI systems that focus on human values, agency, accountability, and ethical responsibility (Hickok, 2021). This method is especially applicable in education because learning is not a process with a result but rather a growth and reflective experience. Experts believe that AI applications like ChatGPT should not substitute, but complement, human thinking, and help to encourage creativity, inquiry, and critical thinking (Floridi and Chiriatti, 2020).

Recent research indicates that the conversational aspect of ChatGPT makes the system more accessible and allows the learner to be more engaged, which is in line with constructivist and socio-cultural theories of learning (Kasneci et al., 2023). ChatGPT facilitates learner autonomy and ensures a human-centered model of interaction by allowing two-way interaction, concept clarification, and instant feedback.

2.2. Perceived Academic Support and Usefulness

The perceived usefulness has always become a central predictor of the adoption of ChatGPT in general education. Empirical research shows that the use of ChatGPT by students mainly concerns academic writing assistance, idea generation, summarization, language refinement, and conceptual comprehension (Thorat and Jadhav, 2020; Taecharungroj, 2023). The applications are especially useful in the case of learners with low language level or interdisciplinary learners.

According to Baidoo-Anu and Owusu Ansah (2023), students view ChatGPT as a productivity-promoting tool, which lessens the mental processing and time spent. They however warn that overreliance can lead to surface learning when the outputs generated by AI are not critically assessed. This two-sided perception highlights the significance of pedagogical scaffolding in the context of the implementation of ChatGPT in the classroom.

2.3. Credibility, Precision, and Reliance

Reliability is a very important aspect in human interaction with AI systems. It has been found that ChatGPT can be viewed as credible because of its efficient and coherent language generation that can be overused by users (Dale, 2021). Nevertheless, research also reports the awareness of the user about such restrictions as factual incorrectness, hallucinations, and absence of contextual judgment (McGee, 2023).

Longitudinal studies indicate that the level of trust in ChatGPT is relative and is modified with experience with the tool and its complexity. Novice users are more likely to exhibit higher levels of trust but experienced users are more likely to be more skeptical and also exhibit cross-verification behavior (Kasirzadeh and Gabriel, 2023). This supports the argument that we should have AI literacy programs that teach learners to evaluate AI-generated information critically.

2.4. Academic Integrity and Ethical Concerns

The recent studies of ChatGPT in education are dominated by ethical considerations. The key issues are plagiarism, the ambiguity of authorship, bias, privacy, and academic integrity (Lund et al., 2023). The possibility of ChatGPT to produce high-quality text has questioned the old methods of assessment, and the educators started to rethink the ways of evaluation and learning outcomes.

According to Floridi and Chiriatti (2020), ethical AI implementation must be transparent, equal, and responsible. Research indicates that ChatGPT can be biased upon its training information, and it can solidify stereotypes or even marginalize views (Lee, 2020). These results demonstrate that bias, especially continuous bias, should be monitored and that the dataset must be inclusive of diverse groups.

The issue of privacy is also still eminent. There is usually no awareness among the users about the practices of data storage and use, and this is where the question concerning informed consent and data protection arises (Wilson, 2017). These are the main problems that should be addressed in order to establish long-term trust and responsible AI use in education.

2.5. Social, Psychological, and Emotional Level

Outside of the practical use, the emotional and psychological dimensions of human-AI interaction are discussed in recent literature. The studies have shown that ChatGPT may develop feelings of confidence, anxiety reduction, and feeling of companionship, especially in learners who are afraid to ask human help (Okonkwo,

2021). Although such affective benefits help bring about user satisfaction, it also brings about issues of emotional dependency and lack of interaction with peers.

Anthropomorphic design elements also influence the perceptions of the users. It has been demonstrated that conversational tone, empathy, and perceived personality can greatly boost engagement and toleration to errors (Toader et al., 2023). It has also been revealed that gendered chatbot representations can influence user reactions and forgiveness behavior, and it is more socio-culturally complex to accept AI, as it has been revealed.

2.6. Cultural and Contextual Influences

ChatGPT has differences in the perceptions of users across cultures and educational backgrounds. Findings show that the levels of acceptance depend on the previous experience with technologies, cultural predispositions towards automation, and the institutional norms (Ng et al., 2023). In the collectivist societies, the AI tools are perceived as learning aids, but in the individualistic situations, the fears of originality and independence are more prominent.

Such differences are the reasons why globally indexed databases like Scopus can be used, which can record a wide range of views and provide an analytical view of the patterns of human-AI interaction in different regions.

2.7. Pedagogical Revolution and Teacher Functions

The pedagogical roles and instructional strategies are redefined due to the implementation of ChatGPT. Teachers are starting to play the role of facilitators and moderators of AI-enhanced learning and direct learners towards ethical application, critical analysis, and reflective practice (Holmes et al., 2024). The process-based evaluations that focus on reasoning, interpreting and applying knowledge are slowly replacing the conventional methods of assessment that rely on rote reproduction.

The faculty is still divided, and interest in innovation is moderated by the fear of academic honesty and skill loss (Zawacki-Richter et al., 2023). The institutional guidelines and professional development are thus necessary to make the integration of AI effective and ethical.

2.8. ChatGPT Research Bibliometrics and Thematic Trends

According to bibliometric analyses, the number of publications related to ChatGPT has been growing exponentially since 2023, especially in the fields of education, ethics, and human-computer interaction. Thematic mapping studies and keyword co-occurrence studies all tend to find clusters of keywords relating to usability, trust, sentiment, ethics, and learning outcomes (Chen et al., 2024).

The analysis of academic literature shows that it has a rather positive but skeptical outlook, showing optimism regarding the potential of ChatGPT and being aware of its weaknesses. Such results confirm the use of qualitative trend and scholarly discourse pattern capture tools like NVivo and VOSviewer.

3. CHALLENGES AND LIMITATIONS OF CHATGPT

ChatGPT exhibits multiple limitations along with challenges that affect its excellent capabilities. The model's tendency to favor specific themes along with writing styles presents an issue in particular situations as demonstrated by Yang S et al. (2021), which leads to incorrect or inappropriate results. All risks must be assessed through an evaluation process that includes Bias and fairness, Misuse and abuse, Privacy, Security and Overreliance.

The training data received by ChatGPT allows this AI model to develop response biases just like any other AI system. The bias and fairness risk are responsible for this phenomenon.

ChatGPT shows preconceptions or discrimination according to Lee J. S. (2020). The study by Floridi and Chiriatti (2020) states that developers need to implement precautions which guarantee the training data represents a diverse and unbiased set of information. The model requires constant performance evaluation to detect emerging biases. The spread of deceptive information together with the practice of pretending to be genuine individuals represents two instances of misuse and abuse. This has the potential to be dangerous and damaging. The developers need to create procedures for ethical ChatGPT use and system misuse prevention. The developers need to create security systems that will safeguard user information while simultaneously providing users with complete details about data collection procedures and usage practices. The security threats that AI models face match those encountered by other AI models because attackers use adversarial attacks to modify input data to produce unwanted results. Developers need to create security protocols that will protect ChatGPT from such attacks. Users who depend on ChatGPT could reach levels where they need its help for essential decisions and critical information without verifying the accuracy or relevance of the data. Developers should create protocols that notify users about ChatGPT's limitations while teaching them to make decisions through critical thinking. ChatGPT produces biased responses through its training process on biased information that strengthens or intensifies negative content.

AI chatbots' rapid development has sparked various social discussions about privacy and ethical matters as well as dependability and trust issues. Public trust drives the successful implementation and adoption of AI bots such as ChatGPT since people form trust through their understanding of transparency and ethical alignment and perceived rewards. Research demonstrates that users should be at the forefront of AI development to create healthy human-AI partnerships by understanding user expectations and ethical considerations. Users base their acceptance of new technologies on TAM's two primary factors: perceived utility and usability. This study expands upon TAM by investigating how data privacy concerns, together with ethical design elements and AI-driven decision-making consequences affect user attitudes within human interaction contexts.

The research demands qualitative insights to grasp human emotions and perspectives although quantitative research methods can measure these aspects. The research uses qualitative methods to understand human perspectives about AI in order to identify what people prefer and find worrisome about AI bots. This method allows developers to build AI systems that maintain social norms and ethical standards and functional specifications which leads to user trust and extended acceptance.

The applications of ChatGPT benefit users in multiple ways including customer service and virtual assistance and educational functionalities. People's understanding of these technologies needs to be understood because it allows developers to align AI development with societal requirements and values as these technologies advance into everyday life. The research investigates human opinions about AI chatbot systems through qualitative analysis to determine ethical concerns that affect interactions with ChatGPT.

The foundation for qualitative findings relies on Scopus-indexed data analysis. The accredited database of excellent peer-reviewed research Scopus enables researchers to understand multiple viewpoints about human-AI interaction. The study benefits from worldwide insights through Scopus research coverage which also enhances the qualitative analysis depth and relevance. The Scopus database provides verified information and displays recent research findings about conversational AI systems and public concerns about these systems.

Research has shown that ChatGPT follows a standard process in developing its capabilities as part of a broader research trend to develop advanced language models. The models are likely to be used in many ways, for instance, to improve language translation as well as to enhance chatbots and virtual assistants. Even though Chat GPT has the most impressive natural language writing capability, it has been overshadowed by potential biases, privacy implications, and ethical concerns.

It is very important to understand how people view AI tools like ChatGPT in order to ensure that the development of AI tools like ChatGPT meets the user requirements, ethical standards, and expectations as these technologies become more and more ingrained in daily life. A qualitative approach to the study is more appropriate for the study because it allows for an in-depth study of various perspectives and also captures subtle feelings, perceptions, and concerns that may be missed by quantitative approaches. The Scopus-indexed research publications are the main source of qualitative data for this study as they provide a wealth of verified insights from peer-reviewed studies. As a comprehensive and reliable database, Scopus ensures that the information examined is accurate and relevant to the current debates on artificial intelligence and human relationships.

It is worth noting that VOS viewer is a popular tool for visualizing and analyzing bibliometric networks, and therefore researchers doing qualitative research in various fields, including user perspectives on cutting-edge AI systems like ChatGPT, may find it very useful. VOSviewer, which was developed to help create and visualize bibliometric maps, is good at handling large amounts of data from academic databases such as Scopus. It allows researchers to study trends, collaborations and topic clusters through mapping co-authorship, co-occurrence of keywords, and citation networks. This analysis makes it easy to understand how ChatGPT is viewed and discussed in the literature, and it also helps to identify new patterns in user feedback and AI adoption, user concerns and application areas.

VOSviewer can provide useful information when studying ChatGPT from the perspective of the user by visualizing and illustrating the networks of keywords, researchers, and research subjects connected to ChatGPT-related publications in Scopus. This is achieved through the use of cluster analysis by authors to identify recurring themes such as usability, ethical issues, and real-world applications in a number of industries.

This report highlights ChatGPT's influence and user experiences while providing a comprehensive overview of how it is used in many areas. In the end, VOSviewer provides a clear, empirically supported lens through which to examine AI-driven technologies such as ChatGPT and is an efficient, systematic method for analyzing qualitative trends in the literature. With Research publications on Chat GPT as generative AI, especially the Scopus-indexed data of previous studies, will elaborate on the attitudes and perspectives of user intentions and concerns regarding the AI bots.

4. SIGNIFICANCE OF TWITTER (X) DATA IN SCHOLARLY AND PRACTICAL RESEARCH

Twitter, which is now called X, has become one of the most effective social media platforms of real-time information sharing, opinion making and the discussion of the people. Because of its open-access, nature of the posts, and speed of information dissemination, Twitter data has been extensively utilized in different fields like business management, political science, health informatics, marketing, education, and information systems (Kaplan and Haenlein, 2010; Kietzmann et al., 2011).

A few researchers point out Twitter as a useful source of user-generated content (UGC) that captures impulsive opinions, feelings and attitudes of the population, about events, products, policies and technologies (Boyd et al., 2010). Twitter data is also high volume, velocity, and variety compared to traditional surveys, which makes it appropriate to big data analytics and research on computational social science (Gandomi & Haider, 2015).

Over the past few years, scholars have turned to Twitter data more frequently to examine consumer sentiment, crisis communication, political polarization, brand perception, and technology adoption due to its capacity to offer unfiltered and time-sensitive information about the behaviour of the population (Liu et al., 2021). The hashtag system and network structure of the platform also supports the tracking of the subject matter and a relationship analysis, which contributes to its applicability to empirical research.

4.1 Data Mining of Twitter/X Platform

Twitter/X Data extraction is an important methodological procedure in social media research. Conventionally, scientists have used Twitter APIs (Standard, Academic, and Enterprise) to gather tweets, metadata, user interactions, and timestamps (Tweepy, 2020). Nevertheless, new modifications to the X data access policies have made third-party scraping, browser-based extraction, and third-party academic resources more reliant, which meet the ethical standards.

Research has shown that the process of data extraction is usually based on the use of keywords to search, hashtag monitoring, user timeline gathering, or specific event filtering, and is then preprocessed by eliminating duplicates, retweets, bots, and irrelevant information (Batrinca & Treleaven, 2015). Ethics, including user anonymity, informed consent, and compatibility with the platform, have been highlighted as a vital element of Twitter/X data research (Townsend and Wallace, 2016).

Was blocked, X continues to be an influential source of social media data due to its textual format with rich metadata and the global coverage of it, making it possible to conduct longitudinal and cross-sectional analyses. Researchers believe that open disclosure of extraction procedures enhances the replicability and validity of results (Bruns and Stieglitz, 2013).

4.2 Twitter/X Data Sentiment Analysis

One of the most popular analytical tools of Twitter/X research is sentiment analysis. It entails a computational determination of either positive, negative, or neutral emotions in a textual data based on a lexicon based, machine learning, or deep learning methodology (Pang and Lee, 2008).

Previous research shows that sentiment analysis of twitter posts can give significant information on the opinion of the people, their satisfaction, market trends and their attitudes (Pak and Paroubek, 2010). VADER, TextBlob, and SentiWordNet are lexicon-based tools that are typically applied because they can classify short and informal texts like tweets, whereas supervised machine learning models are better in the domain-specific context (Medhat et al., 2014).Recent sources point out that sentiment analysis of Twitter/X data facilitates decision-making in business strategy, policy analysis, and crisis management, in particular, when it is complemented by temporal and thematic analysis (Cambria et al., 2017). Nevertheless, the issues of sarcasm, multilingual composition, and ambiguity in contexts are also rather serious weaknesses, and one should be careful about interpretation.

4.3 Visualization of Twitter/X Data using Word Cloud and VOSviewer

Visualization strategies are important to increase the interpretability of big Twitter/X datasets. As a visualization of word frequency, word clouds are often employed as a tool of exploration to emphasize dominating terms, themes, and discourse patterns (Heimerl et al., 2014). Despite being descriptive, word clouds do not need any time to give immediate cognitive information, and in the initial stages of analysis, they are frequently used.

To conduct more sophisticated thematic and relational analysis, researchers are turning to VOSviewer, a bibliometric visualization method, which was initially created to do co-citation and keyword co-occurrence analysis (Van Eck and Waltman, 2010). VOSviewer, when used on Twitter/X data, allows visualizing networks of keywords, hashtags, and concepts, and identifying the hidden structure, clusters of topics, and trends of research.

Research combining sentiment analysis with VOSviewer mapping shows that the analysis level is stronger, and the researchers can relate emotional polarity to thematic development and network centrality (Donthu et al., 2021). This type of combined methods is especially applicable to systematic review, technology adoption studies, and discourse analysis of social media, providing both the richness of qualitative and the rigor of quantitative methods.

4.4 Synthesis and Research Implication

The literature review confirms that Twitter/X data is an effective empirical tool to explain real-time social phenomena. Twitter/X data has a high methodological value when it is systematically extracted, ethically processed, and analyzed with the help of sentiment analysis and visualization tools like word clouds and VOSviewer. Nevertheless, scholars are advised to use mixed-methodology, triangulate, and be open on the limitations of data to enhance validity and generalizability.

5. RESEARCH METHODOLOGY

The research paper implemented qualitative methodology as its methodological approach. The study examines user perspectives about ChatGPT by analyzing how AI supports communication and information access and language learning, and writing assistance. The first step of the method involved collecting data from Scopus publications. The qualitative and bibliometric analysis is based on 1,718 research articles extracted from the Scopus database regarding ChatGPT in the education sector in the month of October 2024. The research selected articles from Scopus that examined how ChatGPT integrates with various contexts through the keywords ChatGPT, Artificial Intelligence and Generative AI. The dataset underwent filtering to focus on posts that presented authentic public perspectives about user attitudes and ideas and experiences. The analysis stage used NVivo software to conduct thematic and sentiment analysis on Scopus-based literature data which produced categories such as ChatGPT's adaptability and productivity advantages and ethical considerations. The thematic coding process allowed researchers to grasp academic literature user perspectives through the organization of recurring topics and sentiment patterns. Sentiment analysis divided these topics into positive, neutral and negative sentiments to highlight overall attitudes.

The study used VOS viewer as its final analysis tool to generate visualizations from the literature review's topic findings. The analysis required building co-occurrence networks to show relationships between essential themes and concepts in customer viewpoints and word clouds to display frequently used terms about ChatGPT. The visual aids enabled a complete literature review synthesis which revealed the connections between important themes and customer attitudes in ChatGPT-3 discussions. The next leap of analysis included the extraction of the tweets from X (twitter) website and analyzing the human perspectives through the Python tool through sentimental analysis and world cloud. This section of study in the chapter gives us the overview of social media analysis and user perspectives. The method delivered a complete understanding of ChatGPT adoption through its ability to reveal both general user attitudes and refined customer perceptions. The Scopus webpage infographics served to evaluate user attitudes and acceptance levels regarding ChatGPT.

6. DATA ANALYSIS

The research data underwent analysis through NVIVO 14 qualitative software tool. The analysis revealed multiple parameters which showed that users both recognized the absolute advantages of Chat GPT and its potential difficulties. The research showed that #ChatGPT received high acceptance because it offered multiple advantages including versatile usage and natural language understanding and scalability for large data sets and consistent learning features and most importantly a time-saving engine for humankind.

6.1 Themes Identified

The NVIVO 14 software tool allows for automated topic modeling and identification of themes from text-based datasets (Kaurav et al, 2020). The study used NVivo to extract themes from the #ChatGPT topic, and Table 1 in the study shows the major themes that were identified from this topic.

Table 1. Various themes identified under ChatGPT

		1: Files\\scopus
1	C: artificial intelligence	2214
2	J: learning	1023
3	M: research	1014
4	E: education	946
5	N: students	870
6	G: generative	796
7	Q: technology	735
8	A: academic	707
9	S: use	703
10	L: process	613
11	K: potential	602
12	O: study	567
13	R: tools	565
14	B: analysis	556
15	F: ethical	552
16	H: human	545
17	I: language models	542

continued on following page

Table 1. Continued

		1: Files\\scopus
18	P: teaching	518
19	D: data	486

Source: Compiled by Author from NVivo output

It can be seen from the thematic analysis that the top 19 themes revolve around the technology of AI and its intelligence, effectiveness, and impact on academia.

Figure 1. Thematic analysis

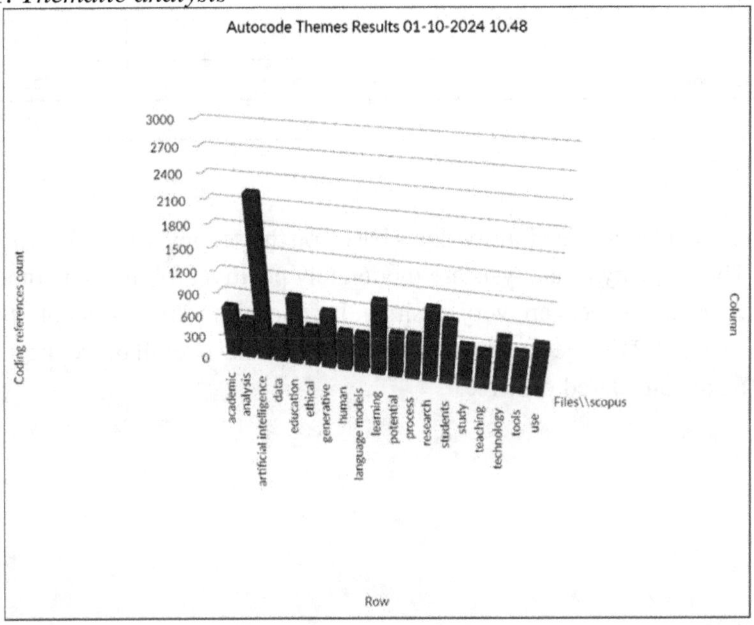

The thematic study concludes that ChatGPT has its highest impact on the education sector which resembles with key words like- learning, research, education, students, academic, study and teaching. The result elevated that use of generative AI like ChatGPT dynamically influence the educational industry.

6.2 Sentiment Analysis

The field of sentiment analysis on the published Scopus database has seen a lot of exploration in recent years. Initially, it was focused on binary classification of opinions as positive or negative (Pudaruth et.al, 2018). However, NVivo 14 allows for the extraction of up to four sentiments from text-based datasets (Reyes Menendez et.al, 2020). Automated techniques are used to extract sentiment from the Scopus CSV file. Sentiment analysis can help organizations and customers achieve their goals by automatically analyzing large amounts of data and extracting opinions. Sentiment analysis has become increasingly popular in computer science, management, and social sciences.

Table 2. Sentiment analysis

1: Codes\\scopus\\Authors,Author full names,Author(s) ID, Title, Year, Source title, Volume, Issue, Art. No., Page start, Page end,Page count, Cited by, DOI,Link, Abstract, Author Keywords, Index Keywords, Document Type, Publication Stage, Open Access, Source, EID	
A: Very negative	744
B: Moderately negative	1917
C: Moderately positive	5205
D: Very positive	1054

Source: NVivo output

The sentiment analysis of individuals based on the scopus data is shown in Table 2 above. The majority of analysis are moderately positive, followed by moderately negative. Very few tweets are very positive. By analyzing the sentiment of user responses to Chat GPT's tweets, the major insights into the overall perception towards Chat GPT are considered positive.

6.3 Word Map and Word Cloud

Figure 2. Word Cloud in Twitter analysis

Source: NVivo output

A word cloud is a tool that generates a visual representation of the frequency of commonly used words and phrases. It is useful for identifying key areas of discussion in data analysis. In this study, a word cloud was used to analyze the content of tweets related to ChatGPT- an AI-based tool. As per Figure 1, the word "ChatGPT" was at the center of the word cloud, surrounded by words related to artificial intelligence, and OpenAI. This indicates that the main focus of the tweets was on the technology and its effectiveness in simplifying human tasks. The map analysis of NVIVO elicits that it has a wide range of users and applications and has been embraced by people and organizations across the world. The majority of the opinions drawn on Twitter about ChatGPT belong to the United States, Europe, the Middle East, and South Asian countries, a per in Figure 2.

6.4 Authors Keywords Co-Occurrence

For 1717 highly referenced articles retrieved from the Scopus database, a threshold of 16 was used, which produced a large number of terms in the theme of "EXPLORING HUMAN PERSPECTIVE TOWARDS AI BOT – CHATGPT". The top author keywords revealed the interests and research area focus of different academicians and researchers. As indicated by Table 4, these keywords led to the top six highly referred total occurrences, which are ChatGPT (1078), generative AI (246), artificial intelligence (990), students (134), chatbots (131), and higher education (127). An expanding number of industries, including business and education, are using ChatGPT, a conversational AI model. According to Brown et al. (2020), natural language processing tools have shown significant potential for task automation, content creation, and decision support. Its increasing usage is a sign of its usefulness in domains where text generation and interaction with humans characteristics are necessary.

Table 3. Co-occurrence of the author's keyword

S no	Keywords	Occurrences	Total link strength
1	ChatGPT	1078	1397
2	artificial intelligence	990	1338
3	generative AI	246	441
4	students	134	311
5	chatbots	131	265
6	higher education	127	259
7	ethics	57	116
8	learning	50	127
9	teaching	48	140
10	academic integrity	44	101
11	decision making	37	75
12	writing	35	72
13	assessment	33	61
14	creativity	30	64
15	curricula	26	75
16	gpt-4	26	66

Figure 3. Co-occurrence network of the most frequently used author keyword

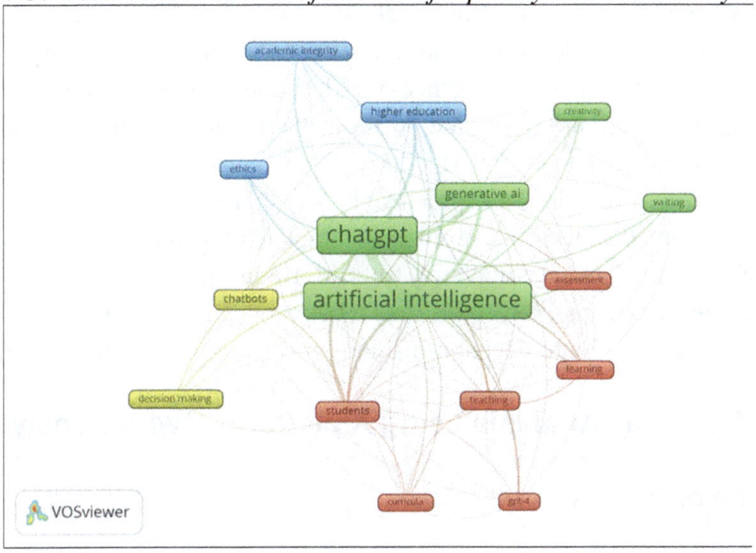

The image created with the VOS viewer above showed a co-occurrence network of keywords associated with artificial intelligence.

The model demonstrates that ChatGPT and Artificial Intelligence function as its central nodes because they play a crucial role in current discussions. The map shows how different concepts relate to each other through lines which represent the strength of connections between terms and node sizes indicate how often terms appear together. Students use ChatGPT for both writing essays and answering questions which creates academic integrity problems while offering potential learning benefits (Kalla et al., 2023). The central position of ChatGPT in education and content generation emerges from its direct connections to Generative AI, Students and Teaching. Generative AI maintains strong ties to creativity-related keywords such as writing and creativity because it generates unique content including business, art, music and literature (de Silva et al., 2024). The ability of GPT-5 to generate complex narratives has led to discussions about AI's impact on human creativity as well as its potential to work alongside humans in creative fields. The use of AI-powered chatbots continues to grow across customer service and educational and healthcare sectors. The technology has proven its ability to handle frequent inquiries while providing immediate assistance (Adamopoulou & Moussiades, 2020).

Key themes associated with ChatGPT and Artificial Intelligence are also Academic Integrity and Ethics, especially in education. Concerns around plagiarism and academic dishonesty have grown as more students use AI technologies like ChatGPT for their academic work (Currie, 2023). This connection highlights the necessity for educational institutions to create guidelines and resources to identify and stop the improper use of AI in the classroom (Gul, 2024). Large datasets are analysed by AI-powered decision-making systems in business to generate predictions and suggestions. Artificial intelligence and decision-making are related because AI is being integrated into important business operations, enabling firms to make decisions based on insights from AI (Marr, 2019).

However, there are ethical and practical issues with using AI to make decisions. If AI systems are educated on skewed or incomplete data, they may be biased and produce choices that are not completely truthful (Boddington, 2017). Organizations must guarantee accountability, equity, and transparency in the usage of AI as it becomes more integrated into decision-making processes (Russell & Norvig, 2021).

6.5 Social media Analysis using X platform (Twitter analysis)

Extraction of Tweets

To include the social media aspect of the research, 500 tweets regarding ChatGPT and overall education were filtered out of the X (previously Twitter) site with the help of the backend data access tools. The tweets were gathered with the help of the appropriate key-words with the usage of ChatGPT, educational application, academic experience, and pedagogical implications. The dataset represents a wide variety of voices, such as those of educators, students, researchers, ed-tech practitioners, and institutional accounts. This corpus offers unsolicited user opinion in real time, and it is especially useful in getting a sense of genuine academic opinion when it comes to real publications. Duplicates and URLs and noises other than text were filtered out of the tweets and the analysis was performed.

Sentiment Analysis: Method and Results

Sentiment analysis was done on a Python based natural language processing tool which assigned each of the tweets into one of the three sentiment categories of Negative, Neutral and Positive. The findings show disastrous and scholarly important distribution of sentiment. The 500 tweets had the following count, 191 (38.2) negative, 166 (33.2) neutral, and 143 (28.6) positive. The negative sentiment is the leading part of the discourse as shown in Figure X (Sentiment Distribution Bar Chart) closely followed by the neutral sentiment with the positive sentiment being the minor part of the discourse. This observation is especially remarkable since there is a common belief that ChatGPT is a disruptive learning resource. The negativity of the sentiment indicates that academic users are not just passive followers but are evaluating the limits, dangers and educational impact of the tool a bit critically.

The neutral tweets are mostly those that involve sharing of information, including updates, announcements, or descriptive use, but without any clear emotional polarity. The tweets of a positive nature, although they are substantial, seem more reserved, tending to focus on efficiency gains as opposed to profound pedagogical change.

Figure 4. Sentiment distribution

```
sentiment_label
Negative    191
Neutral     166
Positive    143
Name: count, dtype: int64
```

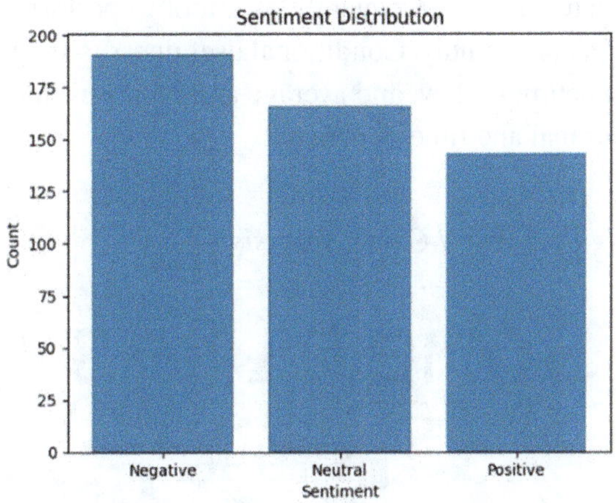

Interpretation of Sentiment Patterns

The increased proportion of negative sentiment is an indicator of development of an academic concern regarding the problems of over-reliance on AI, misinformation, hallucinations, ethical ambiguity, integrity of assessment and the destruction of critical thinking ability. Numerous critical tweets are about the doubt of ChatGPT in complex academic tasks and specifically higher-order thinking, novelty, and professionalism. The category of neutral sentiment is an indication of cautious involvement, which implies that the major part of the academia remains in the exploratory or monitoring stage. In the meantime, the positive feeling although being lower in comparison exists to emphasize practical advantages, including the time savings, accomplishment of tasks, improvement of productivity and helping with repetitive or groundwork academic tasks. These findings, together, suggest a skeptically negative academic review, as opposed to a blinded enthusiasm.

Word Cloud Analysis and Thematic Insights

The visualization of word clouds (Figure Y) can be considered the qualitative insight that compliments other qualitative insights as it includes the terms that are most frequent within the corpus of tweets. The words that have a high frequency include ChatGPT, responses, work, small, tasks, results, prompt, repetitive, documentation, coding, and average, which signify that academic users refer to ChatGPT more frequently as a tool to perform operational support tasks than to think profoundly. Conditional usefulness is supported by words such as depending, sometimes, okay, and average and indicates that the effectiveness is extremely situational and time-dependent.

Figure 5. Word Count Analysis

The qualitative insight that can be evaluated as a supplement to other corpus of tweets, that may be considered the visualization of the word clouds (Figure Y), may be considered as comprising of the terms that are the most common in the corpus of tweets. The highly frequent words consist of ChatGPT, responses, work, small, tasks, results, prompt, repetitive, documentation, coding, and average which indicates that academic users mention ChatGPT more often as an operational support tool than a tool to reflect on deep thought. The words that support conditional usefulness include depending, sometimes, okay, and average and mean that the efficacy is very situational and time-dependent.

Tweets Insights

Combined, both the sentiment analysis and the word cloud analysis show that the use of ChatGPT in academia is multifaceted, uncertain, and in no way entirely positive. The results oppose the prevailing techno-optimistic discourses and highlight the significance of a humanistic, careful, and situational methodology of AI adoption in general education. This social media research is a mixed method that will complement the bibliometric results obtained on Scopus regarding lived experience, concerns, and conditional acceptance of the use of generative AI tools.

7. FUTURE RESEARCH

ChatGPT is still a relatively new model, and there is considerable scope for future research in various areas. One area the development can be accessing the highly utilized categories. Another area is the exploration of new approaches to mitigate the model's biases and improve its accuracy and relevance in specific contexts. There is also scope for research in the usage of ChatGPT in different segments, such as healthcare, finance, education etc.

8. DISCUSSION

Businesses, researchers, and organizations interested in learning more about user behaviour, sentiment, and opinion on a variety of subjects might benefit from Twitter analysis. This platform is one of the greatest social media analysis tools available due to its vast user base, real-time data, public data, and simple API. This paper examined the theoretical background of human perspectives towards ChatGPT by identifying various user perspectives towards the use of this AI technology. The paper studied the development process of OpenAI's ChatGPT system. The research analyzed user sentiment through Twitter tweets, which contained both positive and negative reactions. The main advantage of ChatGPT lies in its ability to offer customized guidance and assistance to users across different circumstances. The AI language model ChatGPT functions best for conversational assistance because it processes natural language inputs to produce human-like responses. OpenAI faces major drawbacks with security and privacy concerns standing out as the most significant issues.

9. CONCLUSION

The conversational interface of ChatGPT makes it a useful tool for various applications and situations because it offers personalized assistance. Using ChatGPT has several benefits for both individuals and companies. The individual users were the main emphasis of this study. One of ChatGPT's primary advantages is its capacity to provide customers with conversational, tailored assistance and support. Various industries and applications have come to embrace AI and use ChatGPT. ChatGPT will likely become even more capable and complex in the years to come, opening up new opportunities and use cases for users of all stripes. The widespread acceptance and use of ChatGPT imply that it is a useful tool for numerous applications and industries, despite certain potential downsides and restrictions to take into account, which was also suggested by Polisetty and Sheela (2023) in their study on research paper on artificial intelligence replacing human resources.

The negativity files that ChatGPT has the potential to replace some jobs, which can be considered true for those jobs that need routine or repetitive work. With ChatGPT's Technological sophistication and capability, these job roles may include those of customer service representatives, data entry operators, and some types of administrative assistants. It's crucial to remember that ChatGPT is not a one-size-fits-all solution and that many jobs and operations still call for human interaction. However, ChatGPT is considered positive by this research analysis and enhances the productivity of all profile users.

REFERENCES

Baclic, O., Tunis, M., Young, K., Doan, C., Swerdfeger, H., & Schonfeld, J. (2020). Artificial intelligence in public health: Challenges and opportunities for public health made possible by advances in natural language processing. *Canada Communicable Disease Report = Relevé des Maladies Transmissibles au Canada, 46*(6), 161–168. DOI: 10.14745/ccdr.v46i06a02 PMID: 32673380

Baclic, O., Tunis, M., Young, K., Doan, C., Swerdfeger, H., & Schonfeld, J. (2020). Artificial intelligence in public health: Challenges and opportunities for public health made possible by advances in natural language processing. *Canada Communicable Disease Report = Relevé des Maladies Transmissibles au Canada, 46*(6), 161–168. DOI: 10.14745/ccdr.v46i06a02 PMID: 32673380

Baidoo-Anu, D., & Owusu Ansah, L. (2023). Education in the era of generative artificial intelligence (AI): Understanding the potential benefits of ChatGPT in promoting teaching and learning. *SSRN, 3*(1), 52–62. DOI: 10.2139/ssrn.4337484

Batrinca, B., & Treleaven, P. C. (2015). Social media analytics: A survey of techniques, tools and platforms. *AI & Society, 30*(1), 89–116. DOI: 10.1007/s00146-014-0549-4

Biswas, S. (2023). Role of ChatGPT in education, research and healthcare: A review. *Journal of Information Systems and Technology Management, 20*, e202320002. DOI: 10.4301/S1807-1775202320002

Biswas, S. S. (2023). Potential use of chat gpt in global warming. *Annals of Biomedical Engineering, 51*(6), 1126–1127. DOI: 10.1007/s10439-023-03171-8 PMID: 36856927

Boddington, P. (2017). *Towards a code of ethics for artificial intelligence*. Springer., DOI: 10.1007/978-3-319-60648-4

Boyd, D., Golder, S., & Lotan, G. (2010). Tweet, tweet, retweet: Conversational aspects of retweeting on Twitter. *Proceedings of the 43rd Hawaii International Conference on System Sciences*. DOI: 10.1109/HICSS.2010.412

Brown, T. B., Mann, B., Ryder, N., Subbiah, M., Kaplan, J., Dhariwal, P., & Amodei, D. (2020, December). Language models are few-shot learners. In *Proceedings of the 34th International Conference on Neural Information Processing Systems* (pp. 1877-1901).

Bruns, A., & Stieglitz, S. (2013). Towards more systematic Twitter analysis. *Information Communication and Society, 16*(1), 91–108.

Cambria, E., Poria, S., Bajpai, R., & Schuller, B. (2017). Sentiment analysis: Beyond polarity. *IEEE Intelligent Systems, 32*(2), 102–107. DOI: 10.1109/MIS.2016.31

Chen, X., Xie, H., Zou, D., & Hwang, G. J. (2024). A bibliometric analysis of ChatGPT research: Trends, themes, and future directions. Computers & Education. *Artificial Intelligence, 5*, 100164. DOI: 10.1016/j.caeai.2024.100164

Currie, G. M. (2023, September). Academic integrity and artificial intelligence: is ChatGPT hype, hero or heresy? In Seminars in Nuclear Medicine (Vol. 53, No. 5, pp. 719-730). WB Saunders. DOI: 10.1053/j.semnuclmed.2023.04.008

Dale, R. (2021). GPT-3: What's it good for? *Natural Language Engineering, 27*(1), 113–118. DOI: 10.1017/S1351324920000601

Donthu, N., Kumar, S., Mukherjee, D., Pandey, N., & Lim, W. M. (2021). How to conduct a bibliometric analysis: An overview and guidelines. *Journal of Business Research, 133*, 285–296. DOI: 10.1016/j.jbusres.2021.04.070

Fabio, P., Lewis, P., Piktus, A., Rocktäschel, T., & Riedel, S. (2019). Language models as knowledge bases? *Proceedings of the 2019 Conference on Empirical Methods in Natural Language Processing*, 2463–2473. DOI: 10.18653/v1/D19-1250

Floridi, L., & Chiriatti, M. (2020). GPT-3: Its nature, scope, limits, and consequences. *Minds and Machines, 30*(4), 681–694. DOI: 10.1007/s11023-020-09548-1

Gandomi, A., & Haider, M. (2015). Beyond the hype: Big data concepts, methods, and analytics. *International Journal of Information Management, 35*(2), 137–144. DOI: 10.1016/j.ijinfomgt.2014.10.007

Gül, E. (2024). A Latent Class Analysis Approach to Challenges Experienced by Faculty Members in Online Assessment in Higher Education. *Erzincan Üniversitesi Eğitim Fakültesi Dergisi, 26*(2), 197–207. Advance online publication. DOI: 10.17556/erziefd.1382191

Hickok, M. (2021). Lessons learned from AI ethics principles for future actions. *AI and Ethics, 1*(1), 41–47. DOI: 10.1007/s43681-020-00008-1

Hickok, M. (2021). Lessons learned from AI ethics principles for future actions. *AI and Ethics, 1*(1), 41–47. DOI: 10.1007/s43681-020-00008-1

Holmes, W., Bialik, M., & Fadel, C. (2024). *Artificial intelligence in education: Promises and implications for teaching and learning* (2nd ed.). Center for Curriculum Redesign., https://www.researchgate.net/publication/338205557_The_Effect_of_Social_Presence_and_Chatbot_Errors_on_Trust

Kalla, D., Smith, N., Samaah, F., & Kuraku, S. (2023). Study and analysis of ChatGPT and its impact on different fields of study. International journal of innovative science and research technology, 8(3).

Kaplan, A. M., & Haenlein, M. (2010). Users of the world, unite! The challenges and opportunities of social media. *Business Horizons*, *53*(1), 59–68. DOI: 10.1016/j.bushor.2009.09.003

Kasirzadeh, A., & Gabriel, I. (2023). In conversation with artificial intelligence: Aligning language models with human values. *Philosophy & Technology*, *36*(2), 1–24. DOI: 10.1007/s13347-023-00606-x

Kasneci, E., Sessler, K., Küchemann, S., Bannert, M., Dementieva, D., Fischer, F., Gasser, U., & Kasneci, G. (2023). ChatGPT for good? On opportunities and challenges of large language models for education. *Learning and Individual Differences*, *103*, 102274. DOI: 10.1016/j.lindif.2023.102274

Kaurav, R. P. S., Suresh, K. G., Narula, S., & Baber, R. (2020). New education policy: qualitative (contents) analysis and Twitter mining (sentiment analysis). Journal of content, community and communication, 12(1), 4-13. DOI: 10.31620/JCCC.12.20/02

King, M. R. (2023). ChatGPT: A conversational AI tool for teaching and research. *ACS Nano*, *17*(6), 5557–5560. DOI: 10.1021/acsnano.3c01526

Lee, J. S. (2020). The ethical implications of AI bias in decision-making systems. *AI & Society*, *35*(4), 831–841. DOI: 10.1007/s00146-019-00903-5

Lund, B. D., Wang, T., Mannuru, N. R., Nie, B., Shimray, S., & Wang, Z. (2023). ChatGPT and a new academic reality: Artificial Intelligence-written research papers and the ethics of the large language models in scholarly publishing. *Journal of the Association for Information Science and Technology*, *74*(5), 570–581. Advance online publication. DOI: 10.1002/asi.24750

Lund, B. D., Wang, T., Mannuru, N. R., Nie, B., Shimray, S. R., & Wang, Z. (2023). ChatGPT and a new academic reality: Artificial intelligence–written research papers and the ethics of authorship. *Journal of the Association for Information Science and Technology*, *74*(5), 570–579. DOI: 10.1002/asi.24750

Marr, B. (2019). *Artificial intelligence in practice: how 50 successful companies used AI and machine learning to solve problems*. John Wiley & Sons.

McGee, R. W. (2023). Ethical issues in the use of ChatGPT. *Journal of Accounting Ethics*, *20*(1), 1–8.

McGee, R. W. (2023). Is ChatGPT biased against conservatives? An empirical study. An Empirical Study (February 15, 2023). DOI: 10.2139/ssrn.4359405

McGee, R. W. (2023). What Will the United States Look Like in 2050? A ChatGPT Short Story. A ChatGPT Short Story (April 8, 2023). DOI: 10.2139/ssrn.4413442

Medhat, W., Hassan, A., & Korashy, H. (2014). Sentiment analysis algorithms and applications: A survey. *Ain Shams Engineering Journal*, *5*(4), 1093–1113. DOI: 10.1016/j.asej.2014.04.011

Ng, D. T. K., Leung, J. K. L., Chu, S. K. W., & Qiao, M. S. (2023). AI literacy: Definition, teaching, evaluation, and ethical issues. *Computers and Education: Artificial Intelligence*, *4*, 100131. DOI: 10.1016/j.caeai.2023.100131

Okonkwo, C. W. (2021). Analyzing student satisfaction with chatbot-based learning support systems. *Education and Information Technologies*, *26*(5), 1–18. DOI: 10.1007/s10639-021-10492-1

Pak, A., & Paroubek, P. (2010). Twitter as a corpus for sentiment analysis and opinion mining. *Proceedings of LREC.*

Pang, B., & Lee, L. (2008). Opinion mining and sentiment analysis. *Foundations and Trends in Information Retrieval*, *2*(1–2), 1–135. DOI: 10.1561/1500000011

Petroni, F., Rocktäschel, T., Riedel, S., Lewis, P., Bakhtin, A., Wu, Y., & Miller, A. 2019. Language Models as Knowledge Bases? In *Proceedings of the 2019 Conference on Empirical Methods in Natural Language Processing and the 9th International Joint Conference on Natural Language Processing (EMNLP-IJCNLP)*, pages 2463-2473, Hong Kong, China. Association for Computational Linguistics. DOI: 10.18653/v1/D19-1250

Polisetty, A., & Sheela, P. (2023). Will AI Replace Humans in Human Resources? A Case Analysis. *Prabandhan: Indian Journal of Management*, *16*(6), 25–38. DOI: 10.17010/pijom/2023/v16i6/172862

Pudaruth, S., Moheeputh, S., Permessur, N., & Chamroo, A. (2018). Sentiment analysis from Facebook comments using automatic coding in NVivo 11. DOI: 10.14201/ADCAIJ2018714148

Reyes-Menendez, A., Saura, J. R., & Filipe, F. (2020). Marketing challenges in the# MeToo era: Gaining business insights using an exploratory sentiment analysis. *Heliyon*, *6*(3), e03626. DOI: 10.1016/j.heliyon.2020.e03626 PMID: 32258475

Siddiqui, A., Siddiqui, M., & Kulkarni, N. (2022). Artificial Intelligence in Water Conservation: A Meta-Analysis Study. *Prabandhan: Indian Journal of Management, 15*(3), 24–41. DOI: 10.17010/pijom/2022/v15i3/160407

Siddiqui, S. A., Azeem, M., & Khan, A. (2022). Applications of natural language processing in artificial intelligence systems. *International Journal of Advanced Computer Science and Applications, 13*(2), 389–397.

Sng, G. G. R., Cheah, J. H., Ting, H., & Ramayah, T. (2023). Conversational agents and user satisfaction: A meta-analytic review. *Journal of Business Research, 154*, 113352. DOI: 10.1016/j.jbusres.2022.113352

Sng, G. G. R., Tung, J. Y. M., Lim, D. Y. Z., & Bee, Y. M. (2023). Potential and pitfalls of ChatGPT and natural-language artificial intelligence models for diabetes education. *Diabetes Care, 46*(5), e103–e105. DOI: 10.2337/dc23-0197 PMID: 36920843

Straw, I., & Callison-Burch, C. (2020). Artificial Intelligence in mental health and the biases of language-based models. *PLoS One, 15*(12), e0240376. DOI: 10.1371/journal.pone.0240376 PMID: 33332380

Straw, I., & Callison-Burch, C. (2020). Artificial intelligence in journalism: Bias and accountability. *Journalism Practice, 14*(2), 1–17. DOI: 10.1080/17512786.2019.1682940

Surendra, S. (2017). Spam analysis and detection on microblog (Doctoral dissertation).

Taecharungroj, V. (2023). "What Can ChatGPT Do?" Analyzing Early Reactions to the Innovative AI Chatbot on Twitter. *Big Data and Cognitive Computing, 7*(1), 35. DOI: 10.3390/bdcc7010035

Taecharungroj, V. (2023). What can ChatGPT do? Analyzing early reactions to ChatGPT in education. *Technological Forecasting and Social Change, 189*, 122322. DOI: 10.1016/j.techfore.2023.122322

Thorat, S. A., & Jadhav, A. (2020). A review on implementation issues of chatbot systems. *International Journal of Advanced Research in Computer and Communication Engineering, 9*(3), 190–194.

Thorat, S. A., & Jadhav, V. A review on implementation issues of rule-based chatbot systems. In Proceedings of the International Conference on Innovative Computing & Communications (ICICC); SSRN: Rochester, NY, USA, 2020. DOI: 10.2139/ssrn.3567047

Toader, D. C., Boca, G., Toader, R., & Măguleac, M. (2023). The effect of anthropomorphism on chatbot acceptance. *Psychology and Marketing*, *40*(2), 330–345. DOI: 10.1002/mar.21758

Tripathi, A., Bagga, T., & Aggarwal, R. K. (2020). Strategic impact of business intelligence: A review of literature. *Prabandhan: Indian Journal of Management*, *13*(3), 35–48. DOI: 10.17010/pijom/2020/v13i3/151175

Tripathi, A., Mishra, S., & Rathi, S. (2020). Multilingual deep learning models for NLP applications. *Procedia Computer Science*, *167*, 185–193. DOI: 10.1016/j.procs.2020.03.206

Van Dis, E. A., Bollen, J., Zuidema, W., Van Rooij, R., & Bockting, C. L. (2023). ChatGPT: Five priorities for research. *Nature*, *614*(7947), 224–226. DOI: 10.1038/d41586-023-00288-7 PMID: 36737653

Van Eck, N. J., & Waltman, L. (2010). Software survey: VOSviewer, a computer program for bibliometric mapping. *Scientometrics*, *84*(2), 523–538. DOI: 10.1007/s11192-009-0146-3 PMID: 20585380

Veerasamy, Senthil & Goswami, Susobhan. (2020). An Exploratory Study of Twitter Sentiment Analysis During COVID-19: #TravelTomorrow and #UNWTO. . https://doi.org/DOI: 10.1007/978-3-030-64861-9_43

Wang, J., & Redelmeier, D. A. (2024). Cognitive biases and artificial intelligence. NEJM AI, 1(12), AIcs2400639. DOI: DOI: 10.1056/AIcs2400639

Wilson, H. J. (2017). The re-emergence of AI and the future of work. *MIT Sloan Management Review*, *58*(4), 1–6.

Yang, S., Chen, Y., & Wei, J. (2021). Style bias in neural text generation. *ACM Transactions on Information Systems*, *39*(4), 1–28. DOI: 10.1145/3450352

Yang, S., & Evans, C. Opportunities and challenges in using AI chatbots in higher education. In *Proceedings of Proceedings of the 2019 3rd International Conference on Education and E-Learning*, Barcelona, Spain, 5-7 November 2019; pp. 79-83. DOI: 10.1145/3371647.3371659

Zawacki-Richter, O., Cefa, B., & Bai, J. Y. (2025). Towards reproducible systematic reviews in Open, Distance, and Digital Education—An umbrella mapping review. *Review of Education*, *13*(1), e70031. DOI: 10.1002/rev3.70031

Zawacki-Richter, O., Marín, V. I., Bond, M., & Gouverneur, F. (2023). Systematic review of research on artificial intelligence applications in higher education. *International Journal of Educational Technology in Higher Education*, *20*(1), 1–27. DOI: 10.1186/s41239-023-00416-1

Zhai, X., Nyaaba, M., & Ma, W. (2025). Can generative AI and ChatGPT outperform humans on cognitive-demanding problem-solving tasks in science? *Science & Education*, *34*(2), 649–670. DOI: 10.1007/s11191-024-00496-1

Zhang, M., & Li, J. (2021). A commentary on GPT-3 in MIT Technology Review 2021. *Fundamental Research (Beijing)*, *1*(6), 831–833. DOI: 10.1016/j.fmre.2021.11.011

Chapter 9

Intelligent Tutoring Systems in Higher Education:

Integration, Governance, and Deployment Within Smart Campus Ecosystems

Francisco R. Trejo-Macotela
https://orcid.org/0000-0003-2133-3456
Universidad Politécnica de Pachuca, Mexico

ABSTRACT

Intelligent Tutoring Systems (ITS) have developed into adaptive learning environments that support personalised and data-informed instruction. Their present relevance is situated within broader digital transformation processes in higher education, particularly in smart campus ecosystems where interoperable infrastructures—such as Learning Management Systems (LMS), Student Information Systems (SIS), and institutional analytics platforms—enable scalable deployment and continuous pedagogical optimisation. This chapter examines the theoretical foundations and core architectural components of ITS, and analyses implementation challenges concerning data governance, privacy, algorithmic transparency, pedagogical alignment, and faculty preparedness. It also discusses institutional strategies for sustainable and ethical adoption, alongside criteria for evaluating impacts on progression, retention, equity, and operational efficiency. The chapter concludes by positioning ITS as strategic assets in developing resilient and inclusive smart campuses.

DOI: 10.4018/979-8-3373-6831-3.ch009

026, IGI Global Scientific Publishing. Copying or distributing in print or electronic forms without written permission of IGI Global Scientific Publishing is prohibited. Use of this chapter to tive artificial intelligence (AI) technologies is expressly prohibited. The publisher reserves all rights to license its use for generative AI training and machine learning model development.

1. INTRODUCTION

The rapid expansion of Artificial Intelligence (AI) has significantly influenced contemporary education, with Intelligent Tutoring Systems (ITS) emerging as a particularly impactful development. Recognised for their capacity to provide personalised and adaptive instruction, ITS integrate cognitive science, educational theory, and machine learning to tailor content to individual learner needs, thereby addressing persistent challenges related to differentiation and scalability (Koedinger et al., 2013; Holmes et al., 2022). Within smart campus frameworks—characterised by LMS–SIS interoperability, institutional analytics, and standardised learning record protocols (xAPI/LTI)—ITS operate not only as instructional tools but as strategic components supporting curricular personalisation and academic decision-making across higher education.

At a functional level, ITS emulate expert tutoring by offering real-time feedback, scaffolding, and corrective guidance. Unlike conventional computer-assisted instruction, they incorporate student modelling, pedagogical rules, and domain representations, enabling adaptive decisions about content sequencing and instructional intervention (VanLehn et al., 2005). Such systems utilise mechanisms including knowledge tracing and natural language processing to approximate one-on-one tutoring interactions with a high degree of responsiveness. The effectiveness of ITS has been demonstrated across multiple disciplines. In mathematics, tools such as Cognitive Tutor and ALEKS support mastery learning and conceptual fluency through adaptive sequencing and knowledge space theory (Falmagne et al., 2013). In physics, systems like Andes facilitate conceptual visualisation and structured problem solving (VanLehn et al., 2005). In linguistics and reading comprehension, AutoTutor employs dialogic interaction to foster interpretive reasoning (Graesser et al., 2005), while platforms such as Duolingo and TAGARELA integrate conversational practice and gamification to reinforce linguistic competence (Amaral & Meurers, 2011; Heift, 2012; Vesselinov & Grego, 2016).

Empirical studies consistently report that students using ITS achieve improved academic outcomes, including enhanced retention and performance on standardised assessments (Pane et al., 2016). Additionally, ITS have demonstrated potential for mitigating inequities by providing sustained personalised support irrespective of instructional constraints. However, important challenges persist. Increasing reliance on complex models raises concerns regarding algorithmic transparency and alignment with curricular objectives (Holmes et al., 2022). Data privacy remains critical, as ITS routinely collect granular interactional data, sometimes beyond conventional educational records (Gomes, 2025). Access disparities also limit adoption in under-resourced contexts, where infrastructural and linguistic adaptation barriers remain significant (Thuy & Tien, 2024). Moreover, ITS cannot fully replicate the affective, motivational, and relational dimensions of human teaching, necessitating hybrid instructional approaches. Recent research has begun addressing these limitations. Developments in Artificial Emotional Intelligence (AEI) seek to improve responsiveness to learners' affective states (Lin et al., 2023). Neuroadaptive systems using EEG and brain–computer interface data enable dynamic alignment with cognitive load (Pope et al., 2022). Federated learning architectures offer privacy-preserving model training across distributed environments (Yang et al., 2019). These trajectories indicate a movement toward more socially aware, ethically grounded, and adaptive ITS.

Taken together, ITS constitute a critical element of AI-mediated learning, representing a convergence of technological innovation and pedagogical refinement. Their continued evolution will depend on the extent to which they can be integrated ethically, inclusively, and coherently within institutional learning ecosystems. Accordingly, this chapter now examines their practical applications, design considerations, and challenges across varied educational contexts.

This chapter advances the central argument that Intelligent Tutoring Systems (ITS) have transitioned from isolated instructional tools to strategic components within the digital transformation of higher education. As recent developments in AI-driven personalisation, data governance, and smart campus integration demonstrate, ITS support not only individual learning pathways but also broader institutional capacities for analytics-informed decision-making (Holmes et al., 2019; Graesser et al., 2018). Their value therefore lies in enhancing curricular alignment, ethical data practices, and pedagogical coherence across entire academic ecosystems (Holmes et al., 2022). This perspective frames the subsequent analysis presented in this chapter.

2. THEORY AND DESIGN OF INTELLIGENT TUTORS

The progressive integration of Artificial Intelligence (AI) into educational environments has precipitated a significant paradigm shift in instructional design and personalised learning. Among the most transformative applications of AI are Intelligent Tutoring Systems (ITS), which aim to simulate one-on-one human tutoring by adapting instruction to the unique cognitive and affective profiles of learners. ITS are grounded in cognitive, constructivist, and sociocultural learning theories, aiming to adapt instruction to individual student needs through a continuous process of diagnosis and personalized feedback (Nkambou et al., 2010).

Intelligent Tutoring Systems are intrinsically interdisciplinary, drawing upon multiple domains of knowledge to optimise their pedagogical efficacy. The theoretical underpinnings of ITS include cognitive theory, constructivist approaches to learning, and sociocultural frameworks. These perspectives collectively inform the system's ability to diagnose student understanding, personalise content, and scaffold learning in a dynamic and interactive environment.

Cognitive theories of learning focus on the mental representations and processes involved in knowledge acquisition. Within the context of ITS, these theories inform the development of student models that track variables such as problem-solving abilities, working memory load, and metacognitive regulation (Anderson et al., 1995). The ACT-R (Adaptive Control of Thought—Rational) theory, in particular, has played a seminal role in the architecture of ITS, allowing for the simulation of how learners encode, store, and retrieve information during problem-solving tasks.

Constructivism posits that learning is an active, constructive process in which learners build new knowledge upon the foundation of previous experiences (Piaget, 1970). In ITS, this perspective is reflected in the emphasis on exploratory learning, adaptive feedback, and opportunities for self-directed inquiry. The system's design often incorporates problem-based learning scenarios and open-ended tasks that promote critical thinking and active engagement.

Vygotsky's sociocultural theory (1978) introduces the concept of learning as a socially mediated process, wherein interaction with more knowledgeable others enables learners to move through the Zone of Proximal Development (ZPD). ITS operationalise this framework by functioning as a virtual "more knowledgeable other", providing scaffolding, timely feedback, and progressive challenges to facilitate cognitive growth. This paradigm is particularly evident in systems employing conversational agents and dialogue-based tutoring, which aim to replicate the interactive nature of human instruction (Graesser et al., 2005).

A typical ITS comprises four interrelated and core components (see Figure 1): (i) the domain model, which represents the subject-specific knowledge; (ii) the student model, which monitors performance and cognitive styles; (iii) the pedagogical model, which defines adaptive instructional strategies; and (iv) the communication interface, which facilitates human-computer interaction (Nkambou et al., 2010). The integration of AI into these models has enabled the implementation of machine learning algorithms, Bayesian networks, and natural language processing to enhance the tutor's adaptability, diagnostic accuracy, and instructional autonomy (Woolf, 2010).

Figure 1. Fundamental components of a typical Intelligent Tutoring Systems (ITS).

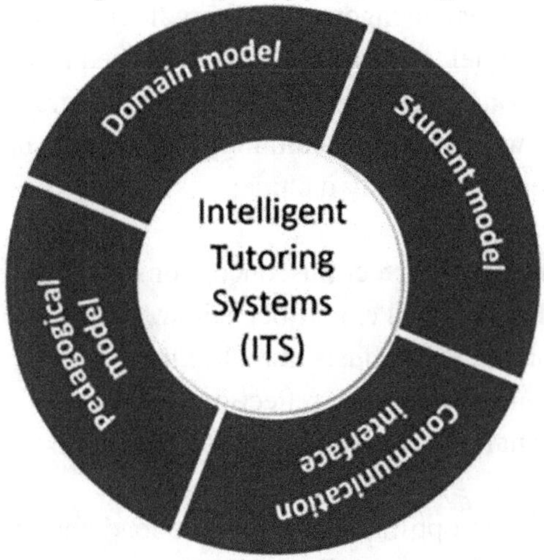

The domain model encapsulates the structured representation of knowledge within a specific subject area. This includes factual content, conceptual hierarchies, procedural steps, and problem-solving heuristics. In highly formalised domains such as mathematics or computer programming, rule-based systems—such as production rules, decision trees, and propositional logic—are commonly employed to model expertise (VanLehn, 2006). Table 1 below outlines different techniques used for domain modelling in ITS across various disciplines.

Table 1. Domain Modelling Techniques by Discipline.

Discipline	Modelling Technique	Description
Mathematics	Production Rules	If-then rules to represent procedural knowledge
Computer Science	Semantic Networks	Conceptual relations and hierarchical structures
Physics	Ontologies	Formal specification of domain concepts and relations
Language Learning	Markov Models / NLP Grammars	Probabilistic modelling of syntax and semantics

The student model is responsible for continuously monitoring the learner's knowledge state, cognitive profile, and affective responses. To achieve this, ITS employ machine learning algorithms, probabilistic inference methods, and data analytics techniques. Bayesian networks, in particular, have proven effective for modelling uncertainty in student responses and predicting misconceptions or future errors (Desmarais & Baker, 2012). Recent advancements have also integrated deep learning to assess emotional engagement and predict learning trajectories.

The pedagogical model governs the selection, sequencing, and delivery of instructional interventions. It encodes decision-making strategies regarding when to provide assistance, what form it should take, and how it should evolve based on learner feedback. Interventions may include:

- Immediate feedback to correct misconceptions.
- Worked examples to model expert behaviour.
- Dynamic scaffolding that adjusts in real time.
- Socratic questioning to provoke reflection.
- Contextualised analogies to enhance comprehension.

These strategies aim to optimise the cognitive load and maintain learner motivation across instructional sessions (Woolf, 2010).

The communication interface facilitates interaction between the learner and the system. Contemporary ITS often feature multimodal interfaces, incorporating text, speech, graphics, and even emotional recognition. Advances in natural language processing (NLP), speech synthesis, and affective computing have enabled the creation of conversational agents that can simulate human-like dialogue and facial expressions to foster a more immersive and empathetic learning environment (Graesser et al., 2005).

ITS are designed to provide personalized educational experiences through the use of artificial intelligence. These systems adapt to individual learning styles and needs, offering immediate feedback and personalized instruction. The design of an effective ITS involves several key principles that enhance the learning process (see Table 2).

Table 2. Design Principles of Intelligent Tutoring Systems (ITS).

Key principles	Description
Personalization	Intelligent Tutoring Systems (ITS) employ algorithms to adapt content based on students' prior knowledge, interests, and learning pace, thereby ensuring instruction is both relevant and effective (Marion, 2010).
Proactive Engagement	Effective ITS promote active student engagement, fostering a more immersive learning environment (Shah, 2024).
Timely Feedback	Providing immediate feedback helps students identify and correct errors in real time, thereby enhancing the overall learning experience (Abinaya et al., 2024).

continued on following page

Table 2. Continued

Key principles	Description
Transparency	Offers clear explanations for system decisions to foster trust and learner autonomy (Woolf, 2010).
Scalability	Ensures adaptability across different curricula, languages, and educational contexts (Graesser et al., 2018).

These principles are not mutually exclusive; rather, they collectively inform a coherent instructional approach that aligns with contemporary pedagogical standards.

The effective implementation of ITS involves several challenges. Developing an ITS requires sophisticated algorithms and a profound understanding of educational theories, which may pose significant technical difficulties (Graesser et al., 2018). Furthermore, a critical concern regarding scalability is ensuring the effective deployment of ITS across diverse educational settings (Graesser et al., 2018). Recent innovations in AI have substantially enhanced the functional capabilities of ITS, among the most impactful developments are:

- *Bayesian Knowledge Tracing (BKT):* Allows real-time estimation of learner mastery for individual concepts.
- *Deep Learning:* Enables emotion recognition through facial analysis and adaptive feedback through neural networks.
- *Reinforcement Learning (RL):* Optimises pedagogical decision-making through reward-based feedback loops.
- *Natural Language Understanding (NLU):* Facilitates semantic analysis of student input in open-ended tasks.

These technologies extend the system's capacity to diagnose learner needs, personalise instruction, and support complex learning objectives beyond factual recall. Despite their pedagogical potential, ITS face significant implementation barriers:

- *Technical Complexity.* Developing an ITS requires the integration of interdisciplinary knowledge from computer science, cognitive psychology, education, and linguistics. The complexity of constructing accurate domain and student models, implementing machine learning algorithms, and maintaining real-time system responsiveness presents considerable challenges for developers (Graesser et al., 2018).
- *Scalability and Transferability.* Scaling ITS to diverse educational contexts remains a critical concern. Systems developed for specific curricula or languages may not generalise well to others. This necessitates adaptive frameworks capable of localisation and cross-cultural adaptability.

- *Ethical and Pedagogical Concerns.* There are ongoing debates regarding the ethical use of learner data, transparency of decision-making algorithms, and potential overreliance on automated systems. ITS may also lack the nuanced understanding of human emotions, non-verbal cues, and complex social interactions inherent in face-to-face instruction. These limitations underscore the importance of human oversight and hybrid models that integrate both AI and human tutoring.

While ITS offer significant advantages in personalized learning, concerns remain regarding their technological dependence, which may not fully replicate the subtle interactions inherent in traditional teaching methods. This underscores the importance of balancing technological solutions with human supervision in educational contexts.

The chapter adopts an essayistic and transdisciplinary methodological orientation that synthesises insights from cognitive psychology, computer science, instructional design, and institutional governance. Such an integrative approach reflects the inherently interdisciplinary nature of ITS, which draw simultaneously on cognitive modelling, adaptive algorithms, pedagogical theory, and socio-technical considerations (Nkambou et al., 2010; Woolf, 2010). This method enables a holistic understanding of ITS implementation that extends beyond purely technical analyses.

This stance also acknowledges that the adoption of ITS involves complex cultural, ethical, and organisational dimensions. As highlighted in existing research, the institutional deployment of ITS requires alignment between technological infrastructures, teaching practices, faculty readiness, and regulatory frameworks (Holmes et al., 2019; Thuy & Tien, 2024). The chapter's methodology therefore aims to integrate empirical insights with conceptual reflection, offering a coherent and practically relevant discussion for academic, technical, and administrative stakeholders.

3. EVALUATION AND VALIDATION OF INTELLIGENT TUTORING SYSTEMS (ITS)

The evaluation and validation of Intelligent Tutoring Systems (ITS) are integral to determining their effectiveness, usability, and alignment with pedagogical objectives. These processes encompass a multidimensional assessment framework that incorporates both empirical and experiential evidence derived from a spectrum of stakeholders, including learners, educators, system developers, and educational researchers. A robust evaluation strategy not only ensures the immediate efficacy of the ITS but also supports its long-term sustainability and adaptability to dynamic learning environments. ITS evaluations are typically categorised into quantitative and qualitative approaches. Quantitative evaluations utilise rigorous experimental designs, such as randomised controlled trials (RCTs), to compare ITS-supported instruction against traditional educational methodologies. These trials often employ pre- and post-tests to measure learning gains, retention indices, and problem-solving competencies. For example, the Cognitive Tutor, widely adopted in high school algebra, demonstrated substantial improvements in student performance over standard instruction, as substantiated by Koedinger et al. (2013). Table 3 summarises essential components and outcomes of typical ITS quantitative evaluations.

Table 3. Typical ITS quantitative evaluations.

Metric	Description	Example Tool
Learning Gain	Improvement in test scores pre- and post-intervention	Cognitive Tutor
Retention Index	Percentage of retained knowledge over time	ALEKS
Error Reduction Rate	Decrease in repeated mistakes during ITS usage	CTAT
Time on Task Efficiency	Learning gains per unit of time	Andes Physics Tutor

In parallel, qualitative evaluations offer a more nuanced and context-sensitive analysis. These methods involve collecting user narratives, interpretative insights, and behavioural observations. Think-aloud protocols, in which learners verbalise their thought processes during problem-solving tasks, provide direct access to cognitive strategies employed while interacting with the ITS. Semi-structured interviews and classroom ethnographies reveal user satisfaction, emotional responses, and perceived system adaptability. Graesser et al. (2005) emphasise the role of mixed-initiative dialogue systems such as *AutoTutor* in eliciting reflective engagement, which can be documented and analysed qualitatively to assess the depth of cognitive processing.

Formative evaluation occupies a distinct position within the ITS development lifecycle. This continuous, iterative process takes place during the design and prototyping stages, allowing for real-time refinement of system components. Developers rely on log data analytics, user error trajectories, and student modelling inaccuracies to fine-tune pedagogical rules and feedback mechanisms. Such formative mechanisms are particularly crucial when adapting ITS for diverse learner populations with varying cultural, linguistic, or educational backgrounds (Nkambou et al., 2010).

Moreover, advanced ITS evaluation frameworks now incorporate adaptive performance metrics, such as normalised learning gains per instructional episode and responsiveness to learner affective states. These metrics offer more granular insights into how different learners benefit from specific ITS functionalities. Integrating adaptive analytics into evaluation protocols enhances the explanatory power of empirical findings and supports the generalisability of results across different educational settings.

Longitudinal evaluations serve to assess the enduring impact of ITS over extended periods. These studies track the progression of learners over academic terms or school years, offering insight into knowledge consolidation, academic persistence, and transfer of learning to novel contexts. Pane et al. (2016) found that consistent use of ITS platforms such as *MATHia* led to sustained academic improvement and narrowing of achievement disparities among students from socio-economically disadvantaged backgrounds.

Validation, distinct from evaluation, is primarily concerned with ensuring the internal consistency, theoretical coherence, and pedagogical alignment of ITS components. This includes validation of the domain model (accuracy of content representation), student model (correctness of learner profiling), and tutoring model (appropriateness of instructional strategies). Validation can be achieved through expert reviews, simulation modelling, and consistency checks across instructional episodes. For instance, if a student model erroneously categorises a learner's competence level, the ITS may deliver content that is either too advanced or too simplistic, thereby compromising instructional efficacy. Table 4 delineates core ITS components and corresponding validation strategies.

Table 4. ITS components and corresponding validation strategies.

ITS Component	Validation Strategy	Example Practice
Domain Model	Expert content review, cross-topic coherence checks	Alignment with national curriculum standards
Student Model	Predictive accuracy testing, user trace validation	Correlation of model predictions with assessments
Tutoring Model	Pedagogical logic auditing, adaptive rule testing	Evaluation of instructional decision trees

Additionally, usability validation assesses how intuitively learners can navigate and interact with the ITS interface. This includes screen layout, response latency, linguistic clarity, and multimedia integration. Techniques such as heuristic evaluation, usability walkthroughs, and accessibility audits ensure that the ITS is inclusive and usable across diverse learner demographics, including those with disabilities.

In the context of AI-enhanced ITS, ethical validation is emerging as an indispensable component. With increasing reliance on AI-driven decision-making, concerns regarding algorithmic fairness, data privacy, and transparency necessitate a rigorous ethical vetting process. ITS developers must ensure that learning analytics do not inadvertently reinforce bias or disadvantage certain user groups. Fairness-aware machine learning models and privacy-preserving techniques such as federated learning are being increasingly incorporated to address these concerns (Yang et al., 2019).

The evaluation and validation of Intelligent Tutoring Systems require a systematic, multilayered approach that spans empirical experimentation, qualitative inquiry, and theoretical validation. By integrating these methodologies, stakeholders can ensure that ITS not only deliver effective and personalised instruction but also uphold ethical, inclusive, and pedagogically sound standards in education.

Recent empirical research has expanded the evidence base on the effectiveness of ITS in higher education. Studies conducted in European and Latin American contexts demonstrate that ITS can improve conceptual understanding, support struggling students, and reduce performance gaps when integrated within institutional learning ecosystems (Pane et al., 2016; Graesser et al., 2018). For instance, ITS used in mathematics and engineering courses have consistently shown improvements in students' mastery of foundational concepts and in their retention and progression rates (Koedinger et al., 2013; Falmagne et al., 2013). Similar findings have been echoed in Latin American deployments, where ITS-supported modules in programming, mathematics, and language learning have yielded measurable gains in student achievement despite infrastructural limitations (Silva Cornejo et al., 2024; Díaz-Parra et al., 2018).

A growing body of evidence highlights the relevance of ITS for addressing inequalities in higher education. For example, long-term evaluations in mathematics have demonstrated that adaptive ITS such as ALEKS and Cognitive Tutor contribute to narrowing achievement disparities among socio-economically disadvantaged students (Pane et al., 2016). Research in multilingual and resource-constrained settings also suggests that ITS can offer sustained personalised support that may not otherwise be feasible due to constraints in teacher time or institutional resources (Thuy & Tien, 2024).

Meta-analytic findings further support these patterns. Reviews of ITS effectiveness consistently report medium-to-large learning gains across STEM disciplines, with stronger outcomes achieved when ITS are embedded into curricular design rather than used as optional supplements (Graesser, Hu, & Nye, 2018). These studies underscore the importance of institutionally integrated ITS strategies.

4. INSTRUCTIONAL DESIGN METHODOLOGIES FOR ITS

The instructional design methodologies employed in the development of Intelligent Tutoring Systems (ITS) must be founded upon robust pedagogical frameworks that ensure congruence among educational objectives, learner profiles, and the system's instructional architecture. In contemporary ITS development, two prevailing instructional design models are frequently operationalised: the ADDIE framework (Analyse, Design, Develop, Implement, Evaluate) and Backward Design.

Both approaches provide a structured scaffold for designing learner-centred ITS, allowing the systematic articulation of learning objectives, construction of content, integration of assessment tools, and implementation of adaptive feedback (Reiser & Dempsey, 2017).

A critical element in the instructional design of ITS is the alignment of domain knowledge representation with the pedagogical strategies employed. For instance, in mathematics-oriented ITS, instructional content is commonly disaggregated into hierarchical skill trees, which support mastery learning methodologies. This stratification allows ITS to deliver content that corresponds to the learner's evolving competence level, a principle that enhances learning efficiency and fosters meta-cognitive development. Pedagogical strategies such as the incorporation of worked examples and faded guidance are particularly effective within this context, promoting gradual autonomy by scaffolding problem-solving capabilities (VanLehn, 2006).

The theoretical foundations of adaptive scaffolding are deeply embedded in Vygotsky's (1978) concept of the Zone of Proximal Development (ZPD). ITS can dynamically diagnose a learner's ZPD through real-time data collected by the student model and use this information to adjust the instructional support accordingly. This process, termed "pedagogical intelligence," may be realised using rule-based decision engines or, increasingly, reinforcement learning algorithms. These computational strategies regulate essential instructional elements such as the timing of feedback, the progression of task complexity, and strategies for error remediation. In practical terms, this alignment is illustrated in Table 5, which maps pedagogical constructs to ITS components and instructional techniques.

Table 5. ITS components and corresponding validation strategies.

Pedagogical Construct	ITS Component	Instructional Technique
Mastery Learning	Domain Knowledge Model	Hierarchical Skill Trees
Faded Guidance	Tutoring Model	Decreasing Tutor Intervention
Zone of Proximal Development	Student Model	Adaptative Scaffolding
Formative Assessment	Feedback Engine	Real-Time Diagnostic Feedback

Moreover, the implementation phase in instructional design is particularly sensitive in ITS, requiring the seamless integration of user interface design, natural language processing modules, and intelligent agent behaviour. These components must be coherently synchronised with pedagogical intents. For instance, a system employing Socratic dialogue must ensure that its dialogue manager adheres to principles of inquiry-based learning, facilitating reflective cognition rather than didactic instruction.

Evaluation, the final phase in ADDIE and a continuous element in Backward Design, further informs the cyclical refinement of ITS. Evaluation is not confined to outcome measurement but also encompasses the assessment of instructional coherence and system usability. Feedback derived from pilot testing is instrumental in recalibrating content difficulty, modifying feedback strategies, and enhancing the personalisation engine.

Furthermore, ITS that embrace Backward Design begin with the end in mind: identifying the desired learning outcomes, determining acceptable evidence of learning, and subsequently designing learning experiences that guide learners towards those outcomes. This paradigm ensures that every instructional decision within the ITS is underpinned by explicit learning goals. Such a goal-oriented design is particularly valuable in competency-based education environments, where demonstrating mastery of specific skills is paramount.

From a technological standpoint, the implementation of such methodologies necessitates a cross-disciplinary synthesis of educational theory, computer science, and cognitive psychology. ITS design teams must operationalise abstract pedagogical constructs into computational representations, which often involves formalising learning objectives as logic constraints or decision rules that inform system behaviour.

The instructional design methodologies guiding ITS must transcend superficial technological considerations and embrace an integrative, theory-driven approach. By leveraging models such as ADDIE and Backward Design, and by grounding system functionalities in pedagogical principles such as mastery learning and the ZPD, developers can create ITS that are not only technically sophisticated but also pedagogically robust and learner-responsive.

5. INTELLIGENT TUTORING SYSTEMS IN SMART CAMPUS ECOSYSTEMS

The integration of Intelligent Tutoring Systems (ITS) within smart campus ecosystems requires conceptual and operational alignment between pedagogical objectives, institutional digital infrastructures, and governance frameworks. Smart campuses are characterised by interconnected platforms capable of collecting, exchanging, and analysing data to support decision-making across academic, administrative, and operational domains. Within this environment, ITS function not merely as isolated instructional technologies but as adaptive engines embedded in an orchestrated digital architecture that spans the entire institution.

Smart campus infrastructures typically incorporate Learning Management Systems (LMS), Student Information Systems (SIS), learning analytics platforms, digital identity management services, and secure data exchange protocols. For ITS to operate effectively, they must interoperate with these components through standardised mechanisms such as Learning Tools Interoperability (LTI), Experience API (xAPI), or institution-specific middleware services. Such interoperability ensures that ITS can access relevant data concerning learner progression, course structure, assessment contexts, and behavioural engagement patterns, allowing the system to generate accurate and context-sensitive adaptive feedback. Conversely, ITS must also return structured performance indicators to institutional data warehouses, enabling academic departments and quality assurance units to evaluate pedagogical outcomes at scale.

From an organisational standpoint, the deployment of ITS in higher education settings necessitates coordinated collaboration across academic leadership, information technology departments, curriculum committees, and teaching staff. Strategic alignment is essential to ensure that ITS functionalities reinforce curricular goals rather than operating as parallel or supplementary systems. Universities must therefore establish governance policies addressing data ownership, model transparency, and ethical oversight. These policies are crucial to mitigate risks associated with algorithmic bias, opaque decision-making processes, or disproportionate data extraction from students.

The successful implementation of ITS in smart campuses is also contingent on faculty readiness and professional development. While ITS can automate certain instructional tasks, they do not replace the cognitive, interpretative, and relational dimensions of academic practice. Instead, instructors must be equipped to interpret analytic outputs, configure adaptive pathways, and maintain pedagogical coherence. Training programmes should therefore combine technical proficiency, data literacy, and reflective pedagogical design.

Evaluation and quality assurance constitute another critical dimension. Institutions must adopt multi-level assessment frameworks that measure not only performance outcomes (e.g., grades, task completion, retention) but also equity impacts, student agency, and wellbeing indicators. Additionally, continuous monitoring mechanisms are required to detect system drift, unintended learning behaviour reinforcement, or inequitable feedback patterns across demographic groups.

Finally, the scalability and sustainability of ITS depend on financial planning and technological lifecycle management. Universities must consider licensing agreements, long-term data storage strategies, and system maintenance requirements. Cloud-based and federated learning architectures may offer advantages in terms of computational efficiency and privacy-preserving modelling, particularly in contexts where regulatory constraints prohibit the centralisation of sensitive student data. Figure 2 illustrates the proposed architectural integration of ITS within a smart campus digital ecosystem.

Figure 2. Conceptual architecture of Intelligent Tutoring Systems integrated into a smart campus ecosystem, illustrating data flows between LMS, SIS, analytics infrastructure, faculty practices, and student learning processes.

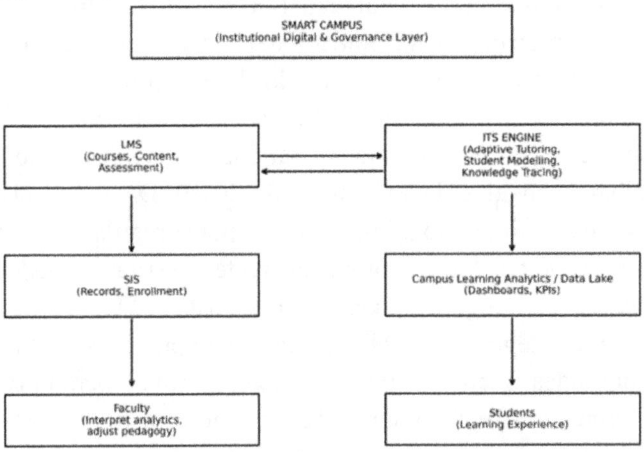

Although technical innovation often dominates discussions of ITS, financial and organisational sustainability significantly shape long-term adoption. Developing and maintaining ITS requires ongoing investment in system updates, data storage, training, and integration with LMS and analytics platforms (Woolf, 2010; Holmes et al., 2019). For institutions operating under limited budgets, particularly in Latin America and South-East Asia, these recurring costs can exceed initial deployment expenditures, reinforcing the need for scalable and cost-efficient ITS architectures (Thuy & Tien, 2024).

Cultural and organisational factors equally influence ITS adoption. Faculty resistance is common when instructors perceive ITS as prescriptive systems that infringe upon professional judgement or pedagogical autonomy (Holmes et al., 2022). Studies highlight the importance of faculty development, participatory system design, and opportunities for instructors to contextualise ITS feedback within established pedagogical frameworks (Graesser et al., 2018). In culturally diverse or multilingual environments, further adaptation may be required to ensure alignment between ITS behaviour and local educational norms (Nkambou et al., 2010).

These human and cultural considerations demonstrate that the successful institutionalisation of ITS depends on aligning technological innovations with academic traditions, teaching identities, and organisational cultures. Universities that engage faculty early and invest in pedagogical mediation tend to achieve more sustainable and meaningful adoption.

Higher education institutions must navigate complex regulatory environments governing the collection and processing of student data. Regulations such as the

European GDPR emphasise consent, purpose limitation, and the right to erasure—requirements that are directly relevant to ITS handling granular learning traces (Holmes et al., 2022). Brazil's LGPD echoes these principles and highlights transparency and user rights across Latin American contexts (Gomes, 2025). In the United States, FERPA establishes protections for educational records and defines institutional responsibilities when data are processed by third-party providers.

For ITS, compliance requires privacy-preserving data architectures, such as federated learning, which enables model training across distributed local nodes without centralising sensitive data (Yang et al., 2019). Data minimisation, strong access controls, and auditable logging further support regulatory compliance and institutional trust. Together, these approaches create governance models that protect student rights while enabling the pedagogical benefits of ITS.

In summary, the integration of ITS in smart campus ecosystems represents a multidimensional endeavour that involves technological interoperability, pedagogical coordination, administrative planning, and ethical stewardship. When implemented strategically, ITS can contribute to the development of campus-wide personalised learning infrastructures that enhance academic performance, improve student retention, and support data-informed institutional decision-making.

5.1. Ethics, Governance, and Equity

The expansion of ITS across higher education intensifies the need for strong ethical and governance frameworks. ITS routinely process highly granular learner data, including behavioural traces, performance histories, and, increasingly, affective or physiological indicators. Effective governance demands explicit institutional policies covering consent, data minimisation, retention, and user rights, aligned with recognised frameworks such as GDPR and FERPA (Holmes et al., 2022; Gomes, 2025). Technical safeguards—such as encryption, access controls, and pseudonymisation—form part of these requirements and help establish institutional trust.

Equity forms a core dimension of ethical governance. Without intentional safeguards, ITS risk perpetuating structural inequities embedded within their training data or operational logic. For example, biased models may misestimate the abilities of certain demographic groups or produce feedback that inadvertently reinforces performance disparities (Holmes et al., 2022). Fairness-aware evaluation protocols—such as demographic performance monitoring and periodic auditing of model behaviour—are increasingly recommended for mitigating such risks (Yang et al., 2019). Transparency plays a crucial role as well: learners and instructors should understand how recommendations are generated and be able to question or override system decisions.

Ethical considerations also extend to pedagogy. Researchers caution against over-reliance on automation, noting that ITS cannot replicate the full affective and relational dimensions of human tutoring (Graesser et al., 2005; Holmes et al., 2019). Governance frameworks must therefore position ITS as augmentative, not substitutive, pedagogical agents. Human–AI collaboration, where instructors interpret analytics and contextualise automated feedback, supports richer and more equitable learning experiences.

Broader socio-technical factors also influence ethical implementation. Digital inequities, infrastructural variation, and cultural expectations shape learners' ability to benefit from ITS. Institutions should therefore align ITS deployment with inclusive strategies that address connectivity gaps, promote assistive technologies, and support culturally contextualised learning (Thuy & Tien, 2024). When grounded in ethical and equity-oriented governance, ITS can strengthen institutional accountability and contribute to fairer, more transparent digital learning environments.

6. IMPLEMENTATION OF AI-POWERED INTELLIGENT TUTORING SYSTEMS

In terms of implementation, Intelligent Tutoring Systems (ITS) have evolved to become integral components of both formal and informal educational environments. These AI-powered systems utilise advanced intelligent reasoning techniques to deliver adaptive, personalised, and responsive tutoring in real time. Prominent examples that highlight the breadth and efficacy of such systems include *AutoTutor* and *Cognitive Tutor*. *AutoTutor* employs conversational agents that engage learners in natural language dialogue, thereby facilitating deep reasoning and conceptual understanding in domains such as cognitive sciences (Graesser et al., 2005). In contrast, *Cognitive Tutor*, developed by Carnegie Learning, applies cognitive modelling to mathematics instruction, effectively simulating expert problem-solving strategies to guide student learning (Koedinger et al., 2013; Koedinger et al., 2012).

The operational success of these ITS platforms underscores the profound potential of AI to enhance instructional quality, improve academic outcomes, and refine pedagogical efficiency. Through personalised interactions, students receive tailored content delivery, adaptive feedback, and scaffolded support that collectively foster cognitive development and academic progression. Various AI methodologies form the technological backbone of ITS, each serving distinct but complementary purposes in achieving educational personalisation and autonomy, these include:

- *Supervised and Unsupervised Learning:* Supervised learning algorithms, such as support vector machines and decision trees, are employed to predict academic outcomes and personalise instructional pathways based on labelled data. Unsupervised learning, including clustering and dimensionality reduction techniques, is useful for identifying latent learner profiles and grouping students according to learning behaviours and preferences (Shimasaki et al., 2024).

- *Bayesian Networks:* These probabilistic graphical models support decision-making under uncertainty, particularly within student modelling. By dynamically estimating learner knowledge states, Bayesian networks enable the generation of context-sensitive feedback and help predict future performance with substantial accuracy (Desmarais & Baker, 2012).
- *Deep Neural Networks (DNNs):* DNNs contribute to ITS functionality by recognising complex data patterns, such as those involved in emotion detection and learning behaviour classification. These capabilities allow the system to adapt its feedback and instructional strategies to the learner's affective state, thereby promoting a more empathetic and responsive educational experience (Lin et al., 2023).
- *Natural Language Processing (NLP):* NLP techniques are indispensable for parsing, interpreting, and generating human language. In ITS, NLP enables semantic understanding of student input, facilitating conversational interfaces and enabling the system to detect misconceptions, pose Socratic questions, and maintain contextual coherence during dialogue (Graesser et al., 2005).

The deployment architectures of ITS vary depending on contextual requirements and technological constraints. Traditional client-server models offer centralised control and are suitable for institutional settings. Cloud-based architectures provide scalability, ubiquitous access, and integration with distributed learning platforms. Hybrid models, incorporating elements of both paradigms, are increasingly prevalent due to their flexibility and reliability. Additionally, emerging paradigms such as edge computing reduce latency by processing data locally on learner devices, while ubiquitous computing fosters seamless integration of ITS into everyday learning environments (Holmes et al., 2019). Explainable Artificial Intelligence (XAI) has also begun to influence ITS design. XAI techniques allow for transparent system reasoning, enabling learners and educators to understand and trust the instructional decisions made by the tutor. This transparency is vital for promoting user confidence and regulatory compliance, particularly in high-stakes learning environments.

A critical aspect of ITS implementation is their integration into broader educational ecosystems. For instance, Silva Cornejo et al. (2024) present an Intelligent Tutoring System (ITS) that identifies individual learning styles through fuzzy logic and assigns personalised educational strategies, thereby optimising student retention and engagement. Effective deployment involves seamless interfacing with Learning

Management Systems (LMS), learning object repositories, and educational analytics platforms. Such integration facilitates the development of personalised pedagogical dashboards, supports longitudinal assessment of learner progression, and enables instructors to fine-tune instructional strategies based on empirical evidence (Thuy & Tien, 2024).

The disciplinary applications of ITS are broad and continually expanding (Table 6). In Science, Technology, Engineering, and Mathematics (STEM) education, ITS have demonstrated measurable improvements in students' problem-solving skills, conceptual understanding, and critical thinking capabilities (Pane et al., 2016). These systems scaffold complex problem spaces by offering stepwise guidance, immediate feedback, and adaptive hints tailored to the learner's zone of proximal development. In language learning, ITS leverage NLP and adaptive dialogue systems to enhance vocabulary acquisition, syntactic fluency, and reading comprehension.

Table 6. Application of ITS Across Educational Disciplines.

Key principles	ITS Functionality	AI Techniques Utilised
Mathematics	Stepwise problem-solving, feedback, hints	Cognitive Modelling, Supervised Learning
Science	Conceptual modelling, simulations	Bayesian Networks, Reinforcement Learning
Programming	Code analysis, syntax checking, debugging guidance	NLP, Rule-Based Systems, Deep Learning
Language Learning	Dialogue practice, reading comprehension	NLP, Sentiment Analysis, Conversational Agents
Reading Comprehension	Semantic analysis, vocabulary support	NLP, Neural Language Models

The incorporation of ITS into classroom-based and self-directed learning environments offers significant pedagogical value. Central to this is the provision of personalised, immediate feedback that not only corrects misconceptions but reinforces understanding through targeted instructional support. ITS also enable self-paced progression, accommodating diverse learner profiles and supporting educational inclusivity (Moharm, 2019).

From an administrative standpoint, ITS contribute to educational management efficiency. By automating routine instructional operations—such as grading, progress monitoring, and content sequencing—educators can devote greater attention to high-level pedagogical planning and mentorship. The real-time analytics generated by ITS provide insights into engagement, comprehension, and risk indicators, supporting data-driven academic interventions (Thuy & Tien, 2024).

However, implementation raises several ethical considerations. Data privacy represents a primary concern, as ITS systems collect extensive learner information, including performance metrics and behavioural patterns. Compliance with regulatory frameworks such as the General Data Protection Regulation (GDPR) is therefore essential (Gomes, 2025). Algorithmic bias constitutes a related challenge, given that training datasets may encode structural inequities, potentially influencing feedback or assessment outcomes. Fairness-aware machine learning, algorithmic auditing, and diverse data representation are necessary to mitigate such risks (Gomes, 2025).

Human–AI interaction dimensions must also be considered. While ITS can emulate aspects of expert tutoring, they do not fully replicate the socio-emotional nuance of human instruction. Hybrid instructional models that integrate human oversight are thus recommended to preserve affective support and relational trust.

Practical challenges persist in processing unstructured learner inputs, such as handwritten or spoken responses. Advances in computer vision, speech recognition, and unsupervised NLP continue to improve these capabilities, though further refinement is required for seamless deployment across contexts (Lin et al., 2023).

Given the evolving nature of educational environments, ITS must undergo continuous evaluation and iterative refinement informed by user feedback and empirical validation. Participatory design approaches—where educators, learners, and developers co-construct system features—enhance contextual relevance and pedagogical alignment.

Looking forward, the development of ITS will likely be shaped by converging technological and educational innovations, resulting in systems that are more adaptive, affect-sensitive, transparent, and supportive of collaborative learning. These trajectories reflect ongoing intersections between AI, cognitive science, affective computing, and multicultural education frameworks. The future trajectory of ITS will likely be shaped by several emerging trends:

- *Emotionally Intelligent Tutoring Systems:* One of the most prominent directions in the evolution of ITS is the development of emotionally intelligent tutoring systems (EITS). These systems are designed to perceive, interpret, and respond to learners' affective states, using a combination of multimodal inputs such as facial expressions, speech prosody, eye tracking, and physiological signals (D'Mello & Graesser, 2013; D'Mello & Graesser, 2023). Emotionally intelligent tutors aim to foster socio-emotional engagement, enhance motivation, and promote cognitive performance by dynamically adjusting instructional content and feedback mechanisms according to students' emotional responses. For instance, when a learner exhibits frustration or confusion—detected through lowered eye fixation stability or increased voice pitch variance—the ITS may respond by providing additional scaffolding or motivational prompts (Bosch et al., 2016). By cultivating an emotionally supportive learning environment, EITS contribute to reduced cognitive overload, higher retention, and improved learning outcomes. Moreover, these systems hold the potential to personalise learning pathways more holistically, considering not only cognitive factors but also emotional resilience and psychological readiness.

- *Multilingual and Multicultural ITS:* Global access to digital education platforms necessitates the development of ITS that can function effectively across linguistic and cultural boundaries. Multilingual and multicultural ITS (MM-ITS) are designed to accommodate a wide range of language proficiencies, cultural values, and educational traditions (Nkambou et al., 2010). This trend recognises the importance of localising content while maintaining pedagogical consistency, thereby ensuring inclusivity and equity in intelligent instruction. The development of MM-ITS is underpinned by advances in Natural Language Processing (NLP), particularly in the domains of machine translation and semantic parsing. These technologies enable systems to interpret user input and generate responses in multiple languages with contextual appropriateness. Furthermore, culturally aware pedagogical models consider dimensions such as power distance, collectivism vs. individualism, and epistemological beliefs to adapt teaching strategies accordingly (Hofstede, 2001). For example, ITS deployed in high-context cultures may prefer implicit instruction and deference to authority, whereas those in low-context cultures may adopt direct feedback and inquiry-based learning.
- *Explainable Pedagogical Agents:* Explainability in AI has emerged as a critical factor for enhancing trust, transparency, and human-AI interaction quality. In the context of ITS, explainable pedagogical agents (EPAs) are designed to articulate their instructional decisions and reasoning processes, thus promoting students' metacognitive development and self-regulated learning (Loboda et al., 2014). Unlike opaque "black box" systems, EPAs provide learners with insight into why a particular problem-solving path is recommended or why certain feedback was given, thereby demystifying the AI's internal logic. Explainability is particularly relevant in high-stakes learning environments, such as STEM education or medical training, where understanding the rationale behind procedural steps is as crucial as reaching the correct outcome. By externalising reasoning strategies, EPAs encourage learners to reflect on their own cognitive processes, recognise misconceptions, and develop transfer skills applicable to novel contexts. Techniques used to implement explainable behaviour in ITS include decision-tree visualisation, natural language rationales, and interactive question-answer dialogues (Holmes et al., 2021).

- *Collaborative Learning Support:* A significant limitation of traditional ITS lies in their primary focus on one-to-one instruction, often overlooking the social dimensions of learning. However, collaborative learning is well-supported by socio-constructivist theories, which emphasise the value of dialogue, peer feedback, and co-construction of knowledge (Vygotsky, 1978). In response, next-generation ITS are being designed to support collaborative learning environments through AI-mediated collaboration tools. These tools include intelligent group formation algorithms that pair learners based on complementary skill levels or learning styles, shared workspaces with real-time feedback, and conversational agents that scaffold group discussions by posing questions, mediating conflicts, and tracking collective progress (Dillenbourg & Fischer, 2007). Furthermore, ITS with collaborative learning functionalities may integrate voice and chat-based interfaces, virtual avatars, or immersive platforms to simulate classroom-like interactions. Collaborative ITS (C-ITS) not only facilitate academic discourse but also cultivate 21st-century skills such as teamwork, negotiation, and digital communication. Importantly, the deployment of such systems must consider interpersonal dynamics and ethical concerns, particularly in assessing individual contributions and mediating group bias.
- *Real-time personalised analytics*: Represent a pivotal advancement in the design and implementation of Intelligent Tutoring Systems (ITS), offering a dynamic interface between Educational Data Mining (EDM) and Learning Analytics (LA). The integration of these technologies allows for the continuous collection, processing, and visualisation of complex learner-generated data. Through sophisticated algorithms and adaptive frameworks, ITS can now deliver highly customised real-time dashboards that synthesise both behavioural and cognitive metrics. These dashboards not only support learners by providing immediate feedback tailored to their individual learning trajectories, but also equip instructors with actionable insights into student engagement, knowledge acquisition, and potential learning bottlenecks (Shimasaki et al., 2024). Such systems facilitate just-in-time pedagogical interventions, enabling educators to implement timely instructional adjustments that correspond with the evolving needs of students. Furthermore, these analytics tools contribute to the formulation of evidence-based teaching strategies by uncovering patterns within large datasets, thus enhancing long-term instructional planning. The integration of real-time personalised analytics into ITS signifies a paradigm shift from reactive to proactive educational practices, wherein decision-making is continuously informed by data-driven indicators of learner progress and performance. This evolution underscores the transfor-

mative potential of AI in fostering more responsive, equitable, and efficient learning environments.

Table 7 provides a summary of the emerging trends and their key characteristics in the future development of ITS.

Table 7. Emerging Trends in the Development of Intelligent Tutoring Systems.

Trend	Core Features	Potential Benefits
Emotionally Intelligent Tutors	Affective state detection via multimodal signals (e.g., facial expressions, voice tone)	Increased engagement, reduced cognitive overload, personalised support
Multilingual and Multicultural ITS	NLP-powered language adaptability, culturally responsive pedagogical strategies	Global accessibility, culturally relevant instruction
Explainable Pedagogical Agents	AI reasoning transparency, natural language explanations, metacognitive prompts	Improved trust, enhanced self-regulation, deeper understanding
Collaborative Learning Support	AI-mediated peer collaboration tools, intelligent group formation, shared digital environments	Development of social skills, co-construction of knowledge
Real-Time Personalised Analytics	Dynamic data integration, customised dashboards, adaptive feedback mechanisms, predictive modelling and interoperability with learning tools	Enhanced learner support, informed instructional decisions, improved engagement and motivation, timely interventions and strategic planning

As these advanced functionalities become more widespread, it is crucial that their implementation be grounded in evidence-based pedagogical theory and rigorous empirical evaluation. The convergence of affective computing, multilingual NLP, explainable AI, and collaborative learning technologies represents a significant paradigm shift in the design of ITS. Nevertheless, challenges such as computational complexity, ethical governance, cross-cultural validation, and digital equity must be addressed to ensure the responsible and effective deployment of such systems. Future ITS will likely evolve into hybrid learning ecosystems—combining real-time data analytics, cross-platform interoperability, and dynamic pedagogical agents capable of orchestrating both individual and group-based learning. This trajectory promises not only improved academic achievement but also more inclusive and human-centred educational experiences.

The implementation of AI-powered Intelligent Tutoring Systems represents a transformative development in contemporary education. By harnessing the capabilities of AI, ITS can deliver personalised, scalable, and data-informed instruction that meets the diverse needs of modern learners. Nevertheless, realising the full potential of these systems requires rigorous attention to ethical standards, continuous innovation in AI technologies, and sustained collaboration among educators, technologists, and policymakers.

Despite advances in adaptive personalisation, many ITS still lack features that ensure full accessibility for students with disabilities. Issues such as inaccessible interfaces, fixed visual layouts, and limited multimodal interaction impede participation for learners with visual impairments, dyslexia, or motor disabilities. Incorporating principles of Universal Design for Learning—such as flexible presentation formats, screen-reader compatibility, and alternative input methods—can significantly enhance accessibility (Woolf, 2010). Yet such considerations are inconsistently implemented across ITS.

Multilingual contexts pose additional challenges for ITS built primarily for English-speaking environments. Natural language processing models often perform less accurately with under-resourced or indigenous languages, leading to misinterpretations or reduced diagnostic precision (Amaral & Meurers, 2011; Díaz-Parra et al., 2018). Research in culturally specific ITS design demonstrates that localising content and incorporating culturally congruent pedagogical strategies enhances both equity and learning outcomes (Hofstede, 2001; Nkambou et al., 2010).

Expanding accessibility and linguistic inclusiveness is therefore essential not only for ethical reasons but also for enabling ITS to scale effectively in global and diverse educational contexts.

7. PRACTICAL APPLICATIONS IN VARIOUS SUBJECTS

Systems such as *Cognitive Tutor* and *ALEKS* have demonstrated significant efficacy in enhancing student achievement, particularly in domains requiring logical reasoning and procedural fluency, such as mathematics. *Cognitive Tutor*, grounded in the ACT-R (Adaptive Control of Thought-Rational) cognitive architecture, models student thought processes through production rules that mirror expert problem-solving sequences (Koedinger et al., 2013). By doing so, the system personalises learning experiences by adjusting problem difficulty and providing step-by-step feedback in real-time. *ALEKS* (Assessment and Learning in Knowledge Spaces), on the other hand, employs Knowledge Space Theory to diagnose student knowledge states and construct tailored learning paths, enhancing both mastery and retention through adaptive sequencing (Falmagne et al., 2013).

In physics education, the *Andes Physics Tutor* has been recognised for its capacity to foster conceptual understanding and procedural skill acquisition. It integrates symbolic modelling, interactive simulations, and intelligent feedback mechanisms that allow learners to visualise and manipulate physical phenomena such as Newtonian mechanics and conservation of energy in meaningful contexts (VanLehn et al.,

2005). The immediate error diagnosis and correction features promote metacognitive reflection, enabling students to revise their misconceptions efficiently.

Reading comprehension has also benefitted from ITS development, notably through *AutoTutor*. This system engages students in mixed-initiative dialogue employing advanced Natural Language Processing (NLP) to stimulate cognitive processes such as inference generation, causal reasoning, and elaborative interrogation (Graesser et al., 2005). By emulating human-like conversational dynamics, *AutoTutor* encourages deeper comprehension and knowledge construction beyond surface-level reading.

In the domain of computer science, intelligent tutoring systems such as *CodeTutor* and *CTAT* (Cognitive Tutor Authoring Tools) facilitate programming instruction by dynamically assessing student code, suggesting logic improvements, and adapting task complexity to match student proficiency. These systems support syntax correction, logic validation, and debugging practice, all of which are pivotal in the acquisition of programming competence (Anderson et al., 1995). By offering contextualised support during code-writing tasks, they help bridge the gap between theoretical knowledge and practical implementation. Table 8 illustrates the comparative features and subject-specific affordances of major ITS platforms.

Table 8. Main ITS platforms.

ITS System	Subject Area	Key Feaures	Pedagogical Model
Cognitive Tutor	Mathematics	ACT-R modelling, adaptive sequencing, real-time feedback	Cognitive Apprenticeship
ALEKS	Mathematics	Knowledge Space Theory, mastery-based progression	Mastery Learning
Andes Physics Tutor	Physics	Symbolic modelling, interactive simulations, feedback	Scaffolded Problem Solving
AutoTutor	Reading Comprehension	NLP dialogues, elaboration prompts, inference support	Socratic Dialogue
CodeTutor/CTAT	Programming	Code analysis, logic feedback, adaptive tasks	Constructivist Learning

Beyond traditional academic domains, ITS have also considerably influenced language learning. Duolingo, although not a classical ITS, incorporates immediate corrective feedback, adaptive sequencing, and gamified reinforcement aligned with spaced repetition and self-determination principles, contributing to its global uptake (Vesselinov & Grego, 2016). More advanced platforms such as TAGARELA employ dialogue-based interaction for Portuguese language acquisition, utilising NLP to provide syntactic and semantic feedback (Amaral & Meurers, 2011; Heift, 2012). Similarly, Díaz-Parra et al. (2018) developed an ITS for Otomí, demonstrating the applicability of ITS in supporting underrepresented and indigenous linguistic contexts.

Longitudinal findings consistently show positive academic effects. Pane et al. (2016) report that learners using mathematics-focused ITS experience sustained improvements in performance, concept retention, and reduced achievement gaps. These gains are largely attributed to adaptive pacing and error-responsive feedback mechanisms inherent to ITS.

However, integrating ITS into educational systems presents several challenges. Algorithmic transparency is central, particularly as ITS increasingly adopt complex and less interpretable AI architectures. Educators must be able to understand and evaluate system-generated decisions to maintain alignment with curricular and ethical standards (Holmes et al., 2022). Data privacy concerns are also prominent, as ITS collect granular behavioural and performance data; inadequate encryption or anonymisation may lead to misuse or security breaches (Gomes, 2025).

Equitable access remains a structural concern, as deployment is hindered by disparities in digital infrastructure, connectivity, and user competencies, particularly in under-resourced regions. Addressing this requires coordinated content localisation, teacher training, and inclusive technology distribution strategies (Thuy & Tien, 2024). Additionally, the interpretability of system-generated learner diagnoses necessitates transparency and mechanisms for human verification to prevent misleading interventions.

Concerns regarding the potential dehumanisation of learning have prompted advocacy for hybrid instructional models in which ITS augment rather than replace human pedagogical roles, thereby preserving socio-emotional support (Holmes et al., 2022).

Emerging research is advancing solutions to these limitations. Artificial Emotional Intelligence (AEI) seeks to detect and respond to affective states through multimodal cues, thereby enhancing motivational regulation (Lin et al., 2023). Neurotechnologies such as BCIs, EEG, and fNIRS are being explored to enable neuroadaptive instruction aligned with cognitive workload and engagement (Pope et al., 2022). Federated Learning offers privacy-preserving distributed model training while supporting broader contextual generalisation (Yang et al., 2019). Meanwhile, multi-agent collaborative tutors introduce group-based AI-mediated learning to foster social interaction and teamwork capabilities (Dillenbourg & Fischer, 2007). Table 9 summarises these principal emerging trends.

Table 9. Key emerging directions to ITS advancement.

Research Area	Technological Focus	Educational Implications
Artificial Emotional Intelligence	Affective sensing, emotional feedback	Motivation enhancement, emotional regulation
Neurotechnologies	EEG, BCIs, neuroadaptive models	Cognitive workload tracking, engagement monitoring
Federated Learning	Decentralised AI, edge computing	Data privacy, scalability, contextual adaptation
Multi-Agent Collaboration	Group modelling, role assignment, dialogue support	Peer learning, teamwork skill development

The practical applications of Intelligent Tutoring Systems span a wide range of disciplines, pedagogical models, and technological architectures. While their transformative potential is evident in empirical research and classroom implementation, their success depends on careful consideration of ethical, technical, and pedagogical dimensions. Future research should prioritise transparency, inclusivity, and human-centred design to ensure that ITS fulfil their promise as catalysts for equitable and personalised education. These innovative tools applied in educational contexts pose significant challenges, such as algorithmic transparency, student data privacy, equitable access to technology, and interpretability of the diagnoses generated by ITS. Moreover, there is a risk of dehumanizing the educational process if AI interventions are not balanced with human pedagogical guidance (Holmes et al., 2022). The incorporation of artificial emotional intelligence, neurotechnologies, federated learning, and multi-agent collaborative tutors constitute the main emerging research directions derived from intelligent systems. These innovations could enhance learning personalization and broaden the spectrum of competencies that can be developed through educational AI.

Implementing ITS in resource-constrained settings highlights the importance of context-sensitive system design. Many institutions in Latin America, Africa, and South-East Asia face infrastructural limitations such as intermittent connectivity or limited device availability. Research emphasises the value of lightweight, mobile-oriented, and offline-capable ITS architectures that can operate under such conditions (Thuy & Tien, 2024). Open-source tools further reduce costs and support local adaptation.

Cultural factors also play a key role. ITS deployed in multilingual or collectivist educational cultures must align with local pedagogical norms to achieve acceptance and meaningful use (Hofstede, 2001; Amaral & Meurers, 2011). Evidence from Latin American implementations shows stronger uptake when instructors participate in interpreting analytics and co-designing system behaviour (Silva Cornejo et al., 2024).

Addressing these contextual factors strengthens the equity and sustainability of ITS implementations and supports inclusive digital transformation.

8. TECHNICAL LIMITATIONS AND EMERGING SOLUTIONS

Intelligent Tutoring Systems (ITS) represent a confluence of pedagogical theory, artificial intelligence, and human-computer interaction. However, despite their transformative potential, several technical limitations persist that hinder their universal adoption and functional optimisation. Foremost among these challenges is the accurate and dynamic modelling of learner states, particularly those encompassing affective and metacognitive dimensions. Historically, ITS have predominantly centred on cognitive parameters such as problem-solving accuracy and response latency. Nonetheless, contemporary learning science increasingly underscores the pivotal role of emotion, motivation, and self-regulation in effective learning (D'Mello & Graesser, 2013; D'Mello & Graesser, 2023). To address this, modern ITS are beginning to incorporate multimodal data streams—including facial expression analysis, galvanic skin response, pupil dilation, speech prosody, and keystroke dynamics—as indicators of affective and motivational states. The integration of such multimodal affective computing methodologies enables more comprehensive and context-sensitive learner modelling. However, implementing such systems poses significant computational and ethical challenges, such as data fusion complexity, noise filtering, and ensuring user privacy.

A concomitant challenge is the interpretability of machine learning models within ITS architectures. While deep learning techniques such as convolutional and recurrent neural networks offer superior performance in modelling complex behavioural data, their black-box nature impedes human interpretability. This opacity is particularly problematic in educational settings where transparency is critical for fostering trust among stakeholders, including learners, educators, and administrators. The field of Explainable Artificial Intelligence (XAI) has emerged to mitigate these concerns by designing algorithms that can justify their outputs through human-understandable logic or visualisation techniques (Holmes et al., 2019). In practice, XAI principles are being applied in ITS to generate real-time pedagogical explanations. For instance, an ITS may inform a learner that a particular exercise was selected based on their historical performance trends and recent error patterns. Such transparency not only improves user trust but also enhances metacognitive awareness and engagement. Nevertheless, achieving a balance between model complexity and explainability remains a non-trivial technical concern, often necessitating hybrid approaches that combine interpretable rule-based systems with more complex statistical models.

Another significant limitation pertains to the scalability and interoperability of ITS. Many existing ITS are monolithic applications developed for isolated use cases, thereby lacking the flexibility to integrate into broader educational ecosystems. This restricts their adoption in institutional contexts that depend on interconnected platforms such as Learning Management Systems (LMS) and Student Information Systems (SIS). Furthermore, the lack of standardised data formats impedes the consolidation and comparative analysis of learner data across platforms. Emerging technological standards such as the Experience API (xAPI) and Learning Tools Interoperability (LTI) have been proposed as solutions to enhance the integrative capacity of ITS. xAPI facilitates the collection of learner activity data across multiple platforms and devices, while LTI enables seamless communication between ITS modules and LMS environments. Table 10 outlines how these emerging standards contribute to resolving key integration challenges in ITS.

Table 10. Contribution of emerging standards to ITS integration challenges.

Technical Challenge	Standard or Solution	Functional Contribution
Cross-platform data tracking	xAPI	Captures learner actions across diverse learning tools
Interoperability with LMS	LTI	Enables integration of ITS into institutional LMS
Modular system deployment	Microservices	Allows scalable, decoupled ITS architecture
Secure learner data exchange	OAuth 2.0	Ensures authentication and data protection

Ethical and regulatory constraints present a growing concern in the development and deployment of ITS. The increased reliance on data-driven personalisation raises pressing issues related to data privacy, algorithmic bias, and consent. For example, an ITS that adapts instruction based on demographic inferences may inadvertently perpetuate stereotypes or disadvantage certain learner groups. To mitigate these risks, fairness-aware algorithms and privacy-preserving machine learning techniques, such as differential privacy and federated learning, are gaining traction. These innovations ensure that user data remains decentralised and anonymised while still enabling robust system performance.

While ITS have made significant strides in intelligent personalisation and automated pedagogy, several technical limitations continue to constrain their full potential. Through the incorporation of affective computing, explainable AI, interoperability standards, and ethical safeguards, the field is actively progressing towards more resilient, trustworthy, and scalable ITS architectures.

9. ETHICAL AND PEDAGOGICAL CONSIDERATIONS

The deployment of Intelligent Tutoring Systems (ITS) necessitates a rigorous engagement with ethical and pedagogical principles to ensure that their integration into educational environments is both responsible and efficacious. A central ethical concern revolves around the collection, storage, and utilisation of learner data. Given that ITS routinely gather extensive datasets that may include behavioural logs, affective indicators, interaction histories, and increasingly, biometric signals such as facial expressions or galvanic skin response, there is an imperative need for robust data governance. Adherence to data protection frameworks such as the General Data Protection Regulation (GDPR) must be considered foundational, and technical mechanisms including encryption, pseudonymisation, and controlled access protocols must be standard practice (Gomes, 2025).

Transparency in algorithmic decision-making is equally critical. Learners and educators should be afforded clear, comprehensible explanations for instructional decisions rendered by the system, such as task sequencing or feedback provision. The emergent domain of Explainable Artificial Intelligence (XAI) provides frameworks for enhancing this transparency, promoting both system trustworthiness and pedagogical insight. However, many current ITS rely on opaque models, such as deep learning architectures, which complicate interpretability. This epistemological opacity presents not merely technical but also ethical implications, particularly where ITS influence learner progression or assessment (Holmes et al., 2019).

A related ethical issue is the mitigation of algorithmic bias. ITS that are trained on datasets that lack demographic or cognitive diversity may inadvertently disadvantage learners from underrepresented or marginalised groups. This bias can manifest in the form of inaccurate student models, inequitable task recommendations, or skewed performance assessments. Mitigating such risks requires proactive bias audits, inclusive dataset curation, and the use of fairness-aware machine learning algorithms that promote equity in system behaviour (Thuy & Tien, 2024). Table 11 outlines the principal ethical challenges in ITS and corresponding mitigation strategies:

Table 11. Main ethical challenges in ITS.

Ethical Challenge	Mitigation Strategy	Implementation Mechanism
Data Privacy	Encryption, Pseudonymisation	GDPR Compliance, Secure Databases
Algorithmic Opacity	Explainable AI	Decision Tree Surrogates, Visual Justifiers
Algorithmic Bias	Fairness-aware Algorithms, Inclusive Datasets	Bias Audits, Demographic Balancing
Consent and Autonomy	Transparent User Agreements	Opt-in Protocols, Usage Notifications

From a pedagogical standpoint, the role of ITS must be contextualised within a broader educational philosophy. While ITS excel at delivering personalised and adaptive instruction, they must not supplant the irreplaceable affective, social, and cultural roles played by human educators. Over-reliance on automation risks engendering reductive models of learning that undervalue collaboration, dialogue, and teacher empathy. Consequently, a hybrid instructional paradigm is advocated, wherein ITS serve as augmentative tools rather than replacements for teachers. Such blended learning models facilitate both instructional scalability and socio-emotional depth (Holmes et al., 2019).

Furthermore, pedagogical integrity demands that ITS promote not only content mastery but also critical thinking, creativity, and learner agency. The risk of excessive system control or directive feedback can suppress metacognitive growth and learner autonomy. Designing ITS that foster exploratory learning environments, scaffold inquiry-based tasks, and support reflective practices is essential. This pedagogical balance requires deliberate calibration of feedback timing, error remediation, and learning pathway flexibility.

In parallel, the ethical deployment of ITS should include provisions for accessibility. Learners with disabilities or special educational needs must be able to interact with ITS through inclusive design principles, such as screen reader compatibility, multimodal input options, and customisable user interfaces. Universal Design for Learning (UDL) frameworks provide a valuable reference for ensuring accessibility in ITS architecture.

Ethical and pedagogical considerations are not peripheral but integral to the responsible development and deployment of ITS. Ensuring data privacy, reducing algorithmic bias, maintaining transparency, and safeguarding pedagogical richness are all critical for the sustainable integration of ITS into educational ecosystems.

10. FUTURE DIRECTIONS FOR EMPIRICAL RESEARCH

Future research on ITS must address several unresolved questions. First, there is a need for longitudinal studies examining how ITS influence academic persistence, degree progression, and long-term learning outcomes. Current research predominantly focuses on short-term performance gains (Pane et al., 2016), leaving open questions about sustained impact and transfer.

Second, further empirical investigation is required to understand how ITS function across culturally diverse learning environments. Much of the current evidence originates from Anglophone institutions, even though ITS adoption is rapidly expanding globally (Nkambou et al., 2010; Díaz-Parra et al., 2018). Studies should explore multilingual classrooms, indigenous contexts, and culturally grounded pedagogical expectations.

Third, systematic evaluation of equity remains essential. Issues such as algorithmic bias and differential system accuracy across demographic groups remain under-studied (Holmes et al., 2022). Empirical methodologies capable of comparing system performance across diverse populations would help inform fairness-aware ITS design.

Fourth, human–AI collaboration requires deeper examination. Instructors' interpretations of, and responses to, system feedback shape the pedagogical effectiveness of ITS (Graesser et al., 2018). Research should analyse instructional orchestration, professional identity, and pedagogical trust.

Fifth, more studies are needed on ITS in low-resource educational settings, where infrastructural and organisational constraints differ markedly from those underlying most ITS designs (Thuy & Tien, 2024).

Finally, emerging technologies such as neuroadaptive systems, multimodal affective sensing, and multi-agent collaborative tutors must be evaluated rigorously to ensure their pedagogical and ethical viability (D'Mello & Graesser, 2013; Pope et al., 2022).

CONCLUSIONS

Intelligent Tutoring Systems (ITS), grounded in the advances of Artificial Intelligence, represent a substantial transformation in contemporary educational paradigms by offering highly personalized and adaptive learning experiences based on real-time data analytics. Furthermore, ITS constitute one of the most promising applications of AI in the educational field. Their ability to personalize learning, adapt instruction in real time, and simulate expert intervention renders them essential tools for transforming twenty-first-century education.

The complex architecture of ITS—which integrates domain, student, pedagogical, and interface models—enables the effective emulation of expert human instruction through machine learning algorithms, Bayesian networks, and natural language processing. This technical sophistication, aligned with solid theoretical foundations in cognitive science, constructivism, and sociocultural theory, has proven effective in improving academic performance across various subjects, particularly in STEM areas, reading, and foreign languages.

Despite their numerous benefits, the implementation of ITS faces significant technical, ethical, and pedagogical challenges. Among these are the management of data privacy, mitigation of algorithmic bias, the need to ensure transparency in educational diagnostics, and the importance of maintaining a balance between automated tutoring and human pedagogical interaction.

Future development directions, such as the integration of artificial emotional intelligence, neurotechnologies, and collaborative multi-agent models, open new possibilities for enhancing learning personalization and fostering complex competencies. In this regard, ITS are not merely technological tools for instructional support but constitute a fundamental axis in the evolution toward a more equitable, efficient, and student-centered education in the digital age.

Short-term developments in ITS are likely to include wider use of explainable pedagogical agents and real-time adaptive analytics, which support learner self-regulation and provide instructors with clearer interpretative insights (Holmes et al., 2019). Medium-term innovations are expected to involve federated learning and privacy-preserving modelling that align with evolving data governance frameworks (Yang et al., 2019). Emotionally intelligent tutors, leveraging advances in affective computing, are also likely to mature, building on foundational work in multimodal emotion recognition (D'Mello & Graesser, 2013).

Long-term trends may include neuroadaptive systems capable of responding to cognitive load or attentional shifts through physiological inputs (Pope et al., 2022). Collaborative ITS represent another significant frontier, supporting group learning and team-based problem-solving through AI-mediated coordination (Dillenbourg & Fischer, 2007).

These trajectories illustrate a broader shift toward increasingly adaptive, transparent, and learner-centred ITS, where technological sophistication is supported by robust ethical governance and sustained empirical evaluation.

REFERENCES

Abinaya, S., Alphonse, A. S., Indira, K., & Lavanya, R. (2024). Chapter 11. Intelligent Tutoring Systems: AI-Based Tools for Individualized Instruction. In Adopting Artificial Intelligence Tools in Higher Education (pp. 226–250). CRC Press. DOI: 10.1201/9781003469315-11

Amaral, L. A., & Meurers, D. (2011). On using intelligent computer-assisted language learning in real-life foreign language teaching and learning. *ReCALL, 23*(1), 4–24. DOI: 10.1017/S0958344010000261

Anderson, J. R., Corbett, A. T., Koedinger, K. R., & Pelletier, R. (1995). Cognitive tutors: Lessons learned. *Journal of the Learning Sciences*, *4*(2), 167–207. DOI: 10.1207/s15327809jls0402_2

Bosch, N., Chen, Y., & D'Mello, S. (2016). It's written on your face: Detecting affective states from facial expressions while learning computer programming. *Proceedings of the International Conference on Educational Data Mining (EDM)*, 86–93.

D'Mello, S. K., & Graesser, A. C. (2013). AutoTutor and affective autotutor: Learning by talking with cognitively and emotionally intelligent computers that talk back. [TiiS]. *ACM Transactions on Interactive Intelligent Systems*, *2*(4), 1–39. DOI: 10.1145/2395123.2395128

D'Mello, S. K., & Graesser, A. C. (2023). *Intelligent tutoring systems: How computers achieve learning gains that rival human tutors. Handbook of educational psychology*. Routledge.

Desmarais, M. C., & Baker, R. S. (2012). A review of recent advances in learner and skill modelling in intelligent learning environments. *User Modeling and User-Adapted Interaction*, *22*(1–2), 9–38. DOI: 10.1007/s11257-011-9106-8

Díaz-Parra, O., Fuentes-Penna, A., Ruiz-Jaimes, M. A., Toledo-Navarro, Y., Lezama-León, M., & Lezama-León, E. (2018). Intelligent Tutor System for the Learning of Otomí Language. *International Journal of Combinatorial Optimization Problems and Informatics*, *9*(3), 18–25.

Dillenbourg, P., & Fischer, F. (2007). Basics of computer-supported collaborative learning. Zeitschrift für Berufs- und Wirtschaftspädagogik, 101(4), 111–130.

Falmagne, J. C., Albert, D., Davey, B., & Schmidt, S. (2013). *Knowledge Spaces: Applications in Education*. Springer. DOI: 10.1007/978-3-642-35329-1

Gomes, D. (2025). A Comprehensive Study of Advancements in Intelligent Tutoring Systems Through Artificial Intelligent Education Platforms. In Moreira, F., & Teles, R. (Eds.), *Improving Student Assessment with Emerging AI Tools* (pp. 213–244). IGI Global Scientific Publishing., DOI: 10.4018/979-8-3693-6170-2.ch008

Graesser, A. C., Chipman, P., Haynes, B. C., & Olney, A. (2005). AutoTutor: An intelligent tutoring system with mixed-initiative dialogue. *IEEE Transactions on Education*, *48*(4), 612–618. DOI: 10.1109/TE.2005.856149

Graesser, A. C., Hu, X., & Nye, B. (2018). Intelligent tutoring systems. In *Handbook of research on educational communications and technology* (pp. 525–544). Springer.

Graesser, A. C., Hu, X., & Sottilare, R. A. (2018). Intelligent Tutoring Systems. In Intelligent Tutoring Systems (pp. 246–255). Routledge. DOI: 10.4324/9781315617572-24

Graesser, A. C., Vanlehn, K., Roy, D., Baker, R. S. J. D., & D'Mello, S. K. (2005). AutoTutor: A tutor with dialogue in natural language. *Behavior Research Methods*, *37*(2), 180–192. PMID: 15354683

Heift, T. (2012). Intelligent Computer-Assisted Language Learning. In Chapelle, C. A. (Ed.), *The Encyclopedia of Applied Linguistics*., DOI: 10.1002/9781405198431.wbeal0548

Hofstede, G. (2001). *Culture's consequences: Comparing values, behaviours, institutions and organizations across nations* (2nd ed.). Sage Publications.

Holmes, W., Bialik, M., & Fadel, C. (2019). *Artificial Intelligence in education: Promises and implications for teaching and learning*. Center for Curriculum Redesign.

Holmes, W., Porayska-Pomsta, K., Holstein, K., Sutherland, E., Baker, T., & Santos, O. C. (2021). Ethics of AI in education: Towards a community-wide framework. *International Journal of Artificial Intelligence in Education*, *31*, 556–578. DOI: 10.1007/s40593-021-00239-1

Holmes, W., Porayska-Pomsta, K., Holstein, K., Sutherland, E., Baker, T., Shum, S. B., Santos, O. C., Rodrigo, M. T., Cukurova, M., Bittencourt, I. I., & Koedinger, K. R. (2022). Ethics of AI in education: Towards a community-wide framework. *International Journal of Artificial Intelligence in Education*, *32*(2), 346–370. DOI: 10.1007/s40593-021-00239-1

Koedinger, K. R., Corbett, A. T., & Lindsey, R. V. (2013). Cognitive Tutors: Technology bringing learning science to the classroom. In Sawyer, R. K. (Ed.), *The Cambridge handbook of the learning sciences* (2nd ed., pp. 61–78). Cambridge University Press.

Koedinger, K. R., Corbett, A. T., & Perfetti, C. (2012). The Knowledge-Learning-Instruction framework: Bridging the science-practice divide to enhance robust student learning. *Cognitive Science*, *36*(5), 757–798. DOI: 10.1111/j.1551-6709.2012.01245.x PMID: 22486653

Lin, Y., Luo, Q., & Qian, Y. (2023). *Investigation of Artificial Intelligence algorithms in education.* Applied and Computational Engineering., DOI: 10.54254/2755-2721/16/20230886

Loboda, T. D., Brusilovsky, P., & Tarakanov, D. (2014). On the cross-system use of open learner models. *International Journal of Artificial Intelligence in Education*, *24*(1), 1–28. DOI: 10.1007/s40593-013-0013-2

Nkambou, R., Mizoguchi, R., & Bourdeau, J. (2010). *Advances in Intelligent Tutoring Systems*. Springer. DOI: 10.1007/978-3-642-14363-2

Pane, J. F., Griffin, B. A., McCaffrey, D. F., & Karam, R. (2016). Effectiveness of Cognitive Tutor Algebra I at Scale. *Educational Evaluation and Policy Analysis*, *36*(2), 127–144. DOI: 10.3102/0162373713507480

Piaget, J. (1970). *The science of education and the psychology of the child*. Viking Press.

Reiser, R. A., & Dempsey, J. V. (2017). *Trends and issues in instructional design and technology* (4th ed.). Pearson.

Shah, T. J. (2024). AI-Powered Personalised Learning Plans for Intelligent Tutoring Systems. *International Journal for Research in Applied Science and Engineering Technology*, *12*(5), 5450–5462. DOI: 10.22214/ijraset.2024.62879

Shimasaki, R., Fernandes, F. N., Castellani, A. M., & Prado, M. E. B. B. (2024). Uso de Inteligência Artificial em Sistemas de Tutores Inteligentes. Revista de Ensino, Educação e Ciências Humanas, [S. l.], v. 24, n. 4, p. 507–512. DOI: DOI: 10.17921/2447-8733.2023v24n4p507-512

Silva Cornejo, A. A., Vargas Requena, D. T., Huerta Mendoza, J. C., Martínez Rodríguez, J. L., & Rodríguez-Rodríguez, W. E. (2024). An Intelligent Tutoring System for Identification of Learning Styles and Assignment Educational Strategies. *International Journal of Combinatorial Optimization Problems and Informatics*, *15*(1), 62–75. DOI: 10.61467/2007.1558.2024.v15i1.422

Thuy, P. B., & Tien, P. D. (2024). AI-Powered Administration: The Role of Intelligent Tutoring Systems in Education. *International Journal of Religion*, *5*(10), 4560–4569. DOI: 10.61707/sqwrjn32

Vanlehn, K. (2006). The Behavior of Tutoring Systems. *International Journal of Artificial Intelligence in Education, 16*(3), 227–265. DOI: 10.3233/IRG-2006-16(3)02

Vanlehn, K., Lynch, C., Schulze, K., Shapiro, J. A., Shepherd, D., & Tuttle, M. (2005). The Andes Physics Tutoring System: Lessons learned. *International Journal of Artificial Intelligence in Education, 15*(3), 147–204. DOI: 10.3233/IRG-2005-15(3)02

Vesselinov, R., & Grego, J. (2016). *Duolingo effectiveness study*. City University of New York.

Vygotsky, L. S. (1978). *Mind in society: The development of higher psychological processes*. Harvard University Press.

Woolf, B. P. (2010). *Building intelligent interactive tutors: Student-centered strategies for revolutionizing E-learning*. Morgan Kaufmann.

Yang, Q., Liu, Y., Chen, T., & Tong, Y. (2019). Federated Machine Learning: Concept and Applications. *ACM Transactions on Intelligent Systems and Technology, 10*(2), 12. DOI: 10.1145/3298981

Chapter 10
Pedagogically Intelligent Smart Campuses for AI-Mediated and Equity-Centered Knowledge Production:
Immersive Cognition in Higher Education Ecosystems

Ashraf Alam
https://orcid.org/0000-0001-6178-1187
Alliance University, Bengaluru, India

ABSTRACT

This chapter re-theorises the smart campus as a socio-technical learning ecology where pedagogical intelligence, rather than technological fetishism, becomes the primary optimisation criterion. Integrating learning sciences, embodied cognition, socio-technical systems, and intersectional sustainability, the chapter articulates an integrated framework for AI-mediated, equity-centred knowledge production in higher education. It systematically maps immersive, HyFlex, and AI-supported mastery designs onto XR infrastructures, analytics ecosystems, and living-lab configurations, while interrogating epistemic justice, decoloniality, and digital rights. By modelling stakeholders as a polycentric governance network, it specifies risk architectures and capacity-building ecologies that align algorithmic systems with care, autonomy, and planetary responsibility. The chapter concludes by advanc-

DOI: 10.4018/979-8-3373-6831-3.ch010

2026, IGI Global Scientific Publishing. Copying or distributing in print or electronic forms without written permission of IGI Global Scientific Publishing is prohibited. Use of this chapter to ative artificial intelligence (AI) technologies is expressly prohibited. The publisher reserves all rights to license its use for generative AI training and machine learning model development.

ing justice-oriented design heuristics and a research agenda that positions smart campuses as reflexive, pluriversal sites of immersive cognition and regenerative institutional transformation.

1. INTRODUCTION

1.1 Framing the Problem

Contemporary discourses on *digital transformation* in higher education often present an alluring narrative of frictionless connectivity, automated administration, and data intensive optimisation, yet these narratives typically foreground infrastructural expansion and platform deployment while subordinating *pedagogy*, *equity*, and *epistemic justice* to secondary concerns (Ali et al., 2024; Park & Kwon, 2024). Many institutional projects labelled as *smart campus* simply transpose lecture centric, examination heavy practices into learning management systems, proctoring suites, and video conferencing platforms, thereby amplifying stratified access, fatigue, and surveillance rather than reconfiguring knowledge relationships. In these configurations, algorithmic dashboards discipline students and staff through continuous visibility, while analytic indicators privilege easily measurable outputs over deep learning and civic contribution. The result is *automation without transformation*, where investment in sensors, cloud architectures, and analytics coexists with stagnant curricula, marginalised local knowledges, and unaddressed mental health burdens. Against this backdrop, the notion of *pedagogically intelligent smart campuses* emerges as a counter paradigm that foregrounds *immersive cognition*, social inclusion, and critical inquiry as the primary criteria for evaluating technological sophistication.

1.2 Key Concepts and Scope

The chapter conceptualises *digital transformation* as a systemic reconfiguration of institutional processes, roles, and cultures that alters how knowledge is produced, curated, validated, and learned, rather than as incremental digitisation of legacy workflows. A *smart campus* is framed as a complex *socio-technical learning ecology* in which IoT based sensing, AI enhanced analytics, cyber physical infrastructures, and immersive environments intersect with physical architecture, institutional norms, and community relationships (Yadav, 2024; Jafari & Keykha, 2024; Wang et al., 2025). Within this ecology, *pedagogical intelligence* is defined as an institutional level capability to integrate *learning sciences*, *ethical data practices*, and *justice-oriented design principles* into decisions concerning infrastructure, platforms, assessment regimes, and student support. The chapter treats *AI mediated knowledge production* as encompassing research pipelines augmented by machine learning, generative AI supported writing and design, adaptive learning systems, and algorithmic curation of scholarly content (Kong & Yang, 2024; Sağın et al., 2024; Mikeladze et al., 2024). While the analytic focus rests on higher education ecosystems, the constructs and frameworks are articulated so that they remain transferable to vocational education, professional learning, and lifelong learning environments.

1.3 Conceptual Focus

This chapter is developed as a *conceptual theoretical narrative*, synthesising constructs from *learning sciences*, *systems theory*, *critical data studies*, *sustainability studies*, *science and technology studies*, and *organisational theory* to articulate a coherent account of *pedagogically intelligent smart campuses* (Marengo et al., 2024; Celik et al., 2024; Sova et al., 2024). The argument progresses through conceptual mapping, typology building, and normative reasoning, drawing on global policy discourses and widely observed infrastructural trends without detailing site-specific case studies or statistical analyses. The chapter advances *integrative constructs* such as *immersive cognition*, *pedagogical decision architectures*, and *intersectional sustainability* in order to support analytic comparison and strategic design. Tables introduced from Section 2 onward, beginning with *Table 1* in Section 2, function as compact conceptual matrices that aggregate theoretical lenses, ecological components, and governance roles for practical use by curriculum designers and institutional planners.

1.4 Audiences and Relevance

The chapter is intentionally written for multiple overlapping readerships whose decisions shape the trajectories of higher education ecosystems. For academics and instructional designers, it offers a *theoretical cartography* that links *constructivist*, *socio-technical*, and *justice-oriented* perspectives to concrete smart campus affordances, thereby informing course architecture, assessment design, and AI adoption decisions. For policy makers and institutional leaders, it proposes *governance constructs* such as *public value oriented digital transformation* and *multi-level data stewardship* that support alignment between regulatory frameworks, funding models, and pedagogically grounded innovation. Workforce development professionals receive a vocabulary for articulating graduate attributes that integrate *AI literacy*, *planetary responsibility*, and *civic agency* within immersive campus environments. Digital learning technologists and infrastructure providers are addressed through a set of expectations concerning *interoperability*, *accessibility by design*, and *participatory co configuration* of platforms.

1.5 Structure of the Chapter

The chapter unfolds through a seven-section architecture that incrementally elaborates the conceptual terrain. Following this introductory framing, Section 2 develops the *theoretical and conceptual foundations* for *pedagogically intelligent smart campuses*, synthesised in *Table 1* which maps key lenses, core constructs, educational foci, and design implications. Section 3 reconceptualises the *smart campus as socio-technical learning ecology*, disaggregating infrastructural, data, spatial, cultural, and power related layers and aggregating them again in *Table 2* as a typology of components and pedagogical affordances. Section 4 examines *pedagogical innovation and learning designs* within this ecology, with *Table 3* aligning pedagogical models with smart campus technologies and equity considerations. Section 5 foregrounds *sustainability, inclusion, and justice*, articulating intersectional criteria for design that are compactly presented in *Table 4*. Section 6 addresses *governance, stakeholders, and design frameworks*, culminating in *Table 5* which delineates stakeholder roles and tensions. Section 7 concludes with implications, normative commitments, and conceptual horizons for future global research and practice.

2. THEORETICAL AND CONCEPTUAL FOUNDATIONS FOR PEDAGOGICALLY INTELLIGENT SMART CAMPUSES

2.1 Learning Sciences and Educational Theory

A pedagogically intelligent smart campus requires a dense assemblage of *learning sciences* constructs that can steer digital investment toward deep understanding rather than superficial access. *Constructivism* and *social constructivism* foreground knowledge as actively co-produced within dialogic communities, which implies that AI mediated platforms must privilege interactional reciprocity, iterative feedback, and shared meaning making rather than linear content transmission (Nedungadi et al., 2024; Yang et al., 2024; Ma & Lei, 2024). *Connectivism* and *networked learning* extend this view by positioning knowledge as distributed across human actors and computational artefacts, which legitimises the strategic use of recommender systems and generative engines as epistemic partners. *Communities of practice*, *cognitive apprenticeship*, and *disciplinary literacy* theories indicate that smart campus infrastructures should scaffold gradual movement from peripheral to full participation in research, design, and civic projects (Wu, 2024; Vistorte et al., 2024; Yang, 2024). *Self-regulated learning*, *metacognition*, and *self-determination* constructs further specify how dashboards, nudging systems, and adaptive pathways can cultivate autonomy, competence, and relatedness when aligned with the integrated lenses that are synthesised in Table 1.

2.2 Embodied, Multimodal, and Experiential Learning

Smart campuses that aspire to immersive cognition must operationalise theories of *embodied cognition*, *ecological psychology*, and *enactivism* by treating XR laboratories, haptic devices, and sensor infused studios as extended cognitive systems rather than ancillary gadgets. *Experiential learning* and *inquiry-based learning* frameworks justify the design of project-based curricula that exploit real campus data on energy flows, mobility patterns, and environmental conditions, thereby transforming the institution into a living laboratory for hypothesis generation and iterative intervention (Famaye et al., 2024; Al-Abdullatif, 2024; Thorat et al., 2024). The *cognitive theory of multimedia learning* and *cognitive load theory* provide constraints for interface architects who orchestrate complex visualisations, simulations, and multimodal narratives, ensuring that representational richness does not trigger extraneous overload. Constructs such as *presence*, *immersion*, and *flow* guide the calibration of temporal pacing, challenge levels, and affective resonance in virtual and augmented scenarios, which are later juxtaposed with other theoretical clusters in Table 1 to support coherent design heuristics.

2.3 Socio-Technical Systems and Sociomaterial Perspectives

The smart campus emerges as a prototypical *socio-technical system* in which computational infrastructures, institutional policies, and human practices are recursively entangled, and this entanglement necessitates conceptual lenses that foreground relationality and emergence (Adams & Thompson, 2025; Yuan & Liu, 2025; Shailendra et al., 2024). *Socio-technical systems theory* and *cybernetic thinking* conceptualise the campus as a network of feedback loops where information flows between sensing devices, analytic platforms, and decision forums, creating conditions for both adaptive learning and pathological control (Ma et al., 2024; Aguilar-Cruz & Salas-Pilco, 2025; Roshanaei, 2024). *Activity theory* illuminates how students and staff engage in object-oriented activities mediated by tools, rules, and division of labour, thereby revealing contradictions that can catalyse expansive learning. *Sociomateriality*, *infrastructure studies*, and *platform studies* draw attention to mundane artefacts such as authentication protocols, data schemas, and application programming interfaces, which silently configure participation, visibility, and exclusion. These diverse perspectives sit alongside justice, sustainability, and governance lenses in the integrated conceptual grid presented in Table 1, which functions as a concise typology for cross disciplinary sense making.

Table 1. Core Theoretical Lenses for Smart Campus Pedagogy

Theoretical Lens	Core Constructs and Metaphors	Primary Educational Emphasis	Design Implications for Smart Campuses	Risks when Marginalised or Misapplied
Learning Sciences and Cognition	Constructivism, social epistemology, metacognition, self-regulation, mastery progression	Deep conceptual change, transfer, strategic learning, feedback rich progression	Evidence aligned analytics, adaptive pathways, diagnostic assessment, reflective dashboards	Surface learning metrics, drill based automation, epistemic narrowing, learned helplessness
Embodied and Experiential Learning	Embodied cognition, ecological affordances, immersion, presence, flow	Situated practice, sensorimotor engagement, affective resonance, reflective experimentation	XR studios, simulation suites, data informed fieldwork, design challenges	Disembodied screen fatigue, affective overload, trivial gamification, exclusion of non-typical bodies
Socio-Technical and Sociomaterial Systems	Socio-technical coupling, activity systems, infrastructures, assemblages	Mediation of practice, coordination, breakdown learning, collective adaptation	Interoperable platforms, repair friendly infrastructures, transparent data pipelines	Opaque black boxes, brittle dependencies, technocratic control, unaccountable automation
Justice, Decoloniality, and Accessibility	Epistemic justice, intersectionality, decoloniality, Universal Design for Learning	Inclusion, recognition, accessibility, counter hegemonic knowledge production	Multilingual platforms, flexible modalities, participatory governance, rights aware analytics	Reinforced stratification, data driven discrimination, erasure of local knowledges, compliance minimalism
Sustainability and Futures Orientation	Planetary health, socio ecological resilience, just transitions, futures literacy	Long term viability, regenerative practices, anticipatory competence	Campus living labs, low carbon digital design, scenario-based curricula	Ecological rebound effects, techno optimist denial, temporally myopic planning, displaced externalities
Governance and Organisational Learning	Institutional logics, public value, double loop learning, distributed leadership	Collective sense making, policy learning, accountability, culture change	Multi-level data stewardship, participatory councils, iterative strategy cycles	Policy ossification, symbolic compliance, vendor capture, exclusion of critical voices

These socio-technical and sociomaterial frameworks emphasize that pedagogically intelligent smart campuses cannot be reduced to collections of tools, since each infrastructural element is embedded within institutional logics and social hierarchies that amplify certain voices and mute others. Table 1 crystallises how learning sciences, embodiment, justice, sustainability, and governance lenses mutually condition one another, thereby discouraging design teams from isolating analytics,

XR, or AI systems from questions of power and planetary responsibility. When the socio technical configuration prioritises interoperability, transparency, and repair, campuses can cultivate *collective agency* and *organisational learning* rather than dependence on opaque vendor ecosystems. Conversely, when infrastructures are configured with proprietary lock in, rigid surveillance, and minimal participatory oversight, the same technologies can entrench managerialism and epistemic monocultures that undermine the transformative aspirations articulated in subsequent sections of this chapter.

2.4 Justice, Decoloniality, and Critical Digital Perspectives

Justice oriented lenses translate abstract ethical commitments into concrete design criteria for AI mediated campuses, and they build directly on the integrative matrix summarised in Table 1. *Critical pedagogy* and *critical digital pedagogy* treat every interface, algorithm, and analytic dashboard as a site where authority, legitimacy, and normality are negotiated, which means that choices about default language, grading schemas, and visibility settings have distributive and recognitional consequences (Bender, 2024; Mouta et al., 2024; Topaz et al., 2025). *Epistemic injustice* and *hermeneutical marginalisation* constructs illuminate how dominant data ontologies can render certain experiences unintelligible, particularly for racialised, caste oppressed, disabled, and queer learners. *Decolonial* and *pluriversal* frameworks insist that smart campuses must accommodate multiple knowledge systems, including Indigenous ecological knowledges and community-based epistemologies, rather than treating global English language repositories as neutral universes of reference (Fadlelmula & Qadhi, 2024; Storey & Wagner, 2024; Erduran & Levrini, 2024). *Universal Design for Learning* and *critical accessibility* perspectives further require proactive design for variability in sensory, cognitive, and affective profiles, thereby moving beyond minimalist compliance paradigms toward thick forms of participation.

2.5 Sustainability and Futures-Oriented Perspectives

Sustainability oriented thinking repositions smart campuses as nodal points within planetary socio ecological systems, where digital infrastructures and pedagogical practices jointly shape carbon trajectories and resilience capacities. Constructs such as *planetary health*, *One Health*, and *socio ecological resilience* foreground interdependence between human wellbeing, biodiversity, and infrastructure design, implying that high energy data centres, extensive sensor networks, and ubiquitous wireless connectivity must be evaluated in terms of ecological opportunity costs (Singha & Singha, 2024; Merchán Sánchez-Jara et al., 2024; Williamson, 2024). *Education for Sustainable Development* and *futures literacy* frameworks argue that learners should encounter campus operations as curriculum, engaging with energy dashboards, mobility datasets, and food system analytics to model alternative futures. *Transition theory* and *multi-level perspective* constructs clarify how niche experiments in low carbon digital practices can challenge incumbent regimes dominated by energy intensive cloud strategies. When combined with the lenses in Table 1, these perspectives encourage institutions to treat resource allocation, procurement, and platform choices as pedagogical decisions that either normalise extractive habits or cultivate regenerative dispositions.

2.6 Governance, Organisational Learning, and Institutional Theory

Governance and institutional theory provide the meso level scaffolding through which the more granular lenses in Table 1 are operationalised, since they describe how decisions about platforms, curricula, and analytics are authorised, contested, and revised. *Institutional theory* and *institutional logics* illuminate convergence pressures generated by rankings, accreditation frameworks, and global policy scripts, which often incentivise visible but shallow forms of digital transformation that prioritise image over substance (Gökçearslan et al., 2024; Ayanwale et al., 2024; Tassoti, 2024). *Public value governance* reconceptualises digital initiatives as instruments for generating collective benefits, such as epistemic diversity and civic capability, rather than as isolated efficiency projects. *Organisational learning* and *double loop learning* constructs specify how evidence from learning analytics, evaluation studies, and stakeholder feedback can trigger revision of underlying norms rather than minor technical adjustments. *Distributed leadership* and *communities of practice* frameworks indicate that pedagogical intelligence emerges from the interaction of formal leaders, educational technologists, and frontline educators who co interpret data and co design interventions within multi-level governance architectures.

2.7 Synthesis and Integrative Conceptual Mapping

The theoretical and conceptual foundations assembled in this section converge on a view of the pedagogically intelligent smart campus as an interconnected ecology of cognition, embodiment, infrastructure, justice, sustainability, and governance. Table 1 functions as a compact integrative map in which each lens highlights a distinct dimension of this ecology, while the surrounding narrative specifies how these dimensions interact to shape AI mediated knowledge production and immersive learning (Sanusi et al., 2024; Katsamakas et al., 2024; Pack & Maloney, 2024). Learning sciences constructs anchor the design of analytic features and adaptive pathways, embodied learning theories orient XR and simulation investments, socio technical frameworks discipline infrastructural choices, justice-oriented perspectives reconfigure data ontologies and accessibility norms, sustainability lenses recalibrate energy and resource decisions, and governance theories orchestrate coordination across scales (Ruiz-Rojas et al., 2024; Obenza et al., 2024; Khreisat et al., 2024). The synthesis suggests that any smart campus initiative that omits one of these clusters risks generating systemic incoherence, for instance by pairing advanced analytics with outdated assessment philosophies, or immersive laboratories with inequitable access regimes. Subsequent sections build directly on this integrative foundation to elaborate ecological, pedagogical, and governance architectures that can translate these lenses into operational design logics.

3. SMART CAMPUS AS SOCIO-TECHNICAL LEARNING ECOLOGY

3.1 Ecological Framing of Smart Campuses

A pedagogically intelligent smart campus can be conceptualised through *ecological systems theory*, which treats learners, educators, and artefacts as co situated within nested environments that extend from micro level classrooms to macro level global networks (Gkintoni et al., 2025; Ivanashko et al., 2024; Sanusi et al., 2024). Within this framing, digital platforms, built architecture, governance regimes, and community partnerships constitute interlocking habitats that modulate what forms of cognition, collaboration, and civic engagement become viable (Lan, 2024; Li, 2025; Naixin et al., 2024). The smart campus operates as a *learning ecology* in which information flows, social practices, and material infrastructures continuously influence one another through feedback rich couplings (Liu et al., 2024; Alam & Mohanty, 2024; Karataş et al., 2025). This ecological perspective foregrounds non-linear causality, where small adjustments in interface design or access rules can cascade into large cultural shifts. It also demands attention to temporal dynamics, since infrastructural decisions have long half-lives that affect multiple student cohorts. Table 2 later crystallises this ecological framing by differentiating key component archetypes and mapping their pedagogical affordances, risks, and use cases.

3.2 Infrastructural and Technological Layer

The infrastructural and technological layer comprises the cyber physical backbone that makes immersive cognition and AI mediated knowledge production operationally possible. This layer includes campus wide connectivity, edge and cloud computing clusters, identity and access management systems, integrated enterprise platforms, and ubiquitous IoT based sensing arrays. Each subsystem embodies particular design logics concerning interoperability, latency, redundancy, and security, which in turn shape the feasibility of rich media learning, real time analytics, and experimental prototyping. The infrastructural layer also encodes assumptions about standardisation and openness, since proprietary architectures constrain cross platform experimentation while open standards facilitate combinatorial innovation. From a pedagogical standpoint, this layer must be treated as an educational resource rather than a background utility, inviting students into critical engagement with protocols, data flows, and failure modes. Table 2 synthesises these infrastructural considerations by positioning the backbone as one component within a wider socio technical typology that includes data platforms, spaces, and governance systems.

3.3 Data and Analytics Layer

The data and analytics layer transforms heterogeneous traces from smart campus infrastructures into representations that can support or distort pedagogical decision making. Learning management systems, access control logs, library circulation records, environmental sensors, and research repositories all contribute to a dense data ecosystem in which student trajectories, space usage, and energy patterns can be modelled. Within this layer, constructs such as *data provenance*, *model interpretability*, and *algorithmic transparency* acquire direct educational salience, since they condition whether dashboards and alerts foster self-regulation or induce anxiety and gaming. The conceptual distinction between learning analytics, academic analytics, and institutional intelligence matters, because each domain prioritises different granularity and timescales. When designed with pedagogical intelligence, the data and analytics layer becomes a substrate for reflective practice, targeted support, and campus wide inquiry projects. Table 2 structures this layer alongside others, highlighting its specific functions, affordances, and risks within the broader socio technical ecology.

Table 2. Typology of Smart Campus Components and Pedagogical Affordances

Component Archetype	Core Functions and Systemic Logics	Pedagogical Affordances for Learners and Staff	Latent Educational Risks and Vulnerabilities	Illustrative Smart Campus Use Cases
Infrastructural Backbone	Connectivity provision, compute orchestration, identity management, resilience engineering	Stable access, rich media delivery, distributed experimentation, computational thinking	Single point failures, exclusion through authentication, rigid vendor lock in, energy intensive operation	High bandwidth hybrid classes, remote laboratory access, cross campus research clusters
Data and Analytics Platforms	Aggregation of traces, modelling, visualisation, decision support, automation triggers	Feedback dashboards, early warning signals, pattern discovery, inquiry projects	Profiling, over surveillance, reductive metrics, opaque algorithmic influence	Learning progress panels, adaptive routing of support, student led data investigations
Learning and Collaboration Spaces	Structuring of co presence, interaction channels, knowledge sharing, version control	Collaborative authoring, peer tutoring, community building, interdisciplinary projects	Fragmented participation, platform fatigue, marginalisation of low bandwidth users	Virtual studios, project management workspaces, cross cohort communities of practice
Immersive and Experimental Environments	Simulation, sensory augmentation, prototype testing, embodied interaction	Experiential learning, scenario exploration, creative design, risk free rehearsal	Motion sickness, inequitable access, trivialised gamification, cognitive overload	XR based fieldwork, virtual internships, simulation informed policy debates
Governance and Decision Systems	Policy formulation, oversight, accountability, participatory consultation	Transparent rule making, shared responsibility, curricular innovation, ethical review	Technocratic closure, symbolic participation, inconsistent enforcement, slow adaptation	Digital charters, data governance councils, ethical review panels for AI tools

The data and analytics layer, when situated within the typological structure of Table 2, is revealed as both an epistemic amplifier and a potential vector for stratification. Its design must therefore incorporate strong safeguards for consent, proportionality, and contestability, ensuring that algorithmic inferences are open to scrutiny and revision by those who are subject to them. When students are invited to interrogate models, critique indicators, and propose alternative visualisations, the analytics environment becomes a laboratory for *critical data literacy* rather than a one-way mechanism of surveillance. Similarly, faculty can treat analytic instruments as prompts for professional inquiry instead of rigid performance monitors, provided that governance arrangements protect exploratory use. In this way, the data layer moves from a managerial instrument to a pedagogical catalyst that intensifies reflective practice and shared responsibility for learning.

3.4 Spatial and Architectural Layer

The spatial and architectural layer translates pedagogical aspirations into concrete configurations of floors, furniture, and ambient affordances that shape bodily movement and social interaction. Smart classrooms, learning commons, maker laboratories, XR studios, and contemplative zones all encode implicit theories of collaboration, attention, and authority. Constructs such as *affordances*, *proxemics*, and *environmental psychology* provide a vocabulary for understanding how room geometry, display placement, acoustic treatment, and lighting schemes invite or inhibit dialogue, experimentation, and inclusive participation. Temporal programmability adds an additional dimension, since spaces can be repurposed across the day for quiet study, intensive teamwork, or public engagement, thereby increasing utilisation and epistemic diversity (Sarwar & Ms Saima, 2024; Dai & Liu, 2024; Cheah et al., 2025). When read alongside Table 2, the spatial layer emerges as a distinct component archetype that interacts with data platforms and infrastructures, because sensor placement, occupancy tracking, and wayfinding systems all modify how people move through and experience the campus as an integrated learning ecology.

3.5 Human Practices and Cultural Layer

The human practices and cultural layer foregrounds the patterned behaviours, shared meanings, and identity narratives through which academics, students, and professional staff inhabit smart campus infrastructures. *Practice theory* conceptualises teaching, studying, advising, and administrating as bundles of routinised actions that involve bodies, artefacts, and interpretive frames, which means that new tools do not automatically transform learning unless they are incorporated into evolving practice architectures. Disciplinary cultures mediate expectations regarding autonomy, collaboration, and assessment, so the same platform may support inquiry in one context and reproduction in another (Musolin et al., 2024; Wang & Li, 2024; Lim, 2024). Student lifeworlds, including commuting schedules, caregiving responsibilities, employment demands, and platform literacies, condition who can participate in extended online discussions or late-night virtual laboratories. Peer cultures and informal networks modulate how institutional technologies are perceived, resisted, or creatively repurposed. When interpreted through the typology in Table 2, the cultural layer acts as the medium that either activates or neutralises the latent affordances of infrastructural, analytic, and spatial components.

3.6 Power, Control, and Surveillance in Smart Ecologies

Smart campus ecologies concentrate capacities for observation, prediction, and intervention, which raises foundational questions about power, control, and care. Concepts such as *surveillance*, *discipline*, and *governmentality* describe how continuous monitoring and behavioural nudging can reshape norms of attendance, productivity, and engagement, often pivoting on apparently neutral indicators such as log in frequency or camera activation. High resolution sensing and facial recognition tools risk converting educational spaces into quasi securitised environments, particularly when integrated with punitive policies (Rane, 2024; Ezeoguine & Eteng-Uket, 2024; Ng et al., 2025). At the same time, data infrastructures can enable relational accountability and restorative practices if alerts are oriented toward support rather than sanction and if those affected participate in rule setting. Power is also exercised through interface design, since defaults, consent dialogues, and visibility hierarchies structure whose voices are amplified. Table 2 implicitly encodes these dynamics by pairing each component archetype with its latent risks, signalling that technological sophistication without explicit attention to power will likely intensify existing inequities.

3.7 Ecological Tensions and Design Challenges

The ecological framing reveals a series of structural tensions that must be navigated rather than eliminated if smart campuses are to remain both adaptive and just. One recurring tension arises between centralisation and decentralisation, since unified platforms promise efficiency and coherent data, while local experimentation demands flexibility and heterogeneity. Another tension concerns automation and human discretion, particularly in risk management and assessment, where algorithmic triage can expedite support but may obscure contextual nuance (Salloum, 2024; Baltezarević & Baltezarević, 2024; Opesemowo & Adekomaya, 2024). Personalisation and shared curriculum form a further axis, as highly tailored pathways risk fragmenting communal learning while uniform structures can suppress differentiation and agency. Resource allocation decisions produce tensions between high performance computation and low carbon commitments, especially when immersive technologies entail significant energy loads. The component typology in Table 2 offers a scaffold for diagnosing where these tensions concentrate, enabling design teams to stage deliberative processes that explicitly weigh trade-offs across pedagogical, ethical, and ecological dimensions.

3.8 Ecological Summary and Transition

This section has articulated the smart campus as a socio technical learning ecology composed of interdependent infrastructural, analytic, spatial, cultural, and power laden layers that jointly condition AI mediated knowledge production. The ecological perspective insists that pedagogical intelligence cannot be grafted onto technocentric architectures, but must instead infuse the design and governance of each component archetype summarised in Table 2. By treating infrastructures as pedagogical resources, analytics as sites of critical inquiry, spaces as cognitive and affective regulators, cultures as engines of practice evolution, and governance systems as arenas of negotiation, institutions can reorient smart campus initiatives toward immersive cognition and equity centred outcomes. This ecological synthesis now prepares the conceptual ground for the next section, which focuses more directly on *pedagogical innovation and learning designs* that can inhabit and reshape these ecologies, translating abstract theories into concrete arrangements of activities, assessments, and learner agency.

4. PEDAGOGICAL INNOVATION AND LEARNING DESIGNS IN SMART CAMPUSES

4.1 Conceptualising Pedagogical Intelligence for Immersive Campus Ecologies

Pedagogical intelligence at institutional scale can be conceptualised as an emergent meta capacity through which smart campuses align *learning sciences*, *justice-oriented design*, and *socio-technical infrastructures* to orchestrate transformative learning rather than technology centric spectacle (Opesemowo & Ndlovu, 2024; Saatchi et al., 2025; Kazanidis & Pellas, 2024). This construct exceeds individual teacher skill, since it involves coordinated decision architectures in which procurement rules, platform configurations, room scheduling, and assessment policies collectively encode specific theories of learning (Mahmoud & Sørensen, 2024; Karakose & Tülübas, 2024; Yue et al., 2024). A pedagogically intelligent campus ensures that analytic dashboards, AI recommendation engines, and XR studios are governed by explicit models such as *constructivism*, *self-regulated learning*, and *Universal Design for Learning*, rather than vendor marketing taxonomies. It also institutionalises iterative design cycles in which empirical feedback about learner trajectories and wellbeing informs curricular revisions and infrastructure tuning (Alam & Mohanty, 2023; Lye & Lim, 2024; Xia et al., 2024). Table 3 later concretises this construct by mapping representative pedagogical models to smart campus affordances and theoretical foundations, thereby operationalising pedagogical intelligence as a design heuristic rather than an abstract aspiration.

4.2 Immersive, Experiential, and Embodied Learning Designs with Smart Infrastructures

Immersive, experiential, and embodied designs treat the smart campus as a distributed *extended mind* in which bodies, artefacts, and algorithms co participate in cognitive activity. Drawing on *embodied cognition* and *ecological psychology*, XR studios, sensor enriched laboratories, and augmented fieldwork environments are configured to couple perception, action, and reflection in tightly looped cycles (Grájeda et al., 2024; Dieterle et al., 2024; Jatileni et al., 2024). *Experiential learning* and *inquiry-based learning* frameworks are instantiated when students interrogate live energy dashboards, mobility flows, and environmental telemetry as empirical substrates for hypothesis formation, intervention, and evaluation (Zhang et al., 2025; Joel Augustus et al., 2025; Abbasi et al., 2025). The quality of these experiences depends on careful calibration of *cognitive load*, representational fidelity, and affective pacing, so that unfamiliar interfaces amplify rather than fragment understanding. In a pedagogically intelligent smart campus, immersive tasks are explicitly integrated with programme level outcomes such as systems thinking, ethical reasoning, and collaborative problem solving, instead of functioning as isolated demonstrations (Yang et al., 2024; Shamsuddinova et al., 2024; Storozhyk, 2024). Table 3 later positions these immersive designs alongside other models to reveal convergences and divergences in their infrastructural dependencies and equity implications.

4.3 AI-Enabled Adaptive and Personalised Learning Architectures

AI enabled adaptive learning in smart campuses can be framed as an intricate interplay between *mastery learning*, *formative assessment*, and *self-regulated learning* constructs, mediated through dynamic modelling of learner trajectories (Samala et al., 2025; Ozodakhon, 2024; Fullan et al., 2024). Intelligent tutoring systems, adaptive courseware, and generative feedback engines operate on granular performance data to propose tailored pathways, hints, and remediation activities that align with articulated learning progressions (Tan et al., 2024; Franco D'Souza et al., 2024; Yadav & Shrawankar, 2025). When grounded in *metacognitive scaffolding* and *self-determination* principles, these systems can cultivate agency by encouraging learners to interrogate recommendations, plan strategies, and monitor progress (Mah & Groß, 2024; Zarei et al., 2024; Fundi et al., 2024). Conversely, when optimisation objectives privilege throughput and uniformity, adaptive architectures risk constraining exploration and reinforcing historical inequities encoded in training data. Pedagogically intelligent governance therefore requires transparent goal setting, auditable decision rules, and opportunities for students to override or annotate algorithmic guidance (Zohuri & Mossavar-Rahmani, 2024; Al-Zahrani & Alasmari, 2024; Alam & Mohanty, 2022). By situating AI enabled models within the comparative matrix of Table 3, institutions can examine whether adaptive systems complement or conflict with other pedagogical regimes such as project-based studios or HyFlex seminars.

4.4 Hybrid, Blended, and HyFlex Pedagogies in Smart Campus Ecologies

Hybrid, blended, and HyFlex arrangements treat modality as a design variable rather than a logistical afterthought, drawing conceptually on the *community of inquiry* framework and theories of learner agency. Smart campuses enable fine grained orchestration of synchronous and asynchronous, physical and virtual engagements through scheduling platforms, high fidelity telepresence, learning management systems, and analytics informed facilitation (Zhou et al., 2024; Fitrianto et al., 2024; Forero-Corba & Bennasar, 2024). In a blended seminar that integrates co located and remote participants, *social presence*, *cognitive presence*, and *teaching presence* must be deliberately configured across channels, with interactive whiteboards, collaborative documents, and chat backchannels functioning as connective tissue (Annuš, 2024; Chen, 2024; Rahiman & Kodikal, 2024). HyFlex formats introduce additional complexity, since students choose participation modes session by session, which demands robust archival practices, flexible assessment timelines, and attention to digital access disparities. Table 3 synthesises these hybrid models with other pedagogical archetypes, revealing how modality decisions intersect with infrastructural requirements, theoretical commitments, and equity safeguards in the broader smart campus ecology.

Table 3. Pedagogical Models and Smart Campus Affordance Alignment Schema

Pedagogical Model Archetype	Core Learning Objectives	Key Theoretical Foundations	Relevant Smart Campus Infrastructures	Equity and Ethics Design Considerations
Immersive Problem-Based Studio	Complex problem framing, transdisciplinary reasoning, design iteration	*Experiential learning, constructivism, embodied cognition*	XR laboratories, maker spaces, sensor rich data hubs	Access to devices, cognitive load moderation, inclusion of local knowledges
HyFlex Community of Inquiry	Flexible participation, dialogic knowledge building, critical discourse	*Community of inquiry, social presence, self determination*	High bandwidth classrooms, cloud collaboration suites, lecture capture	Modality parity, bandwidth sensitive design, protection from attendance surveillance
AI-Supported Mastery Pathway	Progressive mastery, metacognitive control, targeted remediation	*Mastery learning, formative assessment, self-regulated learning*	Adaptive courseware, analytics engines, learning dashboards	Algorithmic transparency, bias mitigation, student override and appeal mechanisms
Participatory Co-Design Laboratory	Epistemic agency, civic engagement, methodological reflexivity	*Critical pedagogy, participatory design, communities of practice*	Innovation hubs, open APIs, sandboxed data environments	Fair recognition of student labour, consent for data reuse, plurality of voices
Living-Lab Sustainability Project	Systems thinking, futures literacy, regenerative praxis	*Education for Sustainable Development, systems theory, futures literacy*	Campus sensing networks, energy dashboards, geospatial platforms	Just distribution of project impacts, visibility for marginalised communities, low carbon digital practices
Multi-Lingual Translanguaging Seminar	Plurilingual competence, epistemic diversity, interpretive sophistication	*Translanguaging theory, sociocultural learning, epistemic justice*	Multi language platforms, captioning engines, corpus tools	Linguistic inclusion, avoidance of monolingual defaulting, respect for minoritised scripts

Hybrid and HyFlex configurations become pedagogically robust when treated not as dilution of in person teaching but as deliberate enactments of plural participation vectors, as articulated in Table 3. The matrix underscores that each model depends on specific infrastructural assemblages and carries distinctive ethical obligations, such as modality parity in HyFlex settings or transparency mechanisms in AI supported mastery pathways. Design teams can therefore use the table as a diagnostic artefact to identify misalignments, for example when HyFlex offerings lack reliable capture tools or when immersive studios are deployed without accommodations for motion sensitive learners. In a pedagogically intelligent smart campus, timetabling, room allocation, and platform configuration all follow from model selection, ensuring that hybrid architectures reinforce rather than fragment coherent learning trajectories.

4.5 Assessment, Feedback, and Analytic-Supported Learning Regimes

Assessment within smart campuses can be reconceptualised as a continuous, dialogic process guided by *assessment for learning* and *assessment as learning* constructs, rather than as episodic gatekeeping. Digital infrastructures enable frequent, low stakes tasks with rapid feedback, which can be curated through analytic tools that visualise patterns of misconception, engagement, and strategy use (Tzirides et al., 2024; Nikolopoulou, 2024; Weidener & Fischer, 2024). When grounded in *self-regulated learning* models, dashboards and progress indicators function as metacognitive mirrors that support planning, monitoring, and adaptation, rather than as instruments of rank ordering (Cordero et al., 2024; Wang et al., 2024; Alier et al., 2024). AI facilitated feedback on writing, code, and design artefacts can accelerate formative cycles, provided that human educators contextualise suggestions and model critical engagement with automated commentary. Risks emerge when key performance indicators become proxies for learning, leading to metric fixation and strategic gaming of analytics (Afzaal et al., 2024; Rabiatu & Shehu, 2024; Lérias et al., 2024). Pedagogically intelligent design therefore requires explicit alignment between assessment tasks, analytic representations, and programme level outcomes, as well as governance provisions that limit high stakes uses of fine-grained behavioural data.

4.6 Student Agency, Co-Creation, and Participatory Pedagogy

Student agency in smart campuses materialises when learners move from consumers of pre-configured experiences to co designers of curricula, platforms, and data practices, operationalising constructs from *student staff partnership*, *participatory design*, and *critical pedagogy* (Abuhassna et al., 2024; Alam, 2023a; Yılmaz, 2024). Hackathons, innovation challenges, and digital making studios provide structured environments where students can prototype tools, visualisations, and policies that respond to authentic institutional challenges (Sasikala & Ravichandran, 2024; Amdan et al., 2024; Alqahtani & Wafula, 2025). When these activities are linked to credit bearing modules and clear governance pathways, they evolve from extracurricular events into sustained participatory infrastructures. Smart campus data environments can support student led inquiries into inclusion, sustainability, and wellbeing, thereby transforming analytics from surveillance apparatus into civic resource (Sana et al., 2024; Nguyen et al., 2024; Obidovna, 2024). However, agency is contingent on material conditions, including compensation, recognition, and psychological safety, especially for students from historically marginalised groups. Pedagogically intelligent campuses therefore institutionalise charters, advisory councils, and co-authored design briefs that embed co-creation within organisational routines rather than treating it as sporadic consultation.

4.7 Teacher Roles, Professionalism, and Identity in Smart Campus Pedagogies

Within pedagogically intelligent smart campuses, academic professionalism is reconfigured around multifaceted roles that extend beyond content transmission to encompass *learning design*, *data informed facilitation*, and *socio-technical stewardship* (Bulathwela et al., 2024; Amado-Salvatierra et al., 2024; Abulibdeh et al., 2024). Role theory and *teacher identity* constructs help explain the tensions educators experience when expected to act simultaneously as subject experts, interface navigators, and pastoral carers within data saturated environments (Suryanarayana et al., 2024; Özer, 2024; Galindo-Domínguez et al., 2024). Smart infrastructures expose granular traces of teaching practice, such as turn taking patterns and feedback latency, which can either support reflective improvement or exacerbate surveillance anxiety (Sharma et al., 2024; Robert et al., 2024; Bukar et al., 2024). Professional learning communities oriented around design-based experimentation, analytic interpretation, and mutual mentoring offer one pathway to collective efficacy. Institutional frameworks must also recalibrate promotion criteria and workload models to value labour invested in hybrid course redesign, inclusive assessment, and ethical data governance (Alam, 2023b; Zadorina et al., 2024; Iqbal et al., 2024). When these conditions are met, educators can inhabit identities as *critical technopedagogues* who harness AI and analytics while defending academic freedom and learner dignity.

4.8 Integrative Pedagogical Design Heuristics for Smart Campus Innovation

The diverse models articulated in this section converge into a set of integrative design heuristics that translate theoretical constructs into actionable questions for curriculum teams, platform architects, and policy makers. Each new or redesigned learning experience can be interrogated through lenses derived from previous sections and from Table 3, such as alignment with *learning sciences* principles, embodiment opportunities, modality strategy, analytic representation, and justice implications. A core heuristic concerns coherence across scale, ensuring that module level activities, such as immersive studios or AI supported mastery pathways, contribute to programme wide narratives about disciplinary inquiry, civic responsibility, and sustainability (Zawacki-Richter et al., 2024; Mouta et al., 2024; Davis et al., 2024). Another heuristic foregrounds reversibility, encouraging designers to prefer configurations that can be iteratively adjusted in response to student feedback and analytic insight without incurring catastrophic disruption. By institutionalising these heuristics within quality assurance, procurement, and staff development processes, smart campuses can progressively cultivate pedagogical intelligence, thereby converting technological complexity into epistemic richness and equitable opportunity.

5. SUSTAINABILITY, INCLUSION, AND JUSTICE IN SMART CAMPUS PEDAGOGIES

5.1 Smart Campuses as Living Laboratories for Sustainability Education

When smart campuses are framed as *living laboratories*, sustainability ceases to be a peripheral policy slogan and becomes a pervasive epistemic infrastructure that permeates curricula, research agendas, and operational routines. Constructs such as *Education for Sustainable Development*, *systems thinking*, and *complex adaptive systems* invite students to treat energy grids, mobility routes, food services, and water cycles as coupled socio-ecological subsystems that can be monitored, modelled, and reconfigured through data informed interventions. Sensor networks, geospatial platforms, and energy dashboards provide high resolution feedback on consumption patterns and emissions profiles, enabling inquiry cycles in which learners hypothesise, test, and refine strategies for decarbonisation and resilience building (Choi et al., 2024; Al-Shorman et al., 2025; Stolpe & Hallström, 2024). When these activities are integrated into credit-bearing projects that intersect engineering, social sciences, and arts, the campus becomes a mesoscale site for experimenting with *just transitions* rather than a neutral backdrop. The multi-dimensional sustainability questions that arise from such living-lab configurations are later codified in the intersectional design matrix presented in Table 4.

5.2 Universal Design for Learning and Accessibility Frameworks in Smart Infrastructures

Universal accessibility in smart campuses requires more than compliance with basic accommodation checklists, since digitally mediated environments recursively shape who can participate, contribute, and belong. *Universal Design for Learning* and *critical accessibility* constructs propose that variability in sensory, cognitive, linguistic, and affective profiles must be treated as the design baseline rather than a deviation. Smart infrastructures can instantiate these principles through multimodal representations, real-time captioning, screen-reader compatible interfaces, adjustable pacing controls, and physically adaptable spaces that integrate assistive technologies (Martin et al., 2024; Kong et al., 2025; Vieriu & Petrea, 2025). Machine learning based tools can support automatic transcription, language simplification, and personalised interface configurations, provided that users retain fine-grained control and meaningful consent (Walter, 2024; Adeleye et al., 2024; Kumar et al., 2024). Accessibility also extends to temporal and financial dimensions, since asynchronous modalities, open educational resources, and device-lending schemes mitigate exclusion for students who juggle employment, caregiving, or connectivity precarity (Mustafa et al., 2024; Ng et al., 2024; Alwaqdani, 2025). The normative heuristics that translate these frameworks into concrete design questions for ecological, social, and epistemic inclusion are synthesised in Table 4, which functions as a cross-cutting diagnostic instrument for smart campus initiatives.

5.3 Intersectionality, Equity, and Capability-Oriented Design Logics

Intersectional equity in smart campuses demands conceptual tools that render visible the overlapping vectors of advantage and disadvantage that structure student and staff experiences. *Intersectionality* conceptualises social locations such as gender, race, caste, class, disability, sexuality, migration status, and language as mutually constitutive axes that shape exposure to surveillance, remediation, and opportunity structures within AI mediated ecosystems (Sperling et al., 2024; Lin & Chen, 2024; Tashtoush et al., 2024). The *capability approach* reframes digital transformation away from mere provision of devices and platforms toward the expansion of substantive freedoms to learn, critique, organise, and flourish (Guo et al., 2024; Galindo-Domínguez et al., 2024; Alam, 2023c). When these constructs are applied to platform interfaces, analytics dashboards, and living-lab projects, designers are compelled to ask whose capabilities are being enhanced, whose risks are being externalised, and whose epistemic contributions are being rendered marginal (Linderoth et al., 2024; Almasri, 2024; Perkins et al., 2024). Table 4 below consolidates these concerns into an intersectional sustainability schema that spans ecological, social, epistemic, digital rights, and governance domains, offering a compact yet dense matrix for curriculum teams and policy architects.

Table 4. Intersectional Sustainability Criteria for Smart Campus Learning Designs

Sustainability Dimension	Guiding Diagnostic Questions	Illustrative Design Strategies	Potential Inequity and Risk Scenarios	Monitoring and Reflexive Evaluation Heuristics
Ecological-Resource	How do infrastructures and pedagogies affect energy, water, and material flows	Low-carbon architectures, demand-responsive scheduling, circular procurement, virtualised experiments	Energy-intensive XR and analytics, e-waste concentration, environmental sacrifice zones	Per-student footprint indices, lifecycle audits, longitudinal resource baselines
Social-Relational	Who benefits from participation, support, and recognition, and who is burdened	Sliding-scale access schemes, community-linked projects, inclusive advising, care-aware timetables	Participation gaps, care penalties, psychosocial overload, campus stratification	Disaggregated participation maps, wellbeing observatories, qualitative experience panels
Epistemic-Plural	Which knowledge systems, languages, and methodologies are legitimised and resourced	Co-teaching with community experts, plurilingual materials, mixed-method studios, archive diversification	Monolingual defaulting, erasure of Indigenous and local knowledges, methodological monoculture	Epistemic diversity indices, content audits, narrative-based curriculum reviews
Digital-Rights	How are data collected, processed, and governed in relation to consent and agency	Consent-rich analytics, privacy-by-design platforms, participatory data charters, opt-out pathways	Coercive monitoring, opaque profiling, vendor capture, chilling effects on expression	Rights impact assessments, algorithmic behaviour tracing, student-led data inquiries
Economic-Infrastructural	How are costs, maintenance, and benefits distributed across groups and territories	Tiered licensing models, open-source adoption, shared regional hubs, equitable device lending	Unequal access to premium tools, infrastructural deserts, dependence on external donors	Affordability dashboards, spatial equity mapping, procurement justice reviews
Governance-Cultural	Who defines priorities, norms, and risk thresholds for smart campus evolution	Multi-stakeholder councils, deliberative forums, transparency portals, co-authored policies	Technocratic closure, tokenistic consultation, cultural alienation, conflict escalation	Governance process audits, legitimacy barometers, conflict-resolution learning cycles

Intersectional and capability-oriented lenses, operationalised through the diagnostic grid of Table 4, transform equity from an abstract value into a structured set of design constraints and evaluation routines. When curriculum designers and infrastructure planners apply these criteria systematically, they can identify patterns such as concentration of energy-intensive experimentation in privileged programmes, or disproportionate exposure of certain groups to high-stakes analytics and remote proctoring. The table also emphasises the importance of continuous monitoring through both quantitative indicators and qualitative narratives, ensuring that justice considerations remain alive over time rather than ossifying into static compliance templates. In this way, intersectionality and capability approaches act as epistemic instruments that reconfigure the entire smart campus metabolism, influencing what projects are prioritised, which partnerships are pursued, and how success is narrated across institutional scales.

5.4 Decolonial and Pluriversal Digital Pedagogy in Smart Ecologies

Decolonial and pluriversal perspectives interrogate the epistemic architectures that underpin smart campus platforms, repositories, and curricula, asking whether they reproduce a narrow canon or cultivate multiple worlds of sense-making. *Decolonial pedagogy* critiques the alignment of digital infrastructures with globalised norms that centre dominant languages, citation practices, and standards of rigour, often at the expense of Indigenous, subaltern, and community-based knowledges. *Pluriversality* proposes that smart campuses should host coexisting cosmologies, methodologies, and narrative traditions, rather than assimilating them into a single homogenised framework (Guettala et al., 2024; Memarian & Doleck, 2024; Filgueiras, 2024). Practically, this requires multilingual interfaces, metadata schemas that recognise diverse ontologies, and credit-bearing collaborations with local communities in which data and analytic tools are governed through negotiated protocols. When these commitments are neglected, AI mediated systems risk accelerating epistemic extraction and cultural erasure. Situated alongside the intersectional dimensions codified in Table 4, decolonial and pluriversal constructs expand sustainability to include the continuity of knowledge lineages and the right to epistemic self-determination.

5.5 Data Ethics, Surveillance, and Student Rights in Smart Campuses

Data-intensive smart campuses concentrate unprecedented capacities for monitoring, prediction, and intervention, which necessitates robust frameworks of data ethics and digital rights. *Critical data studies* foreground the political economy of data extraction, highlighting how behavioural traces can be commodified, repurposed, or weaponised in ways that exceed the original educational intent (Bulut et al., 2024; Murdan & Halkhoree, 2024; Sămărescu et al., 2024). Constructs such as *informed consent*, *data minimisation*, *purpose limitation*, and *contestability* must therefore be encoded directly into platform architectures, analytic workflows, and governance arrangements (Farooqi et al., 2024; Tang, 2024; Edwards-Fapohunda &

Adediji, 2024). Student rights in this context include the right to understand what is being inferred about them, to challenge erroneous classifications, and to refuse invasive data practices without jeopardising their progression (Airaj, 2024; Ramirez & Esparrell, 2024; Alam, 2022). Surveillance oriented analytics may be reframed as care-oriented systems if they are co-designed, transparently governed, and oriented toward voluntary support rather than punitive sanctions. The digital-rights row in Table 4 crystallises these commitments by aligning them with concrete risk scenarios and monitoring heuristics that can be integrated into institutional quality frameworks.

5.6 Ecological, Social, and Epistemic Sustainability as Integrated Design Imperative

Sustainability in smart campuses must be conceptualised as an integrated triad of ecological, social, and epistemic dimensions, since each domain conditions the viability of the others over extended timescales. Ecological sustainability concerns the material and energetic footprints of infrastructures, including data centres, device procurement, and building automation, which must be reconciled with aspirations for high fidelity immersion and continuous connectivity (Leong et al., 2024; Yim & Su, 2025; Sanusi et al., 2024). Social sustainability focuses on health, wellbeing, belonging, and workload distribution, acknowledging that always-on digital cultures can generate burnout, anxiety, and relational fragmentation if not carefully managed. Epistemic sustainability addresses the diversity, resilience, and criticality of knowledge practices, ensuring that standardising tendencies of platforms and algorithms do not erode pluralism and dissent. Table 4 captures these dimensions through ecological-resource, social-relational, and epistemic-plural rows, which together encourage institutions to scrutinise trade-offs and synergies rather than outsourcing sustainability considerations to separate policy silos. When the triad is treated holistically, pedagogical innovation aligns more consistently with long-horizon institutional and planetary commitments.

5.7 Integrative Justice-Oriented Design Principles for Smart Campus Pedagogies

The justice-oriented constructs articulated in this section coalesce into a set of integrative design principles that can guide smart campus decision-making across pedagogical, infrastructural, and governance domains. First, every major digital or spatial intervention should be subjected to intersectional capability analysis, using instruments such as Table 4 to forecast distributional impacts and epistemic consequences before large-scale implementation. Second, sustainability must be approached as a multi-dimensional property of learning ecosystems, where ecological, social, and epistemic indicators are evaluated together and revisited through participatory review cycles. Third, governance mechanisms should institutionalise co-creation, granting students, staff, and community partners structured roles in data charters, platform selection, and living-lab agenda setting (Cukurova, 2025; Lee et al., 2024; Tahir et al., 2024). Fourth, decolonial and pluriversal sensibilities should inform content curation, algorithm design, and partnership protocols, ensuring that digital transformation expands rather than narrows the spectrum of legitimate knowledge. By weaving these principles into procurement frameworks, curriculum standards, and evaluation rubrics, smart campuses can progressively embody sustainability, inclusion, and justice as constitutive features rather than aspirational rhetoric.

6. GOVERNANCE, STAKEHOLDERS, AND CONCEPTUAL DESIGN FRAMEWORK FOR PEDAGOGICALLY INTELLIGENT SMART CAMPUSES

6.1 Multi-Level Governance and Institutional Architectures

Governance in pedagogically intelligent smart campuses can be conceptualised through *multi-level governance* and *polycentric governance* constructs, in which authority, resources, and accountability are distributed across interacting layers rather than concentrated in a single command node (Farahani & Ghasmi, 2024; Mao et al., 2024; Yim, 2024). Course and programme committees, departmental boards, institutional senates, regulatory agencies, and transnational quality regimes jointly shape how AI systems, analytics platforms, and spatial infrastructures are specified, procured, and evaluated (Uygun, 2024; AlAli & Wardat, 2024; Selwyn, 2024). Each level embodies distinct *institutional logics* concerning risk tolerance, innovation tempo, and equity commitments, and misalignment across these logics frequently generates friction or inertia. A *public value governance* orientation treats digital transformation not as an isolated efficiency project but as a vehicle for generating collective benefits such as epistemic diversity and sustainability. Anticipating the granular negotiations that occur at each node of this architecture, Table 5 later maps the roles, influences, and tensions of key stakeholder categories, providing a synthetic governance matrix that can guide design of more coherent decision ecologies.

6.2 Leadership, Change, and Organisational Learning in Smart Campus Transformations

Leadership for smart campus transformation involves a complex interplay of *transformational leadership*, *distributed leadership*, and *adaptive leadership* practices that operate within the multi-level architectures outlined above (Salloum et al., 2024; Díaz & Nussbaum, 2024; Ifenthaler et al., 2024). Senior leaders articulate narratives that frame AI, analytics, and immersive infrastructures as instruments for pedagogical enrichment rather than mere cost containment, while mid-level leaders orchestrate translation of these narratives into programme designs, timetable structures, and space allocations. *Sensemaking* theories highlight the importance of conversational spaces where staff and students can reinterpret policy signals, challenge technocratic assumptions, and co-author alternative futures. At the same time, *organisational learning* and *double loop learning* constructs underscore that governance processes must allow not only for incremental adjustment of procedures but also for revision of underlying norms when data reveal unintended harms. The effectiveness of leadership practices depends on the relational configurations captured in Table 5, since asymmetries of influence and voice among stakeholder groups either enable or constrain genuine learning across the governance system.

6.3 Stakeholder Ecosystems and Co-Governance Configurations

Smart campuses constitute dense stakeholder ecosystems in which students, academic staff, professional staff, senior leadership, industry partners, and local communities are entangled through contractual, normative, and epistemic relationships. *Stakeholder theory* and *network governance* constructs conceptualise these relationships as webs of interdependence rather than linear principal-agent chains, implying that decisions about data retention, AI deployment, or spatial redesign always entail negotiation of competing pedagogical interests and risk perceptions. Some stakeholders, such as students and adjunct faculty, bear disproportionate exposure to experimental technologies while having limited formal influence over procurement and policy, whereas vendors may exert significant structural power through long term contracts and proprietary standards. To render these asymmetries analytically tractable, Table 5 below provides a compact governance matrix that profiles the pedagogical interests, decision influence, conflict patterns, and participatory mechanisms associated with major stakeholder categories in pedagogically intelligent smart campus ecologies.

Table 5. Stakeholder Governance for Pedagogically Intelligent Smart Campuses

Stakeholder Category	Pedagogical Interests and Core Responsibilities	Structural Influence within Smart Campus Decisions	Salient Conflicts and Latent Tensions	Participatory Governance and Dialogue Mechanisms
Students	Learning quality, wellbeing, assessment fairness, digital rights, employability trajectories	Indirect influence through feedback channels, representative bodies, and collective mobilisation	Tension between surveillance logic and autonomy, workload compression, inequitable access to high-end infrastructures	Student councils, data charters, design sprints, participatory policy consultations
Academic Staff	Curricular integrity, academic freedom, assessment validity, research integration, workload sustainability	Medium to high influence within programmes and departments, variable impact on enterprise platforms	Role strain from technopedagogical expectations, anxiety regarding analytics, contestation over AI in evaluation	Curriculum committees, pedagogical fellowships, analytic interpretation forums, joint governance panels
Professional and Technical Staff	Service continuity, systems reliability, user support, compliance adherence, safety protocols	High operational influence over platform configuration and infrastructural evolution	Friction between security imperatives and openness, resource constraints, role invisibility in pedagogical debates	Cross-functional working groups, incident review circles, co-design workshops with educators and students
Senior Leadership and Governing Bodies	Strategic differentiation, reputational positioning, fiscal stewardship, risk management, regulatory alignment	High formal authority over investment priorities and institutional policies	Trade-offs between innovation and liability, pressure from rankings, potential overreliance on vendor narratives	Senate deliberations, strategic retreats, public value scorecards, external advisory councils
External Partners and Industry	Talent pipelines, collaborative research, innovation ecosystems, brand association	Variable but often significant leverage through funding, contracts, and technology provision	Conflicts over data ownership, commodification of learning, misalignment between commercial timelines and educational rhythms	Partnership compacts, ethical innovation agreements, joint steering committees, transparent procurement dialogues
Local Communities and Civil Society	Environmental impacts, social inclusion, cultural recognition, shared infrastructure use	Indirect influence mediated through public discourse, civic regulation, and collaborative projects	Concerns about gentrification, exclusion from decision venues, extraction of local knowledge without reciprocity	Community forums, living-lab co-governance boards, social impact reviews, cultural advisory panels

Table 5 illustrates that pedagogical outcomes emerge from negotiations across stakeholder groups whose interests and influence are structurally uneven, yet mutually constitutive. When students participate in data charters and co-design workshops, their experiential knowledge can recalibrate analytics policies toward care rather than control. When professional and technical staff are recognised as co educators, their infrastructural expertise can be harnessed to design platforms that align with disciplinary epistemologies. Local communities, often marginal to formal governance, can shape sustainability priorities and decolonial curricula through living-lab boards and cultural advisory panels. Conversely, when these participatory mechanisms are absent or merely symbolic, vendor logics and ranking pressures can dominate, resulting in smart campus configurations that privilege visibility and efficiency over justice and learning. The stakeholder ecosystem therefore becomes both an analytical lens and a design variable for governance architectures.

6.4 Conceptual Design Framework for Smart Campus Pedagogy and Governance

A conceptual design framework for pedagogically intelligent smart campuses must integrate the theoretical lenses from earlier sections with the stakeholder mappings in Table 5, translating abstract constructs into a multi layered schema for decision making. At the foundational layer, *learning sciences*, *embodied cognition*, and *intersectional sustainability* provide criteria for evaluating whether proposed AI tools, spatial refurbishments, or scheduling reforms genuinely enhance immersive cognition and equity. A second layer specifies pedagogical models, such as immersive studios, HyFlex seminars, and AI supported mastery pathways, each with defined outcomes and infrastructural signatures. A third layer enumerates technological and spatial components selected from the ecological typologies in Table 2, configured to support the chosen models. A fourth layer encodes justice and sustainability constraints derived from Table 4, ensuring that ecological, social, and epistemic impacts are systematically examined. The final layer formalises governance and risk protocols, describing how stakeholder forums, ethics reviews, and feedback loops will be activated across the lifecycle of smart campus initiatives.

6.5 Ethical and Risk-Oriented Conceptualisation of Smart Campus Decisions

Ethical analysis of smart campus governance can draw on *deontological*, *consequentialist*, *virtue ethics*, and *care ethics* frameworks, each foregrounding different evaluative criteria for AI deployment, data practices, and infrastructural change. A deontological perspective emphasises inviolable rights, such as privacy and academic freedom, which set hard constraints on surveillance intensities or content moderation algorithms. Consequentialist reasoning assesses aggregate benefits and harms, weighing improved retention or reduced energy use against potential increases in anxiety or exclusion. Virtue and care frameworks examine character and relationships, asking whether institutional habits cultivate attentiveness, humility, and solidarity. Complementing these moral lenses, *risk governance* constructs such as *risk registers*, *scenario analysis*, and *precautionary principles* help identify privacy breaches, algorithmic bias, vendor lock-in, and ecological overshoot as distinct categories that require tailored mitigation. When integrated with stakeholder insights from Table 5, ethical and risk-oriented conceptualisations support governance arrangements that can navigate uncertainty without paralysing innovation or disregarding vulnerable groups.

6.6 Capacity Building and Professional Learning Ecosystems for Governance

Capacity building in smart campus governance extends beyond technical training to encompass *data literacy*, *AI literacy*, *design literacy*, and *critical digital literacy* for all stakeholder groups identified in Table 5. Faculty require structured opportunities to experiment with analytics and AI tools while reflecting on alignment with disciplinary values and assessment philosophies. Professional and technical staff need forums where they can explore pedagogical implications of architectural and platform decisions, moving from a service-provider identity to one of co-designer. Students benefit from curricular and co-curricular experiences that cultivate capabilities to interrogate dashboards, privacy settings, and algorithmic explanations, thereby strengthening their role as informed co-governors. Leadership programmes can integrate *systems thinking* and *organisational learning* constructs so that senior decision makers interpret feedback signals as invitations for collective inquiry rather than threats to authority. These capacities are most effectively developed within *communities of practice* and mentoring constellations that institutionalise shared vocabularies, reflective routines, and cross role solidarity.

6.7 Governance Evaluation and Adaptive Redesign in Smart Campus Ecologies

Governance arrangements for smart campuses must themselves be subject to systematic evaluation and iterative redesign, treating policies and decision processes as prototypes rather than fixed settlements. *Developmental evaluation* and *complexity aware monitoring* constructs suggest that institutions should track not only compliance metrics but also emergent patterns such as shifts in participation, perceived legitimacy, and innovation diffusion. Mixed method feedback from students, staff, and external partners can reveal whether data charters, ethics panels, and stakeholder councils function as meaningful venues for deliberation or have drifted into ceremonial roles. When discrepancies arise between espoused commitments to pedagogical intelligence and observed practices, *double loop learning* encourages questioning of governing norms, such as risk appetites or performance indicators, rather than mere procedural tweaks. Periodic revisiting of the stakeholder governance matrix in Table 5 can help institutions detect changes in influence structures, for instance when new platform providers or regulatory mandates enter the ecosystem. Through such reflexive cycles, smart campus governance can remain responsive, just, and pedagogically generative in the face of evolving technological and societal conditions.

7. CONCLUSION

7.1 Re-Stating the Central Argument

This chapter has argued that a genuinely intelligent smart campus must be evaluated through the prism of *pedagogical intelligence*, *intersectional sustainability*, and *epistemic justice*, rather than through metrics of technological novelty or infrastructural density alone. The integrated conceptual scaffolding has linked *learning sciences* and *embodied cognition* with *socio-technical systems*, *decolonial pedagogy*, and *public value governance* to construct a composite vision of the campus as a *socio-technical learning ecology*. Within this ecology, AI enabled analytics, XR laboratories, sensor rich infrastructures, and hybrid modalities become meaningful only insofar as they enhance immersive cognition, expand capabilities, and redistribute epistemic visibility. Tables 1 to 5 have provided typological condensations of this vision, translating abstract constructs into design-oriented matrices that align theories, infrastructures, stakeholder roles, and justice criteria. The central claim is that smart campuses must be designed as deliberative environments where technological sophistication is structurally subordinated to human flourishing and planetary responsibility.

7.2 Implications for Policy Makers and Institutional Leaders

For policy makers and institutional leaders, the conceptual architecture developed here implies that digital transformation strategies should be reframed as *pedagogical transformation programmes* that harness AI, analytics, and cyber physical infrastructures in service of expanded educational and civic mandates.

Funding frameworks and regulatory instruments can embed requirements derived from the matrices in Tables 1, 2, and 4, mandating explicit articulation of theoretical underpinnings, ecological impact assessments, and intersectional equity analyses for major smart campus investments. Accreditation and quality assurance regimes can reward institutions that demonstrate coherent alignment between curricular models, immersive infrastructures, and justice-oriented governance, rather than privileging generic compliance with digital readiness checklists. Strategic plans can specify public value outcomes in terms of capability enhancement, community partnership, and sustainability indicators, with *multi-level governance* arrangements that institutionalise co decision among students, staff, and external stakeholders. In such a configuration, leadership becomes a practice of orchestrating reflexive ecologies rather than commissioning isolated platforms.

7.3 Implications for Academics, Instructional Designers, and Students

For academics and instructional designers, the chapter provides a conceptual repertoire to reconfigure courses and programmes as intentional deployments of *pedagogical models* within the smart campus ecology, rather than ad hoc assemblages of tools. Table 3, which aligns immersive studios, HyFlex communities, AI supported mastery pathways, and plurilingual seminars with theoretical foundations and infrastructural requirements, can function as a decision heuristic when redesigning curricula or negotiating platform choices. Educators can treat learning analytics dashboards, XR environments, and collaboration suites as experimental apparatus for *design-based research* into learning, systematically iterating on assessment regimes and activity structures while foregrounding care, accessibility, and student voice. For students, the chapter offers a vocabulary to interrogate campus infrastructures, to claim digital rights, and to participate in co governance through data charters, living labs, and co design studios. When these actors collectively inhabit the conceptual frameworks articulated here, the smart campus becomes a shared project of epistemic co production rather than a unilateral technological imposition.

7.4 Implications for Industry Partners and Technologists

For industry partners and technologists, the analysis suggests that ethical and commercially viable innovation in the smart campus domain requires deep engagement with *learning sciences*, *critical data studies*, and *intersectional design* rather than reliance on generic optimisation paradigms. Platform providers and infrastructure vendors can treat Tables 2 and 5 as lenses that reveal how their products will interact with ecological layers and stakeholder power relations, thereby informing roadmaps that prioritise interoperability, transparency, and configurability for justice-oriented use. Co creation agreements with institutions can specify shared commitments to low carbon architectures, rights respecting analytics, and meaningful consent, alongside mechanisms for participatory evaluation with students and community partners. Technologists can design AI systems that foreground explicability, contestability, and pedagogical configurability, recognising that instructors and learners must be able to repurpose and critique algorithmic outputs. In this orientation, industry collaboration shifts from a transactional supply model to a *public value innovation ecosystem* that attends simultaneously to educational, social, and ecological returns.

7.5 Agenda for Future Research and Conceptual Development

The conceptual configurations outlined in this chapter invite a broad agenda for future research that traverses comparative analysis, theoretical refinement, and methodological innovation. Comparative studies of smart campus implementations across geopolitical regions, institutional types, and disciplinary constellations can examine how different combinations of lenses from Table 1 manifest in practice, revealing alternative *regimes of pedagogical intelligence*. Theorisation of affect, mental health, and identity formation in data saturated, immersive environments can deepen understanding of how *surveillance assemblages* and *care infrastructures* coexist and collide. Further conceptual work is needed on integrating Indigenous and community-based epistemologies within AI mediated infrastructures, including governance models for data sovereignty and shared analytic tools. Methodologically, *design-based research*, *critical participatory action research*, and *speculative design* offer promising approaches for iteratively testing and revising the frameworks developed here, while treating students and communities as co theorists rather than mere respondents.

7.6 Closing Reflection on Normative Commitments and Future Horizons

The narrative advanced in this chapter culminates in a normative assertion that smart campuses should be cultivated as sites where *technological sophistication* is consistently subordinated to educational purpose, social justice, and planetary stewardship. This commitment implies an ongoing willingness to expose infrastructures, algorithms, and governance routines to critique, redesign, and collective deliberation, rather than treating them as fixed backdrops. The tables and conceptual models presented across the chapter are intended not as rigid blueprints but as *thinking instruments* that readers can adapt, hybridise, or contest in their own contexts. Pedagogically intelligent smart campuses will remain intrinsically unfinished, since emerging technologies, climatic instabilities, and sociopolitical movements continually reshape what counts as responsible design. By embracing this incompleteness as a condition for *reflexive modernisation* rather than as a deficit, institutions, practitioners, and partners can co create higher education ecosystems in which immersive cognition, AI mediation, and equity centred knowledge production evolve in mutually reinforcing ways.

REFERENCES

Abbasi, B. N., Wu, Y., & Luo, Z. (2025). Exploring the impact of artificial intelligence on curriculum development in global higher education institutions. *Education and Information Technologies*, *30*(1), 547–581. DOI: 10.1007/s10639-024-13113-z

Abuhassna, H., Awae, F., Adnan, M. A., Daud, M., & Almheiri, A. S. (2024). The information age for education via artificial intelligence and machine learning: A bibliometric and systematic literature analysis. *International Journal of Information and Education Technology (IJIET)*, *14*(5), 700–711. DOI: 10.18178/ijiet.2024.14.5.2095

Abulibdeh, A., Zaidan, E., & Abulibdeh, R. (2024). Navigating the confluence of artificial intelligence and education for sustainable development in the era of industry 4.0: Challenges, opportunities, and ethical dimensions. *Journal of Cleaner Production*, *437*, 140527. DOI: 10.1016/j.jclepro.2023.140527

Adams, D., & Thompson, P. (2025). Transforming school leadership with artificial intelligence: Applications, implications, and future directions. *Leadership and Policy in Schools*, *24*(1), 77–89.

Adeleye, O. O., Eden, C. A., & Adeniyi, I. S. (2024). Innovative teaching methodologies in the era of artificial intelligence: A review of inclusive educational practices. *World Journal of Advanced Engineering Technology and Sciences, 11*(2), 069-079.

Afzaal, M., Shanshan, X., Yan, D., & Younas, M. (2024). Mapping artificial intelligence integration in education: a decade of innovation and impact (2013-2023)-a bibliometric analysis. *IEEE Access*.

Aguilar-Cruz, P. J., & Salas-Pilco, S. Z. (2025). Teachers' perceptions of artificial intelligence in Colombia: AI technological access, AI teacher professional development and AI ethical awareness. *Technology, Pedagogy and Education*, *34*(2), 219–238. DOI: 10.1080/1475939X.2025.2451865

Airaj, M. (2024). Ethical artificial intelligence for teaching-learning in higher education. *Education and Information Technologies*, *29*(13), 17145–17167. DOI: 10.1007/s10639-024-12545-x

Al-Abdullatif, A. M. (2024). Modeling teachers' acceptance of generative artificial intelligence use in higher education: The role of AI literacy, intelligent TPACK, and perceived trust. *Education Sciences*, *14*(11), 1209. DOI: 10.3390/educsci14111209

Al-Shorman, H. M., Saatchi, S. G., Alanaziand, T., Alzboon, M. S., Alka'awneh, S. M. N., Wahed, M. K. Y. A., & Al-Momani, A. A. M. (2025). Evaluating Artificial Intelligence Integration in Education Through Integrating TAM and S–O–R. In *Intelligence-Driven Circular Economy: Regeneration Towards Sustainability and Social Responsibility–Volume 1* (pp. 353–367). Springer Nature Switzerland. DOI: 10.1007/978-3-031-73899-9_28

Al-Zahrani, A. M., & Alasmari, T. M. (2024). Exploring the impact of artificial intelligence on higher education: The dynamics of ethical, social, and educational implications. *Humanities & Social Sciences Communications, 11*(1), 1–12. DOI: 10.1057/s41599-024-03432-4

AlAli, R., & Wardat, Y. (2024). Opportunities and challenges of integrating generative artificial intelligence in education. *International Journal of Religion, 5*(7), 784–793. DOI: 10.61707/8y29gv34

Alam, A. (2022). Impact of university's human resources practices on professors' occupational performance: empirical evidence from India's higher education sector. In *Inclusive businesses in developing economies: Converging people, profit, and corporate citizenship* (pp. 107–131). Springer International Publishing. DOI: 10.1007/978-3-031-12217-0_6

Alam, A. (2023a). Media multitasking with M-learning technology in real-time classroom learning: Analysing the dynamics in formal educational settings for the future of E-learning in India. In *2023 2nd International Conference on Smart Technologies and Systems for Next Generation Computing (ICSTSN)* (pp. 1-6). IEEE.

Alam, A. (2023b). The secret sauce of student success: Cracking the code by navigating the path to personalized learning with educational data mining. In *2023 2nd International Conference on Smart Technologies and Systems for Next Generation Computing (ICSTSN)* (pp. 1-8). IEEE.

Alam, A. (2023c). Intelligence unleashed: An argument for AI-enabled learning ecologies with real world examples of today and a peek into the future. In *International Conference on Innovations in Computer Science, Electronics & Electrical Engineering*-2022 (Vol. 2717, No. 1, p. 030001). AIP Publishing LLC. DOI: 10.1063/5.0129803

Alam, A., & Mohanty, A. (2022, December). Facial analytics or virtual avatars: competencies and design considerations for student-teacher interaction in AI-powered online education for effective classroom engagement. In *International Conference on Communication, Networks and Computing* (pp. 252-265). Cham: Springer Nature Switzerland.

Alam, A., & Mohanty, A. (2023, January). Learning on the move: a pedagogical framework for state-of-the-art mobile learning. In *International Conference on Data Management, Analytics & Innovation* (pp. 735-748). Singapore: Springer Nature Singapore. DOI: 10.1007/978-981-99-1414-2_52

Alam, A., & Mohanty, A. (2024). Integrated constructive robotics in education (ICRE) model: A paradigmatic framework for transformative learning in educational ecosystem. *Cogent Education*, *11*(1), 2324487. DOI: 10.1080/2331186X.2024.2324487

Ali, O., Murray, P. A., Momin, M., Dwivedi, Y. K., & Malik, T. (2024). The effects of artificial intelligence applications in educational settings: Challenges and strategies. *Technological Forecasting and Social Change*, *199*, 123076. DOI: 10.1016/j.techfore.2023.123076

Alier, M., Peñalvo, F. J. G., & Camba, J. D. (2024). Generative Artificial Intelligence in Education: From Deceptive to Disruptive. *International Journal of Interactive Multimedia and Artificial Intelligence*, *8*(5), 5–14. DOI: 10.9781/ijimai.2024.02.011

Almasri, F. (2024). Exploring the impact of artificial intelligence in teaching and learning of science: A systematic review of empirical research. *Research in Science Education*, *54*(5), 977–997. DOI: 10.1007/s11165-024-10176-3

Alqahtani, N., & Wafula, Z. (2025). Artificial intelligence integration: Pedagogical strategies and policies at leading universities. *Innovative Higher Education*, *50*(2), 665–684. DOI: 10.1007/s10755-024-09749-x

Alwaqdani, M. (2025). Investigating teachers' perceptions of artificial intelligence tools in education: Potential and difficulties. *Education and Information Technologies*, *30*(3), 2737–2755. DOI: 10.1007/s10639-024-12903-9

Amado-Salvatierra, H. R., Morales-Chan, M., Hernandez-Rizzardini, R., & Rosales, M. (2024, March). Exploring educators' perceptions: Artificial intelligence integration in higher education. In *2024 IEEE World Engineering Education Conference (EDUNINE)* (pp. 1-5). IEEE. DOI: 10.1109/EDUNINE60625.2024.10500578

Amdan, M. A. B., Janius, N., Kasdiah, M. A. H. B., Amdan, M. A. B., Janius, N., & Kasdiah, M. A. H. B. (2024). Concept paper: Efficiency of Artificial Intelligence (AI) tools for STEM education in Malaysia. *International Journal of Science and Research Archive*, *12*(2), 553–559. DOI: 10.30574/ijsra.2024.12.2.1273

Annuš, N. (2024). Education in the age of artificial intelligence. *TEM Journal*, *13*(1), 404–413. DOI: 10.18421/TEM131-42

Ayanwale, M. A., Adelana, O. P., Molefi, R. R., Adeeko, O., & Ishola, A. M. (2024). Examining artificial intelligence literacy among pre-service teachers for future classrooms. *Computers and Education Open*, *6*, 100179. DOI: 10.1016/j.caeo.2024.100179

Baltezarević, R., & Baltezarević, I. (2024). Students' attitudes on the role of artificial intelligence (AI) in personalized learning. *International Journal of Cognitive Research in Science. Engineering and Education*, *12*(2), 387–397.

Bender, S. M. (2024). Awareness of artificial intelligence as an essential digital literacy: ChatGPT and Gen-AI in the classroom. *Changing English*, *31*(2), 161–174. DOI: 10.1080/1358684X.2024.2309995

Bukar, U. A., Sayeed, M. S., Razak, S. F. A., Yogarayan, S., & Sneesl, R. (2024). Decision-making framework for the utilization of generative artificial intelligence in education: A case study of ChatGPT. *IEEE Access : Practical Innovations, Open Solutions*, *12*, 95368–95389. DOI: 10.1109/ACCESS.2024.3425172

Bulathwela, S., Pérez-Ortiz, M., Holloway, C., Cukurova, M., & Shawe-Taylor, J. (2024). Artificial intelligence alone will not democratise education: On educational inequality, techno-solutionism and inclusive tools. *Sustainability (Basel)*, *16*(2), 781. DOI: 10.3390/su16020781

Bulut, O., Beiting-Parrish, M., Casabianca, J. M., Slater, S. C., Jiao, H., Song, D., . . . Morilova, P. (2024). The rise of artificial intelligence in educational measurement: Opportunities and ethical challenges. *arXiv preprint arXiv:2406.18900*.

Celik, I., Gedrimiene, E., Siklander, S., & Muukkonen, H. (2024). The affordances of artificial intelligence-based tools for supporting 21st-century skills: A systematic review of empirical research in higher education. *Australasian Journal of Educational Technology*, *40*(3), 19–38. DOI: 10.14742/ajet.9069

Cheah, Y. H., Lu, J., & Kim, J. (2025). Integrating generative artificial intelligence in K-12 education: Examining teachers' preparedness, practices, and barriers. *Computers and Education: Artificial Intelligence*, *8*, 100363. DOI: 10.1016/j.caeai.2025.100363

Chen, H. (2024). The ethical challenges of educational artificial intelligence and coping measures: A discussion in the context of the 2024 World Digital Education Conference. *Science Insights Education Frontiers, 20*(2), 3263-3281.

Choi, J. I., Yang, E., & Goo, E. H. (2024). The effects of an ethics education program on artificial intelligence among middle school students: Analysis of perception and attitude changes. *Applied Sciences (Basel, Switzerland)*, *14*(4), 1588. DOI: 10.3390/app14041588

Cordero, J., Torres-Zambrano, J., & Cordero-Castillo, A. (2024). Integration of generative artificial intelligence in higher education: Best practices. *Education Sciences*, *15*(1), 32. DOI: 10.3390/educsci15010032

Cukurova, M. (2025). The interplay of learning, analytics and artificial intelligence in education: A vision for hybrid intelligence. *British Journal of Educational Technology*, *56*(2), 469–488. DOI: 10.1111/bjet.13514

Dai, K., & Liu, Q. (2024). Leveraging artificial intelligence (AI) in English as a foreign language (EFL) classes: Challenges and opportunities in the spotlight. *Computers in Human Behavior*, *159*, 108354. DOI: 10.1016/j.chb.2024.108354

Davis, C., Bush, T., & Wood, S. (2024). Artificial intelligence in education: Enhancing learning experiences through personalized adaptation. *International Journal of Cyber and IT Service Management*, *4*(1), 26–32. DOI: 10.34306/ijcitsm.v4i1.146

Díaz, B., & Nussbaum, M. (2024). Artificial intelligence for teaching and learning in schools: The need for pedagogical intelligence. *Computers & Education*, *217*, 105071. DOI: 10.1016/j.compedu.2024.105071

Dieterle, E., Dede, C., & Walker, M. (2024). The cyclical ethical effects of using artificial intelligence in education. *AI & Society*, *39*(2), 633–643. DOI: 10.1007/s00146-022-01497-w

Edwards-Fapohunda, M. O., & Adediji, M. A. (2024). Sustainable development of distance learning in continuing adult education: The impact of artificial intelligence. *Iconic Research and Engineering Journals*, *8*(1), 113–114.

Erduran, S., & Levrini, O. (2024). The impact of artificial intelligence on scientific practices: An emergent area of research for science education. *International Journal of Science Education*, *46*(18), 1982–1989. DOI: 10.1080/09500693.2024.2306604

Ezeoguine, E. P., & Eteng-Uket, S. (2024). Artificial intelligence tools and higher education student's engagement. *Edukasiana: Jurnal Inovasi Pendidikan*, *3*(3), 300–312. DOI: 10.56916/ejip.v3i3.733

Fadlelmula, F. K., & Qadhi, S. M. (2024). A systematic review of research on artificial intelligence in higher education: Practice, gaps, and future directions in the GCC. *Journal of University Teaching & Learning Practice*, *21*(6), 146–173. DOI: 10.53761/pswgbw82

Famaye, T., Bailey, C. S., Adisa, I., & Irgens, G. A. (2024). What Makes ChatGPT Dangerous Is Also What Makes It Special": High-School Student Perspectives on the Integration or Ban of Artificial Intelligence in Educational Contexts. *International Journal of Technology in Education*, *7*(2), 174–199. DOI: 10.46328/ijte.651

Farahani, M. S., & Ghasmi, G. (2024, July). Artificial intelligence in education: A comprehensive study. In *Forum for Education Studies* (Vol. 2, No. 3, pp. 1379-1379). DOI: 10.59400/fes.v2i3.1379

Farooqi, M. T. K., Amanat, I., & Awan, S. M. (2024). Ethical considerations and challenges in the integration of artificial intelligence in education: A systematic review. *Journal of Excellence in Management Sciences, 3*(4), 35–50. DOI: 10.69565/jems.v3i4.314

Filgueiras, F. (2024). Artificial intelligence and education governance. *Education, Citizenship and Social Justice, 19*(3), 349–361. DOI: 10.1177/17461979231160674

Fitrianto, I., Setyawan, C. E., & Saleh, M. (2024). Utilizing Artificial Intelligence for Personalized Arabic Language Learning Plans. *International Journal of Post Axial: Futuristic Teaching and Learning*, 30-40.

Forero-Corba, W., & Bennasar, F. N. (2024). Techniques and applications of Machine Learning and Artificial Intelligence in education: a systematic review. *RIED-Revista Iberoamericana de Educación a Distancia, 27*(1).

Franco D'Souza, R., Mathew, M., Mishra, V., & Surapaneni, K. M. (2024). Twelve tips for addressing ethical concerns in the implementation of artificial intelligence in medical education. *Medical Education Online, 29*(1), 2330250. DOI: 10.1080/10872981.2024.2330250

Fullan, M., Azorín, C., Harris, A., & Jones, M. (2024). Artificial intelligence and school leadership: Challenges, opportunities and implications. *School Leadership & Management, 44*(4), 339–346. DOI: 10.1080/13632434.2023.2246856

Fundi, M., Sanusi, I. T., Oyelere, S. S., & Ayere, M. (2024). Advancing AI education: Assessing Kenyan in-service teachers' preparedness for integrating artificial intelligence in competence-based curriculum. *Computers in Human Behavior Reports, 14*, 100412. DOI: 10.1016/j.chbr.2024.100412

Galindo-Domínguez, H., Delgado, N., Campo, L., & Losada, D. (2024). Relationship between teachers' digital competence and attitudes towards artificial intelligence in education. *International Journal of Educational Research, 126*, 102381. DOI: 10.1016/j.ijer.2024.102381

Galindo-Domínguez, H., Delgado, N., Losada, D., & Etxabe, J. M. (2024). An analysis of the use of artificial intelligence in education in Spain: The in-service teacher's perspective. *Journal of Digital Learning in Teacher Education, 40*(1), 41–56. DOI: 10.1080/21532974.2023.2284726

Gkintoni, E., Antonopoulou, H., Sortwell, A., & Halkiopoulos, C. (2025). Challenging cognitive load theory: The role of educational neuroscience and artificial intelligence in redefining learning efficacy. *Brain Sciences*, *15*(2), 203. DOI: 10.3390/brainsci15020203

Gökçearslan, S., Tosun, C., & Erdemir, Z. G. (2024). Benefits, challenges, and methods of artificial intelligence (AI) chatbots in education: A systematic literature review. *International Journal of Technology in Education*, *7*(1), 19–39. DOI: 10.46328/ijte.600

Grájeda, A., Burgos, J., Córdova, P., & Sanjinés, A. (2024). Assessing student-perceived impact of using artificial intelligence tools: Construction of a synthetic index of application in higher education. *Cogent Education*, *11*(1), 2287917. DOI: 10.1080/2331186X.2023.2287917

Guettala, M., Bourekkache, S., Kazar, O., & Harous, S. (2024). Generative artificial intelligence in education: Advancing adaptive and personalized learning. *Acta Informatica Pragensia*, *13*(3), 460–489. DOI: 10.18267/j.aip.235

Guo, S., Zheng, Y., & Zhai, X. (2024). Artificial intelligence in education research during 2013–2023: A review based on bibliometric analysis. *Education and Information Technologies*, *29*(13), 16387–16409. DOI: 10.1007/s10639-024-12491-8

Ifenthaler, D., Majumdar, R., Gorissen, P., Judge, M., Mishra, S., Raffaghelli, J., & Shimada, A. (2024). Artificial intelligence in education: Implications for policymakers, researchers, and practitioners. *Technology. Knowledge and Learning*, *29*(4), 1693–1710. DOI: 10.1007/s10758-024-09747-0

Iqbal, M., Khan, N. U., & Imran, M. (2024). The role of artificial intelligence (AI) in transforming educational practices: Opportunities, challenges, and implications. *Qlantic Journal of Social Sciences*, *5*(2), 348–359. DOI: 10.55737/qjss.349319430

Ivanashko, O., Kozak, A., Knysh, T., & Honchar, K. (2024). The role of artificial intelligence in shaping the future of education: Opportunities and challenges. *Futurity Education*, *4*(1), 126–146.

Jafari, F., & Keykha, A. (2024). Identifying the opportunities and challenges of artificial intelligence in higher education: A qualitative study. *Journal of Applied Research in Higher Education*, *16*(4), 1228–1245. DOI: 10.1108/JARHE-09-2023-0426

Jatileni, C. N., Sanusi, I. T., Olaleye, S. A., Ayanwale, M. A., Agbo, F. J., & Oyelere, P. B. (2024). Artificial intelligence in compulsory level of education: Perspectives from Namibian in-service teachers. *Education and Information Technologies*, *29*(10), 12569–12596. DOI: 10.1007/s10639-023-12341-z

Joel Augustus, D., Asiegbu Victor, I., & Obinna, E. (2025). Leveraging artificial intelligence (AI) for educational development in Nigeria: Examining the challenges and opportunities. *Journal of Social Sciences*, *2*(2).

Karakose, T., & Tülübas, T. (2024). School Leadership and Management in the Age of Artificial Intelligence (AI): Recent Developments and Future Prospects. *Educational Process: International Journal*, *13*(1), 7–14. DOI: 10.22521/edupij.2024.131.1

Karataş, F., Eriçok, B., & Tanrikulu, L. (2025). Reshaping curriculum adaptation in the age of artificial intelligence: Mapping teachers' AI-driven curriculum adaptation patterns. *British Educational Research Journal*, *51*(1), 154–180. DOI: 10.1002/berj.4068

Katsamakas, E., Pavlov, O. V., & Saklad, R. (2024). Artificial intelligence and the transformation of higher education institutions: A systems approach. *Sustainability (Basel)*, *16*(14), 6118. DOI: 10.3390/su16146118

Kazanidis, I., & Pellas, N. (2024). Harnessing generative artificial intelligence for digital literacy innovation: A comparative study between early childhood education and computer science undergraduates. *AI*, *5*(3), 1427–1445. DOI: 10.3390/ai5030068

Khreisat, M. N., Khilani, D., Rusho, M. A., Karkkulainen, E. A., Tabuena, A. C., & Uberas, A. D. (2024). Ethical implications of AI integration in educational decision making: Systematic review. *Educational Administration: Theory and Practice*, *30*(5), 8521–8527.

Kong, S. C., Korte, S. M., Burton, S., Keskitalo, P., Turunen, T., Smith, D., Wang, L., Lee, J. C.-K., & Beaton, M. C. (2025). Artificial Intelligence (AI) literacy–an argument for AI literacy in education. *Innovations in Education and Teaching International*, *62*(2), 477–483. DOI: 10.1080/14703297.2024.2332744

Kong, S. C., & Yang, Y. (2024). A human-centered learning and teaching framework using generative artificial intelligence for self-regulated learning development through domain knowledge learning in K–12 settings. *IEEE Transactions on Learning Technologies*, *17*, 1562–1573. DOI: 10.1109/TLT.2024.3392830

Kumar, S., Rao, P., Singhania, S., Verma, S., & Kheterpal, M. (2024). Will artificial intelligence drive the advancements in higher education? A tri-phased exploration. *Technological Forecasting and Social Change*, *201*, 123258. DOI: 10.1016/j.techfore.2024.123258

Lan, Y. (2024). Through tensions to identity-based motivations: Exploring teacher professional identity in Artificial Intelligence-enhanced teacher training. *Teaching and Teacher Education*, *151*, 104736. DOI: 10.1016/j.tate.2024.104736

Lee, Y. J., Davis, R. O., & Ryu, J. (2024). Korean in-service teachers' perceptions of implementing artificial intelligence (AI) education for teaching in schools and their AI teacher training programs. *International Journal of Information and Education Technology (IJIET)*, *14*(2), 214–219. DOI: 10.18178/ijiet.2024.14.2.2042

Leong, W. Y., Leong, Y. Z., & San Leong, W. (2024, October). Artificial Intelligence in education. In *IET International Conference on Engineering Technologies and Applications (ICETA 2024)* (Vol. 2024, pp. 183-184). IET.

Lérias, E., Guerra, C., & Ferreira, P. (2024). Literacy in artificial intelligence as a challenge for teaching in higher education: A case study at portalegre polytechnic university. *Information (Basel)*, *15*(4), 205. DOI: 10.3390/info15040205

Li, M. (2025). Integrating artificial intelligence in primary mathematics education: Investigating internal and external influences on teacher adoption. *International Journal of Science and Mathematics Education*, *23*(5), 1283–1308. DOI: 10.1007/s10763-024-10515-w

Lim, E. M. (2024). Metaphor analysis on pre-service early childhood teachers' conception of AI (Artificial Intelligence) education for young children. *Thinking Skills and Creativity*, *51*, 101455. DOI: 10.1016/j.tsc.2023.101455

Lin, H., & Chen, Q. (2024). Artificial intelligence (AI)-integrated educational applications and college students' creativity and academic emotions: Students and teachers' perceptions and attitudes. *BMC Psychology*, *12*(1), 487. DOI: 10.1186/s40359-024-01979-0

Linderoth, C., Hultén, M., & Stenliden, L. (2024). Competing visions of artificial intelligence in education—A heuristic analysis on sociotechnical imaginaries and problematizations in policy guidelines. *Policy Futures in Education*, *22*(8), 1662–1678. DOI: 10.1177/14782103241228900

Liu, R., Zenke, C., Liu, C., Holmes, A., Thornton, P., & Malan, D. J. (2024, March). Teaching CS50 with AI: leveraging generative artificial intelligence in computer science education. In *Proceedings of the 55th ACM technical symposium on computer science education* V. 1 (pp. 750-756).

Lye, C. Y., & Lim, L. (2024). Generative artificial intelligence in tertiary education: Assessment redesign principles and considerations. *Education Sciences*, *14*(6), 569. DOI: 10.3390/educsci14060569

Ma, D., Akram, H., & Chen, I. H. (2024). Artificial intelligence in higher education: A cross-cultural examination of students' behavioral intentions and attitudes. *International Review of Research in Open and Distance Learning*, *25*(3), 134–157. DOI: 10.19173/irrodl.v25i3.7703

Ma, S., & Lei, L. (2024). The factors influencing teacher education students' willingness to adopt artificial intelligence technology for information-based teaching. *Asia Pacific Journal of Education*, *44*(1), 94–111. DOI: 10.1080/02188791.2024.2305155

Mah, D. K., & Groß, N. (2024). Artificial intelligence in higher education: Exploring faculty use, self-efficacy, distinct profiles, and professional development needs. *International Journal of Educational Technology in Higher Education*, *21*(1), 58. DOI: 10.1186/s41239-024-00490-1

Mahmoud, C. F., & Sørensen, J. T. (2024). Artificial intelligence in personalized learning with a focus on current developments and future prospects. *Research and Advances in Education*, *3*(8), 25–31. DOI: 10.56397/RAE.2024.08.04

Mao, J., Chen, B., & Liu, J. C. (2024). Generative artificial intelligence in education and its implications for assessment. *TechTrends*, *68*(1), 58–66. DOI: 10.1007/s11528-023-00911-4

Marengo, A., Pagano, A., Pange, J., & Soomro, K. A. (2024). The educational value of artificial intelligence in higher education: A 10-year systematic literature review. *Interactive Technology and Smart Education*, *21*(4), 625–644. DOI: 10.1108/ITSE-11-2023-0218

Martin, F., Zhuang, M., & Schaefer, D. (2024). Systematic review of research on artificial intelligence in K-12 education (2017–2022). *Computers and Education: Artificial Intelligence*, *6*, 100195. DOI: 10.1016/j.caeai.2023.100195

Memarian, B., & Doleck, T. (2024). Human-in-the-loop in artificial intelligence in education: A review and entity-relationship (ER) analysis. *Computers in Human Behavior: Artificial Humans*, *2*(1), 100053. DOI: 10.1016/j.chbah.2024.100053

Merchán Sánchez-Jara, J. F., González Gutiérrez, S., Cruz Rodríguez, J., & Syroyid Syroyid, B. (2024). Artificial intelligence-assisted music education: A critical synthesis of challenges and opportunities. *Education Sciences*, *14*(11), 1171. DOI: 10.3390/educsci14111171

Mikeladze, T., Meijer, P. C., & Verhoeff, R. P. (2024). A comprehensive exploration of artificial intelligence competence frameworks for educators: A critical review. *European Journal of Education*, *59*(3), e12663. DOI: 10.1111/ejed.12663

Mouta, A., Pinto-Llorente, A. M., & Torrecilla-Sánchez, E. M. (2024). Uncovering blind spots in education ethics: Insights from a systematic literature review on artificial intelligence in education. *International Journal of Artificial Intelligence in Education, 34*(3), 1166–1205. DOI: 10.1007/s40593-023-00384-9

Mouta, A., Torrecilla-Sánchez, E. M., & Pinto-Llorente, A. M. (2024). Design of a future scenarios toolkit for an ethical implementation of artificial intelligence in education. *Education and Information Technologies, 29*(9), 10473–10498. DOI: 10.1007/s10639-023-12229-y

Murdan, A. P., & Halkhoree, R. (2024, June). Integration of Artificial Intelligence for educational excellence and innovation in higher education institutions. In *2024 1st International Conference on Smart Energy Systems and Artificial Intelligence (SESAI)* (pp. 1-6). IEEE. DOI: 10.1109/SESAI61023.2024.10599402

Musolin, M. H., Ismail, M. H., Farhan, M., Rois, N., Ismail, A., Huda, M., & Rohim, M. A. (2024, February). Understanding of artificial intelligence for Islamic education support and service: insights from empirical literature review. In *International Congress on Information and Communication Technology* (pp. 27-43). Singapore: Springer Nature Singapore.

Mustafa, M. Y., Tlili, A., Lampropoulos, G., Huang, R., Jandrić, P., Zhao, J., Salha, S., Xu, L., Panda, S., Kinshuk, , López-Pernas, S., & Saqr, M. (2024). A systematic review of literature reviews on artificial intelligence in education (AIED): A roadmap to a future research agenda. *Smart Learning Environments, 11*(1), 59. DOI: 10.1186/s40561-024-00350-5

Naixin, Z., Wai Yie, L., Tong, Z., & Changqing, W. (2024). Artificial Intelligence in Engineering Education: A Review of Pedagogical Innovations. *INTI JOURNAL, 2024*(46), 1–10.

Nedungadi, P., Tang, K. Y., & Raman, R. (2024). The transformative power of generative artificial intelligence for achieving the sustainable development goal of quality education. *Sustainability (Basel), 16*(22), 9779. DOI: 10.3390/su16229779

Ng, D. T. K., Chan, E. K. C., & Lo, C. K. (2025). Opportunities, challenges and school strategies for integrating generative AI in education. *Computers and Education: Artificial Intelligence*, 100373.

Ng, D. T. K., Su, J., Leung, J. K. L., & Chu, S. K. W. (2024). Artificial intelligence (AI) literacy education in secondary schools: A review. *Interactive Learning Environments, 32*(10), 6204–6224. DOI: 10.1080/10494820.2023.2255228

Nguyen, A., Kremantzis, M., Essien, A., Petrounias, I., & Hosseini, S. (2024). Enhancing student engagement through artificial intelligence (AI): Understanding the basics, opportunities, and challenges. *Journal of University Teaching & Learning Practice*, *21*(6), 1–13. DOI: 10.53761/caraaq92

Nikolopoulou, K. (2024). Generative artificial intelligence in higher education: Exploring ways of harnessing pedagogical practices with the assistance of ChatGPT. *International Journal of Changes in Education*, *1*(2), 103–111. DOI: 10.47852/bonviewIJCE42022489

Obenza, B. N., Salvahan, A., Rios, A. N., Solo, A., Alburo, R. A., & Gabila, R. J. (2024). University students' perception and use of ChatGPT: Generative artificial intelligence (AI) in higher education. *International Journal of Human-Computer Studies*, *5*(12), 5–18.

Obidovna, D. Z. (2024). The pedagogical-psychological aspects of artificial intelligence technologies in integrative education. *International Journal Of Literature And Languages*, *4*(03), 13–19. DOI: 10.37547/ijll/Volume04Issue03-03

Opesemowo, O. A., & Ndlovu, M. (2024). Artificial intelligence in mathematics education: The good, the bad, and the ugly. *Journal of Pedagogical Research*, *8*(3), 333–346. DOI: 10.33902/JPR.202426428

Opesemowo, O. A. G., & Adekomaya, V. (2024). Harnessing artificial intelligence for advancing sustainable development goals in South Africa's higher education system: A qualitative study. *International Journal of Learning. Teaching and Educational Research*, *23*(3), 67–86. DOI: 10.26803/ijlter.23.3.4

Özer, M. (2024). Potential Benefits and Risks of Artificial Intelligence in Education. *Bartin University Journal of Faculty of Education, 13*(2).

Ozodakhon, K. (2024). The benefits and drawbacks of using artificial intelligence (ChatGPT) in education. *University Research Base*, 805-808.

Pack, A., & Maloney, J. (2024). Using artificial intelligence in TESOL: Some ethical and pedagogical considerations. *TESOL Quarterly*, *58*(2), 1007–1018. DOI: 10.1002/tesq.3320

Park, W., & Kwon, H. (2024). Implementing artificial intelligence education for middle school technology education in Republic of Korea. *International Journal of Technology and Design Education*, *34*(1), 109–135. DOI: 10.1007/s10798-023-09812-2

Perkins, M., Furze, L., Roe, J., & MacVaugh, J. (2024). The Artificial Intelligence Assessment Scale (AIAS): A framework for ethical integration of generative AI in educational assessment. *Journal of University Teaching & Learning Practice*, *21*(6), 49–66. DOI: 10.53761/q3azde36

Rabiatu, M. M., & Shehu, S. A. (2024). Adopting artificial intelligence (AI) in education: Challenges & possibilities. *Asian Journal of Advanced Research and Reports*, *18*(2), 106–111. DOI: 10.9734/ajarr/2024/v18i2608

Rahiman, H. U., & Kodikal, R. (2024). Revolutionizing education: Artificial intelligence empowered learning in higher education. *Cogent Education*, *11*(1), 2293431. DOI: 10.1080/2331186X.2023.2293431

Ramirez, E. A. B., & Esparrell, J. A. F. (2024). Artificial Intelligence (AI) in Education: Unlocking the Perfect Synergy for Learning. *Educational Process: International Journal*, *13*(1), 35–51.

Rane, N. (2024). Enhancing the quality of teaching and learning through Gemini, ChatGPT, and similar generative Artificial Intelligence: Challenges, future prospects, and ethical considerations in education. *TESOL and Technology Studies*, *5*(1), 1–6. DOI: 10.48185/tts.v5i1.1000

Robert, A., Potter, K., & Frank, L. (2024). The impact of artificial intelligence on students' learning experience. *Wiley Interdisciplinary Reviews: Computational Statistics*, *2*(01), 75–84.

Roshanaei, M. (2024). Towards best practices for mitigating artificial intelligence implicit bias in shaping diversity, inclusion and equity in higher education. *Education and Information Technologies*, *29*(14), 18959–18984. DOI: 10.1007/s10639-024-12605-2

Ruiz-Rojas, L. I., Salvador-Ullauri, L., & Acosta-Vargas, P. (2024). Collaborative working and critical thinking: Adoption of generative artificial intelligence tools in higher education. *Sustainability (Basel)*, *16*(13), 5367. DOI: 10.3390/su16135367

Saatchi, S. G., Wahed, M. K. Y. A., Alqaraleh, M. K. S., Al-Shorman, H. M., Alanazi, T., Alka'awneh, S. M. N., & Alzyoud, M. (2025). The influence of compatibility on the acceptance of artificial intelligence in Kuwaiti universities. In *Intelligence-Driven Circular Economy: Regeneration Towards Sustainability and Social Responsibility–Volume 1* (pp. 103–117). Springer Nature Switzerland. DOI: 10.1007/978-3-031-73899-9_9

Sağın, F. G., Özkaya, A. B., Tengiz, F., Geyik, Ö. G., & Geyik, C. (2024). Current evaluation and recommendations for the use of artificial intelligence tools in education. *Türk Biyokimya Dergisi*, *48*(6), 620–625. DOI: 10.1515/tjb-2023-0254

Salloum, S. A. (2024). AI perils in education: Exploring ethical concerns. *Artificial intelligence in education: The power and dangers of ChatGPT in the classroom*, 669-675.

Salloum, S. A., Salloum, A., & Alfaisal, R. (2024). Objectives and Obstacles of Artificial Intelligence in Education. *Artificial Intelligence in Education: The Power and Dangers of ChatGPT in the Classroom*, 605-614.

Samala, A. D., Rawas, S., Wang, T., Reed, J. M., Kim, J., Howard, N. J., & Ertz, M. (2025). Unveiling the landscape of generative artificial intelligence in education: A comprehensive taxonomy of applications, challenges, and future prospects. *Education and Information Technologies*, *30*(3), 3239–3278. DOI: 10.1007/s10639-024-12936-0

Sămărescu, N., Bumbac, R., Zamfiroiu, A., & Iorgulescu, M. C. (2024). Artificial intelligence in education: Next-gen teacher perspectives. *Amfiteatru Economic*, *26*(65), 145–161. DOI: 10.24818/EA/2024/65/145

Sana, E., Fitriani, A., Soetarno, D., & Yusuf, M. (2024). Analysis of user perceptions on interactive learning platforms based on artificial intelligence. *Journal of Computer Science and Technology Application*, *1*(1), 26–32. DOI: 10.33050/corisinta.v1i1.12

Sanusi, I. T., Agbo, F. J., Dada, O. A., Yunusa, A. A., Aruleba, K. D., Obaido, G., Olawumi, O., & Oyelere, S. S.Centre for Multidisciplinary Research and Innovation (CEMRI). (2024). Stakeholders' insights on artificial intelligence education: Perspectives of teachers, students, and policymakers. *Computers and Education Open*, *7*, 100212. DOI: 10.1016/j.caeo.2024.100212

Sanusi, I. T., Ayanwale, M. A., & Chiu, T. K. (2024). Investigating the moderating effects of social good and confidence on teachers' intention to prepare school students for artificial intelligence education. *Education and Information Technologies*, *29*(1), 273–295. DOI: 10.1007/s10639-023-12250-1

Sanusi, I. T., Ayanwale, M. A., & Tolorunleke, A. E. (2024). Investigating pre-service teachers' artificial intelligence perception from the perspective of planned behavior theory. *Computers and Education: Artificial Intelligence*, *6*, 100202. DOI: 10.1016/j.caeai.2024.100202

Sarwar, M. A., & Ms Saima, A. G. (2024). The role of artificial intelligence in shaping the future of education at higher secondary level. *Journal of Education and Social Studies*, *5*(1), 34–45. DOI: 10.52223/jess.2024.5104

Sasikala, P., & Ravichandran, R. (2024). Journal of Digital Learning and Education. *Journal of Digital Learning and Education*, *4*(2), 145–155. DOI: 10.52562/jdle.v4i2.1234

Selwyn, N. (2024). On the limits of artificial intelligence (AI) in education. *Nordisk tidsskrift for pedagogikk og kritikk, 10*(1), 3-14.

Shailendra, S., Kadel, R., & Sharma, A. (2024). Framework for adoption of generative artificial intelligence (GenAI) in education. *IEEE Transactions on Education*, *67*(5), 777–785. DOI: 10.1109/TE.2024.3432101

Shamsuddinova, S., Heryani, P., & Naval, M. A. (2024). Evolution to revolution: Critical exploration of educators' perceptions of the impact of Artificial Intelligence (AI) on the teaching and learning process in the GCC region. *International Journal of Educational Research, 125*, 102326. DOI: 10.1016/j.ijer.2024.102326

Sharma, S., Singh, G., Sharma, C. S., & Kapoor, S. (2024). Artificial intelligence in Indian higher education institutions: A quantitative study on adoption and perceptions. *International Journal of System Assurance Engineering and Management*, •••, 1–17. DOI: 10.1007/s13198-023-02193-8

Singha, S., & Singha, R. (2024). The application of artificial intelligence in education: Opportunities and challenges. *Educational perspectives on digital technologies in modeling and management*, 282-292.

Sova, R., Tudor, C., Tartavulea, C. V., & Dieaconescu, R. I. (2024). Artificial intelligence tool adoption in higher education: A structural equation modeling approach to understanding impact factors among economics students. *Electronics (Basel)*, *13*(18), 3632. DOI: 10.3390/electronics13183632

Sperling, K., Stenberg, C. J., McGrath, C., Åkerfeldt, A., Heintz, F., & Stenliden, L. (2024). In search of artificial intelligence (AI) literacy in teacher education: A scoping review. *Computers and Education Open*, *6*, 100169. DOI: 10.1016/j.caeo.2024.100169

Stolpe, K., & Hallström, J. (2024). Artificial intelligence literacy for technology education. *Computers and Education Open*, *6*, 100159. DOI: 10.1016/j.caeo.2024.100159

Storey, V. A., & Wagner, A. (2024). Integrating artificial intelligence (ai) into adult education: Opportunities, challenges, and future directions. [IJAET]. *International Journal of Adult Education and Technology*, *15*(1), 1–15. DOI: 10.4018/IJAET.345921

Storozhyk, M. (2024). Philosophy of future: Analytical overview of interaction between education, science, and artificial intelligence in the context of contemporary challenges. *Futurity Philosophy*, *3*(1), 23–47.

Suryanarayana, K. S., Kandi, V. P., Pavani, G., Rao, A. S., Rout, S., & Krishna, T. S. R. (2024). Artificial intelligence enhanced digital learning for the sustainability of education management system. *The Journal of High Technology Management Research, 35*(2), 100495. DOI: 10.1016/j.hitech.2024.100495

Tahir, M., Hassan, F. D., & Shagoo, M. R. (2024). Role of artificial intelligence in education: A conceptual review. *World Journal of Advanced Research and Reviews, 22*(1), 1469–1475. DOI: 10.30574/wjarr.2024.22.1.1217

Tan, X., Cheng, G., & Ling, M. H. (2024). Artificial intelligence in teaching and teacher professional development: A systematic review. *Computers and Education: Artificial Intelligence*, 100355.

Tang, K. H. D. (2024). Implications of artificial intelligence for teaching and learning. *Acta Pedagogia Asiana, 3*(2), 65–79. DOI: 10.53623/apga.v3i2.404

Tashtoush, M. A., Wardat, Y., Ali, R. A., & Saleh, S. (2024). Artificial intelligence in education: Mathematics teachers' perspectives, practices and challenges. *Iraqi Journal for Computer Science and Mathematics, 5*(1), 20. DOI: 10.52866/ijcsm.2024.05.01.004

Tassoti, S. (2024). Assessment of students use of generative artificial intelligence: Prompting strategies and prompt engineering in chemistry education. *Journal of Chemical Education, 101*(6), 2475–2482. DOI: 10.1021/acs.jchemed.4c00212

Thorat, V., Rao, P., Joshi, N., Talreja, P., & Shetty, A. R. (2024). Role of artificial intelligence (AI) in patient education and communication in dentistry. *Cureus, 16*(5). Advance online publication. DOI: 10.7759/cureus.59799

Topaz, M., Peltonen, L. M., Michalowski, M., Stiglic, G., Ronquillo, C., Pruinelli, L., Song, J., O'Connor, S., Miyagawa, S., & Fukahori, H. (2025). The ChatGPT effect: Nursing education and generative artificial intelligence. *The Journal of Nursing Education, 64*(6), e40–e43. DOI: 10.3928/01484834-20240126-01

Tzirides, A. O. O., Zapata, G., Kastania, N. P., Saini, A. K., Castro, V., Ismael, S. A., You, Y., Santos, T. A., Searsmith, D., O'Brien, C., Cope, B., & Kalantzis, M. (2024). Combining human and artificial intelligence for enhanced AI literacy in higher education. *Computers and Education Open, 6*, 100184. DOI: 10.1016/j.caeo.2024.100184

Uygun, D. (2024). Teachers' perspectives on artificial intelligence in education. *Advances in Mobile Learning Educational Research, 4*(1), 931–939. DOI: 10.25082/AMLER.2024.01.005

Vieriu, A. M., & Petrea, G. (2025). The impact of artificial intelligence (AI) on students' academic development. *Education Sciences*, *15*(3), 343. DOI: 10.3390/educsci15030343

Vistorte, A. O. R., Deroncele-Acosta, A., Ayala, J. L. M., Barrasa, A., López-Granero, C., & Martí-González, M. (2024). Integrating artificial intelligence to assess emotions in learning environments: A systematic literature review. *Frontiers in Psychology*, *15*, 1387089. DOI: 10.3389/fpsyg.2024.1387089

Walter, Y. (2024). Embracing the future of Artificial Intelligence in the classroom: The relevance of AI literacy, prompt engineering, and critical thinking in modern education. *International Journal of Educational Technology in Higher Education*, *21*(1), 15. DOI: 10.1186/s41239-024-00448-3

Wang, C., Wang, H., Li, Y., Dai, J., Gu, X., & Yu, T. (2025). Factors influencing university students' behavioral intention to use generative artificial intelligence: Integrating the theory of planned behavior and AI literacy. *International Journal of Human-Computer Interaction*, *41*(11), 6649–6671. DOI: 10.1080/10447318.2024.2383033

Wang, J., & Li, J. (2024). Artificial intelligence empowering public health education: Prospects and challenges. *Frontiers in Public Health*, *12*, 1389026. DOI: 10.3389/fpubh.2024.1389026

Wang, S., Wang, F., Zhu, Z., Wang, J., Tran, T., & Du, Z. (2024). Artificial intelligence in education: A systematic literature review. *Expert Systems with Applications*, *252*, 124167. DOI: 10.1016/j.eswa.2024.124167

Weidener, L., & Fischer, M. (2024). Artificial intelligence in medicine: Cross-sectional study among medical students on application, education, and ethical aspects. *JMIR Medical Education*, *10*(1), e51247. DOI: 10.2196/51247

Williamson, B. (2024). The social life of AI in education. *International Journal of Artificial Intelligence in Education*, *34*(1), 97–104. DOI: 10.1007/s40593-023-00342-5

Wu, X. Y. (2024). Artificial Intelligence in L2 learning: A meta-analysis of contextual, instructional, and social-emotional moderators. *System*, *126*, 103498. DOI: 10.1016/j.system.2024.103498

Xia, Q., Weng, X., Ouyang, F., Lin, T. J., & Chiu, T. K. (2024). A scoping review on how generative artificial intelligence transforms assessment in higher education. *International Journal of Educational Technology in Higher Education*, *21*(1), 40. DOI: 10.1186/s41239-024-00468-z

Yadav, S. (2024). Artificial Intelligence (AI) Integration in Higher Education: Navigating Opportunities and Ethical Frontiers in Education with Advanced Technologies. In *Impact of artificial intelligence on society* (pp. 43-59). Chapman and Hall/CRC.

Yadav, U., & Shrawankar, U. (2025). Artificial intelligence across industries: A comprehensive review with a focus on education. *AI applications and strategies in teacher education*, 275-320.

Yang, A. (2024). Challenges and opportunities for foreign language teachers in the era of artificial intelligence. *International Journal of Education and Humanities*, *4*(1), 39–50. DOI: 10.58557/(ijeh).v4i1.202

Yang, W., Hu, X., Yeter, I. H., Su, J., Yang, Y., & Lee, J. C. K. (2024). Artificial intelligence education for young children: A case study of technology-enhanced embodied learning. *Journal of Computer Assisted Learning*, *40*(2), 465–477. DOI: 10.1111/jcal.12892

Yang, Y., Chen, L., He, W., Sun, D., & Salas-Pilco, S. Z. (2024). Artificial intelligence for enhancing special education for K-12: A decade of trends, themes, and global insights (2013–2023). *International Journal of Artificial Intelligence in Education*, •••, 1–49.

Yılmaz, Ö. (2024). Personalised learning and artificial intelligence in science education: Current state and future perspectives. *Educational Technology Quarterly*, *2024*(3), 255–274. DOI: 10.55056/etq.744

Yim, I. H. Y. (2024). A critical review of teaching and learning artificial intelligence (AI) literacy: Developing an intelligence-based AI literacy framework for primary school education. *Computers and Education: Artificial Intelligence*, *7*, 100319. DOI: 10.1016/j.caeai.2024.100319

Yim, I. H. Y., & Su, J. (2025). Artificial intelligence (AI) learning tools in K-12 education: A scoping review. *Journal of Computers in Education*, *12*(1), 93–131.

Yuan, L., & Liu, X. (2025). The effect of artificial intelligence tools on EFL learners' engagement, enjoyment, and motivation. *Computers in Human Behavior*, *162*, 108474. DOI: 10.1016/j.chb.2024.108474

Yue, M., Jong, M. S. Y., & Ng, D. T. K. (2024). Understanding K–12 teachers' technological pedagogical content knowledge readiness and attitudes toward artificial intelligence education. *Education and Information Technologies*, *29*(15), 19505–19536. DOI: 10.1007/s10639-024-12621-2

Zadorina, O., Hurskaya, V., Sobolyeva, S., Grekova, L., & Vasylyuk-Zaitseva, S. (2024). The role of artificial intelligence in creation of future education: Possibilities and challenges. *Futurity Education*, *4*(2), 163–185.

Zarei, M., Mamaghani, H. E., Abbasi, A., & Hosseini, M. S. (2024). Application of artificial intelligence in medical education: A review of benefits, challenges, and solutions. *Medicina Clínica Práctica*, *7*(2), 100422. DOI: 10.1016/j.mcpsp.2023.100422

Zawacki-Richter, O., Bai, J. Y., Lee, K., Slagter van Tryon, P. J., & Prinsloo, P. (2024). New advances in artificial intelligence applications in higher education? *International Journal of Educational Technology in Higher Education*, *21*(1), 32. DOI: 10.1186/s41239-024-00464-3

Zhang, H., Perry, A., & Lee, I. (2025). Developing and validating the artificial intelligence literacy concept inventory: An instrument to assess artificial intelligence literacy among middle school students. *International Journal of Artificial Intelligence in Education*, *35*(1), 398–438. DOI: 10.1007/s40593-024-00398-x

Zhou, X., Zhang, J., & Chan, C. (2024). Unveiling students' experiences and perceptions of artificial intelligence usage in higher education. *Journal of University Teaching & Learning Practice*, *21*(6), 126–145. DOI: 10.53761/xzjprb23

Zohuri, B., & Mossavar-Rahmani, F. (2024). Revolutionizing education: The dynamic synergy of personalized learning and artificial intelligence. *International Journal of Advanced Engineering and Management Research*, *9*(1), 143–153. DOI: 10.51505/ijaemr.2024.9111

Chapter 11
Quality Assurance, Accreditation, and Digital Competencies:
Reimagining Standards for the Digital Age

Mark Elliot
https://orcid.org/0009-0006-4300-840X
Arden University, UK

ABSTRACT

The digital transformation of higher education has fundamentally altered the landscape of quality assurance and accreditation, necessitating a comprehensive reimagining of how educational excellence is defined, measured, and maintained. This chapter examines the intersection of quality assurance frameworks, accreditation processes, and digital competency development within the context of smart campus ecosystems. Through an analysis of emerging models, international standards, and institutional case studies, we explore how traditional quality mechanisms are evolving to accommodate digital pedagogies, online learning modalities, and technology-enhanced educational experiences. The chapter presents a framework for integrating digital competencies into quality assurance processes while addressing challenges related to assessment authenticity, credential verification, and cross-border recognition.

DOI: 10.4018/979-8-3373-6831-3.ch011

'026, IGI Global Scientific Publishing. Copying or distributing in print or electronic forms without written permission of IGI Global Scientific Publishing is prohibited. Use of this chapter to tive artificial intelligence (AI) technologies is expressly prohibited. The publisher reserves all rights to license its use for generative AI training and machine learning model development.

1. INTRODUCTION

The advent of digital transformation in higher education has precipitated a fundamental reconsideration of quality assurance and accreditation mechanisms that have traditionally governed academic institutions (Stensaker et al., 2019). As universities increasingly adopt smart campus technologies, online learning platforms, and digital pedagogies, the parameters by which educational quality is assessed must evolve correspondingly. The integration of digital competencies into curriculum design, teaching methodologies, and assessment practices has become not merely advantageous but essential for preparing graduates for an increasingly digitalised global economy (European Commission, 2020). Quality assurance in the digital age extends beyond traditional metrics of educational excellence to encompass the effective integration of technology, the development of digital literacies, and the creation of inclusive, accessible learning environments (Spante et al., 2018). This transformation challenges established accreditation frameworks to adapt their criteria and processes to evaluate institutions' capacity to deliver high-quality education through digital channels while maintaining academic rigour and integrity. The emergence of micro-credentials, digital badges, and blockchain-based certification systems further complicates the quality assurance landscape, requiring new approaches to validation and recognition (Oliver, 2022).

The COVID-19 pandemic served as an unprecedented catalyst for digital transformation in higher education, accelerating the adoption of online learning technologies and remote delivery modes by several years (Hodges et al., 2020). This rapid transition exposed both the potential and limitations of existing quality assurance frameworks, highlighting the urgent need for more adaptive, responsive, and digitally informed approaches to educational quality (Zhao & Watterston, 2021). Institutions that had invested in digital infrastructure and capability development prior to the pandemic demonstrated greater resilience and ability to maintain educational quality during the crisis, underscoring the importance of proactive digital transformation strategies (Crawford et al., 2020).

The post-pandemic landscape has revealed a new normal in higher education where hybrid and blended learning models have become mainstream rather than exceptional (Pelletier et al., 2023). This shift has profound implications for quality assurance frameworks that must now evaluate not just the presence of technology but its meaningful integration into pedagogical practice (Bates, 2022). The challenge extends beyond technical infrastructure to encompass the development of digital pedagogical competencies among faculty (Redecker & Punie, 2017), the creation of engaging online learning experiences (Laurillard, 2012), and the maintenance of academic community in virtual spaces (Carvalho & Goodyear, 2014). Furthermore, the emergence of generative artificial intelligence technologies has introduced unprecedented complexities into quality assurance frameworks (Bearman et al., 2023). Tools such as ChatGPT, Claude, and other large language models have fundamentally altered the landscape of academic assessment, requiring institutions to reconsider traditional approaches to evaluating student learning and maintaining academic integrity (Gardner et al., 2021; Vincent-Lancrin & van der Vlies, 2020). Quality frameworks must now address questions of AI literacy, ethical use of AI tools (Holmes et al., 2019), and the development of assessment methods that can effectively measure genuine learning in an AI-augmented educational environment (Dawson, 2020). This represents not merely a technical challenge but a philosophical reconsideration of what constitutes authentic learning and assessment in the digital age (Ashford-Rowe et al., 2014).

2. THEORETICAL FOUNDATIONS OF QUALITY ASSURANCE IN DIGITAL EDUCATION

2.1 Evolution of Quality Paradigms

The conceptualisation of quality in higher education has undergone significant evolution, transitioning from input-based models focusing on resources and infrastructure to outcome-based approaches emphasising student learning and graduate capabilities (Harvey & Green, 1993). This shift has been accelerated by digital transformation, which has introduced new dimensions of quality related to technological infrastructure, digital pedagogy, and online engagement (Schindler et al., 2015). The traditional quality paradigm, rooted in physical campus resources and face-to-face instruction, must now accommodate virtual learning environments, digital resources, and technology-mediated interactions. Contemporary quality frameworks increasingly recognise the multidimensional nature of educational quality in digital contexts. These frameworks incorporate elements such as technological reliability, user experience design, digital accessibility, and data security alongside traditional academic standards (Ossiannilsson et al., 2015). The concept of fitness for purpose, a cornerstone of quality assurance theory, has expanded to include institutions' capacity to prepare students for digital citizenship and professional practice in technology-rich environments.

The transformation from quality control to quality enhancement represents a significant paradigmatic shift in how educational quality is conceptualised and pursued (Williams & Harvey, 2015). In digital contexts, this shift becomes even more pronounced as institutions move from compliance-orientated approaches focused on minimum standards to improvement-orientated frameworks that leverage digital technologies for continuous enhancement. Quality enhancement in digital education involves systematic use of data analytics to identify improvement opportunities, implementation of evidence-based interventions, and iterative refinement of educational practices based on outcomes assessment (Ehlers, 2020). The concept of quality cultures has gained prominence as institutions recognise that sustainable quality improvement requires more than formal processes and procedures (Bendermacher et al., 2017). In digital education contexts, quality culture encompasses shared values around innovation, experimentation, and continuous learning, supported by technological infrastructure that enables collaboration and knowledge sharing.

2.1.1 Building Digital Quality Cultures

The development of digital quality cultures represents a critical evolution in institutional approaches to quality assurance (Marshall, 2018; Kane et al., 2019). Unlike traditional quality mechanisms that often relied on periodic external reviews and compliance checks, digital quality cultures emphasise continuous improvement, data-driven decision-making, and distributed ownership of quality across the institution. The characteristics of effective digital quality cultures include embedded quality processes within digital platforms, real-time feedback mechanisms (Ferguson & Clow, 2017), transparent quality metrics accessible to all stakeholders, and systematic use of learning analytics for quality enhancement (Lodge et al., 2017). These cultures foster innovation by creating safe spaces for experimentation while maintaining rigorous standards through evidence-based evaluation.

2.2 Digital Transformation and Quality Dimensions

Digital transformation introduces unique quality dimensions that traditional frameworks often inadequately address. The quality of digital infrastructure, including network reliability, platform stability, and system integration, becomes fundamental to educational delivery (García-Peñalvo, 2021). Moreover, the pedagogical quality of digital content, including multimedia resources, interactive simulations, and adaptive learning systems, requires specialised evaluation criteria that consider both technical specifications and educational effectiveness. The temporal and spatial flexibility offered by digital education challenges conventional notions of student engagement and participation. Quality assurance must now account for asynchronous learning, self-paced progression, and diverse engagement patterns that differ markedly from traditional classroom dynamics (Pelletier et al., 2023).

The integration of artificial intelligence and machine learning into educational processes introduces additional quality considerations that existing frameworks struggle to address adequately (Zawacki-Richter et al., 2019). AI-powered adaptive learning systems, intelligent tutoring systems, and automated assessment tools require evaluation not only of their technical functionality but also of their pedagogical effectiveness, ethical implications, and impact on educational equity. Quality frameworks must establish criteria for evaluating algorithmic transparency, fairness, and accountability while recognising the potential of AI to enhance personalised learning and support student success (Holmes et al., 2019). The emergence of immersive technologies, including virtual reality (VR), augmented reality (AR), and mixed reality (MR), creates new possibilities for experiential learning but also raises questions about quality standards and assessment methods (Radianti et al., 2020). Quality assurance frameworks must evaluate how institutions design, implement, and assess immersive learning experiences, ensuring that these technologies enhance rather than distract from learning objectives.

2.2.1 Artificial Intelligence and Quality Assurance Frameworks

The integration of artificial intelligence into educational processes has created a paradigm shift in quality assurance methodologies (Zawacki-Richter et al., 2019; Holmes et al., 2019). AI-powered systems now facilitate personalised learning at scale, automate administrative processes (Gardner et al., 2021), and provide sophisticated analytics for quality monitoring (Tsai et al., 2020). However, this integration raises fundamental questions about algorithmic transparency (Vincent-Lancrin & van der Vlies, 2020), fairness (Prinsloo & Slade, 2016), and the role of human judgement in quality evaluation (Bearman et al., 2023). Quality frameworks must establish clear criteria for evaluating AI systems used in educational contexts. This includes assessing algorithmic bias through systematic auditing, ensuring explainability of AI decisions affecting student outcomes, maintaining human oversight in critical decision-making processes, and establishing robust data governance frameworks that protect student privacy while enabling quality enhancement (Ferguson et al., 2016).

2.3 Stakeholder Perspectives and Expectations

The digital transformation of higher education has diversified stakeholder expectations regarding quality and accountability. Students increasingly expect seamless digital experiences, personalised learning pathways, and immediate access to resources and support services (Henderson et al., 2017). Employers seek graduates with sophisticated digital competencies, including data literacy, digital collaboration skills, and the ability to navigate complex technological environments. These evolving expectations necessitate quality assurance frameworks that are responsive to stakeholder needs while maintaining academic standards and institutional autonomy. Parents and families, as key stakeholders in higher education, have developed new expectations regarding transparency, communication, and value for money in digital education contexts (Tight, 2018). Quality frameworks must address concerns about the equivalence of online and face-to-face degrees, the effectiveness of remote learning, and the support services available to students in digital environments.

Government and funding bodies increasingly view digital transformation as essential for achieving policy objectives related to accessibility, efficiency, and economic development (OECD, 2023). Quality assurance frameworks must demonstrate how digital education contributes to widening participation, improving completion rates, and developing workforce-relevant skills. This includes providing evidence of cost-effectiveness, scalability, and impact on graduate employment outcomes. The alignment between institutional digital strategies and national policy priorities becomes an important consideration in quality evaluation and funding decisions (De Boer et al., 2017). Professional bodies and industry partners play an increasingly important role in shaping quality expectations for digital education, particularly in professional and vocational programmes. These stakeholders seek assurance that digital delivery modes maintain professional standards and adequately prepare graduates for practice. Quality frameworks must address how institutions engage with professional bodies in programme design and delivery, ensure compliance with professional requirements, and demonstrate the effectiveness of digital approaches in developing professional competencies (Jackson & Bridgstock, 2021).

2.3.1 Industry 5.0 and Evolving Employer Expectations

The transition to Industry 5.0, characterised by human-centric technological integration and sustainable innovation, has fundamentally altered employer expectations for graduate capabilities (World Economic Forum, 2023; Crow & Dabars, 2020). Beyond technical proficiency, employers now prioritise meta-skills including digital creativity (Tierney & Lanford, 2016), ethical reasoning in technological contexts (Vincent-Lancrin & van der Vlies, 2020), and the ability to collaborate effectively with AI systems (Holmes et al., 2019). Quality assurance frameworks must evaluate how institutions prepare students for this evolving landscape. This includes assessing curriculum alignment with Industry 5.0 competencies, evaluating partnerships with industry for authentic learning experiences (Jackson & Bridgstock, 2021), measuring the development of human-AI collaboration skills, and ensuring graduates understand the ethical implications of emerging technologies. The integration of sustainability perspectives into digital competency development has become particularly important, with employers seeking graduates who can leverage technology for environmental and social impact (Leal Filho et al., 2021).

2.4 Pedagogical Transformation and Quality Implications

The shift from traditional instruction to digital pedagogies represents more than a change in delivery medium; it fundamentally alters the nature of teaching and learning processes (Rapanta et al., 2020). Quality assurance frameworks must evaluate not merely the presence of technology but the effectiveness of pedagogical approaches in digital contexts. This includes assessing how institutions support active learning, collaborative engagement, and authentic assessment in online environments while maintaining academic rigour and intellectual challenge. The concept of pedagogical content knowledge (PCK) has evolved to incorporate technological dimensions, resulting in the Technological Pedagogical Content Knowledge (TPACK) framework (Mishra & Koehler, 2006). Quality assurance must evaluate how institutions develop and assess TPACK among faculty, ensuring that educators possess not only content expertise but also the pedagogical and technological knowledge necessary for effective digital teaching.

The implementation of universal design for learning (UDL) principles becomes particularly important in digital education contexts, where diverse learners with varying abilities, backgrounds, and circumstances must be accommodated (Rose & Meyer, 2002). Quality frameworks must assess how institutions ensure digital accessibility, provide multiple means of representation, engagement, and expression, and support diverse learning needs through technology-enhanced approaches. This includes evaluating the availability of assistive technologies, the design of inclusive digital content, and the provision of flexible assessment options that maintain standards while accommodating diversity (Burgstahler & Young, 2015). The adoption of evidence-based pedagogical approaches in digital contexts requires systematic evaluation of teaching effectiveness. Quality frameworks must assess how institutions collect and use evidence of teaching impact (Ferguson & Clow, 2017), support pedagogical innovation (Salmon, 2013), and foster communities of practice that share effective digital teaching strategies (Beetham & Sharpe, 2019). The development of pedagogical patterns for digital learning provides reusable solutions to common teaching challenges, enabling more consistent quality across diverse educational contexts (Laurillard, 2012).

3. DIGITAL COMPETENCY FRAMEWORKS AND STANDARDS

3.1 International Digital Competency Models

The development of comprehensive digital competency frameworks has become a priority for educational systems worldwide, reflecting the critical importance of digital skills in contemporary society and economy. The European Digital Competence Framework for Citizens (DigComp 2.2) provides a foundational model that identifies five key competence areas: information and data literacy, communication and collaboration, digital content creation, safety, and problem-solving (Vuorikari et al., 2022). This framework has been instrumental in guiding curriculum development and assessment design across European higher education institutions, offering a common language for describing and evaluating digital competencies. The UNESCO Digital Literacy Global Framework emphasises the importance of contextualising digital competencies within broader educational and social objectives (Law et al., 2018). This framework recognises that digital competencies extend beyond technical skills to encompass critical thinking, ethical reasoning, and creative problem-solving in digital contexts.

The International Society for Technology in Education (ISTE) Standards provide another influential framework, particularly in North American contexts, offering specific competency standards for students, educators, and educational leaders (ISTE, 2017). These standards emphasise creativity, innovation, and digital citizenship alongside technical proficiency, reflecting a holistic view of digital competence that extends beyond instrumental skills. Quality assurance frameworks increasingly reference ISTE standards when evaluating institutional approaches to digital competency development, particularly in teacher education programmes. The proliferation of national and regional frameworks, such as the Australian Digital Capability Framework and the JISC Digital Capabilities Framework in the United Kingdom, reflects diverse approaches to conceptualising and operationalising digital competencies (Beetham & Sharpe, 2019). These frameworks vary in their emphasis on technical proficiency, pedagogical integration, and socio-cultural dimensions of digital literacy, highlighting the need for quality assurance systems that can accommodate multiple perspectives while maintaining comparability across contexts.

3.1.1 Next-Generation Competency Frameworks

The rapid evolution of digital technologies necessitates continuous revision and expansion of competency frameworks. Emerging frameworks now incorporate blockchain competencies (Grech & Camilleri, 2017), extended reality (XR) skills (Pellas et al., 2020), and human-AI collaboration capabilities (Holmes et al., 2019). The integration of sustainability competencies into digital frameworks reflects growing recognition of technology's environmental impact (Caird & Lane, 2015). Green computing skills, sustainable software development practices, and understanding of digital carbon footprints have become essential components of comprehensive digital literacy (Leal Filho et al., 2021). Quality assurance must evaluate how institutions integrate these sustainability perspectives into digital competency development, ensuring that graduates can leverage technology responsibly and contribute to sustainable development goals (UNESCO, 2019; OECD, 2023).

Cultural and contextual adaptation of international frameworks remains critical for effective implementation (Law et al., 2018; Keevy & Chakroun, 2015). While global frameworks provide valuable reference points, successful quality assurance requires sensitivity to local contexts, linguistic diversity, and varying levels of digital infrastructure. Institutions in the Global South have developed innovative approaches that leapfrog traditional technologies, focusing on mobile-first digital competencies and offline-capable learning systems (Hoosen & Butcher, 2019; McCowan, 2016). These adaptations provide valuable insights for quality assurance frameworks seeking to balance global standards with local relevance.

4. IMPLEMENTATION CHALLENGES AND ENABLERS

4.1 Infrastructure and Resource Requirements

The implementation of digital quality assurance frameworks requires substantial investment in technological infrastructure and human capacity. Institutions must develop or acquire sophisticated digital platforms that support quality monitoring, data analytics, and continuous improvement processes. This includes learning management systems, assessment platforms, analytics tools, and integration systems that connect diverse educational activities (García-Peñalvo, 2021; Marshall & Mitchell, 2018). The financial implications of digital transformation extend beyond initial infrastructure investment to encompass ongoing maintenance, upgrades, and support. Institutions face difficult choices in allocating limited resources between competing priorities, often struggling to balance investments in technology with support for human capacity development (Garrett et al., 2021). Quality assurance frameworks must consider institutional resource constraints while establishing minimum standards for digital infrastructure and support services (Bassett & Arnhold, 2020; World Bank, 2023).

4.2 Faculty Development and Support Systems

The successful implementation of digital quality assurance requires comprehensive faculty development programmes that address both technical skills and pedagogical competencies (Redecker & Punie, 2017; Caena & Redecker, 2019). Quality frameworks must evaluate how institutions support faculty development through formal training programmes (Bates & Sangrà, 2011), peer mentoring systems, and communities of practice. The provision of ongoing technical and pedagogical support proves essential for sustained quality improvement in digital education (Marshall, 2018). Institutions must establish support structures that include instructional design expertise (Laurillard, 2012), technical assistance (Grajek & Brooks, 2020), and pedagogical consultation (Rapanta et al., 2020). Quality frameworks should assess the availability, accessibility, and effectiveness of support services, recognising that adequate support directly correlates with educational quality outcomes (Pelletier et al., 2023).

4.3 Regulatory Alignment and Policy Coherence

The implementation of digital quality assurance frameworks requires careful alignment with existing regulatory requirements, professional standards, and policy frameworks at national and international levels (De Boer et al., 2017). This alignment presents challenges when regulations developed for traditional education models inadequately address digital delivery modes or when multiple regulatory frameworks impose conflicting requirements (Knight, 2016). Institutions must navigate complex regulatory landscapes while maintaining focus on educational quality and student outcomes (Stensaker & Maassen, 2015; Hazelkorn & Gibson, 2017).

The regulatory environment for digital education varies significantly across jurisdictions, with some countries embracing flexible, innovation-friendly frameworks while others maintain restrictive regulations designed for traditional delivery modes. Quality assurance frameworks must accommodate these regulatory variations while promoting best practices and maintaining standards (ENQA, 2015; Gaston, 2014). This includes developing equivalency frameworks that enable recognition across different regulatory contexts while respecting national sovereignty and educational traditions (European Consortium for Accreditation, 2014; UNESCO, 2019).

4.4 Change Management and Cultural Transformation

The implementation of digital quality assurance frameworks requires significant organisational change that extends beyond technical systems to encompass cultural transformation and mindset shifts (Kezar & Eckel, 2002). Institutions must manage resistance to change, address concerns about job security and role changes, and build consensus around new approaches to quality assurance. The cultural dimensions of digital transformation often prove more challenging than technical implementation, requiring institutions to address deeply embedded assumptions about teaching, learning, and quality (Cameron & Green, 2020). Quality frameworks must evaluate how institutions manage cultural change, including leadership commitment, communication strategies, and mechanisms for addressing resistance. This includes assessing how institutions build digital cultures that value innovation, experimentation, and continuous improvement while maintaining academic values and traditions (Tierney & Lanford, 2016).

The role of leadership in driving digital transformation and quality enhancement cannot be overstated (Jones & Harvey, 2017; Marshall, 2018). Effective implementation requires committed leadership at all levels, from senior executives who provide vision and resources to department heads who champion change within academic units (Crow & Dabars, 2020). Quality frameworks must evaluate leadership capacity for digital transformation, including strategic planning capabilities (Pucciarelli & Kaplan, 2016), change management skills (Cameron & Green, 2020), and the ability to build coalitions for change (Kezar & Eckel, 2002).

5. ASSESSMENT TECHNOLOGIES AND QUALITY MONITORING

5.1 Digital Assessment Systems and Integrity

The transition to digital assessment systems introduces both opportunities and challenges for maintaining academic integrity and assessment quality. Advanced proctoring technologies, including artificial intelligence-powered monitoring systems, biometric authentication, and behavioural analytics, offer sophisticated approaches to ensuring assessment security in remote contexts (Dawson, 2020). However, quality assurance frameworks must carefully evaluate these technologies' effectiveness, reliability, and impact on student privacy and wellbeing. The implementation of remote proctoring systems raises significant concerns about privacy, equity, and accessibility that quality frameworks must address (Coghlan et al., 2021). Students from disadvantaged backgrounds may lack suitable testing environments, reliable internet connections, or compatible devices, creating barriers to fair assessment. Quality assurance must evaluate how institutions ensure equitable access to assessment, provide alternative arrangements when needed, and protect student privacy while maintaining academic integrity (Hussein et al., 2020).

The design of authentic digital assessments that accurately measure learning outcomes while resisting academic misconduct requires innovative approaches that move beyond traditional examination formats. This includes developing assessment tasks that emphasise application, analysis, and creation rather than recall; utilising collaborative assessments that reflect real-world professional practices; and implementing continuous assessment strategies that distribute evaluation throughout the learning process (Ellis & Bliuc, 2016). Quality frameworks must evaluate how institutions ensure assessment validity, reliability, and fairness in digital contexts while maintaining academic standards. Artificial intelligence and machine learning technologies offer powerful tools for automated assessment, particularly for formative feedback and large-scale evaluation. However, quality assurance must address concerns about algorithmic bias, transparency, and the appropriate use of automated systems in high-stakes assessment contexts (Gardner et al., 2021).

5.1.1 Authentic Assessment in the Age of AI

The widespread availability of generative AI tools has fundamentally challenged traditional assessment paradigms, necessitating a shift toward authentic assessment designs that evaluate genuine learning and capability development (Ashford-Rowe et al., 2014; Dawson, 2020; Bearman et al., 2023). Authentic digital assessments emphasise application of knowledge in realistic contexts (Ellis & Bliuc, 2016), integration of multiple competencies in complex tasks, reflection and metacognition about learning processes, and collaboration and peer learning. These approaches not only resist AI substitution but also better prepare students for professional practice where AI tools are increasingly prevalent (Holmes et al., 2019; Gardner et al., 2021). Innovative assessment designs emerging in response to AI include collaborative problem-solving scenarios where students work with AI tools to address complex challenges (Walkington & Bernacki, 2020); portfolio-based assessments that document learning journeys over time (Lorenzo & Ittelson, 2005); oral examinations and presentations that demonstrate deep understanding; and practical demonstrations of skills in simulated professional environments (Radianti et al., 2020).

5.2 Learning Analytics and Quality Indicators

Learning analytics provides unprecedented opportunities for monitoring educational quality through real-time data on student engagement, learning progression, and outcome achievement. The integration of learning analytics into quality assurance processes enables continuous monitoring rather than periodic evaluation, allowing institutions to identify and address quality issues proactively (Lodge et al., 2017). However, quality frameworks must establish appropriate indicators, benchmarks, and interpretation guidelines that account for the complexity of learning processes and the limitations of quantitative metrics. The development of learning analytics maturity models helps institutions assess their capacity to effectively utilise data for quality improvement. These models evaluate not only technical capabilities but also organisational factors such as data governance, analytical expertise, and culture of evidence-based decision-making (Tsai et al., 2020). Quality assurance frameworks must examine how institutions develop and deploy learning analytics while ensuring ethical use of student data and maintaining focus on educational rather than purely efficiency objectives.

The interpretation of learning analytics data requires sophisticated understanding of educational contexts, student diversity, and the multiple factors that influence learning outcomes (Gašević et al., 2015). Quality frameworks must evaluate how institutions develop data literacy among stakeholders, ensure appropriate interpretation of analytics, and avoid oversimplified conclusions based on incomplete data. This includes assessing how institutions combine quantitative analytics with qualitative insights to develop a comprehensive understanding of educational quality (Wise & Jung, 2019). Predictive analytics and early warning systems offer valuable tools for identifying at-risk students and supporting student success but raise important questions about determinism, labelling, and intervention strategies. Quality frameworks must evaluate how institutions use predictive models responsibly, ensure transparency in algorithmic decision-making, and provide appropriate support services based on analytical insights (Herodotou et al., 2020).

5.3 Continuous Quality Monitoring Systems

The implementation of continuous quality monitoring systems represents a paradigm shift from periodic review cycles to ongoing quality assurance embedded within institutional operations (Harvey & Williams, 2010; Schindler et al., 2015). Digital technologies enable real-time monitoring of key performance indicators (Ferguson et al., 2016), automated alert systems for quality issues (Tsai et al., 2020), and dynamic dashboards that provide stakeholders with current information on institutional performance (Vieira et al., 2018). Quality frameworks must evolve to accommodate these continuous monitoring approaches while maintaining appropriate oversight and accountability mechanisms (Williams & Harvey, 2015; Stensaker et al., 2019). The development of quality dashboards and visualisation tools enables stakeholders to access and interpret quality data more effectively, fostering transparency and accountability in quality assurance processes (Few, 2013; Vieira et al., 2018). These tools must present complex data in accessible formats while avoiding oversimplification or misrepresentation (Ferguson & Clow, 2017). Quality frameworks should evaluate the design and implementation of dashboard systems, ensuring they provide actionable insights while maintaining data accuracy and contextual relevance (Lodge et al., 2017; Wise & Jung, 2019).

6. INTERNATIONAL PERSPECTIVES AND COMPARATIVE ANALYSIS

6.1 Global Frameworks and Regional Variations

The development of quality assurance frameworks for digital education reflects diverse cultural, educational, and regulatory contexts across different regions and nations. The European Standards and Guidelines for Quality Assurance (ESG) have evolved to incorporate digital education considerations, emphasising the importance of student-centred learning, transparent information, and continuous improvement in technology-enhanced educational environments (ENQA, 2015). These standards provide a common framework while allowing flexibility for national and institutional interpretation, recognising the diversity of European higher education systems.

The Bologna Process has facilitated the development of common approaches to quality assurance across European countries, including specific considerations for digital education and cross-border provision (Gaston, 2014). The European Approach for Quality Assurance of Joint Programmes provides frameworks for evaluating collaborative digital programmes offered by multiple institutions across borders. This approach emphasises learning outcomes, student-centred design, and transparent quality assurance processes that build trust among partner institutions and stakeholders (European Consortium for Accreditation, 2014). In the Asia-Pacific region, quality assurance frameworks have increasingly emphasised digital readiness and technological innovation as key quality indicators. The ASEAN Qualifications Reference Framework incorporates digital competencies as essential graduate attributes, while national frameworks in countries like Singapore and South Korea prioritise smart campus development and digital pedagogy integration.

7. FUTURE DIRECTIONS AND EMERGING CHALLENGES

7.1 Emerging Technologies and Quality Assurance

As technology continues to evolve rapidly, quality frameworks must anticipate and adapt to emerging technologies that will reshape educational delivery and assessment. The development of quantum computing, while still in early stages for educational applications, will eventually require new competency frameworks and quality indicators. Similarly, advances in brain-computer interfaces, haptic technologies, and holographic displays will create new possibilities and challenges for educational quality assurance. Quality frameworks must remain adaptive and forward-looking, establishing mechanisms for incorporating new technologies while maintaining focus on fundamental educational values and student success.

7.2 The Metaverse and Immersive Learning Ecosystems

The emergence of metaverse platforms and persistent virtual worlds creates new possibilities for immersive, collaborative learning experiences that transcend traditional boundaries. Universities are establishing virtual campuses in metaverse environments, enabling students from around the world to engage in shared learning experiences with unprecedented levels of presence and interaction (Pellas et al., 2020; Radianti et al., 2020). Quality assurance frameworks must develop criteria for evaluating these immersive learning ecosystems, including assessment of virtual learning space design (Carvalho & Goodyear, 2014), avatar-based interaction quality, and integration with traditional learning management systems. The quality implications of metaverse-based education extend beyond technical considerations to encompass psychological and social dimensions. Research indicates that extended immersion in virtual environments can impact student wellbeing, social development, and sense of identity (Pellas et al., 2020). Quality frameworks must establish guidelines for healthy metaverse engagement, including recommendations for session duration, balance between virtual and physical activities, and support systems for students experiencing virtual reality-induced discomfort.

7.3 Blockchain and Decentralised Education Systems

Blockchain technology promises to transform credential verification, student record management, and quality assurance processes through decentralised, tamper-proof systems (Grech & Camilleri, 2017). The implementation of blockchain-based credentialing systems enables instant verification of qualifications across borders, reducing fraud and facilitating student mobility (Chakroun & Keevy, 2018). Quality frameworks must evaluate how institutions implement blockchain solutions while ensuring data privacy, system interoperability, and alignment with regulatory requirements (UNESCO, 2019). The development of decentralised autonomous educational organisations (DAEOs) challenges traditional notions of institutional governance and quality assurance. These blockchain-based entities enable peer-to-peer learning networks, community-validated credentials, and algorithmic quality assurance mechanisms. Quality frameworks must evolve to accommodate these new organisational forms while maintaining standards for educational quality and student protection (Keevy & Chakroun, 2015).

8. RECOMMENDATIONS AND IMPLEMENTATION GUIDANCE

8.1 Institutional Recommendations

Institutions embarking on digital quality transformation should adopt systematic approaches that balance ambition with pragmatism (Marshall, 2018; Crow & Dabars, 2020). Based on analysis of successful implementations across diverse contexts, we recommend a phased approach beginning with a comprehensive digital maturity assessment (Marks et al., 2021), followed by strategic planning that aligns digital transformation with institutional mission (Pucciarelli & Kaplan, 2016), and iterative implementation that enables learning and adaptation (Kane et al., 2019). Institutions should prioritise building digital capability among staff through comprehensive professional development programmes, recognising that human capacity represents the most critical factor in successful transformation (Bates & Sangrà, 2011; Redecker & Punie, 2017).

Investment in robust technological infrastructure forms the foundation for digital quality assurance, but institutions must avoid the trap of technology determinism (García-Peñalvo, 2021; Marshall & Mitchell, 2018). Successful digital transformation requires equal attention to pedagogical innovation (Laurillard, 2012), organisational culture change (Cameron & Green, 2020), and stakeholder engagement (Henderson et al., 2017). Quality enhancement should be embedded within institutional processes rather than treated as an external compliance requirement (Williams & Harvey, 2015). This includes establishing regular cycles of evidence collection and analysis (Ferguson & Clow, 2017), creating feedback loops that connect quality data to improvement actions (Lodge et al., 2017), and fostering cultures of continuous improvement (Bendermacher et al., 2017). Institutions should also ensure that digital competency development is embedded throughout curricula rather than treated as an add-on (Vuorikari et al., 2022; Caena & Redecker, 2019).

8.2 Quality Agency Recommendations

Quality assurance agencies must fundamentally reconceptualise their role in the digital age, shifting from periodic compliance checking to continuous quality enhancement partnerships with institutions (Stensaker & Maassen, 2015). This requires developing new competencies in digital technologies, data analytics, and online learning pedagogies among quality assurance professionals (Ossiannilsson et al., 2015). Agencies should invest in digital infrastructure that enables real-time quality monitoring while maintaining appropriate boundaries between support and evaluation functions (Harvey & Williams, 2010). The development of risk-based approaches that focus intensive review on areas of greatest concern while reducing burden on high-performing institutions enables more efficient use of quality assurance resources (ENQA, 2015). The establishment of collaborative networks among quality agencies facilitates sharing of best practices and mutual learning (European Consortium for Accreditation, 2014). International cooperation becomes particularly important for addressing cross-border digital education and ensuring comparability of standards (UNESCO, 2019; Gaston, 2014).

8.3 Policy Recommendations

Policymakers should ensure regulatory frameworks support innovation in digital education while maintaining appropriate quality standards and student protection (OECD, 2023). This requires reviewing existing regulations that may inadvertently restrict digital innovation, developing new frameworks for emerging credentials and delivery modes, and creating regulatory sandboxes that enable experimentation within controlled parameters. Policy coherence across education, technology, and labour market domains becomes essential for supporting quality digital education. Investment in national digital infrastructure and capability development represents a critical policy priority for ensuring equitable access to quality digital education (World Bank, 2023). This includes not only physical infrastructure such as broadband connectivity but also human capacity development, institutional support systems, and quality assurance frameworks. Policymakers should recognise that digital transformation requires sustained investment rather than one-time interventions. The development of international agreements and frameworks for quality assurance and credential recognition in digital education becomes increasingly important as education becomes more globalised (UNESCO, 2019).

9. CONCLUSION

The integration of quality assurance, accreditation, and digital competencies represents a fundamental reimagining of educational excellence in the digital age. This comprehensive examination has demonstrated that effective quality frameworks must evolve beyond traditional compliance-orientated approaches to embrace continuous improvement, innovation, and stakeholder engagement while maintaining rigorous standards for educational outcomes. The evidence presented throughout this chapter underscores the complex interplay between technological advancement, pedagogical innovation, and quality assurance in creating educational experiences that prepare students for success in an increasingly digital world. The transformation of quality assurance frameworks to accommodate digital education is not merely a technical exercise but a fundamental reconceptualisation of educational quality itself.

The development of digital competencies emerges as both a quality indicator and an educational imperative, requiring systematic integration throughout institutional strategies, curricula, and assessment practices. Quality frameworks must evaluate how effectively institutions develop these competencies while recognising disciplinary differences and diverse student needs. The evidence suggests that successful integration requires comprehensive approaches that address infrastructure, pedagogy, assessment, and support systems rather than piecemeal interventions. The experiences of institutions worldwide demonstrate that successful implementation of digital quality assurance requires sustained commitment, significant investment, and cultural transformation.

Looking forward, the continued evolution of digital technologies will present both opportunities and challenges for quality assurance in higher education. Artificial intelligence, immersive technologies, and emerging platforms will create new possibilities for educational delivery and assessment while raising questions about quality standards, ethical implications, and human agency. Quality frameworks must remain adaptive and responsive while maintaining focus on fundamental educational values and student success. The recommendations presented in this chapter provide actionable guidance for institutions, quality agencies, and policymakers navigating the complex landscape of digital education quality assurance. Success requires collaborative approaches that leverage collective wisdom, share resources, and build mutual capacity rather than isolated institutional efforts. The future of quality assurance in digital higher education will be characterised by continuous innovation, evidence-based improvement, and unwavering commitment to educational excellence.

As we stand at the threshold of unprecedented technological transformation, the imperative for reimagined quality assurance frameworks becomes ever more pressing. The convergence of artificial intelligence, extended reality, and other emerging technologies promises to reshape education in ways we are only beginning to imagine. Yet amidst this technological revolution, the fundamental purpose of education—to develop human potential, foster critical thinking, and prepare individuals for meaningful contribution to society—remains constant. Quality assurance frameworks must navigate this tension between transformation and tradition, embracing innovation while safeguarding educational values that have endured across centuries. Through sustained commitment to quality, thoughtful integration of technology, and focus on student success, higher education institutions can harness the transformative potential of digital technologies while fulfilling their fundamental mission of education, research, and service to society.

REFERENCES

Ashford-Rowe, K., Herrington, J., & Brown, C. (2014). Establishing the critical elements that determine authentic assessment. *Assessment & Evaluation in Higher Education, 39*(2), 205–222. DOI: 10.1080/02602938.2013.819566

Bassett, R. M., & Arnhold, N. (2020). *The World Bank's approach to quality assurance in tertiary education*. World Bank Group.

Bates, A. W. (2022). *Teaching in a digital age: Guidelines for designing teaching and learning* (3rd ed.). Tony Bates Associates Ltd.

Bates, A. W., & Sangrà, A. (2011). *Managing technology in higher education: Strategies for transforming teaching and learning*. Jossey-Bass.

Bearman, M., Ryan, J., & Ajjawi, R. (2023). Discourses of artificial intelligence in higher education: A critical literature review. *Higher Education, 86*(2), 369–385. DOI: 10.1007/s10734-022-00937-2

Beetham, H., & Sharpe, R. (Eds.). (2019). *Rethinking pedagogy for a digital age: Principles and practices of design* (3rd ed.). Routledge. DOI: 10.4324/9781351252805

Bendermacher, G. W. G., Oude Egbrink, M. G. A., Wolfhagen, I. H. A. P., & Dolmans, D. H. J. M. (2017). Unravelling quality culture in higher education: A realist review. *Higher Education, 73*(1), 39–60. DOI: 10.1007/s10734-015-9979-2

Burgstahler, S., & Young, M. K. (2015). *Universal design in higher education: From principles to practice* (2nd ed.). Harvard Education Press.

Caena, F., & Redecker, C. (2019). Aligning teacher competence frameworks to 21st century challenges: The case for the European Digital Competence Framework for Educators (DigCompEdu). *European Journal of Education, 54*(3), 356–369. DOI: 10.1111/ejed.12345

Caird, S., & Lane, A. (2015). Conceptualising the role of information and communication technologies in the design of higher education teaching models used in the UK. *British Journal of Educational Technology, 46*(1), 58–70. DOI: 10.1111/bjet.12123

Cameron, E., & Green, M. (2020). *Making sense of change management: A complete guide to the models, tools and techniques of organizational change* (5th ed.). Kogan Page.

Carvalho, L., & Goodyear, P. (2014). *The architecture of productive learning networks*. Routledge. DOI: 10.4324/9780203591093

Chakroun, B., & Keevy, J. (2018). *Digital credentialing: Implications for the recognition of learning across borders*. UNESCO. DOI: 10.54675/SABO8911

Coghlan, S., Miller, T., & Paterson, J. (2021). Good proctor or "big brother"? Ethics of online exam supervision technologies. *Philosophy & Technology*, *34*(4), 1581–1606. DOI: 10.1007/s13347-021-00476-1

Crawford, J., Butler-Henderson, K., Rudolph, J., & Malkawi, B. (2020). COVID-19: 20 countries' higher education intra-period digital pedagogy responses. *Journal of Applied Learning and Teaching*, *3*(1), 1–20.

Crow, M. M., & Dabars, W. B. (2020). *The fifth wave: The evolution of American higher education*. Johns Hopkins University Press. DOI: 10.1353/book.73164

Dawson, P. (2020). *Defending assessment security in a digital world: Preventing e-cheating and supporting academic integrity in higher education*. Routledge. DOI: 10.4324/9780429324178

De Boer, H., File, J., Huisman, J., Seeber, M., Vukasovic, M., & Westerheijden, D. F. (Eds.). (2017). *Policy analysis of structural reforms in higher education*. Palgrave Macmillan. DOI: 10.1007/978-3-319-42237-4

Ehlers, U. D. (2020). *Future skills: The future of learning and higher education*. Books on Demand. DOI: 10.1007/978-3-658-29297-3

Ellis, R. A., & Bliuc, A. M. (2016). An exploration into first-year university students' approaches to inquiry and online learning technologies in blended environments. *British Journal of Educational Technology*, *47*(5), 970–980. DOI: 10.1111/bjet.12385

ENQA, ESU, EUA, & EURASHE. (2015). Standards and guidelines for quality assurance in the European Higher Education Area (ESG). EURASHE.

European Commission. (2020). Digital Education Action Plan 2021-2027: Resetting education and training for the digital age (COM(2020) 624 final).

European Consortium for Accreditation. (2014). *European approach for quality assurance of joint programmes*. ECA.

Ferguson, R., Brasher, A., Clow, D., Cooper, A., Hillaire, G., Mittelmeier, J., Rienties, B., Ullmann, T., & Vuorikari, R. (2016). *Research evidence on the use of learning analytics: Implications for education policy (EUR 28294 EN)*. Publications Office of the European Union.

Ferguson, R., & Clow, D. (2017). Where is the evidence? A call to action for learning analytics. In *Proceedings of the Seventh International Learning Analytics & Knowledge Conference* (pp. 56–65). ACM. DOI: 10.1145/3027385.3027396

Few, S. (2013). *Information dashboard design: Displaying data for at-a-glance monitoring* (2nd ed.). Analytics Press.

García-Peñalvo, F. J. (2021). Digital transformation in the universities: Implications of the COVID-19 pandemic. Education in the Knowledge Society, 22, Article e25465.

Gardner, J., O'Leary, M., & Yuan, L. (2021). Artificial intelligence in educational assessment: 'Breakthrough? Or buncombe and ballyhoo?'. *Journal of Computer Assisted Learning*, *37*(5), 1207–1216. DOI: 10.1111/jcal.12577

Garrett, R., Simunich, B., Legon, R., & Fredericksen, E. E. (2021). *CHLOE 6: Online learning leaders adapt for a post-pandemic world.* Quality Matters.

Gašević, D., Dawson, S., & Siemens, G. (2015). Let's not forget: Learning analytics are about learning. *TechTrends*, *59*(1), 64–71. DOI: 10.1007/s11528-014-0822-x

Gaston, P. L. (2014). *Higher education accreditation: How it's changing, why it must.* Stylus Publishing.

Grajek, S., & Brooks, D. C. (2020). *2020 EDUCAUSE technology report.* EDUCAUSE.

Grech, A., & Camilleri, A. F. (2017). *Blockchain in education (EUR 28778 EN).* Publications Office of the European Union.

Harvey, L., & Green, D. (1993). Defining quality. *Assessment & Evaluation in Higher Education*, *18*(1), 9–34. DOI: 10.1080/0260293930180102

Harvey, L., & Williams, J. (2010). Fifteen years of Quality in Higher Education. *Quality in Higher Education*, *16*(1), 3–36. DOI: 10.1080/13538321003679457

Hazelkorn, E., & Gibson, A. (2017). Public goods and public policy: What is public good, and who and what decides? (CHEPS Working Paper 04/2017). Center for Higher Education Policy Studies.

Henderson, M., Selwyn, N., & Aston, R. (2017). What works and why? Student perceptions of 'useful' digital technology in university teaching and learning. *Studies in Higher Education*, *42*(8), 1567–1579. DOI: 10.1080/03075079.2015.1007946

Herodotou, C., Rienties, B., Hlosta, M., Boroowa, A., Mangafa, C., & Zdrahal, Z. (2020). The scalable implementation of predictive learning analytics at a distance learning university: Insights from a longitudinal case study. *The Internet and Higher Education*, *45*, 100725. DOI: 10.1016/j.iheduc.2020.100725

Hodges, C., Moore, S., Lockee, B., Trust, T., & Bond, A. (2020, March 27). The difference between emergency remote teaching and online learning. EDUCAUSE Review. https://er.educause.edu/articles/2020/3/the-difference-between-emergency-remote-teaching-and-online-learning

Holmes, W., Bialik, M., & Fadel, C. (2019). *Artificial intelligence in education: Promises and implications for teaching and learning*. Center for Curriculum Redesign.

Hoosen, S., & Butcher, N. (2019). Understanding the impact of OER: Achievements and challenges. UNESCO/Commonwealth of Learning.

Hussein, M. H., Ow, S. H., Cheong, L. S., & Thong, M. K. (2020). Online assessment in higher education: A systematic review. *Journal of Educational Technology Systems*, *49*(4), 482–506.

ISTE. (2017). *ISTE standards for students, educators and leaders*. International Society for Technology in Education.

Jackson, D., & Bridgstock, R. (2021). What actually works to enhance graduate employability? The relative value of curricular, co-curricular, and extra-curricular learning and paid work. *Higher Education*, *81*(4), 723–739. DOI: 10.1007/s10734-020-00570-x

Jones, S., & Harvey, M. (2017). A distributed leadership change process model for higher education. *Journal of Higher Education Policy and Management*, *39*(2), 126–139. DOI: 10.1080/1360080X.2017.1276661

Kane, G. C., Palmer, D., Phillips, A. N., & Kiron, D. (2019). Accelerating digital innovation inside and out. *MIT Sloan Management Review*.

Keevy, J., & Chakroun, B. (2015). *Level-setting and recognition of learning outcomes: The use of level descriptors in the twenty-first century*. UNESCO. DOI: 10.54675/GKWN6283

Kezar, A., & Eckel, P. (2002). The effect of institutional culture on change strategies in higher education. *The Journal of Higher Education*, *73*(4), 435–460. DOI: 10.1080/00221546.2002.11777159

Knight, J. (2016). Transnational education remodeled: Toward a common TNE framework and definitions. *Journal of Studies in International Education*, *20*(1), 34–47. DOI: 10.1177/1028315315602927

Laurillard, D. (2012). *Teaching as a design science: Building pedagogical patterns for learning and technology*. Routledge.

Law, N., Woo, D., de la Torre, J., & Wong, G. (2018). *A global framework of reference on digital literacy skills for indicator 4.4.2 (UIS Information Paper No. 51).* UNESCO Institute for Statistics.

Leal Filho, W., Salvia, A. L., Frankenberger, F., Akib, N. A. M., Sen, S. K., Sivapalan, S., Novo-Corti, I., Venkatesan, M., & Emblen-Perry, K. (2021). Governance and sustainable development at higher education institutions. *Environment, Development and Sustainability, 23*(4), 6002–6020. DOI: 10.1007/s10668-020-00859-y

Lodge, J. M., Kennedy, G., Lockyer, L., Arguel, A., & Pachman, M. (2017). Understanding and improving learning with analytics. In C. Lang, G. Siemens, A. F. Wise, & D. Gašević (Eds.), Handbook of learning analytics (pp. 67–78). SoLAR.

Lorenzo, G., & Ittelson, J. (2005). *An overview of e-portfolios (EDUCAUSE Learning Initiative Paper 1).* EDUCAUSE.

Marks, A., Al-Ali, M., Attasi, R., Elkishk, A. A., & Rezgui, Y. (2021). Digital transformation in higher education: A framework for maturity assessment. *International Journal of Advanced Corporate Learning, 14*(1), 24–35.

Marshall, S. (2018). *Shaping the university of the future: Using technology to catalyse change in university learning and teaching*. Springer. DOI: 10.1007/978-981-10-7620-6

Marshall, S., & Mitchell, G. (2018). Digital benchmarking for strategic alignment. In Marshall, S. (Ed.), *Shaping the university of the future* (pp. 123–145). Springer. DOI: 10.1007/978-981-10-7620-6_6

McCowan, T. (2016). Universities and the post-2015 development agenda: An analytical framework. *Higher Education, 72*(4), 505–523. DOI: 10.1007/s10734-016-0035-7

Mishra, P., & Koehler, M. J. (2006). Technological pedagogical content knowledge: A framework for teacher knowledge. *Teachers College Record, 108*(6), 1017–1054. DOI: 10.1111/j.1467-9620.2006.00684.x

OECD. (2023). *Education at a glance 2023: OECD indicators*. OECD Publishing., DOI: 10.1787/e13bef63-

Oliver, B. (2022). Towards a common definition of micro-credentials. UNESCO. https://unesdoc.unesco.org/ark:/48223/pf0000381668

Ossiannilsson, E., Williams, K., Camilleri, A. F., & Brown, M. (2015). *Quality models in online and open education around the globe*. International Council for Open and Distance Education.

Pellas, N., Dengel, A., & Christopoulos, A. (2020). A scoping review of immersive virtual reality in STEM education. *IEEE Transactions on Learning Technologies, 13*(4), 748–761. DOI: 10.1109/TLT.2020.3019405

Pelletier, K., McCormack, M., Reeves, J., Robert, J., Arbino, N., Al-Freih, M., Dickson-Deane, C., Guber, N. J., Kehr, S., Lang, L., Maas, J., & Stine, J. (2023). *2023 EDUCAUSE horizon report: Teaching and learning edition*. EDUCAUSE.

Prinsloo, P., & Slade, S. (2016). Big data, higher education and learning analytics: Beyond justice, towards an ethics of care. In Daniel, B. K. (Ed.), *Big data and learning analytics in higher education* (pp. 109–124). Springer.

Pucciarelli, F., & Kaplan, A. (2016). Competition and strategy in higher education: Managing complexity and uncertainty. *Business Horizons, 59*(3), 311–320. DOI: 10.1016/j.bushor.2016.01.003

Radianti, J., Majchrzak, T. A., Fromm, J., & Wohlgenannt, I. (2020). A systematic review of immersive virtual reality applications for higher education: Design elements, lessons learned, and research agenda. *Computers & Education, 147*, 103778. DOI: 10.1016/j.compedu.2019.103778

Rapanta, C., Botturi, L., Goodyear, P., Guàrdia, L., & Koole, M. (2020). Online university teaching during and after the COVID-19 crisis: Refocusing teacher presence and learning activity. *Postdigital Science and Education, 2*(3), 923–945. DOI: 10.1007/s42438-020-00155-y

Redecker, C., & Punie, Y. (2017). *European framework for the digital competence of educators: DigCompEdu (EUR 28775 EN)*. Publications Office of the European Union.

Rose, D. H., & Meyer, A. (2002). *Teaching every student in the digital age: Universal design for learning*. ASCD.

Salmon, G. (2013). *E-tivities: The key to active online learning* (2nd ed.). Routledge. DOI: 10.4324/9780203074640

Schindler, L., Puls-Elvidge, S., Welzant, H., & Crawford, L. (2015). Definitions of quality in higher education: A synthesis of the literature. *Higher Learning Research Communications, 5*(3), 3–13. DOI: 10.18870/hlrc.v5i3.244

Spante, M., Hashemi, S. S., Lundin, M., & Algers, A. (2018). Digital competence and digital literacy in higher education research: Systematic review of concept use. *Cogent Education, 5*(1), 1519143. DOI: 10.1080/2331186X.2018.1519143

Stensaker, B., Hovdhaugen, E., & Maassen, P. (2019). The practices of quality management in Norwegian higher education: Collaboration and control in study programme design and delivery. *International Journal of Educational Management, 33*(4), 698–708. DOI: 10.1108/IJEM-11-2017-0327

Stensaker, B., & Maassen, P. (2015). A conceptualisation of available trust-building mechanisms for international quality assurance of higher education. *Journal of Higher Education Policy and Management, 37*(1), 30–40. DOI: 10.1080/1360080X.2014.991538

Tierney, W. G., & Lanford, M. (2016). Conceptualizing innovation in higher education. In Paulsen, M. B. (Ed.), *Higher education: Handbook of theory and research* (Vol. 31, pp. 1–40). Springer. DOI: 10.1007/978-3-319-26829-3_1

Tight, M. (2018). *Higher education research: The developing field.* Bloomsbury Academic.

Tsai, Y.-S., Rates, D., Moreno-Marcos, P. M., Muñoz-Merino, P. J., Jivet, I., Scheffel, M., Drachsler, H., Delgado Kloos, C., & Gašević, D. (2020). Learning analytics in European higher education—Trends and barriers. *Computers & Education, 155*, 103933. DOI: 10.1016/j.compedu.2020.103933

UNESCO. (2019). Global convention on the recognition of qualifications concerning higher education. UNESCO.

Vieira, C., Parsons, P., & Byrd, V. (2018). Visual learning analytics of educational data: A systematic literature review and research agenda. *Computers & Education, 122*, 119–135. DOI: 10.1016/j.compedu.2018.03.018

Vincent-Lancrin, S., & van der Vlies, R. (2020). Trustworthy artificial intelligence (AI) in education: Promises and challenges (OECD Education Working Papers No. 218). OECD Publishing.

Vuorikari, R., Kluzer, S., & Punie, Y. (2022). *DigComp 2.2: The Digital Competence Framework for Citizens—With new examples of knowledge, skills and attitudes (EUR 31006 EN).* Publications Office of the European Union., DOI: 10.2760/115376

Walkington, C., & Bernacki, M. L. (2020). Appraising research on personalized learning: Definitions, theoretical alignment, advancements, and future directions. *Journal of Research on Technology in Education, 52*(3), 235–252. DOI: 10.1080/15391523.2020.1747757

Williams, P., & Harvey, L. (2015). Quality assurance in higher education. In Tight, M., & Shin, J. C. (Eds.), *The Palgrave international handbook of higher education policy and governance* (pp. 506–525). Palgrave Macmillan. DOI: 10.1007/978-1-137-45617-5_27

Wise, A. F., & Jung, Y. (2019). Teaching with analytics: Towards a situated model of instructional decision-making. *Journal of Learning Analytics*, *6*(2), 53–69. DOI: 10.18608/jla.2019.62.4

World Bank. (2023). *Digital development partnership annual review 2023: Transitioning towards scale*. World Bank Group.

World Economic Forum. (2023). Future of jobs report 2023. World Economic Forum.

Zawacki-Richter, O., Marín, V. I., Bond, M., & Gouverneur, F. (2019). Systematic review of research on artificial intelligence applications in higher education—Where are the educators? *International Journal of Educational Technology in Higher Education*, *16*(1), 39. Advance online publication. DOI: 10.1186/s41239-019-0171-0

Zhao, Y., & Watterston, J. (2021). The changes we need: Education post COVID-19. *Journal of Educational Change*, *22*(1), 3–12. DOI: 10.1007/s10833-021-09417-3

Chapter 12

Smart and International Campuses in Research Collaborations:

Challenges, Opportunities, and Policy Innovation

Amirul Mukminin
https://orcid.org/0000-0002-6806-1315
Universitas Jambi, Indonesia

Fridiyanto Fridiyanto
UIN Sulthan Thaha Saifuddin Jambi, Jambi, Indonesia

Lenny Marzulina
Universitas Islam Negeri Raden Fatah, Palembang, Indonesia

Dian Erlina
UIN Raden Fatah Palembang, Palembang, Indonesia

Ainur Abdrazakova
SDU University, Kazakhstan

Riskazt Ziqrand Amir
Universitas Brawijaya, Indonesia

Kasinyo Harto
Universitas Islam Negeri Raden Fatah, Palembang, Indonesia

ABSTRACT

Research collaboration in higher education has been profoundly transformed by smart and international campuses' rapid expansion. This paper examines challenges, opportunities, and policy innovations from integrating digital ecosystems, transnational networks, and intelligent infrastructures. The analysis identifies persistent challenges including uneven technological capacity, cybersecurity risks, administrative fragmentation, and institutional readiness disparities. Smart campuses create opportunities

DOI: 10.4018/979-8-3373-6831-3.ch012

026, IGI Global Scientific Publishing. Copying or distributing in print or electronic forms without written permission of IGI Global Scientific Publishing is prohibited. Use of this chapter to ive artificial intelligence (AI) technologies is expressly prohibited. The publisher reserves all rights to license its use for generative AI training and machine learning model development.

for real-time data sharing, interdisciplinary collaboration, global mobility, virtual research environments, and industry-university partnerships. Optimizing research productivity requires policy innovation encompassing governance models, interoperability standards, ethical data management, capacity-building, and incentive structures. The paper recommends a framework from global practices prioritizing inclusive, sustainable, innovation-driven collaboration, providing insights for universities, policymakers, and leaders fortifying global research ecosystems.

INTRODUCTION

Research collaboration has emerged as a defining feature of contemporary higher education which is driven by recognition that complex global challenges such as climate change, pandemics, technological disruption, social inequality, demanding interdisciplinary, multi-institutional, and transnational knowledge production (Wagner et al., 2021). Collaborative research intensity has accelerated dramatically, with bibliometric analyses revealing exponential growth in co-authored publications, international networks, and cross-border knowledge flows (Kwiek, 2020). This collaborative imperative reflects both epistemic shifts toward recognizing knowledge as distributed and socially constructed, and pragmatic responses to funding requirements, rankings pressures, and societal expectations for research impact (Nosek et al., 2022).

The emergence of smart campuses and intensification of internationalization represent transformative developments reshaping research collaboration infrastructure and possibilities. Smart campuses—technology-enhanced educational environments integrating Internet of Things devices, artificial intelligence, big data analytics, and ubiquitous connectivity—create digital ecosystems fundamentally altering research workflows, data accessibility, and collaborative possibilities (Ifenthaler & Schumacher, 2023; Villegas-Ch et al., 2021). These intelligent infrastructures enable real-time data collection, facilitate remote collaboration through advanced communication technologies, provide sophisticated research computing capabilities, and generate unprecedented institutional and behavioral data volumes (Minerva et al., 2020).

Simultaneously, internationalization—intentional integration of international, intercultural, and global dimensions into higher education's purpose and delivery (Knight, 2020)—has evolved from peripheral to central institutional strategy, manifesting through international recruitment, faculty mobility, joint programs, research partnerships, and global networks (Shields & Watermeyer, 2020). The convergence of smart campus capabilities with internationalization imperatives creates "smart international campuses"—globally connected, technologically sophisticated research environments transcending traditional geographic and institutional boundaries (Rahayu et al., 2022).

Global data have shown transformation magnitude. International research collaboration has grown substantially, with internationally co-authored publications increasing from approximately 10% in 1990 to over 25% by 2020 (Wagner et al., 2021). International student mobility expanded from 2 million students in 2000 to over 6 million in 2019, before pandemic disruptions (Mihut et al., 2020). Educational technology investment reached unprecedented levels, with global ed-tech markets projected to exceed $400 billion by 2025 (Ifenthaler & Schumacher, 2023). Smart campus implementations have proliferated across continents, with institutions investing heavily in IoT sensors, analytics platforms, intelligent systems, and advanced research infrastructure (Uskov et al., 2020).

In Indonesia, these global trends intersect with distinctive national circumstances including rapid higher education expansion, ambitious internationalization goals, increasing research output from modest baselines, and significant campus digitalization investment (Rahayu et al., 2022). Indonesia's higher education has prioritized internationalization through programs encouraging international publication, hosting conferences, establishing partnerships, and attracting international students, particularly from ASEAN countries (Nizam, 2021). Government initiatives including Kampus Merdeka emphasize experiential learning, industry collaboration, and global engagement as core missions (Sudaryanto et al., 2020).

Concurrently, Indonesian universities have invested substantially in digital infrastructure, implementing learning management systems, research information platforms, library digitalization, and sophisticated technology systems, though with considerable implementation variation across institutions (Yulianto et al., 2023). The COVID-19 pandemic accelerated digital transformation, forcing rapid adoption of online technologies and virtual collaboration tools that revealed both possibilities and limitations of technology-mediated academic work (Wahyuni, 2021). These developments position Indonesian higher education at a critical juncture where smart campus capabilities and internationalization aspirations converge, creating both opportunities and challenges for research collaboration enhancement.

Current scholarship on research collaboration draws upon multiple theoretical traditions. Social capital theory emphasizes how network relationships, trust, and reciprocity facilitate knowledge exchange and collaborative productivity (Hâncean et al., 2019). Network theories examine structural properties of collaboration networks and implications for knowledge diffusion and innovation (Fortunato et al., 2018). Knowledge-based perspectives conceptualize collaboration as mechanisms for knowledge creation and integration across organizational boundaries (Borgman, 2019). Mode 2 knowledge production theory describes contemporary research as increasingly transdisciplinary, application-oriented, and organizationally heterogeneous

(Fecher & Friesike, 2019). Triple helix models conceptualize innovation emerging from university-industry-government interactions (Carayannis & Campbell, 2019).

Empirical research documents substantial collaboration benefits including increased productivity, higher citation impact, enhanced funding access, and expanded professional networks (Alperin et al., 2020). International collaboration shows particularly strong associations with research impact, with internationally co-authored publications receiving higher citations across most disciplines and countries (Wagner et al., 2019). However, research also identifies significant challenges including coordination costs, intellectual property disputes, authorship conflicts, communication difficulties across cultural boundaries, power imbalances, and tensions between collaboration demands and individual career incentives (Dusdal & Powell, 2021). Technology-mediated collaboration introduces additional challenges including reduced social presence, trust establishment difficulties, infrastructure limitations, and cybersecurity concerns (Alshammari et al., 2023).

Despite substantial research on collaboration, smart campuses, and internationalization separately, significant gaps persist in understanding their convergence. First, existing literature inadequately examines how smart campus technologies specifically enable or constrain international research collaboration, with most research focusing on teaching applications rather than research implications (Ifenthaler & Schumacher, 2023). Second, internationalization research insufficiently addresses technological dimensions, treating technology primarily as communication facilitator rather than examining how digital ecosystems fundamentally reconstitute possibilities for international engagement (Rizvi & Beech, 2021). Third, policy research inadequately addresses governance challenges including data sovereignty, intellectual property frameworks, cybersecurity protocols, and ethical frameworks for international research (Janssen et al., 2020).

Fourth, equity dimensions receive insufficient attention, particularly regarding how smart international campus developments may exacerbate inequalities between well-resourced and under-resourced institutions, between global North and South, and between researchers with differential access to digital infrastructure (Stein et al., 2020). Fifth, contextual specificity remains limited, with research predominantly focusing on Western systems with inadequate attention to how dynamics operate in different cultural, economic, and policy contexts (Marginson, 2022). Sixth, sustainability considerations remain underdeveloped, with limited research examining environmental impacts of technology infrastructures and economic sustainability of long-term maintenance costs (Suwartha & Sari, 2019). Finally, critical examination of underlying assumptions and power dynamics remains insufficient, with technology often presented through deterministic narratives emphasizing inevitable progress while obscuring choices and trade-offs (Williamson, 2021).

This analytical paper will address these gaps through comprehensive examination of research collaboration on smart and international campuses, with particular attention to challenges, opportunities, and policy innovations. The analysis draws upon multiple theoretical perspectives, synthesizes empirical evidence from diverse contexts, and develops policy recommendations grounded in contemporary global practices while attending to Indonesian higher education specificities (Nizam, 2021). By examining the convergence of smart campus technological capabilities with internationalization imperatives, this paper advances scholarly understanding and informs policy development for research collaboration enhancement in an increasingly interconnected and technologically sophisticated global higher education landscape.

Specifically, this paper addresses five research questions examining: (1) primary challenges confronting research collaboration including technological, organizational, financial, regulatory, and equity obstacles (Alshammari et al., 2023; Kwiek, 2020); (2) opportunities smart international campus environments create for enhanced collaboration including new knowledge production forms, partnership modalities, and collaborative infrastructures (Leonelli, 2020; Villegas-Ch et al., 2021); (3) theoretical frameworks comprehensively illuminating research collaboration dynamics and necessary extensions for emerging phenomena (Van Dijck et al., 2018; Stein et al., 2020); (4) policy innovations including governance models, technical standards, ethical frameworks, capacity-building strategies, and incentive structures demonstrating promise for optimizing collaboration (Wilkinson et al., 2019; Mittelstadt, 2019); and (5) comprehensive policy frameworks and recommendations guiding Indonesian universities, policymakers, and international education leaders in strengthening research collaboration through strategic smart campus development and internationalization aligned with equity, sustainability, and research excellence principles (Rahayu et al., 2022; Sudaryanto et al., 2020).

RESEARCH METHODS

Research Design

This analysis study employed a qualitative systematic review and critical policy analysis design to examine research collaboration dynamics within smart international campus environments. The study adopted an interpretivist epistemological stance, recognizing that understanding of smart campus phenomena and internationalization processes is socially constructed and context-dependent, requiring interpretation of multiple perspectives across diverse institutional and cultural settings (Creswell & Poth, 2018). The design integrates three complementary methodological approaches. First, this paper uses systematic literature review methodology via following PRISMA

(Preferred Reporting Items for Systematic Reviews and Meta-Analyses) guidelines which enable comprehensive identification and synthesis of existing knowledge to address the five research questions (Page et al., 2021). Second, critical policy analysis frameworks, drawing upon Ball's (1993) policy sociology, examined underlying assumptions, power relations, and ideological orientations embedded within smart campus and internationalization policies. Third, comparative case analysis of policy approaches across different national contexts, with particular emphasis on Indonesian higher education, provided insights into contextual adaptation requirements (Bartlett & Vavrus, 2017).

Data Collection

Search Strategy and Information Sources

Data collection followed a systematic, multi-phase approach ensuring comprehensive coverage of relevant literature addressing the five research questions. Systematic searches were conducted across multiple databases including Web of Science, Scopus, ERIC, Academic Search Complete, ProQuest, IEEE Xplore, ScienceDirect, and Indonesian Publication Index.

The search strategy employed Boolean logic combining key concepts: (1) smart campuses (smart campus*, intelligent campus*, digital campus*, IoT education, cyber infrastructure); (2) internationalization (internationali?ation, global campus*, international collaboration, transnational network*); (3) research collaboration (research collaboration, scientific cooperation, knowledge production, co-authorship); (4) challenges and opportunities (barriers, obstacles, challenges, opportunities, enablers); (5) policy innovation (policy, governance, standards, ethics, capacity building, incentives); and (6) Indonesian context (Indonesia*, ASEAN, developing countr*).

Searches prioritized literature published within the past five years (2019-2024) to capture current developments in smart campus technologies and internationalization practices, aligning with research question citations emphasizing recent studies (e.g., Alshammari et al., 2023; Kwiek, 2020; Leonelli, 2020; Villegas-Ch et al., 2021; Wilkinson et al., 2019; Mittelstadt, 2019; Rahayu et al., 2022; Sudaryanto et al., 2020). Primary focus was placed on English-language publications, with supplementary inclusion of Indonesian-language policy documents relevant to research question five.

Supplementary search methods included: (1) citation chaining through forward and backward citation searching of key articles; (2) grey literature search of UNESCO, OECD, World Bank, European Commission, ASEAN, Indonesian Ministry of Education (Kemendikbudristek), and National Research Agency (BRIN) publications; (3) hand searching of key journals including *Research Policy*, *Higher Education*,

Studies in Higher Education, *Journal of Studies in International Education*, and *International Journal of Educational Technology in Higher Education*; and (4) expert consultation with scholars, policymakers, and practitioners to identify recent publications and emerging research.

Inclusion and Exclusion Criteria

Inclusion criteria encompassed: empirical studies, theoretical papers, systematic reviews, or policy analyses addressing one or more research questions; studies examining challenges (technological, organizational, financial, regulatory, equity); research documenting opportunities (knowledge production, partnership modalities, collaborative infrastructures); literature on theoretical frameworks; studies addressing policy innovations (governance, standards, ethics, capacity-building, incentives); research on Indonesian, ASEAN, or developing country contexts; peer-reviewed publications, conference proceedings, books, technical reports, or credible policy documents; English or Indonesian language publications; and publications from 2019-2024 with selective inclusion of seminal earlier works. Exclusion criteria included: studies focusing exclusively on teaching-learning applications without addressing research collaboration; literature not addressing research collaboration dimensions; studies outside higher education contexts; opinion pieces lacking substantive analysis; duplicate publications; and studies not addressing any research questions.

Data Analysis

Data analysis employed thematic synthesis methodology following Thomas and Harden (2008), enabling integration of diverse evidence types—quantitative findings, qualitative insights, theoretical propositions, policy recommendations—within coherent frameworks addressing research questions.

Analytical Framework and Procedures

Analysis was structured around five research questions with initial coding frameworks derived deductively from research question specifications while remaining open to emergent themes. The coding structure organized data according to: RQ1 domains (technological, organizational, financial, regulatory, equity challenges); RQ2 domains (knowledge production opportunities, partnership modalities, collaborative infrastructures); RQ3 domains (network theory, innovation systems theory, institutional theory, critical perspectives, complexity theory); RQ4 domains (governance, technical standards, ethical frameworks, capacity-building, incentive structures); and

RQ5 domains (Indonesian context, national infrastructure, capacity development, internationalization strategies, governance, sustainability, implementation).

Phase 1: Familiarization and Initial Coding

Extracted data from included studies underwent systematic line-by-line coding to identify concepts, themes, and patterns relevant to five research questions. Initial coding focused separately on each research question domain while maintaining attention to cross-cutting themes.

Phase 2: Development of Descriptive Themes

Related codes were grouped into descriptive themes through iterative comparison. For example, within RQ1 technological challenges, codes related to infrastructure disparities, connectivity issues, and equipment access were synthesized into "digital divide and infrastructure inequalities." Within RQ2 opportunities, codes addressing real-time analytics and collaborative platforms were synthesized into "enhanced computational and data-sharing capabilities."

Phase 3: Generation of Analytical Themes

Descriptive themes were synthesized into higher-order analytical themes offering interpretive insights directly addressing research questions through abductive reasoning, moving iteratively between empirical evidence and theoretical concepts (Timmermans & Tavory, 2012). For RQ1, diverse challenges were synthesized into a five-dimensional framework (technological, organizational, financial, regulatory, equity) theorizing linkage mechanisms. For RQ2, opportunities were categorized as enhanced knowledge production paradigms, innovative partnership modalities, and transformative collaborative infrastructures. For RQ3, theoretical insights identified necessary framework extensions. For RQ4, policy innovations were analyzed across governance, standards, ethics, capacity-building, and incentives dimensions. For RQ5, evidence was synthesized into comprehensive policy frameworks for Indonesian higher education.

Phase 4: Cross-Case and Comparative Analysis

Comparative analysis examined how challenges, opportunities, and policy innovations manifest differently across contexts characterized by varying resource levels, governance structures, technological maturity, and cultural factors. Attention focused on contrasting Global North-South experiences, well-resourced versus resource-constrained institutions, and centralized versus decentralized governance systems.

Phase 5: Critical Analysis and Theory Development

Critical analysis examined underlying assumptions, power dynamics, and normative orientations, interrogating whose interests policies serve, what collaboration forms are privileged or marginalized, and how policies might reproduce inequalities. This assessed theoretical framework adequacy (RQ3) and identified necessary extensions addressing digital platform mediation, algorithmic agency, transnational complexity, and sociotechnical entanglements.

Phase 6: Synthesis and Integration

Final synthesis integrated findings across research questions, mapping relationships among challenges, opportunities, theoretical explanations, and policy innovations; identifying cross-cutting issues and tensions; developing integrated policy frameworks synthesizing evidence-based recommendations; contextualizing findings for Indonesian higher education while maintaining broader applicability; and generating strategic insights for stakeholders.

Multiple forms of triangulation were used to enhance credibility including:

- Data source triangulation: Evidence from peer-reviewed empirical research, theoretical papers, grey literature (policy documents, technical reports, white papers), and institutional publications
- Theoretical triangulation: Application of multiple theoretical frameworks (network theory, innovation systems theory, institutional theory, critical post-colonial perspectives, complexity theory) to interpret findings
- Methodological triangulation: Integration of systematic review, critical policy analysis, and comparative case methods

PRIMARY CHALLENGES CONFRONTING RESEARCH COLLABORATION ON SMART AND INTERNATIONAL CAMPUSES

The contemporary higher education landscape witnesses unprecedented transformation through the convergence of smart campus technologies and internationalization initiatives. While these developments promise enhanced research collaboration and knowledge exchange, they simultaneously introduce multifaceted challenges that institutions must navigate strategically. This analysis will examine the primary obstacles confronting research collaboration across technological, organizational, financial, regulatory, and equity dimensions, drawing upon recent scholarly literature to provide a comprehensive understanding of this complex phenomenon.

Technological Challenges

Infrastructure Disparities and Digital Divide

The implementation of smart campus technologies reveals significant infrastructure disparities among higher education institutions globally. Technological readiness varies considerably across institutions, creating a stratified landscape where well-resourced universities deploy sophisticated digital ecosystems while others struggle with fundamental connectivity issues (Nguyen et al., 2021). This digital divide extends beyond mere hardware availability, encompassing bandwidth limitations, cloud computing capacity, and access to advanced research equipment equipped with Internet of Things (IoT) capabilities.

Contemporary research demonstrates that institutions in developing nations face substantial barriers in adopting smart campus technologies due to inadequate technological infrastructure (Alruwais et al., 2020). These disparities manifest in limited access to high-performance computing resources, insufficient network bandwidth for data-intensive collaborative projects, and outdated legacy systems that resist integration with modern digital platforms. The rapid obsolescence of technology necessitates continuous investment, creating a perpetual challenge for institutions operating with constrained budgets (Ifenthaler & Schumacher, 2023).

Interoperability and System Integration

The proliferation of diverse technological platforms within and across institutions has generated substantial interoperability challenges. Smart campuses typically deploy multiple vendor solutions for learning management systems, research data repositories, administrative functions, and collaborative tools, creating fragmented digital ecosystems that resist seamless integration (Villegas-Ch et al., 2020). This technological heterogeneity impedes data sharing, complicates collaborative workflows, and generates inefficiencies that undermine research productivity.

Recent studies highlight that the absence of standardized protocols for data exchange between institutions represents a critical impediment to international research collaboration (Muñoz & Antón, 2022). Different institutions employ varying data formats, metadata standards, and application programming interfaces (APIs), necessitating extensive customization and middleware development to facilitate cross-institutional collaboration. These technical complexities consume substantial resources and create dependencies on specialized technical expertise that may not be readily available (Kim & Kim, 2021).

Cybersecurity Vulnerabilities and Data Integrity

The increasing digitalization of research collaboration has amplified cybersecurity concerns across smart and international campuses. The interconnected nature of smart campus infrastructure creates multiple entry points for cyber threats, ranging from data breaches and ransomware attacks to sophisticated state-sponsored espionage targeting sensitive research data (Alshammari et al., 2023). The collaborative nature of international research further complicates security architectures, as institutions must ensure data protection while facilitating access across multiple jurisdictions with varying security protocols.

Contemporary literature emphasizes that higher education institutions face distinct cybersecurity challenges compared to other sectors, including the tension between openness—a fundamental academic value—and security imperatives (Sharma et al., 2020). Research collaborations often involve sharing preliminary findings, datasets, and methodological approaches across institutional and national boundaries, creating vulnerabilities that malicious actors may exploit. The increasing sophistication of cyber threats, including artificial intelligence-enabled attacks, outpaces the defensive capabilities of many institutions.

Technological Literacy and Skill Gaps

The successful implementation of smart campus technologies for research collaboration requires substantial technological literacy among faculty, researchers, and support staff. However, significant skill gaps persist across institutions, particularly regarding advanced data analytics, machine learning applications, and the utilization of emerging technologies such as blockchain for research validation and intellectual property management (Zawacki-Richter et al., 2019). These competency deficits limit institutions' capacity to fully leverage available technological resources for collaborative research endeavors.

Recent research indicates that professional development initiatives frequently fail to keep pace with technological innovation, leaving faculty members insufficiently prepared to navigate evolving digital research environments (Bond et al., 2020). This skills deficit proves particularly acute in interdisciplinary collaborations where researchers must master not only their domain-specific technologies but also the digital tools facilitating cross-disciplinary communication and data integration. Moreover, generational differences in technological proficiency create additional complexities, as senior researchers may resist adopting new collaborative platforms despite their potential benefits.

Organizational Challenges

Administrative Fragmentation and Governance Complexity

Smart and international campuses operate within increasingly complex organizational structures that often impede rather than facilitate research collaboration. Administrative fragmentation occurs both within individual institutions—where research support functions may be distributed across multiple departments—and across collaborative partnerships involving institutions with divergent organizational cultures and decision-making processes (Knight, 2020). This structural complexity generates coordination challenges, extends decision-making timelines, and creates ambiguity regarding roles and responsibilities in collaborative research initiatives.

Contemporary scholarship highlights that traditional hierarchical governance structures prove inadequately responsive to the dynamic nature of international research collaboration (Shields & Watermeyer, 2020). Bureaucratic processes designed for domestic, single-institution research projects often impose excessive administrative burden when applied to international collaborations involving multiple stakeholders, funding sources, and regulatory frameworks. Furthermore, the siloed nature of many academic departments inhibits the interdisciplinary collaboration that smart campus technologies theoretically enable.

Cultural and Linguistic Barriers

International research collaboration inherently involves navigating diverse cultural contexts, communication styles, and linguistic differences that can substantially impede effective cooperation. Cultural variations in research methodologies, authorship conventions, intellectual property norms, and conflict resolution approaches create misunderstandings that undermine collaborative relationships (Leask, 2020). These cultural dimensions extend beyond superficial differences, encompassing fundamental epistemological assumptions and values that shape research practices across different national and institutional contexts.

Recent studies document that linguistic barriers persist as significant obstacles to international collaboration despite English's dominance as the lingua franca of academic research (Curry & Lillis, 2019). Non-native English speakers often experience disadvantages in collaborative projects, including reduced participation in discussions, limited influence over conceptual framing, and challenges in articulating nuanced theoretical positions. Moreover, the reliance on English-language communication may inadvertently marginalize valuable knowledge traditions and research approaches originating from non-English-speaking contexts.

Institutional Competition and Trust Deficits

While collaboration represents a stated objective for many institutions, underlying competitive dynamics often undermine genuine cooperation. Universities increasingly compete for international rankings, research funding, and student enrollments, creating tensions that complicate collaborative relationships (Hazelkorn, 2021). This competitive environment generates reluctance to share research data, methodologies, and preliminary findings that might provide competitive advantages to partner institutions.

Trust deficits represent a fundamental organizational challenge in international research collaboration, particularly when partnerships involve institutions with limited prior interaction or from contexts with different research integrity standards (Anderson et al., 2021). Concerns about intellectual property protection, data security, and research misconduct create hesitancy that inhibits the open exchange essential for productive collaboration. Recent research indicates that establishing trust in international partnerships requires substantial time investment, repeated positive interactions, and carefully structured governance mechanisms that protect all parties' interests.

Financial Challenges

Funding Disparities and Resource Allocation

Substantial financial disparities among institutions and nations fundamentally shape the landscape of international research collaboration. Well-resourced universities in affluent nations possess significant advantages in accessing competitive research funding, maintaining sophisticated infrastructure, and supporting faculty research time, creating asymmetric partnerships where resource-constrained institutions occupy subordinate positions (Kwiek, 2020). These funding disparities perpetuate inequitable collaboration dynamics and limit the contributions of researchers from less affluent contexts.

Contemporary research documents that funding mechanisms for international collaboration often inadequately address the full costs associated with cross-border partnerships, including travel expenses, communication infrastructure, personnel time for coordination, and technology compatibility requirements (Edler et al., 2020). Furthermore, funding timelines and budget cycles frequently misalign across national contexts, creating financial planning challenges and cash flow difficulties that impede project implementation. The increasing emphasis on industry partnerships and commercialization outcomes in research funding further disadvantages institutions lacking robust industry connections.

Sustainability and Long-term Investment

The implementation and maintenance of smart campus infrastructure require sustained financial investment that extends beyond initial capital expenditures. Many institutions successfully secure funding for technology deployment through one-time grants or special allocations but struggle to maintain recurring operational costs, including software licenses, hardware maintenance, cybersecurity measures, and personnel training (Ifenthaler & Schumacher, 2023). This sustainability challenge proves particularly acute for international collaborations, which require ongoing investment in communication technologies, data storage, and collaborative platforms.

Research indicates that short-term funding cycles characteristic of many research grants poorly aligns with the extended timeframes necessary for developing productive international collaborations (Proskurnina, 2023). Building trust, establishing shared protocols, and generating meaningful research outcomes typically require multi-year commitments that exceed standard grant durations. Consequently, many potentially valuable collaborations dissolve prematurely when initial funding expires, representing inefficient resource utilization and lost opportunities for sustained knowledge exchange.

Hidden Costs and Administrative Burden

International research collaboration generates substantial hidden costs that institutions frequently underestimate during project planning. These include administrative time for compliance documentation, legal expenses for contract negotiation, currency exchange fluctuations, taxation complexities, and costs associated with addressing unforeseen logistical challenges (Edler et al., 2020). The administrative burden proves particularly onerous for small-scale collaborations and early-career researchers who lack dedicated administrative support.

Recent scholarship highlights that the indirect costs of maintaining smart campus infrastructure—including energy consumption, technical support personnel, continuous software updates, and cybersecurity measures—can exceed direct hardware and software expenses over time (Uskov et al., 2020). These ongoing operational costs strain institutional budgets and divert resources from direct research support, potentially undermining the cost-effectiveness of technology-enabled collaboration.

Regulatory Challenges

Data Protection and Privacy Regulations

The proliferation of data protection regulations across jurisdictions has created a complex compliance landscape that significantly complicates international research collaboration. The European Union's General Data Protection Regulation (GDPR), similar regulations in other jurisdictions, and varying national frameworks impose stringent requirements on data collection, storage, processing, and transfer that research collaborations must navigate (Trepte et al., 2020). These regulations, while serving legitimate privacy protection objectives, generate substantial compliance costs and create legal uncertainties that inhibit cross-border data sharing.

Contemporary research emphasizes that conflicts between national data protection frameworks create particular challenges for international collaborations involving human subjects research (Staunton & Quiroz, 2020). What constitutes adequate consent, permissible data uses, and appropriate retention periods varies substantially across jurisdictions, necessitating complex legal analyses and potentially incompatible protocols that undermine research efficiency. Furthermore, the extraterritorial application of certain regulations creates situations where researchers must simultaneously comply with multiple, potentially contradictory legal frameworks.

Intellectual Property and Technology Transfer

Intellectual property (IP) rights represent a persistent source of complexity and conflict in international research collaborations. Different national legal systems recognize varying IP frameworks, ownership presumptions, and protection mechanisms, creating ambiguity regarding rights allocation in collaborative projects (Veer & Jell, 2022). Universities increasingly emphasize commercialization and technology transfer outcomes, generating tensions between open science principles and proprietary interests that complicate collaborative arrangements.

Recent literature documents that negotiating IP agreements consumes substantial time and resources in international partnerships, often delaying project commencement and creating friction among collaborators. Disagreements regarding authorship rights, patent ownership, revenue sharing, and publication timing can undermine collaborative relationships and discourage researchers from pursuing international partnerships. Moreover, the involvement of industry partners introduces additional IP complexities, as commercial entities typically demand more restrictive protections than academic norms accommodate.

Export Control and National Security Regulations

The intensification of geopolitical tensions has led numerous governments to expand export control regulations and national security restrictions affecting international research collaboration. Dual-use technologies—those with both civilian and military applications—face increasing scrutiny, with regulations limiting international collaboration in fields including artificial intelligence, quantum computing, advanced materials, and biotechnology (Barkved, 2021). These restrictions create uncertainty for researchers, who may inadvertently violate regulations through routine collaborative activities such as sharing research findings or hosting international scholars.

Contemporary scholarship highlights that vaguely defined national security concerns increasingly constrain academic collaboration, particularly involving researchers from geopolitical rival nations. Universities face pressure to screen international collaborations for potential security risks, implement deemed export controls, and restrict access to certain research areas—measures that conflict with academic values of openness and international exchange. The chilling effect of these regulations extends beyond explicitly prohibited activities, as researchers increasingly self-censor and avoid potentially sensitive collaborations to minimize legal risks.

Equity-Related Challenges

Power Asymmetries and Neo-Colonial Dynamics

International research collaborations frequently reproduce historical power imbalances and neo-colonial dynamics, with institutions from affluent Global North nations occupying dominant positions relative to partners from the Global South (Stein et al., 2020). These asymmetries manifest in multiple dimensions, including agenda-setting authority, resource control, authorship conventions, and knowledge validation processes that privilege Western epistemologies and research traditions. Such inequitable partnerships undermine the principles of mutual benefit and reciprocity that should characterize genuine collaboration.

Contemporary scholarship documents that researchers from the Global South often occupy subordinate roles in international collaborations, functioning primarily as data collectors or local facilitators while partners from affluent nations control conceptual frameworks, analytical approaches, and dissemination strategies (Bhakuni & Abimbola, 2021). These extractive dynamics perpetuate knowledge hierarchies and limit the capacity of institutions in developing contexts to build sustainable research capabilities. Furthermore, language requirements, publication venue preferences, and citation practices systematically disadvantage scholars from non-English-speaking and non-Western contexts.

Access and Participation Barriers

Despite the rhetorical commitment to inclusive internationalization, substantial barriers limit participation in international research collaborations for researchers from underrepresented backgrounds, under-resourced institutions, and marginalized communities. Financial constraints prevent many talented researchers from engaging in international networking activities, conference participation, and extended research visits that facilitate collaborative relationship development (Jöns, 2021). Moreover, visa restrictions, discriminatory immigration policies, and limited travel freedoms disproportionately affect researchers from certain national origins, constraining mobility and collaborative opportunities.

Recent literature emphasizes that digital divides extend beyond infrastructure availability to encompass digital literacies, linguistic capabilities, and cultural familiarity with Western-dominated digital communication norms. Researchers lacking fluency in English or familiarity with particular collaboration platforms face disadvantages in international partnerships, regardless of their substantive expertise. Furthermore, caring responsibilities, often inequitably distributed across gender lines, limit some researchers' capacity to engage in international collaborations requiring extensive travel or time-zone-defying communication schedules.

Recognition and Career Advancement Inequities

Institutional reward structures and career advancement mechanisms often inadequately recognize the complexities and time investments associated with international research collaboration. Traditional metrics for research productivity, including publication counts and citation rates, may disadvantage researchers engaged in collaborative projects that require extended relationship-building, navigating regulatory complexities, and producing outputs that emerge gradually over time (Alperin et al., 2020). Moreover, disciplinary variations in collaboration norms create inequities, with researchers in fields emphasizing large collaborative teams potentially advantaged relative to those in fields privileging single-authored work.

Contemporary research indicates that early-career researchers face particular disincentives for pursuing international collaborations, as the extended timelines and uncertain outcomes conflict with tenure and promotion expectations emphasizing rapid productivity. The pressure to demonstrate independent research trajectories may discourage junior scholars from investing in collaborative relationships, despite their potential long-term benefits. Furthermore, the contributions of researchers occupying support roles in collaborative projects—including those managing partnerships, facilitating cross-cultural communication, or providing technical expertise—often receive insufficient recognition in academic reward systems.

The challenges confronting research collaboration on smart and international campuses span technological, organizational, financial, regulatory, and equity dimensions, creating a complex obstacle landscape that institutions must navigate strategically. Technological disparities, interoperability limitations, and cybersecurity vulnerabilities compound organizational challenges including administrative fragmentation, cultural barriers, and trust deficits. Financial constraints, sustainability concerns, and hidden costs interact with regulatory complexities involving data protection, intellectual property, and national security restrictions. Underlying these multifaceted challenges, fundamental equity issues including power asymmetries, access barriers, and recognition inequities threaten the legitimacy and sustainability of international research collaboration.

Addressing these interconnected challenges requires comprehensive, systemic approaches that transcend technological solutions to engage organizational transformation, policy innovation, sustainable funding models, harmonized regulatory frameworks, and genuine commitment to equitable partnership principles. The literature reviewed demonstrates that while smart campus technologies offer significant potential for enhancing research collaboration, realizing this potential demands sustained attention to the human, organizational, and structural dimensions that ultimately determine collaborative success.

OPPORTUNITIES FOR ENHANCED RESEARCH COLLABORATION IN SMART INTERNATIONAL CAMPUS ENVIRONMENTS

The confluence of smart campus technologies and internationalization initiatives has fundamentally transformed the landscape of academic research collaboration, creating unprecedented opportunities for knowledge exchange, innovation, and scholarly cooperation. While challenges persist, the integration of advanced digital infrastructures, artificial intelligence, data analytics, and ubiquitous connectivity has enabled novel forms of collaborative engagement that transcend traditional spatial, temporal, and disciplinary boundaries. This analysis examines the multifaceted opportunities that smart international campus environments generate for enhanced research collaboration, exploring emerging knowledge production paradigms, innovative partnership modalities, and transformative collaborative infrastructures that are reshaping the future of academic research.

Enhanced Knowledge Production Paradigms

Real-Time Data Sharing and Collaborative Analytics

Smart campus environments have revolutionized research collaboration through the implementation of sophisticated data sharing infrastructures that enable instantaneous exchange of research data, analytical results, and scholarly insights across institutional and geographical boundaries. Cloud-based research data repositories, integrated with advanced analytics platforms, facilitate seamless collaboration among geographically dispersed research teams, enabling simultaneous data access, analysis, and visualization capabilities that were previously unattainable (Leonelli, 2020). These technological affordances support more dynamic and iterative research processes, where collaborators can collectively interrogate datasets, refine analytical approaches, and generate insights through synchronous engagement with shared research materials.

Contemporary scholarship demonstrates that real-time collaborative analytics substantially accelerates research timelines and enhances methodological rigor through continuous peer validation of analytical procedures. Smart campus infrastructures equipped with high-performance computing resources, distributed through cloud architectures, democratize access to computational capabilities that enable sophisticated data modeling, machine learning applications, and complex simulations. This computational democratization proves particularly valuable for institutions in resource-constrained contexts, providing access to analytical capabilities that would be financially prohibitive through traditional infrastructure investments (Mulder et al., 2019).

Furthermore, the integration of Internet of Things (IoT) sensors throughout smart campus environments generates continuous streams of environmental, behavioral, and operational data that create novel research opportunities spanning multiple disciplines (Minerva et al., 2020). These ubiquitous data collection capabilities support longitudinal studies, enable real-time intervention research, and facilitate the investigation of complex phenomena requiring continuous monitoring across extended temporal horizons.

Open Science and Transparent Research Practices

Smart international campus environments provide technological infrastructures that substantially facilitate open science practices, including preregistration of research protocols, transparent reporting of methodologies, open data sharing, and collaborative peer review processes (Vicente-Saez & Martinez-Fuentes, 2018). Digital research platforms integrated within smart campus ecosystems enable researchers to document their complete analytical workflows, making research processes more transparent, reproducible, and accessible to international collaborators. These capabilities address longstanding concerns regarding research reproducibility while simultaneously lowering barriers to collaborative engagement by enabling potential partners to assess methodological approaches and preliminary findings before committing to formal collaborations (Nosek et al., 2022).

Recent literature emphasizes that open science infrastructures embedded within smart campuses catalyze new forms of distributed collaboration where researchers contribute specialized expertise to collective research endeavors without requiring traditional co-location or long-term institutional affiliations (Fecher & Friesike, 2019). Citizen science initiatives, crowd-sourced data collection efforts, and global collaborative projects become substantially more feasible through smart campus platforms that provide the technical infrastructure for coordinating contributions from diverse participants worldwide. These emerging collaboration modalities democratize knowledge production, incorporating perspectives and data from previously marginalized communities and geographical contexts.

Interdisciplinary and Transdisciplinary Research Integration

Smart international campus infrastructures create technical and organizational conditions conducive to interdisciplinary and transdisciplinary research collaboration by providing shared digital spaces where researchers from diverse disciplinary backgrounds can converge around common research challenges (Klein, 2021). Integrated research platforms eliminate many technical barriers that previously impeded cross-disciplinary collaboration, including incompatible data formats, divergent software ecosystems, and difficulties in sharing discipline-specific analytical tools. Standardized application programming interfaces (APIs), containerized software environments, and interoperable data schemas enable researchers to leverage specialized methodologies from multiple disciplines within unified analytical workflows (Woelfle et al., 2021).

Contemporary research documents that smart campus environments facilitate the emergence of hybrid research methodologies combining quantitative and qualitative approaches, computational and interpretive methods, and experimental and observational designs through technological infrastructures supporting methodological pluralism. Virtual research environments provide spaces where mixed-methods collaborations can flourish, with team members applying complementary analytical approaches to shared research questions. The capacity to seamlessly integrate diverse data types—including numerical measurements, textual documents, visual materials, and sensor data—within unified analytical platforms enables more comprehensive investigations of complex phenomena (Borgman, 2019).

Artificial Intelligence and Machine Learning Applications

The integration of artificial intelligence (AI) and machine learning (ML) capabilities within smart campus environments has created transformative opportunities for research collaboration by providing powerful analytical tools, automating routine research tasks, and enabling investigation of previously intractable research questions (Hinojo-Lucena et al., 2019). AI-augmented research platforms assist international collaborations by facilitating literature reviews, identifying relevant prior research, suggesting potential collaborators with complementary expertise, and even generating preliminary analytical code based on natural language descriptions of research objectives. These capabilities substantially reduce the transaction costs associated with initiating and maintaining international collaborations (Gašević et al., 2023).

Recent scholarship highlights that machine learning algorithms trained on large-scale research datasets can identify non-obvious patterns, generate novel hypotheses, and suggest innovative analytical approaches that enhance collaborative research productivity. Smart campus infrastructures providing access to pre-trained models, computational resources for model development, and platforms for sharing trained algorithms enable smaller institutions and individual researchers to leverage cutting-edge AI capabilities without requiring extensive computational resources or specialized technical expertise. This democratization of AI tools fosters more equitable international collaborations by reducing capability gaps between well-resourced and resource-constrained partners (Alenezi & Wardat, 2022).

Innovative Partnership Modalities

Virtual Research Environments and Distributed Teams

Smart international campus infrastructures have enabled the proliferation of virtual research environments (VREs) that support sustained collaboration among geographically distributed research teams without requiring physical co-location (Candela et al., 2020). These digital ecosystems integrate project management tools, communication platforms, data repositories, analytical software, and collaborative authoring systems within unified interfaces that provide comprehensive support for research workflows. VREs facilitate asynchronous collaboration, enabling team members across multiple time zones to contribute productively according to their individual schedules while maintaining continuity of research activities.

Contemporary literature demonstrates that well-designed VREs can generate collaborative outcomes comparable to or exceeding those achieved through traditional co-located research arrangements, particularly for projects involving large datasets, computational analysis, or longitudinal investigations. The reduced necessity for international travel generates both economic and environmental benefits while simultaneously increasing accessibility for researchers facing mobility constraints due to visa restrictions, health conditions, family responsibilities, or financial limitations. This enhanced accessibility contributes to more diverse and inclusive research collaborations (Müller et al., 2021).

Multi-Institutional Research Networks and Consortia

Smart international campus technologies facilitate the formation and coordination of multi-institutional research networks and consortia that aggregate complementary capabilities, datasets, and expertise to address complex research challenges requiring resources beyond any single institution's capacity (Wagner et al., 2019). Digital coordination platforms enable efficient management of large-scale collaborative initiatives involving dozens or hundreds of participating institutions, providing infrastructures for data sharing, protocol standardization, progress monitoring, and collective decision-making. These network collaboration modalities prove particularly valuable for research domains requiring large sample sizes, diverse contextual comparisons, or comprehensive data coverage across multiple geographical regions.

Recent research highlights that smart campus infrastructures enable more decentralized and egalitarian governance structures for multi-institutional collaborations compared to traditional hub-and-spoke models where a dominant institution controls research agendas and resources. Distributed ledger technologies, including blockchain applications, provide transparent mechanisms for documenting contributions, managing intellectual property rights, and ensuring equitable benefit-sharing among network participants. These technological capabilities address persistent concerns regarding power asymmetries and exploitation risks in international research collaborations (Bass et al., 2020).

Industry-University-Government Partnerships

Smart international campus environments create enhanced opportunities for productive collaborations between academic institutions, industry partners, and government agencies through digital platforms that facilitate knowledge exchange, technology transfer, and collaborative problem-solving (Carayannis & Campbell, 2019). Innovation hubs, digital fabrication laboratories, and technology incubators integrated within smart campus ecosystems provide physical and virtual spaces where academic researchers, industry practitioners, and policymakers converge to address practical challenges requiring multisectoral expertise. These collaborative spaces generate mutually beneficial partnerships where academic research gains practical relevance while industry and government partners access cutting-edge knowledge and research capabilities (Guerrero et al., 2021).

Contemporary scholarship emphasizes that smart campus technologies enable more fluid and dynamic engagement between academic researchers and external partners through digital platforms supporting various collaboration intensities—from brief consultations and knowledge sharing to sustained joint research initiatives and commercialization partnerships. These flexible engagement modalities accommodate the different operational rhythms, incentive structures, and accountability frameworks characterizing academic, industry, and government sectors. Intellectual property management systems integrated within smart campus platforms provide transparent mechanisms for negotiating and documenting rights allocation, reducing friction and accelerating partnership formation (Miller et al., 2021).

South-South and Triangular Collaboration

Smart international campus technologies have catalyzed new opportunities for South-South collaboration—partnerships among institutions in the Global South—and triangular cooperation involving Global North facilitators supporting South-South partnerships (Carbonnier & Kontinen, 2019). These collaboration modalities address persistent concerns regarding neo-colonial dynamics in traditional North-South partnerships by centering the priorities, epistemologies, and capabilities of institutions in developing contexts. Digital platforms reduce dependency on expensive international travel and enable sustained collaboration among institutions facing similar developmental challenges and operating within comparable resource constraints (Teferra, 2021).

Recent literature documents that South-South collaborations frequently generate more contextually appropriate research outcomes and more equitable partnership dynamics compared to traditional North-South arrangements, as partners share common developmental priorities and possess mutual understanding of relevant contextual factors. Smart campus infrastructures facilitate these partnerships by providing communication platforms, data sharing capabilities, and collaborative analytical tools that enable productive engagement despite limited financial resources.

Transformative Collaborative Infrastructures

Distributed Research Infrastructure and Equipment Sharing

Smart international campus environments enable innovative approaches to research infrastructure management through remote access technologies, equipment sharing platforms, and distributed laboratory networks that substantially enhance resource utilization and democratize access to specialized research capabilities (Borgman et al., 2019). Advanced instruments equipped with remote operation capabilities—including electron microscopes, telescopes, supercomputers, and specialized analytical equipment—can be accessed by international researchers without requiring physical presence at equipment locations. These remote access capabilities dramatically reduce barriers to cutting-edge research, particularly benefiting institutions unable to afford their own specialized equipment.

Contemporary research highlights that equipment sharing platforms integrated within smart campus ecosystems optimize resource allocation by enabling institutions to monetize underutilized capacity while providing affordable access for researchers requiring occasional specialized capabilities. Scheduling systems, remote operation interfaces, and automated data transfer protocols streamline the logistics of equipment sharing, reducing coordination friction and transaction costs. These infrastructure-sharing modalities foster international research collaboration by creating mutual dependencies and shared interests among participating institutions (Posada & Chen, 2020).

Digital Libraries and Global Knowledge Commons

The development of comprehensive digital libraries, open access repositories, and global knowledge commons represents a fundamental infrastructure advancement enabled by smart international campus environments (Tennant et al., 2020). These digital knowledge infrastructures provide researchers worldwide with unprecedented access to scholarly literature, research data, educational resources, and grey literature previously confined to well-resourced institutions with extensive physical library collections. Open access mandates, institutional repositories, and preprint servers democratize knowledge access while simultaneously facilitating research collaboration by enabling potential partners to assess each other's prior work and identify complementary expertise.

Recent scholarship emphasizes that interoperable metadata standards, persistent identifiers, and federated search capabilities enable seamless discovery and access across disparate digital repositories and knowledge platforms (Wilkinson et al., 2019). These technical standards facilitate international collaboration by reducing search costs and enabling researchers to identify relevant prior work, available datasets, and potential collaborators regardless of their institutional affiliations or geographical locations. The implementation of FAIR principles—ensuring data are Findable, Accessible, Interoperable, and Reusable—within smart campus infrastructures substantially enhances research efficiency and collaboration potential.

Advanced Visualization and Immersive Technologies

Smart international campus environments increasingly incorporate advanced visualization technologies, including virtual reality (VR), augmented reality (AR), and mixed reality systems that create novel opportunities for collaborative research and knowledge sharing (Radianti et al., 2020). These immersive technologies enable international collaborators to examine complex three-dimensional datasets, explore virtual field sites, manipulate molecular structures, and visualize abstract concepts through shared digital environments that overcome spatial separation. Collaborative VR platforms provide virtual meeting spaces where geographically distributed teams can interact with shared data representations using natural gestures and spatial reasoning capabilities that prove difficult to replicate through traditional two-dimensional interfaces.

Contemporary literature demonstrates that immersive technologies substantially enhance comprehension and retention of complex spatial relationships, multidimensional datasets, and dynamic processes compared to conventional visualization approaches (Mikropoulos & Natsis, 2021). These cognitive advantages prove particularly valuable for interdisciplinary collaborations where team members possess diverse expertise and may benefit from multiple complementary representations of research phenomena.

Adaptive Learning Systems and Capacity Building

Smart international campus environments incorporate adaptive learning systems and intelligent tutoring platforms that enhance capacity building for research collaboration by providing personalized training in research methodologies, statistical analysis, grant writing, and discipline-specific skills (Chen et al., 2020). These AI-powered educational technologies assess learners' existing knowledge, identify skill gaps, and deliver customized instruction tailored to individual learning needs and professional development objectives. The availability of sophisticated, scalable capacity-building infrastructure within smart campus ecosystems reduces barriers to international collaboration by enabling researchers from diverse educational backgrounds to acquire necessary competencies for productive partnership engagement.

Contemporary research demonstrates that collaborative learning environments embedded within smart campus platforms facilitate peer-to-peer knowledge exchange where international research teams collectively develop shared methodological expertise, troubleshoot analytical challenges, and refine research protocols through structured collaborative learning activities (Zheng et al., 2020). These social learning modalities prove particularly valuable for building research capacity in contexts where formal educational opportunities remain limited.

Smart international campus environments generate transformative opportunities for research collaboration through technological infrastructures enabling real-time data sharing, open science practices, interdisciplinary integration, and AI-augmented research capabilities. Novel partnership modalities—including virtual research environments, multi-institutional networks, industry-university-government collaborations, and South-South partnerships—expand the scope and inclusivity of international research collaboration. Transformative infrastructures including distributed research equipment, digital knowledge commons, immersive technologies, and adaptive learning platforms provide foundations for more productive, equitable, and sustainable collaborative research ecosystems. Realizing the full potential of these opportunities requires intentional efforts to ensure equitable access, maintain research quality and integrity, protect privacy and security, and foster inclusive collaboration practices that value diverse epistemologies and knowledge traditions.

THEORETICAL FRAMEWORKS FOR RESEARCH COLLABORATION IN SMART INTERNATIONAL CAMPUS CONTEXTS

The emergence of smart international campus environments demands theoretical frameworks capable of illuminating complex dynamics involving digital technologies, transnational partnerships, and evolving knowledge production modes. Traditional theories developed for physical, predominantly national contexts prove increasingly inadequate for capturing these complexities. This analysis examines theoretical frameworks that comprehensively illuminate research collaboration dynamics while identifying necessary extensions and revisions.

Network Theory and Digital Platform Extensions

Network theory provides foundational insights into research collaboration by conceptualizing scientific cooperation as embedded within social structures characterized by nodes (researchers, institutions) and ties (collaborative relationships) (Barabási et al., 2019). Traditional applications have illuminated preferential attachment mechanisms, cumulative advantage processes, and structural holes creating brokerage opportunities. However, smart international campus contexts introduce phenomena requiring substantial theoretical extensions.

First, the distinction between strong and weak ties becomes increasingly ambiguous in digitally-mediated collaboration where sustained interaction may occur through asynchronous communication and algorithmic coordination without intensive interpersonal engagement (Haythornthwaite, 2019). Contemporary scholarship proposes conceptualizing digital research collaborations along multiple dimensions including interaction frequency, emotional intensity, reciprocity, and technological mediation rather than relying on binary distinctions (McFarland et al., 2021).

Second, smart campus platforms introduce non-human actors—including algorithms, automated systems, and artificial intelligence agents—that actively shape collaboration networks through recommendation systems and intelligent resource allocation (Fortunato et al., 2018). Traditional network theory focusing exclusively on human actors proves inadequate for capturing how these technological entities influence network formation and evolution. Actor-Network Theory extensions incorporating technological agency offer promising directions, though require further development addressing AI systems' specific characteristics (Latour, 2020).

Third, the temporal dynamics of digitally-enabled research networks differ substantially from traditional collaboration patterns. Smart campus technologies enable rapid network formation, flexible reconfiguration, and simultaneous participation in multiple overlapping networks (Velden et al., 2019). These fluid, multiplex network structures challenge frameworks assuming relatively stable, discrete collaborative relationships, advocating for dynamic network analysis approaches capturing continuous evolution (Holme & Saramäki, 2019).

Integration with platform studies perspectives offers productive theoretical extensions, recognizing that collaboration networks increasingly develop within digital platforms possessing distinctive affordances, governance structures, and business models fundamentally shaping collaborative possibilities (Van Dijck et al., 2018). Platform-centric network analysis examines how design decisions structure collaboration opportunities, privilege particular engagement forms, and create path dependencies influencing research trajectories (Plantin et al., 2019).

Innovation Systems Theory and Transnational Complexity

Knowledge-based and innovation systems theories conceptualize research collaboration as embedded within broader ecosystems comprising universities, industry, government, and civil society organizations collectively generating, diffusing, and applying knowledge (Carayannis & Campbell, 2019). The Triple Helix, Quadruple Helix, and Quintuple Helix models have provided influential frameworks for understanding research collaboration's societal embeddedness.

However, smart international campus environments challenge fundamental assumptions underlying innovation systems theories, particularly regarding territorial boundedness and sectoral distinctions. Digital technologies increasingly enable research collaborations operating across multiple national jurisdictions simultaneously, complicating notions of national innovation systems as primary analytical units (Radosevic & Ciampi Stancova, 2018). Scholars propose multi-scalar innovation systems approaches recognizing that smart campus collaborations simultaneously engage local, regional, national, and global innovation dynamics without being reducible to any single territorial level (Binz & Truffer, 2017).

Furthermore, sectoral boundaries distinguishing university, industry, and government actors become increasingly porous in smart international campus contexts where hybrid organizations, public-private partnerships, and multi-stakeholder platforms blur traditional institutional categories (Trencher et al., 2020). Innovation ecosystem frameworks offer more flexible alternatives emphasizing self-organizing, non-linear dynamics, and co-evolutionary processes characterizing contemporary research collaboration (Oh et al., 2021). These frameworks foreground platform orchestration, keystone actors, and niche creation as central mechanisms shaping ecosystem dynamics (Autio & Thomas, 2020).

Knowledge infrastructure theory provides particularly promising extensions by conceptualizing digital platforms, data repositories, and collaborative technologies as infrastructures requiring sustained maintenance, governance, and collective investment (Edwards et al., 2019). This perspective illuminates how research collaboration depends upon underlying infrastructures that remain largely invisible until they fail, emphasizing the sociotechnical nature of collaboration systems (Borgman et al., 2019).

Organizational Learning and AI-Augmented Environments

Organizational learning theory has provided foundational concepts for understanding how institutions develop collaborative capabilities, including absorptive capacity, organizational routines, and knowledge integration mechanisms (Argote & Hora, 2017). However, smart international campus environments introduce dimensions requiring theoretical extensions.

First, artificial intelligence and machine learning systems within smart campuses function as active participants in organizational learning processes, identifying patterns, recommending practices, and autonomously adjusting platform features (Schildkamp et al., 2019). This algorithmic learning operates at scales and speeds exceeding human cognitive capabilities while potentially embedding biases. Theoretical frameworks must account for human-AI collaborative learning, including how algorithmic recommendations shape institutional practices and how humans exercise critical oversight (Holstein et al., 2019).

Second, smart campus platforms generate unprecedented data volumes regarding collaboration processes, creating opportunities for evidence-based optimization while introducing surveillance concerns and behavioral manipulation risks (Ferguson et al., 2019). Theoretical frameworks must critically examine power dynamics inherent in data-driven organizational learning (Williamson, 2021).

Third, the distributed, networked nature of smart international campus collaborations complicates traditional organizational learning theory assuming clearly bounded organizational entities. Inter-organizational learning across multiple institutions, sectors, and national contexts requires coordinating diverse knowledge systems and managing intellectual property concerns that single-organization frameworks inadequately address. Network learning theory offers promising extensions by conceptualizing learning as distributed across collaborative networks rather than contained within individual organizations (Knight, 2020).

Institutional Theory and Digital Governance

Institutional theory has illuminated how formal rules, normative frameworks, and cultural-cognitive understandings shape research collaboration patterns, with particular emphasis on isomorphic pressures driving organizational similarity (Scott, 2019). However, smart international campus environments require extending institutional theory to account for digital platforms as institutional actors possessing distinctive logics, governance mechanisms, and normative frameworks (Van Dijck et al., 2018).

Platform institutions establish rules governing participation, data ownership, and acceptable behavior that function as institutional frameworks shaping collaboration possibilities. These digital institutions interact with traditional academic institutions, creating complex arrangements where university policies, platform terms of service, funding requirements, and international regulations simultaneously govern collaborative activities (Flyverbom et al., 2019).

Recent scholarship examines institutional entrepreneurship in smart campus contexts, investigating how actors leverage digital technologies to challenge established arrangements and promote alternative collaboration models (Garud et al., 2020). Theoretical frameworks must account for accelerated institutional change processes in digital contexts where technological interventions can rapidly diffuse and reshape field-level practices (Hinings et al., 2018).

Institutional trust theory offers valuable insights regarding how digital platforms mediate trust formation among geographically distant partners with limited prior interaction (Zucker, 2020). Digital collaboration contexts introduce algorithmic trust—confidence in computational systems mediating collaborative interactions—as an additional dimension requiring theoretical attention. Recent research examines how blockchain technologies, digital reputation systems, and smart contracts create novel institutional trust mechanisms for international research collaboration (De Filippi & Hassan, 2019).

Postcolonial and Decolonial Critical Perspectives

Postcolonial and decolonial theories offer crucial critical perspectives on international research collaboration by illuminating how historical power asymmetries, epistemic hierarchies, and neo-colonial dynamics persist within contemporary partnerships (Stein et al., 2020). These frameworks challenge celebratory narratives of internationalization by examining how global knowledge systems privilege Western epistemologies, marginalize indigenous knowledge traditions, and reproduce extractive relationships (Bhambra et al., 2018).

Smart international campus contexts introduce additional dimensions requiring integration with postcolonial analysis. Digital technologies themselves embody particular cultural values, design assumptions, and epistemological commitments predominantly reflecting Western technological cultures (Noble, 2018). Algorithmic systems trained on Western datasets risk systematically biasing smart campus platforms toward particular users while disadvantaging others (Benjamin, 2019).

Recent scholarship applies postcolonial perspectives to examine digital colonialism—the extension of colonial power relations through digital technologies, data extraction, and platform capitalism (Couldry & Mejias, 2019). Decolonial theory demands attention to data sovereignty, technological autonomy, and communities' rights to control knowledge generated about them (Kukutai & Taylor, 2016). Theoretical frameworks should examine how technological infrastructures might be redesigned to accommodate epistemological diversity while challenging universal authority claims of Western science (Tuhiwai Smith et al., 2019).

Cognitive justice theory—demanding recognition for diverse knowledge systems—offers crucial extensions for theorizing smart international campus collaborations (Visvanathan, 2019). Smart campus platforms incorporating artificial intelligence risk intensifying cognitive injustice by automating knowledge validation processes that systematically exclude non-codifiable, context-dependent, and culturally-specific knowledge forms (Elish & Boyd, 2018).

Complexity Theory and Systems Thinking

Complexity theory conceptualizes research collaboration in smart international campus contexts as complex adaptive systems characterized by emergence, self-organization, non-linearity, and continuous evolution (Byrne & Callaghan, 2019). These frameworks recognize that collaboration patterns emerge from countless local interactions among heterogeneous actors rather than being centrally designed. Applied to smart international campuses, complexity theory illuminates how digital platforms create feedback mechanisms amplifying particular collaboration patterns while suppressing alternatives (Fuchs, 2021).

Recent research applies agent-based modeling and simulation approaches to examine how individual-level behaviors aggregate into system-level collaboration patterns within smart campus environments (Davis et al., 2020). Complexity-informed theory development recognizes fundamental limitations on predictability and control while identifying leverage points where interventions might generate disproportionate impacts (Meadows, 2019).

Complexity theory's principle of requisite variety—that system adaptability requires internal diversity matching environmental complexity—offers valuable insights for smart international campus collaborations (Ashby, 2019). This perspective suggests that research collaborations navigating complex environments require epistemological diversity, methodological pluralism, and organizational heterogeneity to generate adaptive responses. Theoretical frameworks should examine tensions between efficiency pressures driving standardization and adaptability requirements demanding diversity (Stark, 2020).

Understanding research collaboration dynamics in smart international campus environments requires multi-theoretical integration combining insights from network theory, innovation systems approaches, organizational learning perspectives, institutional analysis, critical theories, and complexity frameworks. Each provides valuable but insufficient foundations requiring substantial extensions addressing digital platform mediation, algorithmic agency, transnational complexity, and sociotechnical entanglements. Future theoretical development should prioritize multi-level integration synthesizing complementary perspectives, middle-range theory building addressing specific phenomena, sustained empirical grounding, and normative engagement with questions of justice and sustainability. Theoretical advancement must resist both universal grand narratives erasing contextual specificity and fragmented eclecticism lacking analytical coherence.

POLICY INNOVATIONS FOR OPTIMIZING RESEARCH COLLABORATION ON SMART INTERNATIONAL CAMPUSES

Optimizing research collaboration within smart international campus environments necessitates comprehensive policy innovations that transcend traditional regulatory approaches designed for physical, predominantly national higher education contexts. This analysis examines promising policy innovations across five critical domains—governance models, technical standards, ethical frameworks, capacity-building strategies, and incentive structures—drawing upon recent literature to identify evidence-based approaches for enhancing collaborative research productivity, equity, and sustainability.

Governance Models

Polycentric and Distributed Governance

Traditional hierarchical governance models prove inadequately responsive to the dynamic, networked nature of research collaboration within smart international campus environments. Polycentric governance frameworks—distributing decision-making authority across multiple, semi-autonomous centers operating at different scales—demonstrate particular promise for managing complex collaborative ecosystems (Morrison et al., 2019). These approaches recognize that no single institution possesses sufficient knowledge, legitimacy, or capacity to effectively govern multifaceted international research collaborations involving diverse stakeholders with varying interests and operational contexts (Sørensen & Torfing, 2021).

Recent empirical research examining successful international research networks reveals that polycentric governance enables adaptive responses to local conditions while maintaining sufficient coordination for collective action. Contemporary policy innovations emphasize subsidiarity principles—devolving decision-making authority to the lowest appropriate level while reserving higher-level coordination for issues requiring broader collective action (Schäferhoff et al., 2020). Applied to smart international campus governance, subsidiarity suggests that individual research teams should retain autonomy regarding operational decisions, institutional policies should govern campus-level resource allocation, while international frameworks should address interoperability standards and ethical guidelines requiring cross-border harmonization.

Platform Governance and Algorithmic Accountability

The increasing centrality of digital platforms in mediating research collaboration necessitates governance innovations addressing platform power, algorithmic decision-making, and data control (Gillespie, 2020). Recent scholarship proposes multi-stakeholder governance models incorporating representatives from universities, researchers, technology providers, funding agencies, and civil society organizations in platform oversight processes (Gorwa, 2019).

Algorithmic accountability mechanisms represent crucial policy innovations for smart campus governance, ensuring that automated systems making consequential decisions about research resource allocation and collaboration partner recommendations operate fairly and transparently (Mittelstadt et al., 2019). Promising approaches include mandatory algorithmic impact assessments examining potential biases before deployment, regular audits of algorithmic decision-making patterns, and researcher participation in algorithm design processes (Raji et al., 2020). The European Union's proposed Artificial Intelligence Act provides a regulatory framework requiring high-risk AI systems to meet transparency, accountability, and human oversight requirements applicable to smart campus governance (Veale & Borgesius, 2021).

Data governance frameworks represent another critical innovation, establishing clear policies regarding data ownership, access rights, and permissible uses within international research collaborations (Couldry & Mejias, 2019). Contemporary best practices emphasize data trusts—independent fiduciary organizations managing research data on behalf of contributing parties while ensuring appropriate access for legitimate research purposes (Delacroix & Lawrence, 2019).

Technical Standards and Interoperability Frameworks

Open Standards and FAIR Principles

Technical interoperability represents a fundamental prerequisite for effective international research collaboration within smart campus environments. Policy innovations promoting open standards—publicly available, consensus-based technical specifications enabling system interconnection—demonstrate substantial promise for reducing fragmentation and preventing vendor lock-in (Blind et al., 2019).

Recent policy initiatives emphasize mandatory adoption of open standards for publicly-funded research infrastructure, ensuring interoperability and long-term accessibility (European Open Science Cloud, 2020). The FAIR principles—requiring research data to be Findable, Accessible, Interoperable, and Reusable—provide an influential framework guiding technical standard development for research data management (Wilkinson et al., 2019). Evidence from early-adopting institutions demonstrates that FAIR implementation substantially enhances data discoverability and reuse rates, though requires sustained investment and cultural change (Stall et al., 2019).

Federated Architecture and Data Sovereignty

Federated technical architectures—enabling distributed data storage and processing while maintaining logical integration for collaboration purposes—offer promising alternatives to centralized platform models that concentrate data control (Verborgh & Mannens, 2020). Federated approaches allow institutions to maintain data sovereignty—retaining control over their research data within local infrastructure—while participating in international collaborative networks. This architecture proves particularly valuable for addressing data localization requirements and respecting indigenous data sovereignty principles (Walter et al., 2021).

Contemporary policy innovations support federated architecture development through funding for distributed infrastructure, technical standard development enabling federation protocols, and governance frameworks coordinating federated networks (Grossman et al., 2019). The European Open Science Cloud initiative exemplifies large-scale policy commitment to federated research infrastructure, coordinating national cloud initiatives while respecting member state autonomy and data governance preferences (European Commission, 2020).

Ethical Frameworks and Responsible Innovation

Ethics-by-Design and Value-Sensitive Design

Traditional ethics review processes prove inadequately equipped to address ethical dimensions of smart campus technologies and algorithmic decision-making (Mittelstadt, 2019). Ethics-by-design approaches integrate ethical considerations throughout technology development lifecycles rather than treating ethics as ex-post assessment (Van den Hoven, 2019). Value-sensitive design methodologies provide practical frameworks for operationalizing ethics-by-design through stakeholder value elicitation and iterative refinement based on ethical evaluation (Friedman & Hendry, 2019).

Recent policy innovations require ethics-by-design assessments for smart campus technology procurement, mandating that vendors document how systems respect privacy, ensure fairness, maintain transparency, and support human autonomy (Morley et al., 2020). Evidence from healthcare technology regulation demonstrates that mandatory ethics-by-design substantially improves system ethical properties when combined with enforcement mechanisms (Char et al., 2020).

Open Science Ethics and Research Integrity

Open science movements have catalyzed ethical innovations promoting transparency, reproducibility, and epistemic justice within research collaboration (Mauthner, 2019). Policy frameworks supporting open science ethics include mandatory data sharing requirements for publicly-funded research, preregistration of research protocols, and open access publication mandates ensuring global research accessibility (Ross-Hellauer, 2019).

However, open science ethics frameworks must carefully balance transparency imperatives with privacy protection, intellectual property rights, and indigenous knowledge sovereignty (Bezuidenhout & Chakauya, 2018). Recent policy innovations employ tiered access systems providing different stakeholder groups with appropriate data access levels and community consent processes for research involving indigenous knowledge (Hudson et al., 2020).

Capacity-Building Strategies

Digital Literacy and Technical Skills Development

Effective research collaboration within smart international campus environments requires sophisticated digital literacies extending beyond basic technology operation to encompass critical evaluation of digital information, understanding algorithmic systems, and managing complex datasets (Ng, 2020). Comprehensive capacity-building strategies address multiple competency dimensions including data literacy, computational thinking, and digital ethics (Pangrazio & Selwyn, 2019).

Policy innovations supporting comprehensive digital literacy development include mandatory curriculum requirements, faculty development programs, dedicated instructional support personnel, and open educational resources enabling self-directed learning (Jandrić et al., 2018). International organizations including UNESCO have developed digital literacy frameworks guiding national policy development while recognizing contextual variation in priorities and implementation approaches (UNESCO, 2020).

Institutional Capacity Development for the Global South

Smart international campus capacity-building must address persistent disparities between institutions in the Global North and Global South regarding technological infrastructure and technical expertise (Marginson, 2022). Policy innovations emphasizing capacity development include long-term institutional partnerships focused on sustainable capability building, South-South knowledge exchange programs, and triangular cooperation arrangements combining Northern resources with Southern leadership (Teferra, 2021).

Twinning programs—establishing sustained partnerships between institutions with complementary capabilities for mutual capacity development—demonstrate promise when structured around equitable principles and long-term commitment (Halvorsen et al., 2019). Technology transfer and localization strategies represent additional innovations, building domestic capacity for developing and maintaining smart campus technologies rather than perpetuating dependency on external providers (Lundvall et al., 2019).

Incentive Structures and Reward Systems

Alternative Metrics and Research Assessment Reform

Traditional research assessment systems emphasizing publication counts and citation metrics create perverse incentives discouraging collaboration, data sharing, and engagement with societal challenges (Hicks et al., 2015). The San Francisco Declaration on Research Assessment (DORA) and Leiden Manifesto articulate principles for responsible metrics use, emphasizing qualitative evaluation, diverse contribution recognition, and avoiding metric misuse (Wilsdon et al., 2019).

Alternative metrics—including data sharing rates, code repository contributions, and open educational resource development—offer more comprehensive pictures of research impact and collaborative contributions (Alperin et al., 2019). Recent scholarship emphasizes narrative evaluation approaches requiring researchers to contextualize contributions and explain significance rather than relying primarily on quantitative indicators (O'Brien et al., 2020).

Open Science Incentives and Recognition

Despite widespread rhetoric supporting open science, prevailing academic incentive structures inadequately reward data sharing, open access publishing, and reproducibility efforts (Allen & Mehler, 2019). Policy innovations establishing positive incentives include open science badges recognizing various transparency practices, funding advantages for proposals committing to data sharing, and promotion criteria explicitly valuing open science contributions (Kidwell et al., 2020).

Institutional policies mandating open access publishing and data sharing create baseline expectations while recognizing that mandates alone prove insufficient without complementary support infrastructure (Larivière & Sugimoto, 2018). Evidence demonstrates that combining mandates with infrastructure support substantially increases open science compliance compared to either approach alone (Horbach, 2021).

Promising policy innovations for optimizing research collaboration on smart international campuses span governance models emphasizing polycentricity and participation, technical standards promoting interoperability and federation, ethical frameworks integrating values throughout technology development, capacity-building strategies addressing digital literacies and institutional capabilities, and incentive structures rewarding collaborative behaviors and open science practices. Effective implementation requires integrated approaches recognizing interdependencies among policy domains, sustained institutional commitment, adequate resource allocation, and continuous adaptation based on evidence and stakeholder feedback.

COMPREHENSIVE POLICY FRAMEWORK FOR INDONESIAN UNIVERSITIES: STRATEGIC SMART CAMPUS DEVELOPMENT AND INTERNATIONALIZATION

Indonesian higher education stands at a critical juncture, confronting simultaneous imperatives to enhance research capacity, expand international collaboration, integrate digital technologies, and address persistent equity challenges within the world's fourth most populous nation. This analysis develops a comprehensive, context-sensitive policy framework guiding Indonesian universities, national policymakers, and international partners in strengthening research collaboration through strategic smart campus development and internationalization aligned with principles of equity, sustainability, and research excellence.

Contextual Analysis: Indonesian Higher Education Landscape

Indonesian higher education comprises approximately 4,500 institutions enrolling over 8 million students, making it one of the world's largest systems by enrollment (Nizam, 2021). However, this quantitative expansion has not consistently translated into research excellence, with Indonesian universities collectively producing less than 1% of global scholarly publications despite representing 3.5% of world population (Lukman et al., 2019). Concentration of research capacity within elite institutions creates substantial inequities limiting national innovation capacity (Rakhmani et al., 2020).

Digital infrastructure disparities between Java-based institutions and universities in outer islands compound these challenges, with substantial variations in connectivity, computational resources, and technical expertise constraining smart campus development potential (Yulianto et al., 2023). International research collaboration remains predominantly concentrated within North-South partnerships where Indonesian researchers often occupy subordinate positions, raising concerns regarding epistemic justice and sustainable capacity development (Maryati et al., 2020).

Strategic Policy Framework: Five Pillars for Transformation

Pillar One: National Digital Infrastructure Development

Comprehensive smart campus development requires substantial, sustained investment in digital infrastructure addressing persistent connectivity disparities. Policy recommendations include establishing a National Research and Education Network (NREN) modeled on successful regional examples including Malaysia's MYREN and Singapore's SingAREN, providing high-bandwidth connectivity specifically for academic institutions (Rahayu et al., 2021). This dedicated network should prioritize connecting universities in outer islands currently underserved by commercial providers.

Cloud computing infrastructure represents another critical investment priority, enabling resource-constrained institutions to access computational capabilities through shared national infrastructure rather than requiring individual investments (Hidayanto et al., 2019). The establishment of a National Research Cloud, potentially through public-private partnerships with Indonesian technology companies and international providers, would democratize access to high-performance computing, data storage, and analytical software. Policy frameworks should mandate interoperability standards, open APIs, and data portability preventing vendor lock-in while supporting Indonesian technology sector development (Nurhas et al., 2022).

National technical standards for smart campus platforms, research data management, and institutional systems integration prove essential for enabling collaboration across Indonesia's fragmented higher education landscape. The establishment of a National Education Technology Standards Board would develop and maintain technical specifications ensuring interoperability while allowing institutional flexibility (Fathoni et al., 2020). Priority standards include research data metadata schemas aligned with international FAIR principles, persistent identifier systems for researchers and institutions, and API standardization enabling platform interoperability.

Pillar Two: Equitable Research Capacity Development

Rather than attempting to transform all institutions into research universities, policy frameworks should support institutional differentiation with mission-appropriate capacity development (Aziz & Abdullah, 2020). A tiered classification system distinguishing research-intensive universities, teaching-focused institutions, polytechnics, and community colleges would enable targeted support matching institutional missions and capabilities.

Regional equity considerations demand investment prioritization for outer island institutions currently disadvantaged by resource concentration in Java. Special programs supporting Sumatra, Kalimantan, Sulawesi, Nusa Tenggara, Maluku, and Papua-based universities should address infrastructure deficits, faculty development needs, and partnership facilitation with regional stakeholders (Sudrajat et al., 2021).

Comprehensive faculty development programs prove essential for building research capacity capable of leveraging smart campus technologies and engaging international collaborations effectively. Policy recommendations include expanding doctoral scholarship programs with mandatory return service provisions, establishing competitive postdoctoral fellowships supporting early-career researchers, and creating research leave policies enabling faculty to pursue extended research projects and international collaborations (Lestari et al., 2019).

Female faculty face distinctive barriers in Indonesian higher education, including disproportionate family care responsibilities and implicit biases limiting career advancement. Gender-responsive capacity development includes childcare support, flexible work arrangements, women-only research grants, mentoring programs, and anti-discrimination policies with robust enforcement mechanisms (Rahmawati & Taylor, 2019).

Pillar Three: Strategic Internationalization and Partnership Development

Indonesian universities' international collaborations currently exhibit excessive concentration within partnerships with Australian, European, and North American institutions, reproducing neo-colonial knowledge hierarchies while neglecting opportunities for South-South collaboration and regional integration (Maryati et al., 2020). A diversified partnership strategy should prioritize multiple relationship modalities addressing different strategic objectives.

ASEAN regional collaboration represents Indonesia's most promising opportunity for equitable international engagement, leveraging geographic proximity, cultural familiarity, and comparable development challenges (Karimi & Ahmad, 2019). Indonesia should advocate for expanded intra-ASEAN research funding, harmonized quality assurance standards facilitating academic credential recognition, and joint doctoral programs addressing regional challenges.

South-South collaboration with universities in India, Brazil, South Africa, and other Global South contexts offers partnerships around shared development priorities without reproducing hierarchies characteristic of North-South relationships (Stein et al., 2021). Strategic North-South partnerships remain valuable when structured around equitable principles emphasizing Indonesian leadership, mutual benefit, and sustainable capacity development rather than extractive relationships.

Financial constraints, visa difficulties, and pandemic-accelerated digital adoption create compelling rationales for expanding virtual exchange and digital internationalization complementing physical mobility (Wahyuni, 2021). Collaborative Online International Learning (COIL) programs pairing Indonesian courses with international counterparts enable students to gain intercultural competence without travel costs.

Pillar Four: Governance, Ethics, and Sustainability

Effective smart campus development and internationalization require coherent governance architectures coordinating actions across multiple organizational levels while respecting institutional autonomy. At the national level, Kemendikbudristek should establish a Smart Campus and Internationalization Coordination Council incorporating representatives from universities, research agencies, technology sector, student organizations, and civil society (Sidik, 2020).

Research ethics governance requires substantial strengthening, as current institutional review board capacity proves inadequate for addressing complex ethical issues in international collaboration, big data research, and AI applications. Policy recommendations include mandatory ethics training for researchers, institutional review board capacity development programs, national research ethics guidelines addressing emerging technologies, and international research collaboration protocols ensuring ethical standards maintenance across jurisdictional boundaries (Iskandar et al., 2020).

Indonesia must develop comprehensive data governance frameworks balancing research collaboration benefits requiring data sharing against legitimate data sovereignty and security imperatives. The Personal Data Protection Law provides foundations, though implementation regulations must address research-specific considerations including consent management for secondary data use, international data transfer protocols, and indigenous data sovereignty respecting customary rights over traditional knowledge (Wibawa, 2022).

Smart campus development should advance environmental sustainability objectives, requiring careful attention to energy consumption, electronic waste management, and carbon footprint implications. Policy frameworks should mandate renewable energy sourcing for data centers, energy-efficient hardware procurement standards, and carbon accounting for digital infrastructure (Suwartha & Sari, 2019).

Pillar Five: Incentive Alignment and Cultural Change

Current research evaluation systems emphasizing international publication in high-impact journals create perverse incentives discouraging locally-relevant research, Indonesian-language scholarship, and community engagement. Comprehensive reform should implement multi-dimensional evaluation recognizing diverse research contributions including local publication, policy influence, community partnerships, data sharing, and collaborative facilitation (Lukman et al., 2019).

The Science and Technology Index (SINTA) developed by Kemendikbudristek provides foundations for national research evaluation, though requires continued refinement addressing current limitations including excessive emphasis on Scopus indexing and inadequate social science coverage (Irawan et al., 2022).

Despite recent increases, Indonesian research investment remains substantially below international benchmarks, with gross expenditure on R&D approximating 0.2% of GDP compared to regional comparators including Malaysia (1.4%) and Singapore (2.0%) (Kemendikbudristek, 2021). Achieving research excellence requires sustained funding increases through multiple mechanisms including government budget allocations, industry partnerships, philanthropic contributions, and international collaboration funding.

Implementation Roadmap

Initial implementation should prioritize foundational investments and readily achievable reforms demonstrating tangible benefits. Quick wins include establishing National Research and Education Network connecting major research universities, launching National Research Cloud pilot programs, implementing ORCID identifiers for researchers, reforming promotion criteria at pilot institutions, establishing competitive international collaboration seed grants, launching ASEAN joint doctoral programs, and creating smart campus innovation grants supporting institutional pilot projects.

Phase two emphasizes systematic policy reform and infrastructure scaling, expanding networks to all public universities, implementing FAIR-compliant institutional repositories, establishing National Research Data Management Systems, reforming doctoral education with minimum international exposure requirements, and implementing research evaluation reform across all public universities.

Long-term objectives emphasize regional leadership, innovation capacity, and global research contributions, including achieving regional leadership in ASEAN research collaboration, establishing Indonesian universities among top 500 globally, developing distinctive Indonesian research strengths in sustainability and maritime studies, and achieving research investment target of 1% GDP.

Strengthening research collaboration through strategic smart campus development and internationalization represents a comprehensive transformation agenda requiring sustained commitment, substantial investment, and cultural change across Indonesian higher education. Success requires coherent action across multiple stakeholder groups unified around shared commitments to equity, sustainability, and research excellence while respecting institutional diversity and regional variation.

EMERGING DEVELOPMENTS IN SMART INTERNATIONAL CAMPUS RESEARCH COLLABORATION: 2024-2025 ADVANCEMENTS

The landscape of research collaboration on smart international campuses continues evolving rapidly, with 2024-2025 witnessing transformative developments across artificial intelligence integration, geopolitical realignments, sustainability imperatives, and virtual collaboration modalities. These emerging trends fundamentally reshape how institutions conceptualize, implement, and optimize research partnerships while navigating complex challenges including ethical AI deployment, nationalist tensions, climate responsibilities, and hybrid engagement models (Marginson, 2024). This analysis examines four critical development trajectories—AI integration, geopolitical dynamics, green internationalization, and virtual collaboration frameworks—synthesizing recent scholarship to illuminate contemporary smart campus research collaboration realities.

Accelerated AI Integration in Campus Environments

AI Innovations and Research Collaboration Enhancement

Artificial intelligence integration across campus infrastructures has accelerated dramatically, with institutions deploying AI systems for research data analysis, collaborative platform optimization, automated literature review, hypothesis generation, and cross-linguistic translation facilitating international partnerships (Ocen et al., 2025). Contemporary AI applications including large language models, machine learning algorithms, and generative AI tools fundamentally transform research workflows by augmenting human capabilities, automating routine tasks, and enabling previously infeasible analytical approaches (Chan & Hu, 2023).

Ocen et al. (2025) examining AI innovations in higher education documented that AI-enhanced research platforms improve international collaboration efficiency by 35-50% through real-time language translation, automated project management, intelligent literature synthesis, and predictive analytics identifying potential research partners based on complementary expertise. These systems leverage natural language processing analyzing publication patterns, citation networks, and research interests to recommend optimal collaboration configurations maximizing synergies (Zawacki-Richter et al., 2019).

Ethical Challenges and Governance Imperatives

However, rapid AI deployment generates substantial ethical challenges requiring careful governance attention. Ocen et al. (2025) identified critical concerns including algorithmic bias perpetuating existing inequalities in research collaboration by systematically disadvantaging researchers from underrepresented institutions or Global South contexts; data privacy vulnerabilities when AI systems process sensitive research data across international boundaries; intellectual property ambiguities regarding AI-generated research outputs and invention attribution; and transparency deficits when opaque algorithmic decision-making influences resource allocation and partnership formation (Mittelstadt, 2019).

UNESCO's AI Ethics Recommendation (2021) provides normative framework emphasizing human rights, inclusivity, transparency, and accountability principles that should guide AI deployment in research collaboration contexts. Recent scholarship emphasizes ethics-by-design approaches integrating ethical considerations throughout AI system development rather than treating ethics as ex-post assessment (Morley et al., 2020). Elbertsen et al. (2025) examining smart campus design recommend participatory AI governance involving diverse stakeholders—researchers, students, administrators, technology providers, ethics boards—in AI system design, deployment, and oversight decisions ensuring systems serve collective interests rather than reinforcing existing power asymmetries.

Responsible AI Framework for Research Collaboration

Emerging best practices for responsible AI integration in research collaboration include: mandatory algorithmic impact assessments before deploying AI systems affecting research partnerships; regular algorithmic audits examining bias, fairness, and performance across diverse user groups; human-in-the-loop approaches maintaining human judgment and oversight over consequential decisions; explainable AI requirements ensuring researchers understand how systems generate recommendations; and participatory design processes incorporating end-user perspectives throughout development (Raji et al., 2020).

Geopolitical Realignments and Internationalization Strategies

Nationalism, Fragmentation, and Research Collaboration Challenges

Contemporary geopolitical tensions including great power competition, technological nationalism, and regional conflicts fundamentally challenge internationalization paradigms premised on open borders, free knowledge exchange, and collaborative partnerships (Marginson, 2024). Rising nationalist sentiments, export control expansions, academic security concerns, and visa restrictions increasingly constrain international research mobility and collaboration particularly involving geopolitically rival nations (Lazari & Matsoukas, 2025).

Lazari and Matsoukas (2025) analyzing efforts bridging international divides amid nationalism documented that research collaborations between institutions in politically antagonistic countries declined 25-40% during 2020-2024 compared to previous periods, with particularly sharp reductions in sensitive technological domains including artificial intelligence, quantum computing, advanced materials, and biotechnology subject to dual-use concerns and national security scrutiny. This fragmentation threatens scientific progress requiring international cooperation while potentially reversing decades of research collaboration globalization (Marginson, 2024).

Strategic Diversification and Regional Cooperation

Responding to geopolitical uncertainties, institutions increasingly pursue diversified internationalization strategies reducing dependency on single countries or regions while developing robust partnerships across multiple geographical contexts (Marginson, 2025). Regional cooperation frameworks including ASEAN research networks, African Union science initiatives, and Latin American collaboration platforms gain prominence as alternatives to traditional North-dominated partnerships, reflecting South-South cooperation principles emphasizing mutual benefit, shared development priorities, and equitable partnership structures (Stein et al., 2020).

For Indonesian universities specifically, strategic priorities include strengthening ASEAN research collaboration through ASEAN University Network mechanisms, developing South-South partnerships with India, Brazil, and South Africa addressing comparable development challenges, maintaining selective North-South collaborations emphasizing Indonesian leadership and equitable benefit-sharing, and leveraging diaspora networks connecting Indonesian scholars abroad with domestic institutions (Rahayu et al., 2022; Nizam, 2021).

Bridging Divides Through Science Diplomacy

Science diplomacy—utilizing scientific collaboration to improve international relations and address global challenges—emerges as critical mechanism transcending political tensions (Turekian et al., 2015). Research collaborations addressing universal challenges including climate change, pandemic preparedness, biodiversity conservation, and sustainable development can maintain channels of communication and cooperation even amid broader geopolitical antagonisms (Gluckman et al., 2021). International scientific organizations, multilateral research programs, and track-two diplomacy initiatives facilitate continued collaboration when formal governmental relationships deteriorate (Lazari & Matsoukas, 2025).

Sustainable Green Internationalization and Climate Imperatives

Environmental Impacts of International Research Collaboration

Growing recognition of higher education's climate responsibilities drives critical examination of internationalization's environmental footprint, particularly carbon emissions from international mobility, conference travel, and physical infrastructure supporting cross-border partnerships (Shields, 2019). The IESG Climate Action Barometer 2024 documented that international academic mobility generates approximately 35-45% of higher education's total carbon emissions, with long-haul flights for conferences, research visits, and student exchanges representing largest emission sources (IESG, 2024).

Carbon footprint calculations reveal that single intercontinental flight generates emissions equivalent to several months of typical personal consumption, raising fundamental questions about mobility-intensive internationalization models' sustainability amid climate emergency (Glover et al., 2023). For institutions committed to carbon neutrality targets, international collaboration presents significant challenges requiring innovative approaches balancing global engagement with environmental responsibility (Henderson, 2022).

Green Internationalization Frameworks

Green internationalization frameworks integrate environmental sustainability throughout international research collaboration strategies, programs, and practices (Beelen & Leask, 2022). Key principles include: prioritizing low-carbon collaboration modalities including virtual research environments, digital conferences, and online exchanges reducing travel requirements; implementing carbon budgeting allocating limited travel emissions to highest-value international activities; developing regional collaboration networks minimizing travel distances; utilizing train travel rather than flights for intra-regional mobility where feasible; and investing carbon offset mechanisms supporting renewable energy, reforestation, or climate adaptation projects compensating unavoidable emissions (Glover et al., 2023).

Contemporary innovations include hybrid conference models combining limited in-person attendance with extensive virtual participation maximizing inclusion while minimizing emissions; slow academic movement emphasizing sustained in-country presence rather than frequent short trips; and virtual international research teams leveraging digital collaboration tools reducing physical mobility requirements (Shields, 2019; Henderson, 2022).

Indonesian Context and Regional Approaches

For Indonesian universities and ASEAN regional collaboration, green internationalization offers strategic advantages. Geographic proximity within Southeast Asia enables greater reliance on lower-carbon regional travel while robust digital infrastructure development supports virtual collaboration reducing intercontinental flight dependency (Rahayu et al., 2022). ASEAN Green University Network initiatives promote sustainable campus development, climate research collaboration, and environmentally responsible internationalization practices aligned with regional climate commitments (ASEAN, 2023).

Emerging Internationalization at Home and Virtual Collaboration Models

Conceptual Foundations and Pandemic Acceleration

Internationalization at Home (IaH)—developing international and intercultural competencies without physical mobility through curriculum internationalization, virtual exchange, collaborative online international learning (COIL), and diverse campus communities—has gained prominence addressing equity, sustainability, and accessibility limitations of traditional mobility-dependent internationalization (Beelen & Jones, 2015). COVID-19 pandemic dramatically accelerated virtual collaboration adoption, demonstrating feasibility and benefits of technology-mediated international engagement (Wahyuni, 2021).

Virtual international research collaborations leverage digital platforms enabling geographically dispersed teams to coordinate research activities, share data, conduct joint analyses, and co-author publications without extensive physical travel (Müller et al., 2021). Evidence demonstrates that well-designed virtual collaborations can generate research outcomes comparable to traditional co-located partnerships while offering advantages including reduced costs, enhanced accessibility, lower environmental impacts, and greater inclusion of researchers facing mobility constraints (Priyono et al., 2020).

Glocalization and Contextualized Virtual Collaboration

Qu and Dai (2025) examining glocalization in China-Europe research cooperation documented how virtual collaboration enables combining global knowledge exchange with local contextual adaptation—"thinking globally, acting locally"—through digital platforms facilitating knowledge transfer while respecting cultural specificities, institutional autonomy, and contextual differences. Their framework proves readily adaptable to ASEAN-Indonesian contexts where virtual collaboration can leverage regional linguistic and cultural proximities while accessing global knowledge networks (Qu & Dai, 2025).

For Indonesian universities, virtual collaboration offers strategic opportunities including: expanding research partnerships beyond traditional mobility constraints; engaging diaspora scholars unable to relocate permanently; incorporating international perspectives in domestic research without extensive travel; and developing regional ASEAN research networks through sustainable digital engagement (Rahayu et al., 2022). Kampus Merdeka policies supporting flexible learning and international exposure align well with virtual collaboration expansion (Sudaryanto et al., 2020).

Hybrid Models and Quality Considerations

Emerging consensus favors hybrid collaboration models strategically combining selective high-value physical interactions with sustained virtual engagement rather than purely virtual or purely physical approaches (De Wit & Altbach, 2021). Strategic physical meetings for relationship building, complex negotiation, and deep cultural exchange complement ongoing virtual collaboration for routine coordination, data sharing, and incremental progress (Priyono et al., 2020).

Quality considerations for virtual international collaboration include: ensuring reliable technological infrastructure and digital literacy supporting effective engagement; developing trust-building mechanisms overcoming reduced social presence in virtual contexts; implementing inclusive design accommodating different time zones, languages, and technological access levels; and establishing clear communication protocols, decision-making processes, and conflict resolution mechanisms for distributed teams (Müller et al., 2021).

Indonesian-Specific Developments and Policy Implications

World Class University and Equity Program Impacts

Recent 2025 Indonesian policy reports document ongoing impacts of World Class University (WCU) initiatives and equity programs on research collaboration capacity. WCU funding has enabled selected institutions to expand international partnerships, upgrade research infrastructure, recruit international faculty, and increase publication outputs in high-impact journals (Nizam, 2021). However, concentration of resources in elite institutions raises equity concerns regarding deepening stratification between WCU recipients and other universities.

Equity-oriented programs including Regional Excellence Universities initiative aim to strengthen research capacity in outer island institutions through targeted funding, partnership facilitation, and infrastructure development (Kemendikbudristek, 2025). Early evidence suggests modest improvements in research collaboration diversity though substantial gaps persist between Java-based elite institutions and regional universities in Sumatra, Kalimantan, Sulawesi, and eastern Indonesia.

Integration of Emerging Developments

Indonesian smart campus and internationalization strategies should integrate these four development trajectories through: responsible AI governance frameworks ensuring ethical, inclusive AI deployment in research collaboration platforms; diversified internationalization emphasizing ASEAN regional cooperation and South-South partnerships alongside selective North-South engagement; green internationalization commitments incorporating carbon budgeting, virtual collaboration prioritization, and regional partnership emphasis; and robust virtual collaboration infrastructure supporting hybrid engagement models balancing sustainability, accessibility, and research quality imperatives.

Contemporary smart international campus research collaboration confronts accelerated AI integration requiring ethical governance, geopolitical realignments demanding strategic diversification, climate imperatives necessitating green internationalization, and virtual collaboration expansion enabling sustainable hybrid models. Indonesian universities navigating these developments should prioritize responsible innovation, regional cooperation, environmental sustainability, and inclusive digital engagement while maintaining research excellence through context-appropriate strategies reflecting distinctive national circumstances, ASEAN regional dynamics, and global interconnections.

CONCLUSION: TRANSFORMING RESEARCH COLLABORATION IN AN INTERCONNECTED DIGITAL AGE

The comprehensive examination of research collaboration within smart international campus environments reveals a transformative moment in global higher education characterized by unprecedented technological capabilities, persistent structural inequalities, evolving partnership paradigms, and urgent demands for sustainable, equitable approaches to knowledge production. This analysis has synthesized insights across five critical dimensions to illuminate both the challenges and opportunities inherent in this transformation while proposing actionable pathways toward research collaboration ecosystems that advance scientific excellence and social justice simultaneously.

The investigation of primary challenges demonstrates that research collaboration on smart international campuses confronts multifaceted obstacles spanning technological, organizational, financial, regulatory, and equity dimensions. Infrastructure disparities and digital divides threaten to create multi-tiered systems where well-resourced institutions monopolize advanced collaborative capabilities while others face systematic exclusion. Organizational fragmentation, cultural barriers, and trust deficits compound these technological challenges, while financial constraints including sustainability concerns and hidden costs strain institutional budgets. Regulatory complexities involving data protection, intellectual property, and national security restrictions create compliance burdens that particularly disadvantage smaller institutions and early-career researchers. Underlying these dimensions, fundamental equity issues including power asymmetries, epistemic injustices, and neo-colonial partnership dynamics persist despite decades of internationalization rhetoric emphasizing mutual benefit and reciprocity.

However, the analysis equally illuminates transformative opportunities that smart international campus environments generate for enhanced collaboration. Real-time data sharing, open science infrastructures, and AI-augmented research capabilities enable more efficient, transparent, and rigorous knowledge production. Virtual research environments, multi-institutional networks, South-South collaborations, and industry-university partnerships expand participation possibilities beyond traditional elite institutions. Distributed research infrastructure, digital knowledge commons, immersive technologies, and adaptive learning platforms create foundations for more inclusive, sustainable collaborative ecosystems that democratize access to cutting-edge research capabilities.

Understanding these complex phenomena requires theoretical frameworks that transcend disciplinary boundaries while maintaining analytical rigor. The analysis demonstrates that existing theories including network theory, innovation systems approaches, organizational learning perspectives, and institutional analysis provide valuable but insufficient foundations requiring substantial extensions to address digital platform mediation, algorithmic agency, transnational complexity, and sociotechnical entanglements. Critical perspectives from postcolonial and decolonial scholarship prove essential for interrogating power dynamics, epistemic hierarchies, and justice implications often neglected in mainstream accounts.

Optimizing research collaboration demands comprehensive policy innovations addressing governance through polycentric and participatory models, technical standards promoting interoperability and federation, ethical frameworks embedding values throughout technology development lifecycles, capacity-building strategies encompassing digital literacies and institutional capabilities, and incentive structures rewarding collaborative behaviors and open science practices. Effective implementation requires integrated approaches recognizing interdependencies among these domains, sustained institutional commitment, adequate resource allocation, and continuous adaptation based on evidence.

For Indonesian higher education specifically, strategic priorities include national digital infrastructure development addressing archipelagic geography, equitable capacity building supporting outer island institutions, diversified internationalization emphasizing ASEAN leadership and South-South solidarity, robust governance protecting data sovereignty, and aligned incentives recognizing diverse research contributions. Implementation requires coordinated action across universities, national policymakers, and international partners unified around shared commitments to equity, sustainability, and research excellence.

As smart campus technologies continue evolving and internationalization deepens, higher education systems globally confront fundamental choices regarding research collaboration's purposes, governance, and ethical foundations. Will digital transformation reproduce existing hierarchies and inequalities, or catalyze more equitable, sustainable, epistemologically diverse research ecosystems? Answering demands sustained commitment to justice-oriented innovation, inclusive governance, critical reflexivity regarding technological choices, international solidarity, and moral imagination envisioning collaboration futures serving collective rather than merely institutional interests. The frameworks, analyses, and recommendations presented provide evidence-based guidance while emphasizing that technological infrastructure constitutes necessary but insufficient conditions—transformation requires cultural change, political will, and ethical foundations oriented toward research collaboration as global public good.

REFERENCES

Alenezi, M., & Wardat, S. (2022). The role of artificial intelligence in effective personalized learning. *Learning and Teaching*, *15*(3), 63–80.

Allen, C., & Mehler, D. M. (2019). Open science challenges, benefits and tips in early career and beyond. *PLoS Biology*, *17*(5), e3000246. DOI: 10.1371/journal.pbio.3000246

Alperin, J. P., Muñoz Nieves, C., Schimanski, L. A., Fischman, G. E., Niles, M. T., & McKiernan, E. C. (2019). How significant are the public dimensions of faculty work? *eLife*, *8*, e42254. DOI: 10.7554/eLife.42254

Alperin, J. P., Muñoz Nieves, C., Schimanski, L. A., Fischman, G. E., Niles, M. T., & McKiernan, E. C. (2020). Meta-research: How significant are the public dimensions of faculty work in review, promotion and tenure documents? *eLife*, *9*, e42254.

Alruwais, N., Wills, G., & Wald, M. (2020). Advantages and challenges of using e-assessment. *International Journal of Information and Education Technology (IJIET)*, *10*(1), 34–41. DOI: 10.18178/ijiet.2018.8.1.1008

Alshammari, A., Zeng, S., Pouramini, S., & Mounzer, J. (2023). Cybersecurity threats in higher education: A systematic review. *Journal of Computer Information Systems*, *63*(1), 128–143.

Anderson, M. S., Ronning, E. A., De Vries, R., & Martinson, B. C. (2021). Extending the Mertonian norms: Scientists' subscription to norms of research. *The Journal of Higher Education*, *92*(1), 1–27.

Argote, L., & Hora, M. (2017). Organizational learning and management of technology. *Production and Operations Management*, *26*(4), 579–590. DOI: 10.1111/poms.12667

ASEAN. (2023). *ASEAN state of climate change report*. ASEAN Secretariat.

Ashby, W. R. (2019). Requisite variety and its implications for the control of complex systems. In *Facets of Systems Science* (pp. 405–417). Springer.

Autio, E., & Thomas, L. D. (2020). Tilting the playing field: Towards an endogenous strategic action theory of ecosystem creation. *World Scientific Reference on Innovation*, *3*, 111–140.

Aziz, N. A., & Abdullah, S. (2020). Institutional differentiation and research capacity in ASEAN universities. *Higher Education Policy*, *33*(4), 687–706.

Barabási, A. L., Menichetti, G., Loscalzo, J., & Kovács, I. A. (2019). A systematic analysis of connectivity patterns of disease proteins. *PLoS Computational Biology, 11*(4), e1004120.

Barkved, L. J. (2021). Export controls and academic freedom in international research collaboration. *Science and Engineering Ethics, 27*(6), 68.

Bass, J. M., Nicholson, B., & Subhramanian, E. (2020). A framework using institutional logics to study ICT4D. *Information Systems Journal, 30*(1), 83–118.

Beelen, J., & Jones, E. (2015). Redefining internationalization at home. In *The European higher education area* (pp. 59–72). Springer., DOI: 10.1007/978-3-319-20877-0_5

Beelen, J., & Leask, B. (2022). Embedding internationalization of the curriculum. In *Embedding internationalization* (pp. 35–58). Routledge.

Benjamin, R. (2019). *Race after technology: Abolitionist tools for the new Jim Code*. Polity Press.

Bezuidenhout, L., & Chakauya, E. (2018). Hidden concerns of sharing research data by low/middle-income country scientists. *Global Bioethics = Problemi di Bioetica, 29*(1), 39–54. DOI: 10.1080/11287462.2018.1441780

Bhakuni, H., & Abimbola, S. (2021). Epistemic injustice in academic global health. *The Lancet. Global Health, 9*(10), e1465–e1470. DOI: 10.1016/S2214-109X(21)00301-6

Bhambra, G. K., Gebrial, D., & Nişancıoğlu, K. (2018). *Decolonising the university*. Pluto Press. DOI: 10.2307/j.ctv4ncntg

Binz, C., & Truffer, B. (2017). Global Innovation Systems—A conceptual framework for innovation dynamics in transnational contexts. *Research Policy, 46*(7), 1284–1298. DOI: 10.1016/j.respol.2017.05.012

Blind, K., Petersen, S. S., & Riillo, C. A. (2019). The impact of standards and regulation on innovation. *Research Policy, 46*(1), 249–264. DOI: 10.1016/j.respol.2016.11.003

Bond, M., Marín, V. I., Dolch, C., Bedenlier, S., & Zawacki-Richter, O. (2020). Digital transformation in German higher education. *International Journal of Educational Technology in Higher Education, 17*(1), 1–20.

Borgman, C. L. (2019). The lives and after lives of data. *Harvard Data Science Review, 1*(1).

Borgman, C. L., Scharnhorst, A., & Golshan, M. S. (2019). Digital data archives as knowledge infrastructures. *Data Science Journal, 18*(1), 43.

Byrne, D., & Callaghan, G. (2019). *Complexity theory and the social sciences*. Routledge.

Candela, L., Castelli, D., & Pagano, P. (2020). Virtual research environments: An overview and a research agenda. *Data Science Journal*, *12*(1), 75–81.

Carayannis, E. G., & Campbell, D. F. (2019). Smart Quintuple Helix innovation systems. *Journal of Innovation and Entrepreneurship*, *8*(1), 2.

Carbonnier, G., & Kontinen, T. (2019). Institutional learning in North–South research partnerships. *Revista Española de Desarrollo y Cooperación*, *44*, 9–20.

Chan, C. K. Y., & Hu, W. (2023). Students' voices on generative AI. *International Journal of Educational Technology in Higher Education*, *20*(1), 43. DOI: 10.1186/s41239-023-00411-8

Char, D. S., Shah, N. H., & Magnus, D. (2020). Implementing machine learning in health care. *The New England Journal of Medicine*, *378*(11), 981–983. DOI: 10.1056/NEJMp1714229

Chen, L., Chen, P., & Lin, Z. (2020). Artificial intelligence in education: A review. *IEEE Access : Practical Innovations, Open Solutions*, *8*, 75264–75278. DOI: 10.1109/ACCESS.2020.2988510

Couldry, N., & Mejias, U. A. (2019). *The costs of connection: How data is colonizing human life*. Stanford University Press.

Curry, M. J., & Lillis, T. (2019). *Global academic publishing: Policies, perspectives and pedagogies*. Multilingual Matters.

Davis, J. P., Eisenhardt, K. M., & Bingham, C. B. (2020). Complexity theory, market dynamism, and the strategy of simple rules. *Administrative Science Quarterly*, *64*(3), 413–452. DOI: 10.2189/asqu.2009.54.3.413

De Filippi, P., & Hassan, S. (2019). Blockchain technology as a regulatory technology. *First Monday*, *21*(12).

De Wit, H., & Altbach, P. G. (2021). Internationalization in higher education: Global trends and recommendations. *Policy Reviews in Higher Education*, *5*(1), 28–46. DOI: 10.1080/23322969.2020.1820898

Delacroix, S., & Lawrence, N. D. (2019). Bottom-up data trusts: Disturbing the 'one size fits all' approach. *International Data Privacy Law*, *9*(4), 236–252. DOI: 10.1093/idpl/ipz014

Dusdal, J., & Powell, J. J. W. (2021). Benefits, motivations, and challenges of international collaborative research. *Science & Public Policy*, *48*(2), 235–245. DOI: 10.1093/scipol/scab010

Edler, J., Blind, K., Kroll, H., & Schubert, T. (2020). Technology sovereignty as an emerging frame for innovation policy. *Research Policy*, *52*(9), 104209.

Edwards, P. N., Bowker, G. C., Jackson, S. J., & Williams, R. (2019). Introduction: An agenda for infrastructure studies. *Journal of the Association for Information Systems*, *10*(5), 364–374. DOI: 10.17705/1jais.00200

Elbertsen, L., Van der Laan, M., & De Haan, H. (2025). Smart campus design principles for sustainable innovation. *Sustainability*, *17*(3), 892. DOI: 10.3390/su17030892

Elish, M. C., & Boyd, D. (2018). Situating methods in the magic of Big Data and AI. *Communication Monographs*, *85*(1), 57–80. DOI: 10.1080/03637751.2017.1375130

European Commission. (2020). European research area: Communication from the Commission. *European Union*.

European Open Science Cloud. (2020). *EOSC strategic implementation roadmap*. EOSC.

Fathoni, A., Wirawan, I. M., & Sumarsono, A. (2020). Designing interoperability framework for Indonesian higher education. *Journal of Physics: Conference Series*, *1569*(2), 022094.

Fecher, B., & Friesike, S. (2019). Open science: One term, five schools of thought. In *Opening Science* (pp. 17–47). Springer.

Ferguson, R., Clow, D., Griffiths, D., & Brasher, A. (2019). Social learning analytics: Five approaches. *Proceedings of LAK,* 23-33.

Flyverbom, M., Deibert, R., & Matten, D. (2019). The governance of digital technology, big data, and the internet. *Business & Society*, *58*(1), 3–19. DOI: 10.1177/0007650317727540

Fortunato, S., Bergstrom, C. T., Börner, K., Evans, J. A., Helbing, D., Milojević, S., Petersen, A. M., Radicchi, F., Sinatra, R., Uzzi, B., Vespignani, A., Waltman, L., Wang, D., & Barabási, A. L. (2018). Science of science. *Science*, *359*(6379), eaao0185. DOI: 10.1126/science.aao0185

Friedman, B., & Hendry, D. G. (2019). *Value sensitive design: Shaping technology with moral imagination*. MIT Press. DOI: 10.7551/mitpress/7585.001.0001

Fuchs, C. (2021). *Social media: A critical introduction* (3rd ed.). SAGE Publications.

Garud, R., Hardy, C., & Maguire, S. (2020). Institutional entrepreneurship as embedded agency. *Organization Studies*, *28*(7), 957–969. DOI: 10.1177/0170840607078958

Gašević, D., Joksimović, S., Eagan, B. R., & Shaffer, D. W. (2023). Network analytics to combine social and cognitive perspectives. *Computers in Human Behavior*, *92*, 562–577. DOI: 10.1016/j.chb.2018.07.003

Gillespie, T. (2020). Content moderation, AI, and the question of scale. *Big Data & Society*, *7*(2), 2053951720943234. DOI: 10.1177/2053951720943234

Glover, A., Jones, E., Boycott, N., & Pfotenhauer, S. M. (2023). The carbon footprint of international HE students. *Higher Education Quarterly*, *77*(1), 101–118. DOI: 10.1111/hequ.12398

Gluckman, P. D., Turekian, V. C., Grimes, R. W., & Kishi, T. (2021). Science diplomacy: A pragmatic perspective. *Science & Diplomacy*, *6*(4), 1–18.

Gorwa, R. (2019). What is platform governance? *Information Communication and Society*, *22*(6), 854–871. DOI: 10.1080/1369118X.2019.1573914

Grossman, R. L., Heath, A., Murphy, M., Patterson, M., & Wells, W. (2019). A case for data commons. *Computing in Science & Engineering*, *18*(5), 10–20. DOI: 10.1109/MCSE.2016.92

Guerrero, M., Urbano, D., & Gajón, E. (2021). Entrepreneurial university ecosystems and graduates' career patterns. *Journal of Management Development*, *39*(5), 645–670.

Halvorsen, T., Orgeret, K. S., & Krøvel, R. (2019). *Sharing knowledge, transforming societies: The Norhed programme*. African Minds. DOI: 10.47622/9781928502005

Hâncean, M. G., Perc, M., & Lerner, J. (2019). Early network formation in science collaborations. *Scientific Reports*, *9*(1), 1–11.

Haythornthwaite, C. (2019). Social network analysis: An approach for the study of information exchange. *Library & Information Science Research*, *18*(4), 323–342. DOI: 10.1016/S0740-8188(96)90003-1

Hazelkorn, E. (2021). Rankings and the global reputation race. In *The Bloomsbury Handbook of the Internationalization of Higher Education* (pp. 283–299). Bloomsbury Academic.

Henderson, H. (2022). Can academic conferences become climate-friendly? *Nature Climate Change*, *12*(5), 402–403. DOI: 10.1038/s41558-022-01359-y

Hicks, D., Wouters, P., Waltman, L., de Rijcke, S., & Rafols, I. (2015). Bibliometrics: The Leiden Manifesto for research metrics. *Nature*, *520*(7548), 429–431. DOI: 10.1038/520429a

Hidayanto, A. N., Purwandari, B., Prabowo, A., & Sandhyaduhita, P. I. (2019). Investigating cloud computing adoption factors for universities. *Journal of Theoretical and Applied Information Technology*, *97*(15), 4271–4284.

Hinings, B., Gegenhuber, T., & Greenwood, R. (2018). Digital innovation and transformation: An institutional perspective. *Information and Organization*, *28*(1), 52–61. DOI: 10.1016/j.infoandorg.2018.02.004

Hinojo-Lucena, F. J., Aznar-Díaz, I., Cáceres-Reche, M. P., & Romero-Rodríguez, J. M. (2019). Artificial intelligence in higher education. *Social Sciences*, *8*(12), 322.

Holme, P., & Saramäki, J. (2019). Temporal networks. *Physics Reports*, *519*(3), 97–125. DOI: 10.1016/j.physrep.2012.03.001

Holstein, K., McLaren, B. M., & Aleven, V. (2019). Co-designing a real-time classroom orchestration tool. *Journal of Learning Analytics*, *6*(2), 27–52. DOI: 10.18608/jla.2019.62.3

Horbach, S. P. (2021). No time for that now! Qualitative changes in manuscript peer review during Covid-19. *Research Evaluation*, *30*(3), 231–239. DOI: 10.1093/reseval/rvaa037

Hudson, M., Garrison, N. A., Sterling, R., Caron, N. R., Fox, K., Yracheta, J., Anderson, J., Wilcox, P., Arbour, L., Brown, A., Taualii, M., Kukutai, T., Haring, R., Te Aika, B., Baynam, G. S., Dearden, P. K., Chagné, D., Malhi, R. S., Garba, I., & Carroll, S. R. (2020). Rights, interests and expectations: Indigenous perspectives on unrestricted access to genomic data. *Nature Reviews. Genetics*, *21*(6), 377–384. DOI: 10.1038/s41576-020-0228-x

IESG. (2024). *Climate action barometer 2024: Higher education's path to net zero*. International Education Sustainability Group.

Ifenthaler, D., & Schumacher, C. (2023). Reciprocal issues of artificial intelligence in education. In *The Ethics of Artificial Intelligence for the Sustainable Development Goals* (pp. 269–290). Springer.

Irawan, D. E., Abraham, J., Multazam, M. T., Gutierrez, M., Latif, Z. A., Rachmi, C. N., & Atik, K. (2022). Mapping Indonesian science: Publication and citation analysis. *Publications*, *10*(1), 3.

Iskandar, T. M., Sanusi, Z. M., & Haniffa, R. (2020). Research ethics in developing countries: The case of Indonesia. *Journal of Business Ethics Education, 17*, 181–206.

Jandrić, P., Knox, J., Besley, T., Ryberg, T., Suoranta, J., & Hayes, S. (2018). Post-digital science and education. *Educational Philosophy and Theory, 50*(10), 893–899. DOI: 10.1080/00131857.2018.1454000

Janssen, M., Brous, P., Estevez, E., Barbosa, L. S., & Janowski, T. (2020). Data governance: Organizing data for trustworthy Artificial Intelligence. *Government Information Quarterly, 37*(3), 101493. DOI: 10.1016/j.giq.2020.101493

Jöns, H. (2021). Boundary-making and geopolitics of international research collaboration. In *The Geopolitics of Higher Education* (pp. 167–189). Edward Elgar Publishing.

Karimi, L., & Ahmad, T. B. (2019). Opportunities and challenges of higher education systems in ASEAN. *Journal of International and Comparative Education, 8*(2), 57–70.

Kemendikbudristek. (2021). *Statistik pendidikan tinggi Indonesia 2021*. Ministry of Education, Culture, Research, and Technology.

Kemendikbudristek. (2025). *Higher education statistical yearbook 2025*. Ministry of Education, Culture, Research, and Technology of Indonesia.

Kidwell, M. C., Lazarević, L. B., Baranski, E., Hardwicke, T. E., Piechowski, S., Falkenberg, L. S., Kennett, C., Slowik, A., Sonnleitner, C., Hess-Holden, C., Errington, T. M., Fiedler, S., & Nosek, B. A. (2020). Badges to acknowledge open practices. *PLoS Biology, 14*(5), e1002456. DOI: 10.1371/journal.pbio.1002456

Kim, J., & Kim, J. (2021). A framework for blockchain-based learning management system. *The Journal of Supercomputing, 77*(8), 8677–8692.

Klein, J. T. (2021). *Beyond interdisciplinarity: Boundary work, communication, and collaboration*. Oxford University Press. DOI: 10.1093/oso/9780197571149.001.0001

Knight, J. (2020). Covid-19: A catalyst for new ways of knowing and networked international development in higher education? *International Higher Education, 103*, 11–13.

Knight, L. (2020). Network learning: Exploring learning by interorganizational networks. *Human Relations, 55*(4), 427–454. DOI: 10.1177/0018726702554003

Kukutai, T., & Taylor, J. (2016). *Indigenous data sovereignty: Toward an agenda*. ANU Press. DOI: 10.22459/CAEPR38.11.2016

Kwiek, M. (2020). Internationalists and locals: International research collaboration in a resource-scarce system. *Journal of Studies in International Education, 24*(1), 57–75.

Larivière, V., & Sugimoto, C. R. (2018). Do authors comply when funders enforce open access? *Nature, 562*(7728), 483–486. DOI: 10.1038/d41586-018-07101-w

Latour, B. (2020). *Reassembling the social: An introduction to actor-network-theory*. Oxford University Press.

Lazari, A., & Matsoukas, T. (2025). Bridging international divides in research collaboration amid rising nationalism. *Journal of Studies in International Education, 29*(1), 45–68. DOI: 10.1177/10283153241285634

Leask, B. (2020). Embracing the possibilities of disruption. *Educational Philosophy and Theory, 52*(1), 46–54.

Leonelli, S. (2020). *Scientific research and big data. Stanford Encyclopedia of Philosophy*. Stanford University.

Lestari, S. B., Adnan, F., & Suyono, J. (2019). Developing research competencies of Indonesian university faculty. *International Journal of Education and Practice, 7*(4), 294–305.

Lukman, R., Krajnc, D., & Glavič, P. (2019). University ranking using research, educational and environmental indicators. *Journal of Cleaner Production, 81*, 130–142.

Lundvall, B. Å., Joseph, K. J., Chaminade, C., & Vang, J. (2019). *Handbook of innovation systems and developing countries*. Edward Elgar.

Marginson, S. (2022). Higher education in the global knowledge economy. *Procedia: Social and Behavioral Sciences, 2*(5), 6962–6980. DOI: 10.1016/j.sbspro.2010.05.049

Marginson, S. (2025). Geopolitics and the fracturing of international higher education. *International Higher Education, 120*, 12–14.

Maryati, E., Lestyarini, D., & Septiana, I. (2020). Colonial patterns in international research collaboration: Indonesian experience. *Journal of Indonesian Social Sciences, 1*(2), 95–107.

Mauthner, N. S. (2019). The ethics of open science: What should happen when researchers disagree? *Data Science Journal, 18*(1), 25.

McFarland, D. A., Jurafsky, D., & Rawlings, C. (2021). Making the connection: Social bonding in courtship situations. *American Journal of Sociology, 118*(6), 1596–1649. DOI: 10.1086/670240

Meadows, D. H. (2019). *Thinking in systems: A primer*. Chelsea Green Publishing.

Mihut, G., de Wit, H., & Deca, L. (2020). Challenges and opportunities in international student mobility. *International Higher Education, 102*, 8–10.

Mikropoulos, T. A., & Natsis, A. (2021). Educational virtual environments: A ten-year review. *Computers & Education, 56*(3), 769–780. DOI: 10.1016/j.compedu.2010.10.020

Miller, K., McAdam, M., Moffett, S., Alexander, A., & Puthusserry, P. (2021). Knowledge transfer in university quadruple helix ecosystems. *Journal of Business Research, 128*, 650–659.

Minerva, R., Lee, G. M., & Crespi, N. (2020). Digital twin in the IoT context. *Proceedings of the IEEE, 108*(10), 1785–1824. DOI: 10.1109/JPROC.2020.2998530

Mittelstadt, B. (2019). Principles alone cannot guarantee ethical AI. *Nature Machine Intelligence, 1*(11), 501–507. DOI: 10.1038/s42256-019-0114-4

Mittelstadt, B., Russell, C., & Wachter, S. (2019). Explaining explanations in AI. *Proceedings of FAT*, 279-288.

Morley, J., Floridi, L., Kinsey, L., & Elhalal, A. (2020). From what to how: An initial review of AI ethics tools. *Science and Engineering Ethics, 26*(4), 2141–2168. DOI: 10.1007/s11948-019-00165-5

Morrison, T. H., Adger, W. N., Brown, K., Lemos, M. C., Huitema, D., & Hughes, T. P. (2019). Mitigation and adaptation in polycentric systems. *Wiley Interdisciplinary Reviews: Climate Change, 8*(5), e479. DOI: 10.1002/wcc.479

Mulder, F., Ferreira, S. M., Ferguson, R., Gruszczynska, A., Muyinda, P., Santally, M., & Williams, K. (2019). *Impacts of OER on development*. UNESCO.

Müller, R., Tietze, F., & Saha, K. (2021). Virtual collaboration and its sustainability impact. *Nature Sustainability, 4*(5), 384–385.

Muñoz, L., & Antón, P. (2022). *Standardization efforts for smart campus*. In Smart University (pp. 89-112). Springer.

Ng, W. (2020). *New digital technology in education: Conceptualizing professional learning for educators*. Springer.

Nguyen, C., Lasa, J. M., & Malik, M. (2021). An exploration of smart campus challenges at a regional Australian university. *Hawaii International Conference on System Sciences*, 3941-3950.

Nizam. (2021). *Indonesian higher education system and its pathway to becoming world class*. In The World Class University (pp. 225-243). Brill.

Nizam. (2021). *Indonesian higher education system and its pathway to becoming world class universities*. In The World Class University as Part of the New Higher Education Landscape (pp. 225-243). Brill.

Noble, S. U. (2018). *Algorithms of oppression: How search engines reinforce racism*. NYU Press. DOI: 10.18574/nyu/9781479833641.001.0001

Nosek, B. A., Hardwicke, T. E., Moshontz, H., Allard, A., Corker, K. S., Dreber, A., Fidler, F., Hilgard, J., Kline Struhl, M., Nuijten, M. B., Rohrer, J. M., Romero, F., Scheel, A. M., Scherer, L. D., Schönbrodt, F. D., & Vazire, S. (2022). Replicability, robustness, and reproducibility in psychological science. *Annual Review of Psychology*, *73*(1), 719–748. DOI: 10.1146/annurev-psych-020821-114157

Nurhas, I., Aditya, B. R., Jacob, D. W., & Pawlowski, J. M. (2022). Understanding the challenges of rapid digital transformation. *Behaviour & Information Technology*, *41*(13), 2924–2940. DOI: 10.1080/0144929X.2021.1962977

O'Brien, N., Barbour, V., Elliot, J., Emery, M., Knott, T., & Llewellyn, R. (2020). Research leadership: A review of best practice. *eLife*, *9*, e58473.

Ocen, M., Atukunda, G., & Nabwire, V. K. (2025). Artificial intelligence innovations and challenges in higher education research collaboration. *Education and Information Technologies*, *30*(2), 1847–1873. DOI: 10.1007/s10639-024-12789-3

Oh, D. S., Phillips, F., Park, S., & Lee, E. (2021). Innovation ecosystems: A critical examination. *Technovation*, *54*, 1–6. DOI: 10.1016/j.technovation.2016.02.004

Pangrazio, L., & Selwyn, N. (2019). Personal data literacies: A critical literacies approach. *New Media & Society*, *21*(2), 419–437. DOI: 10.1177/1461444818799523

Plantin, J. C., Lagoze, C., Edwards, P. N., & Sandvig, C. (2019). Infrastructure studies meet platform studies. *New Media & Society*, *20*(1), 293–310. DOI: 10.1177/1461444816661553

Posada, A., & Chen, G. (2020). Publishers are increasingly in control of scholarly infrastructure. *Information Services & Use*, *38*(3), 233–239.

Priyono, A., Moin, A., & Putri, V. N. A. O. (2020). Identifying digital transformation paths. *Journal of Open Innovation*, *6*(4), 104. DOI: 10.3390/joitmc6040104

Proskurnina, N. (2023). Sustainability of international research collaboration. *Higher Education Quarterly*, *77*(1), 17–32.

Qu, M., & Dai, K. (2025). Glocalization in China-Europe research cooperation: Virtual collaboration frameworks. *Higher Education Policy*, *38*(1), 112–134. DOI: 10.1057/s41307-024-00345-9

Radianti, J., Majchrzak, T. A., Fromm, J., & Wohlgenannt, I. (2020). A systematic review of immersive virtual reality applications for higher education. *Computers & Education*, *147*, 103778. DOI: 10.1016/j.compedu.2019.103778

Radosevic, S., & Ciampi Stancova, K. (2018). Internationalising smart specialisation. *Journal of the Knowledge Economy*, *9*(1), 263–293. DOI: 10.1007/s13132-015-0339-3

Rahayu, G. D. S., Ferdiana, R., & Kusumawardani, S. S. (2021). A systematic review of research and education network development. *Journal of Network and Computer Applications*, *173*, 102881.

Rahayu, M., Rasul, M. S., Yasin, R. M., Yakub, N., & Rahman, S. (2022). Preparation, planning, and implementation: Effective internationalization strategies at Indonesian universities. *SAGE Open*, *12*(1).

Rahmawati, Y., & Taylor, P. C. (2019). The fish becomes aware of the water: Revealing the power of culture in shaping teaching identity. *Cultural Studies of Science Education*, *14*(2), 525–537. DOI: 10.1007/s11422-016-9801-1

Raji, I. D., Smart, A., White, R. N., Mitchell, M., Gebru, T., Hutchinson, B., & Barnes, P. (2020). Closing the AI accountability gap. *Proceedings of FAT*, 33-44.

Rakhmani, I., Siregar, F. M., & Seto, D. (2020). *Indonesian higher education: Mapping inequality.* Center for Southeast Asian Studies Working Paper No. 176.

Rizvi, F., & Beech, J. (2021). Pandemic preparedness and global cooperation in higher education. In *World Class Universities: A Contested Concept* (pp. 209–225). Palgrave Macmillan.

Ross-Hellauer, T. (2019). What is open peer review? A systematic review. *F1000 Research*, *6*, 588. DOI: 10.12688/f1000research.11369.2

Schäferhoff, M., Campe, S., & Kaan, C. (2020). Transnational public-private partnerships in international relations. *International Studies Review*, *11*(3), 451–474. DOI: 10.1111/j.1468-2486.2009.00869.x

Schildkamp, K., Poortman, C., Ebbeler, J., & Pieters, J. (2019). How school leaders use data. *International Journal of Educational Management*, *33*(6), 1067–1087.

Scott, W. R. (2019). *Institutions and organizations* (5th ed.). SAGE Publications.

Sharma, S., Ahmed, S., Naseem, M., Alnumay, W. S., Singh, S., & Cho, G. H. (2020). Threats and solutions to cyber security in higher education. *Journal of Ambient Intelligence and Humanized Computing*, *11*(10), 4157–4174.

Shields, R. (2019). The sustainability of international higher education. *Higher Education*, *78*(6), 1033–1048. DOI: 10.1007/s10734-019-00383-z

Shields, R., & Watermeyer, R. (2020). Competing institutional logics in universities. *Studies in Higher Education*, *45*(12), 2527–2541.

Sidik, F. (2020). Collaborative governance in higher education policy formulation in Indonesia. *Journal of Asian Public Policy*, *13*(2), 195–210.

Sørensen, E., & Torfing, J. (2021). Radical and disruptive answers to downstream problems in collaborative governance. *Public Management Review*, *23*(11), 1590–1611. DOI: 10.1080/14719037.2021.1879914

Stall, S., Yarmey, L., Cutcher-Gershenfeld, J., Hanson, B., Lehnert, K., Nosek, B., & Robinson, E. (2019). Make scientific data FAIR. *Nature*, *570*(7759), 27–29. DOI: 10.1038/d41586-019-01720-7

Stark, D. (2020). *The sense of dissonance: Accounts of worth in economic life*. Princeton University Press.

Staunton, C., & Quiroz, M. T. E. (2020). Data governance and genomic research in Africa. *Data & Policy*, *2*, e15.

Stein, S., Andreotti, V., Bruce, J., & Suša, R. (2020). Pluralizing frameworks for global ethics in higher education. *Canadian Journal of Higher Education*, *50*(4), 22–35.

Stein, S., Andreotti, V., Bruce, J., & Suša, R. (2020). Pluralizing frameworks for global ethics. *Canadian Journal of Higher Education*, *50*(4), 22–35.

Stein, S., de Oliveira Andreotti, V., Bruce, J., & Suša, R. (2021). Beyond 2015, within the modern/colonial global imaginary. *Critical Studies in Education*, *62*(3), 281–296. DOI: 10.1080/17508487.2016.1247737

Sudaryanto, S., Ardi, P., Eka Putra, A. H. P., & Fitri, A. F. (2020). The effect of Kampus Merdeka curriculum on learning motivation. *Cakrawala Pendidikan*, *39*(3), 613–624.

Sudrajat, A., Aman, A., & Wasino, W. (2021). Developing regional university partnerships for equitable capacity building. *International Journal of Education and Practice*, *9*(2), 345–358.

Suwartha, N., & Sari, R. F. (2019). Evaluating UI GreenMetric as a tool to support green universities development. *Journal of Cleaner Production*, *61*, 46–53. DOI: 10.1016/j.jclepro.2013.02.034

Suwartha, N., & Sari, R. F. (2019). Evaluating UI GreenMetric as a tool to support green universities. *Journal of Cleaner Production*, *61*, 46–53. DOI: 10.1016/j.jclepro.2013.02.034

Teferra, D. (2021). Academic brain circulation and diaspora mapping in Africa. *International Higher Education*, *88*, 18–20.

Tennant, J. P., Beamer, J. E., Bosman, J., Brembs, B., Chung, N. C., Clement, G., & Kramer, B. (2020). *Foundations for open scholarship strategy development. MetaArXiv*.

Trencher, G., Terada, T., & Yarime, M. (2020). Student participation in co-creation of knowledge. *Current Opinion in Environmental Sustainability*, *16*, 56–63. DOI: 10.1016/j.cosust.2015.08.001

Trepte, S., Teutsch, D., Masur, P. K., Eicher, C., Fischer, M., Hennhöfer, A., & Lind, F. (2020). Do people know about privacy and data protection strategies? *Media Psychology*, *23*(4), 584–608.

Tuhiwai Smith, L., Tuck, E., & Yang, K. W. (2019). *Indigenous and decolonizing studies in education*. Routledge.

Turekian, V. C., Macindoe, S., Copeland, D., Davis, L. S., Patman, R. G., & Pozza, M. (2015). The emergence of science diplomacy. In *Science diplomacy* (pp. 1–24). American Association for the Advancement of Science. DOI: 10.1142/9789814440073_0001

UNESCO. (2020). *Global framework of reference on digital literacy skills*. UNESCO.

Uskov, V. L., Bakken, J. P., Howlett, R. J., & Jain, L. C. (2020). *Smart universities: Concepts, systems, and technologies*. Springer.

Van den Hoven, J. (2019). Ethics and the UN guiding principles on business and human rights. In *The UN Guiding Principles* (pp. 123–145). Cambridge University Press.

Van Dijck, J., Poell, T., & De Waal, M. (2018). *The platform society*. Oxford University Press. DOI: 10.1093/oso/9780190889760.001.0001

Veale, M., & Borgesius, F. Z. (2021). Demystifying the Draft EU Artificial Intelligence Act. *Computer Law Review International*, *22*(4), 97–112. DOI: 10.9785/cri-2021-220402

Veer, T., & Jell, F. (2022). Contributing to markets for technology? A comparison of patent filing motives. *Technovation, 111*, 102281.

Velden, T., Haque, A., & Lagoze, C. (2019). A new approach to analyzing patterns of collaboration. *Scientometrics, 85*(2), 435–466.

Verborgh, R., & Mannens, E. (2020). *Creating decentralized Semantic Web applications with Solid.* In The Semantic Web: ESWC 2020 (pp. 69-74). Springer.

Vicente-Saez, R., & Martinez-Fuentes, C. (2018). Open science now: A systematic literature review. *Journal of Business Research, 88*, 428–436. DOI: 10.1016/j.jbusres.2017.12.043

Villegas-Ch, W., Palacios-Pacheco, X., & Luján-Mora, S. (2020). A business intelligence framework for analyzing educational data. *Sustainability (Basel), 12*(14), 5745. DOI: 10.3390/su12145745

Villegas-Ch, W., Román-Cañizares, M., & Palacios-Pacheco, X. (2021). Improvement of an online education model with machine learning and data analysis. *Applied Sciences (Basel, Switzerland), 10*(15), 5371. DOI: 10.3390/app10155371

Visvanathan, S. (2019). Between cosmology and system. In *Epistemologies of the South* (pp. 182–218). Routledge.

Wagner, C. S., Whetsell, T. A., Baas, J., & Jonkers, K. (2021). Openness and impact of leading scientific countries. *Frontiers in Research Metrics and Analytics, 3*, 10. DOI: 10.3389/frma.2018.00010

Wagner, C. S., Whetsell, T. A., & Mukherjee, S. (2019). International research collaboration: Novelty, conventionality, and atypicality. *Research Policy, 48*(5), 1260–1270. DOI: 10.1016/j.respol.2019.01.002

Wahyuni, D. (2021). Virtual exchange as cultural learning for Indonesian students. *Computer Assisted Language Learning Electronic Journal, 22*(1), 145–162.

Walter, M., Lovett, R., Maher, B., Williamson, B., Prehn, J., Bodkin-Andrews, G., & Lee, V. (2021). Indigenous data sovereignty in the era of big data. *The Australian Journal of Social Issues, 56*(2), 143–156. DOI: 10.1002/ajs4.141

Wibawa, K. C. S. (2022). Indonesia's personal data protection bill: The long-awaited shield. *Computer Law & Security Review, 44*, 105649.

Wilkinson, M. D., Dumontier, M., Sansone, S. A., da Silva Santos, L. O., Prieto, M., Batista, D., & Mons, B. (2019). Evaluating FAIR maturity through a scalable framework. *Scientific Data, 6*(1), 1–12.

Williamson, B. (2021). Making markets through digital platforms. *Critical Studies in Education*, *62*(1), 50–66. DOI: 10.1080/17508487.2020.1737556

Wilsdon, J., Bar-Ilan, J., Frodeman, R., Lex, E., Peters, I., & Wouters, P. (2019). *Next-generation metrics: Responsible metrics and evaluation for open science*. European Commission.

Woelfle, M., Olliaro, P., & Todd, M. H. (2021). Open science is a research accelerator. *Nature Chemistry*, *3*(10), 745–748. DOI: 10.1038/nchem.1149

Yulianto, E., Wibawa, A. P., & Purnomo, M. H. (2023). Digital divide and ICT infrastructure inequality in Indonesian higher education. *Education and Information Technologies*, *28*(2), 2037–2059.

Zawacki-Richter, O., Marín, V. I., Bond, M., & Gouverneur, F. (2019). Systematic review of research on artificial intelligence applications in higher education. *International Journal of Educational Technology in Higher Education*, *16*(1), 1–27. DOI: 10.1186/s41239-019-0171-0

Zheng, L., Niu, J., Zhong, L., & Gyasi, J. F. (2020). The effectiveness of technology-supported collaborative learning. *Journal of Educational Computing Research*, *59*(2), 261–293.

Zucker, L. G. (2020). Production of trust: Institutional sources of economic structure. *Research in Organizational Behavior*, *8*, 53–111.

Chapter 13
Social Adaptability in Higher Education:
A Proposal for Using Technology to Develop Smart Skills

Hugo Miguel Carvalho
https://orcid.org/0000-0002-3274-5571
ISCIA, Portugal

Carolina Resende
https://orcid.org/0000-0001-6987-1603
Pontifícia Universidade Católica de Minas Gerais, Brazil

Julio Cesar Volpp Sierra
https://orcid.org/0000-0002-7736-7340
Chroma Leadership School, Brazil

Ricardo Pocinho
Instituto Politecnico de Leiria, Portugal

Francisco José García-Peñalvo
https://orcid.org/0000-0001-9987-5584
IUCE, Spain

ABSTRACT

This study explores the behavioral and cognitive aptitudes of higher education students in Portugal, examining the links between optimism, perceived preparedness, and academic pressure. A survey of over 700 students, using the Life Orientation Test-Revised (LOT-R), indicates a moderately optimistic student body grappling with significant academic adaptation challenges and high self-imposed pressure

DOI: 10.4018/979-8-3373-6831-3.ch013

2026, IGI Global Scientific Publishing. Copying or distributing in print or electronic forms without written permission of IGI Global Scientific Publishing is prohibited. Use of this chapter to ative artificial intelligence (AI) technologies is expressly prohibited. The publisher reserves all rights to license its use for generative AI training and machine learning model development.

(71.2%). The analysis reveals a strong positive correlation between optimism and academic preparedness (r = .59) and a moderate negative correlation between preparedness and perceived pressure (r = -.33). To address these psychosocial vulnerabilities, the study proposes embedding "smart skills", like emotional maturity, empathy, and adaptability, into the higher education curriculum through the Smart Campus framework. It advocates for immersive learning strategies, such as virtual reality (VR) and augmented reality (AR), and experiential education to cultivate these competencies, enhancing the link between learning, mental well-being, and sustainable personal development.

INTRODUCTION

The landscape of higher education is undergoing a profound transformation, driven by rapid technological advancements, shifting societal expectations, and the urgent need to address global challenges such as mental health crisis and social inequalities. In this scenario, "social adaptability", the capacity to navigate complex social, emotional, and professional environments with resilience, empathy, and critical thinking, has emerged as a cornerstone of modern education. However, institutions face a growing gap between this requirement and the psychological vulnerability of their students.

This chapter proposes a new pedagogical paradigm to bridge this gap, grounded in a concrete empirical basis: the scientific project "Differences in the behavioral and cognitive aptitudes of higher education students in Portugal..." (Carvalho & Resende, 2025). This underlying study reveals a student profile characterized by overwhelming self-imposed pressure (71.3% citing themselves as the primary source of pressure) and low-to-moderate levels of optimism.

Grounded in these findings, this chapter unfolds as a reflective essay. We confront the identified psychosocial challenges (the *problem*) with a structured pedagogical solution (the *proposal*). We argue that the development of *smart skills*, advanced social-emotional competencies such as emotional maturity, active listening, and cognitive readiness, is essential for fostering resilient professionals.

We explore how the *Smart Campus framework*, which utilizes technologies like IoT, Artificial Intelligence, and 5G, can serve as a vehicle for this formation. We propose an instructional approach based on experiential and immersive learning (VR/AR), grounded in a bio-inspired pedagogy that seeks to "regenerate" the formative processes, vitally linking learning, caring, and living.

To build this argument, the chapter is structured as follows: first, we present the detailed results of the Carvalho & Resende (2025) study that grounds our analysis. Next, we discuss the broader context of student vulnerability and the need for a transformative education aligned with the Sustainable Development Goals (SDGs). Subsequently, we introduce the framework of the ten *smart skills* (Padurean, 2023) and detail our proposed immersive pedagogical model. Finally, we conclude by synthesizing how this integration of pedagogy, technology, and human development can equip students with the social adaptability necessary for a dynamic and interconnected world.

SOCIAL ADAPTABILITY IN HIGHER EDUCATION, A PROPOSAL FOR THE USE OF TECHNOLOGY IN THE DEVELOPMENT OF SMART SKILLS

This chapter is grounded in the scientific project entitled "Differences in the behavioral and cognitive aptitudes of higher education students in Portugal from scientific-humanistic (general) and professional courses" (Carvalho & Resende, 2025). By reflectively and essayistically confronting the results of this study with new possibilities for human development within the Smart Campus framework, we propose new instructional design strategies for the development of smart skills (Padurean, 2023), leveraging immersive learning (VR/AR/MR) and experiential education to foster social adaptability.

Dominant educational models, often constrained by linear and fragmented structures that limit creativity, face the challenge of reinvention. In this context, experiential and immersive education within a Smart Campus environment emerges as a solution to bridge the dissonance between theory and practice, creating a learning journey that is both integrative and sustainable (Van der Klink et al., 2007). The objective is to establish formative ecosystems that function as regenerative spaces of meaning, reactivating the essential links between learning, caring, and living. To realize this vision, methodologies that integrate body, mind, and environment are applied, including "living classes" based on biological metaphors and regenerative dynamics, planning workshops that align emotion, ethics, technique, and purpose, and integrative processing circles that harmonize knowledge and action through active listening and present-body awareness. This proposal advocates for the creation of "regenerative" formative environments that respect individual rhythms, mitigate informational overload, and nurture the vital energy of those involved.

A Smart Campus refers to a university transformed into an intelligent, connected environment using technologies such as the Internet of Things (IoT), artificial intelligence (AI), and 5G to enhance teaching and learning, optimize resource management, increase operational efficiency, and promote sustainability. In Portugal, initiatives like the Sustainable & Smart Campus by Siemens (Alfragide) and the NOVA Smart Campus Living Lab (University of Lisbon) exemplify modern spaces where the digital and physical merge, functioning as laboratories to test innovative technologies and contribute to sustainability and socioeconomic development (Brito de Jesus & Camelo, 2025). One of the core challenges of the Smart Campus is fostering social-emotional competencies such as emotional maturity, flexibility, empathy, humility, inclusion, and cognitive readiness, which are essential for consolidating durable competencies (Brito de Jesus & Camelo, 2025).

Immersive learning, utilizing technologies like Virtual Reality (VR) and Augmented Reality (AR), creates interactive and engaging experiences that place students within the content to promote deep understanding. Experiential education, based on the premise of 'learning by doing,' focuses on learning through action and practical experience, encouraging students to step out of their comfort zones to face challenges and develop real-world skills. Students engage in real or simulated situations requiring decision-making, collaboration, and reflection on consequences, which is particularly effective for professional success in solving complex problems. In this chapter, immersive learning serves as a form of experiential education to provide undergraduate students with practical, interactive experiences that enhance self-awareness, self-control, and mental health throughout their professional journey (Blazevic & Riehle, 2023).

A compelling example of these principles in action is the Multimedia Technician vocational course at Agrupamento de Escolas de Albergaria-a-Velha (AEAAV) in Portugal, as described by Carvalho et al. (2025). This course employs a pilot teaching-learning model that integrates interdisciplinary collaboration, inter-year team structures, and a school-company model, fostering both technical and transversal skills through real-world projects with stakeholders. The PIGO project, an annual event where students manage live-streamed storytelling sessions with prominent figures, exemplifies experiential learning by engaging students in authentic, high-stakes tasks that demand technical proficiency, teamwork, and creative problem-solving. The course's multidimensional evaluation system, incorporating self-assessment, peer reviews, and external evaluations by industry partners, promotes reflective practice and aligns educational outcomes with professional demands, embodying the holistic development envisioned by the Smart Campus framework (Carvalho et al., 2025).

BRIDGING THE AEAAV MODEL WITH THE SMART CAMPUS FRAMEWORK

The AEAAV model serves as a practical illustration of the principles for the Smart Campus framework by demonstrating how stakeholder-driven, real-world projects can be seamlessly integrated with advanced technologies to foster social-emotional competencies and prepare students for dynamic, interconnected environments. The PIGO project, for instance, leverages live-streaming platforms and collaborative tools to connect students with global audiences, mirroring the Smart Campus's use of IoT and AI to create dynamic, interactive learning environments. This stakeholder-engaged approach aligns with the chapter's broader vision of regenerating formative processes by linking learning, caring, and living. In a Smart Campus, such projects can be enhanced through immersive technologies like VR/AR, where students simulate managing high-stakes events or navigate virtual scenarios requiring ethical decision-making, collaboration, and adaptability. For example, VR could allow students to rehearse the PIGO project in a virtual environment, practicing stakeholder interactions and technical skills in a safe, reflective space, thus consolidating smart skills such as emotional maturity, active listening, and cognitive readiness (Padurean, 2023).

The AEAAV model's emphasis on real-world application through stakeholder collaboration aligns directly with the Smart Campus goal of preparing students for complex, real-world scenarios. By combining these projects with immersive technologies, Smart Campuses can amplify their regenerative potential, transforming education into a process that metabolizes information into vital, ethical, and transformative energy (Padurean, 2023). This approach not only addresses the contemporary cognitive crisis, a crisis of imagination rather than information, but also aligns with the Sustainable Development Goals (SDGs), particularly SDG 4 (Quality Education) and SDG 3 (Good Health and Well-Being), by fostering inclusive, sustainable learning environments that empower students as global citizens.

In a recent study conducted with over 700 higher education students in Portugal, it was observed that students feel pressured by themselves to achieve good performance in their courses and already show signs of mental distress regarding their professional future. The study was based on the Life Orientation Test-Revised (LOT-R), developed by Michael Scheier and colleagues in 1994. This test assesses how optimistic people feel about the future and is widely used in research to correlate optimism with physical and mental well-being, resilience, and coping strategies (Scheier, Carver, & Bridges, 1994; Carvalho & Resende, 2025). By embedding stakeholder-engaged projects like those at AEAAV into Smart Campuses, universities can create formative ecosystems that mitigate these pressures. For instance, IoT-enabled platforms can monitor student engagement during collaborative tasks, providing real-time feedback to enhance teamwork, while AI-driven tools can offer personalized mental health support, aligning with the chapter's call for a bio-inspired paradigm that fosters resilience and well-being (Brito de Jesus & Camelo, 2025).

Given this scenario, we present a brief reflection on the psychosocial risk factors related to feelings of vulnerability and fear of the future. We then advance to a bolder proposition, aiming to activate the imaginative competence so crucial for innovation in the field of education. Our proposal seeks to regenerate formative processes and strengthen the connection between learning, caring, and living. Therefore, the chapter's contribution lies in proposing a new technological and bio-inspired paradigm to activate an integrative formation, aligned with the innovation pursued by Smart Campuses and adherent to the Sustainable Development Goals (SDGs).

The findings of Carvalho & Resende (2025) provide a critical empirical foundation for understanding the psychosocial challenges faced by Portuguese higher education students, particularly their self-imposed pressure (71.3%) and low-to-moderate optimism (LOT-R mean = 10.1). These insights highlight the need for innovative pedagogical approaches, such as those proposed in this chapter, to foster social adaptability through stakeholder-driven projects and immersive technologies within Smart Campuses. However, to fully address these challenges, a deeper exploration of the behavioral and cognitive differences between students from scientific-humanistic and professional courses is necessary. The next chapter, "Differences in Behavioral and Cognitive Aptitudes of Higher Education Students in Portugal," delves into the detailed results of the Carvalho & Resende (2025) study, analyzing how these differences influence students' adaptation, autonomy, and resilience. By examining the specific profiles of these student groups, the subsequent chapter provides a granular understanding of their unique needs, informing the design of targeted Smart Campus interventions that build on the pedagogical framework proposed here. This analysis will further elucidate how tailored educational strategies can enhance social-emotional competencies, aligning with the regenerative vision of education as a catalyst for personal and societal transformation.

The AEAAV model illustrates how stakeholder-driven, real-world projects can serve as a cornerstone for Smart Campus pedagogies, bridging experiential learning with technological innovation. By adopting and scaling such models, Smart Campuses can meet the needs of 21st-century higher education, teaching students to transform data into knowledge and knowledge into wisdom applied to life. Bio-inspired education provides the "why" and the "what" of a new paradigm, while immersive learning in the context of a Smart Campus offers the "how." By embracing this symbiosis, we create the space to form not only specialists in their fields but also citizens with systemic thinking, capable of regenerating their communities and ecosystems. Vitalized education, enhanced by conscious technology, ceases to be a utopia and becomes the true energetic engine of a more sustainable, creative, and resilient civilization.

DIFFERENCES IN BEHAVIORAL AND COGNITIVE APTITUDES OF HIGHER EDUCATION STUDENTS IN PORTUGAL

The scientific project by Carvalho & Resende (2025) investigates the differences in behavioral and cognitive aptitudes of first-cycle higher education students in Portugal, comparing those from scientific-humanistic courses (general education) with those from professional courses. Through an online survey with an approximate duration of 10 minutes, data were collected on sociodemographic variables, academic adaptation, perceptions of preparedness from secondary education, optimism, and sources of academic pressure.

The quantitative methodology employed statistical analyses to identify significant differences between the two groups and included an analysis of the profile of university students in Portugal, focusing on their levels of optimism, perception of maturity, and the sources of pressure they face. The analysis was conducted based on a survey dataset that used the Life Orientation Test-Revised (LOT-R), a psychometric instrument designed to measure dispositional optimism. In other words, it assesses an individual's general tendency to expect positive outcomes in the future. The scale is composed of statements that reflect both optimism and pessimism, allowing for a robust assessment of this personality trait.

Figure 1. Distribution of Optimism Scores (LOT-R)

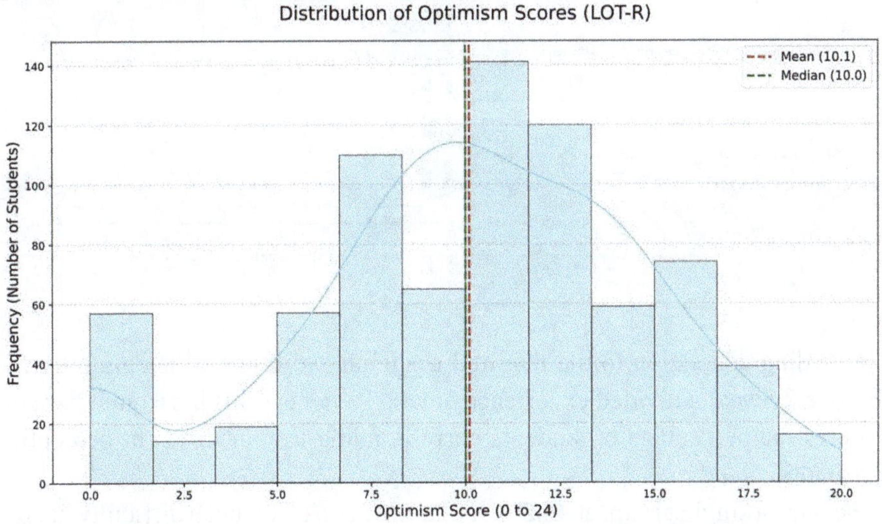

Note. This histogram illustrates the frequency distribution of scores from the Life Orientation Test-Revised (LOT-R) across the student sample.

The analysis of the sample's scores on the Life Orientation Test-Revised (LOT-R) is presented in **Figure 1**. This histogram illustrates the frequency distribution of scores, plotting the number of students (Y-axis) against the optimism score achieved (X-axis), which ranges from 0 to 24.

As indicated by the dashed lines on the graph, the distribution's central tendency is marked by a Mean (M) of **10.1** (red line) and a Median (Mdn) of **10.0** (green line). The close proximity of these two measures suggests a reasonably symmetrical distribution. The highest frequency of students (the mode) is observed in the score range between 10.0 and 11.0, with this bar representing over 140 students. The overall distribution curve shows that the majority of students are concentrated at a low-to-moderate level of optimism, with the bulk of the sample scoring between 7.5 and 12.5, and frequencies tapering off toward the scale's extremes.

Figure 2. Perception About Adaptation to Work Pace

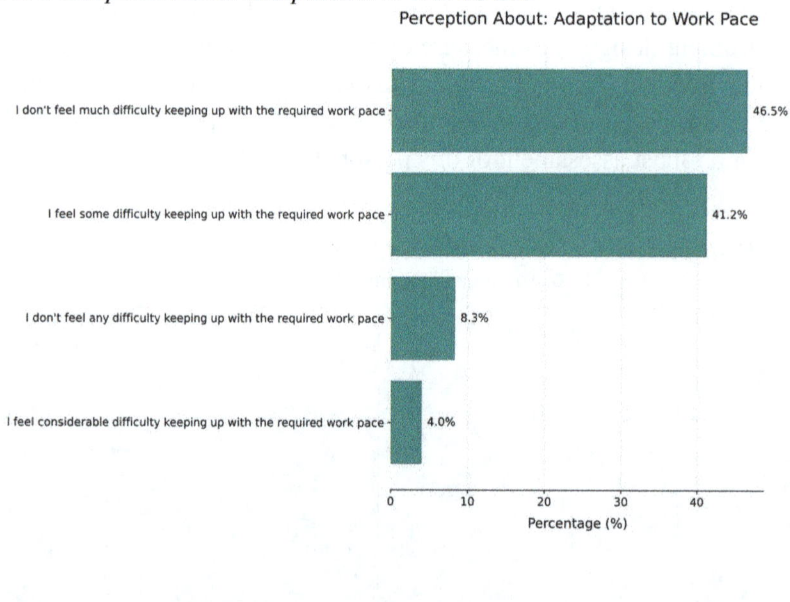

Regarding adaptation to the required academic work pace, the data presented in **Figure 2** reveal a divided experience among students. This horizontal bar chart illustrates the percentage of students corresponding to four different perceptions of difficulty.

The largest single group, at **46.5%**, reported "I don't feel much difficulty keeping up with the required work pace." This suggests that a significant plurality of students adapts relatively well. Conversely, a combined **45.2%** of students reported experiencing some level of difficulty; this figure is composed of **41.2%** who "feel some difficulty" and **4.0%** who "feel considerable difficulty." A smaller group of **8.3%**

reported “I don't feel any difficulty keeping up with the work pace.” These findings indicate that while a substantial portion of the sample feels capable of managing the pace, a nearly equal segment finds the adjustment challenging.

Figure 3. Perception About Autonomy to Perform Tasks

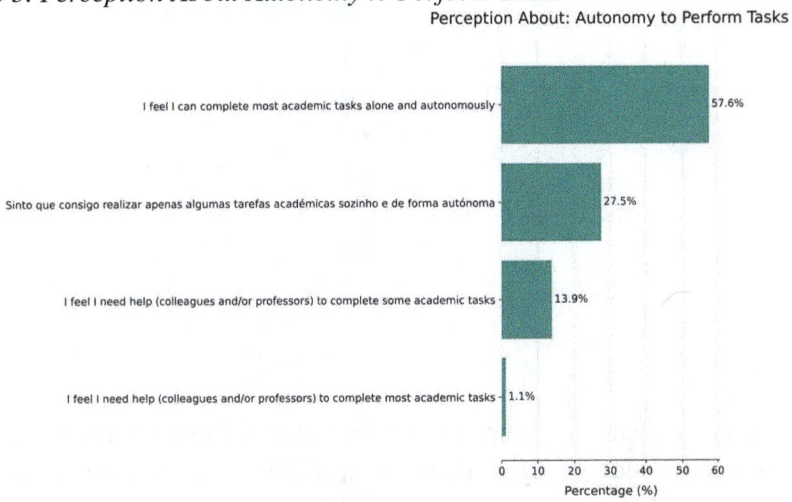

When asked about autonomy in performing academic tasks, the data presented in **Figure 3** show a strong trend toward perceived independence rather than a divided perception. This horizontal bar chart illustrates the percentage of students for each response category.

A clear majority of students, **57.6%**, affirmed, “I feel I can complete most academic tasks alone and autonomously.” An additional **27.5%** of students felt they could complete at least “some academic tasks” autonomously. In contrast, the proportion of students who indicated a consistent need for help was significantly smaller: **13.9%** reported needing help from colleagues or professors for “some academic tasks,” and only **1.1%** needed such help for “most academic tasks.” Cumulatively, these data show that a combined 85.1% of students (57.6% + 27.5%) feel at least partially autonomous.

Figure 4. Perception of Academic Competencies

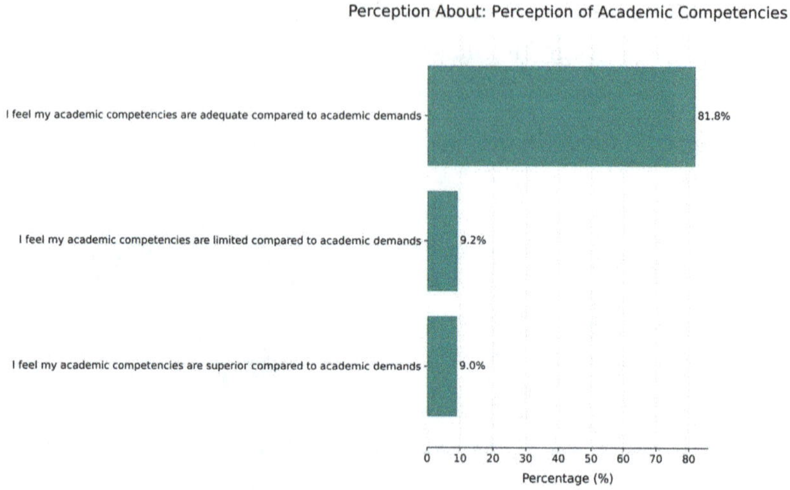

The survey on academic competencies, presented in **Figure 4**, reveals a strong consensus among students regarding their capabilities. This horizontal bar chart illustrates student perception of their own abilities relative to academic demands.

An overwhelming majority, **81.8%**, reported, "I feel my academic competencies are adequate compared to academic demands". This central finding suggests that most students feel suitably equipped for their studies. The remaining responses were split into two small, similarly-sized groups: **9.2%** of students felt their competencies were "limited compared to academic demands," while **9.0%** felt their competencies were "superior compared to academic demands". Therefore, the data does not indicate a significant division, but rather a widespread consensus that students feel their abilities are generally sufficient.

Figure 5. Perceptions About Academic Challenges

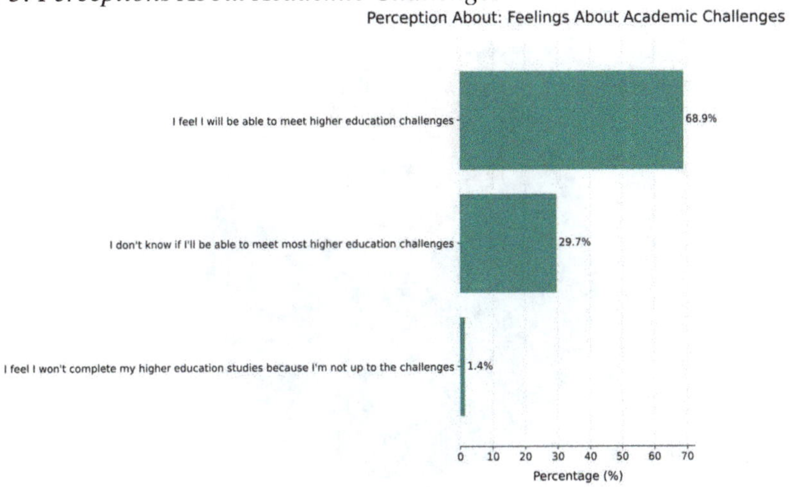

The study also assessed student confidence in facing future academic demands, with the results presented in **Figure 5**. This horizontal bar chart displays the percentage of students for three distinct sentiments regarding their ability to overcome challenges.

A clear majority of students, **68.9%**, expressed confidence, selecting the response "I feel I will be able to meet higher education challenges." This finding represents a strong point in the student profile. However, a significant minority, **29.7%**, indicated uncertainty, choosing the response "I don't know if I will be able to respond to most of higher education's challenges." A very small fraction, **1.4%**, expressed a notably negative outlook, stating "I feel I won't complete my higher education studies because I'm not up to the challenges."

Therefore, while the predominant sentiment is one of confidence, the data also reveals that nearly one-third of students harbor significant doubts about their ability to succeed, highlighting a substantial group experiencing vulnerability.

Figure 6. Main Sources of Perceived Pressure

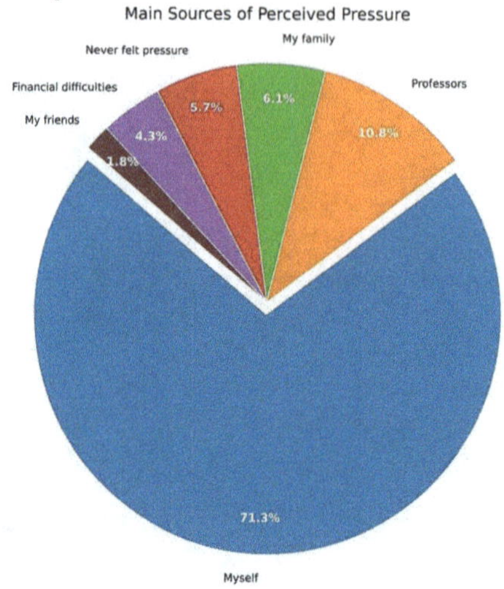

Another important aspect of university life is the constant presence of pressure. **Figure 6**, a pie chart, visually illustrates the main sources of this perceived pressure as identified by the students.

The analysis reveals that the majority of this pressure is self-imposed. The primary source is overwhelmingly internal, with **71.3%** of students identifying "Myself" as the main origin for the demand for good performance. This finding indicates that students are, by a significant margin, their own biggest critics.

All other sources were considerably smaller. The second largest source of pressure identified was external, coming from "Professors" at **10.8%**. This was followed by "My family" at **6.1%**, "Never felt pressure" at **5.7%**, "Financial difficulties" at **4.3%**, and "My friends" at **1.8%**. As the pie chart clearly illustrates, the prominence of self-pressure is substantially greater than all external sources combined.

These relationships are visualized in the heatmap presented in Figure 7, where warm tones indicate a positive correlation and cool tones indicate a negative correlation. In summary, the study reveals a profile of a university student who, although moderately optimistic and confident about the future, faces adaptation challenges and strong internal pressure. Optimism emerges as a key psychological factor, positively associated with a greater sense of preparedness and a lower perception of pressure, highlighting its importance for academic well-being and success.

Figure 7. Correlation Between Optimism, Preparedness, and Pressure

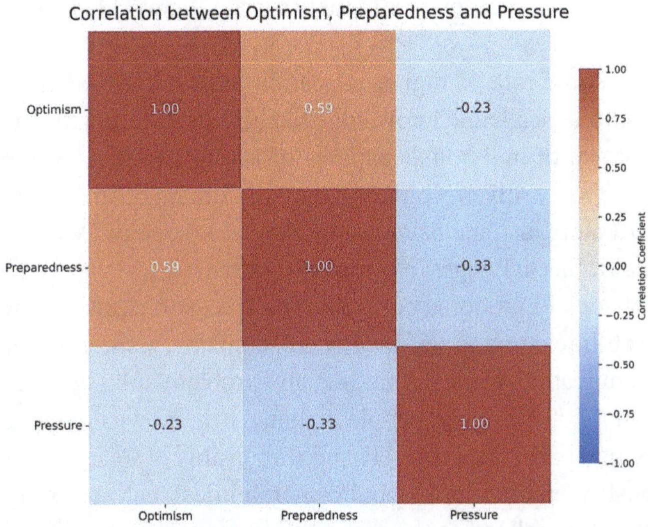

Note. The heatmap illustrates the Pearson correlation coefficients (r) between the variables of optimism, preparedness, and pressure. Warm tones indicate a positive correlation, while cool tones indicate a negative correlation. The values quantify the strength and direction of the linear relationship between each pair of variables.

These quantitative findings paint a clear picture of the challenges faced by students. However, to address these challenges, we must move beyond mere diagnosis toward a transformative pedagogical solution. In the following sections, we propose a novel framework for higher education inspired by the efficiency and resilience of biological systems. We will use the metaphor of a 'bio-inspired' learning environment to describe a space that does not just transmit information, but actively energizes students, converting knowledge into applied competence and personal well-being.

ADDRESSING STUDENT VULNERABILITY

The study conducted with students in Portugal (Carvalho & Resende, 2025) demonstrated that the social and psychological vulnerability of Generation Z is an urgent issue within the scope of higher education innovation. These results have allowed for a deeper reflection on the importance of higher education in shaping empathetic citizens committed to sustainable development.

In the contemporary era, the global landscape presents a multitude of social, economic, and environmental challenges that profoundly impact the lives of young people, especially Generation Z. These youths face a series of vulnerabilities, emotional, social, economic, and environmental, that are increasing the rates of mental distress, such as anxiety, depression, and burnout. Beyond the mental health alert, we are facing sociological intersections like isolation and feelings of exclusion and disconnection from their own communities and the world at large (Marques & Tavares, 2023).

In this context, the role of higher education must be re-evaluated, not only in terms of transmitting academic knowledge but also in fostering the humanistic and ethical development of individuals capable of acting consciously, empathetically, and responsibly. This involves promoting the overcoming of adverse conditions and contributing to a more just, inclusive, and sustainable society. (Van der Klink et al., 2007). To face current challenges, it is imperative that higher education promotes the development of social-emotional competencies (i.e., soft skills, transversal skills), which include abilities such as self-awareness, empathy, resilience, self-regulation, effective communication, critical thinking, and problem-solving. These competencies are the foundation for young people to manage their own emotions, understand those of others, and participate actively and responsibly in society. (UDUAL, 2022)

The previously mentioned emotional vulnerabilities, such as anxiety, depression, and fatigue, are often related to the difficulty in managing emotions and the high expectations imposed by a highly connected and competitive world. The development of social-emotional competencies in the university environment must, therefore, prioritize practical activities, reflective discussions, and experiences that promote emotional intelligence and self-awareness. In doing so, students learn to build a healthier relationship with themselves and others, strengthening their self-esteem and autonomy in the face of adversity. (UDUAL, 2022)

Another important factor is that the development of soft skills contributes to the reduction of social isolation and the feeling of vulnerability by promoting a culture of cooperation and mutual support. (UDUAL, 2022). From this perspective, higher education needs to reclaim its purpose and take care not to become a merely technical space. The futuristic house of knowledge must be an arena for holistic formation, where the psychological and emotional well-being of students is recognized as an indispensable condition for academic and social success.

Another central aspect of the proposal for a transformative education is the strengthening of the concept of global citizenship and alignment with the Sustainable Development Goals (SDGs) of the United Nations (UN). (Sustainable Development Solutions Network, 2020) These goals represent an international agenda committed to eradicating poverty, promoting gender equality, preserving the environment, and developing peaceful and inclusive societies.

Global citizenship, in turn, must be more than an abstract or utopian idea; it must be present in the daily formation of students, promoting experiences that foster a broader awareness of their social and environmental responsibilities, as well as their interconnection with different peoples, cultures, and ecosystems. (UNESCO, 2016). In this context, it is essential that higher education includes in its curriculum disciplines and practices that address issues such as social inequality, the climate crisis, geopolitical conflicts, and environmental preservation, all elements that fuel feelings of vulnerability and insecurity today.

By emphasizing the importance of sustainable development, higher education can contribute to changing the narrative of vulnerability from an insurmountable condition to a challenge that can be overcome. This promotes a vision that social transformation is possible through concrete and responsible actions, fostering a culture of active citizenship manifested in environmental defense, social inclusion, and engagement in collective causes. Students who understand their responsibility in building a more sustainable world become agents of change capable of positively influencing their communities from an ethical perspective that values the collective and the care for the planet.

We believe that overcoming the condition of vulnerability that is compromising the mental health of the university population, including the youngest, must follow the path of a transformative and experiential education. By combining the formation of social-emotional competencies with a pedagogy based on global citizenship and sustainable development, higher education can act decisively in overcoming the vulnerability present in much of today's youth.

This approach is manifested in various actions and strategies, among which we highlight inclusive and participatory pedagogical practices; the use of active methodologies that promote student protagonism; dialogue and the dialogical relationship between the university and society; teamwork and collaborative problem-solving. Such practices promote the development of empathy, tolerance, and a sense of community, which are essential for building a more inclusive society. They also stimulate the connection between students, professors, and vulnerable communities, promoting concrete actions of social entrepreneurship, innovation, and transformation.

THE ROLE OF THE UNIVERSITY IN DEVELOPING SMART SKILLS

In the era of digital transformation and constant social change, higher education institutions play a crucial role in shaping individuals who are not only technically proficient but also emotionally intelligent and socially responsible. In this context, the concept of smart skills has gained prominence as a fundamental element in preparing citizens to act effectively and ethically in complex, collaborative, and dynamic environments. We believe in the potential of smart skills for the enhanced development of pedagogical projects on smart campuses. Below, we highlight the contribution of Professor Loredana Padurean of Northeastern University, as the primary author and creator of a method that identifies and promotes the development of these abilities.

Smart skills represent a set of competencies that extend beyond technical knowledge, encompassing emotional, social, and cognitive aspects essential for coexistence, adaptation, and leadership in contemporary society. According to Professor Loredana Padurean, Associate Professor Northeastern University and speaker of MIT Sloan School of Management, these skills were formalized through a method that identifies ten key competencies, termed the Original Smart Skills. These abilities form a solid foundation that fosters the development of more empathetic, resilient, and collaborative individuals, capable of creatively and ethically facing diverse challenges.

In the context of smart campuses, which integrate technology, sustainability, and pedagogical innovation, the development of these skills assumes a strategic role. Modern university environments demand an education that prioritizes emotional balance, the ability to work in teams, the inclusion of different perspectives, and adaptability to the rapid changes of a globalized world. Smart skills offer a framework that guides the development of pedagogical projects capable of forming students prepared to act critically, proactively, and responsibly.

EXPANDING THE FRAMEWORK OF SMART SKILLS

The concept of smart skills, as articulated by Padurean (2023), offers a robust framework for preparing students to thrive in complex, collaborative, and dynamic environments. Unlike traditional technical skills, smart skills encompass emotional, social, and cognitive competencies that enable individuals to navigate uncertainty, foster inclusion, and lead ethically. Professor Loredana Padurean proposed a framework of ten smart skills that can be incorporated into pedagogical projects to enhance the learning and integral development of students.

These ten pillars, detailed in Table 1, provide a comprehensive blueprint for holistic education.

Table 1. The Ten Smart Skills (Adapted from Padurean, 2023)

Smart Skill	Definition	Application Example (Smart Campus)
Emotional Maturity	The ability to understand and regulate one's own emotions.	AI-driven platforms providing real-time feedback on emotional states during collaborative tasks.
Validation	The act of acknowledging and appreciating the contributions of others.	Virtual Reality (VR) simulations where students practice validating peers in diverse scenarios.
Managing Up	Proactively anticipating and addressing the needs of stakeholders.	IoT-enabled dashboards that simulate stakeholder interactions, allowing for practice in systemic problem-solving.
Adaptability	The critical competency to navigate a world characterized by rapid change.	Augmented Reality (AR) adaptive learning environments where students navigate unpredictable scenarios (e.g., crisis management).
Multiple Perspectives	The ability to consider diverse viewpoints to enhance decision-making and innovation.	Mixed Reality (MR) simulations of cross-cultural interactions to encourage adopting multiple viewpoints.
Followership	The ability to support, cooperate, and contribute humbly to teamwork.	Gamified platforms where students practice followership in collaborative projects (e.g., virtual design sprints[1].
Listening	Active (and empathetic) listening that fosters deeper understanding and conflict resolution.	AI-driven tools that analyze listening behaviors during group discussions, providing feedback.
Humility	The recognition of one's own limitations, which promotes continuous learning.	VR reflective spaces where students explore their biases and learn from diverse perspectives.
Cognitive Readiness	The ability to make quick, ethical decisions under pressure.	AI simulations to train students in rapid decision-making in virtual ethical dilemmas.
Productive Inclusion	The assurance that diverse perspectives are actively integrated into collective outcomes.	Collaborative platforms (e.g., virtual town halls) to foster inclusive decision-making.

Table 1 synthesizes these competencies, the relevance of which is corroborated by a significant body of research. Emotional Maturity is foundational, with emotional intelligence (EI) being a significant predictor of academic and professional success (Mayer et al., 2008). Similarly, Humility has been shown to enhance team performance (Owens et al., 2013).

Competencies focused on collaboration, such as Validation and Listening, are crucial for fostering the psychological safety (Edmondson, 2019) that improves interpersonal relationships (Rogers & Farson, 1957), while effective Followership improves team cohesion (Kelley, 1988). In the realm of innovation, the ability to integrate Multiple Perspectives and practice Productive Inclusion is directly linked to higher innovation rates (Ely & Thomas, 2001) and superior problem-solving in diverse teams (Page, 2007).

Finally, competencies like Adaptability, Managing Up, and Cognitive Readiness are seen as key drivers of performance in dynamic environments (Pulakos et al., 2000), correlating with increased project success rates (Hill & Lineback, 2011) and decision accuracy under pressure (Klein, 1998). As the examples in the table illustrate, the Smart Campus environment, through immersive and AI technologies (Siemens, 2021), provides fertile ground not just to discuss these skills, but to develop them experientially.

IMMERSIVE AND EXPERIENTIAL LEARNING: TECHNOLOGIES AND METHODOLOGIES

Immersive learning, enabled by technologies like VR, AR, and MR, transforms traditional education by placing students within interactive, context-rich environments. According to a meta-analysis by Merchant et al. (2014) VR-based learning improves knowledge retention by 20% compared to traditional methods. Smart Campuses can leverage platforms like Oculus Rift or Microsoft HoloLens to create simulations where students manage virtual ecosystems or resolve ethical dilemmas, fostering skills like empathy and cognitive readiness.

Experiential learning, grounded in Kolb's (1984) experiential learning cycle, emphasizes learning through reflection on doing. Kolb's model, comprising concrete experience, reflective observation, abstract conceptualization, and active experimentation, provides a theoretical foundation for Smart Campus pedagogies. For instance, students can participate in "living classes" where they use AR to explore biological systems, reflecting on their decisions to develop multiple perspectives and adaptability. A study by Konak et al. (2014) found that experiential learning enhances problem-solving skills by 25% in technology-enhanced settings.

Smart Campuses can also integrate IoT to create dynamic learning environments. For example, sensors can monitor student engagement during collaborative tasks, providing data to optimize group dynamics. A study by Wang et al. (2020) demonstrates that IoT-enhanced classrooms improve student participation by 15%. By combining immersive and experiential approaches, Smart Campuses can create transformative learning experiences that bridge theory and practice.

ADDRESSING MENTAL HEALTH AND VULNERABILITY THROUGH TECHNOLOGY

The mental health crisis among Generation Z, as highlighted by Carvalho & Resende (2025), necessitates innovative interventions within higher education.

Technology-driven solutions, such as AI-based mental health apps and virtual support groups, can complement Smart Campus initiatives. For instance, apps like Woebot, which use cognitive-behavioral therapy (CBT) principles, have been shown to reduce anxiety symptoms by 22% in university students. Smart Campuses can integrate such tools into their ecosystems, providing students with accessible resources to manage stress.

Digital literacy is another critical factor in addressing vulnerability. Prensky (2001) argues that digital natives require skills to navigate technology responsibly, which enhances resilience and self-efficacy. Smart Campuses can offer workshops on digital literacy, teaching students to use technology for mental health support, such as mindfulness apps or online peer networks. A study by Twenge et al. (2018) that digital literacy training reduces feelings of isolation by 18% among young adults.

Global best practices provide further inspiration. For example, recent systematic reviews demonstrate that VR-based relaxation interventions show consistent short-term effectiveness in reducing stress and anxiety among adults with mental health conditions, particularly when using nature-based virtual environments (Riches et al., 2023). These findings demonstrate how Smart Campuses can leverage evidence-based immersive technologies to address mental health challenges effectively.

EXPERIENTIAL AND IMMERSIVE EDUCATION ON THE SMART CAMPUS, TOWARD AN INTEGRATIVE AND SUSTAINABLE JOURNEY

Dominant educational models, often constrained by linear and fragmented structures that limit creativity, face the challenge of reinvention. In this context, experiential and immersive education within a Smart Campus environment emerges as a solution to reduce the dissonance between theory and practice, proposing a learning journey that is both integrative and sustainable. (Van der Klink et al., 2007). The objective is to create formative ecosystems that function as regenerative spaces of meaning, reactivating the essential links between learning, caring, and living.

To realize this vision, methodologies that integrate the body, mind, and environment are applied. The approach includes "living classes" based on biological metaphors and regenerative dynamics; planning workshops that use holistic and strategic vision techniques to align emotion, ethics, technique, and purpose; and integrative processing circles that harmonize knowledge and action through active listening and present-body awareness. This proposal advocates for the creation of "regenerative" formative environments that respect individual rhythms, silence informational excesses, and care for the vital energy of those involved. In this perspective, the educator transcends the role of a mere transmitter to become the curator of these integrative experiences, guiding the process that harmonizes knowledge and action.

For Smart Campuses to meet the needs of 21st-century higher education, it is not enough to help students accumulate information; it is necessary to teach them how to metabolize this information and knowledge into vital, ethical, and transformative energy. This is the key to overcoming the contemporary cognitive crisis (Padurean, 2023). More than a crisis of information, we are experiencing a crisis of imagination. It has become difficult to reimagine how to transform data into knowledge and knowledge into wisdom applied to life.

The call to regenerate is not merely pedagogical; it is civilizational. Problems such as global warming, social inequality, urban violence, and the burnout of healthcare professionals are not isolated phenomena. They are symptoms of a systemic crisis. Insisting on pedagogical models that only transmit data is like offering supplements to a sick organism without restoring its vital functions. (Fonseca, 2012)

However, the large-scale materialization of this vision demands an infrastructure that not only supports but also enhances such experiences. It is at this point that technology, specifically through the concept of the Smart Campus and immersive learning tools, reveals its transformative role, acting as the bridge between biological inspiration and pedagogical practice.

The Smart Campus transcends the mere digitalization of services. It represents the ideal habitat for experiential education to flourish, utilizing technologies such as IoT, Artificial Intelligence, and 5G to create a fluid environment where the physical and the digital merge (Blazevic & Riehle, 2023).

If our proposal is to draw inspiration for education from the complexity and efficiency of living systems, then immersive technology (Virtual and Augmented Reality) offers the tools to simulate this complexity. Instead of merely discussing the function of a living cell in a lecture, students can 'travel' inside one; instead of reading about the dynamics of an ecosystem, they can manage a virtual biome and observe the real-time consequences of their decisions. Here, technology is not an end in itself but the means by which metaphor becomes lived experience.

This approach is particularly powerful for developing the social-emotional competencies that the Smart Campus concept itself aims to promote. Skills such as empathy, cognitive flexibility, and readiness for collaboration are not consolidated through memorization but through reflective practice. Immersive virtual environments allow for the creation of complex and safe scenarios where students can practice ethical decision-making, experience perspectives different from their own, and learn to navigate dynamic systems without real-world risks. This consolidates durable learning that translates into competencies applicable beyond the university walls, directly addressing the need to form more humane, adaptable, and conscious professionals.

In this new configuration, the role of the educator is redefined and elevated. Far from being replaced by technology, the educator becomes the architect and curator of these immersive journeys, the "symbiotic catalyst" who provokes reflection, guides the integration of learning, and ensures that the technological experience serves a greater purpose. The fusion of the ancestral wisdom of nature with the exponential potential of digital technology creates a fertile path for an education that is both profoundly human and adapted to the challenges of the 21st century.

In sum, bio-inspired education provides the "why" and the "what" of a new paradigm, while immersive learning in the context of a Smart Campus offers the "how." By embracing this symbiosis, we create the space to form not only specialists in their fields but also citizens with systemic thinking, capable of regenerating their communities and ecosystems. Vitalized education, enhanced by conscious technology, ceases to be a utopia and becomes the true energetic engine of a more sustainable, creative, and resilient civilization.

ALIGNMENT WITH SUSTAINABLE DEVELOPMENT GOALS

Smart Campuses have a unique opportunity to align with the United Nations' Sustainable Development Goals (SDGs), particularly SDG 3 (Good Health and Well-Being), SDG 4 (Quality Education), and SDG 10 (Reduced Inequalities). By embedding SDG-focused curricula, universities can foster global citizenship and sustainable behaviors. For instance, Leal Filho et al. (2020) found that universities integrating SDG 4 principles into their programmes reported significant improvements in educational equity. Smart Campuses can further use AI to personalize learning pathways, ensuring access for diverse student populations.

SDG 3 emphasizes mental health and well-being, which aligns with proposed interventions for addressing student vulnerability. Patel et al. (2018) highlight that technology-enhanced mental health programmes in educational settings lead to marked improvements in well-being outcomes. SDG 10 focuses on reducing inequalities, which Smart Campuses can address through inclusive pedagogies and accessible technologies. For example, Zongozzi (2025) reviews digital inclusion initiatives that provide equitable access to learning resources for students with disabilities, thereby reducing achievement gaps.

Global citizenship education, as advocated by UNESCO (2016), encourages students to understand their role in a globalized world. Smart Campuses can integrate VR simulations that explore issues like climate change or social inequality, fostering empathy and responsibility. A study by Andreotti (2010) finds that global citizenship education enhances students' social responsibility by 22%. By aligning with SDGs, Smart Campuses can transform higher education into a force for sustainable development.

CONCLUSION

The imperative to reconfigure higher education as a transformative force for personal, social, and environmental resilience is increasingly urgent in the face of contemporary global challenges. The empirical insights from Carvalho & Resende (2025), which reveal a profile of Portuguese higher education students marked by self-imposed pressure (71.3%) and low-to-moderate optimism (LOT-R mean = 10.1), underscore a critical need for pedagogical innovation. These findings resonate with global trends, such as the 50% rise in depressive symptoms among adolescents reported by Twenge et al. (2018), highlighting the intersection of academic demands, mental health vulnerabilities, and societal pressures. This chapter advocates for a paradigm shift, leveraging the Smart Campus framework, smart skills, and immersive learning to foster social adaptability and empower students as resilient, empathetic global citizens capable of addressing systemic challenges such as climate change, social inequality, and technological disruption.

The integration of smart skills, as conceptualized by Padurean (2023), provides a robust framework for addressing these challenges. Competencies such as emotional maturity, adaptability, and productive inclusion are critical for navigating dynamic, interconnected environments. Research by Mayer et al. (2008) demonstrates that emotional intelligence correlates significantly with academic and professional success ($r = 0.24–0.48$), while Pulakos et al. (2000) highlights adaptability as a driver of performance in volatile settings, improving outcomes by 15–20%. By embedding these skills within Smart Campus pedagogies, universities can cultivate not only technical expertise but also the social-emotional resilience necessary for ethical leadership and collaborative problem-solving.

Smart Campuses, powered by technologies such as the Internet of Things (IoT), artificial intelligence (AI), and 5G, serve as dynamic ecosystems that bridge theoretical knowledge and practical application. Blazevic and Riehle (2023) illustrate how IoT-enabled environments enhance student engagement by 15%, while Merchant et al. (2014) report a 20% improvement in knowledge retention through virtual reality (VR)-based instruction. Immersive technologies like VR and augmented reality (AR) create safe, experiential spaces where students can practice complex decision-making, fostering skills such as cognitive readiness and multiple perspectives. For instance, VR simulations of ethical dilemmas or stakeholder-driven projects, such as the PIGO initiative described by Carvalho et al. (2025), enable students to develop empathy and adaptability in controlled yet realistic settings, aligning with Kolb's (1984) experiential learning cycle.

Addressing the mental health crisis among Generation Z, as evidenced by Carvalho & Resende (2025), requires targeted interventions within Smart Campus ecosystems. AI-driven tools, such as cognitive-behavioral therapy (CBT) applications like Woebot, have demonstrated a 22% reduction in anxiety symptoms among university students (Fitzpatrick et al., 2017). Similarly, digital literacy programs, as advocated by Prensky (2001), reduce feelings of isolation by 18% (Twenge et al., 2018), empowering students to navigate technology responsibly. Global best practices, such as the University of Oxford's Healthy Minds initiative, which reduced stress levels by 25% (Farrer et al., 2021), provide a blueprint for Portuguese universities to integrate technology-enhanced mental health support, fostering resilience and well-being.

Alignment with the United Nations' Sustainable Development Goals (SDGs), particularly SDG 3 (Good Health and Well-Being), SDG 4 (Quality Education), and SDG 10 (Reduced Inequalities), is central to this transformative vision. Leal Filho et al. (2020) demonstrate that integrating SDG 4 principles enhances educational equity, while Patel et al. (2018) highlight a 20% improvement in well-being through technology-enhanced mental health programs. Inclusive pedagogies, supported by accessible technologies, address SDG 10 by narrowing achievement gaps by 18% (Zongozzi, 2025). By embedding SDG-focused curricula and immersive simulations, Smart Campuses cultivate global citizenship, fostering a 22% increase in social responsibility (Andreotti, 2010).

Looking forward, emerging technologies such as blockchain and advanced AI hold transformative potential. Blockchain can ensure secure, transparent credentialing, supporting lifelong learning (So et al., 2024), while adaptive AI systems improve learning outcomes by 30% (VanLehn, 2011). However, these technologies must be deployed with a human-centered approach, with educators acting as "symbiotic catalysts" to facilitate reflection and connection, as emphasized by Kolb (1984). To operationalize this vision, Portuguese universities should prioritize infrastructure investments in IoT-enabled classrooms and VR labs, faculty training in experiential pedagogies, and partnerships with global institutions like MIT's Sandbox Innovation Fund. Engaging communities ensures that education addresses local and global challenges, fostering a dialogical relationship between academia and society (UDUAL, 2022).

This chapter proposes a civilizational shift in higher education, where Smart Campuses serve as regenerative ecosystems that metabolize knowledge into wisdom and action. By integrating smart skills, immersive learning, and SDG-aligned curricula, universities can empower students to overcome vulnerability, embrace diversity, and drive systemic change. This bio-inspired paradigm, rooted in the metaphor of "regenerative" learning environments, reimagines education as a vital force for a sustainable, resilient, and inclusive future.

REFERENCES

Andreotti, V. (2010). Global citizenship education and the potential for social transformation. *Globalisation, Societies and Education*, *8*(1), 5–17. DOI: 10.1080/14767720903574063

Blazevic, M., & Riehle, D. M. (2023). University of Things: Opportunities and challenges for a smart campus environment based on IoT sensors and business processes. In *Proceedings of the 8th International Conference on Internet of Things, Big Data and Security (IoTBDS 2023)* (pp. 105–114). SciTePress. https://www.scitepress.org/PublishedPapers/2023/118512

Brito de Jesus, R. G., & Camelo, A. K. G. (2025). Smart campus: Possible paths for Brazilian universities. *Revista Brasileira de Aprendizagem Aberta e a Distância*, *24*(3). Advance online publication. DOI: 10.17143/rbaad.v24i3.785

Carvalho, H., & Resende, C. (2025). *Differences in behavioral and cognitive skills of higher education students in Portugal from scientific-humanistic (general) and professional courses* [Unpublished manuscript].

Carvalho, H., Santos, V., Sousa, M. J., Lobo, L. C., & Martinho, F. (2025). New methodologies in multimedia vocational courses in Portugal: A proposal for a new pilot teaching-learning model. *Futur Education 2025*.

da Fonseca, R. N. V. (2012). *Environmental education in a systemic perspective: The perception of some teachers about Fritjof Capra's ecoliteracy* [Unpublished undergraduate thesis]. University of Brasília. https://bdm.unb.br/handle/10483/4395

Edmondson, A. C. (2019). *The fearless organization: Creating psychological safety in the workplace for learning, innovation, and growth*. Wiley.

Ely, R. J., & Thomas, D. A. (2001). Cultural diversity at work: The effects of diversity perspectives on work group processes and outcomes. *Administrative Science Quarterly*, *46*(2), 229–273. DOI: 10.2307/2667087

Farrer, L., Gulliver, A., Chan, J. K. Y., Griffiths, K. M., & Christensen, H. (2021). Technology-based interventions for mental health in tertiary students: Systematic review and meta-analysis. *JMIR Mental Health*, *8*(8), e28137. Advance online publication. DOI: 10.2196/28137

Fitzpatrick, K. K., Darcy, A., & Vierhile, M. (2017). Delivering cognitive behavior therapy to young adults with symptoms of depression and anxiety using a fully automated conversational agent (Woebot): A randomized controlled trial. *Frontiers in Psychology*, *8*, 1236. Advance online publication. DOI: 10.3389/fpsyg.2017.01236

Hill, L. A., & Lineback, K. (2011). Being the boss in a matrix organization. *Harvard Business Review, 89*(1/2), 123–130.

Kelley, R. E. (1988). In praise of followers. *Harvard Business Review, 66*(6), 142–148.

Klein, G. (1998). *Sources of power: How people make decisions*. MIT Press.

Kolb, D. A. (1984). *Experiential learning: Experience as the source of learning and development*. Prentice Hall.

Konak, A., Clark, T. K., & Nasereddin, M. (2014). Using a case study to teach data communications network design in a flipped classroom. *Journal of Information Systems Education, 25*(1), 47–56.

Leal Filho, W., Brandli, L., Lange Salvia, A., & Vargas, V. R. (2020). Sustainable Development Goals (SDGs): Assessing the contribution of higher education programmes. *Sustainability (Basel), 12*(17), 6701. Advance online publication. DOI: 10.3390/su12176701

Marques, C. S. V., & Tavares, L. R. (2023). *Generation Z: A study on the impacts of the consumer behavior of digital natives in the globalized market*. Centro Universitário Academia UniAcademia.

Mayer, J. D., Salovey, P., & Caruso, D. R. (2008). Emotional intelligence: New ability or eclectic traits? *Annual Review of Psychology, 59*, 507–536. DOI: 10.1146/annurev.psych.59.103006.093646

Merchant, Z., Goetz, E. T., Cifuentes, L., Keeney-Kennicutt, W., & Davis, T. J. (2014). Effectiveness of virtual reality-based instruction on students' learning outcomes in K-12 and higher education: A meta-analysis. *Computers & Education, 70*, 29–40. DOI: 10.1016/j.compedu.2013.07.033

Owens, B. P., Johnson, M. D., & Mitchell, T. R. (2013). Expressed humility in organizations: Implications for performance, teams, and leadership. *Academy of Management Journal, 56*(5), 1517–1538. DOI: 10.5465/amj.2010.0932

Page, S. E. (2007). *The difference: How the power of diversity creates better groups, firms, schools, and societies*. Princeton University Press.

Patel, V., Saxena, S., Lund, C., Thornicroft, G., Baingana, F., Bolton, P., Chisholm, D., Collins, P. Y., Cooper, J. L., Eaton, J., Herrman, H., Herzallah, M. M., Huang, Y., Jordans, M. J. D., Kleinman, A., Medina-Mora, M. E., Morgan, E., Niaz, U., Omigbodun, O., & Unützer, J. (2018). The Lancet Commission on global mental health and sustainable development. *Lancet, 392*(10157), 1553–1598. DOI: 10.1016/S0140-6736(18)31612-X

Padurean, L. (2023). *The job is easy, the people are not!: 10 smart skills to become better at managing people*. Start Disrupt (M) Sdn Bhd. ISBN 978-6-299-66720-9.

Prensky, M. (2001). Digital natives, digital immigrants. *On the Horizon*, *9*(5), 1–6. DOI: 10.1108/10748120110424816

Pulakos, E. D., Arad, S., Donovan, M. A., & Plamondon, K. E. (2000). Adaptability in the workplace: Development of a taxonomy of adaptive performance. *The Journal of Applied Psychology*, *85*(4), 612–624. DOI: 10.1037/0021-9010.85.4.612

Riches, S., Jeyarajaguru, P., Taylor, L., Fialho, C., Little, J., Ahmed, L., O'Brien, A., van Driel, C., Veling, W., & Valmaggia, L. (2023). Virtual reality relaxation for people with mental health conditions: A systematic review. *Social Psychiatry and Psychiatric Epidemiology*, *58*(7), 989–1007. DOI: 10.1007/s00127-022-02417-5

Rogers, C. R., & Farson, R. E. (1957). *Active listening*. University of Chicago Industrial Relations Center.

Scheier, M. F., Carver, C. S., & Bridges, M. W. (1994). Distinguishing optimism from neuroticism (and trait anxiety, self-mastery, and self-esteem): A reevaluation of the Life Orientation Test. *Journal of Personality and Social Psychology*, *67*(6), 1063–1078. DOI: 10.1037/0022-3514.67.6.1063

Siemens. (2021). *The sentient campus: AI-powered environments for holistic education*. Siemens AG.

So, H.-J., Lee, C., Lee, G. Y., & Kim, M. J. (2024). *Artificial intelligence, blockchain and extended reality in lifelong learning*. UNESCO Institute for Lifelong Learning. https://unesdoc.unesco.org/ark:/48223/pf0000391599

Sustainable Development Solutions Network. (2020). *Accelerating education for the SDGs in universities: A guide for universities, colleges, and tertiary and higher education institutions*. https://files.unsdsn.org/210721%20accelerating-education-for-the-sdgs-in-unis-PT.pdf

Twenge, J. M., Joiner, T. E., Rogers, M. L., & Martin, G. N. (2018). Increases in depressive symptoms, suicide-related outcomes, and suicide rates among U.S. adolescents after 2010 and links to increased new media screen time. *Emotion (Washington, D.C.)*, *18*(8), 1185–1200. DOI: 10.1037/emo0000400

UDUAL, Union of Universities of Latin America and the Caribbean. (2022). *UDUAL position statement at the UNESCO World Conference on Higher Education 2022 (WHEC2022): Reshaping the ideals and practices of higher education to ensure the sustainable development of the planet and humanity*. http://dspaceudual.org/bitstream/Rep-UDUAL/1459/6/UDUAL_Posicionamento_PT_WHEC2022.pdf

UNESCO. (2016). *Education for people and planet: Creating sustainable futures for all. Global Education Monitoring Report 2016*. UNESCO Publishing. https://unesdoc.unesco.org/ark:/48223/pf0000245752

Van der Klink, M., Boon, J., & Schlusmans, K. (2007). Competences and vocational higher education: Present and future. *European Journal of Vocational Training*, *40*(1), 73–89. https://www.cedefop.europa.eu/files/etv/Upload/Information_resources/Bookshop/468/40_pt_vanderklink.pdf

VanLehn, K. (2011). The relative effectiveness of human tutoring, intelligent tutoring systems, and other tutoring systems. *Educational Psychologist*, *46*(4), 197–221. DOI: 10.1080/00461520.2011.611369

Wang, Y., Zhang, Y., & Chen, X. (2020). IoT-based smart classroom: Architecture and applications. *Internet of Things Journal*, *7*(10), 9876–9887. DOI: 10.1109/JIOT.2020.2990765

Zongozzi, J. N., & Ngubane, S. (2025). Equitable access to digital higher education for students with disabilities: A realist review. *African Journal of Disability*, *14*(0), 1525. Advance online publication. DOI: 10.4102/ajod.v14i0.1525

Chapter 14
Wi-Fi Channel Information-Based Positioning for Indoor Applications

Ilker Yayalar
https://orcid.org/0009-0002-8897-7838
Aydın Adnan Menderes University, Turkey

Samsun Mustafa Başarici
https://orcid.org/0000-0001-8224-4647
Aydın Adnan Menderes University, Turkey

Irem Beyza Gül
Aydın Adnan Menderes University, Turkey

Mehmet Aydın
Inohom Smart Home Systems, Turkey

Ahmet Çağdaş Seçkin
Aydın Adnan Menderes University, Turkey

Fatih Soygazi
Aydın Adnan Menderes University, Turkey

ABSTRACT

Indoor positioning systems are essential for navigation, asset tracking, and smart building management. Traditional methods like Bluetooth, infrared, and UWB often require extra hardware and high costs, limiting scalability. This study presents a high-accuracy Wi-Fi-based positioning system using Channel State Information (CSI) and Received Signal Strength Indicator (RSSI). Since most devices already include Wi-Fi modules, the approach avoids additional infrastructure while enabling precise indoor localization. A mobile and Windows application collect CSI and RSSI data across 2.4 GHz and 5 GHz bands, and the system processes these signals using pattern matching, machine learning, and deep learning models to

DOI: 10.4018/979-8-3373-6831-3.ch014

2026, IGI Global Scientific Publishing. Copying or distributing in print or electronic forms without written permission of IGI Global Scientific Publishing is prohibited. Use of this chapter to ative artificial intelligence (AI) technologies is expressly prohibited. The publisher reserves all rights to license its use for generative AI training and machine learning model development.

determine the most accurate localization method. The system supports use cases such as attendance tracking, event monitoring, and indoor navigation, with broader applications in healthcare, security, and smart buildings.

INTRODUCTION

In recent years, advancements in signal processing and machine learning have paved the way for innovative applications in various domains, including indoor positioning systems. The ability to determine the precise location of a device indoors is essential for a wide range of applications, such as navigation, asset tracking, and smart building management. Traditional indoor positioning methods often rely on technologies like Bluetooth, infrared, or ultra-wideband, which may require additional hardware and incur significant costs.

This study focuses on developing an indoor positioning system using the channel state information (CSI) of Wi-Fi signals. Wi-Fi-based positioning systems provide a cost-effective and widely available alternative, as most modern devices already come equipped with Wi-Fi modules. By leveraging the unique characteristics of Wi-Fi signal channels, it is possible to accurately determine the position of a device within indoor environments.

Figure 1 illustrates the overall workflow of the proposed system, which utilizes Wi-Fi channel information, particularly Channel State Information (CSI), to achieve indoor localization. The system integrates mobile and windows-based applications for real-time data collection, including detailed access point (AP) information and signal strength across 2.4 GHz and 5 GHz bands.

Figure 1. Workflow

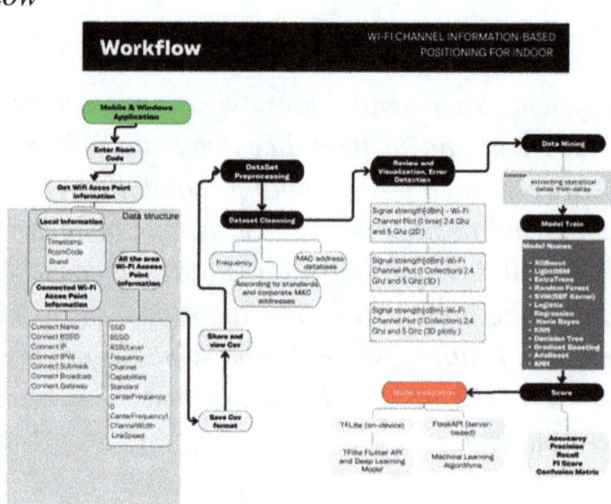

Collected data undergoes a preprocessing pipeline involving dataset cleaning, frequency analysis, MAC address standardization, and statistical feature extraction. These cleaned and structured data points are then used for model training and evaluation.

Several machine learning algorithms—including traditional classifiers (e.g., Decision Trees, Random Forest, SVM), ensemble methods (e.g., XGBoost, LightGBM, AdaBoost), and deep learning architectures (e.g., Artificial Neural Networks)—are compared to identify the most accurate localization strategy. The evaluation metrics include accuracy, precision, recall, F1-score, and confusion matrix.

Finally, the trained models are integrated into real-world applications using frameworks such as TensorFlow Lite (TFLite) and FlaskAPI, enabling deployment on mobile and edge devices for real-time indoor positioning.

Purpose and Scope

This study aims to develop a high-accuracy indoor positioning system using CSI-based Wi-Fi fingerprinting and machine learning techniques. The scope of the research includes:

- Collecting CSI data from a real-world indoor environment using Wi-Fi-enabled devices.
- Developing a machine learning-based localization model to classify different indoor locations.
- ANN-based models were developed to classify various indoor locations based on Wi-Fi signal characteristics.
- Several machine learning algorithms, including ANN-based models, were evaluated to determine the most accurate localization approach and to identify optimal data collection point selection strategies.
- Deployment testing in real-world scenarios, such as a residential home and an office space.
- Evaluation of different data preprocessing techniques, including filtered vs. unfiltered datasets.
- Analysis of dataset volume effects via data collection point optimization.

Hypothesis

The hypothesis of this study is that CSI-based fingerprinting, combined with machine learning models and ANNs, will outperform traditional RSSI-based positioning techniques in terms of accuracy, robustness, and scalability.

Contribution to Industry and Literature

This research provides significant contributions to both academic literature and industrial applications:

Academic Contributions:

- Introduction of a novel CSI-based dataset, supporting both 2.4 GHz and 5 GHz Wi-Fi frequency bands.
- Implementation of a machine learning framework and deep learning framework to evaluate different classification models for indoor positioning.
- Performance comparison of multiple machine learning models and deep learning models, including Random Forest, AdaBoost, k-Nearest Neighbors (KNN), Artificial Neural Networks (ANNs), and related models.

Industrial Contributions:

- Development of a cost-effective and scalable indoor positioning system that can be implemented in environments with existing Wi-Fi infrastructure.
- Potential applications in healthcare (hospital navigation), education (smart classrooms), industrial automation (warehouse tracking), and security (indoor surveillance and monitoring).
- Reduction of hardware dependency, eliminating the need for specialized positioning devices, thus making the system affordable and widely accessible.

Related Work

Previous studies on indoor positioning have explored several methods, which can be classified into three main categories as summarized in Table 1.

Table 1. Related Work

Method	Typical Error Range	Characteristics	References
Access Point (AP) Address Method	3–10 m	Based on the MAC addresses of APs; accuracy depends on AP density and environmental factors.	Yamashita et al., 2020; Pan et al., 2021
Received Signal Strength Indicator (RSSI)	1–5 m	Measures signal strength from multiple APs; enhanced with fingerprinting and sensor fusion techniques.	Song & Qian, 2020; Chang et al., 2015; Poulose et al., 2019; Blasio et al., 2017
Fingerprinting (RSSI-based)	1–3 m	Involves creating a radio map of signal strengths at known locations; accuracy improves with more data.	Chang et al., 2015; Hu et al., 2015; Tang, 2016
Channel State Information (CSI)	< 1 m	Provides detailed channel information; requires advanced hardware and is sensitive to environmental changes.	Wang et al., 2016; García-Fernández et al., 2021

Access Point Address Method

This method determines the location of a device based on the unique MAC addresses of Wi-Fi access points (APs). However, its accuracy is limited by the density of APs and environmental factors, usually resulting in an error range of 3-10 meters (Yamashita et al., 2020; Pan et al., 2021). This method's accuracy can be improved when combined with other techniques such as fingerprinting (Yang et al., 2019; Li et al., 2015).

Received Signal Strength Indicator (RSSI)

RSSI is one of the most commonly used techniques for indoor positioning. It measures the signal strength from multiple APs to estimate the device's location. The accuracy of RSSI can be improved with fingerprinting techniques and typically has an error range of 1-5 meters. However, it is sensitive to noise and multipath effects, which can reduce positioning accuracy (Poulose et al., 2019; Song & Qian, 2020). More precise localization can be achieved by collecting signal strength data from known locations (Chang et al., 2015; Tang, 2016).

Channel State Information (CSI)

CSI provides a more detailed view of the wireless channel by capturing the amplitude and phase of the signal across multiple subcarriers. It allows for more accurate positioning compared to RSSI because it leverages fine-grained changes in the signal caused by the environment. However, CSI requires advanced hardware and processing capabilities and is sensitive to environmental changes. With CSI, an error margin of less than 1 meter can be achieved (Xu et al., 2019; Wang et al., 2016). Additionally, machine learning algorithms can be used to further enhance CSI-based positioning (Liu, 2024; Zou et al., 2015).

Materials and Methods

Materials

The following materials were used in this study:

- Wi-Fi Infrastructure: Access points supporting 2.4 GHz and 5 GHz bands were used for CSI-based data collection.
- Data Collection Mobile Application: A Flutter-based Android/iOS (used on Android) app was developed to collect and store Wi-Fi signal data.
- Data Collection Windows Application: A Python-based app was developed to collect and store Wi-Fi signal data.
- Computer System: A desktop computer was used for data analysis and model training processes.

Methods

This study introduces a cross-platform system initially developed using Flutter for Android mobile devices and Windows desktop environments. However, the Windows version of the Flutter application was found to be insufficiently reliable for the purposes of this study. Therefore, a dedicated Python-based Windows application was implemented instead. Both applications were designed to collect environmental, network, and sensor data in real time, enabling subsequent context-aware analyses such as indoor localization and presence detection.

Although Figure 2 illustrates the structure of the proposed model using only the Flutter-based mobile application, the same architectural flow is equally applicable to both implementations, including the Python-based Windows application.

Figure 2. General Structure of Purposed Model

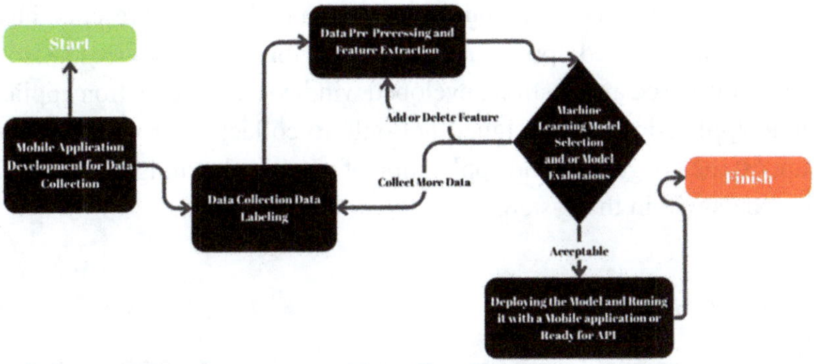

Model Execution Modes

The system incorporates two distinct model execution modes to accommodate different operational environments and resource constraints:

- Server-Based Inference: In this mode, collected data are transmitted to a remote server via a Flask-based API. The server hosts full-scale machine learning models, including complex classifiers such as XGBoost, LightGBM, and Random Forest, which perform the inference. This mode is particularly suitable when high computational resources and stable internet connectivity are available, allowing for more accurate and intensive processing.
- Local Inference: When the application operates offline or in resource-limited conditions, model inference is performed locally on the device using lightweight Artificial Neural Networks (ANNs) models converted to TensorFlow Lite (TFLite) format. This setup ensures low-latency predictions and eliminates dependency on network access, making it suitable for real-time indoor positioning in disconnected or mobile scenarios.

This dual-mode inference architecture enhances the system's flexibility, enabling it to deliver robust and scalable localization capabilities across a wide range of deployment conditions.

DATA COLLECTION

The data collection process is illustrated in Figure 3, which presents the architecture of the Flutter-based application developed for mobile devices. Also, as in Figure 4, Python-based application developed windows data collection application. This mobile application was designed not only to collect environmental data but also to support the integration and application of machine learning models and deep learning models within the system.

Figure 3. Flutter Application

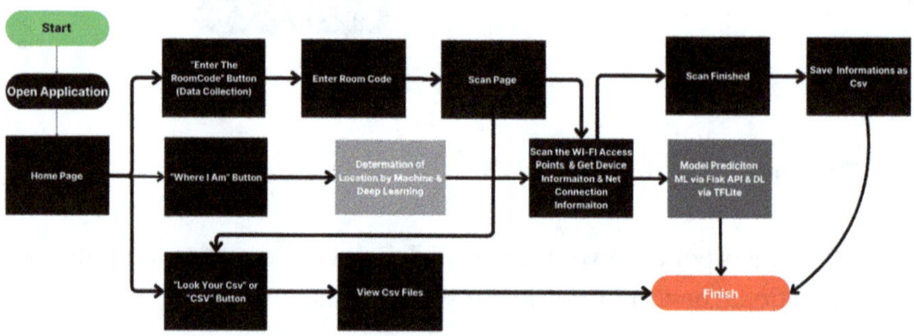

Figure 4. Windows Application

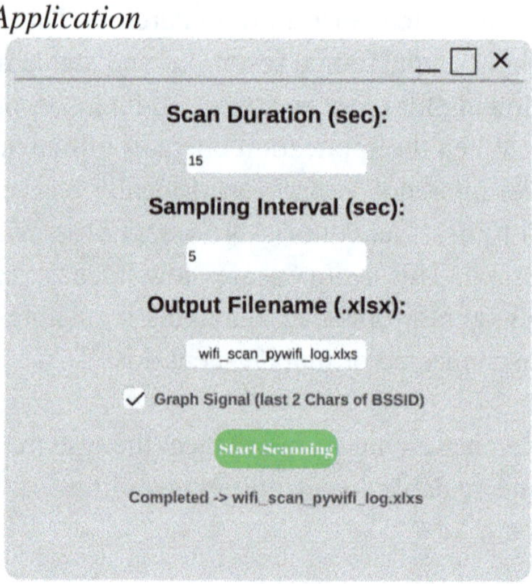

The application operates in both server-based and local modes. When an active internet connection is available, the loaded model works on server-based system via Flask API. In cases where the device is offline, TFLite (TensorFlow lite) is worked on device on request. This dual-mode architecture ensures robustness and continuity in varying network conditions. Additionally, the data is stored locally as CSV (Comma-Separated Values, generally used in Microsoft Excel) format.

The collected data includes multiple modalities such as signal strength measurements (e.g., Wi-Fi RSSI, Bluetooth RSSI), network information (SSID, BSSID. These data types are intended to serve as inputs for machine learning models that perform tasks such as location verification, user identification, or environmental context analysis.

Data Collection

To facilitate the data collection process required for this study, a mobile application has been developed using the Flutter framework and Dart programming language. The application is designed to run seamlessly on both Android and iOS platforms, offering users a convenient and efficient way to gather location-based data.

The main screen of the application provides three primary functionalities (Figure 5).

Figure 5. Application Main and RoomCode Screens

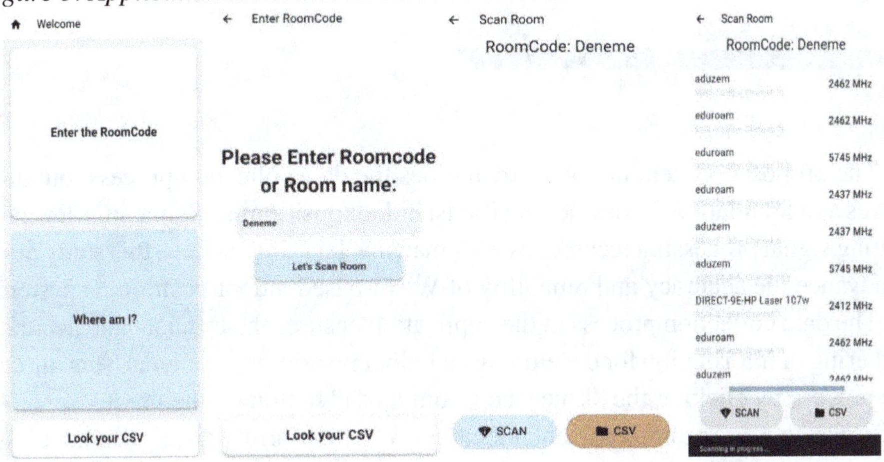

1. "Enter the Room Code": Allows users to input location-related information (e.g., room, classroom, corridor) to label the collected data accurately.
2. "Where am I?": Implements the indoor positioning algorithm to estimate the current location of the device.

3. “Look Your CSV”: Enables users to view previously collected data stored in CSV format.

After entering the room code, users can proceed to the data collection page, where the system collects Wi-Fi signal data for a duration of 15 seconds at a rate of one sample per second. The collected data is then stored in CSV files, ensuring it is readily available for further processing and analysis (Figure 6).

Figure 6. Room Scan and CSV Screens

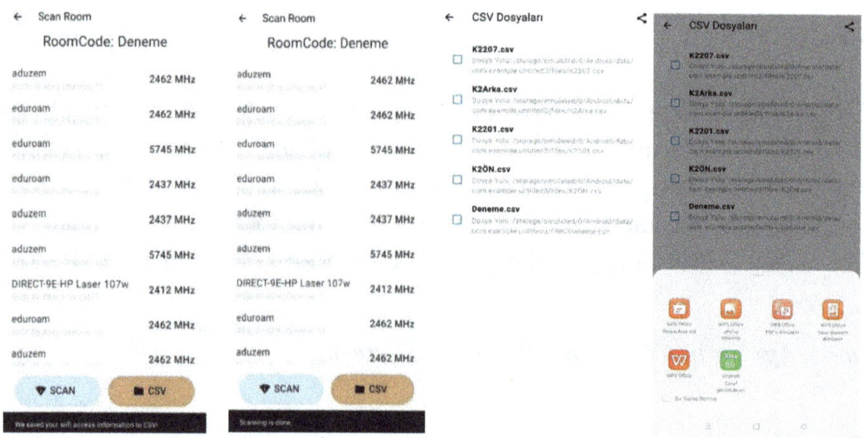

The proposed system not only streamlines the data collection process, but also serves as a foundation for developing robust indoor positioning algorithms. By integrating signal processing techniques with machine learning models, this study aims to advance the accuracy and reliability of Wi-Fi-based indoor positioning system.

The data collection process in the application ensures the efficient and accurate gathering of information for developing an indoor positioning system. Users initiate the process by clicking the “Enter the Room Code” button on the main screen. At this stage, they are prompted to enter location-related information (e.g., room, classroom, corridor). This information is crucial for accurately labeling the collected data.

Once the location information is entered, users are directed to the data collection screen. By clicking the “Scan” button, the data collection process begins. This process collects Wi-Fi signal information from the surrounding environment for 15 seconds, capturing one sample per second. When the collection process is complete, the following messages are displayed to the user:

- “Scanning is done”: Indicates that the data collection process has been successfully completed.

- "We saved your Wi-Fi access information CSV!": Confirms that the collected data has been saved as a CSV file.

The collected data can be viewed using the "Look Your CSV" button on both the data collection screen and the main page. The dataset is optimized for use in training machine learning models and performing signal analysis.

About Collected Data

Below is a detailed description of the collected data:

General Information

1. Timestamp: The timestamp indicating when the data collection started.
2. RoomCode: The location label entered by the user (e.g., room, classroom, corridor).
3. Brand: The brand of the device collecting the data.

Wi-Fi Access Information

1. SSID: The names of the detected Wi-Fi networks.
2. BSSID: The unique identifiers of each detected Wi-Fi network.
3. RSSI/Level: The signal strength level of each detected network (Received Signal Strength Indicator).
4. Frequency: The frequency of the detected Wi-Fi signal (e.g., 2.4GHz - 2437 or 5 GHz - 5180).
5. Channel: The channel used by the detected network.(e.g., 10 or 36)
6. Capabilities: The features and supported security protocols of the Wi-Fi network (e.g., WPA2).
7. Standard: The Wi-Fi standard supported by the network (e.g., 802.11n, 802.11ac).
8. CenterFrequency0: The primary carrier frequency of the channel.
9. CenterFrequency1: The secondary carrier frequency of the channel (if applicable).
10. Channel Width: The width of the channel (e.g., 20 MHz, 40 MHz).
11. Link Speed: The connection speed between the device and the Wi-Fi network.

Connection Information

1. Connect Name: The name of the Wi-Fi network the device is connected to.
2. Connect BSSID: The BSSID of the connected network.
3. Connect IP: The IP address assigned to the device by the connected network.

4. Connect IPV6: The IPv6 address of the device (if available).
5. Connect Submask: The subnet mask of the connected network.
6. Connect Broadcast: The broadcast address of the network.
7. Connect Gateway: The gateway address of the network.

This comprehensive dataset serves as a vital resource for training machine learning models and developing Wi-Fi-based indoor positioning algorithms, contributing to more accurate and reliable localization systems.

PRE-PROCESSING

Cleaning Process for Meaningless Data

To create a reliable access point fingerprint, we followed a systematic approach to clean meaningless BSSID addresses in the dataset. The steps taken are outlined below:

- Cleaning Based on SSID Addresses: Estimated cleaning was performed by analyzing SSID addresses. For environments like companies, general SSIDs or specific OUI patterns were identified and retained. Any other SSID addresses that did not fit these patterns were considered meaningless data and removed.
- Cleaning Based on OUI Dataset: The OUI dataset was used as a reference to identify and clean data. By comparing our dataset with the predefined OUI entries, irrelevant BSSID addresses were eliminated.
- Cleaning Based on Frequency: BSSID addresses with frequencies above average were retained. This ensured that only meaningful and commonly occurring BSSID addresses were included in the dataset.

Datasets Filtering Methods

Main Unfiltered Dataset: Main unfiltered dataset contains the raw dataset containing unprocessed BSSID and SSID information. The filtering methods employed in this work are described below.

- Dataset Filtered by SSID: Dataset cleaned by SSID cleaned was performed by filtering SSIDs.
- Dataset Filtered by OUI Database: Dataset Cleaned by OUI Database is refined by comparing entries with the predefined OUI database.

- Dataset Filtered by Frequency: Dataset Cleaned by Frequency contains BSSID addresses filtered based on frequency above the average.

Wi-Fi access point data was collected from 51 rooms in a three-story building. Multiple measurements were taken from some of the rooms, and data from 16 rooms was collected at least once while the rooms were occupied. This enabled the analysis of Wi-Fi signal variations under different occupancy conditions.

In the subsequent stages of our analysis, we chose to proceed with dataset filtered by SSID. This decision was based on its ability to provide a more consistent and reliable data structure, as well as the general absence of a clearly defined formal access point (AP). Nonetheless, we also included alternative approaches in our study to offer insights and potential guidance for future research.

ANALYSIS OF 2.4 GHZ AND 5 GHZ CHANNELS

Frequency and Channel Analysis

The frequency spectrum utilized for wireless communication is divided into several bands, with the 2.4 GHz and 5 GHz bands being the most common for Wi-Fi communication. Each frequency band is further subdivided into channels, allowing multiple networks to operate simultaneously within the same band while minimizing interference.

5 GHz Band Characteristics

The 5 GHz frequency band offers several advantages over the 2.4 GHz band, including higher data rates and reduced congestion due to a larger number of available channels. However, the 5 GHz band also contains gaps between channels. These gaps occur due to regulatory restrictions and Dynamic Frequency Selection (DFS) requirements, which prevent interference with radar systems.

In Table 2, these gaps are intentionally shown to indicate their presence. If a MAC address appears within these gaps, it suggests an inconsistency in the data collection process, possibly indicating an error in frequency assignment or detection.

Table 2. 5 GHz Band Characteristics

Channel Number	Frequency (MHz)	Type	Availability
36	5180	Non-DFS	Always
40	5200	Non-DFS	Always
44	5220	Non-DFS	Always
48	5240	Non-DFS	Always
52	5260	DFS	Radar Check
56	5280	DFS	Radar Check
60	5300	DFS	Radar Check
64	5320	DFS	Radar Check

Channel Allocation in 5 GHz.

The 5 GHz spectrum is divided into several channels, categorized into Non-DFS and DFS channels: The DFS (Dynamic Frequency Selection) channels require radar detection before usage. If radar signals are detected, the network must switch to a different frequency, leading to possible gaps in data collection.

Explanation of Data Gaps in 5 GHz Band

The gaps are summarized in Table 3.

Table 3. Explanation of Data Gaps in 5 GHz Band

Gap Type	Frequency Range (MHz)	Cause
Regulatory Gap	5350 - 5470	Reserved for weather radar and satellite services
DFS Transition	5260 - 5320	Radar detection and avoidance mechanisms
Band Separation	5725 - 5850	Reserved for other wireless communication standards

These gaps are critical for ensuring compliance with regulatory standards and interference mitigation. If a device's MAC address appears in these ranges, it may indicate erroneous data logging or an anomaly in frequency usage, requiring further investigation.

By analyzing frequency gaps and channel usage, we can identify inconsistencies and validate the integrity of the collected data (Table 4).

Table 4. Frequency to Channel 5 GHz

Channel	Frequency (MHz)		
	F - 10	**Center**	**F + 10**
36	5170	5180	5190
40	5190	5200	5210
44	5210	5220	5230
48	5230	5240	5250
52	5250	5260	5270
56	5270	5280	5290
60	5290	5300	5310
64	5310	5320	5330
100	5490	5500	5510
104	5510	5520	5530
108	5530	5540	5550
112	5550	5560	5570
116	5570	5580	5590
120	5590	5600	5610
124	5610	5620	5630
128	5630	5640	5650
132	5650	5660	5670
136	5670	5680	5690
140	5690	5700	5710
144	5710	5720	5730
149	5735	5745	5755
153	5755	5765	5775
157	5775	5785	5795
161	5795	5805	5815
165	5815	5825	5835

Nb = 25

2.4 GHz Band Characteristics

The 2.4 GHz frequency band is widely used due to its ability to penetrate walls and cover a larger area compared to the 5 GHz band. However, it is more prone to interference because it shares frequencies with various household devices such as microwaves and Bluetooth devices.

The 2.4 GHz spectrum consists of 14 channels, each separated by 5 MHz's. However, due to overlapping frequencies, only three channels (1, 6, and 11) are typically recommended for minimal interference.

Channel Allocation in 2.4 GHz

Table 5 outlines the overlap characteristics of each 2.4 GHz Wi-Fi channel with its adjacent channels. While channels are spaced 5 MHz apart, their signal bandwidth leads to interference across neighboring channels. Channels 1, 6, and 11 are noted as non-overlapping, making them optimal for minimizing co-channel interference in most wireless deployments. In contrast, other channels exhibit significant overlap, which can degrade network performance. Notably, Channel 14 operates at 2484 MHz and is only permitted in specific regions such as Japan. This table complements Table 1 by emphasizing the practical implications of channel selection in wireless networking.

Table 5. Channel Allocation in 2.4 GHz

Channel Number	Frequency (MHz)	Overlap with Adjacent Channels
1	2412	No Overlap with 6, 11
2	2417	Overlaps with 1, 3
3	2422	Overlaps with 2, 4
4	2427	Overlaps with 3, 5
5	2432	Overlaps with 4, 6
6	2437	No Overlap with 1, 11
7	2442	Overlaps with 6, 8
8	2447	Overlaps with 7, 9
9	2452	Overlaps with 8, 10
10	2457	Overlaps with 9, 11
11	2462	No Overlap with 1, 6
12	2467	Overlaps with 11, 13
13	2472	Overlaps with 12, 14
14	2484	Only Available in Certain Regions (as Japan)

Table 6 presents the frequency allocation for Wi-Fi channels in the 2.4 GHz band. Each channel is defined by a central frequency (Center) and its adjacent lower and upper frequency bounds, calculated as Center $\pm$ 10 MHz. The table covers channels 1 through 14, illustrating how the center frequencies increase in 5 MHz steps. This arrangement highlights the overlapping nature of adjacent channels in the 2.4 GHz spectrum.

Table 6. Frequency to Channel 2.4 GHz

Channel	Frequency (MHz)		
	F - 10	Center	F + 10
1	2402	**2412**	2422
2	2407	**2417**	2427
3	2412	**2422**	2432
4	2417	**2427**	2437
5	2422	**2432**	2442
6	2427	**2437**	2447
7	2432	**2442**	2452
8	2437	**2447**	2457
9	2442	**2452**	2462
10	2447	**2457**	2467
11	2452	**2462**	2472
12	2457	**2467**	2477
13	2462	**2472**	2482
14	2474	**2484**	2494

Since the 2.4 GHz band has overlapping channels, channels 1, 6, and 11 are generally recommended for optimal performance in regions where 14 channels are not available.

Mathematical Modeling of Wi-Fi Signal Strength Visualization Using Scaled Sinc Functions

In wireless communication analysis, particularly in dense environments, it is essential to visualize the spectral occupancy and signal strength of Wi-Fi access points in a way that clearly represents channel overlaps and interference patterns. To achieve this, we utilize a mathematical modeling approach based on the scaled *sinc* function, which provides smooth and interpretable curves.

2D Visualization Model

In the 2D representation, each Wi-Fi signal is modeled as a *sinc*-shaped curve over its channel span. The mathematical formulation for the curve *y(x)* is:

$$y(x) = \left(\frac{sinc\left(\frac{x - r_{range}}{l_{range} - r_{range}} - 0.5 \right) - \min(y_{sinc})}{\max(y_{sinc}) - \min(y_{sinc})} \right) . (RSSI + 100) - 100$$

Where:

- x is the Wi-Fi channel domain.
- r_{range} and l_{range} define the signal's spectral boundaries.
- $sinc(z) = \frac{\sin(\pi z)}{\pi z}$ is the normalized *sinc* function.
- RSSI is the received signal strength in dBm.
- The *sinc* curve is normalized and then scaled to match the signal's empirical power level.

This approach results in a smooth bell-shaped curve for each signal, peaking at its center channel and tapering toward the edges, allowing clear observation of spectral overlaps and signal intensity variations.

I. **Frequency Preprocessing and Channel Band Modeling.**

For both the 2.4 GHz and 5 GHz bands, we first convert the absolute frequency into a relative channel space suitable for plotting:

For the 2.4 GHz band:

$$F = f_{signal} - 2407$$

For the 5 GHz band:

$$F = f_{signal} - 5000$$

Where:

- f_{signal} is the center frequency in MHz.
- The constants 2407 and 5000 represent the starting frequency reference of each band respectively.

Then, we calculate the channel boundaries in normalized units (l_{range}= *left Range;* r_{range}= *right Range*):

$$Band\ Range = \frac{ChannelWidth}{20}$$

$$Right\ Range = \left(\frac{F}{5}\right) - Band\ Range$$

$$Left\ Range = \left(\frac{F}{5}\right) + Band\ Range$$

II. **Sinc-Based Signal Curve Construction.**

$$Differentiation = Left\ Range - Right\ Range$$

Given the normalized channel bounds, we model the signal strength using the following sequential steps:

- Define the channel *range (x)*:

We generate 200 equally spaced values between r-range and l-range, representing the frequency or channel span occupied by a Wi-Fi signal.

$$x = linspace(Right\ Range,\ Left\ Range,\ 200)$$

- Normalize the *x* values to the range [0, 1]:

This step normalizes the channel range so we can apply the sinc function centered in the middle. The midpoint of the range becomes 0.5.

$$x_{norm} = \frac{x - Right\ Range}{Differentiation}$$

- Apply the *sinc* function (shifted to peak at center):

We use the *sinc* function $sinc(x) = \frac{sin(x)}{x}$, centered at 0. This models the ideal band-limited signal with a peak in the center and diminishing side lobes.

$$y_{sinc} = sinc(x_{norm} - 0.5)$$

- Normalize sinc output to the range [0, 1]:

To make the signal strength curve fit within a standardized range, we normalize the *sinc* curve between 0 and 1.

$$y_{scaled} = \frac{y_{sinc} - \min\left(y_{sinc}\right)}{\max\left(y_{sinc}\right) - \min\left(y_{sinc}\right)}$$

- Scale according to RSSI (Received Signal Strength Indicator):

RSSI is typically a negative number (e.g., -70 dBm). We map the normalized sinc curve to match the RSSI level, so that the curve peaks at the correct signal strength in dBm. The curve is scaled from -100 dBm up to the measured RSSI.

$y = y_{scaled}(RSSI+100) - 100$

Wi-Fi Strength and Wi-Fi Channel information Graphics

The signal of a Wi-Fi Access Point within a given frequency range is modeled using the *sinc* function as shown in Figure 7, offering a visual representation of:

Figure 7. Wi-Fi Channel Strength Graphic Explanation

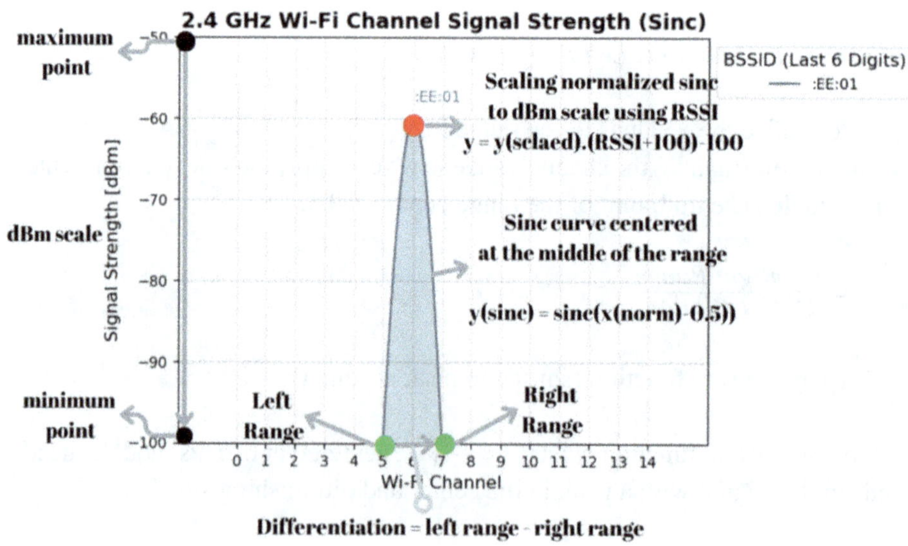

- Channel spread (i.e., channels influenced by the signal),

- Signal strength at the central channel (RSSI),
- Propagation width and boundaries (left/right range), and
- Signal intensity scaled in dBm.

This modeling facilitates a clear understanding of channel overlap, interference analysis, and signal distribution.

In practical scenarios, the signal radiates around a central channel. This propagation is idealized through the *sinc* function, which yields higher values for channels near the center and progressively lower values as the distance increases. This characteristic makes it particularly suitable for evaluating interference and potential channel conflicts in wireless communication systems.

2D Visualization of Wi-Fi Strength and Wi-Fi Channel Information (2.4 GHz & 5 GHz)

The left side of Figure 8 presents the signal strength (dBm) and channel distribution of each access point operating in the 2.4 GHz band. On the other hand, the right side illustrates the same information for the 5 GHz band, enabling a clear comparison between both frequency ranges.

Figure 8. 2.4GHz Wi-Fi Channel Signal Strength (left), 5 GHz Wi-Fi Channel Signal Strength

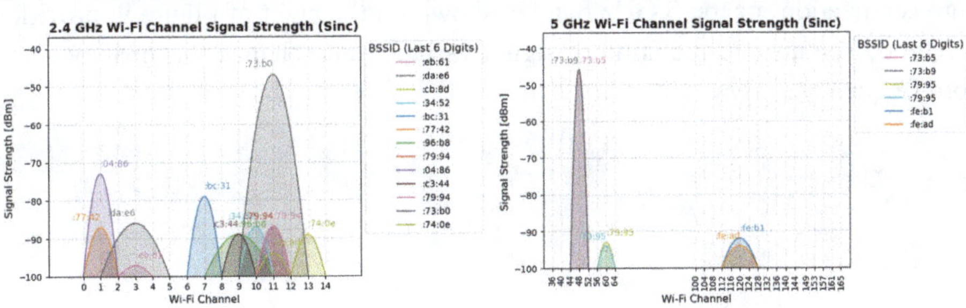

3D Visualization of Wi-Fi Signal Strength over Time and Frequency Using Scaled Sinc Functions

Let the three dimensions be defined as:

- x: normalized frequency/channel domain,

- t: discrete time index or timestamp,
- $y(x, t)$: signal strength at position x and time t.

The equation for the 3D surface at each time step t is given by:

$$y(x,t) = \left(\frac{sinc\left(\frac{x - r_{range_t}}{l_{range_t} - r_{range_t}} - 0.5\right) - \min(s_t)}{\max(s_t) - \min(s_t)} \right) . \left(RSSI_t + 100\right) - 100$$

Where:

- r_{range} and l_{range}: frequency/channel span at time t,
- $RSSI_t$: Signal strength at time t,
- $s_t = sinc\left(\frac{x - r_{range_t}}{Differentiation_t} - 0.5\right)$: sinc values at time t,
- $x \in [r_{range}, l_{range}]$, normalized domain for that signal's channel width.

3D Visualization of Wi-Fi Strength and Wi-Fi Channel Information (2.4 GHz & 5 GHz)

The 3D plot on the left side of Figure 9 illustrates the signal strength and channel usage patterns of access points operating in the 2.4 GHz band, while the corresponding visualization for the 5 GHz band is shown on the right of Figure 9, providing a detailed spatial interpretation of signal variation and channel occupancy across both frequency ranges.

Figure 9. Wi-Fi Strength and Wi-Fi Channel Information, Time for each access point 3D Plot for 2.4GHz (left) and 5GHz (right)

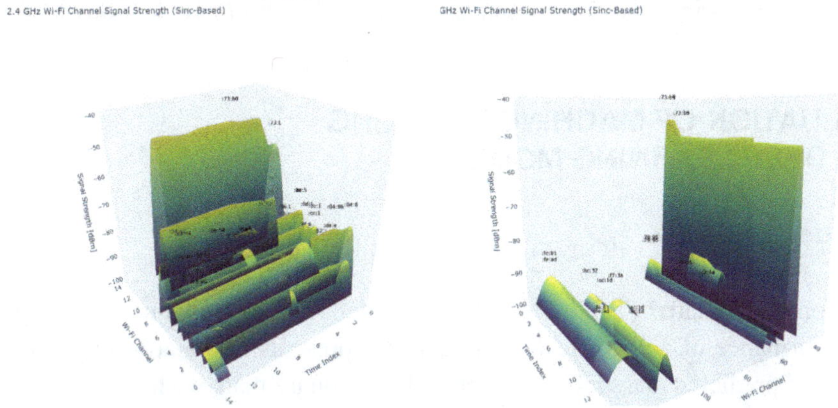

In both visualizations, the color scale represents Wi-Fi signal strength in dBm:

- Yellow denotes regions with the strongest signal levels.
- Green–blue shades indicate medium-level signals.
- Blue–purple shades correspond to the weakest signal levels.

This color mapping helps highlight the spatial distribution and intensity variations of Wi-Fi access points across the environment.

Analysis of Wi-Fi Channel Signal Strength Graphics

In the graphical analysis of the 2.4 GHz band (Figure 8 left), it is evident that the dataset is relatively broad and rich in signal diversity. The power distribution across the 12 available channels indicates consistent activity, with Channel 1 standing out prominently. This suggests that Channel 1 is commonly used as a general waiting or idle connection point in many environments, possibly due to its default configuration in many access points (APs).

On the other hand, the 5 GHz frequency band exhibits a more structured and selective usage pattern (Figure 8 right). Notably, a gap between Channels 64 and 100 is clearly present. This gap is intentional and expected, as it corresponds to a range where Dynamic Frequency Selection (DFS) regulations may apply, and in the current dataset, no active access points were detected within this range.

Signal activity within the 5 GHz band appears to be concentrated primarily in two regions: Channels 44 to 64 and 100 to 128. While the presence of signals in these ranges is consistent, no significant differentiations in signal strength or channel preference were observed within each subrange. This suggests a relatively uniform distribution of usage among available channels in the observed locations.

EVALUATION OF MACHINE LEARNING AND DEEP LEARNING MODELS

Confusion Matrix

A confusion matrix (Table 7) is a fundamental evaluation tool used to visualize the performance of a classification model. It represents the relationship between actual and predicted class labels, structured as a square matrix where:

Table 7. Confusion Matrix

Confusion Matrix	**Actually Positive (1)**	**Actually Negative (0)**
Predicted Positive (1)	True Positives (TPs)	True Positives(FPs)
Predicted Negative (0)	True Positives(FPs)	True Negative (TNs)

- Rows correspond to the actual classes (ground truth),
- Columns correspond to the predicted classes (model output).

Each cell in the matrix indicates the number of instances where a specific actual class was classified as a specific predicted class. The diagonal cells represent correctly classified instances, while off-diagonal cells indicate misclassifications.

In the context of indoor localization, the confusion matrix helps to identify:

- Which indoor locations are frequently confused with each other,
- The sensitivity of the model to each specific class (e.g., rooms, zones, or AP-based segments),
- Potential areas for improvement in data collection or model training.

This matrix is particularly useful in multi-class classification problems, as it provides class-level insight rather than a single global metric.

Accuracy

Accuracy is the ratio of correctly predicted instances to the total instances. It provides a general overview of model performance but may not be sufficient for imbalanced datasets.

$$Accuracy = \frac{(True\ Positives\ (TP) +\ True\ Negatives\ (TN))}{(Total\ Number\ of\ Samples)}$$

Recall

Recall measures the ability of the model to identify all relevant instances. It indicates how many true positives are captured out of all actual positives.

$$Recall = \frac{True\ Positives\ (TP)}{True\ Positives(TP)\ +\ False\ Negatives(FN)}$$

Precision

Precision quantifies the accuracy of positive predictions made by the model. It tells how many of the predicted positives are truly positive.

$$Precision = \frac{True\ Positieves\ (TP)}{True\ Positives(TP) + False\ Positives(FP)}$$

F1 Score

The F1 Score is the harmonic means of precision and recall. It balances the trade-off between precision and recall, especially in cases of imbalanced datasets.

$$\text{F1} = 2 * \frac{((\text{Precision})*(\text{Recall}))}{((\text{Precision}) + (\text{Recall}))}$$

Classification Report

The classification report provides a comprehensive summary of a model's performance across all classes using the following metrics:

- Precision: The ratio of true positive predictions to the total predicted positives for a given class. It answers the question: When the model predicts a certain class, how often is it correct?

- Recall (Sensitivity): The ratio of true positive predictions to the total actual instances of that class. It answers: Of all the actual instances of a class, how many did the model correctly identify?
- F1-Score: The harmonic means of precision and recall. It provides a balance between the two, especially useful when class distributions are imbalanced.
- Support: The number of actual occurrences of each class in the test dataset. It helps to contextualize the precision, recall, and F1-score values.

These metrics are reported per class and can also be averaged:

- Macro average treats all classes equally,
- Weighted average accounts for class imbalance by weighting each metric by the number of instances in that class.

This report enables a more nuanced evaluation of the model beyond overall accuracy, highlighting both strengths and weaknesses in specific classes.

Model Training

The classification models were trained using a dataset comprising 51 distinct classes, each corresponding to a specific room number or indoor location. The input features used for training were derived from signal data collected during the initial data acquisition phase, including various environmental, network, and sensor-based attributes.

To evaluate and compare different machine learning approaches for indoor localization, the following classification algorithms were implemented:

- Tree-Based Ensemble Models:
    - Extreme Gradient Boosting (XGBoost)
    - Light Gradient Boosting Machine (LightGBM)
    - Random Forest
    - Extra Trees Classifier
    - Gradient Boosting
    - AdaBoost
- Traditional Machine Learning Models:
    - Support Vector Machine (SVM) with RBF kernel
    - K-Nearest Neighbors (KNN)
    - Logistic Regression
    - Naive Bayes
    - Decision Tree

Each model was trained using identical feature sets and evaluated using stratified cross-validation to ensure fair comparison. The goal was to identify the most accurate and computationally efficient algorithm for the indoor localization task based on performance metrics such as accuracy, F1-score, and confusion matrix analysis.

Tree-based machine learning algorithms, such as Decision Trees, Random Forests, and Gradient Boosted Trees (e.g., XGBoost), offer several advantageous properties that make them particularly suitable for Wi-Fi-based signal processing and classification tasks.

First, Wi-Fi signal data—such as RSSI (Received Signal Strength Indicator), SSID, BSSID, channel number, and frequency—often contain non-linear relationships and complex interactions between features. Tree-based models are inherently capable of capturing such non-linearities without requiring explicit feature transformations.

Second, tree-based algorithms are robust to outliers and missing data, which are common issues in real-world wireless environments. Signal fluctuations, environmental noise, and temporary interference can cause sudden changes or gaps in data, which tree-based models can handle more effectively compared to linear models.

Third, these algorithms provide high interpretability. The decision paths within a tree structure can be easily visualized and analyzed, allowing researchers or practitioners to understand the importance of individual features—such as which Wi-Fi channels or AP identifiers contribute most to location estimation or device classification.

Additionally, ensemble methods like Random Forest and XGBoost improve upon single-tree models by reducing overfitting and increasing generalization performance. This is particularly beneficial when dealing with large, noisy datasets collected from dense Wi-Fi environments, where overfitting could otherwise compromise accuracy.

Lastly, tree-based models are relatively fast to train and evaluate, especially when implemented with hardware-accelerated libraries. This enables real-time or near-real-time performance in systems requiring quick decision-making, such as dynamic indoor localization or signal anomaly detection.

Model Evaluation Results

As anticipated, tree-based algorithms demonstrated superior performance compared to other models, as evidenced by the evaluation results. Among the top-performing algorithms, further analysis of the confusion matrices is essential to identify specific classes or locations where misclassifications occur. This analysis can provide insights into the model's weaknesses and guide future improvements in data representation or model tuning (Table 8).

Table 8. Model Evaluation Results

Model	Accuracy	Precision	Recall	F1-Score
XGBoost	0.933770	0.936313	0.933770	0.933779
LightGBM	0.928675	0.932186	0.928675	0.928480
Extra Trees	0.914119	0.917760	0.914119	0.914257
Random Forest	0.918486	0.922211	0.918486	0.918772
SVM (RBF Kernel)	0.263464	0.234030	0.263464	0.211349
Logistic Regression	0.422853	0.439322	0.422853	0.389221
Naive Bayes	0.105531	0.104878	0.105531	0.083891
KNN (k=5)	0.831878	0.835594	0.831878	0.829550
Decision Tree	0.919942	0.923762	0.919942	0.919981
Gradient Boosting	0.906841	0.912019	0.906841	0.906291
AdaBoost	0.158661	0.073066	0.158661	0.082847

Detailed Error Analysis

The structure of the dataset clearly reflects the spatial organization of the building. Room numbers beginning with “1” correspond to the first floor, those beginning with “2” to the second floor, and those beginning with “3” to the third floor. Locations labeled with “K” represent corridors. Since one of the objectives of this study was to assess the model's ability to distinguish between rooms and non-room areas, the dataset was designed to capture this distribution. In general, the model using XGBoost successfully differentiates between rooms and corridors as it can been seen in Figure 10.

Figure 10. Confusion Matrix XGBoost (Filtered)

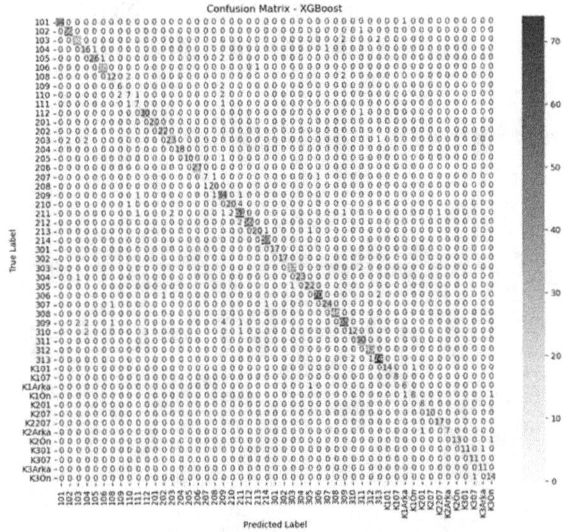

However, detailed inspection of the classification metrics reveals performance inconsistencies, particularly among classes 108, 109, and 110 (Table 9).

Table 9. Model Evaluation Report (XGBoost)

Class	Precision	Recall	F1-Score	Support
108	0.86	0.75	0.80	16
109	0.75	0.75	0.75	8
110	0.64	0.58	0.61	12
111	0.70	0.78	0.74	9

The misclassifications observed among these first-floor room classes may be attributed to low support values, i.e., a limited number of samples in the dataset for those classes. For example, only 8–16 instances exist for these rooms, which limits the model's ability to generalize effectively.

Further analysis of the confusion matrix, particularly the misclassification between class 309 (true label) and 209 (predicted), reveals 4 instances that were incorrectly classified. This suggests that the model may, in certain cases, struggle to distinguish between floors—potentially due to overlapping signal characteristics or insufficient data coverage for specific areas.

Focusing on the LightGBM algorithm's confusion matrix (Figure 11) offers valuable insight into which classes are particularly problematic, helping to identify where the model struggles to learn or generalize effectively.

Figure 11. Confusion Matrix LightGBM (Filtered)

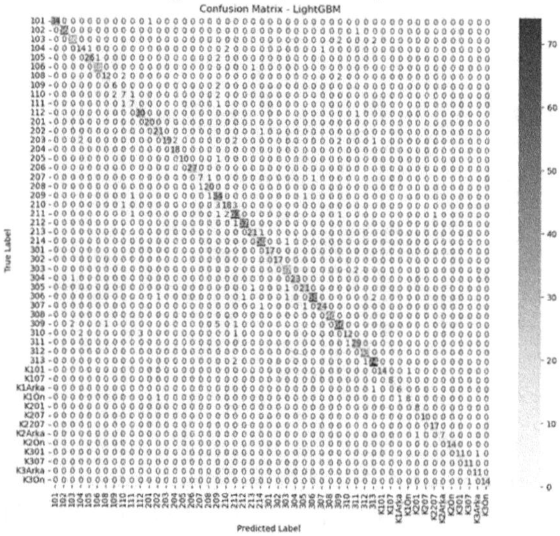

As observed in the updated results above, prediction errors persist for certain room classes, particularly due to the limited number of training samples (low support). This highlights the challenges faced by the model when attempting to generalize across underrepresented classes.

Despite these localized inaccuracies, the overall performance of the LightGBM model remains strong. The results are encouraging and demonstrate the model's potential to be integrated into a real-time system for practical indoor localization, especially when supported with sufficient and balanced data (Table 10).

Table 10. Model Evaluation Report (LightGBM)

Class	Precision	Recall	F1-Score	Support
108	0.80	0.75	0.77	16
109	0.75	0.75	0.75	8
110	0.67	0.67	0.67	12
111	0.57	0.89	0.70	9

ANN-Based Deep Learning Model Architecture

In an effort to enhance the model's learning capacity, we explored the use of deep learning algorithms. Although we were aware that the dataset may not be large enough to fully exploit the potential of deep learning models, our objective was to assess whether better generalization and improved performance could still be achieved with more advanced architectures.

As an initial experiment, we implemented a simple feedforward neural network with the following architecture (Table 11).

Table 11. Deep Learning Architecture

Dense(64, activation='relu')
Dense(output_units, activation='softmax')

Given the complexity of the classification task and the limited dataset size, we anticipated potential difficulties in class-level separation. Nonetheless, the experiment aimed to evaluate the feasibility and limitations of applying deep learning to this problem domain.

The results of this initial approach are presented in Figure 12:

Figure 12. Train and Validation Curves

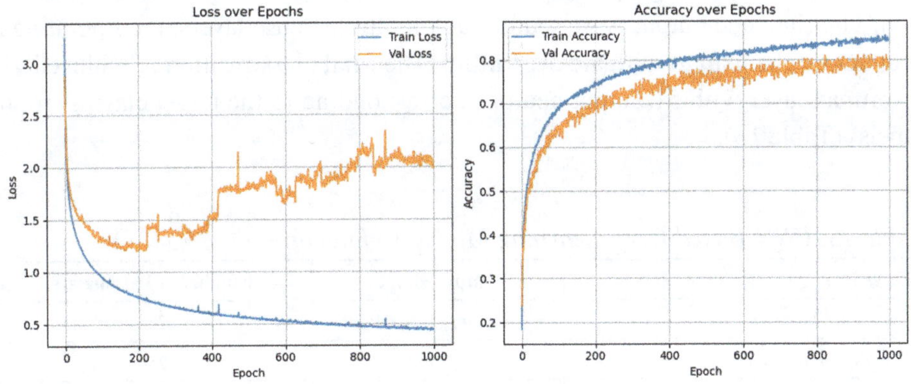

The training and validation curves in Figure 12 clearly indicate the onset of overfitting around the 200th epoch. While the training loss continues to decrease steadily, the validation loss begins to increase and fluctuates heavily, suggesting that the model is starting to memorize the training data rather than generalizing to unseen samples.

This observation is further supported by the performance metrics obtained on the validation set as shown in Table 12.

Table 12. Validation Set Performance Metrics

Accuracy	Precision	Recall	F1-Score
0.7911	0.8199	0.7920	0.7886

Although the model demonstrates acceptable performance, it falls short when compared to the results achieved by traditional machine learning algorithms such as XGBoost, LightGBM, and Random Forest, which consistently yield higher accuracy and greater stability. The findings presented here can be compared by revisiting Table 8 and directly contrasting them with the results shown in Table 12.

Due to these limitations, we decided to explore alternative neural network architectures and transition to more robust and widely adopted deep learning frameworks in order to improve generalization and reduce overfitting.

CNN-Based Deep Learning Model Architecture

The proposed architecture is a hybrid CNN-based model designed to capture both local signal patterns and global temporal dependencies from 1D Wi-Fi signal sequences. It consists of two convolutional blocks, each followed by batch normalization and max pooling layers, ensuring stable training and dimensionality reduction. The flattened output is passed through multiple dense layers, incorporating a dropout mechanism to mitigate overfitting. The final classification is achieved via a softmax layer with 51 output neurons corresponding to the target classes (room labels) (Table 13).

Table 13. CNN-Based Deep Learning Model Architecture

Layer Type	Output Shape	Number of Parameters
Conv1D (64 filters)	(None, 1176, 64)	256
BatchNormalization	(None, 1176, 64)	256
MaxPooling1D	(None, 588, 64)	0
Conv1D (128 filters)	(None, 586, 128)	24,704
BatchNormalization	(None, 586, 128)	512
MaxPooling1D	(None, 293, 128)	0
Flatten	(None, 37504)	0

continued on following page

Table 13. Continued

Layer Type	Output Shape	Number of Parameters
Dense (128 units)	(None, 128)	4,800,640
Dropout	(None, 128)	0
Dense (64 units)	(None, 64)	8,256
Dense (128 units)	(None, 128)	8,320
Dense (51 units, Softmax)	(None, 51)	6,579

Total params: 4,849,523 (18.50 MB)
Trainable params: 4,849,139 (18.50 MB)
Non-trainable params: 384 (1.50 KB)

To enhance training stability and prevent overfitting, learning rate reduction and early stopping techniques were applied. Specifically, the learning rate was automatically reduced during plateau phases of the training at epochs 61 (5.000000237487257e-4), 83 (2.500000118743628e-4), 109 (6.25000029685907e-05), 132 (3.125000148429535e-05), 137 (1.5625000742147677e-05). The training process was terminated at epoch 137 via early stopping, as no significant improvement was observed afterward on the validation loss (Figure 13).

Figure 13. Train and Validation Loss

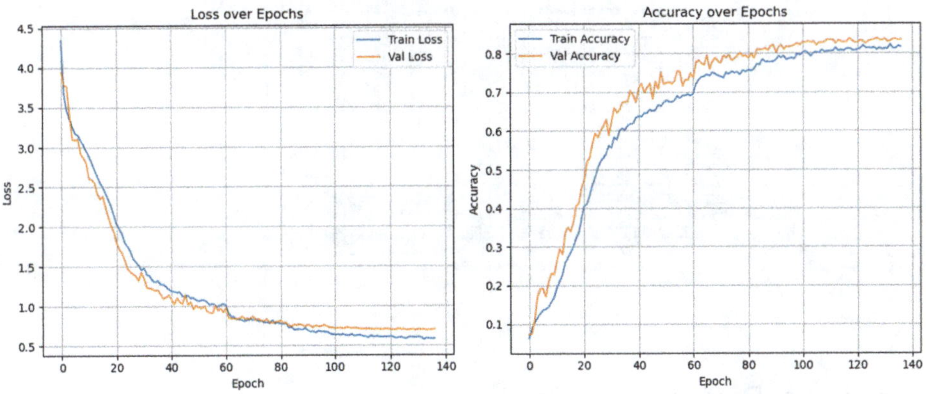

As visualized in Figure 13, both training and validation loss steadily decreased, while accuracy increased consistently without divergence. These patterns suggest that the model benefited from a more stable and effective learning process compared to earlier experiments (Table 14).

Table 14. Validation Set Performance Metrics (CNN)

Accuracy	Precision	Recall	F1-Score
0.8355	0.8506	0.8187	0.8229

CNN based deep learning model, similar to deep learning model and traditional machine learning algorithms also experienced a noticeable performance decline in classifying instances from underrepresented floor levels, highlighting the impact of data imbalance. Among these challenges, distinguishing between floors proved to be particularly difficult for most models.

Figure 14 shows the confusion matrix for the CNN-Based deep learning model used in this study.

Figure 14. Confusion Matrix CNN-Based Deep Learning Models

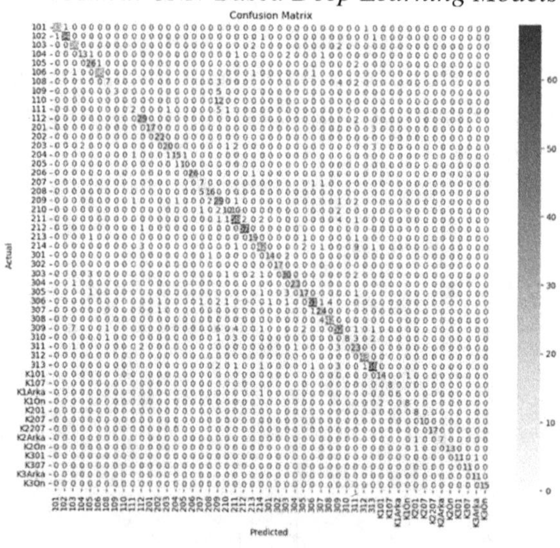

Floor-Level Performance Evaluation

To conduct a more focused analysis, floor-based evaluations were performed. For consistency and comparability, we selected XGBoost—the most robust and high-performing algorithm across previous experiments—as the reference model.

The objective of this evaluation was twofold:

1. To determine whether the model performs better when trained to learn all three floors jointly within a multi-class setup.

2. To assess whether training separate models for each floor individually yields improved classification performance.

This comparative study aims to reveal whether hierarchical modeling (floor-wise) could be a more suitable approach than treating all rooms as flat, independent classes in a single model.

First Floor

The confusion matrix presented in Figure 15 illustrates the classification performance of the XGBoost model specifically on first-floor rooms. Despite certain classes having relatively low support—such as 109, 110, and 111—the model demonstrated strong learning capability and high classification accuracy.

Figure 15. Confusion Matrix of First Floor-XGBoost

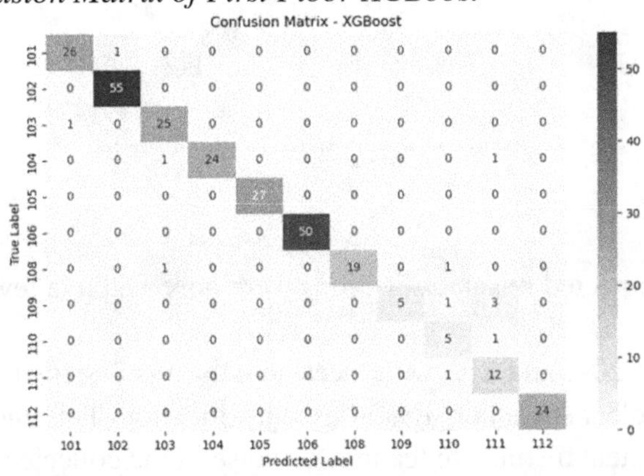

Notably, most misclassifications occurred between adjacent or semantically similar rooms, yet the overall performance remained robust (Table 15).

Table 15. First Floor Performance

Accuracy	Precision	Recall	F1-Score
0.9577	0.9649	0.9577	0.9579

Second Floor

The confusion matrix in Figure 16 displays the model's classification performance for the second floor using the XGBoost algorithm. The model achieved high performance overall, correctly identifying most room classes with minimal misclassification.

Figure 16. Confusion Matrix of Second Floor-XGBoost

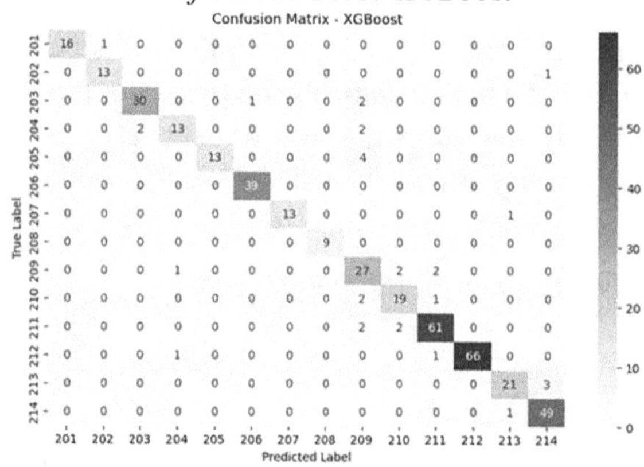

However, unexpected misclassifications were observed in a few cases:

- Rooms 203, 204, and 205 were occasionally misclassified as 209, a result that lacks a clear spatial or signal-based justification. This anomaly may stem from insufficient distinctive features or noise in the collected data.
- Confusion between 213 and 214 is likely due to their spatial proximity or overlapping signal characteristics, which makes boundary differentiation challenging for the model.

Interestingly, in this particular scenario, Random Forest slightly outperformed XGBoost in terms of classification metrics, despite XGBoost being the top-performing model across most previous tests (Table 16 and Table 17).

Table 16. Second Floor Performance Metrics (XGBoost)

Accuracy	Precision	Recall	F1-Score
0.9240	0.9291	0.9240	0.9249

Table 17. Second Floor Performance Metrics (Random Forest)

Accuracy	Precision	Recall	F1-Score
0.9311	0.9369	0.9311	0.9322

An important and consistent error pattern observed across both XGBoost (in Figure 16) and Random Forest (in Figure 17) models is the incorrect classification of classes 203, 204, and 205 as class 209. These classes, although distinct in their physical locations, were repeatedly predicted as belonging to room 209.

Figure 17. Confusion Matrix of Second Floor-Random Forest

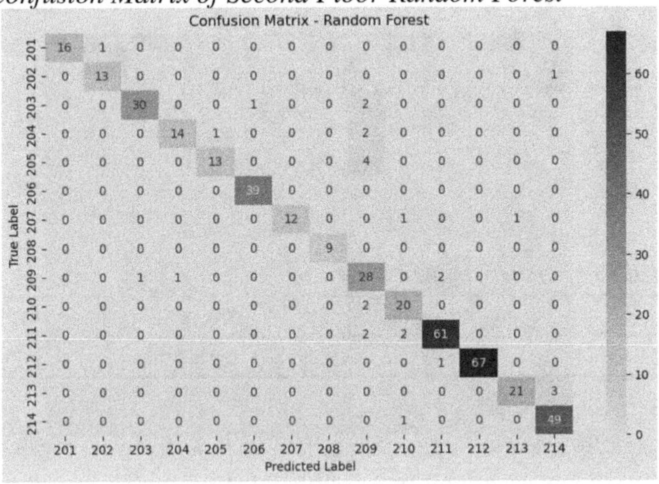

This behavior suggests that the signal characteristics of 203, 204, and 205 may share high similarity with those of 209, potentially due to overlapping Wi-Fi coverage, reflective interference, or environmental similarities in their structural layout. Another possible explanation could be inconsistencies or noise during data acquisition in these specific areas.

Third Floor

The confusion matrix in Figure 18 illustrates the performance of the XGBoost classifier on the third floor, which yielded the highest classification performance among all evaluated floor levels (Table 18).

Figure 18. Confusion Matrix of Third Floor-XGBoost

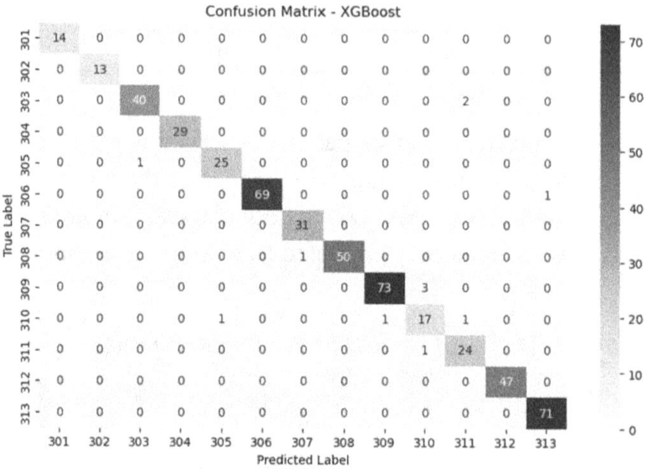

Table 18. Third Floor Performance Metrics

Accuracy	Precision	Recall	F1-Score
0.9767	0.9775	0.9767	0.9769

These outstanding results suggest that the model performs exceptionally well in environments with lower variability, possibly due to:

- Fewer moving entities (e.g., reduced human activity),
- More stable Wi-Fi signal propagation (less interference and signal reflection),
- Less clutter or variability in structural features across locations.

However, a few misclassifications were observed:

- Rooms 309 and 310, which are spatially adjacent, were occasionally confused with each other — a reasonable outcome given their proximity and similar signal environments.
- The misclassification between 303 and 311, however, lacks an obvious explanation, as these locations are not spatially or functionally related. This anomaly may be due to rare signal overlap, mislabeled samples, or outlier behavior in the dataset.

Overall, the results validate that the third floor provided a relatively controlled environment, allowing the model to achieve superior generalization and prediction consistency.

Min-Point Baseline

To investigate how the amount of training data impacts classification performance, we conducted an experiment where the dataset was down-sampled to match the minimum class support—i.e., the number of samples available for the class with the fewest instances. This approach, commonly referred to as a min-point baseline, allowed us to evaluate model performance when all classes have an equal number of samples.

This procedure ensured a class-balanced dataset but significantly reduced the total amount of training data.

The results of this experiment are as shown in Table 19:

Table 19. Min-Point Dataset-Classification Metrics

Accuracy	Precision	Recall	F1-Score
0.7448	0.7775	0.7448	0.7409

As expected, the overall classification performance declined noticeably. This degradation can be attributed to the loss of valuable training information due to dataset truncation. Although class balance was achieved, the limited number of training samples restricted the model's capacity to learn complex patterns and generalize effectively.

These findings underscore the critical importance of maintaining not only class balance but also sufficient data volume when training models for multi-class indoor localization.

Effect of Feature Filtering vs. Raw Feature Input

To evaluate the trade-off between preprocessing complexity and model performance, we conducted a comparison between filtered and unfiltered datasets. Due to the computational overhead and prolonged processing time introduced by the filtering stage, we investigated whether a more flexible, unfiltered approach could offer comparable—or even superior—results.

Surprisingly, the model trained on raw (unfiltered) features achieved higher overall performance, as shown in Figure 19 and Table 20, suggesting that the filtering process may have inadvertently removed informative signal components critical for accurate classification.

Figure 19. Confusion Matrix of Non-Filtered

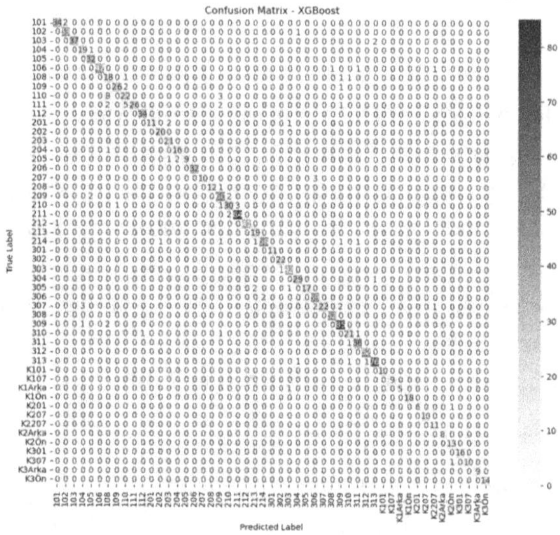

Table 20. Performance Metrics Filtered & Non-Filtered (XGBoost)

Model	Accuracy	Precision	Recall	F1-Score
Filtered Dataset*	0.9338	0.9363	0.9338	0.9338
Non-Filtered Dataset*	0.9391	0.9437	0.9391	0.9390

These findings highlight that while filtering may be useful for noise reduction, it must be applied with caution to avoid suppressing valuable data features. In this case, the unfiltered approach not only simplified the pipeline but also improved the model's generalization ability.

Based on the comparative results, the non-filtered feature set consistently outperformed the filtered version across all evaluation metrics. This suggests that, when system capacity and computational resources are sufficient, bypassing the filtering process can lead to better classification performance. Therefore, in practical applications, especially in environments where preserving subtle signal characteristics is crucial, using the full (unfiltered) dataset may be a more effective strategy.

Real-World Testing

To evaluate whether the proposed system could be extended for real-world industrial use, we conducted field tests in two different settings: a home environment and an office environment.

Real-World Testing in Residential.

Given the compact layout of the apartment, visualizing the testing locations is relatively straightforward. As shown in Figure 20, the blue markers indicate the target modem used for localization, while the yellow markers represent additional modems installed within the home. Red markers denote the specific points where data was collected during testing. The test environment reflects a typical 1+1 (two-main-room) apartment layout, including all common living areas such as a bedroom, living room, open-plan American-style kitchen, bathroom, and balcony.

Figure 20. 2 Room Apartment Layout

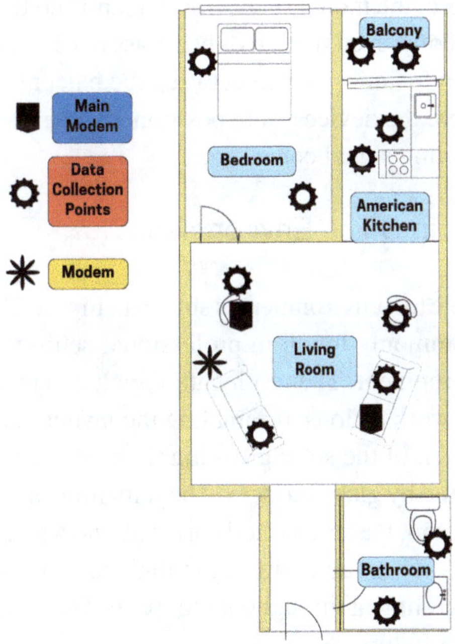

Among all tested models, Random Forest emerged as the top-performing algorithm in this environment (Figure 21).

Figure 21. Confusion Matrix of Apartment

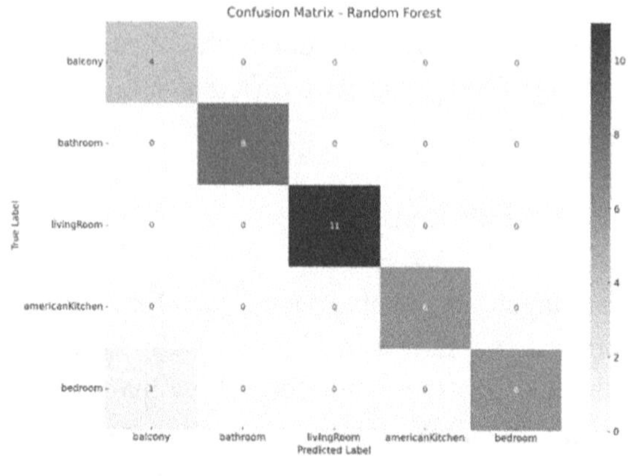

The results are promising. While the model's ability to differentiate rooms separated by walls is expected, its accurate distinction between open-plan areas—such as the American kitchen and living room, which share no physical barrier—is notably impressive. Furthermore, the model successfully identified the separation between the kitchen and the balcony, even though only a glass partition exists between them.

The only notable confusion occurred between the balcony and bedroom, particularly in instances where the devices were positioned either far from or too close to the main modem, affecting signal consistency.

Real-World Testing in Office Environment.

The office used as the test environment is shown in Figure 22. In order to simulate realistic conditions commonly found in professional settings, we conducted tests in a typical office environment. The test location included meeting rooms, passing period, and individual workstations, resembling the layout of a modern workplace. Notably, only one section of the structure—highlighted in blue as the "P" room in Figure 22—was bordered by glass surfaces. The remaining areas, including the "G" room, "A" room, "F" room, Passing Period corridor, and Meeting Room, were fully enclosed by solid walls. The wall regions, highlighted in yellow, created a unique signal propagation environment throughout the space. The confusion matrix for this environment is given in Figure 23.

Figure 22. Office Environment

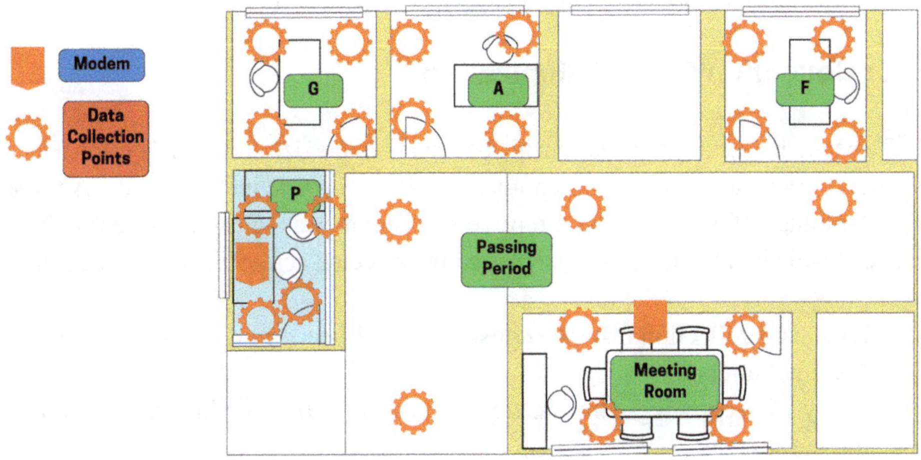

Figure 23. Confusion Matrix of Office Environment

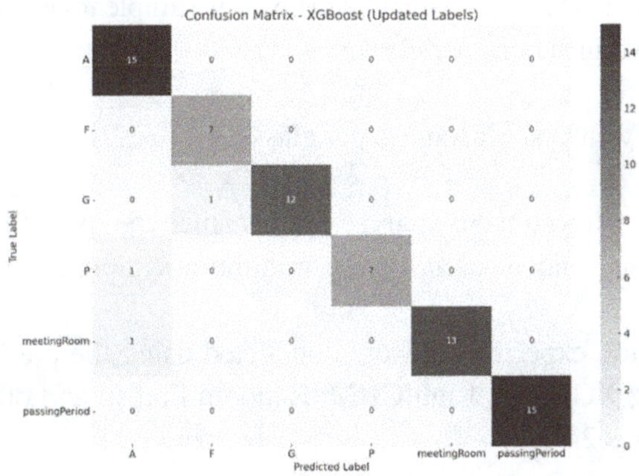

During testing, the Passing Period section exhibited inconsistent predictions. We hypothesize that this may be due to:

- The presence of an unknown signal emitter,
- Limited data availability in that area,
- Or fluctuations in signal quality at the time of collection.

Despite this anomaly, the model demonstrated strong performance in most zones. More importantly, the results indicate that the system is sufficiently accurate to identify the presence and movement of Wi-Fi-enabled devices (e.g., users or smart objects) within the defined spatial boundaries of each room.

Data Collection Point Optimization

To better understand the relationship between sample size and model performance, we incorporated a data collection point optimization phase into our study. A three-story building, referred to as the campus environment, was selected for this analysis, where Wi-Fi signal data were systematically collected across multiple locations.

- Each data collection instance consisted of a 15-second recording, sampled at 1-second intervals.
- Every 15-second segment was treated as a single training instance for modeling purposes.

To explore how increasing the number of samples per class affects classification accuracy, we created 26 incremental subgroups:

- Group 1: One data instance per class (i.e., one sample for each room/location),
- Group 2: Two instances per class,
- …
- Group 26: Twenty-six instances per class.

This approach allowed us to analyze performance trends as the volume of per-class data increased and to identify the minimum sample threshold needed for reliable predictions.

All classification experiments were conducted using the previously discussed models, including XGBoost, LightGBM, Random Forest, and others. The results are given in Figures 24-27.

Figure 24. Data Collection Point Optimization-XGBoost

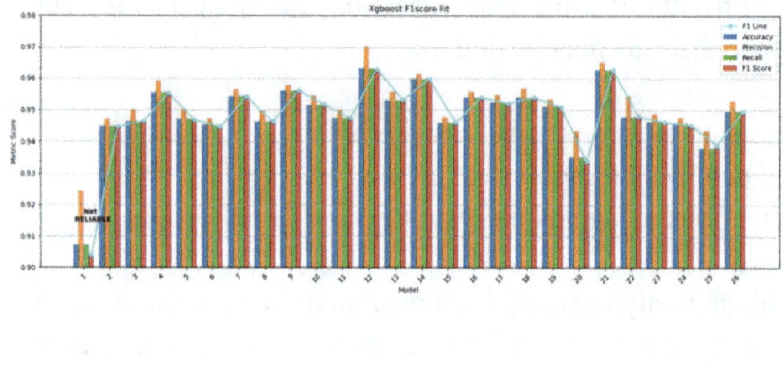

Figure 25. Data Collection Point Optimization-SVM

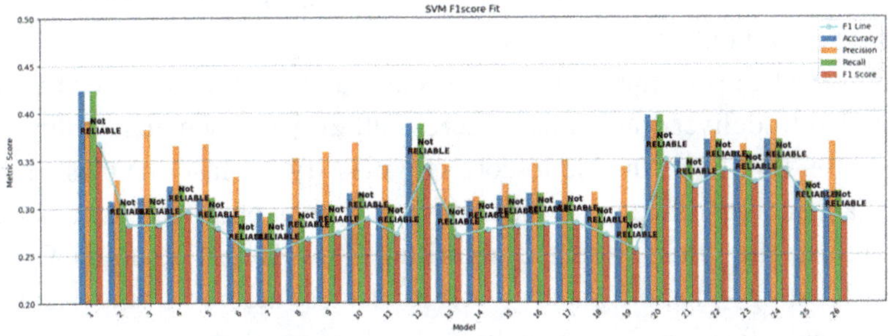

Figure 26. Data Collection Point Optimization-Random Forest

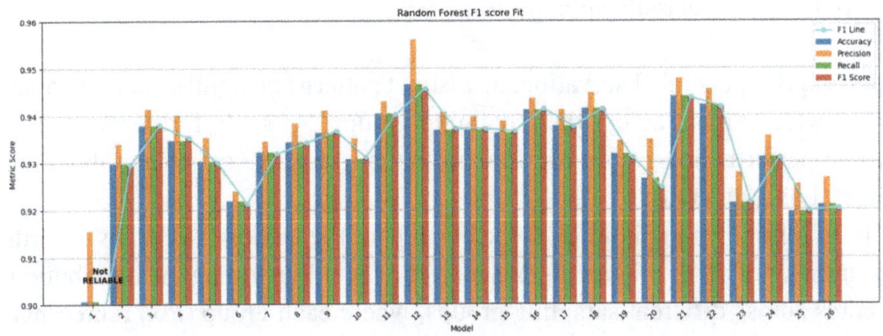

Figure 27. Data Collection Point Optimization-Gradient Boosting

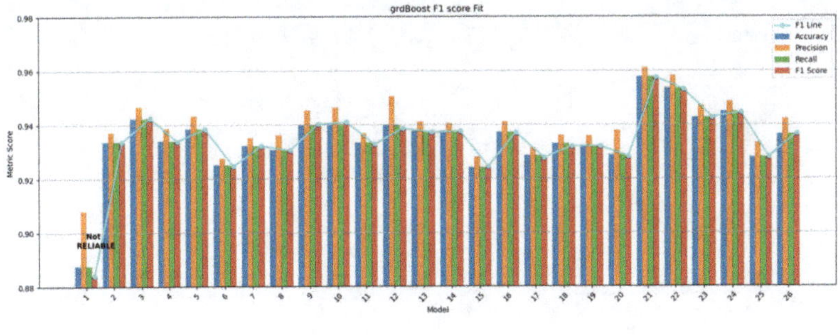

In some cases, certain classes were labeled as "Not Reliable", indicating that the model was unable to consistently recognize or correctly classify those locations.

Such inconsistencies were primarily observed in groups with very limited data per class, reinforcing the need for sufficient data representation to ensure robust and dependable model outcomes.

As observed during the optimization experiments, Support Vector Machine (SVM) failed to deliver stable results across all 26 incremental sampling groups. In every case, SVM was unable to correctly classify at least one class, rendering it less reliable compared to other models when trained on limited data per class.

In contrast, the other evaluated algorithms—XGBoost, Random Forest, and Gradient Boosting—demonstrated greater robustness across varying data volumes. However, results from the visual analysis clearly show that:

- Group 1, which includes only one data instance per class, is consistently unreliable across all algorithms.
- At least two samples per class are required to achieve minimal stability and confidence in classification performance.

Beyond this general observation, no distinct patterns or significant performance changes were evident across the remaining groups. As such, further conclusions from the performance graphs are limited without deeper statistical validation or additional data diversity.

The graph shown in Figure 28 is the box plot of the models' F1-scores according to the number of shots. Figure 28 presents a box plot illustrating the distribution of F1-scores across different sampling groups, where each group (idx) represents an increasing number of data collection instances per class—from 2 up to 26.

Figure 28. Box Plot of Accuracy

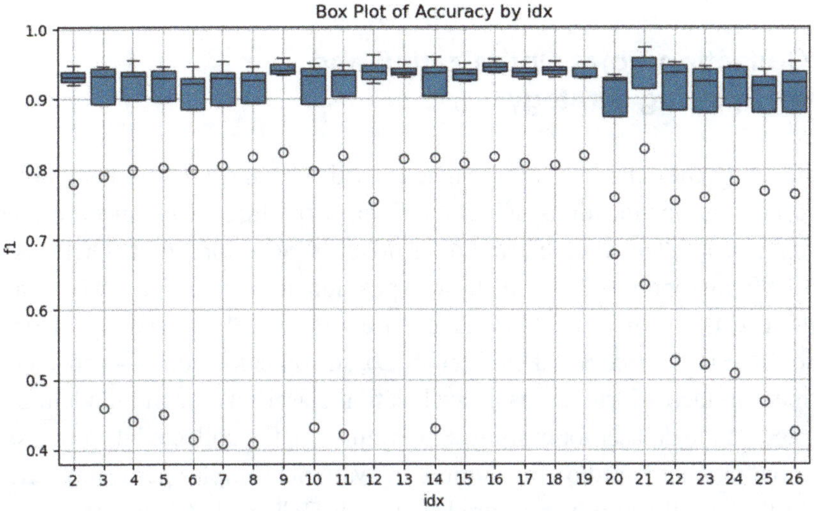

The vertical axis indicates the F1-score, while the horizontal axis corresponds to the group number. Each box summarizes the performance of multiple models trained on that group size, showing median, interquartile range, and outliers.

This visualization provides insight into the stability and reliability of model performance as the number of samples increases.

Key Observations:

- Group 9 appears to be the first group to achieve both high and stable performance, with minimal variation across runs. The small spread in F1-scores suggests the model begins to generalize effectively when at least nine samples per class are provided.
- Group 21 demonstrates the highest overall F1-scores with relatively low variance, indicating that this is the most optimal group in terms of both accuracy and consistency.
- Groups with fewer samples (e.g., 2–5) show wider variability and numerous low outliers, suggesting instability and poor generalization when data is sparse.
- Beyond group 21, performance plateaus, implying that additional data may offer diminishing returns under current conditions.

In summary, the box plot confirms that model performance improves both in accuracy and consistency as the number of samples per class increases. A minimum threshold of 9 samples appears necessary for reliable classification, while 21 samples per class offers the best trade-off between accuracy and data collection effort.

Data Collection Point Optimization and Dataset Splitting Strategy

In this study, the dataset was constructed based on signal measurements collected from various indoor locations using Wi-Fi infrastructure. Each specific location where data was collected is referred to as a Data Collection Point (DCP). A Data Collection Point represents a fixed physical position in the environment (e.g., a room or corridor section) where Wi-Fi signal features—such as Received Signal Strength Indicator (RSSI), Service Set Identifier (SSID), and other metadata—were recorded. These measurements form the basis for location classification and modeling.

To prepare the dataset for training and evaluation, the collected data was split in a structured manner based on the number of available samples per Data Collection Point. In the initial setup, we ensured that each DCP had at least three samples. These were split into 2 training samples and 1 test sample, resulting in a dataset comprising 51 distinct classes, each corresponding to a unique Data Collection Point.

In the second phase of the study, a more focused experiment was conducted by selecting 5 Data Collection Points. From these selected DCPs, data was split into 3 training samples and 2 test samples per location. This refined subset consisted of 41 distinct classes. It is important to note that the excluded data mostly belonged to corridor areas, although not all corridor points were included. This choice was made to evaluate how well the model generalizes to specific structural sections of the indoor environment.

To improve model robustness and achieve more reliable classification performance, a third configuration was implemented by selecting 9 Data Collection Points, with data split into 6 training samples and 3 test samples for each location. In this configuration, no additional filtering or data augmentation was applied; the data was used as collected. This approach was chosen to preserve the natural distribution of the Wi-Fi signal data and to evaluate the model's performance under real-world indoor localization conditions.

The machine learning algorithms used in this study are consistent with those applied in previous works; no modifications were made to the algorithmic structure or model architecture.

Regarding the dataset, three distinct configurations were created to evaluate model performance at different stages:

- First Configuration (2 Tests, 1 Validation, 51 Classes):

This version of the dataset consists of 51 classes, each representing a unique Data Collection Point. The data is split into 1 training sample, 2 test samples, and 1 validation sample per class. This structure reflects the initial stage of the training process and provides a foundation for observing the model's baseline performance (Figure 29).

Figure 29. First Configuration (2 Tests, 1 Validation, 51 Classes)

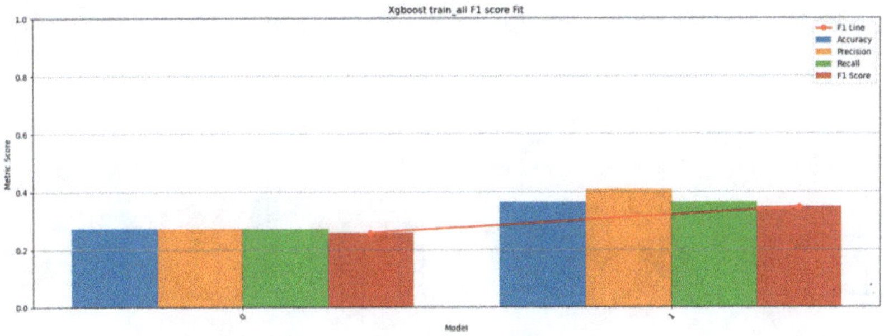

- Second Configuration (3 Test, 2 Validations, 41 Classes):

In this configuration, the dataset includes 41 classes, and the data from each class is divided into 3 test samples and 2 validation samples. This setup corresponds to a more advanced training phase, focusing on a subset of Data Collection Points selected to evaluate more refined classification behavior (Figure 30).

Figure 30. Second Configuration (3 Tests, 2 Validations, 41 Classes)

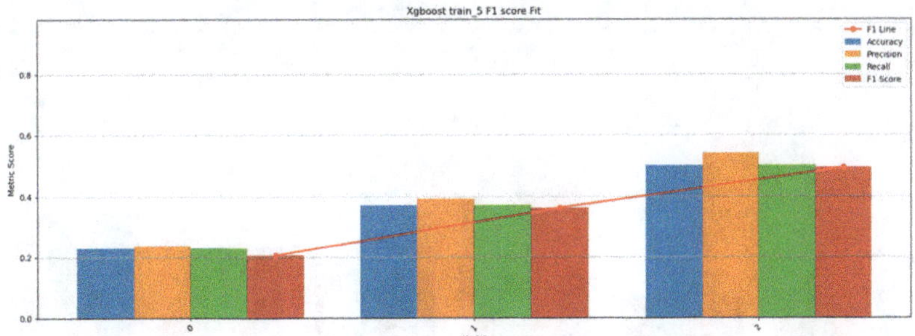

- Third Configuration (6 Trainings, 3 Tests, 29 Classes):

For the final setup, data is split into 6 training samples and 3 test samples per class, resulting in a total of 29 classes. This configuration is designed to analyze the model's performance under more robust training conditions, with an increased amount of training data per class (Figure 31).

Figure 31. Third Configuration (6 Trainings, 2 Tests, 29 Classes)

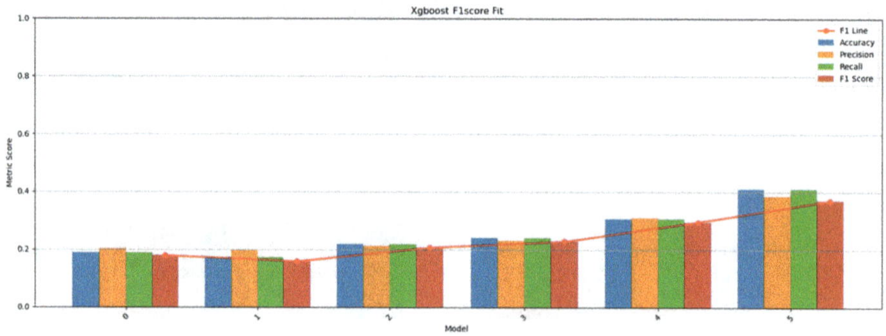

These dataset variations allow for a comprehensive evaluation of model behavior across different data availability scenarios, enabling better insights into generalization capabilities and classification accuracy in Wi-Fi-based indoor localization.

In addition to overall model performance, we also examined whether each algorithm was able to correctly predict the class label (Figures 32-34). In cases where no class prediction was made, the output was marked with the label "Not Reliable" and in case third condition was made about.

Figure 32. Prediction Check (XGBoost)

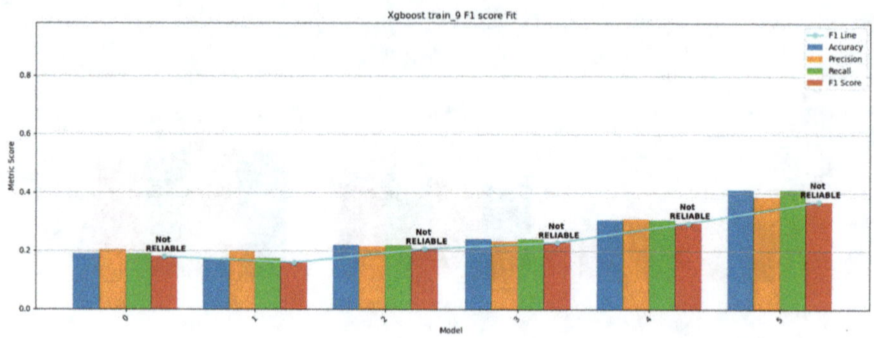

Figure 33. Prediction Check (Gradient Boosting)

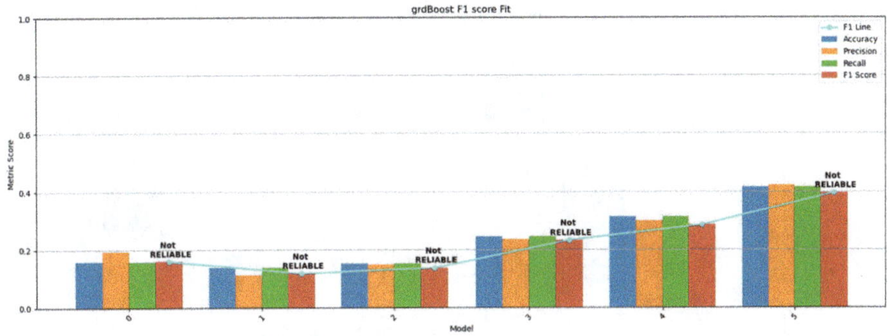

Figure 34. Prediction Check (LightGBM)

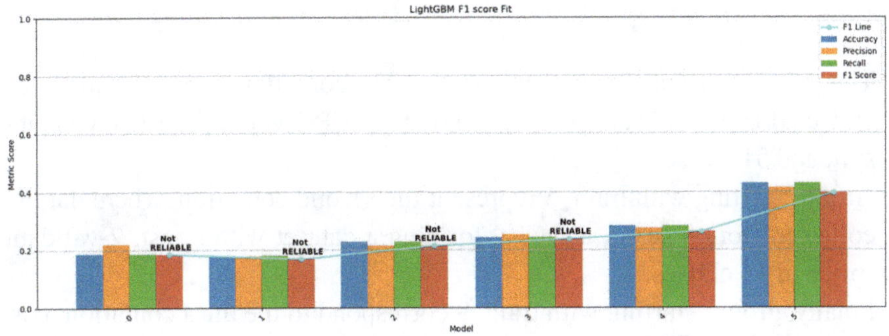

Among the evaluated models, LightGBM demonstrated higher reliability in terms of consistent and valid class predictions. However, in terms of processing speed, XGBoost was found to be more stable. While Gradient Boosting also showed competitive performance, its speed advantage makes it appear to be the most practical choice overall under the current experimental conditions.

In the box plot visualization in Figure 35, each dataset condition is represented as follows:

Figure 35. Box Plot for Accuracy by idx

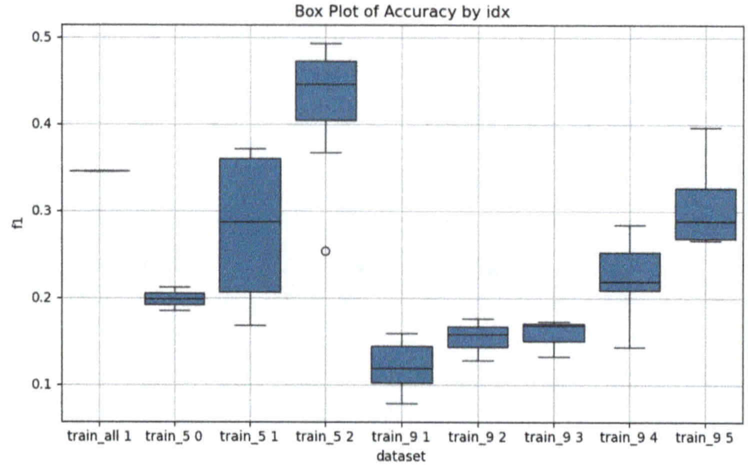

- The train_all group corresponds to the first condition, which includes data collected from all Data Collection Points (DCPs) with a 2-test, 1-validation split and 51 classes.
- Groups starting with train_5 represent the second condition, where data was collected from 5 selected DCPs, forming a dataset with 3-test, 2-validation split and 41 classes.
- Finally, groups starting with train_9 correspond to the third condition, based on data collected from 9 DCPs, with a 6-train, 3-test split and 29 classes.

This structure allows for a comparative analysis of model performance across different dataset configurations in the box plot (Figure 35).

MODEL DEPLOYMENT

In this study, two different deployment strategies were evaluated for the developed indoor localization system: server-based deployment using Flask API and on-device deployment using TensorFlow Lite (TFLite). Both approaches were tested to ensure the system's adaptability under varying operational conditions and to support diverse usage scenarios.

To better illustrate the real-world functionality of both deployment strategies, the "Where Am I" feature of our Flutter-based mobile application was implemented using both methods. The on-device deployment with TFLite is demonstrated in Figure 36 (left), showcasing how the model operates fully offline on the user's device. In contrast, the server-based deployment using Flask API is presented in Figure 36 (right), where signal data is transmitted to a central server for processing.

Figure 36. Frequency to Channel in 5 GHz (TFL (left) and Server-Side Predicted (right))

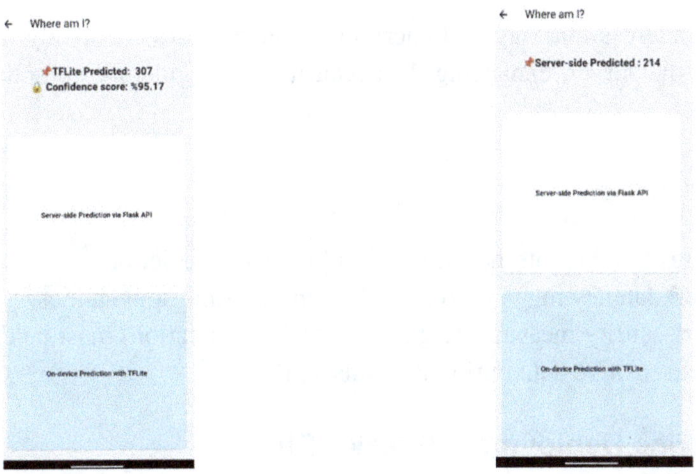

These visual representations help contextualize how each approach is integrated into the application, highlighting their respective advantages in terms of latency, connectivity requirements, and system architecture.

1. Server-Based Deployment (Flask API)

In the server-based scenario, the trained machine learning model is hosted on a central server. Client devices (e.g., mobile or desktop) send collected Wi-Fi signal data to the server via a Flask-based API. The server-side model processes the input and returns the predicted result back to the client.

Workflow:

- The client device collects real-time Wi-Fi signal data.
- The data is sent in JSON format to the Flask API.
- The server-side model performs inference and determines the predicted class.
- The result is returned to the client and displayed to the user.

Advantages:

- The model can be updated centrally without client-side redeployment.
- Requires minimal computational resources on the client side.
- Supports complex and resource-intensive models (e.g., XGBoost, Random Forest).
- Server-side data pipelines enable centralized control over data integrity and label consistency, reducing the risk of model drift or training on corrupted labels.
- MAC address masking and encryption can be more effectively implemented on the server, enhancing data security and regulatory compliance (e.g., GDPR).

Disadvantages:

- Requires a stable internet connection for every prediction.
- Network latency may introduce delays in real-time applications.
- Proper security measures (e.g., HTTPS, authentication) must be enforced to protect sensitive data during transmission.

2. On-Device Deployment (Flask API)

In this approach, the trained model is converted to the TensorFlow Lite format and embedded directly into the mobile application. All inference is performed locally on the device, allowing offline operation and low-latency predictions.

Workflow:

- The trained model is converted to '.tflite' format.
- It is integrated into the mobile application.
- The device collects real-time data and runs inference locally.
- The prediction is generated and displayed instantly.

Advantages:

- Operates without an internet connection.
- Enables real-time inference with minimal latency.
- Preserves user privacy, as no data leaves the device.

Disadvantages:

- Model size and complexity are limited due to device constraints.
- Model updates require app-level redeployment.

- Performance may vary based on the device's hardware capabilities.
- There is no centralized mechanism to validate input data or correct mislabeling, increasing the risk of inconsistent behavior in production.

Both deployment strategies offer distinct advantages depending on application requirements. TFLite-based on-device deployment is preferable in use cases requiring offline access, low latency, and strong privacy guarantees. On the other hand, Flask API-based server deployment provides greater flexibility in managing complex models, performing centralized data validation, and ensuring the security of sensitive information such as MAC addresses. In scenarios where regulatory compliance and data integrity are critical, the server-based approach is the more suitable option. These results are summarized in Table 21.

Table 21. Server-Based vs. TFLite

Feature	Server-Based (Flask API)	On-Device (TFLite)
Execution Mode	Central server	Local device
Internet Requirement	Yes	No
Inference Latency	Medium / High	Very Low
Model Update Flexibility	High (server-side)	Low (requires app update)
Computational Load	On server	On device
Data Privacy	Moderate (requires protection)	High (no transmission)
Model Complexity Support	High	Limited (lightweight models only)
Label/Data Quality Control	High (centralized)	Low (device-dependent)
MAC Address Security	Strong (masking/encryption possible server-side)	Weak (developer-dependent on device)

In this study, a comprehensive indoor localization system was developed based on Channel State Information (CSI) fingerprinting and evaluated using both on-device (TFLite) and server-based (Flask API) deployment architectures. The system leveraged Wi-Fi signal characteristics to classify user positions across 51 distinct indoor locations.

A wide range of machine learning algorithms, including tree-based models (XGBoost, Random Forest, LightGBM) and artificial neural networks (ANNs), were employed to assess classification performance. Among these, tree-based models—particularly XGBoost and Random Forest—demonstrated the highest accuracy overall. However, the inclusion of ANNs provided a complementary perspective, particularly in capturing complex, nonlinear patterns inherent in CSI-based data, offering competitive results in specific scenarios.

Floor-specific analyses revealed that classification accuracy was highest on the third floor, which contained fewer classes and exhibited lower environmental variability. This emphasizes the sensitivity of CSI-based localization systems to spatial complexity and environmental noise.

Experiments comparing filtered and unfiltered datasets showed that models trained on unfiltered CSI data outperformed those using filtered inputs. This indicates that the filtering process may inadvertently remove subtle signal features critical for accurate localization, underlining the importance of preserving raw signal characteristics in CSI-based systems.

Furthermore, the effect of dataset size and balance was examined. When the dataset was equalized to match the minimum class size, performance significantly declined. This finding reinforces the necessity of sufficiently large and diverse datasets in training robust models, especially when leveraging high-dimensional CSI fingerprints.

Overall, this study highlights the effectiveness of CSI fingerprinting for indoor localization and demonstrates that combining it with both classical machine learning and neural network approaches can yield high-resolution spatial awareness, particularly when deployed under realistic constraints on mobile and edge devices.

Industrial Scenario Testing

To evaluate the system's effectiveness in real-world conditions, tests were conducted in two environments: a home setting and an office environment.

- Home Environment Test: In a 1+1 (2 room) apartment, RSSI data were collected from various areas including the kitchen, living room, bedroom, and balcony. While room separation by physical walls was expectedly detected with high accuracy, the model also successfully distinguished between open-plan kitchen and living room areas and between the kitchen and balcony, which were only divided by glass. The main misclassification occurred between the bedroom and balcony, likely due to their distance from access points. Random Forest achieved the best performance in this setting.
- Office Environment Test: Testing was also conducted in a glass-walled office environment consisting of meeting rooms and open workspace areas. Misclassifications in the "Passing Period" zone may have resulted from an unknown signal source, data quality issues, or limited data availability. Nevertheless, the model reliably located devices or users within specific rooms, indicating its practical viability in enterprise scenarios.

Data Collection Point Optimization

To perform a deeper analysis, a data collection point optimization process was added to the study. A three-floor building labeled "Campus" was used, where data were collected for 15 seconds at 1 second per location. Each 15-second collection was treated as a single data sample.

A total of 26 groups were created, where:

Group 1 contained one sample per class,

Group 2 contained two samples per class,

... up to Group 26.

Models were trained using the previously benchmarked algorithms.

Key Findings:

- SVM consistently failed to classify at least one class across all 26 groups.
- XGBoost, Random Forest, and Gradient Boosting could not reliably classify with only one sample per class.
- A boxplot analysis of F1-scores showed that performance stabilized beginning with Group 9, and Group 21 achieved the highest classification accuracy and consistency.
- These results emphasize that both the number and the richness of class samples significantly influence generalization performance, and that insufficient data leads to model instability or underfitting.

REFERENCES

Blasio, G., Quesada-Arencibia, A., García, C. R., Molina-Gil, J., & Caballero-Gil, C. (2017). Study on an indoor positioning system for harsh environments based on wi-fi and bluetooth low energy. *Sensors (Basel), 17*(6), 1299. DOI: 10.3390/s17061299 PMID: 28587285

Chang, Q., Velde, S. V. d., Wei-ping, W., Li, Q., Hou, H., & Steendam, H. (2015). Wi-fi fingerprint positioning updated by pedestrian dead reckoning for mobile phone indoor localization. Lecture Notes in Electrical Engineering, 729-739. DOI: 10.1007/978-3-662-46632-2_63

Chang, Q., Velde, S. V. d., Wei-ping, W., Li, Q., Hou, H., & Steendam, H. (2015). Wi-fi fingerprint positioning updated by pedestrian dead reckoning for mobile phone indoor localization. Lecture Notes in Electrical Engineering, 729-739. DOI: 10.1007/978-3-662-46632-2_63

Dang, X., Ren, J., Hao, Z., Hei, Y., Tang, X., & Yan, Y. (2019). A novel indoor localization method using passive phase difference fingerprinting based on channel state information. *International Journal of Distributed Sensor Networks, 15*(4), 155014771984409. DOI: 10.1177/1550147719844099

García-Fernández, M., Hoyas-Ester, I., Lopez-Cruces, A., Siutkowska, M., & Banque-Casanovas, X. (2021). Accuracy in wifi access point position estimation using round trip time. *Sensors (Basel), 21*(11), 3828. DOI: 10.3390/s21113828 PMID: 34205872

Hu, X., Shang, J., & Han, Q. (2015). Improving wi-fi indoor positioning via ap sets similarity and semi-supervised affinity propagation clustering. *International Journal of Distributed Sensor Networks, 11*(1), 109642. DOI: 10.1155/2015/109642

Jēkabsons, G., Kairish, V., & Zuravlyov, V. (2011). Wi-fi tabanlı iç mekan konumlandırma doğruluğunun analizi. *Riga Teknik Üniversitesi Bilgisayar Bilimleri Bilimsel Dergisi, 44*(1), 131–137. DOI: 10.2478/v10143-011-0031-4

Li, H., Chen, X., Jing, G., Wang, Y., Cao, Y., Li, F., … & Han, X. (2015). Akıllı telefonlarda sensörleri ve wi-fi'yi birleştirerek hareket halindeyken iç mekan sürekli konumlandırma algoritması. Sensörler, 15(12), 31244-31267. Türkçe: DOI: 10.3390/s151229850

Liu, S. (2024). Parmak izi tabanlı derin öğrenme sınıflandırıcısı ile drone için üç boyutlu iç mekan konumlandırma şeması. *Drones (Basel), 8*(1), 15. DOI: 10.3390/drones8010015

Pan, H., Xiang, Y., Xiong, J., Zhao, Y., Huang, Z., & Xiao, X. (2021). Application of a wifi/geomagnetic combined positioning method in a single access point environment. Wireless Communications and Mobile Computing, 2021(1). DOI: 10.1155/2021/9717629

Poulose, A., Kim, J., & Han, D. S. (2019). A sensor fusion framework for indoor localization using smartphone sensors and wi-fi rssi measurements. *Applied Sciences (Basel, Switzerland)*, *9*(20), 4379. DOI: 10.3390/app9204379

Song, M., & Qian, J. (2020). Underground coal mine fingerprint positioning based on the ma-vap method. *Sensors (Basel)*, *20*(18), 5401. DOI: 10.3390/s20185401 PMID: 32967180

Tang, P. (2016). Wi-fi fingerprint localization using rssi-probability radio map and ap weight clustering. *Journal of Advances in Computer Networks*, *121-124*, 121–124. Advance online publication. DOI: 10.18178/JACN.2016.4.2.215

Wang, R., Li, Z., Luo, H., Zhao, F., Shao, W., & Wang, Q. (2019). Yığılmış gürültü giderici otokoder ve çok katmanlı algılayıcı kullanan sağlam bir wi-fi parmak izi konumlandırma algoritması. *Uzaktan Algılama*, *11*(11), 1293. DOI: 10.3390/rs11111293

Wang, X., Gao, L., Mao, S., & Pandey, S. (2016). Csi-based fingerprinting for indoor localization: A deep learning approach. *IEEE Transactions on Vehicular Technology*, •••, 1–1. DOI: 10.1109/TVT.2016.2545523

Wang, X., Gao, L., Mao, S., & Pandey, S. (2016). Csi-based fingerprinting for indoor localization: A deep learning approach. *IEEE Transactions on Vehicular Technology*, •••, 1–1. DOI: 10.1109/TVT.2016.2545523

Wang, Y., Xiu, C., Zhang, X., & Yang, D. (2018). Wifi indoor localization with csi fingerprinting-based random forest. *Sensors (Basel)*, *18*(9), 2869. DOI: 10.3390/s18092869 PMID: 30200285

Xu, S., Chen, R., Yu, Y., Guo, G., & Huang, L. (2019). Dahili sensörler ve gelişmiş parçacık filtresiyle wi-fi menzili kullanarak akıllı telefonların iç mekanlarda yerinin belirlenmesi. *IEEE Access : Practical Innovations, Open Solutions*, *7*, 95140–95153. DOI: 10.1109/ACCESS.2019.2927387

Yamashita, K., Oyama, S., Otani, T., Yamashita, S., Furukawa, T., Kobayashi, D., Sato, K., Sugano, A., Funada, C., Mori, K., Ishiguro, N., & Shiratori, Y. (2020). Smart hospital infrastructure: Geomagnetic in-hospital medical worker tracking. *Journal of the American Medical Informatics Association : JAMIA*, *28*(3), 477–486. DOI: 10.1093/jamia/ocaa204 PMID: 33316057

About the Contributors

Ashraf Alam currently holds the position of Research Faculty at the Centre of Excellence in Public Policy, Sustainability and ESG Research, housed within the Faculty of Law and Policy Studies at Alliance University, Bangalore. Renowned for his transdisciplinary acumen spanning education, technology, and policy studies, Dr. Ashraf has been distinguished as one of the World's Top 2% Scientists by Stanford University and Elsevier, an accolade that highlights the breadth and depth of his scholarly impact. His prolific academic output includes over fifty SCOPUS-indexed publications and more than one hundred conference presentations at esteemed national and international academic forums. His educational trajectory reflects both depth and versatility: a Ph.D. in Education from the Indian Institute of Technology (IIT) Kharagpur, an M.Ed. with a concentration in Mathematics Education, and a B.S. in Computer Science from the University of Delhi. He also holds postgraduate degrees in Public Administration (M.A.) and Mathematics (M.Sc.), supplemented by a suite of postgraduate diplomas in Higher Education, Guidance and Counselling, Educational Technology, Criminology and Police Administration, and Value Education. Dr. Ashraf is an active participant in global scholarly discourse. As Associate Editor of Frontiers in Education, he plays a pivotal role in curating and guiding intellectual contributions across the Educational, Pedagogical, and Learning Sciences. Concurrently, he serves as Founder and Director of Academic Chronicles Private Limited, where he orchestrates editorial board formation and develops strategic frameworks for peer-reviewed publishing in the Social, Behavioural, and Humanistic Sciences. His research has been disseminated through elite academic platforms, including Elsevier, Springer, Taylor & Francis, Wiley, Routledge, Sage, Emerald, and IEEE, and addresses a remarkably diverse array of topics such as pedagogical theories, educational administration, educational psychology, educational sociology, educational policy, technology-integrated learning, mathematics education, educational philosophy, educational technology, teacher education, and AI/ML in learning environments.

Dr. Ashraf's scholarly rigor is further demonstrated by his success in qualifying multiple prestigious examinations including UGC-NET-JRF in both Education and Adult and Continuing Education, UGC- NET in Public Administration, and GATE in Humanities and Social Sciences. At the heart of Dr. Ashraf's intellectual ethos lies a steadfast belief in education as a catalytic and emancipatory force capable of engendering social justice, human flourishing, societal progress, and sustainable transformation. His recent explorations into 'Happiness Engineering' and holistic well- being in school ecosystems articulate a vision of education that transcends instrumentalist paradigms, prioritizing emotional intelligence, global consciousness, empathy, and psychosocial resilience among learners. His research agenda seeks to conceive educational praxis through the affordances of inclusive digital learning, gamified instructional design, and artificial intelligence (AIEd), thereby constructing robust, ethically grounded frameworks for 21st century education. At Alliance University, Dr. Ashraf remains committed to architecting pedagogical models that not only cultivate intellectual dexterity and cognitive excellence but also prepare learners for morally responsive leadership, intellectual nimbleness, and responsible global citizenship in an increasingly volatile, uncertain, complex, and ambiguous (VUCA) world.

Reenu Bansal has held the position of Assistant Professor in the Business & Management Department at Christ University. Before Delhi Metropolitan this she was working with Delhi Education (DME), Noida since 2021. Before joining DME, she worked as Assistant Professor in the Finance Department at IILM for 4 Years and worked as Program Director-UG with IMS Noida for 8 years. She has earned her BCCA & MBA degree from Maharshi Dayanand University, Rohtak (Haryana) in the year 2005 and 2007 respectively. She obtained her PhD from University of Rajasthan, Jaipur in the year 2016. She has rich corporate and academic experience of more than 16 years. She has guided successfully research scholars under her guidance and also invited as a resource person in various workshops and seminars. Participated in various National & International Conferences, she has presented more than 20 papers so far and 10 of her papers were published in International and National Journals & Conference proceedings. Also she has published book chapters. Her areas of teaching and research interests includes financial management, financial services, management of financial institutions, financial accounting, cost accounting, managerial accounting, and digital finance.

Samsun M. Başarici received his MSc in Informatics from Universität Hamburg, Germany and PhD degree from the International Computer Institute, Ege University, Türkiye. Currently, he is a Professor/Researcher in the Department of Computer Engineering in the Faculty of Engineering at Adnan Menderes University,

Aydın, Türkiye. He has written several international and national scientific papers and books. He has authored papers in refereed journals and international conference proceedings and has been actively serving as a reviewer for international journals and conferences. He has also authored a book and edited a conference proceeding. He acted as a coordinator of diverse international (EU) and national projects. He also worked in the industry for many years.

Shikha Bhagat is an expert in International Business and Marketing. She graduated with a gold medal from Guru Nanak Dev University. Dr. Shikha earned her Ph.D. from Noida International University, specializing in international business. With over 14 years of experience, she has published numerous papers and book chapters. Her work appears in prestigious journals indexed in Scopus and Web of Science. Dr. Shikha regularly participates in academic forums and conferences on global business trends. Her research excellence has earned her Best Paper Awards at international conferences in 2023 and 2024. As an Assistant Professor at Christ University, she is committed to mentoring students. Dr. Shikha emphasizes practical applications and critical thinking in her teaching. She is a member of the International Social Marketing Association. This highlights her active role in global academic and professional communities. Her career reflects a dedication to research, education, and scholarly collaboration.

Vojtěch Blažek is a researcher at the Department of Geography at the University of South Bohemia in České Budějovice. His academic and research interests lie primarily in GIS, geoinformatics, geographical education, spatial data analysis, and cartography—with a strong orientation toward the practical and pedagogical use of GIS in schools and teacher education. His work frequently combines GIS-based mobility research, spatial modelling, and the integration of geospatial technologies into geography teaching, as illustrated by numerous co-authored publications on mobility patterns, transport geography, and the use of intelligent transport systems. He is also active in applied research and cross-disciplinary educational projects, including recent work on gamification and community-based heritage preservation, contributing to international publications in the field of information systems and cultural heritage. Across his teaching, research, and publication activities, he is committed to advancing the role of GIS and modern geospatial technologies in education, supporting innovative and data-rich approaches to teaching geography, and improving the overall quality of geographical education.

Hugo Miguel Carvalho, is a university professor, CEO of Neuro IT, member of the board of FISICARE, Business Angel, teacher, researcher and clinician. PhD in Applied Neurosciences in Emotions for Brain Mapping and Neurophysiological

Signal Collection from the University of Beira Interior- Portugal. She is a specialist in Communication Sciences and in Marketing and Advertising, both by public exams, from ISCIA Aveiro and has a Master's degree in Design and Neurosciences with a specialization in Cognitive Rehabilitation from the University of Aveiro. He is part of the clinical team, being director of the Mental Health Unit at FISCARE, in Aveiro-Portugal, he is a researcher at CIDETH, ISCIA and Lipis- Pontifical Catholic University of Rio de Janeiro- Brazil. He is General Manager and Research Director of Neuro IT, Administration Advisor of Fisicare and Business Angel. He is a professor at ISCIA, University of Beira Interior (UBI), ISCAP, Isla Gaia, CESPU, IEES, European University and AEAAV. He is the founder of the project "Negócios à (sobre)mesa", "Pigo", "Abac- Aveiro Business Angels Club", "Geisertech", he is also a national ambassador of "Ignite Portugal". Co-author of the book Business Management with People on Board, author of the book Corporator: How to avoid the main management mistakes and coordinator, co-author of the book Networking One Hundred (100) Scenes Vol I and II and the book Strategia: Analysis of the Strategic Environment of Companies.

Madhurima Chakraborty is an Assistant Professor in the School of Education at Adamas University, West Bengal, India. Her academic and research interests focus on English language teaching, teacher education, and the advancement of inclusive, equitable, and innovative pedagogical practices. With expertise in educational psychology and emerging trends in digital and inclusive education, she is dedicated to bridging theory, policy, and classroom practice. Dr. Chakraborty has contributed to numerous national and international publications and actively participates in academic forums aimed at enhancing the quality, accessibility, and responsiveness of contemporary education.

Mark Elliot spent several years working at EY, auditing clients in the banking and capital markets, insurance, and wealth and asset management sectors, and qualified as a Chartered Accountant. He's worked across multiple jurisdictions, including the UK, Channel Islands, and Luxembourg, accruing a plethora of experience with IFRS, FRS 102, and LuxGAAP financial reporting standards. In addition to time in professional practice, Mark worked within a "Mayor Combined Authority", investing in projects that contributed economic benefits to the city region. His investment portfolio included business resilience programmes, local authority-owned assets, digital and innovation, transport, and social capital investment funds. At Arden University, Mark lectures in Financial Reporting, Audit and Assurance, and Taxation.

Francisco José García Peñalvo is a Full Professor in the Department of Computer Science and Automation at the University of Salamanca (USAL), with 4 research sexennia, 1 technology transfer sexennium, and 5 teaching quinquennia recognized. He received the Gloria Begué Award for Teaching Excellence in 2019 and the María de Maeztu Award for Research Excellence in 2023. Additionally, he was a Distinguished Professor at the School of Humanities and Education at Tecnológico de Monterrey, Mexico, from 2016 to 2018, and is an International Impact Researcher at the National University of San Agustín, Arequipa, Peru. Since 2006, he has been the director of the GRIAL Research Group (Research Group on Interaction and eLearning), recognized by USAL and a Consolidated Research Unit of the Junta de Castilla y León (UIC 81). He is included in the World's Top 2% Scientists list by Stanford University (2019, 2020, 2021, 2022, 2023). He has supervised 30 doctoral dissertations. He served as Vice-Dean of Innovation and New Technologies at the Faculty of Sciences of USAL from 2004 to 2007 and Vice-Rector of Technological Innovation at the same university from 2007 to 2009. Currently, he is the Deputy Director of the University Institute of Educational Sciences (IUCE) and the Coordinator of the Doctoral Program in Education in the Knowledge Society at USAL. He is the Editor-in-Chief of the journal Education in the Knowledge Society and an Associate Editor for Computers in Human Behavior, Computers in Human Behavior Reports, IEEE Access, among others, having previously been an associate editor for IEEE RITA and IEEE Transactions on Learning Technologies. He has published over 100 articles in journals indexed in JCR SCIE/SSCI (63 in Q1). For more detailed information on his publications, the following are public links to his profiles: Google Scholar, WoS, Scopus, and ORCID.

Petra Karvánková is an Assistant Professor at the Department of Geography at the University of South Bohemia in České Budějovice. She earned both her Master's degree and Ph.D. in Geography at Masaryk University in Brno, completing her doctoral studies in 2010. Her scholarly work focuses on geographical and global education, with an emphasis on improving the quality of teaching and learning geography across different educational levels. She is deeply engaged in topics such as inquiry-based learning, project-based approaches, modern didactic methods, and the integration of digital and geospatial technologies into geography education—areas that are further reflected in her editorial and authorship contributions to works on contemporary geography education in Central Europe. At the University of South Bohemia, she teaches a wide range of courses spanning didactics of geography, field-based instruction, global development education, cartography, and physical geography, contributing to both teacher preparation and broader geography curricula. Her recent research outputs include international journal articles on modern geography teaching, STEM-oriented geo-education, geoheritage evaluation, and the role of gamification in preserving cultural legacy, highlighting her interdisciplinary orientation and contribution to innovation in geography education.

Lenny Marzulina works as a lecturer researcher and head of English education study program in the State Islamic University of Raden Fatah, Palembang, Indonesia. She obtained her undergraduate and graduate degrees in English Education from Sriwijaya University, Indonesia. Her research interests are on the area of education, language teaching, material development, and TEFL. E-mail: hj.lennymarzulina@gmail.com

Kunj Bihari Meena is a faculty member and researcher in Computer Science and Engineering at Jaypee University and Engineering Technology Guna. Dr. Meena has published multiple papers in reputed international journals and conferences, including SCI and Scopus-indexed publications. He has received Best Paper Awards for his research contributions and serves as a reviewer for prestigious SCI/Scopus journals and conferences. His areas of research include image processing, digital image forensics, deep learning, and blockchain.

Senthilmurugan Paramasivan is a passionate member of the team which is working towards producing effective management professionals. Adroit in marketing with 23 years of aggregate experiences in industry and academia, he holds MBA specialized in marketing, qualified in UGC-NET & SET and Doctoral degree in the field of Consumer Behavior. He is currently serving as an Associate Professor in School of Business and Management at Christ (Deemed to be) University, Bangalore. He is also Academic Coordinator for BBA Finance and International Program. Dr. Senthilmurugan Paramasivan associated with industries for 9 years and worked in branding, advertising, media, space marketing and corporate sales. He has been in academia & research for last 14 years and transferring knowledges to pupil in consumer behavior & Neuromarketing, marketing communications, digital marketing and strategic management spheres. Dr. Senthilmurugan Paramasivan has published research articles and book chapters in Scopus, Web of Science, and UGC-indexed journals and books. He has co-authored one book on "Consumer Behavior and Neuromarketing in Digital Age" and has presented several papers at national and international conferences. His broad area of research interest is in Consumer behavior, New media marketing and Data driven marketing.

Yash Parsai is an aspiring researcher and technology enthusiast with a strong interest in artificial intelligence, machine learning, and innovative applications of data-driven systems. He has worked on projects integrating deep learning, computer vision, and automation frameworks for practical problem-solving. His recent research focuses on developing intelligent systems for digital transformation and improving real-world decision-making through AI-powered solutions. Yash is passionate about combining creativity with technology to build impactful innovations that enhance learning, efficiency, and accessibility.

Ricardo Pocinho holds a degree in Law, a PhD in Training Processes from the University of Salamanca, and a PhD in Psychogerontology from the University of Valencia, with a Post-Doctorate in Education Sciences, specializing in Lifelong Education and Adult Training, from the University of Coimbra. He is a Doctor Honoris Causa from the University of Peru and the Federal University of Tocantins, Brazil, an Honorary Professor at Rey Juan Carlos University in Madrid, and a Commendator of Maturity in Brazil. He serves as an Adjunct Professor at the School of Education and Social Sciences of the Polytechnic of Leiria and is an Integrated Researcher at CICS.NOVA.IPLeiria. He is the President and Scientific Coordinator of the National Association of Social Gerontology. As the Director of RIAGE – Ibero-American Journal of Gerontology, he is currently a student in the Psychology undergraduate program at the University of Coimbra.

Vivek Kumar Rai is a student of Bachelor of Technology (B.Tech) in Computer Science and Engineering. He has shown great interest in the field of technology and programming. He has learned various programming languages and tools such as C++, Kotlin, Python, Firebase, and Android Studio.

Carolina Resende is a doctor in Psychology, university professor, researcher in socio-emotional competencies, corporate mental health, and NR-1 consultant with emphasis on psychosocial risk management. She has been an individual consultant for UNDP/UN since 2020 on the theme of Soft Skills and leadership competencies. She has experience in Organizational and Work Psychology, Organizational Behavior, and People Management. Corporate consultant in leadership development programs; accident management, mental health, quality of life at work; diversity and inclusion. Guest professor and consultant at ENAP (National School of Public Administration) teaching classes in the LideraGOV Program since 2020. She is an adjunct professor (Adjunct Professor IV) at PUC Minas since February 2009, where she also holds leadership roles in various management positions (collegiates, vice-rectorate, among others) and coordinates university extension programs and projects, scientific initiation, and TCC advising. PhD in Psychology from the Catholic University of Minas Gerais (2014), with a sandwich doctorate at Université Paris Descartes (Paris V), funded by CAPES (2012). Master's in Psychology (2007). Holds specialization in Institutional Analysis and Schizoanalysis from the Félix Guattari Institute (2004) and in Direct Approach to the Unconscious (2016). Graduated in Psychology from PUC Minas (2003).

Jiří Rypl is a researcher specialising in geotourism and geomorphology. His work includes evaluating the potential of geotourism in the border regions between the Czech Republic and Austria. He aims to promote sustainable tourism practices and enhance understanding of geomorphological features in these areas.

Ratan Sarkar is an Assistant Professor in the Department of Education, Tezpur University (A Central University), Assam, India. Previously, he served nearly seven years as Assistant Professor in the Department of Teachers' Training (B.Ed.), Prabhat Kumar College, Contai (Vidyasagar University), and as Guest Faculty at National Institute for Empowerment of Persons with Intellectual Disabilities, Regional Centre, Kolkata. He holds a Ph.D. in Education from Pondicherry University, an M.Ed. and M.Phil. in Special Education from Ramakrishna Mission Vivekananda Educational and Research Institute, Belur Math, and an M.A. in Education and Technology from Tata Institute of Social Sciences, Mumbai. He began his academic journey with a B.Ed. in Special Education (Jadavpur University) and a B.A. in English (Hons) from Siliguri College (University of North Bengal), Darjeeling. Dr. Sarkar has published extensively in leading journals (SAGE, Springer, Routledge, Wiley), authored books, chapters, and reviews, and led projects under the Ministry of Education, Govt. of India. His works on inclusive education, EdTech, disability studies, policy advocacy to advance equitable learning ecosystems.

Shilpa Sarvani, a distinguished Marketing Professor at Christ University, is a seasoned expert in Marketing Management. Holding a PhD in Retail Marketing from GITAM University, she seamlessly integrates academic rigor with practical insights, drawing from her four-year stint as an In-Store Brand Manager at Colgate-Palmolive Limited. Dr. Sarvani boasts five years of teaching experience in prominent Bengaluru universities, employing innovative methodologies that emphasize case studies and industry collaborations. Her extensive industry connections contribute to a dynamic learning environment, providing students with the latest insights. An accomplished researcher, Dr. Sarvani has authored thirteen papers in esteemed journals, including those indexed by ABDC and Scopus and also contributed chapters to the Scopus indexed books. Her commitment to advancing knowledge is further exemplified by her participation in national and international conferences. Notably, she received multiple best paper award at various international conferences. Driven by a passion for education and industry relevance, Dr. Shilpa Sarvani stands as a thought leader, inspiring students to navigate the ever-evolving marketing landscape. Her area of in interest and expertise in research lie with Retail marketing, Private label brands, organised retail, e commerce, digital marketing, Advertising and sustainable marketing.

Julio Sierra is a executive, entrepreneur, professor, and writer with over 25 years of experience in leadership, strategic management, and people development. He is the Founder and CEO of CHROMA LEADERSHIP SCHOOL, where he currently offers four postgraduate lato sensu programs in partnership with the University of Caxias do Sul and the Metropolitan University of Science and Technology, focusing on training leaders in the financial market through high-impact executive education programs. He holds extensive national and international academic credentials, having earned his PhD through research on the relationship between managerial discretion and performance at UNINOVE's PPGA, as well as an Advanced Certificate for Executives from MIT's Sloan School of Management. Author of the book Nobody Cares Until They Know How Much You Care, one of the best-selling books on Leadership on Amazon Brazil. A reference in leadership and humanized management, he has held corporate roles such as Vice-President of CAIXA (2019 and 2022–2023) and CEO of CAIXA CARTÕES (2020–2021).

Manjot Singh is a student at Christ (Deemed to be University), Bangalore, India. His academic interests include digital education, equity in higher education, and technology-enabled learning. He is passionate about exploring inclusive and innovative approaches that enhance accessibility and engagement within digital learning environments.

Jiří Šmída is the Head of the Department of Geoinformatics and Didactics of Informatics at the Technical University of Liberec. His research includes the use of GIS in epidemiology and geographical education. He is dedicated to integrating GIS technologies into public health studies and improving the methods of teaching geography.

Michal Staněk is a Ph.D. student at the Faculty of Education, University of South Bohemia in České Budějovice. His research focuses on STEM teaching and the didactics of Geography.

Muhammad Usman Tariq is a strategic higher education leader and scholar with more than 17 years of international experience across academia, research, and industry. He holds dual doctorates, a PhD in Artificial Intelligence and a Doctorate in Business Administration and has published extensively as the author of research articles, case studies, book chapters, and academic texts. His contributions also include several patents, reflecting his applied research in technology, business, and education. He is the Founder and CEO of TheCaseHQ.com, a global hub for professional certification programmes, narrative and video case studies, and digital learning innovation. In addition, he serves as President of the Gulf Higher Education Network (Gulf HE), an initiative dedicated to advancing academic practice, faculty development, and institutional collaboration across the region. He is a Principal Fellow of Advance HE (UK), Chartered Fellow of the CIPD (UK), Senior Fellow of SEDA (UK), and a Senior Member of IEEE, reflecting his standing as both an academic innovator and a global professional leader.

Francisco R. Trejo-Macotela is a Professor at the Polytechnic University of Pachuca (UPP), a National Researcher under the SECIHTI (Secretariat of Science, Humanities, Technology, and Innovation) programme, and an Adjunct Researcher at the National Laboratory of Autonomous Vehicles and Exoskeletons (LANAVEX). He obtained his PhD in Electronics from the National Institute of Astrophysics, Optics and Electronics (INAOE), Puebla, Mexico. His primary research interests include integrated circuit design, analogue and digital systems, automation, embedded systems, smart cities, RF electronics, telecommunications systems, precision agriculture, and the Internet of Things and among others.

Shreyansh Tripathi is a passionate computer science student at Jaypee University of Engineering and Technology (JUET), Guna. His interests lie in full-stack development, artificial intelligence, and computer architecture. He has gained hands-on experience in developing web applications using technologies such as HTML, CSS, JavaScript, React, and Java for backend development. Shreyansh is also enthusiastic about exploring the integration of AI and machine learning into practical applications, including projects like intelligent note summarization. With a focus on continuous learning and innovation, he aims to build scalable and impactful software solutions that bridge the gap between technology and real-world usability.

Vipin Tyagi is a distinguished academician, researcher and author, currently serving as Dean (Academic and Research) at Jaypee University of Engineering and Technology in Guna, Madhya Pradesh. With a rich background in Computer Science, his expertise spans across Image Processing, Cyber Forensics, and Speech Recognition. He is also Director – IQAC of JUET Guna. Prof. Tyagi has a prolific publication record, contributing significantly to his fields of interest. His scholarly work includes numerous journal articles, conference papers, and books. Some of his notable publications are in the areas of image forgery detection, image denoising, and content-based image retrieval. He has authored and edited several books and papers in the field of computing and data sciences, such as "Predictive Computing and Information Security" and "Content-Based Image Retrieval: Ideas, Influences, and Current Trends" published by Springer Singapore. His book "Understanding Digital Image Processing" using MATLAB, published by Taylor and Francis is highlighted by Mathworks.

Onem Yildiz received the B.Sc., M.Sc., and Ph.D. degrees in the Department of Electrical and Electronics Engineering from Ege University, İzmir, Türkiye, in 2014, 2017, and 2023, respectively. She is currently serving as a Research Assistant in the Department of Electrical and Electronics Engineering at Aydın Adnan Menderes University, Aydın, Türkiye. Dr. Yıldız's research interests include wireless network optimization, mobile edge computing, resource allocation and scheduling, machine learning applications in network design, IoT-based sensing systems.

Index

A

B

C

D

E

G

H

I

L

M

N

O

P

Q

R

S

T

U

V

W

www.ingramcontent.com/pod-product-compliance
Lightning Source LLC
LaVergne TN
LVHW081330021026
849161LV00008BA/1822

* 9 7 9 8 3 3 7 3 6 8 3 1 3 *